Multicultural Education in a Pluralistic Society

SEVENTH EDITION

Donna M. Gollnick

National Council for Accreditation of Teacher Education

Philip C. Chinn

California State University, Los Angeles

PEARSON

Merrill
Prentice Hall

Upper Saddle River, New Jersey
Columbus, Ohio

Library of Congress Cataloging-in-Publication Data

Gollnick, Donna M.
  Multicultural education in a pluralistic society / Donna M. Gollnick, Philip C. Chinn.—
7th ed.
    p. cm.
  Includes bibliographical references and index.
  ISBN 0-13-119719-3
  1. Multicultural education—United States. 2. Social sciences—Study and teaching
(Elementary)—United States. 3. Pluralism (Social sciences)—Study and teaching
(Elementary)—United States. 4. Social sciences—Study and teaching (Secondary)—United
States. 5. Pluralism (Social sciences)—Study and teaching (Secondary)—United States. I.
Chinn, Philip C., II. Title.

LC1099.3.G65 2006
370.117—dc22

2005041552

Vice President and Executive Publisher: Jeffrey W. Johnston
Executive Editor: Debra A. Stollenwerk
Development Editor: Amy Nelson
Senior Editorial Assistant: Mary Morrill
Production Editor: Kris Roach
Production Coordination: Carlisle Publishers Services
Design Coordinator: Diane C. Lorenzo
Cover Designer: Jeff Vanik
Cover Image: Getty Images, SuperStock, Corbis
Photo Coordinator: Sandy Schaefer
Production Manager: Pam Bennett
Director of Marketing: Ann Castel Davis
Marketing Manager: Darcy Betts Prybella
Marketing Coordinator: Brian Mounts

This book was set in Stone Serif Medium by Carlisle Communications, Ltd. It was printed and bound by R.R. Donnelley & Sons Company. The cover was printed by R.R. Donnelley & Sons Company.

Photo Credits: Richard Haynes/Prentice Hall School Division: p. 2; Michael J. Doolittle/The Image Works: p. 12; New York Convention & Visitors Bureau: p. 18; Alex Wong/Getty Images, Inc.–Liaison: p. 26; Anne Vega/Merrill: pp. 35, 157, 197, 234, 268, 359, 382; Louisiana Office of Tourism: p. 46; Prentice Hall High School: p. 55; Laima Druskis/PH College: p. 60; Peter Buckley/ PH College: p. 76; Todd Yarrington/Merrill: p. 90; David Young-Wolff/PhotoEdit: p. 97; AP World Wide Photos: p. 99; Jeff Greenberg/PhotoEdit: p. 103; Scott Cunningham/Merrill: pp. 128, 186, 194, 207, 354, 373, 375; Barbara Schwartz/ Merrill: p. 132; Larry Hamill/Merrill: p. 138; Laimute Druskis/PH College: p. 144; Anthony Magnacca/Merrill: p. 167; Jim Bourg/Getty Images, Inc.–Liaison: p. 172; Patrick Wilson/PH College: p. 176; Bill Aron/PhotoEdit: pp. 214, 232 (left); Victor Bracamontes: p. 232 (right); Courtesy of the Fo Kuang Shan Hsi Lai Temple: p. 239; Robert Brenner/PhotoEdit: p. 276; Richard Hutchings/PhotoEdit: p. 286; Michael Newman/PhotoEdit: p. 298; M. Antman/The Image Works: p. 306; Dan Floss/Merrill: p. 313; Shirley Zeiberg/PH College: p. 321; Tony Freeman/PhotoEdit: p. 344.

Pearson Education Ltd.
Pearson Education Singapore Pte. Ltd.
Pearson Education Canada, Ltd.
Pearson Education—Japan
Pearson Education Australia Pty. Limited
Pearson Education North Asia Ltd.
Pearson Educación de Mexico, S.A. de C.V.
Pearson Education Malaysia Pte. Ltd.

To my late husband, Willard C. Loftis, for supporting my work in multicultural education for 17 years.

DMG

To Frances Kuwahara Chinn, my best friend and daily inspiration to make a difference.

PCC

Preface

Introduction

The seventh edition of *Multicultural Education in a Pluralistic Society* introduces students to diversity, helps them understand the issues involved with a diverse nation, and guides them to think critically and reflectively regarding their decisions as a teacher in a diverse classroom.

Diversity in the Twenty-First Century

As we begin the twenty-first century, the United States is considerably more diverse than it was at the beginning of the last century. The country is a multicultural nation comprised of indigenous peoples, such as the American Indians, Aleuts, Eskimos, and Hawaiians, and those who themselves or whose ancestors arrived as immigrants from other countries. These groups of individuals represent different classes, religions, and native languages. In addition, the people differ in gender, sexual orientation, age, and physical and mental abilities. As we move further into the new millennium, the population will become increasingly more diverse. By 2040, the U.S. Census Bureau predicts that children of color will comprise 50% of the school-aged population. As the ethnic composition of the United States changes, so will the religious landscape as new immigrants bring their religions from abroad. They will also bring diverse languages, values, and ideas that will help reshape U.S. society.

The culture and the society of the United States are dynamic. They are in a continuous state of change. Unless teachers are able to understand the diverse needs of their students, it will be difficult if not impossible to teach them effectively.

What Impact Does Multicultural Education Have on Teaching?

Education that is multicultural provides an environment that values diversity and portrays it positively. Gender, age, race, ethnicity, native language, religion, class, or disability should not limit students' educational and vocational options. Educators have the responsibility to help students contribute to and benefit from our democratic society. Effective instructional strategies for all students in the classroom should not evolve solely from the teacher's culture; they should be drawn primarily from the cultures of students and their communities. The integration of multicultural education throughout the curriculum helps students and teachers think critically about institutional racism, classism, sexism, ablism, ageism, and homophobia. Hopefully, educators will help their students develop both individual and group strategies to overcome the debilitating effects of these society scourges.

About the Seventh Edition

Students in undergraduate, graduate, and in-service courses will find this text helpful in examining social and cultural conditions that influence education and in understanding diversity and how to use this knowledge effectively in the classroom and schools. Other professionals in the social services will find it helpful in understanding the complexity of cultural backgrounds and experiences as they work with families and children.

MICROCULTURAL APPROACH

As in previous editions, we approach multicultural education with a broad perspective of the concept. Using culture as the basis for understanding multicultural education, we present descriptions of seven cultural groups to which students and teachers belong: class, ethnicity and race, gender, exceptionality, religion, language, and age. At this time, we believe that these groups are the most critical to include in order to understand pluralism and multicultural education. Thus, this text examines these group memberships and the ways in which educators can develop education programs to meet the needs of diverse groups and the nation.

TEACHING TO CREATE EQUITABLE ENVIRONMENTS

We also emphasize that educators can deliver an equitable education for all students. We believe that educators cannot attack sexism without also fighting racism, classism, homophobia, and discrimination based on abilities, age, and religion. Schools can eradicate discrimination in their own policies and practices if educators are willing to confront and eliminate their own racism and sexism. To rid our schools of such practices takes a committed and strong faculty. It is a task that can no longer be ignored. The seventh edition helps students to develop the habit of self-reflection that will help them become more effective teachers in the classroom.

FOCUS OF THE SEVENTH EDITION AND ITS INTEGRATED PACKAGE

The seventh edition places an even greater emphasis on engaging students in exploring diversity by inviting and encouraging students to think reflectively and giving them access to real classrooms. Students must begin to develop skills for reflection while they are preparing to teach and practice the habit of reflecting on their practice now and throughout their teaching career in order to make informed decisions. This edition also includes application opportunities for students through a debate feature and portfolio activities. In addition, students are given the opportunity to see what culturally responsive teaching looks like in a real classroom when they view and analyze the examples on the *Exploring Diversity* booklet's CD that is packaged with every copy of this text.

Self-Reflection Opportunities. Self-understanding influences a teacher's practice in the classroom, and developing the habit of self-reflection helps students make informed decisions regarding multicultural issues. The seventh edition introduces reflection in Chapter 1 and encourages students to continue this habit of reflection in each chapter through the chapter narrative and in-chapter features.

- *Chapter-Opening Classroom Scenarios.* Each chapter opens with a classroom scenario to place chapter content in an educational setting. Questions at the end of each scenario encourage students to think about the scenario and guide them to reflect on the decisions they would make.

 *Opportunities for Reflection*

1. *What factors contribute to racial and ethnic conflict in some schools?*
2. *What racial groups are most likely to see themselves in the school curriculum?*
3. *How can a classroom reflect the diversity of its students so that they all feel valued and respected?*
4. *What were the positive and negative outcomes of the steps taken by Ms. Williams?*
5. *What would you have done to improve cross-cultural relations among class members?*

To answer these questions online, go to this chapter's Opening Scenario module of the Companion Website.

- *NEW! Opportunities for Reflection Margin Note.* Located in every chapter, the questions within the narrative guide students to think critically about chapter content and issues and are connected to the text Companion Website at **www.prenhall.com/gollnick**. These questions help students learn skills for reflection while they are preparing to teach and to develop the habit of reflecting on their practice now and throughout their teaching career. Students are encouraged to answer the questions online via the Companion Website to promote reflection and group discussion.

 *Opportunities for Reflection*

Today, 1.9 million citizens identify themselves as Native American only; over half a million people identify themselves as Alaska Native only. Another 1.5 million indicate they are partially Native American or Alaska Native. Forty percent of the Native American population belongs to one of six tribes: Cherokee, Navajo, Latin Native American, Choctaw, Sioux, and Chippewa (U.S. Census Bureau, 2003). *What do you know about American Indians? Where did you learn about them? How accurate is your knowledge base?*

- *Critical Incidents in Teaching.* This feature, which occurs twice or more in each chapter, reflects both real-life and hypothetical situations that occur in schools or classrooms. Students have the opportunity to examine their feelings, attitudes, and possible actions or reactions to each scenario. Linked to the Companion Website, these problem-solving exercises help facilitate and sharpen students' critical thinking skills and their ability to reflect when they need to make informed decisions.

Example of *Critical Incidents in Teaching* feature.

 **CRITICAL INCIDENTS IN TEACHING**

Student Conflict Between Family and Peer Values

Wing Tek Lau is a sixth-grade student in a predominantly white and African American Southern community. He and his parents emigrated from Hong Kong 4 years ago. His uncle, an engineer at a local high-tech company, had encouraged Wing Tek's father to immigrate to this country and open a Chinese restaurant. The restaurant is the only Chinese restaurant in the community, and it was an instant success. Mr. Lau and his family have enjoyed considerable acceptance in both their business and their neighborhood. Wing Tek and his younger sister have also enjoyed academic success at school and appear to be well liked by the other students.

One day when Mrs. Baca, Wing Tek's teacher, calls him by name, he announces before the class, "My American name is Kevin. Please, everybody call me Kevin from now on." Mrs. Baca and Wing Tek's classmates honor this request, and Wing Tek is "Kevin" from then on.

Three weeks later, Mr. and Mrs. Lau make an appointment to see Mrs. Baca. When the teacher makes reference to "Kevin," Mrs. Lau says, "Who are you talking about? Who is Kevin? We came here to talk about our son, Wing Tek."

"But I thought his American name was Kevin. That's what he asked us to call him from now on," Mrs. Baca replies.

"That child," Mrs. Lau says in disgust, "is a disgrace to our family."

"We have heard his sister call him by that name, but she said it was just a joke," Mr. Lau adds. "We came to see you because we are having problems with him in our home. Wing Tek refuses to speak Chinese to us. He argues with us about going to his Chinese lessons on Saturday with the other Chinese students in the community. He says he does not want to eat Chinese food anymore. He says that he is an American now and wants pizza, hamburgers, and tacos. What are you people teaching these children in school? Is there no respect for family, no respect for our culture?"

Mrs. Baca, an acculturated Mexican American who was raised in East Los Angeles, begins to put things together. Wing Tek, in his attempt to ensure his acceptance by his classmates, has chosen to acculturate to an extreme, to the point of rejecting his family heritage. He wants to be as "American" as anyone else in the class, perhaps more so. Like Wing Tek, Mrs. Baca had acculturated linguistically and in other ways, but she had never given up her Hispanic values. She knows the internal turmoil Wing Tek is experiencing.

Questions for Discussion

1. *Is Wing Tek wrong in his desire to acculturate?*
2. *Are Mr. and Mrs. Lau wrong in wanting their son to maintain their traditional family values?*
3. *What can Mrs. Baca do to bring about a compromise?*
4. *What can Mrs. Baca do in the classroom to resolve the problem or at least to lessen the problem?*

To answer these questions online, go to the Critical Incidents in Teaching module for this chapter of the Companion Website.

■ ***Pause to Reflect.*** Located in every chapter, this feature encourages students to think more deeply about the topic being discussed. This feature either asks students to complete an activity or collect data or poses questions about the topic. This feature will help students learn how to reflect on how the issue being discussed relates to their everyday life. Feature questions are linked to the Companion Website.

Pause to Reflect

Some U.S. citizens trace their roots to the indigenous Native Americans; some are first generation immigrants who were born outside the U.S. However, most of the population has lived in the country for generations although their ancestors emigrated from another country.

■ *How closely do you identify with your ethnicity?*

■ *Do you have any relatives in your family's countries of origin with whom you or your parents communicate?*

■ *How has your ethnic background influenced your behavior, attitudes, and values?*

To answer these questions online, go to the Pause to Reflect module for this chapter of the Companion Website.

Application Opportunities. The seventh edition gives students the ability to practice what they have learned regarding multicultural education.

■ *NEW! Portfolio Activities.* Linked to INTASC standards and located at the end of every chapter, these activities encourage students to begin to think reflectively and to begin to construct professional portfolio entries tied to each chapter's content.

Example of *Portfolio Activities* feature.

- ■ ***NEW! Focus Your Cultural Lens: Debate.*** Located in every chapter, this feature presents a controversial school issue with *for* and *against* statements for students to consider. Questions guide students to critically analyze both sides of the issue and encourage them to take a side by posting their responses on the message board on the Companion Website.

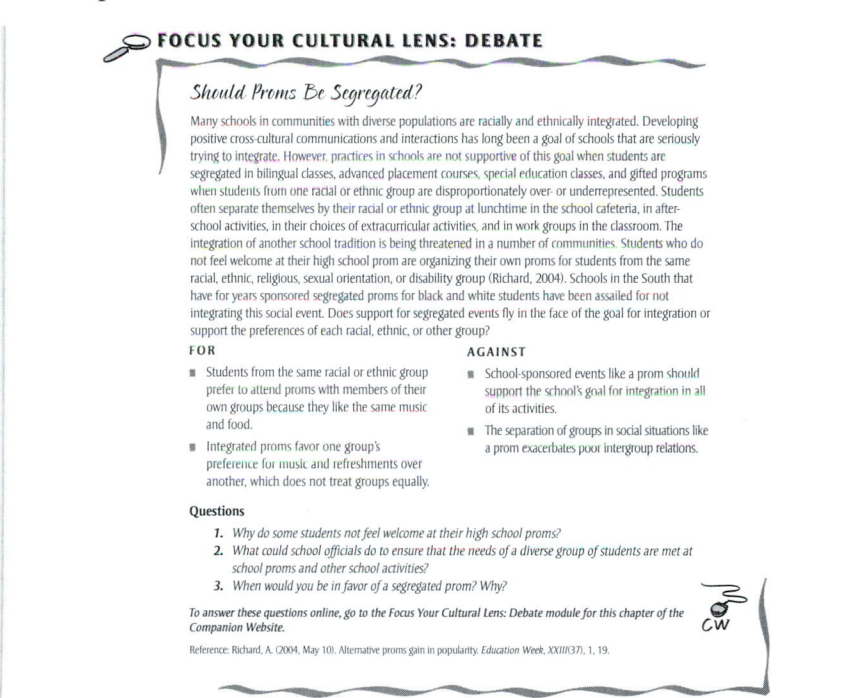

- ■ ***Attitude Inventories.*** Located on the Companion Website and linked to chapter content, these inventories allow students to reflect on their attitudes regarding their individual feelings toward topics, issues, and other content.

- ■ ***Responding to Hate, Southern Poverty Law Activities.*** Through this feature located on the Companion Website, students are encouraged to sign up for a free monthly newsletter. Activities guide them to explore issues and topics.

- ■ ***Integration Activities.*** This module on the Companion Website includes both Class Activities and Class Websites for students to work on and explore.

Seeing Diversity in Action. This edition gives students a glimpse into the real-life world of culturally responsive teaching and learning.

■ *Explore Diversity.* Packaged with every copy of this text, the *Exploring Diversity* activity guide and CD-ROM provide immediate access to living classroom examples of culturally responsive teaching. Culturally responsive teaching reflects the knowledge, skills, and dispositions of the INTASC (Interstate New Teacher Assessment and Support Consortium) standards. The activity guide provides discussion of various concepts, including culturally responsive teaching, instructional planning, classroom climate, and how to engage families; it offers activities and questions that guide students toward understanding, analyzing, and synthesizing the video cases. Additional CD activities are also located the Companion Website at **http://www.prenhall.com/gollnick**. Chapters 3, 4, 8, and 9 include an in-chapter feature, *Explore Diversity,* that directs students to the CD and its chapter-related content. The CD, student activity guide, and the directives in the text work together as a field experience for students where they can view quality examples of culturally responsive teaching and learning in a classroom setting.

 EXPLORE DIVERSITY Go to the *Exploring Diversity* CD located in the accompanying booklet for the perspective of one Native American in the case called *Majority Culture.*

■ *Five New ABC News Video Insights.* In order to explore even more current issues in multicultural education today, the seventh edition includes the videos on DVD (*Critical Issues in Multicultural Education*) in the back of this text. Five new videos have been added, for a total of 18. Each video feature in the text provides a synopsis of the video segment, along with thought-provoking questions that challenge students to consider the real-life experiences presented. Students are invited to submit their responses online via the Companion Website. See page xviii for a complete description of all ABC News videos.

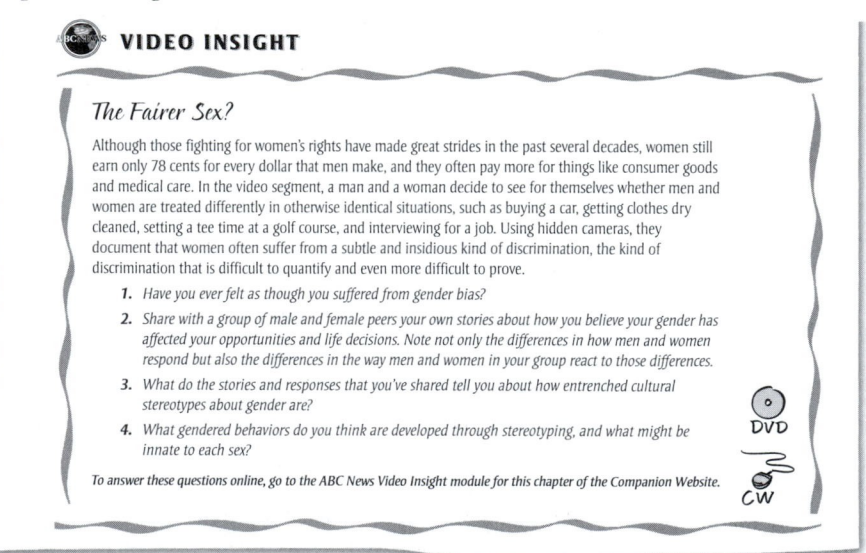

VIDEO INSIGHT

The Fairer Sex?

Although those fighting for women's rights have made great strides in the past several decades, women still earn only 78 cents for every dollar that men make, and they often pay more for things like consumer goods and medical care. In the video segment, a man and a woman decide to see for themselves whether men and women are treated differently in otherwise identical situations, such as buying a car, getting clothes dry cleaned, setting a tee time at a golf course, and interviewing for a job. Using hidden cameras, they document that women often suffer from a subtle and insidious kind of discrimination, the kind of discrimination that is difficult to quantify and even more difficult to prove.

1. *Have you ever felt as though you suffered from gender bias?*
2. *Share with a group of male and female peers your own stories about how you believe your gender has affected your opportunities and life decisions. Note not only the differences in how men and women respond but also the differences in the way men and women in your group react to those differences.*
3. *What do the stories and responses that you've shared tell you about how entrenched cultural stereotypes about gender are?*
4. *What gendered behaviors do you think are developed through stereotyping, and what might be innate to each sex?*

To answer these questions online, go to the ABC News Video Insight module for this chapter of the Companion Website.

WHAT ELSE IS NEW IN THE SEVENTH EDITION?

- *Chapter Cross-Reference Margin Notes.* Located in every chapter, margin notes direct students to other chapters in the text that discuss related topics and issues. The learning and understanding of multicultural education occurs throughout all cultural groups. These margin notes will help students connect to the text's overall message.

 *Please refer to Chapter 2 for a more extensive discussion of intelligence testing and how it impacts all students with exceptionalities.*

- *Key Terms and Glossary.* Key terms are boldfaced in every chapter and a comprehensive glossary is located at the back of the text, helping students build their multicultural education vocabulary and identify terms during class and in their future classrooms.

- *New Topics.* New topics on racism, the Civil Rights movement, Islam, multicultural proficiencies, and reflection have been added to the seventh edition for currency and to emphasize the world's constantly changing diverse society.

Supporting Materials

FOR STUDENTS

- *Exploring Diversity Booklet and CD-ROM,* packaged with every copy of this text and part of the *Explore Diversity* feature. See page xxi for a complete description of this integrated package.

- *ABC News Videos: Critical Issues in Multicultural Education on DVD,* packaged in the back of every text and connected to the text's ABC News *Video Insights* feature. Students are able to view the videos as they read the chapter. See page xvii for more information.

- *Companion Website.* Provides students with resources and immediate feedback on exercises and other activities linked to the text. These activities, projects, and resources enhance and extend chapter content to real-world issues and concepts. Each chapter on the Companion Website contains the following modules or sections:

  - *Chapter Summary.* Outlines key concepts and issues in the chapter.

  - *Chapter-Opening Classroom Scenario.* Includes questions from the scenario giving students the opportunity to submit their responses via e-mail for viewing by the instructor or members of student discussion groups.

  - *(NEW!) Explore Diversity Activities.* These activities extend beyond the activity guide and give students the ability to gain understanding of culturally responsive teaching and learning in the classroom.

- **(NEW!) Opportunities for Reflection.** Students submit their responses to questions from each chapter's reflection margin notes. They are encouraged to answer the questions online to promote reflection and group discussion.
- **(NEW!) Attitude Inventories.** See page ix for a complete description.
- **(NEW!) Portfolio Activities.** INTASC-linked activities encourage students to begin constructing professional portfolio entries tied to each chapter's content.
- **Responding to Hate, Southern Poverty Law Activities.** See page ix for a complete description.
- **Self-Assessment.** Multiple choice and true/false questions are provided with automatic grading to provide immediate feedback to students. Each question includes a hint button to guide students in their learning.
- **Discussion Questions.** Additional questions help students test their knowledge of chapter content. A hint button helps students to guide their learning.
- **Questions for Discussion.** Each end-of-chapter review question is provided online for students to submit their responses electronically.
- **Web Resources.** Links to World Wide Web sites that relate to and enhance chapter content.
- **Integration Activities.** See page ix for a complete description.
- **Pause to Reflect.** Includes discussion questions for reflection to encourage exploration of issues and ideas. These questions are from the text's feature of the same name.
- **Critical Incidents in Teaching.** Classroom-based scenarios provide problem-solving exercises to facilitate and sharpen students' critical thinking skills.
- **ABC News Video Insight.** Connects to thought-provoking questions presented within the text feature of the same name.
- **Focus Your Cultural Lens: Debate.** Includes questions and online resources that encourage students to explore the issue, research the issue, take a stand, and share their ideas and beliefs with others online.
- **Other Resources.** Includes a complete list of INTASC and NCATE standards.
- **Message Board.** Serves as a virtual bulletin board to post or respond to questions or comments to/from a national audience.

- **OneKey.** OneKey is Prentice Hall's exclusive new resource for students and instructors. OneKey is an integrated online course management resource featuring everything students and instructors need for work in or outside of the classroom, available in the nationally hosted CourseCompass platform, as well as WebCT and Blackboard.
- **SafariX.** SafariX is Prentice Hall's exciting new digital platform where students can subscribe to textbooks at savings of up to 50% of the suggested list price of print editions. SafariX will help meet the needs of students who are looking for lower-cost alternatives to print editions.

For more information about OneKey or SafariX, please contact your local Merrill representative prior to placing your textbook order.

FOR INSTRUCTORS

- *Instructor's Manual and Media Guide.* This manual provides concrete suggestions to actively involve students in learning and to promote interactive teaching using the PowerPoints, ABC Videos, and the *Exploring Diversity* CD and Activity Guide. Chapters in the manual parallel the organization and content of the text. This manual will help teach chapter topics and integrate the accompanying media to the fullest extent. Each chapter contains chapter objectives, key terms, a comprehensive test bank containing multiple choice and short-answer discussion questions, and a number of individual and group activities.

- *Computerized Test Bank Software.* This software gives instructors electronic access to the test questions printed in the Instructor's Manual and allows them to create and customize exams on their computer. The PC and MacIntosh-compatible software can help professors manage their courses and gain insight into their students' progress and performance.

- *PowerPoint Slides.* Designed as an instructional tool, the PowerPoint presentations for each chapter can be used to present and elaborate on chapter content and can be found on the Companion Website.

- *ABC News Videos: Critical Issues in Multicultural Education.* Free to professors who adopt this text, these ABC News videos feature 18 thought-provoking video segments that are tied to each chapter's content. They provide you with discussion questions to challenge your students to consider the real-life experiences presented. The DVD is packaged with the text, but VHS is available also.

- *Syllabus Manager*™. An online syllabus creation and management instrument located on this text's Companion Website at **http://www.prenhall.com/gollnick.** Syllabus Manager has the following capabilities:

  - Syllabus Manager provides the instructor with a step-by-step process for creating and revising syllabi, with direct links into the Companion Website and other online content.

  - Your completed syllabus is hosted on our servers, allowing convenient updates from any computer on the Internet. Changes you make to your syllabus are immediately available to your students at their next logon.

  - Students may log on to your syllabus at any time. All they need to know is the web address for this text's Companion Website and the password you've assigned to your syllabus.

  - Clicking on a date, the student is shown the list of activities for that day's assignment. The activities for each assignment are linked directly to text content, saving time for students.

  - Adding assignments consists of clicking on the desired due date, then filling in the details of the assignment.

  - Links to other activities can be created easily. If the activity is online, a URL can be entered in the space provided, and it will be linked automatically in the final syllabus.

Instructor supplements can also be accessed at our Instructor Resource Center located at **http://www.prenhall.com**. The Instructor Resource Center opens the door to a variety of print and media resources in downloadable, digital format. Resources available for instructors include:

- Instructor Manual/Media Guide
- Computerized Test Bank
- PowerPoint slides
- Request and/or review Gollnick's OneKey WebCT and Blackboard course content
- Obtain instructions for downloading a Blackboard cartridge or WebCT e-Pack

Your one-time registration opens the door to Prentice Hall's premium digital resources. You will not have additional forms to fill out or multiple usernames and passwords to remember to access new titles and/or editions. Register today and maximize your time at every stage of course preparation.

How the Text Is Organized

Multicultural Education in a Pluralistic Society provides an overview of the different cultural groups to which students belong. The first chapter examines the pervasive influence of culture and the importance of understanding our own cultural backgrounds and experiences, as well as those of our students. The following seven chapters examine class, ethnicity and race, gender, exceptionality, religion, language, and age. The final chapter contains recommendations for using culturally responsive and social justice pedagogies in the implementation of multicultural education. All of the chapters in this edition have been revised and reorganized to reflect current thinking and research in the area. In particular, the first chapter provides the foundational framework that supports our thinking about multicultural education. The final chapter integrates critical pedagogy with research on teaching effectively. Each chapter opens with a scenario to place the topic in an educational setting.

MULTIPLE PERSPECTIVES

We have tried to present different perspectives on a number of issues in the most unbiased manner possible. We are not without strong opinions or passion on some of the issues. However, in our effort to be equitable, we do attempt to present different perspectives on the issues and allow the reader to make his or her own decisions. There are some issues related to racism, sexism, handicapism, and so on, that are so important to the well-being of society that we do provide our positions, which we recognize to be our biases.

AN ATTENTION TO LANGUAGE

Readers should be aware of several caveats related to the language used in this text. Although we realize that the term *American* is commonly used to refer to the U.S. population, we view *American* as including other North and South Americans as well. Therefore, we have tried to limit the use of this term when referring to the United States. Although we have tried to use the terms *black* and *white* sparingly, data about groups often have been categorized by the racial identification, rather than by national origin such as African or European American. In many cases, we were not able to distinguish ethnic identity and have continued to use *black, white,* or *persons of color.* We have limited our use of the term *minority* and have focused more on the power relationships that exist between groups. In previous editions we used the term *Hispanic.* In this edition we have tried to use *Latino,* which appears to be the preferred term for individuals from a group with many ethnic origins.

FOR MORE INFORMATION

To request a complimentary copy of *Multicultural Education in a Pluralistic Society*, Seventh Edition, or any of its supplements, please contact your Prentice Hall sales representative, call Faculty Services at 1-800-526-0485, or e-mail us at **merrillmarketing@prenhall.com.** We look forward to hearing from you.

Acknowledgments

The preparation of any text involves the contributions of many individuals in addition to those whose names are found on the cover. We wish to thank the following reviewers, whose recommendations were used to improve this edition: Rod Janzen, Fresno Pacific University; Bob Gustafson, Warner Southern College; Mark J. Guillette, Valencia Community College; Janice Dinsmore, Wayne State University; Helen Hoffner, Holy Family University; and Valerie Janesick, Roosevelt University.

We wish to thank William Howe, Sandra Winn, and Pauline Chinn for their contributions to the critical incidents. The research assistance of Maria Gutierrez and Michele Clarke is also acknowledged and very much appreciated. A special thanks to Dr. Muzammil H. Siddiqi, Director of the Islamic Society of Orange County, California, for his review of and helpful suggestions on the section on Islam. The assistance, patience, encouragement, and guidance of our editors, Debra A. Stollenwerk and Amy Nelson, are sincerely appreciated.

The Johns Hopkins University Digital Portfolio and Guide

THE JOHNS HOPKINS UNIVERSITY CENTER FOR TECHNOLOGY IN EDUCATION

Students, would you like...

. . . a dynamic way to create a digital portfolio for your first job interview?

. . . an easy way to connect your course work with federal, state, and professional standards?

. . . to keep a running online journal of student teaching that you can easily convert into evidence for your portfolio illustrating your growth over time?

. . . to add a live Web page link within your portfolio?

If you answered yes to any or all of these questions, then you need the online, digital portfolio created by The Johns Hopkins University, a nationally recognized leader in the use of portfolios in teacher education. This digital portfolio allows you to collect and display artifacts such as lesson plans, audio and video clips, samples of your students' work, and Web-based materials.

An accompanying portfolio guide introduces you to portfolio development and provides you with a step-by-step user guide for accessing and using *The Johns Hopkins University Digital Portfolio.*

To take a tour, visit **www.prenhall.com/JHUportfolio**

If you would like to use *The Johns Hopkins University Digital Portfolio* in this course or any other courses, you may purchase the guide with an online access code for only $33.33* at **www.prenhall.com/JHUportfolio**

Professors:

To package *The Johns Hopkins University Digital Portfolio and Guide* with *Multicultural Education in a Pluralistic Society & Exploring Diversity Package,* Seventh Edition, at a discount the next time you teach this course, please use ISBN 0132245507 when completing your book order for the bookstore.

Price subject to change without notice.

ABC News/Prentice Hall Video Library

The ABC News/Prentice Hall Video Library titled "Critical Issues in Multicultural Education, Volume III" is packaged on DVD in the back of this text. This video library is also available on VHS for professors.

This video library challenges students to explore chapter topics through ABC News segments focusing on multicultural issues. Video Insights features within each chapter offer a short summary of each episode and ask students to think about and respond to questions relating to the video and chapter content.

A Teen's Video of Growing Up in the City

This video is narrated by a young African teenager (Leon) living in one of the crime and drug infested areas of Chicago. You will see the difficult life that these students face in their daily experiences with life and with school. One of Leon's close friends is "Sticks," who has just had a new baby with his girlfriend, Pat, a very young teen. Sticks is determined to support the baby and to complete school. These are too often the experiences that young inner city youth face as they struggle to complete their education and survive the harshness of the inner city.
Chapter 1, Page 6
Running Time: 12:43 minutes

School Busing

In this video segment, you will see proponents of this movement in Oklahoma City and in other cities across the country who say their children have been subjected to segregated settings within integrated schools. African American children are often assigned to remedial classes or lower academic tracks and do not get exposure to the services and resources that other students receive. In addition, because these schools are not close to home, it is difficult for parents to be involved or even be present if there is a problem or an emergency at school.
Chapter 1, Page 36
Running Time: 6:32 minutes

Looking for a Chance in Appalachia

This video shows how most Appalachian counties have unemployment and poverty rates well above the national average. These once-vibrant communities are now shrinking because many people can simply not find work in their hometowns. In this video segment, you will see that there are a number of factors contributing to this problem, but one of the biggest is education. Things are appearing to change, however. Federal programs are helping to educate workers, giving them the opportunity to get their diploma and receive job training in different vocations.
Chapter 2, Page 59
Running Time: 5:33 minutes

Smart Kid, Tough School

This ABC News video segment discusses how students who are educated in deteriorating schools do not receive an education equal to the education given to students who attend schools with greater financial and community resources. This segment features Cedric Jennings, a star student from a high school in the poorest section of Washington, DC. Cedric saw this confirmed when he enrolled in a summer program for gifted minority students, only to

find that the students from higher-income neighborhoods were better prepared academically. Yet, when scholarship offers to attend expensive prep schools came his way, Cedric refused and returned to his old high school for his senior year.
Chapter 2, Page 76
Running Time: 19:09 minutes

America in Black and White: The Search for Common Ground

This video segment explores how society forms impressions of people every day based solely on appearance. Many people make judgments about intelligence, happiness, and earning potential without any real information. In this video segment, you will see people working in different industries, and they are all saying the same thing: it's easier to get a job if you are a lighter skinned African American than if you are a darker skinned African American. In addition, this segment shows the disparity between salaries of lighter versus darker skinned men and women and the judgments people make about them simply based on the color of their skin.
Chapter 3, Page 110
Running Time: 18:37 minutes

Acting White

This ABC News video segment discusses how African American students in any school can define "acting white." The concept of "acting white" is one of the greatest problems in the education of African American students. Underachieving African American students often attack achieving students for excelling in school, speaking Standard English, listening to the "wrong" music, or having white friends. African American students (particularly those who are underachieving) may perceive the achieving students as being traitors or disloyal to their race because of these behaviors. By adopting values common to the dominant culture, they are seen as trying to behave like whites (who have been demonized by some blacks). Latino students have indicated that they too have experienced this same phenomenon. This is a major problem

for students of color who want to achieve, improve their life, or to go on to higher education.
Chapter 3, Page 113
Running Time: 14:03 minutes

America in Black and White: South Carolina High School Drug Raid

This segment focuses on how school drug searches have unfortunately become commonplace across the United States. Many across the country saw video clips on the national news of police with drawn guns, snarling dogs, and frightened students in the hallway of a South Carolina high school searching for drugs. In an effort to rid the school of what the principal considered a drug problem, the principal arranged a surprise raid with the local police. While the school is predominantly white, the students detained in the raid were mostly black. No drugs or weapons were found in the raid. As soon as the video clips were shown locally and across the nation, the backlash was instantaneous.
Chapter 3, Page 115
Running Time: 19:30 minutes

The Secret Life of Boys

In this video segment, you will see that boys have a more difficult time showing emotion and feelings. By the age of 5 it's often difficult to tell if something is bothering a little boy, because he has already learned to mask his feelings. In addition, while boys are conditioned to keep their feelings and emotions inside, girls are supported and expected to share and discuss their feelings with others. Does this difference have an outward effect? Some researchers say yes; this emotional repression leads to boys acting out more in school and being labeled with learning disorders and behavior problems more often than girls. Often, culture determines the appropriate activities in which boys and girls participate.
Chapter 4, Page 141
Running Time: 15:34 minutes

The Fairer Sex?

In this video segment, a man and a woman decide to see for themselves whether men and women are treated differently in otherwise identical situations, such as buying a car, getting clothes dry cleaned, setting a tee time at a golf course, and interviewing for a job. Using hidden cameras, they document that women often suffer from a subtle and insidious kind of discrimination, the kind of discrimination that is difficult to quantify and even more difficult to prove.

Chapter 4, Page 160
Running Time: 17:05 minutes

Jessica Parks Surmounts Her Obstacles

In this video, the accomplishments of a truly remarkable young woman, Jessica Parks, are highlighted. Born without arms, she has accomplished more than many individuals without disabilities, and far more than her parents, physicians, and educators could have imagined. Educators (including special educators) often predetermine in their minds what children with disabilities will or will not be able to accomplish, and limit their access to educational programs. This is often a mistake, which can even lead to lawsuits. In this video, we can see why the courts will almost always side with the student and his or her parents if the schools refuse to allow the student the opportunity to demonstrate the ability to perform in a general education class.

Chapter 5, Page 190
Running Time: 10:41 minutes

Against the Odds: Three Children with Autism

This ABC News video segment introduces us to a family with three children with autism. The family has found a highly specialized treatment program, which has had a profoundly positive impact on these children. However, the program requires tuition of more than $170,000 a year for the three children. The family has exhausted their life savings on tuition. The Individuals with Disabilities Education Act (IDEA) requires schools to provide for the educational needs of children with disabilities. The U.S. Supreme Court has ruled that the schools are required to provide a basic floor of opportunity for children with disabilities, but are not required to provide them with the best possible education. With the private schooling, these three children seem to be thriving. The public schools are reluctant to pay the tuition to the private clinic.

Chapter 5, Page 193
Running Time: 22:29

God and Evolution in Kansas Classrooms

This video segment shows how and why the State Board of Education in Kansas decided in the late 1990s to side with creationists and not require the teaching of evolution in their schools. To the opponents of creationism, this seemed an irresponsible move in the education of Kansas' children. Proponents of creationism say it should be taught in schools because it is a more scientifically valid theory than evolution. To these people, it is not an issue of religious fundamentalism versus science; it's an issue of science versus science.

Chapter 6, Page 254
Running Time: 17:46 minutes

Standing Alone

Although the Supreme Court voted in 1963 to remove prayer from schools, the issue is still not settled. In some areas of the country, where religious diversity is minimal, this ruling is effectively ignored. Other districts have agreed to a "moment of silence" for the purpose of moral reflection. Still others are locked in battle over this issue, like the high school choir in Utah, an area with a large Mormon population, that refused to honor the wishes of Rachel, its single Jewish member, to sing fewer religious songs.

Chapter 6, Page 258
Running Time: 12:53 minutes

American Spoken Here

This ABC News video segment discusses American accents. In this information age where everyone is a phone call, an e-mail, or a flight away from another, it would seem logical that the different accents and dialects around the country might merge into one, but research from the University of Pennsylvania tells a dif-

ferent story. In this video segment, you will see how American accents are becoming more and more distinct from one another.
Chapter 7, Page 277
Running Time: 7:10 minutes

Girl Gangsters—The Queens of Armed Robbery

In this segment, four girls in an affluent Houston, Texas, suburb apparently found themselves bored one summer. Few are surprised when they hear of urban street gang members involved in armed robberies. But what would possess four white middle-class girls from an upscale suburban community to rob several stores at gunpoint? Between their boredom and their drug use, they turned a flippant remark about robbing a store into a crime spree that eventually ended in prison sentences. It may be difficult to understand why children from privileged backgrounds would engage in such high-risk behavior that would leave an indelible stain on their lives.
Chapter 8, Page 329
Running Time: 22:33 minutes

A Closer Look

In this video segment, you will see that according to the Census Bureau, 34 million people over the age of 65 are still working, and 50,000 of those who are over the age of 90 are still cashing a paycheck. If medicine and technology continue at the rate they are moving now, by the year 2030, one third of our lifetimes will be spent in retirement. Right now, individuals who make it past the age of 65 can expect to live until they are approximately 83. Often in our culture, the aged are seen as useless, noncontributing burdens for their younger family members and society to shoulder.
Chapter 8, Page 341
Running Time: 5:36 minutes

Survival Lessons

In this video segment, you are introduced to Francis Scott Key Elementary and other schools that present models for helping troubled youth. Kids are faced with more and more violence and tragedy every day. To combat this, some schools across the country have set up full-time mental health programs to identify and help troubled children before the trouble gets out of control.
Chapter 9, Page 365
Running Time: 18:41 minutes

Children and Race

This video segment explores the relationship between our children and race. It has been more than fifty years since the U.S. Supreme Court mandated school desegregation. As you watch the segment think about the following: Is this nation any closer to integrating children of different backgrounds in its schools? Do the generations of children who are growing up in schools today experience less prejudice than past generations? Is the nation any closer to melding relationships of racially and ethnically diverse people in this pluralistic society?
Chapter 9, Page 374
Running Time: 9:50 minutes

Exploring Diversity CD-ROM Video Cases

The **Explore Diversity** feature located in Chapters 3, 4, 8, and 9 directs students to the interactive *Exploring Diversity: A Video Case Approach* CD-ROM and accompanying activity guide (packaged free with every copy of this text) that provide examples of culturally responsive teaching related to chapter content.

Second Grade Literacy in an Urban School

In the first case, Janice Glaspie and Darwin Henderson are working with literate, inner-city, African American children. In this classroom every child is challenged, feels safe, and experiences the joy of learning. Though well-meaning individuals may emphasize the need for direct instruction with young children in inner urban settings, these two teachers demonstrate the use of literature to enhance literacy learning. As Ms. Glaspie contends, these children are literate.
Chapter 3, page 126

The Emerging Competence of Youth in 7th Grade

At first glance, the second video case appears to present a homogeneous classroom. The socio-economic diversity and developmental needs of these middle school students, however, have a significant effect on the interactions in the classroom. In this science classroom, Cathy Burton works with students to make connections to other content areas, as well as worldwide issues using poster projects and presentations.
Chapter 4, page 166
Chapter 8, page 320

One Teacher's Influence

In the third case, a secondary school teacher, Joy Lohrer, saw a need for diversity in the school. Rather than impose structure, she turned to the students for ideas and suggestions. Ms. Lohrer initially provided the specific agenda of the tolerance training videos and then generated a list of student-desired activities. This educator made a commitment to meet each Thursday. Her goal was to listen to students. In this video case, Ms. Lohrer provides an example of "what one teacher can do" to bring diversity into a school.
Chapter 4, pages 162, 166
Chapter 9, pages 366, 369, 380

Majority Culture

In the final case, Guy Jones, Hunkpapa Lakota and a full-blood member of the Standing Rock Sioux Nation, discusses assumptions that may have an impact on the self-concept of young children. In this conversation with his colleague, Sally Moomaw, they illustrate how classroom practices—some of which are embedded in our own experiences as students and teachers—are laid bare in view of another culture.
Chapter 3, page 93
Chapter 9, page 363

Brief Contents

Contents

Special Features

Explore Diversity

Pause to Reflect

Multicultural Education in a Pluralistic Society

Equality is the heart and essence of democracy, freedom, and justice.

A. PHILIP RANDOLPH, 1942

Chapter 1

Foundations of Multicultural Education

You are just beginning your first teaching position in a nearby urban area. Like many new teachers in an urban area, you were offered the job only a few weeks before school started. You had never been to that part of the city but were sure you could make a difference in the lives of students there. Soon you learn that many students have single parents, many of whom work two jobs to make ends meet. More than half of the students are eligible for free lunch. The families of some students do not speak English at home, but the principal says the students speak English. You are disappointed in the condition of the school, and your classroom in particular, but have been assured it will be repainted during one of the vacation periods.

When students arrive on the first day, you are not surprised that a large proportion of them are from families who immigrated from Central America during the past two decades. The population includes some African American students and a few European American students. You did not realize that the class would include a student who had just moved from Bulgaria and spoke no English and that the native language of two students was Farsi. You have taken a few Spanish courses but know little or nothing about the language or cultures of Bulgaria and Iran. You wonder about the white boy with the black eye but guess that he has been in a fight recently.

Opportunities for Reflection

1. *What assumptions about these students did you make as you read this brief description?*
2. *How has your own cultural background prepared you to teach this diverse group of students?*
3. *What might you want to learn about students' cultural backgrounds to ensure that they learn?*
4. *What kind of challenges are you likely to confront during this year?*
5. *What do you wish you had learned in college to help you be a better teacher in this school?*
6. *Where could you go for assistance in working with students who speak little English?*
7. *Are you glad that you accepted this teaching assignment? Why or why not?*

To answer these questions online, go to this chapter's Opening Scenario module of the Companion Website.

Diversity in the Classroom

Educators today are faced with an overwhelming challenge to prepare students from diverse populations and backgrounds to live in a rapidly changing society and a world in which some groups have greater societal benefits than others because of race, ethnicity, gender, class, language, religion, ability, or age. Schools of the future will become increasingly diverse. Demographic data on birthrates and immigration indicate that there will be more Asian American, Latino (but not Cuban American), and African American children, but fewer children who are European American. Students of color comprise more than one third of the school population today. However, the race and sex of their teachers match neither the student population nor the general population; 84% of the teachers are white and 75% are female (U.S. Department of Education, 2003). By 2020, students of color will represent nearly half of the elementary and secondary population.

Latino, Asian Americans, American Indians, and African Americans already comprise more than half of the student population in California, the District of Columbia, Hawaii, Mississippi, New Mexico, New York, and Texas (U.S. Department of Education, 2004). Whites make up less than one fourth of the student population in the nation's largest cities. Although the U.S. Census Bureau (2003) reports that only 16% of U.S. children live below the official poverty level, 40% of the fourth graders are eligible for free or reduced-price lunch programs in the nation's schools. African American and Latino students are more likely than other students to be concentrated in high poverty schools (U.S. Department of Education, 2004). The number of students with disabilities who are being served by special programs has increased from 4.4 million in 1991 to 5.7 million—15% of enrolled students—in 2000 (U.S. Census Bureau, 2003).

See Chapter 2 for more information about African American and Latino students and Chapter 3 for details on students from low-income families.

It is not only ethnic and racial diversity that is challenging schools. During the past 35 years, new waves of immigrants have come from parts of the world unfamiliar to many Americans. With them have come their religions, which seem even stranger to many Americans than these new people. While small groups of Muslims, Hindus, Buddhists, and Sikhs have been in the country for many decades, only recently have they and their religions become highly visible. Even Christians from Russia, Hong Kong, Taiwan, Korea, and the Philippines bring their own brand of worship to denominations that are well rooted in this country. The United States has not only become a multicultural nation, but it has also become a multireligious society. In earlier years, most religious minority groups maintained a low and almost invisible profile. As the groups have become larger, they have become more visible, along with their houses of worship (Eck, 2000).

For more information on the religions that students bring to schools, see Chapter 6.

These religious differences raise a number of challenges for educators. The holidays to be celebrated must be considered, along with religious codes related to the curriculum, appropriate interactions of boys and girls, dress in physical education classes, and discipline. Parents value the importance of education for their children, but they do not always agree with the school's approaches to teaching and learning, nor accept the secular **values** as appropriate for their family. Values are the qualities that parents find desirable and important in the education of their children, and include areas such as morality, hard work, and caring, often with religious overtones. Working collaboratively with parents and communities will become even more critical in providing education equitably to all students.

To work effectively with the heterogeneous student populations found in schools, educators need to understand and feel comfortable with their own cultural roots. *How would you describe your cultural background? From what countries did you or your ancestors come? How long has your family lived in the United States? How would you describe the experiences your family has had in the United States?*

Opportunities for Reflection

Educators also must understand the cultural setting in which the school is located to develop effective instructional strategies. They must help their students become aware of cultural differences and inequalities in the nation and in the world. One goal is to help students affirm cultural differences while realizing that individuals across **cultures** have many similarities.

Teachers will find that students have individual differences, even though they may appear to be from the same cultural group. These differences extend far beyond intellectual and physical abilities. Students bring to class different historical backgrounds, religious beliefs, and day-to-day experiences that guide the way students behave in school. The cultural background of some students will be mirrored in the school culture. For others, the differences between the home and school cultures will cause dissonance unless the teacher can integrate the cultures of the students into the curriculum and develop a supportive environment for learning. If the teacher fails to understand the cultural factors in addition to the intellectual and physical factors that affect student learning and behavior, it will be near impossible to help students learn.

Multicultural education is an educational strategy in which students' cultural backgrounds are used to develop effective classroom instruction and school environments. It supports and extends the concepts of culture, diversity, equality, social justice, and democracy in the school setting. An examination of the theoretical precepts and practical applications of these concepts will lead to an understanding of the development and practice of multicultural education.

 **VIDEO INSIGHT**

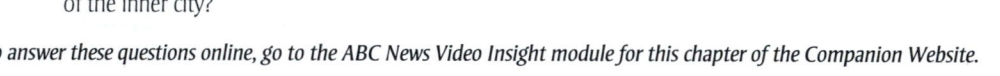

Multicultural Education

Not all students can be taught in the same way because they are not the same. Their cultures and experiences influence the way they learn and respond to schooling. They have different needs, skills, and experiences that must be recognized in developing educational programs. Each student is different because of physical and mental abilities, gender, ethnicity, race, language, religion, class, sexual orientation, and age. Students behave differently in school and toward authority because of cultural factors and their relationship to the dominant society. As educators, we behave in certain ways toward students because of our own cultural experiences within the power structure of the country. Multicultural education is a concept that addresses cultural diversity and **equality** in schools. Equality ensures that students are provided the same access to the benefits of society regardless of their group memberships.

When educators are given the responsibilities of a classroom, they need the knowledge and skills for working effectively in a diverse society. The following fundamental beliefs and assumptions support multicultural education, the strategy for accomplishing this goal:

- Cultural differences have strength and value.
- Schools should be models for the expression of human rights and respect for cultural differences.
- Social justice and equality for all people should be of paramount importance in the design and delivery of curricula.
- Attitudes and values necessary for the continuation of a democratic society can be promoted in schools.
- Schooling can provide the knowledge, skills, and **dispositions**—values, attitudes, and commitments—to help students from diverse groups learn.
- Educators working with families and communities can create an environment that is supportive of multiculturalism.

Many concepts undergird multicultural education. The relationships and interactions among individuals and groups are essential to understanding and working effectively with different cultural groups. Educators should understand racism, sexism, prejudice, discrimination, oppression, powerlessness, power, inequality, equality, and stereotyping. Multicultural education includes various components that often manifest themselves in courses, units of courses, and degree programs. These components include ethnic studies, global studies, bilingual education, women's studies, human relations, special education, and urban education.

For multicultural education to become a reality in schools, the total environment must reflect a commitment to multicultural education. Sleeter and Grant (2002) refer to this commitment as education that is multicultural.

CHARACTERISTICS OF A SCHOOL THAT IS MULTICULTURAL

- The composition of the faculty, administration, and other staff accurately reflects the pluralistic composition of the United States.
- Differences in academic achievement levels disappear between males and females, dominant and oppressed group members, and upper-middle-class and low-income students.
- The school curriculum incorporates the contributions of many cultural groups and integrates multiple perspectives throughout it.
- Instructional materials are free of biases, omissions, and stereotypes.
- Cultural differences are treated as differences, rather than as deficiencies that must be addressed in compensatory programs.
- Students are able to use their own cultural resources and voices to develop new skills and to critically explore subject matter.
- Students learn to recognize and confront inequities in school and society.
- The faculty, administrators, and other staff see themselves as learners enhanced and changed by understanding, affirming, and reflecting cultural diversity.
- Teachers and administrators are able to deal with questions of race, intergroup relations, and controversial realities on an objective, frank, and professional basis.

Multicultural educators believe that all students have the right to learn and can learn. Each subject area is taught from a multicultural perspective. Teachers draw representations from students' cultures and experiences to engage them actively in learning. Skills to function effectively in different cultural settings are taught. For students to function effectively in a democratic society, they must learn about the inequities that currently exist. As teachers, counselors, and principals, we serve as the transmitters of our culture to children and youth. We cannot afford to blame the children and their parents for not learning. We must take responsibility for what and how we teach. We should have the courage to try new methods and techniques, the courage to challenge ineffective and inequitable procedures and policies, and the strength to change schools to ensure learning and equity for all students.

Refer to Chapter 9 for strategies on providing culturally responsive instruction that promotes equity for all students.

EVOLUTION OF MULTICULTURAL EDUCATION

Multicultural education is not a new concept. Its roots are the work of African American scholars who established the National Association for the Study of Negro Life and History in 1915 to focus on the history and culture of African Americans (Banks, 2004). Soon afterwards educators were writing about and training others in intercultural education and ethnic studies.

The intercultural movement during the first two decades had an international emphasis with antecedents in the pacifist movement. Some textbooks were rewritten with an international point of view. Proponents encouraged teachers to make their disciplines more relevant to the modern world by being more issue oriented. The goal was to make the dominant population more tolerant and accepting toward first- and second-generation immigrants in order to maintain national unity and social control (Montalto, 1978). However, issues of power and inequality in society were ignored. The interculturalists supported understanding and appreciation of diverse groups, but did not promote collective ethnic identities that were the focus of ethnic studies. Historian David Tyack (2003) found this movement to be one in which "oppression became reduced to stereotyping and separate ethnic identity was to be dissolved as painlessly as possible" (p. 81).

By the 1960s desegregation was being enforced in the nation's schools. At the same time, cultural differences were being described as deficits. Students of color and whites from low-income families were described as culturally deprived. Their families were blamed for not providing them with the **cultural capital** (that is, advantages such as wealth and education) that would help them succeed in schools. Programs like Head Start, compensatory education, and special education were developed to compensate for these shortcomings. Not surprisingly, those classes were filled with students of color, in poverty, or with disabilities—the children and youth who had not been privileged in society and whose own cultures seldom found their way into textbooks and the school's curriculum.

By the 1970s, oppressed groups were described as culturally different to acknowledge that they did have a culture but that it was different from the culture of the dominant group. The goal of this approach was to teach the exceptional and culturally different to develop the cultural patterns of the dominant society so that they could fit into the mainstream (Sleeter & Grant, 2002).

The civil rights movement brought a renewed interest in ethnic studies, discrimination, and intergroup relations. Racial and ethnic pride emerged from oppressed groups, creating a demand for African American and other ethnic studies programs in colleges and universities across the country. Later, similar programs were established in secondary schools. However, students and participants in ethnic studies programs of the 1960s and early 1970s were primarily members of the group being studied. Programs focused on the various ethnic histories and cultures, with the main objective of providing students with insight and instilling pride in their own ethnic backgrounds. Most of these programs were ethnic-specific, and only one ethnic group was studied. Sometimes the objectives included an understanding of the relationship and conflict between the ethnic group and the dominant population, but seldom was a program's scope multi-ethnic.

Concurrent with the civil rights movement and the growth of ethnic studies, emphasis on intergroup or human relations again emerged. Often, these programs accompanied ethnic studies content for teachers. The objectives were again to promote intergroup, and especially interracial, understanding to reduce or eliminate stereotypes. This approach emphasized the affective level—teachers' attitudes and feelings about themselves and others (Sleeter & Grant, 2002).

With the growth and development of ethnic studies came a realization that those programs alone would not guarantee support for the positive affirmation of cultural diversity and differences in this country. Students from the dominant culture also needed to learn about the history, culture, and contributions of other groups. Thus, ethnic studies expanded into multiethnic studies. Teachers were encouraged to develop curricula that included the contributions of oppressed groups along with those of the dominant group. Textbooks were to be rewritten to represent more accurately the multiethnic nature of the United States. Students were to be exposed to perspectives of oppressed groups through literature, history, music, and other disciplines integrated throughout the general school program. The curriculum and instructional materials were to reflect multiple perspectives, not just the single master narrative of the dominant group.

During this period, other groups that had suffered from institutional discrimination called their needs to the attention of the public. These groups included women, persons with low incomes, persons with disabilities, English language learners, and the elderly. Educators responded by expanding multiethnic education to the more encompassing concept of multicultural education. This broader concept focused on the different cultural groups to which individuals belong, with an emphasis on the interaction of race, ethnicity, class, and gender in their cultural identities. It also called for the elimination of discrimination based on group membership. No longer was it fashionable to fight sexism without simultaneously attacking racism, classism, homophobia, and discrimination against all children, the elderly, and persons with disabilities.

General Multicultural Education

Esther Greenberg is a teacher with Asian and African American students in an alternative education class. Ms. Greenberg's college roommate was Chinese American and she remembers fondly her visit to her roommate's home during the lunar New Year. She remembers how the parents and other Chinese adults had given all the children, including her, money wrapped in red paper, which was to bring all of the recipients good luck in the New Year. Ms. Greenberg thought that it would be a nice gesture to give the students in her class the red paper envelopes as an observance of the upcoming lunar New Year. Since she was unable to give the students money, she took gold-foil covered coins (given to Jewish children) and wrapped these coins in red paper to give to her students.

Unfortunately, on the lunar New Years Day, all of the African American students were pulled out of class for a full day of testing. All of the remaining students were her Asian students. When she passed out the red envelopes, the students were surprised and touched by her sensitivity to cherished custom.

When her administrator was told what Ms. Greenberg had done, he became enraged. He accused her of favoritism to the Asian students and of deliberately leaving out the African American students. When she tried to convince him otherwise, he responded that she had no right to impose Asian customs on African American students. She responded that this was an important Asian custom, and that the Asian students had participated in the observance of Martin Luther King's birthday. However, he continued his attack saying that this was Asian superstition bordering on a religious observance. She was threatened with discipline.

Questions for Discussion

1. *Were Esther Greenberg's actions inappropriate for a public school classroom? If so, why? If no, why not? Was this a violation of the principles of church and state?*
2. *Did Ms. Greenberg create problems for herself by giving out the red envelopes when the African American students were absent from class? Did this create an appearance of favoritism of one racial group over the other?*
3. *How could Ms. Greenberg have handled the situation to make it a pleasing experience to all concerned?*
4. *Was the administrator the one who was out of line, and was Ms. Greenberg simply a victim?*

To answer these questions online, go to the Critical Incidents in Teaching module for this chapter of the Companion Website.

MULTICULTURAL EDUCATION TODAY

The 1990s were characterized by the d3evelopment of standards, which again led to debates between fundamentalists and multiculturalists. The fundamentalists argued that history standards should stress what they believed are the foundations of democracy—patriotism and historical heroes. The multiculturalists promoted the inclusion of diverse groups and multiple perspectives in the standards. The U.S. Senate was drawn into the history standards fray in 1995, voting 99 to 1 to abort the history standards developed by a widely respected group of historians who had promoted the inclusion of diverse groups. In English language arts, groups disagreed about the literature to which students should be exposed, some arguing for multiple perspectives and others arguing that such literature might promote values that they could not support.

Multicultural education is sometimes criticized as focusing narrowly on differences among ethnic groups and not adequately addressing issues of power and oppression that keep a number of groups from participating equitably in society. At least three schools of thought push multiculturalists to think critically about these issues: critical pedagogy, antiracist education, and critical race theory (Sleeter & Bernal, 2004). Critical pedagogy focuses on the culture of everyday life and the interaction of class, race, and gender in contemporary power struggles. Antiracist education is the strategy supported in Canada and a number of European countries to eliminate racist practices in schools such as tracking, inequitable funding, and school desegregation. Critical race theory also focuses on racism in challenging racial oppression, racial inequities, and white privilege (Ladson-Billings, 2004). Multicultural education as presented in this text attempts to incorporate critical pedagogy, antiracist education, and critical race theory as different cultural groups are discussed. The authors believe that multicultural education must include such critical thinking about the issues in order to ensure education serves the needs of all groups equitably.

Still, after eight decades of concern for civil and human rights in education, racism persists. Educators struggle with the integration of diversity into the curriculum and provision of equality in schools. Some classrooms may be desegregated and mainstreamed, and both boys and girls may now participate in athletic activities. However, students are still labeled as at risk, developmentally delayed, underprivileged, lazy, and slow (Tyack, 2003). They are tracked in special classes or groups within the classroom based on their real and perceived abilities. A disproportionate number of students who are African American, Mexican American, Puerto Rican, American Indian, and some

Although the Supreme Court ruled that schools should be desegregated in 1954, students in many classrooms today are from the same racial, ethnic, or language group.

Asian American groups score below European American students on national standardized tests. The number of female, students of color, and low-income students participating in advanced science and mathematics classes is not proportionate to their representation in schools. They too often are offered little or no encouragement to enroll in advanced courses that are necessary to be successful in college.

Some reformers are calling a good education a fundamental civil right (Spring, 2001; Tyack, 2003). In a country that champions equal rights and the opportunity for an individual to improve his or her conditions, educators are thus challenged to help all students achieve academically. At the beginning of the twenty-first century, the standards movement focused on identifying what every student should know and be able to do. The federal legislation for elementary and secondary schools, *No Child Left Behind* (NCLB), requires standardized testing of students to determine how effective a school is in helping students learn. It mandates that test scores be reported to the public by "race, gender, English language proficiency, disability, and socio-economic status" (U.S. Department of Education, 2001, p. 10). The goal of NCLB is to improve the academic achievement of all students. Students in low-performing schools may transfer to a higher-performing school to improve their chances of passing tests if their school is low-performing for three years.

Education Trust (2003) reports that a large number of students are not meeting proficiency standards in the current high-stakes testing environment. Only 39% of black, 43% of Latino, and 47% of American Indian fourth graders scored at the basic level or higher on the reading test of the National Assessment of Educational Progress (NAEP) in 2003 as compared to 74% of white fourth graders. Forty-four percent of low-income students scored at the basic level or higher as compared to 75% of students from families with higher incomes. The pattern is similar on the eighth-grade mathematics test as shown in Figure 1.1.

Figure 1.1

NAEP eighth grade mathematics 2003 by race and ethnicity.

Source: Education Trust. (2003). *Achievement in America.* Retrieved August 15, 2004, from http://www2.edtrust.org/NR/rdonlyres/14FB5D33-31EF-4A9C-B55F-33184998BDD8/0/masterach2003.ppt

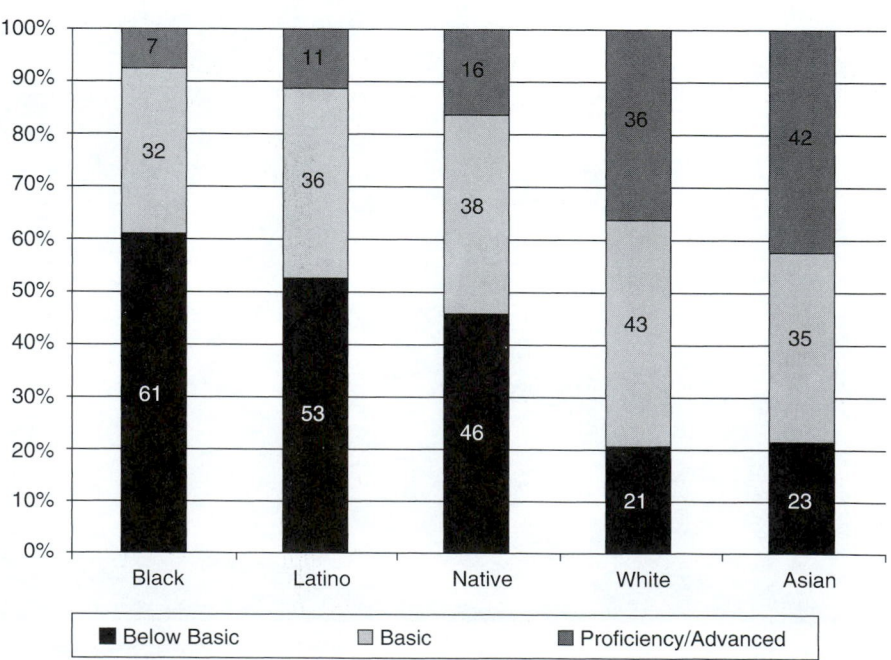

MULTICULTURAL PROFICIENCIES FOR TEACHERS

States and school districts expect new teachers to have **proficiencies** (that is, the specific knowledge, skills, and dispositions) related to multicultural education by the time they finish a teacher education program. With *No Child Left Behind*, they are obligated to hire teachers who can help low-income students, students of color, English language learners, and students with disabilities meet state standards. Just like standards for K–12 students, state agencies have identified what teachers should know and be able to do. State teacher standards for licensure reflect the national standards developed by the Interstate New Teacher Assessment and Support Consortium (INTASC).

Each of the 10 INTASC standards in Table 1.1 is further explicated by statements of the knowledge, dispositions, and performances that new teachers should be able to demonstrate for a state license to teach. Many of these multicultural proficiencies are discussed in this text; others should be addressed in other teacher education courses. For example, the INTASC standards (1992) that address multicultural proficiencies state that new teachers should:

- know about areas of exceptionality in learning—including learning disabilities, visual and perceptual difficulties, and special physical or mental challenges. (Standard 3)

Table 1.1 INTASC* Standards for New Teachers

1. The teacher candidate understands the central concepts, tools of inquiry, and structures of the discipline(s) he or she teaches and can create learning experiences that make these aspects of subject matter meaningful for students.

2. The teacher candidate understands how children learn and develop, and can provide learning opportunities that support their intellectual, social, and personal development.

3. The teacher candidate understands how students differ in their approaches to learning and creates instructional opportunities that are adapted to diverse learners.

4. The teacher candidate understands and uses a variety of instructional strategies to encourage students' development of critical thinking, problem solving, and performance skills.

5. The teacher candidate uses an understanding of individual and group motivation and behavior to create a learning environment that encourages positive social interaction, active engagement in learning, and self-motivation.

6. The teacher candidate uses knowledge of effective verbal, nonverbal, and media communication techniques to foster active inquiry, collaboration, and supportive interaction in the classroom.

7. The teacher candidate plans instruction based upon knowledge of subject matter, students, the community, and curriculum goals.

8. The teacher candidate understands and uses formal and informal assessment strategies to evaluate and ensure the continuous intellectual, social, and physical development of the learner.

9. The teacher candidate is a reflective practitioner who continually evaluates the effects of his/her choices and actions on others (students, parents, and other professionals in the learning community) and who actively seeks out opportunities to grow professionally.

10. The teacher candidate fosters relationships with school colleagues, parents, and agencies in the larger community to support students' learning and well-being.

*Interstate New Teacher Assessment and Support Consortium

- know about the process of second language acquisition and about strategies to support the learning of students whose first language is not English. (Standard 3)
- understand how students' learning is influenced by individual experiences, talents, and prior learning, as well as language, culture, family, and community values. (Standard 3)
- have a well-grounded framework for understanding cultural and community diversity and know how to learn about and incorporate students' experiences, cultures, and community resources into instruction. (Standard 3)
- understand how social groups function and influence people, and how people influence groups. (Standard 5)
- understand how cultural and gender differences can affect communication in the classroom. (Standard 6)
- understand how factors in the students' environment outside of school (e.g., family circumstances, community environments, health and economic conditions) may influence students' life and learning. (Standard 10)

In working with students who come from different ethnic, racial, language, and religious groups than the teacher, the development of dispositions that are supportive of diversity and differences is also very important. Students quickly become aware of the educators who respect their cultures, believe they can learn, and value the differences in the classroom. Examples of dispositions that the INTASC standards (1992) have outlined as important for new teachers include:

- The teacher appreciates multiple perspectives and conveys to learners how knowledge is developed from the vantage point of the knower. (Standard 1)
- The teacher believes that all children can learn at high levels and persists in helping all children achieve success. (Standard 3)
- The teacher is sensitive to community and cultural norms. (Standard 3)
- The teacher makes students feel valued for their potential as people, and helps them learn to value each other. (Standard 3)
- The teacher understands how participation supports commitment, and is committed to the expression and use of democratic values in the classroom. (Standard 5)
- The teacher appreciates the cultural dimensions of communication, responds appropriately, and seeks to foster culturally sensitive communication by and among all students in the class. (Standard 6)
- The teacher is committed to using assessment to identify student strengths and promote student growth rather than to deny students access to learning opportunities. (Standard 8)

As a new teacher, you should be able to demonstrate in your teaching the knowledge and dispositional proficiencies outlined above. The portfolio activities at the end of each chapter will provide opportunities for you to begin to collect artifacts related to your proficiency for working with a diverse student population and delivering education that is multicultural. An icon will identify the portfolio activities that could show evidence that you are meeting, in part, an INTASC standard. These artifacts could become part of the portfolio that you are developing in your teacher education program. They may be a valuable part of the portfolio that you present to a future employer, showing that you have developed the knowledge, skills, and dispositions appropriate for working effectively with a diverse student population. Finally, you may be able to further develop and refine these portfolio entries for national certification later in your teaching career.

REFLECTING ON MULTICULTURAL TEACHING

Throughout these chapters you will have the opportunity to pause and reflect on issues related to diversity and multicultural education. You may want to respond to the questions in your journal or on the book's Companion Website (**http://www. prenhall.com/gollnick**). Teachers who reflect on and analyze their own practice report that their teaching improves over time (National Board for Professional Teaching Standards, 2001). The authors encourage you to begin to develop the habit of reflecting on your practice now and to include in that reflection the multicultural proficiencies mentioned above.

From the first day of student teaching, you should begin to reflect on your effectiveness as a teacher. Are you actually helping students learn the subject and skills you are teaching? An important part of teaching is to ask what is working and what is not. Good teachers are able to change their teaching strategies when students are not learning. They do not leave any student behind, drawing on the experiences and cultures of their students to make the subject matter relevant to them. Self-reflection will be a critical skill in improving your teaching.

You can begin to develop skills for reflection while you are preparing to teach. Many teacher education programs require teacher candidates to keep journals and develop portfolios that include reflection papers. Videotaping lessons that you teach will allow you to critique your knowledge of the subject matter, interactions with students, and managing a class. The critique could be expanded to look for multicultural proficiencies. You may find it valuable to ask a colleague to periodically observe you teaching and to provide you feedback on your multicultural proficiencies. Honest feedback can lead to positive adjustments in our behavior and attitudes. *Do you interact differently with your African American and Latino students than your white students? Do you support male and female students in appropriate ways to support their learning? Do you help English language learners interact with the content? Are your expectations for the academic achievement of students from low-income families the same as students from middle-class families? How effectively are you including the student with a hearing disability in classroom activities? Are you allowing students to segregate themselves by race and/or gender in small-group work? Could your interactions with students or the content you are teaching be perceived as racist or sexist?*

Multicultural education requires an understanding of five basic concepts that support it: culture, cultural identity, pluralism, equality, and social justice. These foundational areas are discussed in the remaining sections of this chapter.

Opportunities for Reflection

Culture

Until early in the twentieth century, the term culture was used to indicate the refined ways of the elite and powerful. People who were knowledgeable in history, literature, and the fine arts were said to possess culture. No longer is culture viewed so narrowly. It helps define who we are. It influences our knowledge, beliefs, and values. It provides the blueprint that determines the way we think, feel, and behave in society. What appears as the natural and only way to learn and to interact with others is determined by our culture. Generally accepted and patterned ways of behavior are necessary for a group of people to live together. Culture imposes order and meaning on our experiences. It allows us to predict how others will behave in certain situations.

Culturally determined norms guide our language, behavior, emotions, and thinking; they are the do's and don'ts of appropriate behavior within our culture. Whereas we are comfortable with others who share the same culture because we know the meaning of their words and actions, we often misunderstand the cultural cues of persons from different cultures. Culture is so much a part of us that we do not realize that not everyone shares our way of thinking and behaving. This may be, in part, because we have never been in cultural settings different from our own. This lack of knowledge often leads to our responding to differences as personal affronts, rather than as cultural differences. These misunderstandings may appear insignificant to an observer, but they can be important to participants. Examples include how loud is too loud, how late one may arrive at an event, and how close one can stand to another without being rude or disrespectful.

Pause to Reflect 1.1

It is normal for people to experience some cultural discontinuity when they visit another country or a new city or a neighborhood in which the inhabitants are ethnically different from themselves.

- *Have you ever found yourself in a setting in which you did not know the cultural norms and were at a loss as to how to fit in?*
- *How often are you in such settings?*
- *Why did you feel uncomfortable?*
- *How were you able to overcome your awkwardness?*

To answer these questions online, go to the Pause to Reflect module for this chapter of the Companion Website.

CHARACTERISTICS OF CULTURE

We all have culture, but how did we get it? One of the characteristics of culture is that it is learned. We were born into the culture of our parents or caretakers. The way a baby is held, fed, bathed, dressed, and talked to is culturally determined and begins the process of learning the family's culture. The process continues throughout life as we interact with members of our own and other cultures.

Two similar processes interact as one learns how to act in society: **enculturation** and **socialization.** Enculturation is the process of acquiring the characteristics of a given culture and becoming competent in its language and ways of behaving and knowing. Socialization is the general process of learning the social norms of the culture. Through this process, we internalize social and cultural rules. We learn what is expected in social roles, such as mother, husband, student, or child, and in occupational roles such as teacher, banker, plumber, custodian, or politician.

Enculturation and socialization are processes initiated at birth by parents, siblings, nurses, physicians, teachers, and neighbors. These varied instructors may not identify these processes as enculturation or socialization, but they demonstrate and reward children for acceptable behaviors. We learn how to behave by observing and participating in society and culture, learning the patterns of the cultures in which we are raised.

The culture in which one is born becomes unimportant unless one is also socialized in that culture. Because culture is so internalized, we tend to confuse biological and cultural heritage. Our cultural heritage identity is not innately based on the culture in which we are born. For example, Vietnamese infants adopted by Italian American, Catholic, middle-class parents will share a cultural heritage with middle-class Italian American Catholics, rather than with Vietnamese. Observers, however, will continue to identify these individuals as Vietnamese Americans, because of physical characteristics and a lack of knowledge about their cultural experiences.

A second characteristic of culture is that it is shared. Shared cultural patterns and customs bind people together as an identifiable group and make it possible for them to live together and function with ease. An individual in the shared culture is provided with the context for identifying with the group that shares that culture. Although there may be some disagreement about certain aspects of the culture, there is a common acceptance and agreement about most aspects. Actually, most points of agreement are outside our realm of awareness. For example, we do not usually realize that the way we communicate with each other and the foods we eat are part of culture. *What are some characteristics of your cultural behavior that are different from other people you have met who do not share the same culture? What are characteristics you have observed in persons who come from a culture different than your own?*

Opportunities for Reflection

Third, culture is an adaptation. Cultures accommodate environmental conditions and available natural and technological resources. Thus, the Eskimo who lives with extreme cold, snow, ice, seals, and the sea develops a culture different from that of the Pacific Islander, who has limited land, unlimited seas, and few mineral resources. The culture of urban residents differs from that of rural residents, in part, because of the resources available in the different settings. The culture of oppressed groups differs from that of the dominant group because of power relationships within society.

Finally, culture is a dynamic system that changes continuously. Some cultures undergo constant and rapid change; others are very slow to change. Some changes, such as a new word or new hairstyle, may be relatively small and have little impact on the culture as a whole. Other changes have a dramatic impact. For instance, the introduction of technology into a culture has often produced changes far broader than the technology itself. Such changes may also alter traditional customs and beliefs. For example, the use of the computer has led to changes in the way we communicate with each other for business and personal purposes. It has even changed the way a number of young people meet each other. Instead of blind dates, they are matched by a computer dating service with people they may want to meet.

MANIFESTATIONS OF CULTURE

The cultural patterns of a group of people are determined by how the people organize and view the various components of culture. Culture is manifested in an infinite number of ways through social institutions, lived experiences, and the individual's fulfillment of psychological and basic needs. To understand how extensively our lives are affected by culture, let's examine a few of these manifestations.

Our values are initially determined by our culture. They influence the importance of prestige, status, pride, family loyalty, love of country, religious belief, and honor. Status symbols differ across cultures. For many families in the United States, accumulation of material possessions is a respected status symbol. For others, the

Our cultures are adapted to the environments in which we live and work. While the environment in rural areas is characterized by space and clean air, urban dwellers adapt to smog, crowded conditions, and public transportation.

welfare of the extended family is of utmost importance. These factors, as well as the meaning of morality or immorality, and the use of punishment and reward, and the need for higher education are determined by the value system of the culture.

Culture also manifests itself in nonverbal communication patterns. The meaning of an act or an expression must be viewed in its cultural context. The appropriateness of shaking hands, bowing, or kissing people on greeting them varies across cultures. Culture also determines the manner of walking, sitting, standing, reclining, gesturing, and dancing. We must remind ourselves not to interpret acts and expressions of people from a different cultural group as wrong or inappropriate just because they are not the same as our own. These behaviors are culturally determined. *How do you feel when someone is very direct with you? How do you feel when a person spends a lot of time finding out how you and your family are before they get down to business? How do you feel when the person with whom you are talking does not look you directly in the eyes?*

Language itself is a reflection of culture and provides a special way of looking at the world and organizing experiences that is often lost in translating words from one language to another. Many different sounds and combinations of sounds are used in the languages of different cultures. Those of us who have tried to learn a second language may have experienced difficulty in verbalizing sounds that were not part of our first language. Also, diverse language patterns found within the same language group can lead to misunderstandings. For example, one person's "joking" is heard by others as serious criticism or abuse of power; this is a particular problem when the speaker is a member of the dominant group and the listener is a member of an oppressed group or vice versa.

Language is discussed in more depth in Chapter 7.

Although we have discussed only a few daily patterns determined by culture, they are limitless. Among them are relationships of men and women, parenting, choosing a spouse, sexual relations, and division of labor in the home and society. These patterns are shared by members of the culture and often seem strange and improper to nonmembers.

ETHNOCENTRISM

Because culture helps determine the way we think, feel, and act, it becomes the lens through which we judge the world. As such, it can become an unconscious blinder to other ways of thinking, feeling, and acting. Our own culture is automatically treated as innate. It becomes the only natural way to function in the world. Even common sense in our own culture is naturally translated to common sense for the world. Other cultures are compared with ours and are evaluated by our cultural standards. It becomes difficult, if not impossible, to view another culture as separate from our own—a task that anthropologists attempt when studying other cultures.

This inability to view other cultures as equally viable alternatives for organizing reality is known as **ethnocentrism.** It is a common characteristic of cultures, whereby one's own cultural traits are viewed as natural, correct, and superior to those of another culture, whose traits are perceived as strange, inferior, or wrong. Although it is appropriate to cherish one's culture, members sometimes become closed to the possibilities of difference. Feelings of superiority over other cultures often develop.

Opportunities for Reflection

The inability to view another culture through its cultural lens, rather than through one's own cultural lens, prevents an understanding of the second culture. This inability can make it impossible to function effectively in a second culture. By overcoming one's ethnocentric view of the world, one can begin to respect other cultures and even learn to function comfortably in more than one cultural group.

Chapter 9 includes recommendations for becoming familiar with cultural groups other than your own.

CULTURAL RELATIVISM

Never judge another man until you have walked a mile in his moccasins. This North American Indian proverb suggests the importance of understanding the cultural backgrounds and experiences of other persons, rather than judging them by our own standards. The principle of cultural relativism is to see a culture as if you are a member of the culture. In essence, it is an attempt to view the world through the other individual's cultural lens. It is an acknowledgement that another person's way of doing things, while perhaps not appropriate for you, may be valid for him or her. This ability becomes more essential than ever in the world today as countries and cultures become more interdependent. In an effort to maintain positive relationships with the numerous cultural groups in the world, the United States cannot afford to ignore other cultures or to relegate them to an inferior status.

Within our own boundaries are many cultural groups that historically have been viewed and treated as inferior to the dominant Western European culture that has been the basis for most of our institutions. These intercultural misunderstandings occur even when no language barrier exists and when large components of the major culture are shared by the people involved. These misunderstandings often occur because one cultural group is largely ignorant about the culture of another group and gives the second culture little credibility. One problem is that members of one group are, for the most part, unable to describe their own cultural system, let alone another. These misunderstandings are common among the various groups in this country and are accentuated by differential status based on race, gender, class, language, religion, and ability.

Cultural relativism suggests that we need to learn more about our own culture than is commonly required. That must be followed by study about, and interaction with, other cultural groups. This intercultural process helps one know what it is like to be a member of the second culture and to view the world from that point of view. To function effectively and comfortably within a second culture, that culture must be learned.

Cultural Identity

Groups in the United States have been called **subsocieties** or **subcultures** by sociologists and anthropologists because they exist within the context of a larger society and share political and social institutions, as well as some traits and values of the dominant culture. These cultural groups provide the social identity for their members, allowing them to have distinctive cultural patterns while sharing some cultural patterns with members of the dominant culture. People who belong to the same group share traits and values that bind them together. At the same time, there is no essential or absolute identity such as female or male, American or recent immigrant, or Buddhist or Jew. Our identities in any single group are influenced by our historical and lived experiences and membership in other groups.

Numerous cultural groups exist in most nations, but the United States is exceptionally rich in the many distinct groups that make up the population. Cultural identity is based on traits and values learned as part of our ethnicity, religion, gender, age, socioeconomic status, primary language, geographic region, place of residence (e.g., rural or urban), and abilities or exceptional conditions, as shown in Figure 1.2. Each of these groups has distinguishable cultural patterns shared with others who identify themselves as members of that particular group. Although they share certain characteristics of the dominant culture with most of the U.S. population, members of these groups also have learned cultural traits, discourse patterns, ways of learning, values, and behaviors characteristic of the groups to which they belong.

Individuals sharing membership in one group may not share membership in other groups. For example, all men are members of the male culture, but not all males belong to the same ethnic, religious, or class group. On the other hand, an ethnic group may be composed of both males and females with different religious and socioeconomic backgrounds.

The interaction of these various group memberships within society begins to determine an individual's cultural identity. Membership in one cultural group can greatly influence the characteristics and values of membership in other groups. For instance, some fundamentalist religions have strictly defined expectations for women and men. Thus, membership in the religious group influences, to a great extent, the way a female behaves as a young girl, teenager, bride,

Figure 1.2

Cultural identity is based on membership in multiple cultural groups that continuously interact and influence each other. Identity within these groups is affected by interaction with the dominant group and power relations among groups in society.

Source: Johnson, J. A., Musial, D., Hall, G. E., Gollnick, D. M., & Dupuis, V. L. (2005). *Introduction to the foundations of American education.* Boston: Allyn & Bacon, p. 47.

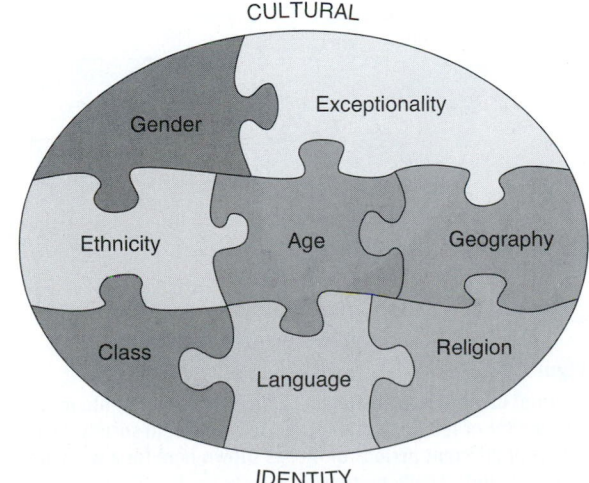

and wife, regardless of her ethnic group. One's economic level will greatly affect the quality of life for families, especially for children and the elderly in that group.

This interaction is most dynamic across race, ethnicity, class, and gender relations. The feminist movement, for example, was primarily influenced early on by white, middle-class women. The labor movement had an early history of excluding minorities and women, and their causes; in some areas, this antagonism continues. Membership in one cultural group often conflicts with the interests of another as is the case when people feel forced to define themselves as black but not a feminist.

One cultural group may have a greater influence on identity than others. This influence may change over time and depends on life experiences. We can shed aspects of our culture that no longer have meaning, and we can also adopt or adapt aspects of other cultures that were not inherent in our upbringing. Identity is not fixed. Alternative views of self and culture can be learned as cultural borders are crossed (Kuper, 2000).

The degree to which individuals identify with their cultural groups and the related cultural characteristics determines, to a great extent, their individual cultural identities. For example, a 30-year-old, middle-class, Catholic, Polish American woman in Chicago may identify strongly with being Catholic and Polish American when she is married and living in a Polish American community. However, other cultural groups may have a greater impact on her identity after she has divorced and becomes totally responsible for her financial well-being. Her femaleness and class status may become the most important representations in her identity. This change in identity is portrayed in Figure 1.3.

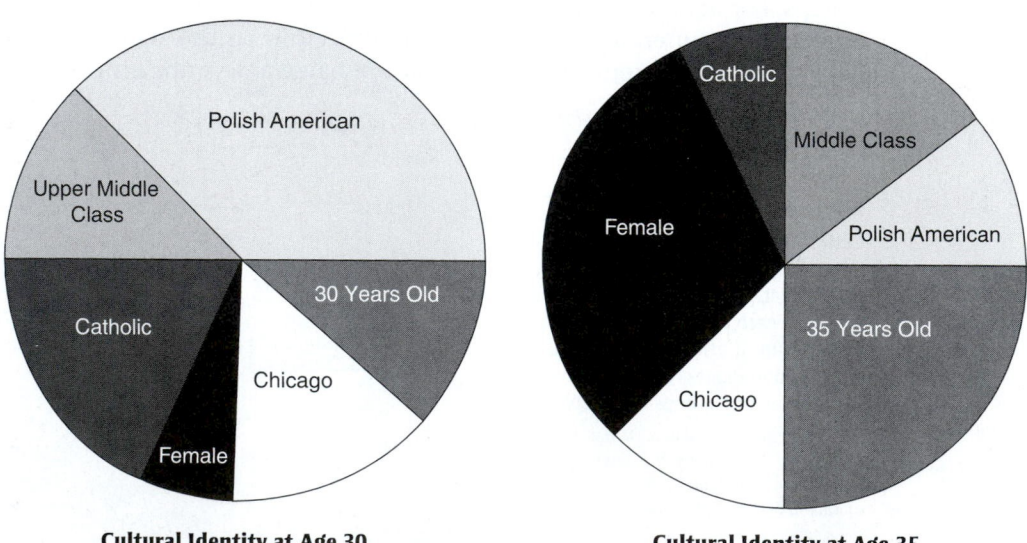

Cultural Identity at Age 30   **Cultural Identity at Age 35**

Figure 1.3

Cultural identity is adapted and changed throughout life in response to political, economic, educational, and social experiences that either alter or reinforce one's status or position in society. Membership in some cultural groups may take on more importance than others at different periods of life, as shown here for a woman when she was 30 years old and married, and again when she was 35, divorced, and a single mother.

The interaction of these cultural groups within society is also important. Most political, business, educational, and social institutions (e.g., the courts, the welfare system, the city government) have been developed and controlled by the dominant group. The values and practices that have been internalized by the dominant group also are inherent within these institutions. Members of oppressed groups are usually beholden to the dominant group to share in that power.

Assimilation policies have been reinforced in schools as the values of the dominant group are reflected in school rules and the **informal curriculum** that guides the expected behaviors and attitudes of students. The children of immigrants and persons of color are expected to learn the dominant culture. To be successful in school they are expected to communicate and behave according to the dominant cultural norms. In the past, Americanization programs for immigrants have not only taught English, but also reinforced the meaning of being American. The virtues of being American and being patriotic continue to be reinforced in many schools, especially in times of crisis such as 9/11 and conflicts with other nations.

The interaction of these cultural groups with each other and with the dominant culture begins to answer the questions "Who am I?" and "Who are my students?" The various cultural groups that educators are likely to confront in a classroom are examined in detail in Chapters 2 through 8.

Pause to Reflect 1.2

Think about the cultural groups to which you belong. How important is your membership in the groups discussed above in your cultural identity? Identify their importance by drawing a circle similar to Figure 1.3 and indicating the degree of importance each has. After you have completed your circle, answer the following questions:

- *What cultural groups are most important in your identity? Why?*
- *Why do some groups have little importance to your identity at this time?*
- *How has discrimination or the lack of it impacted the group memberships that are most important to you? Why?*

To answer these questions online, go to the Pause to Reflect module for this chapter of the Companion Website.

CW

CULTURAL BORDERS

Each of us belongs to multiple cultures (e.g., ethnic, religious, and socioeconomic groups) that help define us. As long as those differences have no status implications in which one group is treated differently from another, conflict among groups is minimal. Unfortunately, **cultural borders** are often erected between groups, and crossing them can be easy or difficult. What is valued on one side of the border may be denigrated on the other side. For example, speaking both Spanish and English may be highly rewarded in the community, but using Spanish in some schools may not be tolerated.

Educators establish cultural borders in the classroom when all activity is grounded in the teacher's culture alone. As we learn to function comfortably in different cultures, we may be able to move away from a single perspective linked to cultural domination. We may be able to cross cultural borders, bringing the students' cultures into the classroom as well. *What cultural borders may exist in a classroom with diverse students? How can you cross the borders that have developed to separate students from different cultural backgrounds in your future classroom? What will you do as a teacher to cross borders between you and your students?*

Opportunities for Reflection

BICULTURALISM AND MULTICULTURALISM

Individuals who have competencies in, and can operate successfully in, two or more different cultures are border crossers; they are bicultural or multicultural and are often bilingual or multilingual as well. Having proficiencies in multiple cultures allows a broad range of abilities on which to draw at any given time, as determined by the particular situation.

Because we participate in more than one cultural group, we have already become proficient in multiple systems for perceiving, evaluating, believing in, and acting according to the patterns of the various groups in which we participate. We often act and speak differently when we are in the community in which we were raised than when we are in a professional setting. We behave differently on a night out with members of our own sex than we do at home with the family. People with competencies in several cultures develop a fuller appreciation of the range of cultural competencies available to all people.

Many members of oppressed groups are forced to become bicultural to work or attend school and to participate effectively in their own ethnic community. Different behaviors are expected in the two settings. To be successful on the job usually requires proficiency in the ways of the dominant group. Because most schools reflect the dominant society, students are forced to adjust (or act white) if they are going to be academically successful. In contrast, most middle-class whites find almost total congruence between the culture of their family, schooling, and work. Most remain monocultural throughout their lives. They do not envision the value and possibilities of becoming competent in a different culture.

In our expanding, diverse nation, it is critical that educators themselves become at least bicultural. Understanding the cultural cues of several ethnic groups, especially oppressed groups, improves our ability to work with all students. It also helps us to be sensitive to the importance of these differences in teaching effectively. *How would you define your cultural competencies? What are your plans for becoming bicultural or multicultural?*

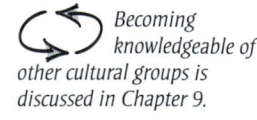 *Becoming knowledgeable of other cultural groups is discussed in Chapter 9.*

Opportunities for Reflection

Pluralism in Society

Although many similarities exist across cultures, differences exist in the ways people learn, the values they cherish, their worldviews, their behavior, and their interactions with others. There are many reasonable ways to organize our lives, approach a task, and use our languages and dialects. It is when we begin to see our cultural norms and behaviors not just as one approach, but as superior to others, that differences become politicized.

Differing and unequal power relations have a great impact on individuals' and groups' ability to define and achieve their own goals. These differences among and within groups can lead not only to misunderstandings and misperceptions, but also to conflict. Cultural differences sometimes result in political alliances that respond to the real and perceived realities of domination or subordination faced by the group. The result may be strong feelings of patriotism or group solidarity that expand into armed conflicts across nations, tribes, religious communities, or ethnic groups. White men sometimes are manifested in anti-Semitic symbols and actions, cross burnings, gay bashing, and sexual harassment.

Conflicts between groups are usually based on the groups' differential status and value in society. The alienation and marginalization that many powerless groups experience can lead to groups accentuating their differences, especially to separate themselves from the dominant group. Groups sometimes construct their own identities in terms of others. For example, whites often do not think of themselves as white, except as different from blacks. Males define themselves in opposition to female. White men have been socialized to see themselves as being at the center of a world in which they are privileging themselves in relation to others—women and African Americans.

In developing an understanding of differences and **otherness,** we can begin to change our simplistic binary approaches of us/them, dominant/subordinate, good/bad, and right/wrong. We begin to realize that a plurality of truths are as reasonable as our own. We seek out others for dialogue and understanding, rather than speak about and for them. We can begin to move from exercising power over others to sharing power with others.

THE DOMINANT CULTURE

U.S. political and social institutions have evolved from an Anglo-Saxon or Western European tradition. The English language is a polyglot of the languages spoken by the various conquerors and rulers of Great Britain throughout history. The legal system is derived from English common law. The political system of democratic elections comes from France and England. The middle-class value system has been modified from a European system. Even our way of thinking, at least the way it is rewarded in school, is based on Socrates' linear system of logic.

Formal institutions, such as governments, schools, social welfare, banks, and businesses, affect many aspects of our lives. Because of the strong Anglo-Saxon

Members of Congress do not yet represent the diversity of the nation's population.

influence on these institutions, the dominant cultural influence on the United States also has been identified as Anglo-Saxon, or Western European. More specifically, the major cultural influence on the United States, particularly on its institutions, has been White, Anglo-Saxon, and Protestant (WASP). But no longer is the dominant group composed only of WASPs. Instead, most members of the ethnically diverse middle class have adopted traditionally WASP characteristics and values that provide the framework for the dominant culture.

Although most of our institutions still function under the strong influence of their WASP roots, many other aspects of American life have been influenced by the numerous cultural groups that have come to comprise the U.S. population. Think about the different food we eat, or at least try: Chinese, Indian, Mexican, soul food, Italian, Caribbean, and Japanese. Young people of many cultures choose clothing that is influenced by hip-hop and black culture. But, more important are the contributions made to society by individuals from different cultural groups in the fields of science, the arts, literature, athletics, engineering, architecture, politics, and all others. *What American Indians, African Americans, Asian Americans, and Latino Americans who have made significant contributions to society can you name? What major contributions have women made? How many Jews and Muslims and their contributions can you identify?*

Opportunities for Reflection

Although the United States has an agrarian tradition, the population now is primarily located in metropolitan areas and small towns. The country has mineral and soil wealth, elaborate technology, and a wealth of manufactured goods. Mass education and mass communication are ways of life. Americans are regulated by clocks and calendars, rather than by seas and the sun. Time is used to organize most activities of life. Most Americans are employees whose salaries or wages are paid by large, complex, impersonal institutions. Work is done regularly, purposefully, and sometimes grimly. In contrast, play is fun—an outlet from work. Money is the denominator of exchange. Necessities of life are purchased, rather than produced. Achievement and success are measured by the quantity of material goods purchased. Religious beliefs are concerned with general morality.

The overpowering value of the dominant group is **individualism,** which is characterized by the belief that every individual is his or her own master, is in control of his or her own destiny, and will advance and regress in society only according to his or her own efforts (Bellah, Madsen, Sullivan, Swidler, & Tipton, 1996). This individualism is grounded in the Western worldview that individuals can control both nature and their destiny. Traits that emphasize this core value include industriousness, ambition, competitiveness, self-reliance, independence, appreciation of the good life, and the perception of humans as separate from, and superior to, nature. The acquisition of such possessions as the latest technology gadget, cars, boats, and homes measures success and achievement.

Another core value is **freedom.** Freedom is defined by the dominant group, however, as not having others determine their values, ideas, or behaviors (Bellah et al., 1996). Relations with other people inside and outside their group are often impersonal. Communications may be very direct or confrontational. Many members of the dominant group rely more on associations of common interest than on strong kinship ties. The nuclear family is the basic kinship unit. Values tend to be absolute (e.g., right or wrong, moral or immoral), rather than range along a continuum of degrees of right and wrong. Personal life and community affairs are based on principles of right and wrong, rather than on shame, dishonor, or ridicule. Youthfulness is also emphasized in advertisements and commercials. Men and women use Botox and have plastic surgery to try to maintain their youthfulness. Many U.S. citizens, especially if they are middle-class, share these traits and values to some degree. They are patterns that are privileged in institutions such as schools. They are values to which the dominant society expects all citizens to adhere.

Privilege.   Most male members of the dominant group do not usually think about themselves as white, financially secure, Christian, English-speaking, or heterosexual. They have not seen themselves as privileged in society and do not view themselves as oppressors of others. Most schools and teachers do not recognize the inequality, racism, and powerlessness that work against the success of students of color, girls, English language learners, non-Christians, students from low-income families, and students with disabilities. Most members of the dominant group have not had the opportunity to explore their own whiteness and other privileged positions in society. They often have not studied or interacted with groups to which they do not belong. Therefore, they have been unable to locate themselves within the continuum of power and inequality in society.

Pause to Reflect 1.3

How much do you know about the power you have because of your race? How do you respond to the following questions?

- *Can you turn on the television or open the newspaper and see people of your race widely represented?*
- *Can you speak in public to a male group without putting your race [or gender] on trial?*
- *Can you perform well on a project without being called a credit to your race?*
- *Are you ever asked to speak for all people of your race?*
- *Can you be pretty much sure that if you ask to talk to "the person in charge" that you will find a person of your same race?*
- *When you are stopped for a traffic violation, do you have to worry that you have been racially profiled?*
- *When you shop, are you followed around by a clerk or security person?*

To answer these questions online, go to the Pause to Reflect module for this chapter of the Companion Website.

Source: McIntosh, P. (2004). White privilege: Unpacking the invisible knapsack. In M. L. Andersen & P. H. Collins (Eds.), *Race, class, and gender* (pp. 103–108). Belmont, CA: Wadsworth.

In contrast to whites, members of oppressed groups are constantly confronted with the difference of their race, language, class, religion, gender, disability, and/or homosexuality. The degree of identification with the characteristics of the dominant culture depends, in part, on how much an individual must interact with society's formal institutions for economic support and subsistence. The more dependence on these institutions, the greater the degree of sharing, or of being forced to adopt, the common traits and values of the dominant group.

These opposing perspectives are situated in one's real or perceived position of privilege or lack of privilege in society. They have led, in recent years, to public debates on college campuses about affirmative action to ensure diversity, and diversity in the common core of the college curriculum. Members of oppressed groups argue that their cultures are not reflected in a curriculum that includes only the great books of Western European thought. The traditionalists, who are predominantly representatives of the dominant group, often invoke nationalism and patriotism in their calls to retain the purity of the Western canon and promote homogeneity in society. Proponents of a common core curriculum that includes the voices of women, people of color, and religions other than Christianity also include many members of the dominant group who value differences and multiple perspectives.

The question appears to be whose culture will be reflected in the elementary and secondary, as well as college, curriculum. Those who call for a curriculum and textbooks that reflect only their history and experiences view their culture as superior to all others. Thus, they and their culture become privileged over others in schools and other institutions in society. They do not see themselves as different; to them, diversity refers only to members of other groups in society. To be successful, members of the dominant group are not required to learn to function effectively in a second culture as are members of oppressed groups. The privileged curriculum reinforces this pattern. It is the members of the oppressed groups who must learn the culture and history of the dominant group without the opportunity to study their own cultural group or to validate the importance of their own history and lived experiences. It is as if they do not belong. This feeling may lead to **marginalization** and **alienation** from school as students are not accepted by the dominant group and do not feel a part of the school culture.

See Chapter 9 for strategies on incorporating diverse groups and multiple perspectives into the curriculum.

Acculturation.   Many groups that immigrated during the twentieth century have become acculturated. **Acculturation** is the process of adopting the dominant group's cultural patterns. Although some groups have tried to maintain the original culture, it is usually in vain as children go to school and participate in the larger society. Continuous and firsthand contacts with the dominant group usually result in subsequent changes in the original cultural patterns of either or both groups. The rapidity and success of the acculturation process depends on several factors, including location and discrimination. If a minority group is spatially isolated and segregated (whether voluntarily or not) in a rural area, as is the case with many American Indians on reservations, the acculturation process is very slow. Unusually marked discrimination such as that faced by oppressed groups, especially African Americans, Native Americans, and Mexican Americans, deprives group members of educational and occupational opportunities and primary relationships with members of the dominant group (Alba & Nee, 2003; Rumbaut & Portes, 2001). The discrimination makes it more difficult to acculturate if they choose to do so.

It is important to note that acculturation is determined, in part, by the individual or family; that is, they can decide how much they want to dress, speak, and behave like members of the dominant group. After conducting a longitudinal study of immigrants in southern California and southern Florida, Rumbaut and Portes (2001) found three acculturation patterns among immigrants: consonant, dissonant, and selective. In consonant acculturation, parents and children learn the language and culture of the community in which they live at approximately the same time. In dissonant acculturation, children learn English and the new culture while parents retain their native language and culture, often leading to conflict within the family and decreasing parental authority. Fluent bilingualism in the second generation is an outcome of selective acculturation in which the children of immigrants learn the dominant culture and language, but retain significant elements of their native culture.

Members of many groups, however, have little choice if they want to share the American dream of success. Many members have had to give up native languages and behaviors or hide them at home. However, acculturation does not guarantee acceptance by the dominant group. Most members of oppressed groups, especially those of color, have not been permitted to assimilate fully into society even though they have adopted the values and behaviors of the dominant group.

ASSIMILATION

Assimilation occurs when a group's distinctive cultural patterns either become part of the dominant culture or disappear as the group adopts the dominant culture. Structural assimilation occurs when the dominant group shares primary group relationships with the second group, including membership in the same cliques and social clubs; members of the two groups intermarry; and the two groups are treated equally within society. Assimilation appears to be relevant for voluntary immigrants, particularly if they are white, but does not apply to **involuntary immigrants** who were forced to come to this country through slavery or conquest of the area in which they lived. These families have been in the country for generations. Except for white European immigrants, only limited **structural assimilation** has occurred as shown by the small number of intermarriages and primary relationships with whites. On the other hand, marriage across groups is fairly common across white ethnic groups and Judeo-Christian religious affiliations. For example, 57% of Jews have married outside of their religion over the past two decades. Only one third of Asian Americans and 30% of Latinos marry outside of their group. Only 2% of whites and 4% of African Americans were marrying outside their group at the end of the twentieth century (Alba, 2000). Thus, success in becoming acculturated has not led to structural assimilation for many groups. Acculturation has neither eliminated prejudice and discrimination nor led to large-scale intermarriage with the dominant group. If the assimilation process is effective, it leads to the disappearance of a cultural group that is distinct from the dominant group, and, in the process, changes the dominant group as well.

As Portes and Rumbaut (2001) studied the second generation of recent immigrants, they found that the degree of their assimilation differed. The history and experiences of the first-generation immigrant varied across and within groups. The pace of acculturation among parents and children as described above influenced assimilation with consonant acculturation being the most rapid. A critical factor is the cultural and economic barriers faced by second-generation youth. Young people who can see upward mobility in their future are more likely to assimilate. Finally, some groups have greater family and community resources for confronting the barriers that society establishes for immigrants. "In a high-technology society, immigrant families who bring large volumes of human and cultural capital obviously have an advantage over low-wage laborers with little formal schooling" (Alba & Nee, 2003, p. 15).

Governmental support of new immigrants also has an influence on a group's desire and ability to assimilate (Portes & Rumbaut, 2001). Some groups have been actively encouraged to immigrate and have been warmly welcomed by society. Favored refugee groups include the Vietnamese and Cubans. Other immigrant groups such as Chinese, Middle Easterners, and Europeans have been passively accepted by society without favoritism, but also with limited discrimination. Discrimination against blacks and Latinos has made it difficult for many Haitians, Mexican Americans, and Central Americans to easily assimilate into the dominant culture. The immigrants and their children in this last group are likely to confront segmented or downward assimilation in which they are not able to improve their economic status (Alba & Nee, 2003; Rumbaut & Portes, 2001). Educational attainment of immigrant children in the excluded groups is affected by the persistence of racial discrimination, the growing inequality of workers, and the consolidation of oppressed populations in the inner city (Portes & Rumbaut, 2001).

Should Patriotism Be a School Requirement?

What does it mean to be an American? Many schools are revitalizing the teaching of patriotism in elementary schools. First graders in some schools are being taught to love their country along with reading and writing. Greenbriar East Elementary School in Fairfax County outside of Washington, DC, hosts an annual Patriotic Salute in which their diverse student population sings "God Bless America," "This Land Is Your Land," and "We're Glad We Live in the U.S.A." Patriotic programs have included essay contests on being an American and assemblies to honor veterans. Other schools avoid interjecting patriotism into their curriculum, viewing it as a personal responsibility.

At times of crisis such as 9/11 and armed conflicts with other nations, state legislators and school board members are sometimes inclined to require students to recite the Pledge of Allegiance, sing the national anthem, or participate in patriotic activities on a daily or regular basis. However, these practices begin to infringe on the rights of groups and do not have unanimous support in many communities. For instance, the Supreme Court declared early last century that Jehovah Witness students could not be forced to say the Pledge of Allegiance.

Do you think patriotism should be required in schools?

FOR

- Students need to understand what it means to be American.

- Schools have an obligation to help students embrace American democracy.

- Students need to learn to appreciate the United States.

AGAINST

- Civics instruction should be about personal responsibility, not instilling patriotism.

- Democracy is about making informed, thoughtful choices.

- Loving your country is not something that should be indoctrinated.

Questions

1. *Why do some school districts feel obligated to push patriotism in their schools?*
2. *How might schools address issues of good citizenship without offending parents who find the focus on patriotism inappropriate?*
3. *What do you think is an appropriate balance between helping students be good citizens and overt patriotism?*

To answer these questions online, go to the Focus Your Cultural Lens: Debate module for this chapter of the Companion Website.

Source: Kalita, S. M. (2004, June 8). A blending of patriotism, native pride: In diverse Fairfax school, civics starts in 1st grade. *The Washington Post*, p. B.01.

Some immigrant groups try to preserve their native cultures; others have assimilation as their goal. Nevertheless, assimilation does not characterize the contemporary U.S. scene. We are a nation of many cultural groups distinguished by our ethnicity, gender, class, language, age, and religion. At the same time, America's desire to assimilate different cultural groups affects the nation's political, social, and educational policies and practices.

CULTURAL PLURALISM

A society organized according to a theory of **cultural pluralism** allows two or more distinct groups to function separately and equally without requiring any assimilation of one into the other. Refusing or not being permitted to assimilate into the dominant American culture, many immigrants and ethnic groups maintain their own unique ethnic communities and enclaves. For most oppressed ethnic and religious groups, primary-group contacts have been maintained within the group, rather than across cultural groups as required in structural assimilation. Cross-cultural contacts occur primarily at the secondary level—in work settings and in interaction with political and civic institutions. Members of oppressed groups develop institutions, agencies, and power structures for services within their ethnic communities. Enclaves such as Little Italy, Chinatown, Harlem, Korea Town, East Los Angeles, Amish and Hutterite communities, and some settlements in rural areas are a few examples. In some places, persons who are blind or deaf have established communities in which they feel comfortable with others of the same cultural group who have the same disability.

The commitment to the value of cultural pluralism is not broadly supported by individuals and groups in society. American Indian nations within the United States come the closest to reflecting cultural pluralism in that they have their own political, economic, and educational systems. For most American Indians, however, the economic, political, and educational opportunities do not approach equality with the dominant group. For a discussion of the relationship of American Indians to dominant society, view the clip on majority culture on the CD, *Culturally Responsive Teaching and Leading: Studies to Improve Awareness and Practice.* In a cultural pluralistic society, the retention of diverse ethnic and religious groups would be promoted in schools and society. In a culturally plural society, power and resources would be shared somewhat equitably across groups.

The problem is that dominant groups are not usually willing to share their power and wealth with others. Some critics of the system believe that the dominant group uses a strategy of divide and conquer to keep ethnic groups segregated and fighting among themselves for the few resources available. Others believe that a societal goal should be integration of cultural groups and the promotion of more equality across groups through a united front. Still others believe that individuals should be able to maintain their ethnic identities while participating in the common culture. These beliefs are not necessarily discrete from one another; for example, society could be integrated, but members would not be required to relinquish their ethnic identities. At the same time, an integrated society can lead to greater assimilation in that primary contacts across cultural groups are more likely.

CULTURAL CHOICE

Neither assimilation nor cultural pluralism adequately addresses the diversity that exists in the United States. While advocates of cultural pluralism treat pluralism and democracy as complements, critics have charged that it does not meet one of the key democratic values—that of calling for free choice for individuals as well as groups. The practice of cultural choice allows individuals the right to choose the importance of their ascribed statuses such as gender, race ethnicity, and age in determining who they are.

As individual choice and mobility across groups increase, discrimination against cultural groups is likely to decrease as well. We will move toward an open society in which cultural group membership may influence who an individual is, but becomes irrelevant in public interactions, especially as the reason for institutional discrimination. Cultural differences will become valued, respected, and encouraged to flourish.

Equality and Social Justice in a Democracy

The United States is a **democracy** in which the people exercise their power directly or indirectly through elected representatives. Schools and the mass media teach us that our democracy is one to be emulated by the rest of the world. A democracy should promote the good of all its citizens. Thus, the Constitution was fashioned with a coherent set of "checks and balances" to limit the systematic abuse of power. **Egalitarianism**—the belief in social, political, and economic rights and privileges for all people—is espoused as a key principle on which democracy is based. All citizens are expected to have a voice. Power should be shared among groups, and no one group should continuously dominate the economic, political, social, and cultural life of the country. Society and government, though not perfect, are promoted as allowing mass participation and steady advancement toward a more prosperous and egalitarian society.

One strength of a democracy is that citizens should be able to bring many perspectives, based on their own histories and experiences, to bear on policy questions and practices. Thus, to disagree is acceptable as long as we are able to communicate with each other openly and without fear of reprisal. Further, we expect that no single right way will be forced on us. For the most part, we would rather struggle with multiple perspectives and actions and determine what is best for us as individuals within this democratic society.

At the same time, a democracy expects its citizens to be concerned about more than just their own individual freedoms. They should be involved in a broader community of interest. In the classic *Democracy and Education,* philosopher and educator John Dewey (1916/1966) suggested that the emphasis should be on what binds us together in cooperative pursuits and results, regardless of the nation or our group alliance and membership. He raised concern about our possible stratification into separate classes and called for "intellectual opportunities [to be] accessible to all on equitable and easy terms" (p. 88).

The emphasis on individualism in the dominant culture provides a dilemma for educators who promote democratic practice. In many classrooms, individualism is supported through competitive activities in which individual achievement is rewarded. A democratic classroom promotes working together across groups. Responsibility and leadership is shared by students and teachers as students practice being active participants in a democratic setting.

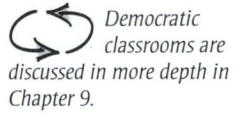 *Democratic classrooms are discussed in more depth in Chapter 9.*

Both individualism and equality have long been central themes of political discourse in a democratic society. The meaning of equality within our society varies according to one's assumptions about humankind and human existence. At least two sets of beliefs govern the ideologies of equality and inequality. The first accepts inequality as inevitable and promotes **meritocracy,** which is a system based on the belief that an individual's achievements are due to their own personal merits and hard work and that the people who achieve at the highest levels deserve the greatest social and financial rewards. It stresses the right of access to society's resources as a necessary condition for equal rights to life, liberty, and happiness. The focus is on individualism and the individual's right to pursue happiness and obtain personal resources. The second set of beliefs supports a much greater degree of equality across groups in society. Persons who believe in equality care about people who have fewer resources and develop policies that allow more people to share in the nation's wealth.

This dilemma forces some people to promote some equality while preventing any real equity from occurring. Affirmative action, for example, is viewed by its critics as evidence of group welfare gaining precedence over individual achievement. The outcry against affirmative action suggests that racism no longer exists and that decisions about employment, promotion, and so forth are no longer influenced by racism and sexism. Whites filing for reverse discrimination decisions believe that their individual rights to an education at a select school, a promotion, or a job should be based solely on their individual achievement. They believe that other factors such as income (or lack of), ethnicity, race, or gender should not be valued in the process. They overlook the fact that they have been privileged throughout their lives because of their race and family income. Even though egalitarianism is an often-espoused goal of democracy in the United States, the inequities that actually exist in society are continually overlooked. Thus, equality must be an essential tenet of multicultural education.

INDIVIDUALISM AND MERITOCRACY

Proponents of meritocracy accept the theories of sociobiology or functionalism or both, in which inequalities are viewed as natural outcomes of individual differences. They believe that everyone has the opportunity to be successful if they just work hard enough. They give little credit to family conditions, such as being born in a wealthy family, as a head start for success. Members of oppressed groups usually are seen as inferior, and their hardships blamed on their personal characteristics rather than societal constraints or discrimination.

A society based on meritocracy ensures that the ablest and most meritorious, ambitious, hardworking, and talented individuals will acquire the most, achieve the most, and become society's leaders. Proponents accept the resulting inequalities as tolerable, fair, and just. They are viewed as a necessary consequence of equality of opportunity and roughly in proportion to inequalities of merit.

The belief system that undergirds meritocracy has at least three dimensions that are consistent with dominant values. First, the individual is valued over the group. The individual has the qualities, ambitions, and talent to achieve at the highest levels in society. Popular stories expound this ideology as they describe the poor im-

Students do not start life with an equal chance to succeed. Because of family income and wealth, some students have access to resources and experiences in their homes, communities, and often schools that are not available to most low-income students.

migrant who arrived on U.S. shores with nothing, set up a vegetable stand to eke out a living, and became the millionaire owner of a chain of grocery stores.

The second dimension stresses differences through competition. IQ and achievement tests are used throughout schooling to help measure differences. Students and adults are rewarded for outstanding grades, athletic ability, and artistic accomplishment.

The third dimension emphasizes internal characteristics, such as motivation, intuition, and character, that have been internalized by the individual. External conditions, such as racism and poverty, are to be overcome by the individual; they are not accepted as contributors to an individual's lack of success.

Equal educational opportunity, or equal access to schooling, applies this principle to education. All students are to be provided with equal educational opportunities that supposedly will give them similar chances for success or failure. Proponents of this approach believe it is the individual's responsibility to use those opportunities to his or her advantage in obtaining life's resources and benefits. Critics of meritocracy would point out that children of low-income families do not start with the same chances for success in life as children from affluent families. Thus, competition is unequal from birth. The chances of the affluent child being educationally and financially successful are much greater than for the low-income child. Those with advantages at birth are almost always able to hold onto and extend those advantages throughout their lives. *Do you believe the above statements are true? Why? Why not? Can you think of examples of how meritocracy has affected your life? As a teacher, what can you do to help low-income students gain some advantages?*

Opportunities for Reflection

EQUALITY

With the persistence of racism, poverty, unemployment, and inequality in major social systems such as education and health, many persons have found it difficult to reconcile daily realities with the publicized egalitarianism that characterizes the public rhetoric. These persons view U.S. society as comprised of institutions and an economic system that represents the interests of the privileged few, rather than the pluralistic majority. Even where institutions, laws, and processes have the appearance of equal access, benefit, and protection, they are almost always enforced in highly discriminatory ways. These patterns of **inequality** are not the product of corrupt individuals as such, but rather are a reflection of how resources of economics, political power, and cultural and social dominance are built into the entire political-economic system.

Even in the optimistic view that some degree of equality can be achieved, inequality is also expected. Not all resources can be redistributed so that every individual has an equal amount, nor should all individuals expect equal compensation for the work they do. The underlying belief, however, is that there need not be the huge disparities of income, wealth, and power that currently exist. Equality does suggest fairness in the distribution of the conditions and goods that affect the well-being of all children and families. It is fostered by policies for full employment, wages that prevent families from living in poverty, and child care for all children.

Critics decry the perceived socialism as being against the democratic foundations that undergird the nation. They believe that equality of resources and societal ben-

 ## VIDEO INSIGHT

School Busing

For decades the remedy for segregation has been school busing. The goals of integrating schools have been racial balance and access to better schools, new equipment, and new opportunities for all students. Now some African American families are criticizing the busing experiment as a failure and are requesting a "separate but equal" education for their children in their own neighborhoods.

In this video segment, you will see proponents of this movement in Oklahoma City and in other cities across the country say their children have been subjected to segregated settings within integrated schools. African American children are often assigned to remedial classes or lower academic tracks and do not get exposure to the services and resources that other students receive. In addition, because these schools are not close to home, it is difficult for parents to be involved or even present if there is a problem or an emergency at school.

1. *After viewing this video segment, how have your views on busing changed?*

2. *Are the people who support this movement to neighborhood schools forsaking the efforts of the countless individuals who have worked so hard for integration in our schools?*

3. *History has shown us that "separate but equal" has not worked. Is this because separate, by definition, is not equal?*

4. *What are your views on the issue of "separate but equal"?*

5. *Do you think we now have the resources, support, and technology to make "separate but equal" a reality?*

To answer these questions online, go to the ABC News Video Insight module for this chapter of the Companion Website.

efits would undermine the capitalist system that allows a few individuals to acquire the great majority of those resources. They warn that equality of results would limit freedom and liberty for individuals.

Equality should mean more than just providing oppressed group members with an equal chance or equal opportunity. One proposal is that equal results should be the goal. These results might be more equal achievement by students of both oppressed and dominant groups and similar rates of dropping out of school, college attendance, and college completion by different ethnic, racial, gender, and class populations.

Traditionally, the belief has been that education can overcome the inequalities that exist in society. The role of education in reducing the amount of occupation and income inequality may be limited, however. School reform has not yet led to significant social changes outside the schools. Equalizing educational opportunity has had very little impact on making adults more equal. Providing equal educational opportunities for all students does not guarantee equal results at the end of high school or college. It does not yet provide equal access to jobs and income across groups. To ensure equality in schools we would guarantee that students in impoverished schools have teachers who are as highly qualified as the teachers in wealthy school districts. Equality requires financial support for providing quality instruction in environments that are conducive to learning to all students. More, not less, money may be needed to ensure equity in educational results by the children of dominant groups and other groups.

To establish equality, major changes in society must take place. This process is very difficult when power is held by those who believe in a meritocratic system. Those in power defend the status quo and are not anxious to relinquish the privileges they have gained. In contrast, the advocates for equality support the dictum: *from each according to his or her ability, to each according to his or her needs.*

Pause to Reflect 1.4

How do you view equality in society and schooling? Check the statements below that best describe your perceptions.

- *The ablest and most meritorious, ambitious, hardworking, and talented individuals should acquire the most, achieve the most, and become society's leaders.*
- *The individual is more important than the group.*
- *The U.S. economic system represents the interests of a privileged few, rather than those of the pluralistic majority.*
- *Huge disparities of income, wealth, and power should not exist in this country.*
- *It is the student's responsibility to get as much out of school as possible.*
- *Differences measured on standardized tests are more important than similarities.*
- *External conditions, such as racism and poverty, should be overcome by the individual.*
- *Students from all cultural groups can be academically successful.*
- *Tracking of students promotes inequality.*
- *Teachers can make a difference in the academic success of students.*

Which of these statements are most related to a belief in meritocracy, and which to a belief in equality?

To answer these questions online, go to the Pause to Reflect module for this chapter of the Companion Website. **CW**

SOCIAL JUSTICE

Social justice is another element of democracy that expects citizens to provide for those persons in society who are not as advantaged as others. To not ensure that they are treated equitably and with dignity is a disservice to democracy. Dewey (1966) called for social justice when he said, "What the best and wisest parent wants for his [or her] own child, that must the community want for all of its children. Any other ideal for our schools is narrow and unlovely; acted upon, it destroys our democracy" (p. 3). In schools, social justice requires a critique of practices that interfere with equity across groups. Social and economic inequities that prevent students from learning and participating effectively in schools must be confronted (Apple, 2004). In a democratic society that is also capitalistic in nature, there are always inequities. In the United States, it would be difficult to recall a period of time when there were no individuals with enormous wealth and none who lived in abject poverty. Most who live in this country do so by choice. The majority of the world's immigrants choose the United States, in part, because it is perceived as the land of opportunities and freedom from oppression.

Enormous disparities exist, however, between the very wealthy and the very poor. The very wealthy have accumulated vast resources. At the same time, the very poor cannot even meet their basic needs. They are unable to obtain the barest essentials for shelter, food, or medical care. Some suffer from lack of heat in the winter and lack of cooling in the very hot summers. Every year, there are reports of elderly, low-income people who die from exposure to excessive heat or cold. This is inconceivable for many Americans who simply turn their thermostats to the precise temperature that will meet their comfort level. Every day, children from poor families come to school with insufficient sleep because of the physical discomforts of their homes, with inadequate clothing, and with empty stomachs. Tens of thousands suffer from malnutrition and no dental care. When they are sick, many go untreated. Under these conditions, it is difficult, at best, to function well in an academic setting.

Civil unrest has almost always been precipitated by the disenfranchised who have no realistic hope of extricating themselves from lives of despair. Children of affluent members of society do not form street gangs; they are typically much too busy enjoying the good life that prosperity brings. The street gangs of New York, Chicago, and Los Angeles are comprised almost exclusively of young individuals who are poor, embittered, and disenfranchised.

Those who have the power to bring about meaningful change in society are usually the more affluent. They have the resources and connections to make things happen. Yet, those who have such power are reluctant to make any significant changes that threaten to diminish their position in society. To bring about truly meaningful change requires paradigm shifts. Even the middle class may be reluctant to make changes if a change in the status quo diminishes their position. Changes are supported only if they provide benefits to the dominant group or do not affect them negatively.

Meaningful change in society requires a universal social consciousness. It requires, to some extent, a willingness of the citizenry to explore the means of redistributing some of the benefits of a democratic society. Effective redistribution would require that some who have considerable wealth provide a greater share in the effort to eliminate poverty and its concomitant effects. Even the middle class would be expected to make proportionate sacrifices. The end result could be a society in which everyone has a decent place to sleep, no child comes to school hungry, and appropriate health care is available to all.

Those who possess special skills and talents will likely continue to accrue, in varying degrees, the benefits of a democratic society. In the United States, most citizens want incentives for achievements. In such a society, however, no one need be disenfranchised, and the allure of gangs and other means of expressing discontent will be diminished.

One of the problems is that people of color, women, and low-income groups have long been recipients of institutional discrimination in the United States. As a result, many exhibit anger at, dissatisfaction with, and alienation from the system. Racism, sexism, and class inequality characterize societies in which the disparities of income, wealth, and power are great. Competition over resources increases conflicts among the various groups. Thus, fundamental changes in the structure of society must accompany changes in attitudes if border crossings are to become a reality. Addressing issues of equality is a key to such changes.

OBSTACLES TO EQUALITY

Prejudice and **discrimination** stem from a combination of several factors related to us and them. Persons who are prejudiced have an aversion to members of a cultural group other than their own. Discrimination leads to the denial of the privileges and rewards to members of oppressed groups. Prejudice can result when people lack an understanding of the history, experiences, values, and perceptions of ethnic groups other than their own. Members of groups are **stereotyped** when others apply to them generalizations about the group without consideration of individual differences within the group. Groups other than our own are often judged according to the standards and values of our own group. Negative attributes are assigned to members of other ethnic groups. The qualities and experiences of other groups are believed to be inferior to one's own. In other words, prejudice and discrimination are forms of ethnocentrism.

Prejudice.   Prejudice manifests itself in feelings of anger, fear, hatred, and distrust about members of a certain group. These attitudes are often translated into fear of walking in the group's neighborhood, fear of being robbed or hurt by group members, distrust of a merchant from the group, anger at any advantages that group members may be perceived as receiving, and fear that housing prices will be deflated if someone from that group moves next door.

Some members of all groups possess negative stereotypes of others. For example, many African Americans and Latinos believe that whites are bigoted, bossy, and unwilling to share power. In a two-year study of teachers in a staff development project, Sleeter (1992) found that many white teachers "associated people of color—and particularly African Americans and Latinos—with dysfunctional families and communities, and lack of ability and motivation" (p. 162). These negative stereotypes may describe some members of most groups, but have been unfairly extended as characteristics of most members of the group.

Although prejudice may not always directly hurt members of a group, it can be easily translated into behavior that does harm them. An ideology based on aversion to a group and perceived superiority undergirds the activities of groups such as the neo-Nazis, Ku Klux Klan, skinheads, and other white racist groups that currently exist in society. A prejudiced teacher may hold high academic expectations for students of one group and low expectations for students of another group. Such prejudice could lead to inappropriate placement of students in gifted or special education programs.

For more information on prejudice and racism, see Chapter 3. The over-representation of students in special education and gifted classes based on their socioeconomic and racial groups is discussed in Chapter 5.

Discrimination. Whereas prejudice focuses on attitudes, discrimination focuses on behavior. Discrimination occurs at two levels: individual and institutional. Individual discrimination is attributed to, or influenced by, prejudice. Individuals discriminate against a member of a group for at least two reasons: (1) either they have strong prejudicial, or bigoted, feelings about the group, or (2) they believe that society demands they discriminate. For example, realtors, personnel managers, receptionists, and membership chairpersons all work directly with individuals. Their own personal attitudes about members of certain groups can influence whether a house is sold, a job is offered, a loan is granted, an appointment is made, a meal is served, or a membership is extended to a member of the group. The action of these individuals can prevent others from gaining the experiences and economic advantages that these activities offer.

An individual has less control in the other form of discrimination; institutional discrimination cannot be attributed to prejudicial attitudes. It refers to the effects of inequalities that have been integrated into the system-wide operation of a society through legislation and practices that ensure benefits to some groups and not to others. Laws that disproportionately limit immigration to people from specific countries are one example. Other examples include practices that lead to a disproportionately large number of African Americans being incarcerated, single low-income mothers being denied adequate prenatal care, and children in low-income neighborhoods suffering disproportionately from asthma as a result of poor environmental conditions in their neighborhoods.

We have grown up in a society that has inherently discriminated against persons of color and women since the first European Americans arrived. Throughout our lives, we have participated in societal institutions, including schools, Social Security, transportation, welfare, and housing patterns. We often do not realize the extent to which members of different groups receive the benefits and privileges of these institutions. Because we may believe that we have never been discriminated against, we should not assume that others do not suffer from discrimination.

Many individuals might argue that institutional discrimination no longer exists because today's laws require equal access to the benefits of society. As a result, they believe that individuals from all groups have had equal opportunities to be successful. They fight against group rights that lead to what is perceived as preferential treatment of the members of one group over them as individuals. The government is usually accused of going too far in eliminating discrimination against historically oppressed groups by supporting affirmative action, contracts set aside for some groups, welfare, special education, and legislation for women's equity. These opponents now charge that such programs lead to reverse discrimination against them.

However, criteria for access to the "good life" are often applied arbitrarily and unfairly. A disproportionately high number of persons of color have had limited opportunities to gain the qualifications for skilled jobs or college entrance or have the economic resources to purchase a home in the suburbs. As businesses and industries move from the city to the suburbs, access to employment by those who live in the inner city is limited. A crucial issue is not the equal treatment of those with equal qualifications, but the accessibility to the qualifications and jobs themselves.

The consequences are the same in individual and institutional discrimination. Members of some groups do not receive the same benefits from society as the dominant group. Individuals are harmed by circumstances beyond their control because of their membership in a specific group. The role of teachers and other professional educators requires that they not discriminate against any student because of his or her cultural group. This consideration must be paramount in assigning students to special education and gifted classes and in giving and interpreting standardized tests. Classroom interactions, classroom resources, extracurricular activities, and counseling practices must be evaluated to ensure that discrimination against students from various ethnic groups does not occur.

Summary

Multicultural education is an educational strategy that incorporates cultural differences and provides equality and social justice in schools. For it to become a reality in the formal school situation, the total environment must reflect a commitment to multicultural education. The diverse cultural backgrounds and cultural memberships of students and families are as important in developing effective instructional strategies as are their physical and mental capabilities. Further, educators must understand the influence of racism, sexism, and classism on the lives of their students and ensure that these are not perpetuated in the classroom.

Culture provides the blueprint that determines the way an individual thinks, feels, and behaves in society. We are not born with culture, but rather learn it through enculturation and socialization. It is manifested through societal institutions, lived experiences, and the individual's fulfillment of psychological and basic needs.

Historically, U.S. political and social institutions have developed from a Western European tradition and still function under the strong influence of that heritage. At the same time, many aspects of American life have been greatly influenced by the numerous cultural groups that make up the U.S. population. The dominant culture is based on its White, Anglo-Saxon, Protestant roots and the core values of individualism and freedom with which many middle-class families identify. Assimilation is the process by which groups adopt and change the dominant culture. Schools have traditionally served as the transmitter of the dominant culture to all students regardless of their cultural backgrounds and differences from the dominant group.

Individuals also belong to a number of cultural groups with cultural patterns that differ from that of the dominant group. Cultural identity is based on the interaction and influence of membership in groups based on ethnic origin, race, religion, gender, age, class, native language, geographic region, and abilities. Membership in one of those groups can greatly affect one's identity with the others. Some religions, for example, dictate the norms for the behavior of men and women, children and adults, as well as the treatment of members of other groups. The theory of cultural pluralism promotes the maintenance of the distinct differences among cultural groups.

A democracy should recognize the differences in society and provide social justice for all of its people. Egalitarianism and equality have long been espoused as goals for society, but they are implemented from two perspectives. The emphasis on individualism is supported in a meritocratic system in which everyone is alleged to start out equally and the most deserving will end up with the most rewards. Equality, in contrast, seeks to ensure that society's benefits and rewards are distributed more equitably among individuals and groups. Prejudice and discrimination continue to be obstacles to equality.

QUESTIONS FOR DISCUSSION

1. How does multicultural education differ from multiethnic studies and intercultural education?

2. What is the danger of stereotyping students on the basis of their membership in only one of their cultural groups?

3. Why is multicultural education as important to students of the dominant culture as to students of other cultures?

4. What impact does culture have on the way one lives?

5. How does ethnicity, gender, and religion interact in determining one's cultural identity? Why might one's cultural identity change over time?

6. What are the implicit and explicit differences between dominant and oppressed cultural groups?

7. How might an understanding of cultural borders help teachers understand differences in classroom settings?

8. How do meritocracy and individualism conflict with the ideal of equality?

ONLINE ACTIVITIES For additional chapter questions and activities, visit this text's Companion Website at http://www.prenhall.com/gollnick.

PORTFOLIO ACTIVITIES

1. Write a reflective paper that describes your cultural identity and the social and economic factors that have influenced your cultural identity. Refer to your circle of cultural identity (Pause to Reflect 1.2) to get you started.

2. Develop a lesson plan for the subject and level you plan to teach that presents the topic from multiple perspectives. Include a summary of the per-

spectives to be presented, why they were selected, and how the different perspectives strengthen the lesson. (INTASC Standard 1)

3. Select one of the schools in which you are observing this semester to develop a case study of the cultural norms prevalent in the community served by the school. In your case study indicate the diversity of the community and the cultural norms that are reflected in the school. Teachers, parents, and students should be interviewed during the development of the case study. In addition, your observations of students should inform your case. (INTASC Standard 3)

SUGGESTED READINGS

Alba, R., & Nee, V. (2003). *Remaking the American mainstream: Assimilation and contemporary immigration.* Cambridge, MA: Harvard University Press.

Exploring the differences between the experiences of European immigrants at the beginning of the twentieth century and the Latino and Asian immigrants since 1968, the authors describe assimilation today and into the future.

Apple, M. W. (2004). *Ideology and curriculum* (3rd ed.). New York: RoutledgeFalmer.

The politics of the school curriculum are the focus of this insightful account of the cultural, political, and economic influences on education. This edition includes a chapter on the challenges facing schools after 9/11.

Banks, J. A., & Banks, C. A. M. (Eds.). (2004). *Handbook of research on multicultural education* (2nd ed.). San Francisco: Jossey-Bass.

This comprehensive handbook provides broad coverage of the history as well as current trends, research issues, and knowledge construction of multicultural education. Well-known scholars address ethnic groups, immigrants, language issues, academic achievement, intergroup education, higher education, and international perspectives.

hooks, b. (1994). *Teaching to transgress: Education as the practice of freedom.* New York: Routledge.

Using passion and politics, this teacher promotes education that helps students cross racial, sexual, and class boundaries in the practice of freedom.

Tyack, D. (2003). *Seeking common ground: Public schools in a diverse society.* Cambridge, MA: Harvard University Press.

Beginning with the establishment of public schools in each township in the eighteenth century, this historian traces the debates that have guided the incorporation of diverse populations in schools into the twenty-first century.

REFERENCES

Alba, R. D. (2000). Assimilations' quiet tide. In Steinberg, S. (Ed.). *Race and ethnicity in the United States: Issues and debates* (pp. 211–222). Malden, MA: Blackwell.

Alba, R. & Nee, V. (2003). *Remaking the American mainstream: Assimilation and contemporary immigration.* Cambridge, MA: Harvard University Press.

Apple, M. W. (2004). *Ideology and curriculum* (3rd edition). New York: RoutledgeFalmer.

Banks, J. A. (2004). Multicultural education: Historical development, dimensions, and practice. In J. A. Banks and C. A. M. Banks (Eds.), *Handbook of research on multicultural education* (2nd edition, pp. 3–29). San Francisco: Jossey-Bass.

Bellah, R. N., Madsen, R., Sullivan, W. M., Swidler, A., & Tipton, S. M. (1996). *Habits of the heart: Individualism and commitment in American life.* Berkeley, CA: University of California Press.

Dewey, J. (1966). *Democracy and education: An introduction to the philosophy of education.* New York: Free Press. (Original work published 1916)

Education Trust. (2003). *Achievement in America.* Retrieved August 15, 2004, from (http://www2.edtrust.org/NR/rdonlyres/14FB5D33-31EF-4A9C-B55F-33184998BDD8/0/masterach2003.ppt).

Eck, D. L. (2000). *Religious pluralism in America in the year 2000.* In E. W. Linder, Yearbook of American and Canadian churches 2000. Nashville, TN: Abingdon Press.

Interstate New Teacher Assessment and Support Consortium. (1992). *Model Standards for Beginning Teacher Licensing, Assessment, and Development: A Resource for State Dialogue.* Washington, DC: Council of Chief State School Officers.

Kuper, A. (2000). *Culture: The anthropologists' account.* Cambridge, MA: Harvard University Press.

Ladson-Billings G. (2004). New directions in multicultural education: Complexities, boundaries, and critical race theory. In J. A. Banks and C. A. M. Banks (Eds.),

Handbook of research on multicultural education (2nd edition, pp. 50–65). San Francisco: Jossey-Bass.

Montalto, N. V. (1978). *The forgotten dream: A history of the intercultural education movement, 1924–1941.* Dissertation Abstracts International, 39A, 1061. (University Microfilms No. 78-13436)

National Board for Professional Teaching Standards. (2001). *The impact of national board certification on teachers: A survey of national board certified teachers and assessors.* Arlington, VA: Author.

Portes, A. & Rumbaut, R. G. (2001). *Legacies: The story of the immigrant second generation.* Berkeley, CA: University of California Press.

Rumbaut, R. G. & Portes, A. (2001). *Ethnicities: Children of immigrants in America.* Berkeley, CA: University of California Press.

Sleeter, C. E. (1992). *Keepers of the American dream: A study of staff development and multicultural education.* London: Taylor & Francis.

Sleeter, C. E. & Bernal, D. D. (2004). Critical pedagogy, critical race theory, and antiracist education. In J. A. Banks and C. A. M. Banks (Eds.), *Handbook of research on multicultural education* (2nd edition, pp. 240–258). San Francisco: Jossey-Bass.

Sleeter, C. E. & Grant, C. A. (2002). *Making choices for multicultural education: Five approaches to race, class, and gender* (4th ed.). New York: John Wiley & Sons.

Spring, J. (2001). *Protecting cultural and language rights: An educational rights amendment to the U. S. constitution.* Keynote Presentation at Annual Meeting of the National Association for Multicultural Education in Arlington, VA.

Tyack, D. (2003). *Seeking common ground: Public schools in a diverse society.* Cambridge, MA: Harvard University Press.

U. S. Census Bureau. (2003). *Statistical Abstract of the United States: 2003* (123rd edition). Washington, DC: U.S. Government Printing Office.

U. S. Department of Education. (2001). *No Child Left Behind Act of 2001.* (http://www.ed.gov/nclb/overview/intro/presidentplan/proposal.pdf). Washington, DC: U. S. Government Printing Office.

U.S. Department of Education, National Center for Education Statistics. (June 2003). *Digest of Education Statistics 2002.* Washington, DC: U.S. Department of Education.

U. S. Department of Education, National Center for Education Statistics. (2004). *The condition of education 2004.* Washington, DC: U. S. Government Printing Office.

We are obliged to make sure that every child gets a healthy start in life. With all of our wealth and capacity, we just can't stand by idly.

SECRETARY OF STATE COLIN POWELL, 2000

Chapter 2

Class

While he was still in college, Tomas Juarez had decided he wanted to work with children from low-income families. He began his teaching career, however, in a culturally diverse suburban school. The school had been built only a few years before and included state-of-the-art science labs. Students were proficient with computers; they even helped Mr. Juarez develop his skills. Most of the students participated in extracurricular activities, and their parents were active in school affairs. More than 90% of the previous graduating class had enrolled in postsecondary programs. It was a pleasure to work with a team of teachers who planned interesting lessons based on a constructivist approach, engaged students in the content, and developed higher-order thinking skills.

After a few years, Mr. Juarez decided that he was ready to take on the challenge of an inner-city school where most students were members of oppressed groups. As soon as he stepped into his new school, he realized that he had been spoiled in the suburbs.

First, the smell wasn't right and the halls were dirty even though it was the beginning of the school year. The room that was to be his classroom did not have enough chairs for all of the students who had been assigned to the class. Not only did the room look as if it had not been repainted for 20 years, but several windowpanes were covered with a cardboard-like material, and numerous ceiling tiles were missing. His first thought was that both he and the students would be exposed to asbestos and lead poisoning. Outside, the playground was uninviting. There was no grass, the stench from local factories was overpowering, and the football field did not even have goalposts.

During Mr. Juarez's first few weeks, he found that the students were terrific. They were enthusiastic about being back in school. He had only enough textbooks for half the class, however, and no money in the budget to purchase more. Supplies were limited, and most of the audiovisual equipment had been stolen the previous year and never replaced.

Opportunities for Reflection

1. *Why were conditions at Mr. Juarez's new school so much different from those in the suburban school?*
2. *How can a teacher overcome environmental conditions that are not supportive of effective learning?*
3. *What are the chances of the new students being academically successful in the same way as the students in the suburban school?*
4. *Why are students in the urban school more likely to drop out, become pregnant, and not attend college?*
5. *Why has society allowed some students to go to school under such appallingly poor conditions?*

To answer these questions online, go to this chapter's Opening Scenario module of the Companion Website.

CW

Class Structure

"**Class** is a system that differentially structures group access to economic, political, cultural, and social resources" (Andersen & Collins, 2004, p. 86). It determines the schools students attend, the stores in which you shop, the restaurants in which you eat, the community in which you live, and the jobs to which you will have access. Class is socially constructed by society and its institutions, determining the relationships between families and persons who have little or limited financial resources and those who are wealthy.

The two views of equality in U.S. society that were outlined in Chapter 1 suggest different class structures in the country. One view accepts the existence of different socioeconomic levels or classes in society. It also strongly supports the notion that one can be socially mobile and can move to a higher class by getting an education and working hard. Groups that have not yet achieved upper-middle-class status are viewed as inferior. The hardships faced by low-income families are blamed on their lack of middle-class values and behaviors. The individual is at fault for not moving up the class ladder—a phenomenon called blaming the victim.

In the second view of U.S. society, distinct class divisions are recognized. Those individuals and families who own and control corporations, banks, and other means of production comprise the privileged upper class. The professional and managerial elite have not only accumulated wealth; they are also able to ensure that their needs are supported by legislative representatives whom they have elected (American Political Science Association, 2004). Persons who earn a living primarily by selling their labor make up other middle and working classes. Another class includes those persons who are unable to work or who can find work only sporadically. Although some individuals are able to move from one class level to another, opportunities for social mobility are limited. Those who control most of the resources and those who have few of the resources are dichotomous groups in a class struggle.

Most people are caught in the socioeconomic strata into which they were born, and the political-economic system ensures they remain there. Certainly some individuals have been socially and economically mobile. Stories about athletes, coaches, movie stars, and singers are recounted during sporting events and in newspaper and television accounts. Few people, however, have abilities that translate into the high salaries of elite stars of the entertainment world. A college education is the most reliable step for moving from a low-income to a middle-class and higher status.

Family background has been found to account for a large part of the variation in educational and occupational attainment. The opportunity to achieve equally is thwarted before one is born. Individuals born into a wealthy family are likely to achieve wealth; individuals born into a low-income family will have difficulty achieving wealth no matter how hard they work. Families usually do everything possible to protect their wealth to guarantee that their children maintain the family's economic status. The inequalities that exist in society often lead to the perpetuation of inequalities from one generation to the next.

Most people, if asked, could identify themselves by class, a distinction based on one's social or economic status. Whereas they do not strongly vocalize their identity with a specific class, they participate socially and occupationally within a class structure. Their behavior and value system may be based on a strong ethnic or religious identification, but that specific identification is greatly influenced by their economic circumstances. The first generation of a group that has moved to the middle class may continue to interact at a primary level with friends and relatives who remain in the working class. Differences in friends, communities, and jobs, however, often lead to the reduction of those cross-class ties over time.

Most U.S. citizens exhibit and articulate less concern about class consciousness than many of their European counterparts. Nevertheless, many have participated in class actions, such as strikes or work stoppages to further the interests of the class to which they belong. Class consciousness, or solidarity with others at the same socioeconomic level, may not be so pronounced here because overall improvement in the standard of living has occurred at all levels, especially during the period from 1940 to the early 1970s and again in the 1990s. In addition, the dominant cultural values and belief systems hold individuals personally responsible for their class position.

Social Stratification

Social stratification ranks individuals and families on the basis of their income, education, occupation, wealth, and power in society. Many people accept and follow socially defined behavior based on their occupation, race, gender, and class. However, civil rights organizations, including women's groups, try to combat the institutionalized acceptance and expectation of unequal status across cultural groups.

Inequality results, in part, from differential rankings within the division of labor. Different occupations are evaluated and rewarded unequally. Some jobs are viewed as more worthy, more important, more popular, and more preferable than others. People who hold high-ranking positions have developed common interests for maintaining their positions and the accompanying power. They have established policies and practices to restrict others' chances of obtaining the same status—a key to establishing and maintaining a system of stratification.

Many people in the United States receive high or low rankings in the social stratification system on the basis of characteristics over which they have no control. Women, people with disabilities, the elderly, children, and people of color often receive low-prestige rankings. **Ascribed status**—one's assignment to groups at birth—affects who is allowed entrance into the higher-ranking socioeconomic positions. However, not all white, able-bodied men achieve a high-ranking position. They are found at all levels of the continuum, from being homeless to being a billionaire, but they and their families are overrepresented at the highest levels. Conversely, members of most oppressed groups can be found at all levels of the continuum, with a few at the top of the socioeconomic scale.

Socioeconomic Status

How is economic success or achievement measured? The economic condition of persons and groups can be measured with a criterion called **socioeconomic status (SES).** It serves as a composite of the economic status of a family or unrelated individuals on the basis of occupation, educational attainment, and income. Related to these three factors are wealth and power, which also help determine an individual's SES but are more difficult to measure.

These five determinants of SES are interrelated. Although inequality has many forms, these factors are probably the most salient for an individual because they affect how one lives. A family's SES is usually observable—in the size of their home and the part of town in which they live, the schools their children attend, or the clubs to which the parents belong. Many educators place their students at specific SES levels on the basis of similar observations about their families, based on the way students dress, the language they use, and their eligibility for free or reduced lunch.

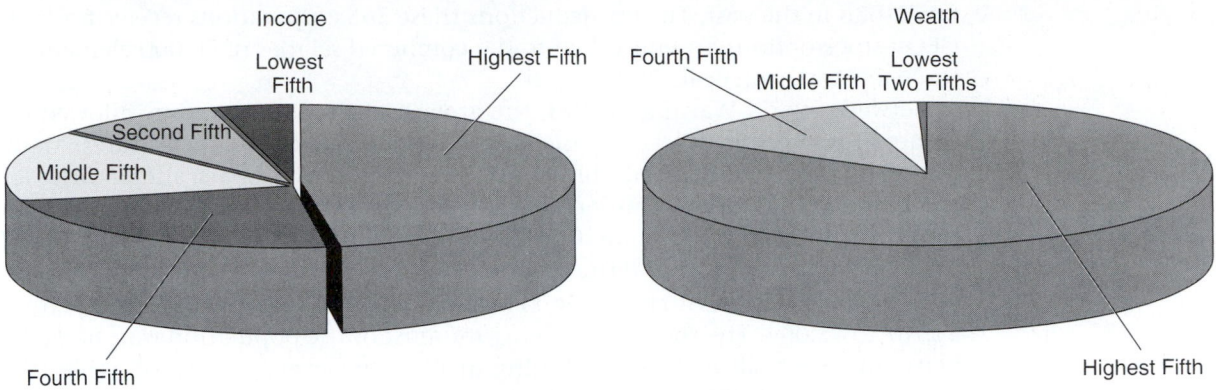

Figure 2.1

Distribution of family income and wealth in the United States by fifths of the population.

Source: (Income) U.S. Census Bureau. (2003). *Statistical abstract of the United States: 2003* (123rd ed.). Washington, DC: U.S. Government Printing Office. (Wealth) Rose, S. J. (2000). *Social stratification in the United States.* New York: New Press.

INCOME

Income is the amount of money earned in wages or salaries throughout a year. One way to look at income distribution is by dividing the population into fifths; the lowest one fifth earns the least income, and the highest one fifth earns the highest income. Figure 2.1 shows the percentage of total income earned in 2001 by each fifth of the population, and the total wealth held by each fifth. The top 20% of the population earned 48% of the total income, whereas the bottom fifth earned 4% of the total income. High incomes are reserved for the privileged few. Five percent of U.S. families earned 21% of the total income received (U.S. Census Bureau, 2003b).

Many people view this income inequity as a natural outcome of the American way. Those people who have worked hard and contributed at high levels to their professions or jobs are believed to deserve to be paid more for their effort. People at the lower end of the continuum are either unemployed or work in unskilled jobs and thus are not expected to receive the same economic rewards. The difference between these two ends of the continuum can be quite large, however. Chief executive officers (CEOs) of the largest 365 U.S. companies earned an average compensation of $8.1 million in 2003, including bonuses and long-term compensation such as stocks (Anderson, Cavanagh, Hartman, Klinger, & Chan, 2004). At the other end of the scale, people earning the minimum wage receive less than $11,000 annually. In this time of tightening budgets and moving jobs outside the United States where salaries are much less, the salaries of most CEOs increased. "If the average production worker's annual pay had increased as quickly as CEO pay since 1990, it would be $15.76 per hour, nearly three times the current minimum wage of $5.15 an hour. Likewise, if the average production worker's annual pay had increased as quickly as CEO pay since 1990, it would today be $75,388 per year, nearly three times the current average of $26,899." (Anderson et al., 2004, p. 22). International studies report that the gap between high and low wages is greater in the United States than in most other industrialized countries. This situation is further exacerbated by the lack of tax policies to readjust somewhat the disparities; in fact, the rich are paying fewer taxes than in the past. The tax deductions these 365 corporations receive for their CEOs' stock options are equivalent to the combined salaries of 70,000 elementary teachers (Anderson et al., 2004).

Between World War II and 1973, the growth of the U.S. economy allowed incomes of workers at all levels to increase at a faster rate than expenditures. Many middle-income families were able to purchase homes, cars, boats, and luxuries for the home; often, money was left over for savings. One way to examine the continuum of income is to use **median income,** which is the number at which half of the group earns more and the other half earns less. During this period, the annual median income of all people 14 years of age and older nearly tripled, from $1,787 to $5,004. The standard of living for most of the population was markedly better in 1973 than in 1940. Beginning in 1973, however, the cost of living (the cost of housing, utilities, food, and other essentials) began to increase faster than income. Except for the wealthy, all families felt the financial pressure. No longer did they have extra income to purchase nonessentials. No longer was one full-time worker in a family enough to maintain the same standard of living. The 1990s brought another upswing in the economy. By 2001, the median annual income of a family was $51,407. When both husband and wife worked full-time and year-round, the median income of married couples was $60,335 (U.S. Census Bureau, 2003b).

Income sets limits on the general lifestyle of a family, as well as on their general welfare. It controls the consumption patterns of a family—the number and quality of material possessions, housing, consumer goods, luxuries, savings, and diet. It allows families to save money for college educations and the purchase of new cars. Most low-income and middle-income families are barely able to cover their expenses from one paycheck to the next, and are only a few paychecks away from homelessness if they lose their job. Higher incomes provide security for families who do not need to worry about paying for the essentials and have access to health care and retirement benefits.

WEALTH

Although the difference in income among families is great, an examination of income alone does not indicate the vast differences in the way families live. Income figures show the amount of money earned by a family for their labors during one year, but the figures do not include the amount of money earned from investments, land, and other holdings. They do not present the **net worth** of a family. The **wealth** of a family includes savings accounts, insurance, corporate stock ownership, and property. Wealth provides a partial guarantee of future income and has the potential of producing additional income and wealth. However, for most families, the majority of family wealth comes from the equity value of homes and the residual value of household goods. Approximately 20% of U.S. households have zero or negative wealth (Collins & Veskel, 2004).

Whereas income can be determined from data gathered on federal income tax forms by the Internal Revenue Service, wealth is difficult to determine from these or any other standard forms. However, the distribution of wealth is concentrated in a small percentage of the population. The wealthiest 10% of the population had a me-

 **CRITICAL INCIDENTS IN TEACHING**

Differences in Socioeconomic Status

The middle school in a rural community of 9,000 residents has four school-sponsored dances each year. At the Valentine's dance, a coat-and-tie affair, six eighth-grade boys showed up in rented tuxedos. They had planned this together, and their parents, among the more affluent in the community, thought it would be "cute" and paid for the rentals. The final dance of the year is scheduled for May, and it, too, is a coat-and-tie dance. This time, rumors are circulating around school that "everyone" is renting a tux and that the girls are getting new formal dresses. The parents of three boys are, according to the grapevine, renting a limousine for their sons and their dates. These behaviors and dress standards are far in excess of anything previously observed at the middle school.

Several students, particularly those from lower socioeconomic backgrounds, have said they will boycott the dance. They cannot afford the expensive attire, and they claim that the ones behind the dress-up movement have said that only the nerds or geeks would show up in anything less than a tux or a formal gown.

Questions for Discussion

1. *Should the school administration intervene? Why or why not?*
2. *Should the limo-renting parents be contacted? Why or why not?*
3. *Should the matter be discussed in the homerooms? In a school assembly? Why or why not?*
4. *Should the May dance be canceled? Why or why not?*
5. *Should limits be set on how dressed up students can be? Could the school legally enforce limits?*
6. *Can and should an issue be made of the hiring of limousine services for middle school students?*

To answer these questions online, go to the Critical Incidents in Teaching module for this chapter of the Companion Website.

dian net worth of $1.3 million in 2001; the median net worth of the bottom fifth of the population was $1,100 (Keenan, 2003). At the other end of the scale, the wealthiest 1% of the population holds 38% of the assets (Rose, 2000). Figure 2.1 shows how wealth is distributed across fifths of the population.

The wealthiest nations in the world are the United States, Canada, and Western Europe, but inequities across groups continue to exist in these countries. The world's wealth is held by a few people. For example, the 225 richest people in the world have a combined wealth equal to the annual income of the poorer half of the world population (Smith, 2000). The difference between the economic lives of populations in the wealthiest and poorest countries in the world is shocking in its magnitude. The average person in the richest countries is more than 100 times wealthier than a person in the poorest countries (Smith, 2003).

Wealth ensures some economic security for its holders even though the amount of security depends on the amount of wealth accumulated. It also enhances the power and prestige of those who possess it. Great wealth accrues power, provides an income that allows luxury, and creates values and lifestyles that are very different from most of the remainder of the population. Wealth also gives great economic advantages to children in these families who can attend the best schools, travel widely, and not worry about medical and health needs.

OCCUPATION

Income, for most people, is determined by their occupation. Generally speaking, it is believed that income is a fair measure of occupational success—both of the importance of the occupation to society and of one's individual skill at the job. In addition to providing an income, a person's job is an activity that is considered important. Individuals who are unemployed often are stigmatized as noncontributing members of society who cannot take care of themselves. Even individuals with great wealth often hold a job, although additional income is unnecessary. Just over half of today's workforce is comprised of white-collar workers—that is, people who do not do manual work. The percentage of service workers is growing, although the percentage of those who are private household workers continues to decline. Between now and 2010, most of the 10 fastest growing occupations are in the following fields, primarily related to computing:

1. computer software engineers, applications,
2. computer support specialists,
3. computer software engineers, systems software,
4. network and computer systems administrators,
5. network systems and data communications analysts,
6. desktop publishers,
7. database administrators,
8. personal and home care aides,
9. computer systems analysts, and
10. medical assistants.

In addition, some education positions are among the fastest growing occupations. Speech-language pathologists are 26th on the list, followed by teachers of special education, preschool, kindergarten, and elementary students (U.S. Census Bureau, 2003b).

The type of job one holds is the primary determinant of income received, providing a relatively objective indicator of a person's SES. The job usually indicates one's education, suggests the types of associates with whom one interacts, and determines the degree of authority and responsibility one has over others. It gives people both differing amounts of compensation in income and differing degrees of prestige in society.

Occupational prestige is often determined by the requirements for the job and by the characteristics of the job. The requirements for an occupation with prestige usually include more education and training. Job characteristics that add to the prestige of an occupation are rooted in the division between mental and manual labor. When the prestige of an occupation is high, fewer people gain entry into that occupation. When the prestige of an occupation is low, employees are allotted less security and income, and accessibility to that occupation is greater. Occupations with the highest prestige generally have the highest salaries.

The type of job one holds impacts one's socioeconomic status. Low-wage jobs make it difficult if not impossible to move into the middle class.

EDUCATION

The best predictor of occupational prestige is the amount of education one acquires. Financial compensation is usually greater for occupations that require more years of education. For example, medical doctors and lawyers remain in school for several years beyond the bachelor's degree program. Many professionals and other white-collar workers have completed at least an undergraduate program at a college or university. Craft workers often earn more money than many white-collar workers, but their positions require specialized training that often takes as long to complete as a college degree.

A great discrepancy exists among the incomes of persons who have less than a high school education and those who have completed professional training after college. The median income of a male who had not completed the ninth grade in 2001 was $14,594; if he had completed four years of college or more, it was $54,069. The differential for a female was $8,846 and $30,973 (U.S. Census Bureau, 2003b).

Education is rightfully viewed as a way to enhance one's economic status. However, impressive educational credentials are more likely to be achieved as a result of family background, rather than other factors. High school graduates whose parents have at least a bachelor's degree are more likely to enroll in postsecondary education (U.S. Department of Education, 2001). The higher the socioeconomic level of students' families, the greater the students' chances of finishing high school and college. Students enrolled in college soon after high school graduation ranged in 2002 from 57% of those from families with annual incomes of less than $35,377 to 83%

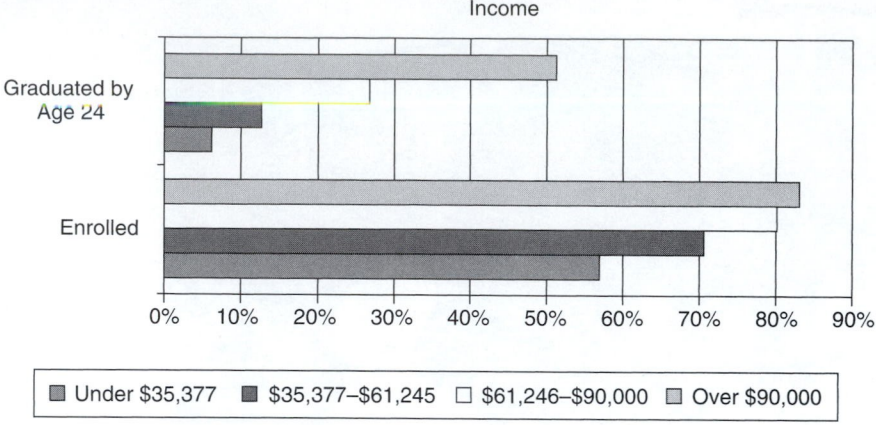

Figure 2.2

High school graduates enrolled and completing college by family.

Source: Family income and higher education opportunity: 1970 to 2002. (2004, May). *Postsecondary Education Opportunity*, No. 143.

of those from families with incomes of more than $90,000. College graduation rates range from 6% for students at the lower income level to 51% for the top income level as shown in Figure 2.2 (Family Income and Higher Education Opportunity, 2004).

The conditions under which low-income students live often make it difficult for them to go to school instead of going to work. They often begin by attending community colleges. The greater the income of families, the greater the chances that their children will have books, magazines, and newspapers available in the home; that they will have attended plays or concerts; and that they will have traveled beyond the region in which they live. Even the colleges that students attend are influenced more by the SES of the family than by the academic ability of the student. Many students simply cannot afford to attend private colleges and instead choose state colleges and universities or community colleges. Thus, a student's socioeconomic origins have a substantial influence on the amount and type of schooling received and, in turn, the type of job obtained.

Education is one of the main ways families pass on class position to their children. One's class position determines, in great part, the material conditions that affect one's lifestyle and the types of jobs one seeks. Thus, educational level is a strong determinant of the future occupation and income of a family's children.

POWER

Individuals and families who are at the upper SES levels exert more power than those at any other level. These individuals are more likely to sit on boards that determine state and local policies, on boards of colleges and universities, and on boards of corporations. They determine who receives benefits and rewards in governmental, occupational, and community affairs. Groups and individuals with power control resources that influence their lives and the lives of others. Groups or individuals with little power do not have the means to get what they need or the access to others who could influence their interests. Powerless groups continually obtain fewer of society's benefits because they lack accessibility to sources of power.

Persons with higher incomes are more likely to participate in national and local politics. They are also much more likely to vote in presidential elections. A study of the American Political Science Association (APSA) (2004) found that 90% of individuals in families with an income over $75,000 vote as compared to half of the individuals in families earning under $15,000. The power that comes with voting and contributing financially to political candidates is described by leading political scientists in this report. They state that "citizens with lower or moderate incomes speak with a whisper that is lost on the ears of inattentive government officials while the advantaged roar with a clarity and consistency that policymakers readily hear and routinely follow" (p. 1). This power is reflected in the actions of legislative action that benefits persons, families, and corporations with money. The APSA reports that "recent research strikingly documents that the votes of U.S. senators far more closely correspond with the policy preferences of each senator's rich constituents than with the preferences of the senator's less-privileged constituents" (p. 14).

The sphere of education is not exempt from the exercise of power. Power relationships between teachers and students are manifested in schools. Teachers and administrators wield power over students by controlling the knowledge dispensed (predominantly grounded in a Western European worldview) and the acceptable behaviors, thoughts, and values for experiencing success in schools. Fewer teachers today are totally authoritarian; a growing number of teachers use cooperative learning rather than lecture and competitive strategies. Nevertheless, the curriculum is controlled by teachers, school boards, and national standards. In high-income schools, families have greater influence on their schools. Parents are able to financially contribute to the hiring of teachers for programs like music and art that many school districts can no longer afford. They will not tolerate the hiring of unqualified or poor teachers. On the other end of the income spectrum, families have little input into who teaches their children and cannot afford to contribute resources to maintain a full and desirable curriculum.

Class Differences

Opportunities for Reflection

Many Americans identify themselves as middle class. It is an amorphous category that often includes everyone who works steadily and who is not accepted as a member of the upper class. It ranges from well-paid professionals to service workers. Most white-collar workers, no matter what their salary, see themselves as middle class. Manual workers, in contrast, may view themselves as working class, rather than as middle class; however, for the most part their incomes and cultural values are similar to those of many white-collar workers. Think about the community in which you grew up. *In which class do the majority of your neighbors fall? What was the class of the majority of students in your high school? How did class influence the educational aspirations of your high school peers?*

Despite the popular myth, most people in the United States are not affluent. A medium budget representing a reasonably comfortable life for a family in the United States would require about $40,000 (Rose, 2000). The family would be buying a home, but would not be able to accumulate any significant savings. This compares to the federal government's poverty line of $9,393 for one person and

$18,725 for a family of four. Nearly 36 million people or 12.5% of the total population live in poverty by federal standards, but 37% of U.S. families earned less than $40,000 in 2003 (U.S. Census Bureau, 2004). Many of these individuals identify themselves as middle class but are unable to obtain the material goods and necessities to live comfortably. The so-called middle class is certainly not homogeneous. The differences in education, occupation, prestige, income, and ability to accumulate wealth vary widely among persons who identify themselves in this group.

THE UNEMPLOYED AND HOMELESS

The portion of the population who suffers the most from the lack of a stable income or other economic resources is the unemployed and homeless. The long-term poor fall into this group; many others are temporarily in poverty because of a job loss or family illness. Of the individuals classified as living in poverty, only 2.2% are persistently poor as measured by living in poverty for at least eight out of the last ten years (Rose, 2000).

The hard-core unemployed have seldom, if ever, worked and often lack the skills to find and maintain a job. The number of unemployed persons was over 8 million in 2002 or 5.8% of the civilian workforce (U.S. Census, 2003b), but this number does not include the discouraged workers who have given up looking for work and are no longer included in the government's report of the unemployed. Disproportionately, these families are headed by single mothers, who are more likely than married women to be in poverty for more than two years.

Members of this group have become socially isolated from the dominant society. They usually are not integrated into, or wanted in, the communities of the other classes. Recommendations to build low-income housing, homeless shelters, or halfway houses in middle- or working-class communities often result in vocal outrage from the residents of these communities. Some analysts think the lack of integration has exacerbated the differences in behavior between members of the underclass and those of other classes.

During the past decade, the number of homeless persons and families has increased dramatically. Children and families live on the streets of our cities, comprising a large portion of today's homeless population as shown in Figure 2.3. Because almost all cities report more homeless people than shelter space, the number housed nightly in shelters would undercount the actual number of homeless people. The National Association for the Education of Homeless Children and Youth (NAEHCY) (2004) estimates that between 2.3 and 3.5 million people have been homeless at some time during a year, and that 900,000 to 1.4 million of them are children. Many of the homeless work, but at such low wages they are unable to afford housing. Half of the homeless have graduated from high school, and approximately one fourth have attended college (Urban Institute, 2000).

Why are people homeless? Poverty and the lack of affordable housing are the primary reasons for homelessness. The federal definition of affordable housing is rent equal to 30% of one's income. If a person makes the minimum wage of $5.15 per hour, his or her household would have to include more than two people earning minimum wage to afford a two-bedroom apartment in most parts of the country. An annual salary of $31,637 is required to rent a two-bedroom rental unit and keep rent

 **VIDEO INSIGHT**

Looking for a Chance in Appalachia

Most Appalachian counties have unemployment and poverty rates well above the national average. These once-vibrant communities are now shrinking because many people can simply not find work in their hometowns. In this video segment you will see that there are a number of factors contributing to this problem, but one of the biggest is education.

The coal mining industry that brought so many jobs to Appalachia has changed over the years. Many coal mines have been shut down, while others have replaced loyal, hard workers with new, efficient technologies. But, because only half of the people in this region have a high school diploma, other big business and industries are hesitant to enter the area.

Things are appearing to change, however. Federal programs are helping to educate workers, giving them the opportunity to get their diploma and receive job training in different vocations. After watching this video segment,

1. *In what ways do you think these programs can make a difference in an area like this?*

2. *What else can be done to reduce poverty in the Appalachian region?*

To answer these questions online, go to the ABC News Video Insight module for this chapter of the Companion Website.

Figure 2.3

Who are the homeless in our cities?

Source: U.S. Conference of Mayors. (2002). *Hunger and homelessness 2002*. Washington, DC: Author.

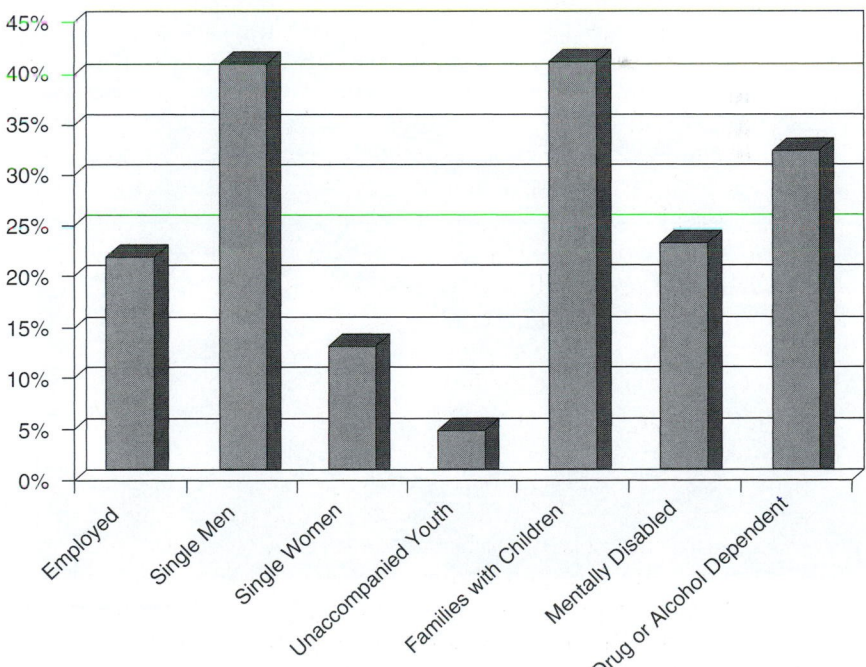

at the recommended 30% of one's income (National Low Income Housing Coalition, 2003). The supply of affordable housing for low-income families does not begin to meet the needs of low-income families; over 14 million families have critical housing needs (National Coalition for the Homeless, 2003). "As a result, these families are living in substandard conditions, are homeless, or are making choices each day to spend money on housing and do without health care, child care, or other basic necessities" (National Low Income Housing Coalition, 2003, p. 6).

Domestic violence is another cause of homelessness because women who are escaping violent relationships do not always have another place to go. Other homeless people are without a place to stay because facilities do not exist to care for persons with mental disabilities. Some persons who are dependent on drugs or alcohol have lost their jobs, can't keep a job that earns enough to pay for their housing, or have become estranged from their families. In 27 cities more than 40% of the homeless are now families with children (U.S. Conference of Mayors, 2002). Some teenagers leave home because of family problems, economic problems, or residential instability, often ending up homeless on city streets. The Urban Institute (2000) found the following characteristics among homeless families:

- Families headed by single mothers predominate.
- Homeless families have, on the average, two children, but they are not all with the homeless parent during the period of homelessness.
- Most homeless students are in school and regularly attending classes.

An increasing number of homeless adults, families, and children are found in communities around the country.

The U.S. Department of Education (2003) reported that 800,000 children and youth were homeless. Some homeless students do not attend school for extended periods of time, and homeless children are not as healthy as other children. Many have not received immunizations that are expected in childhood. They experience higher rates of asthma, ear infections, stomach problems, and speech problems than other children (Books & Polakow, 2001). They have more mental health problems such as anxiety, depression, and withdrawal. They suffer from hypothermia and are often hungry. Further, they are more likely to have been abused or neglected by parents and other adults.

The **McKinney-Vento Homeless Assistance Act** requires public schools to provide educational rights and protections for homeless children and youth, including students who are living with relatives or friends because they have lost their housing. The law requires school districts to provide transportation for homeless students to stay in their schools of origin if requested by their parents. A school cannot deny enrollment to homeless students because they do not have their school records, immunization records, proof of residency, or other documents. The McKinney-Vento Act ensures that homeless students have access to schooling and are not denied services because of circumstances beyond their control. The school district's liaison for homeless students should serve as an advocate for them, assisting them in accessing the available services in the school system and community.

The unemployed and homeless suffer from economic insecurity and from social, political, and economic deprivation. When they hold full-time jobs, they are of the lowest prestige and income levels. The jobs are often eliminated when economic conditions tighten or jobs move to the suburbs, resulting in unemployment again. The work for which they are hired is often the dirty work—not only physically dirty but also dangerous, menial, undignified, and degrading. The jobs are the least desirable ones in society, and they are often performed by persons with no other options if they are to work.

Too often, this group is blamed for its own condition. The members are generally unnoticed when they remain isolated from the majority and work sporadically. In many cities they are isolated as much as possible from others. Homeless citizens and others hanging on corners are moved to areas where they will not be visible to tourists. Members on welfare are subjected to the pejorative and inaccurate opinions of many other Americans. They are often thought of as dishonest and having loose morals. They are stereotyped as lazy and unwilling to work. Economic and political reasons for landing in this class are given little credence by those in power.

Many stereotypical notions about the poor need to be overcome for teachers to effectively serve students who come from this background. Such students should not be blamed if they show acceptance, resignation, and even accommodation to their poverty as they learn to live with their economic disabilities. *Should they be blamed for lethargy when their diets are inadequate to sustain vigor, for family instability when they are under torturing financial stress, for low standardized test scores when their education has been sporadic and of low quality, or for loose workforce attachments when they are in dead-end jobs that cannot lift them out of poverty? How will you support a homeless student who is assigned to your classroom?*

Opportunities for Reflection

Some anthropologists and sociologists who have studied the relationship between cultural values and poverty status have proposed a theory of a culture of poverty. They assert that the poor have a unique way of life that has developed as a reaction to their impoverished environment. This thesis suggests that people in poverty have a different value system and lifestyle that is perpetuated and transmitted to other generations.

Critics of the culture of poverty thesis believe that the cultural values of this group are much like those of the rest of the population but have been modified in practice because of situational stresses. This explanation suggests that the differences in values and lifestyles are not passed from one generation to the next, but rather are the adaptations by them to the experience of living in poverty.

THE WORKING CLASS

The occupations pursued by the **working class** are those that require manual work for which income varies widely, depending on the skill required in the specific job. The factor that is most important in the description of the working class is the subordination of members to the capitalist control of production. These workers do not have control of their work. They do not give orders; they take orders from others. Included in the working class are craft and precision workers (11% of all workers) and operators, fabricators, and laborers (13%). This latter group has been hurt the most because of job losses resulting from technological advances and the movement of jobs to other countries. When farm laborers and service workers are added to this group, the working class comprises 38.4% of the employed population (U.S. Census Bureau, 2003b).

Over the past few decades, jobs have shifted from the manufacturing sector to service jobs in private households, protective services (police and firefighters), food services, health services, cleaning services, and personal services (hairdressers and early childhood assistants). The number of temporary, part-time, and contract jobs is expanding. Most of these jobs provide low wages and no health care or retirement benefits (Collins & Veskel, 2004).

In 2002, the median income of these workers varied from $14,352 for female private household workers and $27,040 for male machine operators to $35,204 for male mechanics and repairers. The median income of female and male workers in farming, forestry, and fishing was $16,016 and $19,552 respectively (U.S. Census Bureau, 2003b). Although the income of the working class is equal to and sometimes higher than that of white-collar workers, the working class has less job security. Work is more sporadic, and unemployment is unpredictably affected by the economy. Jobs are uncertain because of displacement as a result of technology, which often results in more stringent educational requirements. Fringe benefits available to these workers are often not as good as those offered to other workers. Vacation time is usually shorter, health insurance is available less often, and working conditions are more dangerous.

People at the low end of the wage scale are the working poor. They do the jobs that most persons with more education refuse to do. Although they sometimes work one or more jobs at minimum wages, they can't pull themselves out of poverty. Critics of current economic and social policies ask why the minimum wage remains so low that people who earn it fall below the government's poverty line (Rank, 2004;

Shipler, 2004; and Shulman, 2003). Although union workers generally receive higher incomes and have negotiated health care and retirement benefits, many low-income workers do not join unions or they work in states or companies that aggressively discourage union membership.

Blue-collar workers are engaged primarily in manual work that is routine and mechanical. The education required for most of these jobs is not as high as for - **white-collar** jobs that are not mechanical and less routine. The better-paying, skilled blue-collar jobs, however, require specialized training and apprenticeships. Without additional training, it becomes difficult to move into a higher-level position. Many factory workers earn little more after 20 years on the job than a beginner does, and within a few years the new worker is earning the same pay as the worker with seniority.

Except for the skilled jobs and some service and farm jobs that allow autonomy to the worker, most jobs at this level are routine and are often perceived as not very meaningful or satisfying to the worker. Some studies report that blue-collar workers are more likely to separate work and social activities than workers at other levels. They tend not to socialize with coworkers to the same degree as other workers but maintain strong kinship ties with parents and siblings for social life.

Blue-collar workers generally perceive themselves as hardworking and honest, and as performing decent and important work for society. They want to be successful and often hope that their children will not have to spend their lives in a factory. Mistakenly, they are often perceived by others as authoritarian and intolerant of civil rights. This image, however, has not proved accurate; blue-collar workers are no more intolerant or prejudiced than members of other classes.

THE MIDDLE CLASS

In the past, the myth of **middle-class** Americans was a married couple with two or three children in a suburban house with a double garage, a television set, and the latest household gadgets. The father was almost always the primary breadwinner. In reality, the male-breadwinner family no longer provides the central experience for the vast majority of children, but it has not been replaced by any new modal category. Most Americans move in and out of a variety of family types over the course of their lives—families headed by a divorced parent, couples raising children out of wedlock, two-earner families, same-sex couples, families with no spouse in the labor force, foster families, and families headed by grandparents. *When you think of a family, what characteristics come to mind? How do you feel about same-sex parents and single mothers? How might your positive or negative feelings about these family structures affect your view of students from those families?*

Opportunities for Reflection

The incomes of Americans who are popularly considered middle class vary greatly. Families generally are classified as middle class if their annual incomes fall between $30,000 and $80,000 (Rose, 2000)—about 44% of those submitting tax returns in 2003. Although some members of the middle class have comfortable incomes, they have virtually no wealth. Many live from paycheck to paycheck, with little cushion against the loss of earning power through catastrophe, recession, layoffs, wage cuts, or old age. At various periods in the life cycle, some members fall into poverty for brief periods of time. Many families have found it necessary for both husband and wife to work to make ends meet. For discussion purposes, the middle class is divided into two distinct groups: white-collar workers and professionals/managers.

Professionals, managers, and administrators are accorded higher prestige in society than other white-collar workers. A major difference between these two groups is the amount of control they have over their work and the work of others. White-collar clerical workers, technicians, and salespersons are usually supervised by the professionals, managers, or administrators.

The jobs held by the middle class differ greatly, especially in income compensation. Overall, middle-class workers earn a median income above that of most blue-collar workers, except for skilled workers and many operatives. The median income of sales workers was $31,792 in 2002; workers who provide administrative support, including clerical work, earned less, with a median income of $26,520. The median income for the technical and related support occupations was $37,232 (U.S. Census Bureau, 2003b). As a group, these workers have greater job security and better fringe benefits than many blue-collar workers. Whereas the formal education required for these jobs varies, more formal education is usually expected than for blue-collar jobs.

As white-collar jobs expanded during the past five decades, many people believed that such jobs were more meaningful and satisfying than jobs in blue-collar occupations. How meaningful and satisfying a job is, however, depends on the particular job. Certainly, many are as routine and boring as many blue-collar jobs; others are highly interesting and challenging. Still others are extremely alienating in that employees cannot control their environments. Some employees perceive their work as meaningless, are socially isolated from coworkers, and develop low levels of self-esteem. The type of job and the environment in which it is performed vary greatly for workers with white-collar jobs. *Think about your future job as a teacher. How interesting, meaningful, challenging, or routine do you expect it to be? How much control will you have over your environment?*

Members of this class appear to believe strongly in the Protestant work ethic. They see themselves as respectable and as adhering to a specific set of beliefs and values that are inherent in the good life. Although they are only slightly better off economically than their blue-collar counterparts, they live or try to live a more affluent lifestyle.

Opportunities for Reflection

Pause to Reflect 2.1

Perceptions of others develop early in life and are corrected or reinforced on the basis of one's experiences throughout life.

- *What images do you conjure up when you think of the homeless, the working class, and the middle class?*
- *Which characteristics are positive, and which are negative?*
- *Why are your perceptions value laden?*
- *What must you watch for in your own perceptions to ensure that you do not discriminate against students from one of these groups?*

To answer these questions online, go to the Pause to Reflect module for this chapter of the Companion Website. **CW**

THE UPPER MIDDLE CLASS

Professionals, managers, and administrators are the elite of the middle class. They represent the status that many who are concerned with upward mobility are trying to reach. Their income level allows them to lead lives that are, in many cases, quite different from those of white-collar and blue-collar workers. They are the group that seems to have benefited most from the nation's economic growth since the 1940s. Although at a level far below the upper class, the **upper middle class** are the affluent middle class. They reflect the middle-class myth more accurately than any of the other groups described.

The professionals who best fit this category include those who must receive professional or advanced degrees and credentials to practice their professions. Judges, lawyers, physicians, college professors, teachers, and scientists are the professionals. Excluding teachers, most professionals earn far more than the median income of $46,644 reported for this category. They may be classified as members of the upper middle class, many earning over $75,000 annually, especially when the family has two wage earners. They usually own a home and a new car and are able to take vacations to other parts of the country and abroad (Rose, 2000).

This group also includes managers and administrators, who make up 16% of the employed population. They are the successful executives and businesspeople, who are very diverse and include the chief executive officers of companies, presidents of colleges, and owners and administrators of local nursing homes. Those who are the most affluent make up the middle and upper management in financing, marketing, and production. The gap between men's and women's earnings is greater for managers and administrators than for professionals. As reported earlier in this chapter, the administrators of large corporations earn salaries far above this level; their salaries and fringe benefits place them in the upper class instead of the middle class.

Educational credentials are more important for the professionals and managers at this level than at any other class level. The prospect of gaining the necessary qualifications to enter this level is severely restricted, because children of parents with college degrees are much more likely to attend and graduate from college than are children of parents who did not attend college. Thus, a position in this status level often is a part of one's inheritance as a result of the advantages that prestige and income bring to members of the upper middle class.

The incomes and opportunities to accumulate wealth are high for this group compared with the bulk of the population. Members of this class play an active role in civic and voluntary organizations. Their occupations and incomes give them access to policymaking roles within these organizations. They are active participants in political processes and thus are major recipients of public benefits. Of all the groups studied so far, this one holds the greatest power.

The occupations of the people in this group play a central role in their lives, often determining their friends as well as their business and professional associates. Their jobs allow autonomy and a great amount of self-direction. Members of this group tend to view their affluence, advantages, and comforts as universal, rather than as unique. They believe that their class includes almost everyone (Rose, 2000). They believe in the American dream of success because they have achieved it.

THE UPPER CLASS

High income and wealth are necessary characteristics for entering the **upper class** as well as for being accepted by those persons who are already members. Within the upper class, however, are great variations in the wealth of individual families.

The upper class is comprised of two groups. One group includes the individuals and families who control great inherited wealth; the other group includes top-level administrators and professionals. Prestige positions, rather than great wealth, allow some families to enter or maintain their status at this level. The upper class includes persons with top-level and highly paid positions in large banks, entertainment corporations, and industrial corporations. It also includes those who serve as primary advisors to these positions and government leaders—for example, corporate lawyers.

The disparity between the income and wealth of members of this class and members of other classes is astounding. In 1982, for example, chief executive officers earned about 42 times as much as the average worker in their companies. In 1990, their pay reached 85 times the average worker's earnings. By 2003, the ratio had increased to 301 (Anderson et al., 2004). The number of people reporting incomes of more than a million dollars has grown dramatically since the 1980s. This increase in the size of the upper class has occurred, in part, because of the income received from increased rent, dividends, and interest payments available to the holders of financial assets, including property and stock.

Wealth and income ensure power. The extremely small portion of the population that holds a vastly disproportionate share of the wealth also benefits disproportionately when resources are distributed. The power of these people allows them to protect their wealth. The only progressive tax in this country is the federal income tax, in which a greater percentage of the income is taxed as the income increases. Loopholes in the tax laws provide benefits to those whose unearned income is based on assets. What does this mean in terms of advantage to the rich? Tax laws in the 1980s were regressive, resulting in a decline in the taxes of higher-income families. The 1990s saw more progressive taxes in which the taxes of higher-income families rose in comparison to the taxes of low-income families. The tax cut of 2001 reduced taxes for everyone, but more so for higher-income families. The tax rate of families in the bottom fifth of income earners dropped by 0.7% for an average tax reduction of $67. However, the wealthiest 1% experienced a 4.17% drop in their tax rate with an average savings of $45,717 (Mishel, Bernstein, & Schmitt, 2003). Thus, tax relief has been more beneficial to the rich than to those with the lowest incomes.

Although families with inherited wealth do not represent a completely closed status group, they do have an overrepresentation of Anglo, Protestant members who were born in the United States. They tend to intermarry with other members of the upper class. They are well-educated, although a college degree is not essential. The educational mark of prestige is attendance at the elite private prep schools. For example, less than 10% of U.S. high school students attend private schools. Less than 1% of the high school population attends the elite prep schools, whose students are overwhelmingly the children of the upper class (Cookson & Persell, 1985). Greater assimilation of lifestyles and values has occurred within this class than in any other. Although diversity exists within the group, members of the upper class may be the most homogeneous group, and they are likely to remain so as long as their cross-cultural and cross-class interactions are limited.

Interaction of Class with Race and Ethnicity, Gender, and Age

Poverty is most likely to be a condition of the young, persons of color, women, full-time workers in the low status jobs, and the illiterate. On the basis of the U.S. government's poverty threshold, nearly 36 million persons are in poverty, or 12.5% of the total population; many of these individuals are members of the 7.6 million low-income families that make up 10% of all families (U.S. Census Bureau, 2003b). The population groups that suffer the most from poverty are shown in Table 2.1.

Many low-income people do have full-time, year-round jobs but are not paid wages high enough to move their families out of poverty. Nearly 1.9 million families have at least one member who works full-time, year-round but the family remains in poverty, and another 3.1 million families below the poverty threshold have one or more family members who work part-time or full-time for part of the year (U.S. Census Bureau, 2003b). The working poor are disproportionately located in service and retail trade occupations. It is difficult for the working poor to rise above poverty when the minimum wage is low and part-time jobs are often all that is available. A growing economy should lead to a decrease in poverty, but inequality between the top and bottom of the income scale continues to grow, contributing to higher poverty rates for people at the low end of the income scale (Mishel et al., 2003).

Income inequality is higher in the United States than any other industrialized countries. International studies of these countries report that the United States has the highest poverty rates and has social policies that limit opportunities for moving out of poverty. Although workers in the United States work more hours per year, low-income families have a lower standard of living than workers in other countries.

Table 2.1 Population Below the Poverty Level

Group	Number	Percentage
All Races	35.9 million	12.5% of U.S. population
Asian American	1.4 million	11.6% of all Asian Americans
Black	8.8 million	24.4% of all blacks
Latino	9.0 million	22.5% of all Latinos
White	15.9 million	8.2% of all whites
Older than 65 years	3.6 million	10.2% of over 65-year-olds
Younger than 18 years	12.9 million	17.6% of children and youth
Female-headed households with no husband present	12.4 million	30.0% of female-headed households

Source: U.S. Census Bureau. (2004). *Current population survey, 2004 annual social and economic supplement.* Washington, DC: http://ferret.bls.census.gov/macro/032004/pov/toc.htm.

Opportunities for Reflection

Other countries have stronger unions, higher minimum wages, and generous benefits, including more vacation days. The social policies of other countries provide a social safety net for families through maternity leave, family leave, universal health care, and child care for its children (Mishel et al., 2003). *Does it surprise you that income inequality is greater in the United States than other industrialized countries? Why or why not?*

Although the ceiling for poverty level is supposed to indicate an income level necessary to maintain an adequate, not comfortable, living, it is misleading to assume that any family near this level can live adequately. Many families who have incomes just above this level find it difficult to pay even for essential food, housing, and clothing, let alone live comfortably by the American standard. Thus, they are economically poor even though they technically earn an income above the poverty level that is set by the federal government.

The poor are a very heterogeneous group. They do not all have the same values or lifestyles. They cannot be expected to react alike to the conditions of poverty. To many, their ethnicity or religion is the most important determinant of the way they live within the economic constraints of poverty. To others, the devastating impact of limited resources is the greatest influence in determining their values and lifestyles. No matter what aspects of the various cultural groups have the greatest impact on the lives of individuals or families, lifestyles are limited severely by the economic constraints that keep people in poverty. Individual choice is more limited for people with low incomes than for any other group studied in this book.

RACE AND ETHNIC INEQUALITY

African Americans, Mexican Americans, Puerto Ricans, and American Indians experience the severest economic deprivation of all ethnic groups in this country. Although the census data on consumer income are not broken down for American Indians, Eskimos, and Aleuts, these groups probably suffer more from economic inequity than any other group.

In 2001, the median income of white families was $54,067; of black families, $33,598; of Latino families, $34,490; and of Asian American and Pacific Islander families, $60,158 (U.S. Census Bureau, 2003b). Therefore, black families had a median income that was 62% of the median income of whites; Latinos earned 64% of the median income of whites; and Asian Americans and Pacific Islanders earned 111% of the median income of whites. When standards of living were compared by UNESCO across nations, the United States was ranked sixth of the nations in the study. If the data had included only whites, the United States would have ranked first. Blacks would have ranked thirty-first—at the same level as an underdeveloped country (Spencer, 1993).

When families with married couples are compared, the gap between groups becomes smaller, but not equal. Black married couples earn 84% and Latinos 67% of the median income of whites (U.S. Census Bureau, 2002). Therefore, when age, education, experience, and other factors are equal to those of white men, the earnings of persons of color and whites become more similar, but the income ratios between the groups still favor whites.

People of color make up a disproportionately high percentage of people in poverty. Of the white population, 8% fall below the poverty level, compared with 24% of the black and 23% of the Latino populations (U.S. Census Bureau, 2004). One of the rea-

Figure 2.4

Percentage of Asian Americans, blacks, Hispanics, and whites in different occupations[1].

[1]The figure shows the percentages of each group employed in an occupational category (e.g., 10% of all employed blacks work as managers or professionals).

Source: U.S. Census Bureau. (2003). *Statistical abstract of the United States: 2003* (123rd ed.). Washington, DC: U.S. Government Printing Office.

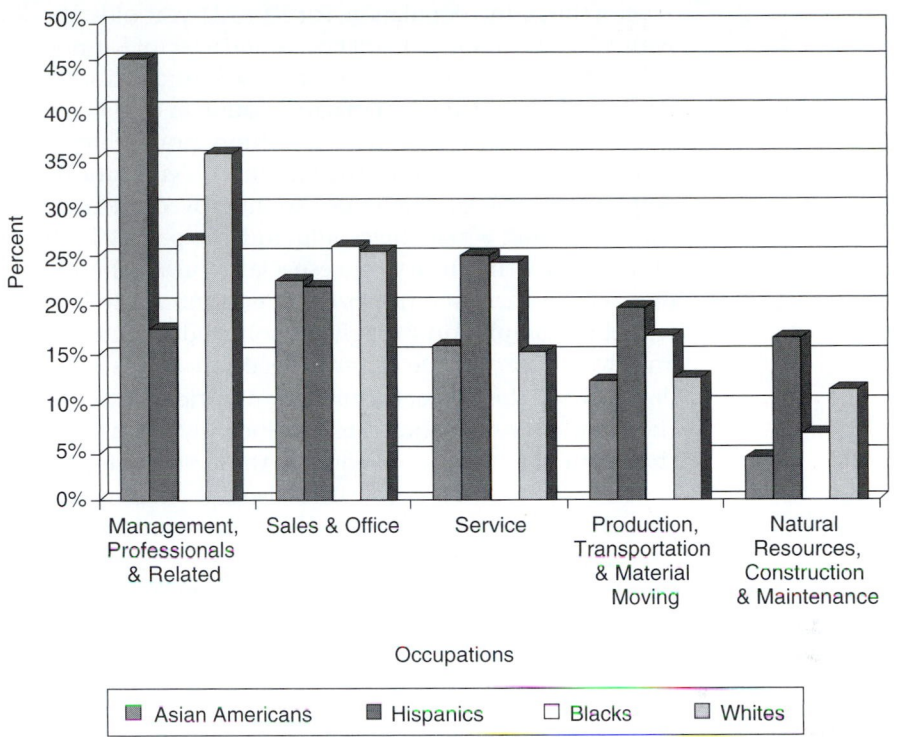

sons is that persons of color are more likely to be concentrated in low-paying jobs as shown in Figure 2.4. The percentage of blacks in the higher-paying and higher-status jobs is much lower than whites. Although both absolute and relative gains in the occupational status of blacks have been made during the past 40 years, blacks and Latinos are still heavily overrepresented in the semiskilled and unskilled positions.

This inequitable condition is perpetuated by several factors. Persons in poverty are more likely not to have graduated from high school. Historically, students of color dropped out of school in greater proportions than white students, limiting their income potential. Although the gap has been greatly reduced over time, it still exists. The U.S. Census Bureau (2003a) reports that 13.2% of white 18- to 21-year-olds had dropped out of high school in 2001 as compared to 13.8% of blacks and 29.7% of Latinos. Two new studies by the Urban Institute and the Civil Rights Project at Harvard University indicate that the dropout rate is much greater than the government reports. They have found that nearly one third of public high school students are not graduating. Students of color have only a 50-50 chance of finishing high school (Edley, 2004; Swanson, 2004). Dropout rates are related to family income. High school graduation rates range from 68% for those from families earning less than $35,377 annually to 91% for those from families earning more than $90,000 (Average Family Income, 2004). *Why do you think so many students of color are dropping out of school? What could a teacher do to encourage more students of color to stay in school? What school policies and practices help prevent students from dropping out?*

Unemployment for people of color is higher than for whites. Five percent of the white population was unemployed in 2002, compared with 10.2% of the black population and

Opportunities for Reflection

7.5% of the Latino population. For 20- to 24-year-olds, the differences were even greater, with 8.1% of whites, 19.1% of blacks, and 9.9% of Latinos unemployed (U.S. Census Bureau, 2003b). Discrimination against blacks and Latinos is still widespread, contributing to unemployment and lack of participation in the labor market.

The historical experiences of ethnic groups have had a great impact on their gains in SES. For example, the absolute class position (income, occupation, rate of employment) of African Americans improved as a result of their migration to America's large cities where they could find jobs paying higher wages during the first half of the twentieth century, and especially during the 1940s. Their educational attainments have narrowed the formerly enormous gap between blacks and whites with regard to completion of high school; median number of school years completed; and, to a lesser degree, standardized test scores and prevalence of college attendance. Since the 1960s, the number of African American families who have entered the middle class has increased significantly. Even so, the jobs that are available and the salaries earned are not equal to those of whites, particularly white males.

Other oppressed groups with a disproportionately low SES have had different historical experiences than blacks but suffer similarly from discrimination. Mexican Americans are highly overrepresented as farm laborers, one of the lowest-status occupations. Many American Indians have been isolated on reservations, away from most occupations except those lowest in prestige, and the numbers of such positions are limited. Asian Americans, who as a group have a high educational level and a relatively high SES, often reach middle-management positions but may then face a glass ceiling that prevents them from moving into upper management.

GENDER INEQUALITY

As a group, women earn less and are more likely to suffer from poverty than any other group, with women of color suffering the greatest oppression. The reasons for such inequality, however, have very different origins from inequality based on race and ethnicity. Institutional discrimination based on gender is based on a patriarchal society in which women have been assigned to traditional roles of mother and wife and, if they had to work outside the home, to jobs in which subordination was expected. This status has limited their job opportunities and has kept their wages low. Overt discrimination against women has resulted in the use of gender to determine wages, hiring, and promotion of individuals by using mechanisms similar to those that promote inequality for members of other oppressed groups.

Refer to Chapter 4 for a more in-depth discussion of the income differences between males and females.

The number of women in the workforce has increased dramatically during the past four decades. Seventy-one percent of women between the ages of 20 and 64 were working in the civilian workforce in 2003, as compared with 91% of the men (U.S. Census Bureau, 2003a). Black women and white women participate in the labor force at about the same rate today; 60% of all women over 16 years of age have jobs. Black women are somewhat more likely to work than others while Latino women are somewhat less likely to work outside the home at rates of 62% and 58%, respectively.

To maintain an adequate or desirable standard of living today, both husband and wife in many families must work. The difference that two incomes make on the family income is obvious. Although the percentages in the workforce of women who are single, widowed, divorced, or separated have increased during the past 50 years, the percentages of married women and white women in the workforce have increased dramatically since 1940. In 1940, only 16.7% of all married women worked outside the home; by 2002, 61% did. Seventy-two percent of married women with children under 18 years of age worked outside the home.

Historically, the sexual division of labor has been fairly rigid. The roles of women were limited to reproduction, childrearing, and homemaking. When they did work outside the home, their jobs were often similar to roles in the home—that is, caring for children or the sick. Jobs were stereotyped by gender. As recently as 2002 women comprised more than 90% and less than 10% of the workforce in the occupations shown in Table 2.2. The jobs in which women predominate are accompanied by neither high

Table 2.2 Occupations in Which Women Are Most Likely and Least Likely to Participate

Traditionally Female Occupations	Percent Participation	Traditionally Male Occupations	Percent Participation
Family child care providers	99.4	Automobile mechanics	1.3
Secretaries	98.6	Aircraft engine mechanics	1.4
Dental hygienists	98.1	Extractive occupations	1.4
Dental assistants	98.0	Carpenters	1.8
Child care workers in private households	97.8	Firefighters	3.4
Prekindergarten & kindergarten teachers	97.7	Airplane pilots and navigators	4.2
Receptionists	97.1	Transportation occupations, except motor vehicles	4.5
Licensed practical nurses	94.9	Material moving equipment operators	4.6
Speech therapists	94.3	Truck drivers	4.9
Typists	93.9	Mechanical engineering	6.9
Early childhood teacher assistants	93.8	Forestry & logging	7.3
Cleaners & servants	93.7	Aerospace engineering	8.1
Registered nurses	92.9	Surveying and mapping technicians	9.1
Bookkeepers, accounting & auditing clerks	92.7		
Teacher aides	91.6		
Billing, posting, & calculating machine operators	91.2		
Dietitians	90.2		

Source: U.S. Census Bureau. (2003). *Statistical abstract of the United States: 2003* (123rd ed.). Washington, DC: U.S. Government Printing Office.

prestige nor high income. People in the category of professionals (teachers and nurses) do not compete in income or prestige with architects and engineers. Women continue to be overrepresented as clerical and service workers and underrepresented as managers and skilled workers. Even within these occupation groups, salaries between women and men differ. Table 2.3 compares the salaries for selected jobs. The difference in the incomes of men and women has declined over the past three decades. In 2002, the income of women was 78% of men's. At the same time, the gap between low-income and high income groups has led to growing inequality among women. Both men and women at the bottom of the income scale are losing ground. Women who enter traditionally male jobs with low-paying jobs at the same salary are not increasing their chances of moving into the middle class. Highly educated women are the ones who have made absolute wage gains during this period.

Below graduate and professional school levels, the percentages of graduates at the various levels of education are similar for men and women, matching closely their percentages of the population. College enrollment is 55% female and 45% male. In 2001, women received 41% of all law degrees, 43% of all medical degrees, and 18% of all engineering degrees (U.S. Census Bureau, 2003b). Compared with the earnings of men with the same education, however, women still earn less. Women with a bachelor's degree earned $30,973 compared to men's $49,985. Men with professional degrees earned $81,602 while women earned only $46,635.

Pause to Reflect 2.2

Throughout the next week, systematically record the types of jobs that men and women hold in your community. You might use a table such as this:

Type of Job	Number of Women	Number of Men

- *What are the similarities?*
- *Were you surprised by your findings?*
- *If so, what in particular surprised you?*

At the end of the week, analyze the data to determine whether men and women hold the same or similar jobs. What are the differences? What are the economic implications for the women and men in your study?

To answer these questions online, go to the Pause to Reflect module for this chapter of the Companion Website. CW

Women, especially those who are the heads of households, are more likely than men to fall below the poverty level. Twenty-eight percent of families maintained by women with no husband present earn an income below the official poverty level (U.S Census Bureau, 2004). The large number of families in this group is a result of a combination of low-paying jobs and an increase in divorces, separations, and out-of-wedlock births.

Table 2.3 Comparison of Women's and Men's Median Salaries in Selected Job Categories

Job Category	Women's Annual Salary	Men's Annual Salary	Women's Salaries as Percentage of Men's
Construction trades	$28,756	$31,512	91%
Executive, administration, & managerial	$38,272	$56,212	68%
Farming, forestry, & fishing	$16,016	$19,552	82%
Mechanics & repairers	$30,836	$35,204	88%
Professional specialty	$40,196	$53,924	75%
Protective services	$26,052	$35,828	73%
Sales	$22,932	$38,584	59%
Technical & related support	$30,732	$43,732	70%

Source: U.S. Census Bureau. (2003). *Statistical abstract of the United States: 2003* (123rd ed.). Washington, DC: U.S. Government Printing Office.

Figure 2.5

Persons in poverty by age, race, and ethnicity.

Source: U.S. Census Bureau. (2003). *Statistical abstract of the United States* (123rd ed.). Washington, DC: U.S. Government Printing Office.

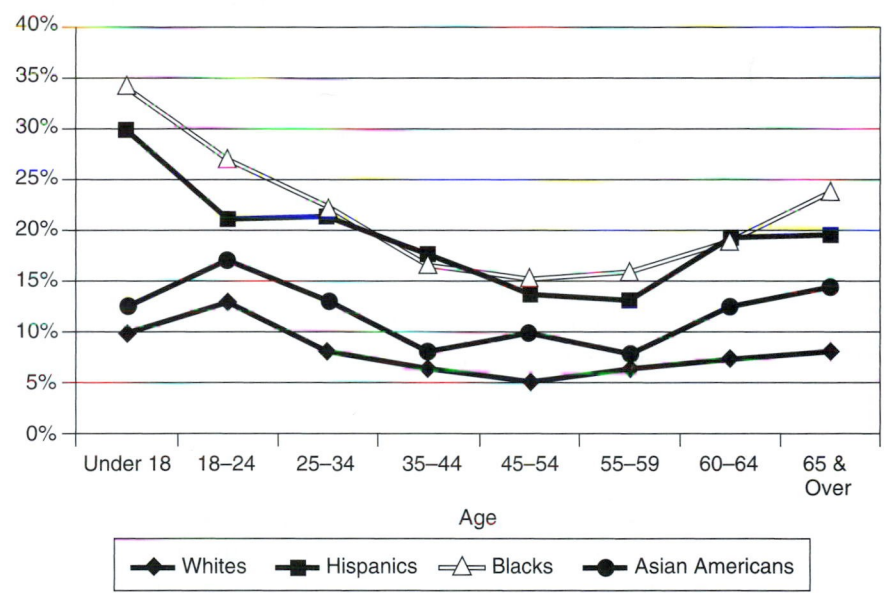

When compared with male households where the wife is absent, women without husbands earn only 65% of the median income of men (U.S. Census Bureau, 2002).

AGE INEQUALITY

The highest incidence of poverty occurs at both ends of the life span. Society has determined that adults over 65 years of age and children are in nonworking periods of their lives. The poverty rate for children is 17.6%, which is much greater than for all other ages, but the differences are greatest for children of color as shown in Figure 2.5.

See Chapters 5 and 7 for more information on students with disabilities and English language learners respectively.

Both women and men earn their maximum income between the ages of 45 and 54. The median income of persons who are 14 to 19 years old is lower than for any other group, primarily because most of these persons are just beginning to enter the workforce at the end of this period and some may not enter for several more years, especially if they attend college. Income then increases steadily for most people until after they reach 55 years of age. The income of women remains fairly constant throughout much of their working lives, whereas the income for a large percentage of men increases dramatically during their lifetimes.

Children's class status depends on their families, and they have little or no control over their destiny during their early years. A higher percentage of children are in poverty in the United States than in European countries (Luxembourg Income Study, 2004). International studies show that U.S. children in high- and middle-income families have a higher standard of living than children in other industrialized countries. However, children in low-income families are at least one third worse off than children in other countries (Rank, 2004). In schools, poverty is tracked by the number of students eligible for free or reduced lunches. In 2003 40% of U.S. fourth graders were eligible for this program, but the percentage of Latino (71%) and black students (70%) was much higher than whites (23%). Black and Latino students are more than 1.5 times as likely to attend high poverty schools in which more than 75% of the students are eligible for free or reduced lunches. (U.S. Department of Education, 2004).

Students from low-income families begin kindergarten with lower cognitive skills than their peers in families with middle and high incomes. To compound the problem, low SES kindergartners begin their schooling in the worst public schools with low-quality teaching and discriminatory practices such as ability grouping (Lee & Burkam, 2002). These children will be disadvantaged in developing their adult earning power by inferior schooling, an oppressive financial environment, and poor health. *Why are children from low-income families entering schools with lower cognitive skills than their peers? How does a family's economic condition influence readiness for school? How can educators begin to overcome the lack of readiness?*

Opportunities for Reflection

To prevent poverty after age 65, individuals must plan throughout their working lives to defer or save income that can be used for support once they stop earning regular incomes. Social Security benefits provide some support to the elderly, and often these benefits are the only support available. Some workers participate in pension plans that provide an income after a lifetime of work, but many employees, especially blue-collar and low-level white-collar workers, still do not have the opportunity to participate in such programs. Ten percent of all persons older than age 65 have an income under the poverty level (U.S. Census Bureau, 2003b).

In a society in which high ranking is given to individuals who either control wealth or are productive in the labor force, persons who do not contribute to this production are assigned a low status. Many elderly persons receive financial and medical support from the government, making them nonproductive drawers on the nation's wealth. Often, they are accorded little deference and instead face impatience, patronization, and neglect by people still in the workforce.

Educational Implications

Many social reformers, educators, and parents view education as a powerful device for achieving social change and the reduction of poverty. From the beginning of the public school movement in the early nineteenth century, low incomes were believed to result from inadequate education. This view was still pervasive in the 1960s as the federal government attempted to eliminate poverty through the establishment of Head Start, Title I (compensatory education), Upward Bound, Job Corps, Neighborhood Youth Corps, and other educational programs. However, test scores of students from low-income groups have not improved as much as expected and racial/ethnic segregation among and within schools has increased.

This lack of progress in overcoming the effects of poverty on students should not suggest that educational reforms are not worthwhile. Some changes make schooling more attractive to students and even increase the achievement of many individual students. In a number of states educational resources have become more equitably distributed as a result of court cases. Nevertheless, the intended goal of increasing income equity and eliminating poverty has not been realized. More than school reform will be required to raise the academic achievement of low-SES students. The social and economic conditions of their lives must be improved through higher wages and social policies that support low-income families (Rothstein, 2004). *What social policies would provide support for children and their families?*

Opportunities for Reflection

Different social-historical interpretations of education explain the role of schools in society and the degree to which this goal and others are met. Two views are prevalent. In one view schools are an agent of social reform that can improve the chances of economic success for its graduates. The second view concludes that schools exist as agents of the larger social, economic, and political context, with the goal of inculcating the values necessary to maintain the current socioeconomic and political systems.

Supporters of the first view are much more benign in their description of the role of schools in helping students become socially mobile. They are optimistic that social reform can be achieved by providing low-income students with more effective schools. The others see schools as preparing students to work efficiently at appropriate levels in corporate organizations. The needs of business and industry are met by preparing students from low-income families for low-wage jobs that will be managed by college graduates from middle- and high-income families. *Which role do you see schools playing? Which would you prefer? Why? Do you believe education can help low SES students be financially successful as adults? What schools serving primarily low-income families do you know whose students are achieving at high academic levels?*

Opportunities for Reflection

Rather than provide equal educational opportunity, many schools perpetuate existing social and economic inequities in society. In this section, we examine four areas that influence the inequities that exist in schools not serving low-income and many working- and middle-class students well: teacher expectations, tracking, developing equitable curriculum, and inequities in the funding of schools.

Some inner-city schools are squeezed between office buildings and housing units, leaving small playgrounds that differ greatly from those in suburban and rural areas.

 VIDEO INSIGHT

Smart Kid, Tough School

In recent years, more and more attention has been given to the deteriorating condition of many of the nation's schools. Surely, students who are educated in such surroundings do not receive an education equal to the education given to students who attend schools with greater financial and community resources. Cedric Jennings, a star student from a high school in the poorest section of Washington, DC, saw this confirmed when he enrolled in a summer program for gifted minority students, only to find that the students from higher-income neighborhoods were better prepared academically. Yet, when scholarship offers to attend expensive prep schools came his way, Cedric refused and returned to his old high school for his senior year. Why do you think Cedric decided to return to Ballou High School?

Imagine you were a teacher at an inner-city school like the high school profiled in the video segment.

1. *How would you try to instill a sense of the value of an education in students in a world where being smart is not always valued by their peers?*

2. *How would your own class background affect your ability to relate to the students?*

3. *What could you do in your classroom on a day-to-day basis to help eradicate the crippling effects of class differences?*

To answer these questions online, go to the ABC News Video Insight module for this chapter of the Companion Website.

DVD

CW

TEACHER EXPECTATIONS

Most classrooms are heterogeneous in terms of student ethnicity, gender, religion, and ability. Unfortunately, many teachers assign academic expectations to students on the basis of their membership in these groups. Students not classified as middle class are often viewed as not able to achieve at high academic levels. Most of these students are greatly harmed by such expectations. In contrast, students from the upper middle class usually benefit from a teacher's judgments because they are expected to perform better in school, are treated more favorably, and perform at a higher level in most cases.

Differences in mathematics and science achievement based on class and race are found by age 9, but are clearly in place by age 13. In junior high school, students from low-income families typically take fewer courses in mathematics and science, which contributes to later differences in college enrollments and vocational choices. In many schools with large numbers of low-income populations, advanced courses in these subjects are often not even offered in their schools. Thus, even those students who are achieving at a level equal to students from the dominant group are stifled in their attempts to achieve equitably at advanced levels. It is no wonder that they score less well on standardized assessments. They have not had the opportunity to take the same high-level courses as their middle-class peers.

Ethnographic studies of schools document how students are classified, segregated, and taught differently, starting with their first days in school. Most teachers can identify the personal characteristics of students that will lead to academic success. They then develop instruction and interactions with their students that ensure that the students will, in fact, behave as the teachers expect—a phenomenon called the **self-fulfilling prophecy.** The kindergarten teacher who divides her class into three reading and mathematics groups by the third week of school has limited knowledge about the academic abilities of the students. Too often, the groups are organized by nonacademic factors. Students in the highest group may be all dressed in clean clothes that are relatively new and well pressed. They interact well with the teacher and other students, are quite verbal, and use standard English. Students in the lower two groupings may be poorly dressed and smell badly. They use black dialect; and their families appear to be less stable than those of students in the highest group. If the teacher's goal is to spend time with students in the lower group to ensure that they develop language and reading skills they will need to be successful in the first grade and their skills become less distinguishable from students in the higher groups, this grouping strategy would be successful. The problem is that many teachers do not expect the students identified at having lower academic ability at the beginning of the year to perform at high levels. The result is that students in the highest group continue to perform better academically and behave in a more acceptable manner than students in the other two groups. As the teacher had projected, these students are more successful throughout their schooling than students from lower socioeconomic levels.

When teachers make such judgments about students, they are taking the first step in preventing students from having an equal opportunity for academic achievement. Rather than ensure that students have access to an egalitarian system, such classification and subsequent treatment of students ensures the maintenance of an inequitable system. This action is not congruent with the democratic belief that all students can learn and should be provided equal educational opportunities.

In helping to overcome the stigma of being poor, educators must consciously review their expectations for students. They should not further exacerbate students' feelings of low esteem that often result because students have already learned that they do not have the same status as their middle-class peers. Seeing students as individuals, rather than as members of a specific socioeconomic group, may assist educators in overcoming the **classism** that exists in the school and the community. Classism allows teachers to view their own class status as superior to that of some or all of their students. Information about a student's family background can be used in understanding the power of environment on a student's expression of self; it must not be used to rationalize stereotypes and label students. Educators must become aware of any prejudices they themselves hold against members of lower socioeconomic groups and work to overcome their biases. Otherwise, discriminatory practices will surface in the classroom in the form of self-fulfilling prophecies that harm students and perpetuate societal inequities. *How will you know if your prejudices are influencing your interactions with students from low-income families? What can you do to become aware of your prejudices and eliminate them so that they do not impact negatively on some of your students?*

In inner-city schools, educators face many low-income and working-class students whose environment outside the school is very different from that of students in most suburban schools. For many students, schools are safe places to go as compared to the abuse and crime they face at home or between home and the school. These students have strengths that are not recognized or supported by many educators. Many are very resilient under conditions that provide almost daily obstacles to their well-being and academic achievement. Isolated rural areas require that families respond to their nonschool environment much differently than families in other areas. Educators should not expect to be able to teach every student effectively in the same way. Although it is essential to ensure that all students learn academics, how the educator teaches these skills should vary, depending on the environment in which students live—a factor greatly dependent on the family's SES. Helping students to achieve academically in many of the schools that serve students from low-income families requires competent educators with "commitment, enthusiasm, compassion, solidarity, and love" (Noguera, 2003, p. 21).

How can the development of negative and harmful expectations for students be prevented? Teachers, counselors, and administrators can unconsciously fall into such behavior because they have learned that poverty is the fault of the individual. As a result, students are blamed for circumstances beyond their control. Instead, educators should see as a challenge the opportunity to provide these students with the knowledge and skills to overcome poverty. Educators should select approaches they would use for the most gifted students. The goal should be to level up the educational experiences for students who previously would have been tracked into the low-ability classes. Too many teachers blame the students, their families, and their communities for students not learning rather than examining and changing their own teaching practices to improve student learning. Effective teachers do make a difference. Students who are lucky enough to have an effective teacher three years in a row have a great academic advantage over students who have not been so lucky (Sanders & Rivers, 1996).

Equality in the achievement of students could be increased by raising the level of instructional content and instructional discourse in all courses at all levels. Achieve-

Opportunities for Reflection

ment is improved when teachers help students interact with the academic content through discussion and **authenticity**—relating the content to students' prior experiences and real-world applications. These strategies work for all students, not just those in the advanced placement and honors courses.

TRACKING

Tracking students into different groups or classes based on their intellectual abilities is a common educational practice. Teachers often divide the class into smaller groups for instructional purposes. These groups could have a heterogeneous makeup with each group containing male and female students from different ethnic groups and students who are currently high and low achievers. These groups are often characterized by students helping each other. In other cases, teachers assign students to a group based on the teacher's perception of the students' academic abilities, which may be based on students' latest standardized test scores. The teacher may use different instructional strategies in these groups and has different expectations for learning outcomes. Tracking also occurs when students are assigned to classes based on their perceived intellectual abilities or other characteristics such as speaking a language other than English or having a disability. Middle and high school students either choose or are assigned to college preparatory, vocational, general, and advanced courses based, in great part, on how their teachers or counselors judge their future potential. Some students are placed in gifted courses or programs and others in courses that are clearly meant for low-ability students.

Opportunities for Reflection

Supporters of tracking argue that separating students based on their perceived abilities allows teachers to better meet the needs of all students. Critics argue that tracking and homogeneous grouping based on ability is discriminatory and prevents many students from developing their intellectual and social potential. *Do you think tracking is an appropriate instructional strategy? Why or why not? How might students in the lowest tracks be harmed by this strategy?*

Tracking is an area in which class matters. High ability appears to be more closely related to family background and SES than intellectual potential (Ball, 2003; Brantlinger, 2003; Welner, 2001). Tracking benefits most the students whose families are already privileged and the most powerful in the community. Students in the gifted and advanced programs are academically challenged in their courses with enrichment activities that encourage them to develop their intellectual and critical thinking skills. At the other end of the learning spectrum, the learning environment is often uninviting, boring, and not challenging. Rather than preparing these students to move to higher-level courses, these courses keep them at the lowest level of academic achievement.

Educational researchers continue to find that simply being in the low-ability group diminishes students' achievement (Lucas, 1999; Welner, 2001). Such students are provided with fewer and less effective opportunities to learn than other students. Critical thinking tasks are reserved for the high-ability groups. Oral recitation and structured written work are common in low-ability groups. Students are exposed to low-status knowledge at a slower pace than their peers in higher-ability groups, helping them fall further behind in subjects like mathematics, foreign languages, and sciences.

Teachers in low-ability classrooms spend more time on administration and discipline and less time actually teaching. As one might expect, student behavior in low tracks is more disruptive than in higher-level groups. However, this probably happens, in part, because students and teachers have developed behavioral standards that are more tolerant of inattention, and not because of students' individual abilities. To compound the problem, the more experienced and more successful teachers are disproportionately assigned to the higher-ability groups. Unfortunately, many teachers generally view high-track students positively and low-track students negatively.

Disproportionately large numbers of students from lower socioeconomic levels are assigned to low-ability groups beginning very early in their school careers. Even more tragic is the fact that the number of students from low-income families who are classified as being mentally challenged is disproportionately high. This inequitable classification places students of color in double jeopardy because they also disproportionately suffer from poverty.

Tracking has become a second-generation segregation issue that has led to the practice being challenged in courts (Welner, 2001). In many schools with diverse student populations, students have been resegregated based on race, class, and language into separate tracks within the school. White middle-class students have disproportionately high representation in gifted and talented programs while African Americans, Latinos, students from low-income families, and English language learners comprise the majority of the students in low-ability classrooms. For the most part, the courts have agreed with the plaintiffs that tracking students into low-ability courses and programs is a discriminatory practice that limits their educational opportunities and potential for later occupational and economic success. Even when students and parents are encouraged to choose courses, a school district may be liable for discriminatory action if parents have not been appropriately informed of required prerequisites for advanced courses. Other discriminatory practices that are being considered by courts today are the inadequate preparation of low-income students and students of color to pass standardized tests and the assignment of unqualified teachers to the schools in which these students are concentrated.

Teachers and administrators in some racially and SES-mixed schools have decided to detrack their schools. Some courts have actually ordered the school district to detrack their schools (Welner, 2001). Other schools have voluntarily made this decision to improve the education of students who have traditionally been assigned to the low tracks. However, dismantling tracking systems in schools is not an easy undertaking. Some teachers fight detracking, in part, because they do not believe that heterogeneous groupings contribute to the learning of all students. They may believe that gifted students will suffer if they are integrated with students who do not perform at the same academic level.

Middle-class parents, especially upper-middle-class parents, often fight efforts to detrack schools. According to Welner (2001), this resistance occurs "because detracking is fundamentally redistributive—altering how schools allocate their most precious resources, including time, teachers, materials, and high-achieving students" (p. xiii). Many parents whose children were most likely to be in the high-ability or gifted tracks fight the integration of their children with others. Students in the advanced placement and gifted programs are disproportionately the children of elite and powerful families in the communities. Many of these parents believe that their achievements should be passed on to their children by ensuring that they receive the highest-quality education possible. To prevent detracking, these parents employ strategies to hold on to the privilege that their children can gain from being in these classes. They use their power to force administrators to respond to their demands. They have been known to threaten to remove their children from public schools and hold out for other special privileges for their children. At times, they co-opt parents from the middle class to support their stand, which supports their children being segregated from low-income students whom they perceive as less able than their own children. Nevertheless, some schools have been able to detrack their schools with the goal of improving the education of all students regardless of the socioeconomic level or race of their parents.

CURRICULUM FOR EQUALITY

The curriculum should also reflect accurately the class structure and inequities that exist in the United States. Too often, the existence of nearly half the population is not validated in the curriculum. The curriculum and the textbooks usually focus on the values and experiences of a middle-class society. They highlight the heroes of our capitalist system and emphasize the importance of developing the skills to earn an income that will enable students to soon own the home, car, furniture, and appliances that have become the symbols of middle-class living. They usually ignore the history and heroes of the labor struggle in this country, in which laborers resisted and endured under great odds to improve their conditions. They do not discuss the role of the working class in the development of the nation. The inequities based on the income and wealth of one's family are usually neither described nor discussed. In classrooms, students should learn of the existence of these discrepancies. They should understand that the majority of the population does not live the middle-class myth.

Often overlooked are the experiences that students bring to the classroom. School is not the only place where students learn about life. Differences in school behavior and knowledge among students from dissimilar socioeconomic levels are strongly dependent on the knowledge and skills needed to survive appropriately in their community environments. Most low-income students, especially those in urban areas, have learned how to live in a world that is not imaginable to most middle-class students or teachers. Yet, the knowledge and skills they bring to school are not valued by teachers in a system with a middle-class orientation. Educators should recognize the value of the community's informal education in sustaining its own culture and realize that formal education is often viewed as undermining that culture.

Students need to see some of their own cultural experiences reflected in the curriculum. They need to see ordinary working people as valued members of society. These students and their families need to be helped to see themselves as desirable and integral members of the school community, rather than as second-class citizens who must learn the ways of the more economically advantaged to succeed in school.

Educators should become cognizant of the materials, films, and books used in class. If students never see their communities in these instructional materials, their motivation and acceptance are likely to be limited. All students should be encouraged to read novels and short stories about people from different socioeconomic levels. When studying historical or current events, they should examine the events from the perspective of the working class and those in poverty, as well as from the

FOCUS YOUR CULTURAL LENS: DEBATE

Detracking

Data in many schools show that the children of upper-middle-class families are overrepresented in high-ability programs for the gifted and talented and underrepresented in low-ability special education and general education courses. School officials are being pushed by the courts to change their practices that segregate students by SES or race. One of the remedies for eliminating these discriminatory practices is detracking or dismantling tracks for students based on ability as determined by standardized tests or teachers' perceptions. Some teachers and middle-class parents resist the move to a single track in which students from different ability groups are mixed.

Opinions about these strategies differ. Some people believe that detracking will provide greater equality of opportunity across economic and racial groups; opponents believe that it will lead to a lower quality of education overall. Some pros and cons for detracking are listed below:

FOR

- Eliminates discrimination against students from low-income families and students of color.

- Integrates students from different ability levels.

- Encourages classroom instruction that is challenging and interesting for low-income as well as upper-middle-class students.

- Supports a classroom environment in which high-ability students learn while assisting peers who may not be at the same academic level.

- Provides low-SES students greater access to good teachers, improving their chances of learning at higher levels.

AGAINST

- Is not fair to high-ability students who need to be challenged at advanced levels.

- Makes it more difficult for teachers to provide appropriate instruction for all students whose abilities differ greatly.

- May lead to pressure from upper-middle-class parents who may withdraw their children from public schools.

- Waters down the curriculum for high-ability students.

- Prevents high-ability students from participating in gifted and talented programs and advanced level courses that will give them the advantage needed to be admitted to elite colleges and universities.

Questions

1. *How do schools ensure that the voices of low- and middle-income families are included in discussions about detracking and the provision of educational equity in schools?*
2. *How does detracking schools contribute to the provision of equal educational opportunity?*
3. *What other steps could school officials take to provide low-income students greater access to advanced courses?*
4. *What are your reasons for supporting or not supporting detracking strategies in schools?*

To answer these questions online, go to the Focus Your Cultural Lens: Debate module for this chapter of the Companion Website.

perspective of the country's leaders. Teaching can be enhanced by drawing examples from experiences with which students are familiar, especially when the experiences are different from the teacher's own.

Instruction should show that not all persons share equally in material goods, but that all persons have potential to be developed. All students, no matter what their SES, should be helped to develop strong and positive self-concepts. Many students do not realize the diversity that exists in this country, let alone understand the reasons for the diversity and the resulting discrimination against some groups. Most middle-class children, especially those from white-collar and professional levels, believe that most persons are as affluent as they are. Educators are expected to expand their students' knowledge of the world, not to hide from them the realities that exist because of class differences.

In a classroom in which democracy and equity are important, social justice should inform the curriculum. Low-income students should receive priority time from teachers and have access to the necessary resources to become academically competitive with middle-class students.

Finally, all students should be encouraged to be critical of what they read, see, and hear in textbooks, through the mass media, and from their parents and friends. The curriculum should encourage the development of critical thinking and problem-solving skills. Unfortunately, schools traditionally have talked about the democratic vision but have been unwilling to model it. Students and teachers who become involved through the curriculum in asking why the inequities in society exist are beginning to practice democracy. *How will you ensure that your low-income students will not be marginalized in the curriculum? How could your classroom model democracy, ensuring that all students participate equitably in classroom activities and decisions? How will your classroom contribute to students knowing how to participate effectively in a democracy?*

Opportunities for Reflection

FINANCIAL SUPPORT FOR SCHOOLS

Inequities are greatly exacerbated by the fact that the current system for funding schools mirrors these inequities. Education is supported by local property taxes, which supply about 44% of all school funds. State support averages about 49%, and federal support around 7% (Karp, 2003). The U.S. spends less on education than many other industrialized countries, ranking 12th in a study by the Organization for Economic Cooperation and Development (Karp, 2003). Another international study rated the United States last among developed countries in the gap between the quality of schools for high- and low-income students (National Commission on Teaching and America's Future, 2004). The few U.S. students who live in high-income communities within generous states attend public schools funded at $15,000 or more per student per year, whereas other students in poor communities within stingy states are supported by $3,000 or less per year in funding for their schools. In a study of schools in the state of New York, for example, researchers found that "New York State has a two-tiered public school system: one for the more affluent, who enjoy the privileges of a relatively sound educational environment, and the other for the least privileged" (National Commission on Teaching and America's Future, 2004, p. 37).

Students in rich schools and poor schools experience very different kinds of education and environments in which learning is to occur. It is little wonder that the gap in academic achievement in such different schools is so great. Through the schools, wealthy and upper-middle-class parents are able to pass on their economic advantages.

Researchers and policymakers disagree as to how much money is needed by schools, to improve academic achievement. In a reanalysis of data from studies on this relationship, University of Chicago researchers concluded that higher per-pupil expenditures, better teacher salaries, more educated and experienced teachers, and smaller class and school sizes are strongly related to improved student learning (Greenwald, Hedges, & Laine, 1996). If we agree that more money would help reduce the inequities across groups in schools and that greater resources are needed in low-wealth school districts, what areas would provide the greatest payoff for improved student achievement? Slavin (1995) recommends smaller class sizes, prekindergarten programs for four-year-olds, tutoring for students having difficulty, cooperative learning, family support systems, and extensive staff and teacher development for delivering effective programs.

Many schools, such as the one that Tomas Juarez entered at the beginning of this chapter, no longer serve students well. *Is there any compelling reason for students not to attend comfortable, clean, and attractive schools? Why shouldn't low-income students have teachers who are qualified to teach and who have high academic expectations for them? More equitable funding of schools would provide low-income students with at least some of the basic opportunities that many middle-class students currently enjoy.*

Opportunities for Reflection

Summary

Socioeconomic status (SES) is a composite of the economic status of a family or unrelated individuals, based on income, wealth, occupation, educational attainment, and power. It is a means of measuring inequalities based on economic differences and the way families live as a result of their economic well-being. Families range from the indigent poor to the very rich. Where a family falls along this continuum affects the way its members live, how they think and act, and the way others react to them. Although a family may actively participate in other cultural groups centered around ethnicity, religion, gender, exceptionality, language, or age, the class to which a family belongs is probably the strongest factor in determining differences among groups.

Social stratification is possible because consistent and recurring relationships exist between people who occupy different levels of the social structure. Persons of color, women, the young, the elderly, and individuals with disabilities are disproportionately represented at the low end of the social stratification system.

The United States can be divided into classes based on income and occupation. In this chapter, the following classes were described: unemployed and homeless, working class, middle class, upper middle class, and upper class. The income and wealth that keep families at one of these levels vary greatly. Individual choice is most limited for those persons who are in poverty and who often can barely meet essential needs. Whereas ethnic and religious diversity exists at all levels, the upper class is the most homogeneous. Persons of color and women who head families are overly represented at the lowest SES level. Class consciousness is strongest among the upper classes, whose members know the value of solidarity in the protection and maintenance of their power and privilege.

Disproportionately large numbers of students from lower levels of SES are assigned to low-ability groups in their early school years. Educators must consciously review their expectations for students and their behavior toward students from different levels of SES to ensure that they are not discriminating. Instructional methods and teaching strategies may vary greatly, depending on the environment in which students live. It is essential that all students be provided with a quality education.

Educators also need to pay attention to the curriculum. Too often, low-income students are placed in remedial programs because of discriminatory testing and placement. In addition, the curriculum does not serve students well if it reflects only the perspective of middle-class America. Students need to see some of their own cultural values reflected in the curriculum, in addition to learning about the cultural values of the dominant group.

Financial support for more equitable funding of schools, no matter where they are located or which students attend them, is likely to reduce the achievement gap between groups of students. The current property tax system for supporting schools gives the advantage to families with high incomes.

QUESTIONS FOR DISCUSSION

1. How does social stratification differentially affect groups in society?

2. Why is social mobility unreal for many members of society?

3. What is the mythical middle class? Why does it not match reality?

4. Which workers are included under the classification of working and middle class?

5. What socioeconomic factors make it difficult for members of the underclass to improve their conditions?

6. Why do the professional and managerial workers, who comprise the upper middle class, have more power in society?

7. Why have schools not been able to eliminate poverty in this country?

8. What is the self-fulfilling prophecy, and how is it affected by the class of families?

9. How might the tracking of students perpetuate inequalities in schools and society?

10. How can teachers ensure that students from low-income and working-class families are able to achieve academically at the same level as other students?

ONLINE ACTIVITIES For additional chapter questions and activities, visit this text's Companion Website at http://www.prenhall.com/gollnick.

PORTFOLIO ACTIVITIES

1. Visit a school in an economically depressed area of your community or a nearby city and another school in a community that serves students from the upper middle class. Record the differences in the physical environment, aesthetics, school climate, resources for students, and attitudes of faculty and students. Write a paper comparing the two schools and analyzing the reasons for any differences you have observed. (INTASC Standard 2)

2. Develop a lesson plan that positively recognizes the socioeconomic differences in society, reflecting the experiences of the working class and other persons who do not have an adequate income to live comfortably. The lesson should be for the subject and level (for example, elementary or secondary) that you plan to teach. (INTASC Standard 3)

3. Volunteer to tutor at a homeless shelter or after-school program for students from low-income families and record your feelings about the children and settings as journal entries. Your entries could include your feelings on going to the shelter or program for the first time, the strengths of the children with whom you work, and your learnings about the obstacles that students face outside of school. (INTASC Standards 2, 3, and 10)

SUGGESTED READINGS

hooks, bell. (2000). *Where we stand: Class matters.* New York: Routledge.

Drawing on her girlhood experiences in Kentucky and later life in New York City, the author reflects on the ways class and race are intertwined in our lives. The meaning of poverty and wealth are explored.

Kozol, J. (1991). *Savage inequalities: Children in America's schools.* New York: Crown.

These descriptions of rich and poor schools are a powerful statement on the class and racial inequities that exist in the United States. Interwoven with the stories of students and educators is an analysis of the inadequacy of the current funding of schools.

Noguera, P. (2003). *City schools and the American dream: Reclaiming the promise of public education.* New York: Teachers College Press.

Drawing on his research in schools in the San Francisco area and Richmond, Dr. Noguera explores what it will take for students in urban schools to achieve at the levels expected in standards. He describes schools that have worked against the odds to succeed.

Rose, S. J. (2000). *Social stratification in the United States.* New York: New Press.

This booklet compiles and analyzes data on income, wealth, race, and marital and occupational status. The accompanying poster and its discussion provide a vivid portrayal of the U.S. social structure.

Shulman, B. (2003). *The betrayal of work: How low-wage jobs fail 30 million Americans.* New York: New Press.

This portrait of workers who are employed full-time in jobs that pay poverty wages provides insights into the struggles of people who work hard, but are not moving up the social mobility ladder.

REFERENCES

American Political Science Association. (2004). *American democracy in an age of rising inequality.* Washington, DC: Author.

Andersen, M. L., & Collins, P. H. (2004). *Race, class, and gender: An anthology* (5th ed.). Belmont, CA: Wadsworth/Thomson.

Anderson, S., Cavanagh, J., Hartman, C., Klinger, S., & Chan, S. (2004, August 31). *Executive excess 2004: Campaign contributions, outsourcing, unexpensed stock options and rising CEO pay* (11th Annual CEO Compensation Survey). Boston, MA: Institute for Policy Studies and United for a Fair Economy.

Average family income by educational attainment 1967–2000. (2004, April). *Postsecondary Education Opportunity*, No. 142.

Ball, S. J. (2003). *Class strategies and the education market: The middle classes and social advantage*. New York: RoutledgeFalmer.

Books, S., & Polakow, V. (2001, Fall). Introduction to special issue: Poverty and schooling. *Educational Studies, 32*(3), 259–263.

Brantlinger, E. (2003). *Dividing classes: How the middle class negotiates and rationalizes school advantage*. New York: RoutledgeFalmer.

Collins, C., & Veskel, F. (2004). Economic apartheid in America. In M. L. Andersen & P. H. Collins (Eds.), *Race, class, and gender: An anthology* (5th ed., pp. 127–139). Belmont, CA: Wadsworth/Thomson.

Cookson, P. W., & Persell, C. H. (1985). *Preparing for power: America's elite boarding schools*. New York: Basic Books.

Edley, C. (2004). *Losing our future: How minority youth are being left behind by the graduation rate crisis*. Cambridge, MA: Civil Rights Project at Harvard University.

Family income and higher education opportunity: 1970 to 2002. (2004, May). *Postsecondary Education Opportunity*, No. 143.

Greenwald, R., Hedges, L. V., & Laine, R. D. (1996, Fall). The effect of school resources on student achievement. *Review of Educational Research, 66*(3), 361–396.

Karp, S. (2003, Fall). Money, schools and justice: State-by-state battle for funding equity gets mixed results. *Rethinking Schools, 18*(1), 26–30.

Keenan, F. (2003, February 3). It's still rich man, poor man. *Business Week Online*. Retrieved November 9, 2004, from http://www.businessweek.com/magazine/content/03_05/c3818066.htm.

Lee, V. E., & Burkam, D. T. (2002). *Inequality at the starting gate: Social background differences in achievement as children begin school*. Washington, DC: Economic Policy Institute.

Lucas, S. R. (1999). *Tracking inequality: Stratification and mobility in American high schools*. New York: Teachers College Press.

Luxembourg Income Study. (2004, July 7). *Poverty rates for children by family type*. Retrieved September 15, 2004, from http://www.lisproject.org/keyfigures/childpovrates.htm

Mishel, L., Bernstein, J., & Schmitt, J. (2003). *The state of working America: 2002/2003*. Armonk, NY: Economic Policy Institute.

National Association for the Education of Homeless Children and Youth. (2004). *Homeless education: An introduction to the issues*. Retrieved September 15, 2004, from http://www.lisproject.org/keyfigures/childpovrates.htm (http://www.naehcy.org/introtoissues.pdf)

National Coalition for the Homeless. (2003). *People need affordable housing*. Retrieved September 15, 2004, from http://www.nationalhomeless.org/facts/housing.html

National Commission on Teaching and America's Future. (2004). *Fifty years after Brown v. Board of Education: A two-tiered education system*. Washington, DC: Author.

National Low Income Housing Coalition. (2003). *Out of reach 2003*. Washington, DC: Author.

Noguera, P. (2003). *City schools and the American dream: Reclaiming the promise of public education*. New York: Teachers College Press.

Rank, R. (2004). *One nation, underprivileged: Why American poverty affects us all*. London: Oxford University Press.

Rose, S. J. (2000). *Social stratification in the United States*. New York: New Press.

Rothstein, R. (2004). *Class and schools: Using social, economic, and educational reform to close the black-white achievement gap*. Washington, DC: Economic Policy Institute.

Sanders, W. L., & Rivers, J. C. (1996). *Cumulative and residual effects of teachers on future academic achievement*. Knoxville, TN: University of Tennessee Value-Added Research and Assessment Center.

Shipler, D. K. (2004). *The working poor: Invisible in America*. New York: Alfred A. Knopf.

Shulman, B. (2003). *The betrayal of work: How low-wage jobs fail 30 million Americans*. New York: New Press.

Slavin, R. (1995, Summer). Making money make a difference. *Rethinking Schools, 9*(4), 10, 23.

Smith, Dan. (2000). *The state of the world atlas*. New York: Penguin.

Smith, Dan. (2003). *The Penguin state of the world atlas* (7th ed.). New York: Penguin.

Spencer, R. (1993, May 18). U.S. ranks 6th in quality of life; Japan is 1st. *The Washington Post*, p. A7.

Swanson, C. B. (2004). *Who graduates? Who doesn't?: A statistical portrait of public high school graduation, class of 2001*. Washington, DC: Urban Institute.

U.S. Census Bureau. (2002). *Current population survey, annual demographic supplements*. Washington, DC: Author.

U.S. Census Bureau. (2003a). *2003 American community survey summary tables*. Washington, DC: Author.

U.S. Census Bureau. (2003b). *Statistical abstract of the United States: 2003* (123rd ed.). Washington, DC: U.S. Government Printing Office.

U.S. Census Bureau. (2004). *Current population survey 2004, annual social and economic supplement*. Washington, DC: Author.

U.S. Conference of Mayors. (2002). *Hunger and homelessness 2002*. Washington, DC: Author.

U.S. Department of Education. (2003, August). *Education for homeless children and youths: Grants for state and local activities*. Retrieved September 15, 2004, from http://www.ed.gov/programs/homeless/index.html

U.S. Department of Education, National Center for Education Statistics. (2001). *The condition of education 2001*. Washington, DC: Author.

U.S. Department of Education, National Center for Education Statistics. (2004). Concentration of enrollment by race/ethnicity and poverty. In *The condition of education 2004*. Washington, DC: Author.

Urban Institute. (2000). *America's homeless II: Populations and services*. Washington, DC: Author.

Welner, K. G. (2001). *Legal rights, local wrongs: When community control collides with educational equity*. Albany, NY: State University of New York Press.

Nobody recognizes I am Vietnamese because when they look at me they think I am Chinese. They cannot recognize who I am.

MY LIEN NGUYEN, 1996

Chapter 3

Ethnicity and Race

Denise Williams had become increasingly aware of the racial tension in the high school in which she teaches, but she did not expect the hostility that erupted between some black and white students that Friday. In the week that followed, the faculty decided they had to do more to develop positive interethnic and interracial relations among students. They established a committee to identify consultants and other resources to guide them in this effort.

Ms. Williams, however, thought that neither she nor her students could wait for months to receive a report and recommendations from the committee. She was ready to introduce the civil rights movement in her social studies class. It seemed a perfect time to promote better cross-cultural communications. She decided that she would let students talk about their feelings.

She soon learned that this topic was not an easy one to handle. African American students expressed their anger at the discriminatory practices in the school and the community. Most white students did not believe that there was any discrimination. They believed there were no valid reasons for the anger of the African American and Latino students and that if they just followed the rules and worked harder, they would not have their perceived problems. She thought the class was getting nowhere. In fact, sometimes the anger on both sides was so intense that she worried a physical fight would erupt. She was frustrated that the class discussions and activities were not helping students understand their stereotypes and prejudices. At times, she thought students were just becoming more polarized in their beliefs. She wondered whether she could do anything in her class to improve understanding, empathy, and communications across groups.

Opportunities for Reflection

1. *What factors contribute to racial and ethnic conflict in some schools?*
2. *What racial groups are most likely to see themselves in the school curriculum?*
3. *How can a classroom reflect the diversity of its students so that they all feel valued and respected?*
4. *What were the positive and negative outcomes of the steps taken by Ms. Williams?*
5. *What would you have done to improve cross-cultural relations among class members?*

To answer these questions online, go to this chapter's Opening Scenario module of the Companion Website.

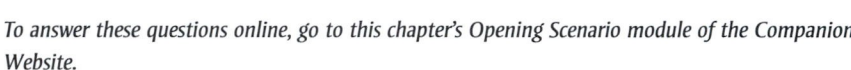

Ethnic and Racial Diversity

The United States is an ethnically and racially diverse nation comprised of nearly 300 **ethnic groups** whose members can identify the national origins of their ancestors. First Americans make up less than 1% of the total U.S. population today with 170 Indian tribes that are **indigenous** or native to the United States (U.S. Census Bureau, 2003). Individuals who were born in Africa, Asia, Australia, Canada, Central America, Europe, Mexico, and South America comprise 11.5% of the population (U.S. Census Bureau, 2003). Family members and ancestors of the remaining 87.5% of the population also immigrated to the United States from around the world over the past 500 years.

Many people forget that the United States was populated when explorers from other nations arrived on its shores. As more and more Europeans arrived, Native Americans were not treated as equal citizens in the formation of the new nation. Eventually, most first Americans were forcibly segregated from the dominant group and, in many cases, forced to move from their geographic homelands to reservations in other parts of the country. This separation led to a pattern of isolation and inequities that remains today. The atrocities and near genocide that resulted from the treatment of Native Americans have been ignored in most historical accounts of U.S. history. Not until 2000 did an official of the U.S. government apologize for the Bureau of Indian Affairs' "legacy of **racism** [that is, the belief that one race is superior to others] and inhumanity that included massacres, forced relocations of tribes and attempts to wipe out Indian languages and cultures" (Kelley, 2000, p. 1).

Today, 1.9 million citizens identify themselves as Native American only; more than half a million people identify themselves as Alaska Native only. Another 1.5 million indicate they are partially Native American or Alaska Native. Forty percent of the Native American population belongs to one of six tribes: Cherokee, Navajo, Latin Native American, Choctaw, Sioux, and Chippewa (U.S. Census Bureau, 2003). What do you know about Native Americans? Where did you learn about them? How accurate is your knowledge base?

EXPLORE DIVERSITY Go to the *Exploring Diversity* CD located in the accompanying booklet for the perspective of one Native American in the case called *Majority Culture.*

Although most of the first European settlers were English, the French, Dutch, and Spanish also established early settlements. After the consolidation and development of the United States as an independent nation, successive waves of Western Europeans joined the earlier settlers. Irish, Swedish, and German immigrants came to escape economic impoverishment or political repression in their countries of origin. These early European settlers brought with them the political institutions that would become the framework for our government. The melding of these Northern and Western European cultures over time became the dominant culture to which other immigrant groups strived or were forced to assimilate.

Africans were also among the early explorers of the Americas and later part of the foreign settlers in the early days of colonization. By the eighteenth century, Africans were being kidnapped and sold into bondage by slave traders. As involuntary immigrants, this group of Africans underwent a process quite different from the Europeans who voluntarily emigrated. Separated from their families and homelands, robbed of their freedom and cultures, Africans developed a new culture out of their different African, European, and Native American heritages and their unique experiences in this country. Initially, the majority of African Americans lived in the South where today they remain the majority population in many counties. In the middle of the twentieth century, industrial jobs in Northern, Eastern, and Western cities began to open up for the first time to African Americans, leading to migration from the South. By the beginning of the twenty-first century, the trend had reversed with a growing number of African Americans from northern states now moving south.

Another factor that contributed to the migration to the North was the racism and political terror that existed in much of the South at that time. Even today, a racial ideology is implicit in the policies and practices of institutions. It continues to block significant assimilation of many African Americans into the dominant society. Although the **civil rights** movement of the 1960s reduced the barriers that prevented many African Americans from enjoying the advantages of the middle class, the number of African Americans, especially children, who remain in poverty is disproportionately high.

Figures on the percentage of African Americans and other groups in poverty are presented in Chapter 2.

Mexican Americans also occupy a unique role in the formation of the United States. Spain was the first European country to colonize Mexico and the Western and Southwestern United States. In 1848, the U.S. government annexed the northern sections of the Mexican Territory, including the current areas of Texas, Arizona, New Mexico, and southern California. The Mexican and Native Americans living within that territory became an oppressed minority in the area in which they had previously been the dominant population. The labor of Mexicans has been persistently sought by farmers and businesses over the past century. Once they arrived, they were treated with hostility, limiting them to low-paying jobs and a subordinate status. Dominant supremacy theories based on color and language have been used against them in a way that, even today, prevents many Mexican Americans from assimilating fully into the dominant culture.

The industrial opening of the West signaled the need for labor that could be met through immigration from Asia. Chinese worked the plantations in Hawaii. Chinese, Japanese, and Phillipinos (Filipinos) were recruited to provide the labor needed on the West Coast for mining gold and building railroads.

By the end of the nineteenth century industries in the nation's cities required more labor than was available. Immigrants from the relatively more impoverished Eastern and Southern European countries were enticed to accept jobs primarily in Midwestern and Eastern cities. Into the early twentieth century, many immigrants arrived from nations such as Poland, Hungary, Italy, Russia, and Greece. The reasons for their immigration were similar to many earlier immigrants: devastating economic and political hardship in the homeland and demand for labor in the United States. Many immigrants came to the United States with the hope of sharing the better wages and living conditions they thought existed here. But many found conditions here worse than they had expected. Most were forced to live in substandard housing near the business and manufacturing districts where they worked, in urban ghettos that grew into ethnic enclaves in which they continued to use the native language and maintain the culture of their native lands. To support their social and welfare needs, ethnic institutions often were established. Many of the dominant racist policies that had been used against African Americans, Mexican Americans, and Native Americans earlier came to be used against these immigrants as well when they first arrived.

IMMIGRATION

At various times, the U.S. Congress has prohibited the immigration of different national or ethnic groups on the basis of the racial superiority of the older, established immigrant groups that had colonized the nation. As early as 1729, immigration was being discouraged. In that year, Pennsylvania passed a statute that increased the head tax on foreigners in that colony. Later that century, Congress passed the Alien and Sedition Acts, which lengthened the time required to become a citizen from 5 years to 14 years. In the nineteenth century, native-born Americans again began to worry about their majority and superiority status over entering immigrant groups. This movement, **nativism,** was designed to restrict immigration and to protect the interests of native-born Americans. It was an extreme form of ethnocentrism and **nationalism,** requiring loyalty and devotion to the United States over all other nations.

 *Ethnocentrism was discussed in greater detail in Chapter 1.*

In 1881, the Chinese Exclusion Act was passed to halt all immigration from China. The Dillingham Commission reported in 1917 that all immigrants should be able to pass a literacy test. The nativists received further support for their views when Congress passed the Johnson-Reed Act in 1924, establishing annual immigration quotas to disproportionately favor immigrants from Western European countries. It also stopped all immigration from Japan. The Johnson-Reed Act was abolished in 1965 when a new quota system was established, dramatically increasing the number of immigrants allowed annually from the Eastern Hemisphere and reducing the number from the Western Hemisphere.

Congressional leaders and presidential candidates during the 1980s promoted a get tough approach to immigration, calling for greater control of the U.S. borders. However, the 1986 Immigration Reform and Control Act ended up expanding immigration by allowing visas to persons born in countries adversely affected by the 1965 law (that is, Europeans).

Congress was not the only group expressing concern about the number of foreigners entering the United States. Sixty percent of California voters in 1994 passed Proposition 187, declaring illegal immigrants as ineligible for public social services, health care services, and education. It also required state and local agencies to report suspected illegals to immigration authorities. Almost immediately after the proposition was passed, a U.S. District Court judge issued an injunction against it because it conflicted with a 1982 Supreme Court decision that required the education of illegal immigrants. The injunction also indicated that the federal government, not states, regulates immigration. It was declared unconstitutional in 1998. Challenges to immigration, especially illegal immigration, continue to be raised today with some people calling for the government to seriously limit all immigration. *Why is immigration such a controversial issue? Why are some businesses not supportive of a strict adherence to preventing illegal immigrants from entering the country?*

Opportunities for Reflection

As people from all over the world joined Native Americans in populating this nation, they brought with them cultural experiences from their native countries. The conditions they encountered, the reasons they came, and their expectations about life in this country differed greatly, causing each ethnic group to view itself as distinct from other ethnic groups. However, just because individuals have the same national origins does not mean that they have the same history and experiences as other individuals and families in that group. The time of immigration, the place in which groups settled, the reasons for emigrating, their socioeconomic status, and the degree to which they are affected by racism and discrimination interact to form a new ethnic group that differs from those who came before and will come afterward.

Changing Patterns. As shown in Figure 3.1, the change in the immigration law has allowed the influx of immigrants from nations that formerly were restricted or

Figure 3.1
Immigration from selected countries and continents since 1981.

Source: U.S. Census Bureau. (2003). *Statistical Abstract of the United States: 2003* (123rd ed.). Washington, DC: U.S. Government Printing Office.

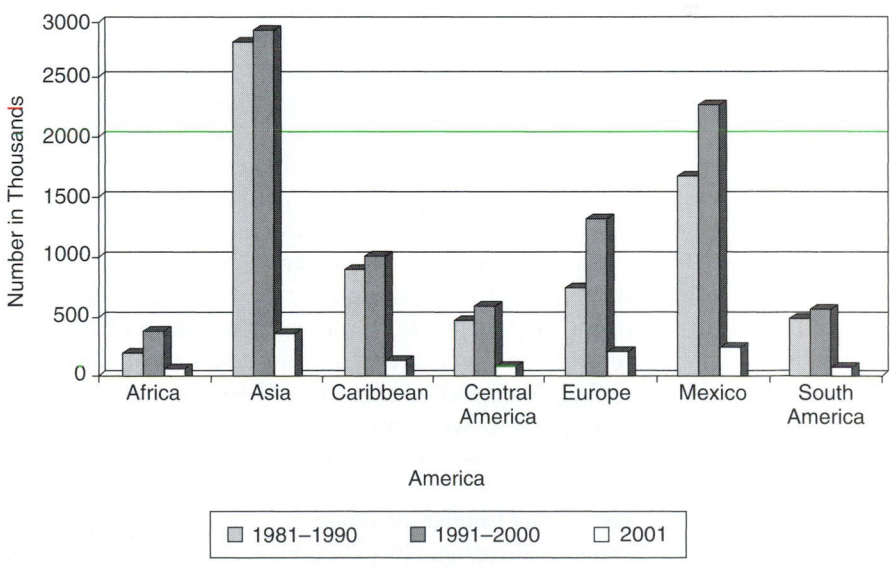

Legend: ☐ 1981–1990   ■ 1991–2000   ☐ 2001

excluded. In 1960, the nations contributing the largest number of legal immigrants were Mexico, Germany, Canada, the United Kingdom, and Italy. By 2001, the five leading countries were Mexico, India, China, the Philippines, and Vietnam. The Asian American population grew dramatically over the past century. Asian Americans were 0.3% of the population in 1920, but had expanded to 4% in 2000. Bosnia and Herzegovina, Russia, and Ukraine contributed the largest number of European immigrants. The immigration rate during the past decade has been nearly 1 million per year (U.S. Census Bureau, 2003). Immigration is worldwide, not just a U.S. phenomenon, with 3% of the world's population living in countries in which they were not born (Smith, 2003).

Favored Status. Favoritism has been granted to **refugees** fleeing countries not supported by the U.S. government. Refugees are the persons recognized by the federal government as being persecuted or legitimately bearing persecution in their home country because of race, religion, nationality, or membership in a specific social or political group. Between 1991 and 2000, more than a million immigrants were admitted as refugees; the largest number came from Vietnam, followed by Cuba, Ukraine, the Soviet Union, Russia, Bosnia and Herzegovina, and Laos. Refugees from some countries, like Haiti, are refused entry as refugees, no matter how oppressive the government may be. As a result of governmental immigration and refugee policies, the U.S. population from various national and ethnic groups has been controlled, but has become increasingly diverse.

The U.S. Bureau of Citizenship and Immigration Services estimates that 7 million unauthorized immigrants lived in the United States in 2000. The status of many of these immigrants later is reclassified as legal because they meet the requirements for employment-based visas, refugees, or being sponsored by a family as allowed by law. They may also become legal immigrants through amnesty programs periodically enacted by Congress. Just over two thirds of the illegal immigrants are from Mexico; only 5% are from outside the Western Hemisphere. California is home to the largest number, with 32% of the undocumented population. The majority of undocumented immigrants settle in the same states as most legal immigrants—California, Texas, New York, Illinois, and Florida.

The border between Mexico and the United States is an ever-present reality in the Southwestern states. Fifty-four percent of the Latino population lives in California, Texas, and Arizona (U.S. Census Bureau, 2003), having an impact on politics and economics in the region. Border patrols search for illegal immigrants. Latinos from all walks of life are regularly stopped and searched by police. Power struggles are common among powerful and oppressed groups and landowners and migrant workers.

In *Plyer v. Doe,* the U.S. Supreme Court ruled in 1982 that undocumented children have the right to seek a public education. Educators are not Immigration and Naturalization Services (INS) officials who enforce immigration laws. In fact, they cannot require students or parents to declare their immigration status, and they cannot make inquiries that might expose such status. For example, parents cannot be forced to provide social security numbers to school districts. Educators should take all possible action to encourage undocumented students to attend school.

Location of Immigrant Groups. The foreign-born population is concentrated in five states: California, New York, Florida, Texas, and Illinois with 40% of them living in the West (Briggs, 2000). More than 80% of the immigrants settle in metropolitan areas, many of them in central cities. New York City, Los Angeles/Long Beach, Chicago, Miami, the Washington, DC area, San Francisco, Orange County (CA), Oakland (CA), Houston, and the Boston area are home to 65% of today's immigrants (Olson, 2000). Immigration to nonmetropolitan areas is often dependent on job availability and perceived quality of life. As a result, schools in Arkansas, Iowa, Nebraska, Montana, North Dakota, and Wisconsin include students from different cultures and with languages other than English.

Education of Immigrants.   The education level of immigrants in 2002 differed greatly. The percent of the foreign-born population with bachelor's degrees was nearly equal to the native-born population at 17% and 18%, respectively. Nearly 10% of the foreign-born population has advanced degrees. At the other end of the economic scale, 33% of foreign-born adults do not have a high school degree—almost three times as many as the native-born population (U.S. Census Bureau, 2003). Studies of immigrants indicate that those with the social or cultural capital of higher education and higher socioeconomic status are more likely to be accepted by dominant society and allowed to assimilate into the middle class (Portes & Rumbaut, 2001).

CIVIL RIGHTS

Members of oppressed groups sometimes coalesce to fight against the harsh economic and political realities and injustices imposed on them. Thus, movements for democratic rights and economic justice develop among different ethnic groups. These movements invariably entail a rise in the concern of the community with its

Members of different ethnic and racial groups join forces to protest for civil rights.

race or national origins, as this aspect of their identity also may have been suppressed and excluded by the dominant majority.

The Civil Rights Movement.   The fight for civil rights by ethnic and racial groups has a long history in the United States. Native Americans fought to maintain their rights as foreigners appropriated their homelands. African slaves revolted against their owners. Free blacks decried the discrimination and violence they faced in the North. Martin Delaney led a Black Nationalist movement in the mid-1800s for black liberation. In the early twentieth century Mexican American miners in Arizona led a strike for better working conditions and pay equal to that of white miners. Across the Southwest, Mexican Americans established ethnic organizations to fight exploitation and support those who were in dire straits. Chinese immigrants used the courts to overturn the 1790 Naturalization Law that excluded them for citizenship (Takaki, 1993).

Although individuals and groups continued to push the government for civil rights throughout the twentieth century, the movement exploded in the 1950s and 1960s when large numbers of African Americans in the South challenged their oppressed status in society. Students sat at lunch counters that were for whites only, challenging **Jim Crow laws** that forced whites and persons of color to use different public accommodations such as water fountains and restrooms to hotels and restaurants. Rosa Parks defied authorities when she sat in the whites-only section at the front of the bus in Montgomery, Alabama. Blacks and whites marched for freedom and established Freedom Schools across the South. Native Americans confronted governmental abuse at Wounded Knee.

The call for "Black Power" followed years of civil rights struggle that led to the passage of the 1964 Civil Rights Act and the 1965 Voting Rights Act, which banned discrimination in schools, employment, and public accommodations and secured the voting rights of African Americans. Yet, changes did not necessarily follow. Although legislation guaranteed equality for all racial groups, many European Americans continued to fight against desegregation of schools and other public facilities. Frustrations with the dominant group led members of oppressed groups to identify strongly with other members of their ethnic group to fight discrimination and inequality with a unified voice. These struggles continue today not only in this country, but throughout the world.

Brown v. Board of Education.   Schools have long been at the center of civil rights movements. At one time children of color were not allowed to attend school. Later they were not allowed to attend schools with white children, leading to a system of desegregated schools in which students of color were delegated to schools without the books and resources to which most white children had access. Desegregation continued in many states until more than a decade after the Supreme Court unanimously declared that separate but equal schooling was not equal in its 1954 *Brown v. Board of Education* decision.

The 1954 decision was the result of four cases making their way through the courts: *Briggs v. Elliott* in South Carolina, *Davis v. County School Board of Prince Edward County* in Virginia, *Gebhart v. Belton* in Delaware, and *Brown v. Board of Education of Topeka* in Kansas. A fifth case, *Bolling v. Sharpe,* settled a year later, declared that the

Linda Brown and her family were the plaintiffs in one of the four cases that led to the Supreme Court decision on *Brown v. Board of Education* in 1954.

federal government could not segregate schools in the District of Columbia. The Supreme Court returned to the implementation of *Brown v. Board of Education* in 1955 when it sent all school integration cases back to the lower courts and asked states to desegregate "with all deliberate speed." Later courts called for the desegregation of metropolitan areas, busing students across city lines to ensure integration. The milestones in the desegregation and resegregation of schools are chronicled in Table 3.1.

Many segregated school districts and universities took years to begin to integrate their schools. The fierce resistance of many whites in many communities required the use of the National Guard to protect African American students who were entering white schools for the first time. Many whites established private schools or moved to the suburbs where the population was primarily white to avoid sending their children to schools with African Americans. As segregated public schools became desegregated, many African American teachers and principals lost their jobs. The composition of schools did change in the three decades following the *Brown* decision. In the mid-1960s only 2% of the African American students in the United States attended integrated schools. By the late 1980s, 45% of them were in integrated schools.

Other ethnic groups also used the courts to demand an equitable education for their children. In *Gong Lum v. Rice* in Mississippi in 1927 a Chinese American girl sought the right to attend a white school by arguing that she was not black. The court ruled she was not white, giving the school the authority to determine the race of their students (Willoughby, 2004). A Mexican American student was allowed to attend an integrated school in California in the 1940s as a result of *Mendez v. Westminster* (Willoughby, 2004). In 1974 Chinese American students in San Francisco won the right to have their first language used in instruction in *Lau v. Nichols*. The

Table 3.1 Milestones in Desegregating and Resegregating Schools

1896 The Supreme Court authorizes segregation in *Plessy v. Ferguson,* finding Louisiana's "separate but equal" law constitutional.

1940 A federal court requires equal salaries for African American and white teachers. (*Alston v. School Board of City of Norfolk*)

1947 In a precursor to the *Brown* case, a federal appeals court strikes down segregated schooling for Mexican American and white students. (*Westminster School Dist. v. Méndez*) The verdict prompts California Governor Earl Warren to repeal a state law calling for segregation of Native American and Asian American students.

1950 Barbara Johns, a 16-year-old junior at Robert R. Moton High School in Farmville, Va., organizes and leads 450 students in an anti-school segregation strike.

1954 In a unanimous opinion, the Supreme Court in *Brown v. Board of Education* overturns *Plessy* and declares that separate schools are "inherently unequal." The Court delays deciding on how to implement the decision and asks for another round of arguments.

The Court rules that the federal government is under the same duty as the states and must desegregate the Washington, D.C., schools. (*Bolling v. Sharpe*)

1955 In *Brown II,* the Supreme Court orders the lower federal courts to require desegregation "with all deliberate speed."

1956 Tennessee Governor Frank Clement calls in the National Guard after white mobs attempt to block the desegregation of a high school.

The Virginia legislature calls for "massive resistance" to school desegregation and pledges to close schools under desegregation orders.

1957 More than 1,000 paratroopers from the 101st Airborne Division and a federalized Arkansas National Guard protect nine black students integrating Central High School in Little Rock, Ark.

1958 The Supreme Court rules that fear of social unrest or violence, whether real or constructed by those wishing to oppose integration, does not excuse state governments from complying with *Brown*. (*Cooper v. Aaron*)

Ten thousand young people march in Washington, D.C., in support of integration.

1959 Prince Edward County, Va., officials close their public schools rather than integrate them.

Twenty-five thousand young people march in Washington, D.C., in support of integration.

1960 In New Orleans, federal marshals shield 6-year-old Ruby Bridges from an angry crowd as she attempts to enroll in school.

1964 The Civil Rights Act of 1964 is adopted. Title IV of the Act authorizes the federal government to file school desegregation cases. Title VI of the Act prohibits discrimination in programs and activities, including schools, receiving federal financial assistance.

The Supreme Court orders Prince Edward County, Va., to reopen its schools on a desegregated basis in 1964.

1965 The Supreme Court orders states to dismantle segregated school systems "root and branch." The Court identifies five factors—facilities, staff, faculty, extracurricular activities and transportation—to be used to gauge a school system's compliance with the mandate of *Brown*. (*Green v. County School Board of New Kent County*)

1969 The Supreme Court declares the "all deliberate speed" standard is no longer constitutionally permissible and orders the immediate desegregation of Mississippi schools. (*Alexander v. Holmes County Board of Education*)

1971 The Court approves busing, magnet schools, compensatory education and other tools as appropriate remedies to overcome the role of residential segregation in perpetuating racially segregated schools. (*Swann v. Charlotte-Mecklenberg Board of Education*)

Brown decision also served as the precursor for federal laws that supported educational equity for girls and women in **Title IX,** passed in 1972, and persons with disabilities in Section 504 of the Rehabilitation Act in 1973.

By the mid-1980s the courts began lifting the federal court sanctions that had forced schools to integrate, stating that the federal requirements were meant to be temporary to overcome **de jure segregation.** Now that schools were no longer

1972 The Supreme Court refuses to allow public school systems to avoid desegregation by creating new, mostly or all-white "splinter districts." (*Wright v. Council of the City of Emporia; United States v. Scotland Neck City Board of Education*)

1973 The Supreme Court rules that states cannot provide textbooks to racially segregated private schools to avoid integration mandates. (*Norwood v. Harrison*)

The Supreme Court finds that the Denver school board intentionally segregated Mexican American and black students from white students. (*Keyes v. Denver School District No. 1*)

The Supreme Court rules that education is not a "fundamental right" and that the Constitution does not require equal education expenditures within a state. (*San Antonio Independent School District v. Rodriguez*)

1974 The Supreme Court blocks metropolitan-wide desegregation plans as a means to desegregate urban schools with high minority populations. (*Milliken v. Bradley*)

The Supreme Court rules that the failure to provide instruction to those with limited English proficiency violates Title VI's prohibition of national origin, race or color discrimination in school districts receiving federal funds. (*Lau v. Nichols*)

1978 A fractured Supreme Court declares the affirmative action admissions program for the University of California Davis Medical School unconstitutional because it set aside a specific number of seats for black and Latino students. The Court rules that race can be a factor in university admissions, but it cannot be the deciding factor. (*Regents of the University of California v. Bakke*)

1982 The Supreme Court rejects tax exemptions for private religious schools that discriminate. (*Bob Jones University v. U.S.; Goldboro Christian Schools v. U.S.*)

1986 For the first time, a federal court finds that once a school district meets the *Green* factors, it can be released from its desegregation plan and returned to local control. (*Riddick v. School Board of the City of Norfolk, Virginia*)

1991 Emphasizing that court orders are not intended "to operate in perpetuity," the Supreme Court makes it easier for formerly segregated school systems to fulfill their obligations under desegregation decrees. (*Board of Education of Oklahoma City v. Dowell*)

1992 The Supreme Court further speeds the end of desegregation cases, ruling that school systems can fulfill their obligations in an incremental fashion. (*Freeman v. Pitts*)

1995 The Supreme Court sets a new goal for desegregation plans: the return of schools to local control. (*Missouri v. Jenkins*)

1996 A federal appeals court prohibits the use of race in college and university admissions, ending affirmative action in Louisiana, Texas and Mississippi. (*Hopwood v. Texas*)

2001 White parents in Charlotte, N.C., schools successfully seek an end to the desegregation process and a bar to the use of race in making student assignments.

2003 The Supreme Court upholds diversity as a rationale for affirmative action programs in higher education admissions, but concludes that point systems are not appropriate. (*Gratz v. Bollinger; Grutter v. Bollinger;*)

A federal district court case affirms the value of racial diversity and race-conscious student assignment plans in K–12 education. (*Lynn v. Comfort*)

Source: Holladay, J. (2004, Spring). *Brown v. Board* Timeline: School Integration in the United States. *Teaching Tolerance, 25*, 42–56.

segregated by race, the easing of sanctions allowed school districts to return to neighborhood schools. Because of **de facto segregation** in communities, many neighborhood schools were comprised of students of the same race, returning integration to pre-1970 levels. At the beginning of the twenty-first century,

Black students are the most likely racial group to attend what researchers call "apartheid schools," schools that are virtually all non-white and where poverty, limited resources, social strife and health problems abound. One-sixth of America's black students attend these schools.

Whites are the most segregated group in the nation's public schools. Only 14% of white students attend multiracial schools (where three or more racial groups are present).

Latino students are the most segregated minority group in U.S. schools. They are segregated by race and poverty; immigrant Latinos also are at risk of experiencing linguistic segregation.

Asian American students are the most integrated group in the nation's public schools. Three-fourths of Asian Americans attend multiracial schools. (Orfield & Frankenberg, 2004, p. 58)

The goal of desegregation has changed from the physical integration of students within a school building to the achievement of equal learning opportunities and outcomes for all students. Court cases today are examining the unequal access of students of color to qualified teachers, advanced mathematics and science classes, gifted classes, and adequately funded schools. Civil rights groups are asking schools why students of color are disproportionately represented in nonacademic and special education classes and why the rates for school suspension and dropping out of school vary for different ethnic groups. As schools become more segregated again, educators have a greater responsibility for ensuring that all students learn regardless of the ethnic and racial composition of the school. Teachers will also have the responsibility for helping students understand that the world in which they are likely to work is multiethnic and multiracial, unlike the school they may be attending.

Ethnic and Racial Group Identity

Children become aware of gender, race, ethnicity, and disabilities between the ages of two and five. At the same time, they become sensitive to the positive and negative biases associated with those groups (Derman-Sparks, Phillips, & Hilliard, 1997). Often, this distinction is made because of the physical characteristics of individuals or the distinct language and shops in a neighborhood. Other times, the distinction may be based on observed behaviors that suggest a particular ethnic background.

Students in a classroom are likely to come from several different racial and ethnic groups, although physical differences are not always identifiable. Two white students who appear to be from similar backgrounds may actually identify strongly with their Irish or Polish backgrounds. The two families may live next door to each other in similar homes, but the insides of the homes may be furnished or decorated differently. The churches they attend may differ, as well as their ideas about raising children and maintaining a family. Their political ideologies may differ markedly. Yet, students often are viewed by teachers as coming from the same cultural background if they have similar racial characteristics, even though their families may be Vietnamese, Hmong, Korean, Cambodian, or Indian American. An educator should not assume that all students who look alike come from the same ethnic background. Factors other than physical characteristics must be used to determine a student's ethnicity. Many intragroup differences exist that may have a great influence on student behavior in the classroom.

Many individuals and families in the United States maintain ties with their national origin or ethnic group by participating in family and cultural traditions.

ETHNICITY

Many definitions have been proposed for the term *ethnic group*. Some writers describe ethnic identity as national origin, religion, and race. In some cases, the definition has been expanded to include gender, class, and lifestyles. The most basic definition focuses on an individual's national origin or origins. Of course, a person's cultural identity is determined by the interaction of one's ethnicity with race, religion, gender, class, language, age, and exceptionalities.

A nation is a historically constituted, stable community of people formed on the basis of a common language, territory, economic life, and culture. Through wars and political realignments, nations change over time because boundaries are moved (or removed) as a result of political negotiations. However, new boundaries do not always translate into new national identities; it may take generations for such a conversion.

Ethnic identity is determined by the native country of your ancestors. The strongest support for the country of origin is usually based on continuing family ties in that country. These ties are especially strong when family members regularly visit relatives and friends in the country of origin. These links often weaken after several generations. Without extensive tracing of the family lineage, most members of ethnic groups who have been in this country for several generations probably could not identify relatives in their country of origin. Yet, support for the country of origin often continues, particularly in the aftermath of natural disasters when ethnic groups across the United States organize to provide relief. When Congressional cuts are being proposed in foreign aid or conflicts develop between groups in other countries, ethnic groups sometimes lobby on behalf of their country of origin.

CRITICAL INCIDENTS IN TEACHING

Student Conflict Between Family and Peer Values

Wing Tek Lau is a sixth-grade student in a predominantly white and African American Southern community. He and his parents emigrated from Hong Kong 4 years ago. His uncle, an engineer at a local high-tech company, had encouraged Wing Tek's father to immigrate to this country and open a Chinese restaurant. The restaurant is the only Chinese restaurant in the community, and it was an instant success. Mr. Lau and his family have enjoyed considerable acceptance in both their business and their neighborhood. Wing Tek and his younger sister have also enjoyed academic success at school and appear to be well liked by the other students.

One day when Mrs. Baca, Wing Tek's teacher, calls him by name, he announces before the class, "My American name is Kevin. Please, everybody call me Kevin from now on." Mrs. Baca and Wing Tek's classmates honor this request, and Wing Tek is "Kevin" from then on.

Three weeks later, Mr. and Mrs. Lau make an appointment to see Mrs. Baca. When the teacher makes reference to "Kevin," Mrs. Lau says, "Who are you talking about? Who is Kevin? We came here to talk about our son, Wing Tek."

"But I thought his American name was Kevin. That's what he asked us to call him from now on," Mrs. Baca replies.

"That child," Mrs. Lau says in disgust, "is a disgrace to our family."

"We have heard his sister call him by that name, but she said it was just a joke," Mr. Lau adds. "We came to see you because we are having problems with him in our home. Wing Tek refuses to speak Chinese to us. He argues with us about going to his Chinese lessons on Saturday with the other Chinese students in the community. He says he does not want to eat Chinese food anymore. He says that he is an American now and wants pizza, hamburgers, and tacos. What are you people teaching these children in school? Is there no respect for family, no respect for our culture?"

Mrs. Baca, an acculturated Mexican American who was raised in East Los Angeles, begins to put things together. Wing Tek, in his attempt to ensure his acceptance by his classmates, has chosen to acculturate to an extreme, to the point of rejecting his family heritage. He wants to be as "American" as anyone else in the class, perhaps more so. Like Wing Tek, Mrs. Baca had acculturated linguistically and in other ways, but she had never given up her Hispanic values. She knows the internal turmoil Wing Tek is experiencing.

Questions for Discussion

1. *Is Wing Tek wrong in his desire to acculturate?*
2. *Are Mr. and Mrs. Lau wrong in wanting their son to maintain their traditional family values?*
3. *What can Mrs. Baca do to bring about a compromise?*
4. *What can Mrs. Baca do in the classroom to resolve the problem or at least to lessen the problem?*

To answer these questions online, go to the Critical Incidents in Teaching module for this chapter of the Companion Website.

We all belong to one or more ethnic groups. For those of us born in the United States, one of our ethnic groups is American. The national origins of our ancestors is reflected in our ethnic identification (e.g., German American or Chinese American). A common bond with an ethnic group is developed through family, friends, and neighbors with whom the same intimate characteristics of living are shared. These are the people invited to baptisms, marriages, funerals, and family reunions. They are the people with whom we feel the most comfortable. They know the meaning of our behavior; they share the same language and nonverbal patterns, traditions, and customs. **Endogamy** (that is, marriage within the group), segregated residential areas, and restriction of activities with the dominant group help preserve ethnic cohesiveness across generations. The ethnic group also allows for the maintenance of group cohesiveness. It helps sustain and enhance the ethnic identity of its members. It establishes the social networks and communicative patterns that are important for the group's optimization of its position in society.

It is important to note, however, that the character of an ethnic group changes over time, becoming different in a number of ways from the culture in the country of origin. Members within ethnic groups may develop different attitudes and behaviors based on their experiences in the United States and the conditions in the country of origin at the time of emigration. Recent immigrants may have little in common with other members of their ethnic group whose ancestors immigrated a century, or even 20 years before. Ethnic communities undergo constant change in population characteristics, locations, occupations, educational levels, and political and economic struggles. All of these aspects affect the nature of the group and its members as they become Americans with ethnic roots in another country.

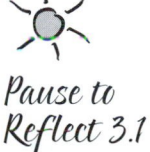

Pause to Reflect 3.1

Some U.S. citizens trace their roots to the indigenous Native Americans; some are first-generation immigrants who were born outside the United States. However, most of the population has lived in the country for generations although their ancestors emigrated from another country.

- *How closely do you identify with your ethnicity?*
- *How would you describe your ethnicity?*
- *Do you participate in any ethnic clubs or activities?*
- *Do you have any relatives in your family's countries of origin with whom you or your parents communicate?*
- *How assimilated is your family into the dominant culture?*
- *What kind of discrimination does your ethnic group face in everyday life?*
- *How has your ethnic background influenced your behavior, attitudes, and values?*

To answer these questions online, go to the Pause to Reflect module for this chapter of the Companion Website. CW

Ethnic Identity.　A person does not have to live in the same community with other members of the ethnic group to continue to identify with the group. Many second-and third-generation children move from their ethnic communities, integrating into the suburbs—a move that is easier to accomplish if they look white and speak standard English. Although many Americans are generations removed from an immigrant status, some continue to consciously emphasize their ethnicity as a meaningful basis of their identity. They may organize or join ethnic social clubs and organizations to revitalize their identification with their national origin. They can be ethnic when they want to be. It is characterized by a nostalgic allegiance to the culture of one's ancestral homeland. As the dominant society allows members of an ethnic group to assimilate, particular ethnic groups become less distinct. Ethnicity then becomes voluntary for group members—a process much more likely to occur when members are no longer labeled as ethnic by society.

In the 2000 census, the European heritages selected by the most people were German (15%), Irish (11%), English (9%), Italian (6%), Polish (3%), and French (3%) (U.S. Census Bureau, 2003). Twenty-two percent of the population reported multiple ancestries because they identify with two or more national origins (U.S. Census Bureau, 2003). They may identify with one ethnic group more than others, or they may view their ethnicity as just American. At the same time, teachers and others with whom students interact may continue to respond to them primarily on the basis of their identifiable race or ethnicity. *What is your ethnic identity? How is your ethnic identity reflected in the way you live or the activities in which you participate? How important is your ethnic group in your cultural identity?*

Opportunities for Reflection

An individual's degree of ethnic identity is influenced early in that person's life by whether or not the family members recognize or promote ethnicity as an important part of their identity. Sometimes, the choice about how ethnic one should be is imposed, particularly for members of oppressed ethnic groups. When the ethnic group believes that strong and loyal ethnic identity is necessary to maintain group solidarity, the pressure of other members of the group makes it difficult to withdraw from the group. For many members of the group, their ethnic identity provides them with the security of belonging and knowing who they are. The ethnic identity becomes the primary source of identification, and they feel no need to identify themselves differently. In fact, they may find it emotionally very difficult to sever their primary identification with the group. Some families fight the assimilative aspects of schooling that draw children into adopting the dress, language, music, and values of their peers from the dominant culture. These are usually immigrant families, families with origins other than Europe, and families who are either not Christian or conservative Christians. They are trying to maintain the values, beliefs, and codes of behavior that are important in their cultures.

Group Assimilation.　Ethnic group identity is reinforced by the political and economic barriers established by the dominant society to prevent the assimilation of oppressed groups. Ethnicity is strongest within groups that develop group solidarity through similar lifestyles, common social and economic interests, and a high degree of interpersonal connections. Historically, oppressed groups have been segregated from the dominant group and have developed enclaves in cities and suburbs that help members maintain a strong ethnic identity.

Chinatown, Little Italy, Harlem, and Little Saigon are examples of ethnic enclaves in the nation's cities. The suburbs also include pockets of families from the same ethnic backgrounds. Throughout the country are small towns and surrounding farmland where the population comes from the same ethnic background, all the residents being African American, German American, Danish American, Anglo American, or Mexican American. These individuals may be culturally encapsulated, so that most of their primary relationships, and many of their secondary relationships, are with members of their own ethnic group. They may not have the opportunity to interact with members of other ethnic groups or to recognize or share the richness of a second culture that exists in another setting. They may never learn how to live with people who speak a different language or dialect, eat different foods, and value things that their own ethnic group does not value. They often learn to fear or denigrate individuals from other ethnic groups primarily because the ways of others seem strange and incorrect. White ethnic groups are particularly vulnerable to knowing only their own group and its culture.

With few exceptions, however, the ethnic enclave does not increase in size. Families move away because of job opportunities and economic rewards that are available outside the community. Children who move away for college often do not return. Yet, some families continue to maintain a strong identity with the ethnic group even after they have moved away. Children are less likely to maintain such a strong identity because many of their primary relationships are with members of other ethnic groups.

Unlike their white counterparts, most people of color are forced out of their ethnic encapsulation to achieve social and economic mobility. Many secondary relationships are with members of other ethnic groups because they work with or for members of the dominant group. Members of the dominant group, however, rarely take the opportunity to develop even secondary relationships with African, Asian, Latino, or Native Americans. Dominant group members could spend their lives not knowing or participating in the culture of another ethnic group.

Identifying the degree of students' assimilation into the dominant culture may be helpful in determining appropriate instructional strategies. Such information can help the educator understand students' values, particularly the students' and their families' expectations for school. It also allows the teacher to more accurately determine the learning styles of students so that the teaching style can be effectively adapted to individual differences. The only way to know the importance of ethnicity in the lives of students is to listen to them. Familiarity and participation with the community from which students come also help the educator know the importance of ethnicity to students and their families.

RACE

Opportunities for Reflection

Are racial groups also ethnic groups? In the United States, many people use the two terms interchangeably. Racial groups include many ethnic groups, and ethnic groups may include members of one or more racial groups. *How has such mixed usage of the terms developed in this country? How do you describe your race? How would others describe your race? What race has the greatest advantage in society?*

Race is a concept that was developed by physical anthropologists to describe the physical characteristics of people in the world more than a century ago—a practice that has now been discredited. It is not a stable category for organizing and differentiating people. Instead, it is a social-historical concept dependent on society's perception that differences exist and that these differences are important. Some theorists suggest that race, as used in the United States, is equivalent to **caste** in other countries. Throughout U.S. history, racial identification has been used by policymakers and much of the population to classify groups of people as inferior or superior to other racial groups, resulting in discrimination, and inequality against persons of color.

Many persons with Northern and Western European ancestry view themselves as the natural, rightful leaders of the United States and the world. Until 1952, immigrants had to be white to be eligible for naturalized citizenship. At one time, slaves and Native Americans were perceived as so inferior to the dominant group that each individual was counted by the government as only a fraction of a person. This phenomenon of racial consciousness in the United States was repeated on the West Coast in the late nineteenth century when Chinese immigrants were charged an additional tax. When Southern and Eastern Europeans immigrated in the late nineteenth and early twentieth centuries, they were viewed as members of an inferior race. However, these Europeans were eligible for citizenship because they were white; persons from most other continents were not eligible. Arab American immigrants, for example, argued in courts that they were white so that they could become citizens.

In 1916, *The Passing of the Great Race* by Madison Grant detailed the U.S. racist ideology. Northern and Western Europeans of the **Nordic race** were considered by the powerful to be the political and military geniuses of the world. Protecting the purity of the Nordic race became such an emotional and popular issue for the majority of U.S. citizens that laws were passed to severely limit immigration from any region except Northern European countries. **Miscegenation** laws in many states legally prevented the marriage of whites to members of other races until the U.S. Supreme Court declared the laws unconstitutional in 1967. However, nativism reappeared in the 1990s in resolutions, referenda, and legislation in a number of states that denied education to illegal immigrants, restricted communication to the English language, and limited the prenatal care and preschool services that were available to low-income families who are disproportionately of color.

Identification of Race.   Once race identification became codified in this country, it was acceptable, even necessary at times, to identify oneself by race. One of the reasons was to be able to track the participation of groups in schools, colleges, and professional fields to determine discriminatory outcomes. Federal forms and reports classify the population on the basis of a mixture of racial and pan-ethnic categorizations as shown in Figure 3.2.

A problem with identifying the U.S. population by such broad categories is that they tell little about the people in these groups. Whether a person is American born or an immigrant may have significance in how he or she identifies himself or herself. These pan-ethnic classifications impose boundaries that do not always reflect how group members see themselves.

Although non-Hispanic whites are numerically dominant, this classification includes many different ethnic groups. Neither the ethnic identification nor the actual racial heritage of African Americans is recognized. Hispanics represent different

Figure 3.2

Pan-ethnic and racial composition of the United States in 2002.

Source: U.S. Census Bureau. (2003). *Statistical Abstract of the United States: 2003* (123rd ed.). Washington, DC: U.S. Government Printing Office.

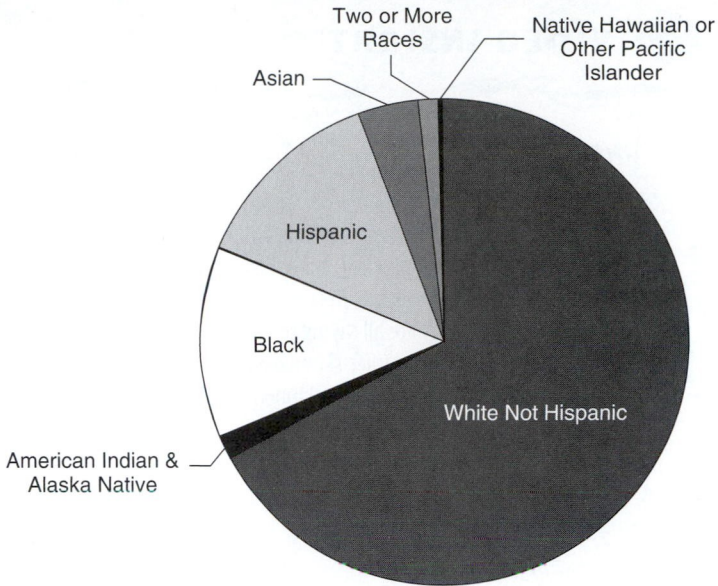

racial groups and mixtures of racial groups, as well as distinct ethnic groups whose members identify themselves as Mexican Americans, Puerto Ricans, Spanish Americans, and Cuban Americans. This category also includes persons with roots in numerous Central and South American countries. When Hispanics were asked to declare their race as black or white in the 2000 census, many rejected the classification and declared their race as Hispanic.

The pan-ethnic classification of Asian and Pacific Islander Americans includes both individuals whose families have been here for generations and those who are first-generation immigrants. Many do not have much more in common than that their countries of origin are part of the same continent. They are "Bangladeshi, Bhutanese, Bornean, Burmese, Cambodian, Celbesian, Cernan, Chamorro, Chinese, East Indian, Filipino, Hawaiian, Hmong, Indonesian, Japanese, Korean, Laotian, Okinawan, Samoan, Sikkimese, Singaporean, Sri Lankan, and Vietnamese" (Young & Pang, 1995, p. 5).

African Americans range in skin color along a continuum from black to white. Thus, it is not the color of their skin that defines them. Their identification is based, in part, on sharing a common origin that can be traced to numerous African tribes and European and Native American nations. They have become a single ethnic group in the United States because they share a common history, language, economic life, and culture that have developed over centuries of living in the United States. They are a cohesive group, in part, because of continuing discrimination as reflected in racial profiling by police, segregated schools and housing, and treatment in shopping centers and on the job (National Conference for Community and Justice, 2000). Because individuals appear to be African American is not an indication that they always identify themselves as African Americans. Some identify themselves as blacks; others with a specific ethnic group—for example, Puerto Rican or Somalian American or West Indian. Africans who are recent immigrants generally identify themselves ethnically by nation or tribe of origin.

America in Black and White: The Search for Common Ground

Society forms impressions of people every day based solely on appearance. Many people make judgments about intelligence, happiness, and earning potential without any real information. Do you think our society in general continues to judge people based on skin tone, consciously or unconsciously?

The issue of colorism is as big an issue now as ever. In this video segment you will see people working in different industries, and they are all saying the same thing: it's easier to get a job if you are a lighter skinned African American than if you are a darker skinned African American. In addition, this segment shows the disparity between salaries of lighter versus darker skinned men and women and the judgments people make about them simply based on the color of their skin.

1. What do you think of the experiment Professor Midge Wilson of DePaul University conducted with her introductory psychology class?

2. Do you think it is fair to say that most college students would respond in the same way as those chosen by Professor Wilson?

3. How do you think college students on your campus would respond? What can you do as an individual to change this way of thinking?

To answer these questions online, go to the ABC News Video Insight module for this chapter of the Companion Website.

The number of persons with multiracial backgrounds is growing. Although multiracial individuals made up only 2.4% of the population in 2002, the number of interracial couples has increased nearly tenfold since 1960 (Tafoya, 2000). Half of the children of Asian immigrants marry non-Asians, and 35% of the children of Latino immigrants marry members of other groups (Diversity Data, 2000). The belief of the racial superiority of whites is reflected in cases of mixed racial heritage. Individuals of black and white parentage are usually classified as black, not white; those of Japanese and white heritage usually are classified as nonwhite.

Many whites see themselves as raceless. They are the norm against which everyone else is "other." They have equated race with European ethnicity in which the social system is viewed as open and individuals can attain success with hard work. This view allows ethnicity to disappear as a determinant of life chances after a group has been in the country for a while. Many whites have their own stories or narratives of the mobility they or their families have experienced. They believe that their mobility was based totally on individual achievement, not assisted by their whiteness. They cannot understand why members of other groups have not experienced the same success. They deny that racial inequality has any impact on their ability to achieve. They seldom acknowledge that white oppression of people of color around the world has contributed to the subordinate status of those groups. Most whites are unable to acknowledge that they are privileged in our social, political, and economic systems. Just as gender studies should not focus solely on girls and women, the study of race should not be limited to persons of color. Whiteness and privilege must be addressed to expose the privilege and power it bestows on its members in the maintenance of an inequitable system.

Racial Diversity. Over the next few decades, whites will comprise less and less of the U.S. population. More than one third of the nation is African American, Latino, Asian American, and Native American. These groups will comprise more than 40% of the population by 2020, and 50% of the population by 2040 (U.S. Census Bureau, 2003). This pattern is not unique to the United States. "Of the 5.7 billion people in the world, only 17% are white, a figure that is expected to drop to 9% by 2010" (Diversity Data, 2000).

Two variables contribute to the significant population growth of persons of color. Half of the 2 million annual increase in the U.S. population can be attributed to immigration. Seventy percent of the immigrants are from Latin America or Asia; 20% are white (U.S. Census Bureau, 2003). The second variable contributing to the changing face of America is the birth rate. In the baby boom years of 1946 to 1964, the U.S. population grew dramatically, with a birth rate of 2.9 children per woman. Today the birth rate is approximately 2.1, the highest among industrialized nations. The differential birth rate among racial and ethnic groups is contributing to differing growth patterns. White women in the United States are having an average of 1.8 children, Asian Americans and Pacific Islanders average 1.9, Native American and Alaska Natives average 2.1, African Americans average 2.2, and Latinos average 2.9.

Race has been important in this country because racial identity singled out certain people who have been treated inferior to whites of Northern and Western Europe heritage. As whites lose their majority status, will the power that some think is their natural right be reduced as well? Will egalitarianism across groups become a more achievable goal? Some white extremists believe that they must fight to maintain their supremacy. This movement could lead to greater conflict among groups if a large number of people actually believe that one group should be superior to all others. Or, the changing demographics could lead to a more equitable sharing of power and societal benefits across all groups.

Although race has no scientific significance in describing people, it is a social construct that endures in the United States to classify groups. It is nearly impossible to be color-blind.

Pause to Reflect 3.2

- *What characteristics do you attribute to whites, blacks, Latinos, Asians, and Native Americans?*
- *Do you view some groups more positively than others?*
- *What has influenced your perceptions of your own group and others?*
- *How will you overcome any negative stereotypes you hold to ensure that you do not discriminate against students in your classroom?*

To answer these questions online, go to the Pause to Reflect module for this chapter of the Companion Website. CW

Racial Identity. Racial identity is influenced by one's family and by reflections of people who look like you in newspapers, on television, and in movies. How racial groups are stereotyped influences the interactions between members of different racial groups. If a group is seen as aggressive and violent, the reaction of the second group may be fear and protection. The construct of whiteness by many students of color may be based on distrust of whites that has grown out of their own or their communities' lived experiences. Unlike most whites, persons of color see the privilege of whiteness and, in many cases, have suffered the consequences of the lack of privilege and power in society. Their oppression by the dominant group is often a unifying theme around which persons of color coalesce (Tatum, 1997).

The racial identity of blacks and whites evolves with education and life experiences, but may be suppressed at any stage before full development (Cross, 1992; Helms, 1990; Tatum, 1997). Psychologist William E. Cross (1992) has identified six stages in the racial development of African Americans. Black children develop a belief that white is better based on their knowledge and interaction with the dominant culture. Adolescent youth often experience an event that makes them acutely aware of racism and more conscious of the significance of race in society. During this period, they are often angry about the stereotyping and racism they are experiencing or see others experience. Acceptance by their African American peers becomes very important, and **acting white** or hanging with whites is frowned upon. In young adulthood—often when in college—an African American develops a "strong desire to surround oneself with symbols of one's racial identity, and actively seek out opportunities to learn about one's own history and culture, with the support of same-race peers" (Tatum, 1997, p. 76). The next stage of development is internalization in which individuals are secure with their own race and able to develop meaningful relationships with whites who respect their racial identity. In the last stage individuals have a very positive sense of their racial identity and develop a commitment to the issues of African Americans as a group.

Whites also go through developmental stages as they develop their racial identity and abandon racism. At the beginning, whites usually do not recognize the significance of race. They accept the common **stereotypes** of persons of color and do not believe that racism pervades society. As they become aware of white racism and privilege, they become uncomfortable and feel guilt, shame, and anger about racism. They begin to recognize that they are prejudice. In the next stage, they become silent about racism and are frustrated at being labeled a member of a group, rather than an individual. As they become more aware of institutional racism, they begin to unlearn their own racism. In this stage they are often self-conscious and feel guilty about their whiteness. The development of a positive white identity allows them to move beyond the role of the victimizer, causing their feelings of guilt and shame to subside. In the last stage, they become an ally to persons of color and are able to confront institutional racism and work toward its elimination (Helms, 1990).

Elementary and secondary students will be at different stages of developing their racial identity. They may be angry, feel guilty, be ethnocentric, or be defensive—behaviors and feelings that may erupt in class as Denise Williams found in the vignette that opened this chapter. Educators must remember that students of color face societal constraints and restrictions that seldom affect white students. Such recognition is essential in the development of instructional programs and schools to effectively serve diverse populations who as yet do not share equally in the benefits that education offers.

Acting White

Almost every black student in any school can define "acting white." Underachieving black students often attribute academic achievement as acting white, and attack achieving students for excelling in school, speaking Standard English, listening to the "wrong" music, or having white friends. Some Black students may perceive the achieving studens as being traitors or disloyal to their race because of these behaviors. By adopting values common to the dominant culture, they are seen as trying to behave like whites and ignoring their own racial history and experiences as a result, many black students do not study as hard as achieving white students and do not choose the more challenging advanced placement courses. Latino students have indicated that they too have experienced this same phenomenon. This is a major problem for students of color who want to achieve academically, or go on to higher education.

DVD

1. *Must these students learn to function biculturally and bidialectally?*

2. *What can we as educators do to address this problem?*

CW

To answer these questions online, go to the ABC News Video Insight module for this chapter of the Companion Website.

Racism

A crucial fact in understanding racism is that whites see themselves as superior to persons and groups of color, and as a result exercise their power to prevent people of color from securing the prestige, power, and privilege held by whites. Many members of the dominant group do not acknowledge the existence of external impingements that make it much more difficult for people of color to shed their subordinate status than it was for their own European ancestors. They ignore the fact that some people of color have adopted the cultural values and standards of the dominant group to a greater degree than many white ethnic groups. Yet, discriminatory policies and practices prevent them from sharing equally in society's benefits with whites. In addition, the opportunities to gain qualifications with which people of color could compete equally with whites have been severely restricted throughout most of U.S. history.

Many whites declare they are not racist. They listen to rap music, dress like black urban youth, and respect African American athletes. They argue that they have never discriminated against a person of color and that they cannot be blamed for events of 40 or 200 years ago. They take no responsibility for society's racism. In a discussion of color-blind privilege, Gallagher (2003) characterizes this dichotomous thinking:

> What are we to make of a young white man from the suburbs who listens to hip-hop, wears baggy hip-hop pants, a baseball cap turned sideways, unlaced sneakers and an oversized shirt emblazoned with a famous NBA player, who, far from shouting racial epithets, lists a number of racial minorities as his heroes? It is

now possible to define oneself as not being racist because of the clothes you wear, the celebrities you like or the music you listen to while believing that blacks or Latinos are disproportionately poor or over-represented in low pay, dead end jobs because they are part of a debased, culturally deficient group. (p. 35)

Whites have little or no experience with discrimination and often do not believe that members of other racial groups are discriminated against. Because it is illegal to deny persons of color access to housing, schools, and jobs, many whites think that segregation and discrimination no longer exist. One reason for this misperception is that whites seldom experience discrimination and think that others have similar experiences to their own. In a national survey by the National Conference for Community and Justice (2000) on the state of intergroup relations in the United States, 42% of the African Americans reported incidents of discrimination in the past month, as compared with 13% of the whites, 16% of the Latinos, and 31% of the Asian Americans. Where the discrimination occurred during the past month differed by group, as shown in Table 3.2.

Blacks and whites have very different perceptions of how persons of color are treated in society. For example, 73% of the whites and 39% of the blacks in a Gallup Poll (2004a) felt that blacks are treated the same as whites in their community. Only 50% of the blacks in the poll, as compared to 81% of the whites, believed that black children had a good chance of receiving a quality education. The fact that whites do not acknowledge the discrimination that blacks know from experience contributes to the racist policies and practices that exist in schools and society.

INTERGROUP RELATIONS

Interethnic and interracial conflict is certainly not new in the United States, although the intensity of such conflicts has been mild compared to that in many other nations. Oppressed people in this country do have a history of resistance, however, as shown in revolts organized by slaves, riots after particularly egregious actions of police or others, and strikes by workers. Native American and white conflicts were common in the European American attempt to subjugate the native peoples.

What are the reasons for continued interethnic conflict? Discriminatory practices have protected the superior status of the dominant group for centuries. When other ethnic groups try to share more equitably in the rewards and privileges of society, the dominant group must concede some of its advantages. Most recently, this concern about giving up some advantages of the dominant group has been reflected in reverse discrimination cases as a reaction to affirmative action programs. As long as one ethnic or racial group has an institutional advantage over others, some intergroup conflict will exist.

Table 3.2 Discrimination in Daily Life by Group

	While Shopping	At Work	In a Restaurant, Bar, or Theater	At Place of Worship	Other
Whites	4%	3%	4%	1%	3%
Blacks	20%	14%	12%	1%	9%
Latinos	8%	6%	3%	1%	3%
Asian Americans	14%	11%	8%	0%	10%

 **VIDEO INSIGHT**

America in Black and White: South Carolina High School Drug Raid

School drug searches have unfortunately become commonplace across the United States. Many across the country saw video clips on the national news of police with drawn guns and snarling dogs frightening students in the hallway of a South Carolina high school while searching for drugs. In an effort to rid the school of what he considered a drug problem, the principal arranged a surprise raid with the local police. While the school is predominantly white, the students detained in the raid were mostly black. No drugs or weapons were found in the raid.

As soon as the video clips were shown locally and across the nation, the backlash was instantaneous. Whites and blacks saw the same video, yet interpreted the incident very differently. African Americans have tended to view the incident as racism with insensitivity on the part of whites. Whites on the other hand see the African Americans as paranoid and overreacting. What is important for educators to understand is while many whites view racism as a thing of the past, individuals of color have different perceptions of life in the United States. Educators must carefully determine the ramifications of their decisions when it relates to race.

1. *Why do some people see this incident as racism and racial profiling of black students?*

2. *Why do many white observers of this incident not see it as a reflection of racism?*

3. *Why do you agree or not agree with the action taken by the principal in the South Carolina high school?*

4. *What are the ramifications of the principal's decision on racial relations in the schools?*

To answer these questions online, go to the ABC News Video Insight module for this chapter of the Companion Website.

DVD

CW

Competition for economic resources can also contribute to intergroup conflict. As economic conditions become tighter, fewer jobs are available. Discriminatory practices in the past have forced people of color into positions with the least seniority. As a result, when jobs are cut back, disproportionately high numbers of persons of color are laid off. The tension between ethnic groups increases as members of specific groups determine that they disproportionately suffer the hardships resulting from economic depression. Conflict sometimes occurs between oppressed groups when they are forced to share limited societal resources, such as affordable housing and access to quality education programs. Conflict as a result of inequitable distribution of economic rewards is likely to continue as long as members of groups can observe and feel those inequities.

Perceptions of intergroup relations differ across racial and ethnic groups. Less than half of young adults believe that race relations in the United States are very good or somewhat good, but more than 70% of persons over 65 rate them as very good or somewhat good (Gallup, 2004b). Fifty-six percent of whites are satisfied with the state of race relations as compared to 49% of persons of color with Latinos being somewhat less satisfied and African Americans the least satisfied (Gallup,

2004a). At the same time, 60% of the Hispanics, 62% of the whites, and 72% of the blacks believe that race relations will always be a problem (Gallup, 2004b). Intergroup tensions and conflicts are often the result of one group receiving more rewards from society than others. Persons of color overwhelmingly perceive whites as having too much power. They also perceive whites as having greater opportunities for job advancement, equal pay, and fair and unbiased treatment by the police and media. Most whites do recognize that persons of color do not have the same opportunities as they do, but the percentage who acknowledge these differences is smaller than any other group.

During the past 50 years, educational strategies have been developed to reduce and overcome intergroup conflicts. These strategies have focused on training teachers to be effective in intergroup or human relations; on attempting to change the prejudicial attitudes of teachers; on fighting institutional discrimination through affirmative action and civil rights legislation; on encouraging changes in textbooks and other resources to more accurately reflect the multiethnic nature of society; and on attempting to remove discriminatory behavior from classroom interactions and classroom practices. All of these strategies are important to combat prejudice and discrimination in the educational setting. Alone or in combination, however, the strategies are not enough, but that does not diminish the need for professional educators to further develop the strategies. It is not a sign of failure, but a recognition that prejudice, discrimination, and racism are diseases that infect all of society.

HATE GROUPS

White privilege is sometimes taken to the extreme as members try to protect their power by preaching hate against other groups that are considered inferior. Since World War II, overt acts of prejudice have decreased dramatically. In the early 1940s, the majority of whites supported segregation of and discrimination against, blacks. Today, most whites support policies against racial discrimination and prejudice.

Nevertheless, intolerance of other groups and violence against their members continue to exist. Many communities have experienced cross burnings, swastika graffiti, and, in some instances, hate crimes against people of color, non-Christians, and gays and lesbians. The Southern Poverty Law Center reports that

- Every hour someone commits a hate crime.
- Every day at least eight blacks, three whites, three gays, three Jews, and one Latino become hate crime victims.
- Every week a cross is burned. (Southern Poverty Law Center, 2000, p. 1)

The FBI reports that hate crimes are increasingly perpetuated against Asian Americans and homosexuals. Although most hate crimes were historically committed in the South against African Americans and Jews, the majority today occur in the North and West (Southern Poverty Law Center, 2000).

The increasing number of individuals of color in the United States, television programming to accommodate new language groups, and new temples and mosques, has forever changed the U.S. landscape. These visible symbols of growth and change have become threatening to some individuals, whose comfort level does not extend beyond white Anglo-Saxon control or Judeo-Christian religious traditions. Some of

FOCUS YOUR CULTURAL LENS: DEBATE

Should Proms Be Segregated?

Many schools in communities with diverse populations are racially and ethnically integrated. Developing positive cross-cultural communications and interactions has long been a goal of schools that are seriously trying to integrate. However, practices in schools are not supportive of this goal when students are segregated in bilingual classes, advanced placement courses, special education classes, and gifted programs when students from one racial or ethnic group are disproportionately over- or underrepresented. Students often separate themselves by their racial or ethnic group at lunchtime in the school cafeteria, in after-school activities, in their choices of extracurricular activities, and in work groups in the classroom. The integration of another school tradition is being threatened in a number of communities. Students who do not feel welcome at their high school prom are organizing their own proms for students from the same racial, ethnic, religious, sexual orientation, or disability group (Richard, 2004). Schools in the South that have for years sponsored segregated proms for black and white students have been assailed for not integrating this social event. Does support for segregated events fly in the face of the goal for integration or support the preferences of each racial, ethnic, or other group?

FOR

- Students from the same racial or ethnic group prefer to attend proms with members of their own groups because they like the same music and food.

- Integrated proms favor one group's preference for music and refreshments over another, which does not treat groups equally.

AGAINST

- School-sponsored events like a prom should support the school's goal for integration in all of its activities.

- The separation of groups in social situations like a prom exacerbates poor intergroup relations.

Questions

1. *Why do some students not feel welcome at their high school proms?*
2. *What could school officials do to ensure that the needs of a diverse group of students are met at school proms and other school activities?*
3. *When would you be in favor of a segregated prom? Why?*

To answer these questions online, go to the Focus Your Cultural Lens: Debate module for this chapter of the Companion Website.

Reference: Richard, A. (2004, May 10). Alternative proms gain in popularity. *Education Week, XXIII*(37), 1, 19.

these extremists have responsibility for public policy. An example is a state board of education member who verbally attacked Buddhists and Muslims and referred to Islam as a cult—worshipers of Lucifer (Eck, 2000).

Because of the increasing adversarial relationship that developed between fundamentalist Muslims in the Middle East and the United States, American Muslims have been the targets of vicious attacks during the Persian Gulf War in the early 1990s and after the 9/11 attacks on the World Trade Center and the Pentagon in 2001. As a part of this violence, mosques have been burned. While it is undeniable that Islamic terrorists have been responsible for some terrorist attacks, the overwhelming majority of American Muslims vigorously condemn terrorism and are model citizens. Nevertheless, they are routinely wrongly accused of being terrorists or sympathizers. Muslims have not been the only victims of religious intolerance. Arsonists have also victimized Jewish synagogues and black churches.

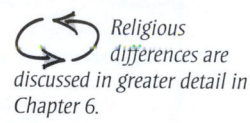 *Religious differences are discussed in greater detail in Chapter 6.*

Hate also occurs on college campuses. The U.S. Department of Education reported 487 hate crimes on campuses in 2001. Many other victims do not report the crimes because of fear or retaliation or the belief that nothing will be done. The Southern Poverty Law Center described a few of the incidents:

> At SUNY Maritime College in the Bronx, 21 Arab students flee after a series of assaults and incidents of racist harassment. At Brown University in Rhode Island, a black senior is beaten by three white students who tell her she is a "quota" who doesn't belong. At the State University of New York at Binghamton, three students are charged in a racially motivated assault that left an Asian American student with a fractured skull. A Harvard resident tutor quits after being subjected to homophobic vandalism. E-mail threats and slurs are sent to 30,000 students and faculty at Stanford University, along with others at many other schools. Holocaust deniers publish their screed in campus newspapers and, in a few cases, are backed up ideologically by professors. (Hate on Campus, 2000, p. 8)

Estimates suggest that there are now more than 751 hate group chapters in the United States with the majority located east of the Mississippi River (Potok, 2004). While freedom of speech, guaranteed by the First Amendment, is one of the most cherished values in the country, it is also one of the variables that contributes to the proliferation of hate groups. Each individual's freedom of speech is guaranteed, and this includes those who express messages of hate in their speeches, writings, and now the Internet. The message of hate groups is attractive to some citizens who want to blame others for their misfortunes. Only 5% of the hate crimes are committed by members of these groups. They are committed by young males who have adopted the hate rhetoric, but don't usually act from a deeply held ideology (Southern Poverty Law Center, 2000).

Recruitment efforts by hate groups often target areas of the country that have experienced economic and racial change, such as a factory layoff or increased diversity in a school as a result of desegregation. Other recruits are sometimes angry about economic conditions that have led to the loss of jobs in their communities. Rather than blaming corporations that are economizing and moving jobs to sources of cheaper labor, they blame African Americans, women, Arabs, Jews, or the government. Hate group organizers convince new recruits that it is members of other groups who are taking their jobs and being pandered to by government programs. Members of the white extremist groups believe that whites are the superior race and that the government and others are emasculating their white power and privilege. A student contact in a school can provide information about the mood and anger of students that might make the school a potential candidate for recruitment (Youth and Hate, 1999).

Many hate groups attract individuals with their appearance of religious affiliation. Leaders are sometimes referred to as pastor. Some use "Church" in their name. Many use Biblical scriptures on their websites. Some use the name of "Jesus" and refer to their efforts as "His work" and themselves as "His People."

Many of the hate groups have developed sophisticated websites and support an ultraviolent white power music industry (Southern Poverty Law Center, 2004). Some hate groups have links on their websites that are developed primarily for school-age youngsters. Some contain cartoons, others crossword puzzles for children. All contain a message of hate. Because so many children have become proficient in the use of computers and in surfing the web, it has become imperative for parents and educators to be able to recognize online hate and to be able to minimize the risks to their children and students. Software that will block or filter hate group websites is available through Internet providers and software dealers.

Educational Implications

At the beginning of the twenty-first century, Latinos replaced African Americans as the largest non-European group in the United States. Within a few years, the number of Latino students will also surpass the number of African American students in schools. Some states and areas of the country are much more diverse than others; for example, the West has the largest concentration of students of color; the Midwest the least. Students of color are more than 60% of the student population in California, Hawaii, New Mexico, and the District of Columbia (U.S. Census Bureau, 2003). They are over half of the student population in Texas, Louisiana, and Mississippi, and more than 40% of the student population in Arizona, Georgia, Maryland, New York, and South Carolina. The highest concentration (25%) of African American students is in the South; Latinos make up 32% of the students in the West (U.S. Department of Education, 2002). The majority of the population in many urban schools is comprised of students of color. Figure 3.3 shows how the diversity of school-aged children and youth has changed over the past 15 years. White students are projected

Figure 3.3

The changing diversity of the school-age population.

Source: National Center for Education Statistics. (2003, June). *Digest of Education Statistics 2002.* Washington, DC: U.S. Department of Education.

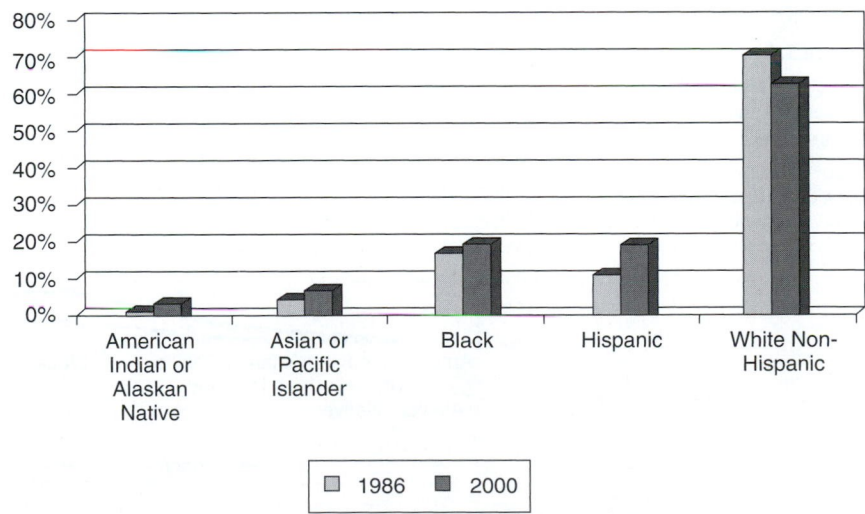

to comprise less than half of the student population by 2050. These demographics obviously have a profound impact on schools throughout the United States.

Schools are the recipients of today's young immigrants. *Education Week* reports, for example, "Broward County, Fla.—the nation's fifth-largest district, with nearly 242,000 students—young people come from at least 52 different countries and speak 52 different languages, ranging from Spanish and Haitian-Creole to Tagalog. The number of children identified as having limited fluency in English has nearly doubled since 1993–94, from 12,039 to 23,459" (Olson, 2000, p. 38). In 2001 5% of all U.S. school-age children were born outside the United States. Many more students were born into first-generation families (U.S. Census Bureau, 2003).

Ethnicity and race play an important role in the lives of many students and communities. Membership in oppressed groups has a significant impact on students' perceptions of themselves and their behavior and performance in school. Ethnicity and race are significant for educators because their cultural background and experiences may be incongruent with the cultural experiences of the students. Teachers themselves may stereotype students who have a racial or ethnic background different than their own. The majority of teachers are white females who are charged with teaching the majority of students of color. Figure 3.4 shows that teachers of color are either not being recruited or retained in our schools. Thus, white teachers must become aware of the cultures of the students in the schools to which they are assigned.

This incongruence may contribute to students not feeling their cultures are reflected in school, sometimes leading to their dropping out of school or not participating in meaningful ways. More students of color than white students are not actively engaged in their schoolwork, too often dropping out of school, in part, because they don't see the payoff in completing high school. Only 77% of 18- to 21-year-olds have graduated from high school with Asian Americans having the highest graduation rates. Seventy-two percent of African American young adults are high school graduates. Native American and Latino students are less likely to graduate from high school (U.S. Census Bureau, 2003).

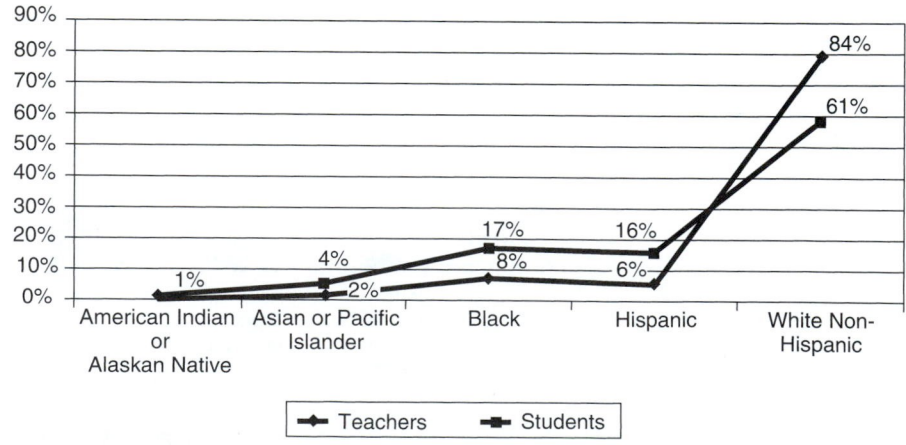

Figure 3.4

Pan-ethnic and racial diversity of elementary and secondary teachers and students.

Source: National Center for Education Statistics. (2003, June). *Digest of Education Statistics 2002.* Washington, DC: U.S. Department of Education.

ACKNOWLEDGING RACE AND ETHNICITY IN SCHOOLS

Opportunities for Reflection

Teachers often declare that they are color-blind, that they do not see a student's color and treat all students equally regardless of race. The problem is that **color blindness** helps maintain white privilege because it fails to recognize the existence of racial inequality in schools (Gallagher, 2003). Teachers do not usually confront issues of race in schools and classrooms, in part because race is not supposed to matter. Teachers' discomfort becomes intertwined with their own uncertainties about race and their possible complicity in maintaining racial inequities. *How comfortable do you feel with handling issues of race in the classroom? How can you ensure that you are not racially discriminating against students of color in your classroom?*

Race and ethnicity do matter to many students and their families, and do have an impact on the communications and interactions with teachers. Students of color are reminded by others of their race on almost a daily basis as they face discriminatory practices and attitudes. Rather than pretending that race and ethnicity do not exist, teachers should acknowledge the differences and be aware of ways culture can influence learning. Equity does not mean sameness; students can be treated differently, as long as the treatment is fair and appropriate, to accomplish the goal of student learning.

The ethnic communities to which students belong provide the real-life examples teachers should draw on to teach. Knowing students' ethnic and cultural experiences and how subject matter interacts with students' reality are important in designing effective strategies to engage students in learning. Successful teachers ensure that students learn the academic skills needed to compete effectively in the dominant workplace. In the process they acknowledge and respect the ethnicity of their students and the community in which the school is located to prevent students from becoming alienated from their homes, their community, and their culture. Too many students of color are not learning what is needed to perform at accepted levels on standardized tests. In fact, the achievement of many students of color decreases the longer they stay in school.

CONFRONTING RACISM IN CLASSROOMS

A first step for educators to confront racism in schools is to realize that racism exists and that, if they are white, they have benefited from it. This is not an easy process as discussed earlier in the section on racial identity. We often resist discussion of race and racism because we must eventually confront our own feelings and beliefs. Once teachers believe that discrimination exists in society and the school, they are more likely to believe students of color when they report incidents of racism or discrimination. They stop making excuses for the perpetrators or explaining that the action of the perpetrator was not really racist.

Students often resist participating in discussions about race and racism. In predominantly white college classrooms, Tatum (1997) found three sources of resistance:

1. Race is considered a taboo topic for discussion, especially in racially mixed settings.
2. Many students, regardless of racial group membership, have been socialized to think of the United States as a just society.

CRITICAL INCIDENTS IN TEACHING

Racial Identification

Roosevelt High School annually celebrates Black History Month in February. The month-long study includes a convocation to celebrate African American heritage. For 10 years, students have organized and conducted this convocation in which the whole student body participates.

The students who have organized the event this year begin the convocation with the black national anthem. The African American students, a few other students, and some faculty members stand for the singing of the anthem. Many of the African American students become very angry with what they perceive to be a lack of respect by the students and faculty who do not stand.

In discussions that follow the convocation, some students and faculty who did not stand for the anthem argue that the only national anthem to which they should be expected to respond is their own national anthem. They say it is unfair to be required to attend a convocation celebrating the heritage of one racial group when there is no convocation to celebrate their own racial or ethnic heritage.

Questions for Discussion

1. *What may have been happening in the school that led to the tensions that surfaced during this convocation?*
2. *How may the African American students perceive the refusal to stand by some of the students and faculty?*
3. *Do you think the reasons for not standing during the anthem are valid? Why or why not?*
4. *If you are meeting with a class immediately after the convocation, how will you handle the tension between students?*
5. *What activities might be initiated within the school to reduce the interracial tensions that have developed?*

To answer these questions online, go to the Critical Incidents in Teaching module for this chapter of the Companion Website.

CW

3. Many students, particularly white students, initially deny any personal prejudice, recognizing the impact of racism on other people's lives but failing to acknowledge its impact on their own.

Opportunities for Reflection

Many teachers do not feel comfortable handling students' resistance to these topics, in part, because they are not always confident of their own stances on race. Because students are at different levels in their own racial identity, many of them cannot address these issues as rationally as the teacher might desire. Some will personalize the discussion. Some will be emotional or confrontive. Others will be uncomfortable or silent. Just because the topic is difficult to address does not mean it should be ignored. Teachers should break the silence about race and develop the courage to work at eliminating racism in their own classrooms and schools. One step is to help students think critically about race and social justice for all students. *How prevalent do you think racism is in your college and home community? How will you help white students understand racism and the privilege that it has given them?*

Teachers should not ignore the racism that exists in the policies and practices of their schools. They should intervene when students call each other names that are racist. Students should be helped to understand that racist language and behavior are unacceptable and will not be tolerated in schools. When students use derogatory terms for ethnic group members or tell ethnic jokes, teachers should use the opportunity to discuss attitudes about those groups. Students should not be allowed to express their hostility to other group members without being confronted by the teacher. When teachers allow students to treat others with disrespect, they are partners in the perpetuation of racism. These overt acts can be confronted and stopped, but the more difficult task will be to identify and eliminate racist practices in schools and by the educators who work in the schools.

A teacher's challenge is to seriously confront these issues at a personal level before entering a classroom. If teachers believe that persons of color are intellectually inferior, they will find it difficult to have high expectations for the academic achievement of those students. We experience stages of racial identity as we learn to accept the existence of racism and to feel comfortable with our own racial identities. Although the developmental stages differ for members of oppressed and dominant groups because of their own lived encounters with racism and oppression (Cross, 1992), it is important that all educators seek opportunities to confront these issues in their own lives. Once in the classroom, they will be in the position to help students grapple with these topics and their own feelings. The goal should be to attack racism and oppression in daily life, rather than reinforce it in the classroom.

RACE AND ETHNICITY IN THE CURRICULUM

School environments should help students learn to participate in the dominant society while maintaining connections to their distinct ethnicities if they choose. Respect for and support of ethnic differences will be essential in this effort. Students know when a teacher or counselor does not respect or value their ethnic backgrounds. As educators, we cannot afford to reject or neglect students because their ethnic backgrounds are different from our own. We are responsible for making sure all students learn to think, read, write, and compute so that they can function effectively in society. We can help accomplish this goal by accurately reflecting ethnicity in the curriculum and positively using it to teach and interact with students.

Traditionally, the curriculum of most schools has been centered in the dominant culture. The curriculum in most schools is based on the knowledge and perspective of the West (Northern and Western Europe). The inherent bias of the curriculum does not encourage candid admissions of racism and oppression within society. In fact, it supports the superiority of Western thought over all others and provides minimal or no introduction to the non-Western cultures of Asia, Africa, and South and Central America. Information on, and perspectives of, other groups are sometimes added as a unit during a school year. Some schools have replaced this traditional curriculum with one based on the culture of students and communities. Multicultural education, on the other hand, encourages a culturally responsive curriculum in which diversity is integrated throughout the courses, activities, and interactions in the classroom.

Ethnic Studies. Ethnic studies courses introduce students to the history and contemporary conditions of one or more ethnic groups. Many universities and

CRITICAL INCIDENTS IN TEACHING

One Person, One Vote

Flint Ridge is a small K–12 private school in a suburb of a major city. The senior class has 47 members. Of that number, three are Asian American, two are Latino, eleven are African American, and the remainder are white. It is February, and plans are being made for the prom. The site has already been selected, and many details must now be determined. One of the most important decisions is who the disc jockey will be for the prom. Suggestions have been made about which DJ is to be hired. Opinions are strong and tend to be drawn along ethnic lines. The African American students want a popular African American DJ who plays music popular to that ethnic group. The white students want a white DJ who plays the type of music they prefer. The chair of the DJ Committee calls for a vote. Not surprisingly, all African American students vote for the black DJ. One Latino student votes with them. The other Latino student and the three Asian American students, however, vote with the white students for the white DJ.

"Twelve to thirty-five," announces the chair. "It's Jerry Smith who will be our DJ for the prom."

"That's not fair," says Tyson Edwards, the captain of the basketball team. "You guys always get your way because there are more of you than us."

"Not fair? What are you talking about?" says Keith Van Fleet, president of the senior class. "How much fairer can you get? It's a democratic election. Everything in this school is done democratically. Every person gets a vote. Jerry Smith got the most votes, and everyone voted and every vote counted."

"You think you can ram everything down our throats just because you outnumber us," says Tyson. "We don't have to listen to you. I'm leaving." As Tyson leaves, so do the other African American students.

The next day, Tyson asks to speak with Shelly Brooks, the senior class advisor. "I don't mean any disrespect, Miss Brooks, but we don't get any respect with the things that matter to black students. Everything is one person and one vote. We never have enough votes to get anything that we want as African Americans. We've decided to boycott the senior prom. We are going to have our own prom. We can't really afford it, but our parents said that we are right, and they will help us hire a DJ who will play our kind of music. This is our last dance at this school, and for just once, we want to hear and dance to our kind of music."

Questions for Discussion

1. *Is "one person, one vote" always the most democratic way of deciding issues?*
2. *Are the white students wrong in holding to the vote outcome?*
3. *Are the black students wrong in protesting so vehemently?*
4. *Are there similar parallel situations in the rest of society?*
5. *What compromises could be made that might be acceptable to both groups?*

To answer these questions online, go to the Critical Incidents in Teaching module for this chapter of the Companion Website.

some high schools have ethnic studies programs, such as African American, Asian American, Native American, and Latino Studies, in which students can major. These courses and programs allow for in-depth exposure to the social, economic, and political history of a specific group. They are designed to correct the distortions and omissions that prevail in society about a specific ethnic group. Events that have been neglected in textbooks are addressed, myths are dispelled, and history is viewed from the perspective of the ethnic group, as well as the dominant group. Prospective teachers and other professional school personnel who have not been exposed to an examination of an ethnic group different from their own should take such a course or undertake individual study.

Traditionally, ethnic studies have been offered as separate courses that students elect from many offerings in the curriculum. Seldom have they been required courses for all students. The majority of students who choose these courses are students from the ethnic groups being studied. Although the information and experiences offered in these courses are important to these students, students from other ethnic groups also need to learn about others and the multiethnic nation and world in which they live. *How have you learned about ethnic groups other than your own? What courses are offered in your college or university that would provide insights into another ethnic group? What groups discussed in this chapter do you know the least about?*

Opportunities for Reflection

Ethnocentric Curriculum. Historically, some immigrant groups have established their own schools, with classes often held in the evenings or on Saturdays, to reinforce their own cultural values, traditions, and the native language. Today other ethnic groups are establishing their own charter or private schools with curriculum that is centered around the history and values of their own ethnic group. Some Native American tribes have established tribal-controlled public schools in which the traditional culture serves as the social and intellectual starting point. Although most of these schools are located in rural Native American communities, some urban areas have created magnet Native American schools with similar goals.

Some African American communities have demanded an **Afrocentric curriculum** to challenge Eurocentrism and tell the truth about black history. They are designed to improve students' self-esteem, academic skills, values, and positive identity with their ethnic group. At the core of this approach is an African perspective of the world and historical events. These schools are often in urban areas with large African American student populations. Afrocentric public schools are now found in Atlanta, Cleveland, Detroit, Kansas City, Milwaukee, Oakland, and Washington, DC.

Another development is the establishment of public school programs for African American male students. These programs are designed to assist African American males in overcoming the harsh realities they face—unemployment, drugs, violence, and poverty. Programs provide a strong gender and cultural identity to assist young men in becoming successful in their academic, occupational, and community pursuits. The programs use strong, positive role models as teachers and focus on an Afrocentric curriculum. The goals are laudable. Such programs may play a role in protecting young African American males against forces that lead to their being murdered, arrested, or unemployed in disproportionate numbers.

Some parents, educators, and community activists who believed that the public schools were not effectively serving their children have established urban, ethnocentric, and grassroots charter schools. Many of these schools have placed the ethnic culture of the enrolled students at the center of the curriculum; they are Afrocentric, Chicano-centric, or Native American-centric, emphasizing what is known, valued, and respected from their own cultural roots. Although a number of these schools have been established within the public system, the schools often do not have the financial support that charter school parents in the suburbs are able to generate. They face the same inequities of other public schools in their communities. *Why do some parents find that the traditional curriculum does not reflect their culture? Why do they think an ethnocentric curriculum would serve their children better? What information would you need to teach in an ethnocentric school?*

Opportunities for Reflection

Multiethnic Curriculum. A **multiethnic curriculum** permeates all subject areas at all levels of education, from preschool through adult education. All courses reflect accurate and positive references to ethnic diversity. The amount of specific content about ethnic groups varies according to the course taught, but an awareness and a recognition of the multiethnic population is reflected in all classroom experiences. No matter how assimilated students in a classroom are, it is the teacher's responsibility to expose them to the ethnic diversity of this nation and the world.

Bulletin boards, resource books, and films that show ethnic diversity should constantly reinforce these realities, although teachers should not depend entirely on these resources for instructional content about groups. Too often, persons of color are studied only during a unit on African American history or Native Americans. Too often, they are not included on reading lists or in the study of biographies, labor unions, or the environment. Students can finish school without reading or seeing anything written or produced by females and males of color. If ethnic groups are included only during a unit or a week focusing on a particular group, students do not learn to view them as an integral part of society. They are viewed as separate, distinct, and inferior to the dominant group. A multiethnic curriculum prevents the distortion of history and contemporary conditions. Without it, the perspective of the dominant group becomes the only valid curriculum to which students are exposed.

EXPLORE DIVERSITY Go to the *Exploring Diversity* CD located in the accompanying booklet to observe a teacher integrating ethnicity into a literacy lesson for second graders in the case called *Second Grade Literacy in an Urban School.*

An educator has the responsibility for ensuring that ethnic groups become an integral part of the total curriculum. This mandate does not require the teacher to discuss every ethnic group. It does require that the classroom resources and instruction *not* focus solely on the dominant group. It requires that perspectives of ethnic groups and the dominant group be examined in discussions of historical and current events. For example, one should consider the perspectives of Mexican and Native Americans as well as the dominant group in a presentation and discussion of the westward movement of European Americans in the eighteenth and nineteenth centuries. It requires students to read literature by authors from different ethnic backgrounds. It expects that mathematics and science be explored from a Native American as well as a Western perspective. The contributions of different ethnic groups are reflected in the books that are used by students, in the movies that they view, and in the activities in which they participate.

Multiethnic education should include learning experiences to help students examine their own stereotypes about and prejudice against ethnic groups. These are not easy topics to address but should be a part of the curriculum beginning in preschool. At all levels, but particularly in junior high and secondary classrooms, students may resist discussion of these issues. Teachers can create a safe classroom climate by establishing clear guidelines for such discussions. *What information about ethnic diversity could be integrated into the subject that you are planning to teach? How have the bulletin boards and display cases in the schools you have visited reflected ethnic diversity? What groups are usually included?*

Opportunities for Reflection

Development of a multiethnic curriculum requires the educator to evaluate textbooks and classroom resources for ethnic content and biases. Although advances have been made in eliminating ethnic biases and adding information about ethnic groups in textbooks, many older textbooks are still used in classrooms. With many textbook revisions, ethnic content has been added to what already existed, rather than being carefully integrated throughout the text. Biased books should not prevent the teacher from providing multiethnic instruction.

Supplementary materials can fill the gap in this area. The biases and omissions in the texts can be used for discussions of the experiences of ethnic groups. None of these instructional activities will occur, however, unless the teacher is aware of and values ethnic differences and their importance in the curriculum.

CLOSING THE ACHIEVEMENT GAPS

After working with African American students in schools for many years, Professor Janice Hale (2001) has concluded that "inferior educational outcomes are tolerated for African American children day in and day out, in inner-city, suburban, and private school settings" (p. xx). The data on student achievement supports Hale's conclusion. African American students, as well as Latino and Native American students, are not meeting standards as measured on the standardized tests required in most states. As a result, a disproportionately large number of students of color are not being promoted to the next grade, not graduating from high school, and dropping out of schools. *Why do educators allow so many students to fail? How can educators ensure that all students are meeting standards? What is the negative impact of standardized testing on students of color?*

Opportunities for Reflection

The Role of Assessment. Schools conduct widespread testing of students to determine if they are meeting the standards established by states. Tests are trumpeted as measures of competence to move from one grade to another, graduate from high school, enter upper-division college courses, earn a baccalaureate, and become licensed to teach. Overwhelmingly, promoters suggest that anyone who cannot pass the appropriate test certainly cannot be qualified to move on to further study. Thus, student performance on state tests has become the primary measure of quality in the nation's schools with sanctions if students are not making **adequate yearly progress (AYP)** or the minimum level of student performance required by the federal legislation, "No Child Left Behind." Teachers and principals are sometimes in jeopardy of losing their jobs if students do not perform at expected levels. Unfortunately, many teachers are teaching to the test, which limits their teaching of a number of subjects that are not tested and limits helping students develop critical thinking skills.

Testing is a mainstay of school culture today as students are required to meet standards as measured by their performance on standardized state tests.

Standardized tests have limited the access of many students from low-income and oppressed ethnic groups to more rigorous study at all educational levels and may prevent students from entering professional schools. Testing has led to the assignment of disproportionately large numbers of these students to special education programs for the mentally retarded, learning disabled, and emotionally disturbed.

Between 1970 and 1990, student performance on national tests improved, with the largest gains being made by students of color (Education Trust, 2003). The progress came to a halt in the 1990s, and the achievement gap between whites and most students of color remains wide. Why do students from oppressed groups score lower than dominant group members on standardized tests? It is not, as the authors of *The Bell Curve* (Hernstein & Murray, 1994) claim, due to genetic differences of intelligence between the races. *Education Watch State and National Data, 2004* (Education Trust, 2004) reports the following disparities between groups:

- Low-income and students of color are more likely to be taught a low-level curriculum with low standards for performance.

- About 62 out of every 100 white students complete Algebra II. Only 52% of African Americans and 45% of Latinos take this course; the pattern is similar for chemistry.

- African American and Latino high-school graduates are much less likely than whites and Asian Americans to go to college.

- Students of color have more unqualified and inexperienced teachers.

- More mathematics courses in high-schools with large numbers of students of color are taught by teachers lacking a major in mathematics.

Should it be a surprise that many students of color do not perform as well as white students when they have not taken advanced mathematics and science courses or had teachers who majored in those subjects? In urban schools in which students of color are overrepresented, teachers are less likely to be fully licensed than in schools with middle-class white students. Advanced courses in mathematics and science are not always available in the schools attended by a large number of students of color. Students must have access to such courses and qualified teachers to study the content on which they will be tested.

As educators, we must be careful not to label students of color intellectually inferior because their standardized test scores are low. These scores too often influence a teacher's expectations for the academic performance of students in the classroom. It is essential that educators maintain high expectations for all students, regardless of test scores. Standardized test scores can help in determining how assimilated into the dominant culture and how affluent one's family may be, but they provide less evidence of how intelligent a person is. Many other factors can be used to provide information about intelligence—for example, the ability to think and respond appropriately in different situations.

What should the purposes of assessments be? Rather than use tests to sort students on the basis of income, ethnicity, and family characteristics, assessments could be used to help understand what students know so that curriculum and activities can be designed to increase their knowledge and skills. Tests should provide information that will help improve student learning. The traditional multiple-choice tests are beginning to be replaced by performance assessments. These assessments use observations, portfolios, projects, and essays for students to demonstrate what they know in many different ways. They are designed to promote complex and engaged learning.

Educators are capable of making valid decisions about ability on the basis of numerous objective and subjective factors about students. If decisions about the capabilities of students of color match exactly the standardized scores, the educator should reevaluate his or her own responses and interactions with these students. This is an area that none of us can afford to neglect. Testing results today are making differences in the life chances for many students, especially those of color and from low-income families.

Who Is Responsible for Closing the Gaps?   When students do not achieve at levels expected, too many teachers do not take responsibility for helping students learn. They blame the students, their parents, or the economic conditions of the community rather than seriously reflecting on why students in their classroom are not learning. A number of research studies are finding that teacher effectiveness is more important in student achievement than a student's race, poverty, or parent's education (Carey, 2004; Sanders & Rivers, 1996). In other words, effective teachers matter. Students who have been assigned the most effective teachers for three years in a row perform at much higher levels than the students who were in the classrooms of the least effective teachers for three years. With effective teachers, low-achieving students become high achievers (Education Trust, 2003). The problem is that low-achieving students are more likely to be assigned ineffective teachers.

Many teachers do not allow students to fail. There are many examples of good teachers who have helped students with low test scores achieve at advanced levels. African American and Latino students have performed at the same level as other students in mathematics and other subjects after teachers raised their expectations and changed their teaching strategies. Project SEED, the Algebra Project, and the Marcus Garvey School in Los Angeles are examples of programs that are successful in ensuring that African American students achieve at high levels (Hilliard, 2003). The Education Trust (2003) has identified a number of schools that are ensuring that their students of color are achieving at high levels. Those schools

1. have clear goals based on standards and benchmarks;
2. provide all students challenging curriculum aligned with standards;
3. provide extra instruction to students when they need it; and
4. know that good teaching matters more than anything else. (p. 2)

Students are not always inactive participants in their academic achievement. They are not always engaged with the schoolwork. They do not always do their homework. Some researchers have found that many working-class boys and students of color develop resistance or oppositional patterns to handle their subordination status within schools (Ogbu, 2003; Solomon, 1988; Willis, 1977). These patterns often take the form of breaking school rules and norms, belittling academic achievement, and valuing manual over mental work. These students may equate schooling with acting white or middle class. Although middle-class African American students perform academically better than their working-class peers, they do not do as well as white students, which some researchers attribute to this oppositional process.

An oppositional identity is accompanied by attitudes and behaviors that are clearly opposed to those of the dominant group (Ogbu, 2003). Some African American, Mexican American, and Native American students equate schooling with acceptance of the culture of the dominant group over their own cultural identity. Some students resist assimilation by developing strategies of resistance, including poor academic achievement (Fordham, 1988; Gibson, 1988; Ogbu, 2003).

Not all students of color adopt an oppositional form, and not all groups are equally affected. As a group, Asian American students have high achievement records in mathematics and science and attend college at rates disproportionately higher than other groups. One explanation is that Asian American adults are overrepresented in professional occupations, which results in incomes above that of most other groups of color. The economic advantages in the home backgrounds of many of these students contribute to their high levels of achievement and participation in mathematics and science. Generally, the cultural group values mathematics and science skills, and families provide experiences that encourage their development.

Many immigrants are less likely to develop the oppositional forms of the long-established groups of color. Students are more willing to accept school norms and succeed academically, in part because they compare the conditions of living in the United States with those in the country they just left. They are motivated to learn and, as a result, expend the necessary effort to learn. However, long-term studies of immigrants find that the longer a child of immigrants lives in the United States, the more their academic engagement and achievement approaches the general student population (Portes & Rumbaut, 2001).

Educators cannot expect that the cultural experiences of all immigrant students will be congruent with the norms of school. An important contributing factor is the status of the immigrant—whether the families are legal immigrants, refugees, migrant workers, or undocumented workers without legal papers (Gibson, 1992/1993). School achievement is dependent on many factors: how long the family has been in the country, the student's age on arrival, the parents' education and economic status in the country of origin, exposure to Western and urban lifestyles, languages spoken in the family, quality of educational experiences before immigrating, and others. It will be important for educators to interact with immigrant families to determine the most effective instructional strategies for ensuring academic achievement.

Students who develop an oppositional identity do not see themselves or their cultures valued in their classrooms and schools. They see few students who look like them in advanced placement classes. They may have few adult role models whose education has led to success and acceptance in dominant society. They may have few teachers of color who have a similar cultural background that allows them to interact and communicate using the same cultural cues. Their teachers often have low expectations for their academic success. Their teachers too often have not majored in the subject they are teaching. *Is it any wonder that many students of color are failing? An effective teacher can overcome these obstacles. Are you willing to accept the challenge to ensure that all of the students in your classroom meet high standards?*

Opportunities for Reflection

DESEGREGATION AND INTERGROUP RELATIONS

Although it has been over 50 years since the *Brown* decision, the nation's schools are now becoming resegregated. The most integrated schools today are in rural and small town areas. The most segregated schools are located in central cities of large metropolitan areas and the suburban rings closest to cities. Segregated schools for students of color usually serve impoverished communities, and, as before 1954, are most often providing unequal educational opportunities to their clientele. Charter and private schools tend to be even more segregated than public schools. This segregation guarantees that most white students have little contact with students of color except in the South and Southwest (Orfield & Lee, 2004).

The emphasis on equal educational opportunity has moved from ensuring that students in a school represent different racial groups to demanding quality education across schools. Courts are beginning to expect states to equalize educational outcomes for all students (Carroll, Fulton, Abercrombie, & Yoon, 2004). The courts continue to hear cases alleging unequal resources for the education of students of color. In a letter to the states, the former U.S. Secretary of Education, Richard W. Riley, expressed his concern about these inequities:

> I am concerned about long standing racial and ethnic disparities in the distribution of education resources, including gaps in access to experienced and qualified teachers, adequate facilities, and instructional programs and support, including technology, as well as gaps in the funding necessary to secure these resources . . . These resource gaps are likely to be particularly acute in high-poverty schools, including urban schools, where many students of color are isolated and where the effect of the resource gaps may be cumulative. In other words, students who need the most may often receive the least, and these students often are students of color. (Riley, 2004, p. 36)

Many middle-class families are very involved in their children's schools, ensuring that they are staffed by highly qualified teachers and offer a challenging curriculum.

The problem is that they tend not to be so concerned about the quality of education for other people's children, particularly the children of parents with whom they never interact. In some communities, parents in upper-middle-class schools are demanding that the money they raise in their fund-raising activities be used in their school and not shared with other schools in the district, even though some of the other schools may be in dire need of additional resources.

While schools are becoming more segregated, the courts are acknowledging the importance of diverse student populations in educational settings. In the most recent affirmative action case regarding the practices at the University of Michigan (*Grutter v. Bollinger*, 2003), Justice Sandra Day O'Conner said in the majority opinion that "Numerous studies show that student body diversity promotes learning outcomes, and better prepares students for an increasingly diverse workforce and society, and better prepares them as professionals" (p. 8). Although this case and other affirmative action cases have addressed colleges and universities, officials in elementary and secondary schools take their cues from them as they decide when it is appropriate to use race to assign students to schools and promote the integration of their schools.

Another outgrowth of *Brown v. Board of Education* was the need for intergroup relations to assist students and teachers in respecting each other and working together effectively. This need continues today. Even within desegregated schools, students are often segregated in classes, the cafeteria, and activities. In a survey of students, Williams (2003) found that schools contributed to placing people into categories. One third of the students said it was hard to make friends with students in other groups. Forty percent of the students said that their group had rejected someone from another group. To ensure that students interact with students from other eth-

When students of different ethnic groups have the opportunity to develop interpersonal relationships, racial and ethnic relations are likely to be improved.

nic and racial groups, educators have to consciously plan for this outcome. A number of national groups have developed programs to encourage cross-cultural communications. The Southern Poverty Law Center's project, Mix It Up at Lunch, for example, challenges schools to mix students from different groups during the lunch hour. More than 3,000 schools are now participating in the project, which is described at **http://www.mixitup.org**.

Small-group teams and cooperative learning should promote both learning and interracial friendships. Educators should be engaging parents in school activities and decision making to decrease the dissonance between school and home. Students from different groups should have equal access to the curriculum, advanced courses, qualified teachers, and activities to develop high-order thinking skills. They should see themselves in the curriculum and in textbooks. Practices such as tracking and pull-out programs are barriers to providing equal access and improving intergroup relations. Multicultural education is a critical component in the continued effort to desegregate schools and improve intergroup relations.

Summary

Almost from the beginning of European settlement, the population of the United States has been multiethnic, with individuals representing many Native American and European nations, later to be joined by Africans, Latinos, and Asians. Primary reasons for immigration were internal economic impoverishment and political repression in the countries of origin and the demands of a vigorous U.S. economy that required a large labor force. The conditions encountered by different ethnic groups, the reasons they came, and their expectations about life here differed greatly and have led ethnic groups to view themselves as distinct from each other.

Persons of color have had to fight for their civil rights throughout U.S. history. During the 1950s and 1960s African Americans were successful in removing Jim Crow laws that allowed states to segregate public schools and accommodations. Their efforts led to the passage of the 1964 Civil Rights Act and 1968 Voting Rights Act and spawned civil rights actions for women, Latinos, Asian Americans, Native Americans, and persons with disabilities.

Ethnicity is a sense of peoplehood based on national origin. Although no longer useful in describing groups of people, the term race continues to be used in this country to classify groups of people as inferior or superior. Its popular usage is based on society's perception that racial differences are important—a belief not upheld by scientific study. Members of oppressed groups experience discriminatory treatment and often are relegated to relatively low-status positions in society.

The school curriculum has traditionally represented the dominant culture as the focus of study. Since the 1970s, ethnic studies have been added to curricula as an extension or special segment that focuses on the in-depth study of the history and contemporary conditions of one or more ethnic groups. Some ethnic groups have established schools, or programs in traditional schools, that center the curriculum on their ethnicity. Afrocentric and Native American schools are examples of ethnocentric curriculum approaches. An integrated approach is broader in scope in that it requires ethnic content to permeate the total curriculum; thus, all courses taught reflect the multiethnic nature of society. Understanding ethnicity is an advantage in developing effective teaching strategies for individual students.

Educators should examine how they are administering and using standardized tests in the classroom. Too often, testing programs have been used for the purpose of identifying native intelligence and thus sorting people for education and jobs. If disproportionately large numbers of students of color are scoring poorly on such tests and being placed in special classes as a result, the program must be reviewed. Many factors can be used to provide information about intelligence and ability—for example, the ability to think and respond appropriately in different situations.

Desegregation is a process for decreasing racial/ethnic isolation in schools. Although early desegregation efforts focused on ensuring that black and white students attended the same schools, increasing numbers of students of color attend predominantly minority schools. The emphasis is on ensuring the academic achievement of all students and eliminating the inequities in educational opportunities. Intergroup activities in schools help students develop cross-cultural communications skills, thus getting to know students from different ethnic and racial groups.

QUESTIONS FOR DISCUSSION

1. Why is membership in an ethnic group more important to some individuals than to others?

2. What factors cause members of oppressed groups to view ethnicity differently from dominant group members?

3. How different and similar were the immigration patterns of Africans, Asians, Central Americans, Europeans, and South Americans during the past four centuries?

4. Why have the changes made during the Civil Rights Movement of the 1950s and 1960s not eliminated the income and educational gaps between groups?

5. Why does race remain such an important factor in the social, political, and economic patterns of the United States?

6. What characteristics might an educator look for to determine a student's ethnic background and the importance it plays in that student's life?

7. How would you use the ethnicity and race of your students to teach a lesson in the subject that you are planning to teach?

8. What are the advantages and disadvantages of the following approaches: ethnic studies, ethnocentric education, and integration of ethnic content?

9. Why is the use of standardized tests so controversial? What are the dangers of depending too heavily on the results of standardized tests?

10. Why do school officials seek teachers who believe that all students can learn?

PORTFOLIO ACTIVITIES

1. Develop a lesson that reflects an integrative approach to incorporating multiethnic content. The lesson should be for the subject and level (for example, elementary or secondary) that you plan to teach. (INTASC Standard 3)

2. As you observe schools, record practices in classrooms, the halls, the cafeteria, extracurricular activities, and the main office that might be perceived as racist by persons of color. Write a paper for your portfolio that describes these practices and why they could be considered racist. (INTASC Standard 3)

3. Analyze the performance of students on required standardized scores in one or more of the schools you are observing. Discuss the results based on the race or ethnicity of students in the school and indicate your conclusions. (Note: Schools are required by the federal legislation, "No Child Left Behind," to disaggregate data by race and ethnicity.) (INTASC Standard 8)

SUGGESTED READINGS

Arboleda, T. (1998). *In the shadow of race: Growing up as a multiethnic, multicultural, and "multiracial" American.* Mahwah, NJ: Lawrence Erlbaum.

This personal chronicle of the author's struggle to identify his ethnicity and race when they do not fit society's categories provides insights into institutionalized notions of race, culture, ethnicity, and class.

Bigelow, B., & Peterson, B. (Eds.). (1998). *Rethinking Columbus: The next 500 years.* Milwaukee, WI: Rethinking Schools.

This book calls for a replacement of the murky legends of Columbus with a more honest sense of who we are and why we are here. It also discusses the courageous struggles and lasting wisdom of indigenous peoples.

Derman-Sparks, L., Gutierrez, M., & Phillips, C. B. (n.d.). *Teaching young children to resist bias: What parents can do.* Washington, DC: National Association for the Education of Young Children.

This pamphlet provides recommendations for helping primary-age students and their parents understand ethnic, race, gender, and disability biases.

Ladson-Billings, G. (1994). *The dreamkeepers: Successful teachers of African American children.* San Francisco: Jossey-Bass.

Eight exemplary teachers of African American students and their approaches to teaching are portrayed. The teachers differ in racial background, personal styles, and methods but affirm and strengthen cultural diversity in their classrooms.

Lee, E., Menkart, D., & Okazawa-Rey, M. (Eds.). (1998). *Beyond heroes and holidays: A practical guide to K–12 anti-racist, multicultural education and staff development.* Washington, DC: Network of Educators on the Americas.

This interdisciplinary guide for educators, students, and parents includes lessons and readings on racism, transforming the curriculum, tracking, parent/school relations, and language policies.

Moses, R. P., & Cobb, C. E. (2002). *Radical equations: Civil rights from Mississippi to the algebra project.* Boston: Beacon Press.

Civil rights leader Robert Moses has transformed the grassroot organizing of parents, teachers, and students into a program that successfully teaches algebra to middle-school students. Building on the civil rights movement in the South, the authors describe the Algebra Project, which has helped students of color create a culture of literacy around algebra.

Slapin, B., & Seale, D. (Eds.). (1998). *Through Indian eyes: The Native experience in books for children.* Los

Angeles: Native American Studies Center, University of California.

This compilation of work by Native parents, educators, poets, and writers is an excellent resource for educators interested in nonbiased material about indigenous people.

Stern-LaRosa, C., & Bettmann, E. H. (2000). *Close the book on hate*. New York: Anti-Defamation League.

This book provides an understanding of the richness and beauty of our multicultural society. It encourages parents and children to discuss the value of diversity and the hurtfulness of hate.

Takaki, R. (1993). *A different mirror: A history of multicultural America*. Boston: Little, Brown.

The history of America is retold from the voices of Native Americans, African Americans, Jews, Irish Americans, Asian Americans, Latinos, and others. It covers the period from the colonization of the New World to the 1992 Los Angeles riots.

Teaching Tolerance. (Published by the Southern Poverty Law Center, 400 Washington Ave., Montgomery, AL 36104)

This semiannual magazine provides teachers with resources and ideas to promote harmony in the classroom. Articles are written from the perspectives of multiple ethnic groups. It is available at no cost to teachers.

Teaching Tolerance. (1999). *Responding to hate at school: A guide for teachers, counselors and administrators*. Montgomery, AL: Southern Poverty Law Center.

These guidelines should help educators in responding promptly and effectively to incidents of bias in schools.

REFERENCES

Briggs, V. M., Jr. (2000). Immigration policy and the U.S. economy: An institutional perspective. In S. Steinberg (Ed.), *Race and ethnicity in the United States: Issues and debates* (pp. 253–266). Malden, MA: Blackwell.

Brown v. Board of Education, 349 U.S. 294, at 300 (1955).

Carey, K. (2004, Winter). *The real value of teachers: Using new information about teacher effectiveness to close the achievement gap*. Washington, DC: The Education Trust.

Carroll, T. G., Fulton, K., Abercrombie, K., & Yoon, I. (2004). *Fifty years after Brown v. Board of Education: A two-tiered education system*. Washington, DC: National Commission on Teaching and America's Future.

Cross, W. E., Jr. (1992). *Shades of black: Diversity in African American identity*. Philadelphia: Temple University Press.

Derman-Sparks, L., Phillips, C. B., & Hilliard, III, A. G. (1997). *Teaching/learning anti-racism: A developmental approach*. New York: Teachers College Press.

Diversity data. (2000). *Principal, 79*(5), 18.

Eck, D. L. (2000). Religious pluralism in America in the year 2000. In E. W. Linder (Ed.), *Yearbook of American and Canadian churches 2000*. Nashville, TN: Abingdon Press.

The Education Trust. (2003). *African American achievement in America*. Washington, DC: Author.

The Education Trust. (2004). *Education watch state and national data, 2004*. Washington, DC: Author.

Fordham, S. (1988). Racelessness as a factor in black students' school success: Pragmatic strategy or pyrrhic victory? *Harvard Educational Review, 58*(1), 54–84.

Gallagher, C. A. (2003). Color-blind privilege: The social and political functions of erasing the color line in post race America. *Race, Gender & Class, 10*(4), 22–37.

The Gallup Organization. (2004a, February 17). *As blacks mark history, satisfaction gap persists*. Princeton, NJ: Author.

The Gallup Organization. (2004b, June 8). *Civil rights and race relations*. Princeton, NJ: Author.

Gibson, M. A. (1988). *Accommodation without assimilation: Sikh immigrants in an American high school*. Ithaca, NY: Cornell University Press.

Gibson, M. A. (1992/1993, Winter). Variability in immigrant students' school performance: The U.S. case. In *The Social Context of Education*. Washington, DC: American Educational Research Association—Division G.

Grutter v. Bollinger. 1235 Ct. 2325 (2003).

Hale, J. E. (2001). *Learning while black: Creating educational excellence for African American children*. Baltimore, MD: The Johns Hopkins University Press.

Hate on campus. (2000, Spring). *Intelligence Report* (Southern Poverty Law Center), *98*, 6–15.

Helms, J. A. (Ed.). (1990). *Black and white racial identity development: Theory, research, and practice*. Westport, CT: Praeger.

Hernstein, R. J., & Murray, C. (1994). *The bell curve: Intelligence and class structure in American life*. New York: Free Press.

Hilliard, III, A. G. (2003). No mystery: Closing the achievement gap between Africans and excellence. In T. Perry, C. Steele, & A. G. Hilliard, III (Eds.), *Young, gifted, and black: Promoting high achievement among African-American students* (pp. 131–165). Boston: Beacon Press.

Holladay, J. (2004, Spring). *Brown v Board* timeline: School integration in the United States. *Teaching Tolerance, 25*: 42–56.

Kelley, M. (2000, September 8). Indian affairs head makes apology. Associated Press.

National Conference for Community and Justice. (2000). *Taking America's pulse II: A survey of intergroup relations*. New York: Author.

Ogbu, J. U. (2003). *Black American students in an affluent suburb: A study of academic disengagement.* Mahwah, NJ: Lawrence Erlbaum.

Olson, L. (2000, September 27). Mixed needs of immigrants pose challenges for schools. *Education Week,* XX(4), 38–39.

Orfield, G., & Frankenberg, E. (2004, Spring). Where are we now? *Teaching Tolerance, 25,* 57–59.

Orfield, G., & Lee, C. (2004, January). *Brown at 50: King's dream or Plessy's nightmare?* Cambridge, MA: The Civil Rights Project, Harvard University.

Plyer v. Doe, 457 U.S. 202 (1982).

Portes, A., & Rumbaut, R. G. (2001). *Legacies: The story of the immigrant second generation.* Berkeley, CA: University of California Press.

Potok, M. (2004, Summer). The year in hate. *Intelligence Report, 113,* 29–32.

Riley, R. W. (2004). Quoted in T. G. Carroll, K. Fulton, K. Abercrombie, & I. Yoon, *Fifty years after Brown v. Board of Education: A two-tiered education system.* Washington, DC: National Commission on Teaching and America's Future.

Sanders, W. I., & Rivers, J. C. (1996). *Cumulative and residual effects of teachers on future student academic achievement.* Knoxville, TN: University of Tennessee Value-Added Research and Assessment Center.

Smith, D. (2003). *The Penguin state of the world atlas* (7th ed.). New York: Penguin Books.

Solomon, R. P. (1988). Black cultural forms in schools: A cross-national comparison. In L. Weis (Ed.), *Class, race, and gender in American education* (pp. 249–265). Albany: State University of New York Press.

Southern Poverty Law Center. (2000). *Ten ways to fight hate.* Montgomery, AL: Author.

Southern Poverty Law Center. (2004). *White power music: Music manufacturer boots Resistance Records.* Retrieved July 15, 2004, from http://www.splcenter.org/intel/intelreport/article.jsp?aid=96.

Tafoya, S. M. (2000, January). Check one or more . . . Mixed race and ethnicity in California. *California Counts, 1*(2), 1–9.

Takaki, R. (1993). *A different mirror: A history of multicultural America.* Boston: Little, Brown.

Tatum, B. D. (1997). *"Why are all the black kids sitting together in the cafeteria?" And other conversations about race.* New York: Basic Books.

U.S. Census Bureau. (2003). *Statistical abstract of the United States: 2003* (123rd ed.). Washington, DC: U.S. Government Printing Office.

U.S. Department of Education, National Center for Education Statistics. (2002). *The condition of education 2004.* Washington, DC: U.S. Government Printing Office.

Williams, D. (2003, Fall). Mixitup: Students bridge social boundaries on mix it up at lunch day. *Teaching Tolerance, 24,* 44–47.

Willis, P. E. (1977). *Learning to labor: How working-class kids get working-class jobs.* Farnborough, UK: Saxon House.

Willoughby, B. (2004, Spring). Beyond black and white. *Teaching Tolerance, 25,* 45.

Young, R. L., & Pang, V. O. (1995, Winter). Asian Pacific American students: A rainbow of dreams. *Multicultural Education, 3*(2), 4–7.

Youth and hate. (1999, Fall). *Intelligence Report* (Southern Poverty Law Center), *96,* 24–27.

No person shall, on the basis of sex, be excluded from participation in, be denied the benefits of, or be subjected to discrimination under any education program or activity receiving federal financial assistance.

TITLE IX (EDUCATION AMENDMENTS, 1972)

Chapter 4

Gender

Abdul Rashid planned to introduce ecology to his science class. Since school began seven months ago, he has not been able to interest most of the girls in the science content. Most of his female students are capable of understanding and using science, but they show little interest. Sometimes he thinks they just do not want to upstage the boys in the class. He knows that some of them should be in an advanced science class because they score extremely well on the written tests, but they show no interest in class discussions and experiments.

To introduce ecology, he decided to try a different approach. Perhaps he could relate the subject to something meaningful in their real lives—maybe even their families' or their own social activities. He wanted to find examples they would care about. He decided to focus on the toxic chemicals found in the creek that runs behind many of their homes.

Premature births in that area are being blamed on the chemical dumping that has been going on for more than 20 years.

Opportunities for Reflection

1. *Why do most of the girls in Mr. Rashid's class appear to be uninterested in science?*
2. *What are the participation rates of females in advanced mathematics and science courses?*
3. *What are the reasons for the lack of participation by girls and young women?*
4. *How might Mr. Rashid's approach to ecology engage the girls?*
5. *What would you do to increase the interest and participation of females in science and mathematics?*

To answer these questions online, go to this chapter's Opening Scenario module of the Companion Website.

Gender Differences

Although some differences exist between males and females, the popular, and sometimes "scientific," beliefs about these differences have often prevented equality across the sexes. At the beginning of the twentieth century, some scientists and many laypersons thought that men, particularly those with ancestors from Northern and Western Europe, were intellectually superior to women and therefore generally more capable of professional and administrative work. They believed that women's nature made it imperative that men give orders and women take orders in the workplace. Because their physical strength was not comparable to that of men, women were also deemed unsuitable for many manual or working-class jobs, except for the most menial and the lowest paid. Well-adjusted women were expected to be married homemakers, performing services for the family without remuneration.

Even though there is now clear evidence that women and men do not differ in intelligence, the percentage of men in the best-paying and most demanding professional jobs is disproportionately higher than the percentage of women in those jobs. Because of technological advances, brute strength is usually no longer a requirement for most manual jobs, but the percentage of women in those jobs still falls far behind that of men. Nevertheless, gender equality still does not exist in many workplaces and homes. Many leaders of the women's movement have blamed the lack of equality on the **patriarchal** arrangements in society that have kept women subordinate to men in the home and in our capitalist system.

BIOLOGICAL DETERMINISM

Opportunities for Reflection

Do biological differences prevent male- and female-assigned roles from being interchanged? Because women have the anatomy to bear children, does that imply that only they can raise children? Do biological differences suggest that males and females do different types of work? Most people today would answer these questions in the negative. However, researchers continue to debate how much of the differences between females and males is due to biology and how much is due to socialization.

Although newborns are described by their sex, they have few observable differences in physical characteristics other than reproductive organs. Boys tend to be slightly longer and heavier than girls. Girls have a lower percentage of total body weight in muscle, and their lungs and hearts are proportionally smaller. Nevertheless, adults describe girls and boys differently. Girls are more likely to be little, beautiful, pretty, and cute, whereas boys are big, strong, and hardy.

Most of us can easily identify physical differences between men and women by appearance alone. Girls tend to have lighter skeletons and different shoulder and pelvic proportions. Although the proportion of different hormones in the body differs by gender, boys and girls have similar hormonal levels and similar physical development during the first eight years of life. The onset of puberty marks the difference in hormonal levels of estrogen and testosterone that control the physical

VIDEO INSIGHT

The Secret Life of Boys

Boys will be boys. This is a belief espoused by many—in schools, in homes, in the media, by society as a whole—but does it ring true? Do boys and girls act differently because of genetics, or are their behaviors learned from society?

In this video segment you will see that boys have a more difficult time showing emotion and feelings. By the age of 5 it's often difficult to tell if something is bothering a little boy, because he has already learned to mask his feelings. In addition, while boys are conditioned to keep their feelings and emotions inside, girls are supported and expected to share and discuss their feelings with others. Does this difference have an outward effect? Some researchers say yes; this emotional repression leads to boys acting out more in school and being labeled with learning disorders and behavior problems more often than girls.

Often, culture determines the appropriate activities in which boys and girls participate. After watching the video segment, where do you stand on this discussion?

1. *Do you notice little boys being treated differently than girls? Give some examples.*

2. *How do you interact with children?*

3. *How will you monitor yourself more closely as you interact with children?*

DVD

CW

To answer these questions online, go to the ABC News Video Insight module for this chapter of the Companion Website.

development of the two sexes. At this time, the proportion of fat to total body weight increases in girls and decreases in boys. The differences in physical structure contribute to a female's diminished strength, lower endurance for heavy labor, greater difficulty in running or overarm throwing, and better ability to float in water. However, environment and culture can also influence the extent of these physical differences for both males and females. Thus, the feminine characteristics listed here can be altered with good nutrition, physical activity, practice, and different behavioral expectations.

Because of society's expectations for different behaviors by males and females, it is difficult to determine how many of the differences are actually biological. Some may result from different cultural expectations and lived experiences, rather than from different biological makeup. For example, gender differences in the incidence of cardiovascular disease may decrease as more women enter jobs associated with stress.

Prior to the twentieth century, intelligence was equated with the size of the brain. Because men's brains were larger than women's, scientists of the time concluded that women were not as intelligent as men, and thus, inferior to them. Today we know that brain size is related to body size, not to intelligence. When Alfred Binet developed the first intelligence test at the beginning of the twentieth century, no differences were found in the general intelligence between the sexes.

However, many studies have found some gender differences in mathematical, verbal, and spatial skills.

Some researchers attribute these differences to biological determinism, especially hormones affecting hemispheric specialization in the brain. The right hemisphere of the cerebral cortex controls spatial relations and the left hemisphere controls language and other sequential skills. Females tend to favor the left hemisphere associated with speaking, reading, and writing. Males are reported to have greater right-hemisphere specialization, which leads to better performance on tests of spatial visualization and higher achievement in mathematics and science. However, some boys and some girls lean toward the hemisphere that is usually identified with the opposite sex (Gurian, 2001).

Proponents of brain-based differences argue that understanding the differences will help teachers understand why boys behave the way they do in classrooms and lead to appropriate instruction. For instance, Gurian (2001) reports that boys are more likely to be **deductive** in their conceptualizations; they begin with the general and move to the details. Girls, on the other hand, are more likely to be **inductive,** beginning with the details to figure out the general. Boys are more easily bored. They need more physical space for learning. Movement stimulates the boys' brains and helps them manage and relieve impulsive behavior. Girls, on the other hand, more easily master **cooperative learning,** in which students work together on a learning project. Table 4.1 outlines the advantages that their favored brain hemisphere gives to boys and girls.

Opportunities for Reflection

Other researchers attribute these differences to socialization patterns in child rearing and schooling, rather than biological factors. They argue that girls and boys can learn to use the other hemisphere of their brain so that they can better perform the skills associated with that hemisphere. These debates focus on the nature versus nurture controversy on what causes the differences between boys and girls. A more balanced view of the causes of sex differences gives credit to the interaction of both nature and nurture. *What do you think is the primary determinant of sex differences? Why?*

Table 4.1 Advantages that Boys and Girls Receive in Schools

Advantages to Boys	Advantages to Girls
Greater athletic support and funding	Greater involvement in extracurricular activities
Attention-getting classroom behavior	Higher academic performance
Mathematics and science test scores	Reading and writing test scores
SAT scores for college admission	Higher educational aspirations
Not prone to eating and other psychological disorders	Fewer learning and behavioral disorders
Few problems caused by teen pregnancy	Fewer discipline problems
Fewer victims of sexual abuse	Fewer victims of school violence
Classrooms that privilege boys	Classroom organization that supports girls' learning

Source: Adapted from Gurian, M. (2001). *Boys and girls learn differently!: A guide for teachers and parents.* San Francisco: Jossey-Bass.

Cultural Influences on Gender

Generally, sex is used to identify an individual as male or female based on biological differences. **Gender**, on the other hand, defines the characteristics of femininity and masculinity that are determined by culture. A factor that complicates discussions about gender differences is the tendency to equate women with nature and men with culture, which controls and transcends nature (Ortner, 1996). Because of their sex, women have traditionally been associated with childbearing, childrearing, and nurturing, which kept them near the home. Men had the freedom to move beyond the home to hunt and seek resources for supporting the family. These patterns have evolved into the current cultural patterns in which women are the predominant workers in the nurturing professions of teaching and health care, whereas men are overrepresented as corporate leaders, engineers, and construction workers. However, no research shows that women cannot do men's work and that men cannot be successful nurturers. Both men and women are active participants in the culture, but the acceptable range of roles and behaviors is more extensive for men than for women, from sexual activity and available jobs to roles assigned by their religious group. A society's image of the two sexes and their appropriate roles and behaviors is determined almost totally by culture, not biology.

Although few differences separate men and women, and they participate in the same or similar everyday activities, the two are often symbolically segregated. Students are sometimes segregated by sex in schools or school activities. Women and men often congregate separately at social gatherings. They dress and groom differently. They participate in gender-specific leisure activities. Most members of each sex have stereotypical perceptions about themselves and the other sex. Men and women disproportionately enter different occupations and have different activities and opportunities in the economic world. *How do you perceive the roles and behavior of men and women? What perceived differences are probably inaccurate stereotypes?*

Opportunities for Reflection

The status and characteristics of males are assigned higher value in society than those of women in all cultures, even though some cultures are more egalitarian than others (Ortner, 1996). The superior status is reflected in the inequities that exist in the prestige of different jobs held by men and women, the difference in wages earned by men and women, and the economic rewards for housework and childrearing compared with nonhousehold work. Of course, the range of social and economic differences within one gender is as great as it is between the genders. There is no doubt that some women are economically and socially better off than many men. Most of the differences that we observe between the sexes result from the lessons we have learned about how females and males should look, act, and think.

Men are also affected by culture's view of gender, which places value on masculinity. In the United States masculinity is measured by a man's independence, assertiveness, leadership ability, self-reliance, and emotional stability. The focus on these masculine characteristics diminishes the importance of the inner lives and feelings of males (Flood, 2001; Kindlon & Thompson, 2000). After researchers focused on the traditional roles of women, some researchers began to examine male identity, defining it in opposition to female and femininity. Real men are supposed to value success, status, and being in charge. They should be tough, confident, and

Culture determines the appropriate activities in which boys and girls should participate.

self-reliant as well as aggressive and daring (Flood, 2001). **Homophobia**—the irrational fear of or aversion to homosexuals—is powerful in pushing boys to meet these stereotypes because they worry about being labeled as gay or a sissy and being harassed (Flood, 2001). As a result, they sometimes go overboard in proving their masculinity.

Many men do not fit the male stereotype. They are empathetic and caring rather than tough and assertive. Even white men sometimes suffer from discrimination, especially in divorce courts and child-custody battles. Some conservatives argue that men are losing their masculinity, and are being harmed as they become more feminine. Life is not easy for young men as shown in the statistics indicating "climbing suicide rate, binge drinking, steroid use, undiagnosed depression, academic underachievement, and the disproportionate representation of boys among car crash victims" (Kindlon & Thompson, 2000). However, psychologists Kindlon and Thompson (2000) do not contribute these problems to a reduction of the differences between the sexes. Instead, they find that boys have not been encouraged to be emotionally literate so that they can be themselves rather than develop a culturally determined identity with little room for divergence.

Sexual Orientation

Heterosexuality is the valued **sexual orientation** or sexual proclivity promoted by the dominant group in the United States. It is so highly valued that laws and social practices used to be written to prohibit **homosexuality.** Laws in most states forbade sexual liaisons between members of the same sex until 2003 when the Supreme Court ruled that all sodomy laws were unconstitutional, overruling the laws that still existed in 13 states (National Gay and Lesbian Task Force, 2004b). In many areas of the country where overt discrimination against homosexuals remains, gays and lesbians may not be able to find housing or jobs. They are not always admitted to "straight" clubs and are vulnerable to attacks on city streets. The National Gay and Lesbian Task Force (2004a) reports that antigay violence is the third most frequent form of bias-motivated crime.

Many people have little knowledge about homosexuality, but they know many myths about it. As a result, they often develop an irrational fear of homosexuals, which is manifested in feelings of disgust, anxiety, and anger. Individuals who harbor these negative feelings usually have had little or no personal contact with gays and lesbians; have participated in little or no homosexual behavior themselves; hold a conservative religious ideology; and/or have little knowledge about the social, medical, and legal issues related to homosexuality (Sears, 1992). In the past, many people viewed homosexuality as a sin, a sickness, or a crime. Even the American Psychological Association defined homosexuality as a mental illness until 1973.

Gay men share with heterosexual men a dominant position in relation to women but are subordinate in relation to heterosexual men. As a result of isolation and discrimination of homosexuals, gay cultural forms have developed. These include gay newspapers, magazines, churches, health clinics, and social clubs. Equality has yet to be extended to many females and males who openly define their sexual orientation against the national norm.

The classroom teacher is likely to find students at different points along the gender identity continuum, both in their beliefs about female and male roles and in their actual behavior. Lesbian and gay adolescents are struggling with their sexual orientation and its meaning in a homophobic climate. Understanding the influence of students' cultural memberships will be important as teachers try to open up the possibilities for all of them, regardless of their gender and sexual orientation.

ACKNOWLEDGEMENT OF SEXUAL ORIENTATION

In 1948, Alfred Charles Kinsey, the American sexologist, estimated that 10% of the population was exclusively homosexual. Other studies suggest that the number is less than 5%. Although experts disagree on the number, most agree that sexual orientation is established early in life, rather than being learned from others in adolescence and adulthood. Many gay and lesbian adults report having attractions to same-sex peers when they were children, but these remembered experiences may be true for some heterosexuals as well. Young people are identifying themselves as gay or lesbian at a younger age than in the past. In the 1960s the average age of self-identification was 20 for gays and 22 for lesbians. Today the average age of self-identification is 16 (National Gay and Lesbian Task Force, 2004c).

Prior to the 1970s, most lesbians and gays hid their homosexuality from their families, landlords, and coworkers because of the fear of rejection and retaliation. Following the 1969 Stonewall Inn riot in Greenwich Village, in which gays fought back

CRITICAL INCIDENTS IN TEACHING

Sexual Orientation

Maureen Flynn is a third-grade teacher in a suburban public school. Each year, she looks forward to Parents' Night, when she can meet the parents of her students. As she inspects her room one final time, the door opens and two nicely dressed women appear. "Good evening," they say, almost in unison. "Good evening. Welcome to the third grade. I'm Maureen Flynn." "We're Amy Gentry and Kirsten Bowers. We're Allison Gentry-Bowers' mothers." "Oh," says Ms. Flynn, trying not to show any surprise. "Let me show you some of Allison's artwork and where her desk is."

The rest of the evening is routine. Ms. Flynn introduces herself, welcomes the parents, and asks them to introduce themselves. As the parents exchange names and greetings, there are a few questioning looks as Allison's two mothers introduce themselves as her mothers. Ms. Flynn explains what the class is currently doing and what the goals and activities are for the remainder of the year. The parents and Ms. Flynn exchange pleasantries and then go home.

The next morning as class begins, Colleen Burke blurts out, "Miss Flynn, my mommy said that Allison has two mommies. How can that be? How can anyone have two mommies? Everyone is supposed to have a father and a mother." All of the students look to Ms. Flynn for her response.

Questions for Discussion

1. What should Maureen Flynn's response be to Colleen's question?
2. Should she just evade the question?
3. Should she use the opportunity to discuss alternative family structures?

To answer these questions online, go to the Critical Incidents in Teaching module for this chapter of the Companion Website.

against police, it became somewhat easier to openly admit their homosexuality. However, many still cannot be open because of community hostility and discrimination. They, like other oppressed groups, have extended the fight for civil rights to include gays and lesbians. As a result, a growing number of companies and government agencies are extending insurance benefits to homosexual partners; nondiscrimination policies have been extended to include sexual orientation, and public support for gay rights is higher. Beginning in 2004, some cities and states allowed gay and lesbian couples to marry. Vermont had set the stage earlier when it passed legislation to allow civil unions.

Nevertheless, discrimination and prejudice against gays and lesbians remain, as evidenced by policies to prevent them from organizing clubs on some college campuses or to openly declare their homosexuality in the armed services. Derogatory terms are used by many adults and students in schools. Much work is still required to overcome prejudices and discrimination against those who are not heterosexual.

Pause to Reflect 4.1

Imagine you are teaching a high school class. You are leading a discussion about current events, and today's topic is AIDS. After several minutes of give-and-take discussion among students in the class, the following dialogue occurs:

Mary: I think it's too bad that all these people are so sick and are going to die. I just think . . .

Paul (interrupting): Those fags get what they deserve. What makes me mad is that we're spending money trying to find a cure. If we just let God and nature take its course, I won't have to worry about any queer bothering me.

Mary: I never thought about it that way before.

Mary then faces you and asks, "What do you think about Paul's comments?" Briefly state how you would respond.

To answer these questions online, go to the Pause to Reflect module for this chapter of the Companion Website.

Source: Sears, J. T. (1992). Educators, homosexuality, and homosexual students: Are personal feelings related to professional beliefs? In K. M. Harbeck (Ed.), *Coming out of the classroom closet: Gay and lesbian students, teachers, and curricula* (pp. 62–64). Binghamton, NY: Harrington Park Press.

Even though a growing number of gays and lesbians are open about their sexual orientation, many of them still fear reprisal. In many areas of the country and in many classrooms, they are harassed and abused if they openly acknowledge their sexual orientation. Unfortunately, it is not just other students who reject gay and lesbian students. A number of families, religious leaders, and teachers not only reject them, but label them as immoral and deviant. Unlike persons whose race can be easily identified by others, gays and lesbians can hide their identities from a hostile society. As a result, many of them suffer loneliness and alienation by not acknowledging their homosexuality.

Gay and lesbian educators are often forced to separate their personal and professional lives for fear of losing their jobs. Because they are silent about their homosexuality, these teachers neither serve as role models for gay and lesbian students nor provide the support needed by a group of students who are usually not recognized by school officials. Heterosexual teachers who are willing to support gay and lesbian students also may face discriminatory retaliation by others.

High school is a difficult time for many adolescents, but it is particularly stressful for gays and lesbians as they struggle with the knowledge that they are members of one of the most despised groups in society. They have few, if any, support systems in their schools or communities. They are alone in making decisions about acknowledging their sexual orientation and facing attacks by others.

HOMOPHOBIA

Homophobia can lead to harassment, which is more common in schools than most educators would like to admit. *The 2003 National School Climate Survey* by the

Gay, Lesbian, and Straight Education Network (GLSEN) found that lesbian, gay, bisexual, and transgender (LGBT) students face violence, bias, and harassment in schools. Nearly 40% of the students in the survey reported that they have been physically harassed at school. A majority of the students feel unsafe in school, and sometimes just don't go to school. The most common harassment among young people is in the form of verbal abuse. Almost all LGBT students report frequently hearing homographic remarks such as "that's so gay," "faggot," or "dyke" from other students. LGBT students of color are harassed because of their race and sexual orientation. *In what situations have you heard or used homophobic language? Why do you think homophobia is so prevalent in schools? What actions could assist in eliminating homophobia from schools?*

Opportunities for Reflection

Thus, hostile climates for LGBT students affect their academic performance and college aspirations. When school officials and teachers are supportive of LGBT students, the students have higher GPAs, feel safer in school, and are more likely to attend college. More than one-third of the students don't feel comfortable talking about LGBT issues with their teachers. The GLSEN (2003) study also found that LGBT students were safer in schools and communities with policies and laws against bias, violence, and harassment of LGBT students. A number of schools have now established student clubs such as GLSEN to provide support for and be allies to LGBT peers.

Professional educators have the responsibility to eliminate homophobia in the classroom and school. Their role requires that they not limit the potential of any student because of sexual orientation. A study of the GLSEN (2003) indicates that most faculty either never intervened or intervened only some of the time when homophobic remarks were being made. Teachers and administrators should confront colleagues and students who engage in name-calling and harassment. Classroom interactions, resources, extracurricular activities, and counseling practices must be evaluated to ensure that students are not being discriminated against because of their sexual orientation.

Gender Identity

Most people take their gender identity for granted and do not question it because it agrees with their biological identity. One's recognition of the appropriate gender identity occurs unconsciously early in life. It becomes a basic anchor in the personality and forms a core part of one's self-identity. By the age of 2 years, children realize that they are either boys or girls and begin to learn their expected behaviors. By the time they enter school, children have clear ideas about gender. Most children know that girls and boys behave differently based on behaviors and language reinforced at home. Many are prepared to strive for conformity with these gender-stereotyped roles.

SOCIALIZATION

Appropriate gender behavior is reinforced in magazines, on television, in play with peers, and with gender-specific toys. In this socialization process, children develop social skills and a sense of self in accordance with socially prescribed roles and expectations. Appropriate gender behavior is reinforced throughout the life cycle by social processes of approval and disapproval, reward and punishment.

Socialization does not end with parents and relatives. When a child enters school, the socialization process continues. Generally, schools convey the same standards for gender roles as the dominant culture. The attitudes and values about appropriate gender roles are embedded in the curriculum of schools. Elementary schools appear to imitate the mothering role, with a predominance of female teachers and an emphasis on obedience and conformity. In classrooms, males and females receive different feedback and encouragement for their work, but the patterns are similar to those used at home.

Gender role expectations are also reflected in schools. Girls and young women are expected to be well-behaved and make good grades. Males are expected to be less well-behaved and not achieve academically as well as females prior to puberty. Many working-class males develop patterns of resistance to school and its authority figures because it is considered feminine and emphasizes mental rather than manual work.

Children are also active participants in the socialization process. Play groups are often determined by the sex of the children. Even when girls and boys play the same game, they often play it differently with the boys being more aggressive. However, not all boys and girls follow the socially acceptable ways of their sex. Not all boys participate in large-group activities and are aggressive; it is usually the most popular boys who participate in these gender-specific activities. The forgotten boys whose voices have been silenced and marginalized may follow behavior patterns generally associated with girls. The same is true for girls; many do not follow the gender-specific behaviors expected of their sex. Nevertheless, most girls and boys do choose to be engaged in separate activities as youngsters. They develop a sense of gender as a dichotomy and opposition when they divide themselves into academic and athletic competitions that pit boys against girls. Cooperative projects in classrooms in which girls and boys work together can undermine this opposition if the students share the work rather than one gender always dominating.

The knowledge required to carry out the traditional roles associated with being female has not been as highly valued by society as the knowledge required to achieve manhood. School playgrounds reflect the importance placed on male as compared to female activities. The space required to play baseball, soccer, basketball, and kickball is much greater than that for girls' jump rope, foursquare, and bar tricks. Some girls may play the boys' sports with them, but almost no boys join the girls' games. When boys do engage in girls' games like jump rope, it is usually to disrupt the game, not to be equal participants.

During socialization, we internalize the social norms considered appropriate for our gender, including gender-appropriate behavior, personality characteristics, emotional responses, attitudes, and beliefs. These characteristics become so much a part of our self-identification that we forget they are learned and are not innate characteristics. Socialization is a lifelong process, and sex-role socialization can be changed as a result of personal experiences or planned interventions during adulthood. *Where do you fall along a continuum of gender identity with traditionally feminine on one end and traditionally masculine on the other? What people have had an influence on the development of your gender identity?*

Opportunities for Reflection

CRITICAL INCIDENTS IN TEACHING

Gender Stereotyping

Jane Irwin is the director of the Model Learning Center at a regional university located in the Southwest. The center is a kindergarten laboratory school located on the university campus to provide observation and practicum opportunities for students in the teacher education program. The children at the center affectionately refer to Ms. Irwin as "Miss Janie." At the end of a lesson on health, Miss Janie dismisses the children for 30 minutes of free play in the classroom. Each child is free to select his or her activity of choice. The Model Learning Center is well equipped with a wide variety of play materials, and the children quickly move to their chosen activities. In the classroom are two undergraduate students in early childhood education who are visiting as part of their required practicum.

Some of the children choose puzzles; some a large playhouse; and others an indoor slide, airplanes, dolls, and various other activities. One of the boys, Tim, moves to an area where two girls are playing with dolls. Tim gently picks up a doll and begins combing its long blonde hair. Shocked by this behavior, one of the practicum students rushes over to Tim, helps him to his feet, takes the doll and comb out of his hands, places them on the floor, and says, "Come with me," as she leads him by the hand to an area where two boys are playing with a model airplane and a helicopter. She picks up an airplane, hands it to Tim, and says, "Here, you play with this. Boys like airplanes, not dolls."

Miss Janie has observed the entire sequence of events as she sits at her desk, watching her students and the university teacher education candidate.

Questions for Discussion

1. *What should Miss Janie do with regard to the child who is now obediently playing with the airplane?*
2. *What should she do with regard to the class because several children observed the incident?*
3. *What should she do with regard to the university student?*

To answer these questions online, go to the Critical Incidents in Teaching module for this chapter of the Companion Website.

In our society, women are supposed to be feminine and men masculine, with society tolerating minimal crossover. Generally, females are allowed more flexibility in their gender identification than males. Even young girls receive positive attributes from acting like boys by being physically active, participating in sports, and rejecting feminine stereotypical behavior. On the other hand, boys are often ostracized by other boys, girls, and adults when they join in girls' games, act effeminate, and don't engage in the same sports as the popular males. Unlike girls who have crossed gender lines, boys suffer loss of prestige.

Gender is no longer being viewed in the traditional bipolar fashion as if masculine and feminine traits never coexist in an individual. We are both male and female, exhibiting the traits of one or the other as appropriate in a specific situation or setting. The dilemma is that not all of us, especially males, are encouraged to be ourselves when our behavior is counter to society's norms of gender identity.

STEREOTYPING OF GENDER ROLES

Although gender roles are gradually changing, they continue to be projected stereotypically in the socialization process. Stereotyping defines the male and female roles narrowly and as quite distinct from one another. It leads children to generalize that all persons within a group behave in the same way. Men and women become automatically associated with the characteristics and roles with which they are constantly endowed by the mass media. Careers are not the only areas in which stereotyping occurs. Female and male intellectual abilities, personality characteristics, physical appearance, social status, and domestic roles have also been stereotyped. Persons who differ from the stereotype of their group, especially gays and lesbians, are often ostracized by the dominant group. Such role stereotyping denies individuals the wide range of human potential that is possible.

Men control political and military apparatus in all societies. Achievement and self-reliance are fostered more in males than females. Males tend to seek dominance more than females do and are significantly more physically and verbally aggressive. No clear evidence suggests, however, that these characteristics are universal gender-role characteristics, rather than a near-universal cultural practice. The fact that these universal practices exist is the result of historical development, rather than the superiority of the male (de Beauvoir, 2003).

In many families today, both wife and husband work. Although a growing number of men assist with childrearing and household chores, working mothers often have the primary responsibility for these activities in addition to their paid employment. Almost half of the nation's workforce is female, and more than 90% of all women will work outside the home at some time (U.S. Census Bureau, 2003). A growing number of women are divorced, widowed, or otherwise alone. Unable to depend on a male wage earner, they are economically forced to fulfill that role alone. Although both men and women now work in a variety of careers and share many roles and activities that were formerly gender-typed, many adults retain their traditional gender roles.

Television is one of the perpetuators of gender stereotyping. Studies show that by 3 years of age, children have already developed tastes in television programs related to age, gender, and race. By the time of high school graduation, the average child will have spent more hours in front of the television than in a classroom. Few children are exempt from this practice because most homes in this country have one or more television sets. The ideals and ideas of dominant America are incorporated into program development as symbolic representations of American society. They are not literal portrayals, yet these representations announce to viewers what is valued and approved in society.

On television, beauty can count for more than intelligence. Adult working women are portrayed, but both they and adolescent women are predominantly rich or middle class. Strong, intelligent, working-class women are generally invisible. Female heroines are not social workers, teachers, or secretaries. On the other hand, today's Olympics project women in a different way. Female athletes compete in the same sports as men, but other than equestrian events, against other women. Nearly half of the athletes in these competitions are now women.

A number of men's and women's magazines portray the two sexes stereotypically. Most newspapers have style pages that include articles on fashion, food, and social events—pages specifically written for what is believed to be the interests of women. Women's magazines often send contradictory messages by indicating that women should both be successful in their chosen professions and exhibit all of the positive feminine attributes of beauty, caring, and housekeeping. Working mothers are supposed to be supermoms who not only work, but are devoted mothers who meet the needs of their children like stay-at-home mothers do. The men's pages of newspapers are the sports and business sections, in which competition and winning are stressed. Men athletes receive the headlines and majority of the print in these sections. The athletic performances of women seldom make the front page.

Whereas adults read newspapers, magazines, and books, children spend much of their reading time with school textbooks. How do the genders fare in the resources used in classrooms across the nation? Studies show that great improvements have been made over the past 30 years. Textbooks are not as racist and sexist as in the past, and perspectives are better balanced. However, teachers still need to be cognizant of the gender and ethnicity of the authors being read by students. *Are they exposing students to the perspectives of women, girls, and diverse ethnic and religious groups? What was the last book that you read that was written by a woman, which was not a textbook? What was the last magazine you read? Was the content of the magazine focused on women's or men's issues?*

Opportunities for Reflection

In contemporary society, the male and female traditional roles are practiced interchangeably in a growing number of families. Both men and women work in nontraditional careers and share many of the formerly gender-typical roles. In many communities, one no longer has to have rigid feminine or masculine characteristics, behavior, or job options; it is becoming easier to have both. More couples are sharing the role of wage earner. It is possible that, in the future, a growing number of men will share more equally in the responsibilities of childrearing and homemaking. Optimistically, both men and women will be able to choose roles with which they are comfortable, rather than have to accept a gender role determined by society.

We are living in an era of changing norms in which old, unequal roles are being rejected by many. These changes are resulting in many new uncertainties in which the norms of the appropriate gender role are no longer so distinct. As new norms develop, more flexible roles, personalities, and behaviors are evolving for both females and males.

INTERACTION OF GENDER WITH ETHNICITY, RACE, AND RELIGION

The degree to which a student adheres to a traditional gender identity is influenced by the family's ethnicity, class, and religion. It is impossible to isolate gender from one's ethnic background. For many women who are not members of the dominant group, racial discrimination has such an impact on their daily lives and well-being that gender is often secondary in their identity. In some religions, gender identity and relations are strictly controlled by religious doctrine. Thus, gender inequality takes on different forms among different ethnic, class, and religious groups.

Ethnic group membership also influences the socialization patterns of males and females. The degree to which traditional gender roles are accepted depends, in large part, on the degree to which the family maintains the traditional patterns and the particular experiences of the ethnic group in this country. Puerto Rican, Mexican American, Appalachian, and Native American families that adhere to traditional religious and cultural patterns are more likely to encourage adherence to rigid gender roles than families that have adopted bicultural patterns.

Women in African American families have developed a different pattern. Historically, they have worked outside the home and are less likely to hold strict traditional views about their roles. They have learned to be both homemakers and wage earners. They are more likely than African American men to complete high school and college. At the same time, African American women have low incomes, are working class and attain less schooling than most other ethnic groups. Unlike many middle-class white women, middle-class black women do not necessarily perceive marriage as a route to upward mobility or a way out of poverty.

African American, Latino, and American Indian women of all classes have current and historical experiences of discrimination based on their race and ethnicity. **Feminists,** who actively support the rights of women, and gays from these groups may feel forced to choose between a racial and a gender identity. The relationship of memberships in multiple groups varies over time and with experience. Identification with one group may be prevalent in one setting, but not another. It is often a struggle to develop an identity that incorporates one's gender, ethnic identity, sexual orientation, class, and religion into a whole with which one feels comfortable and self-assured.

 *For a more in-depth discussion of racial discrimination, see Chapter 3.*

It is dangerous to assume that students will hold certain views or behave in gender-typical ways because of their ethnicity or class level. Individual families within those two cultural groups vary greatly in their support of gender-typical roles for men and women and their subsequent behavior along a continuum of gender identity.

Religions generally recognize and include masculine and feminine principles as part of their doctrines. Regardless of the specific religion, rituals usually reflect and reinforce systems of male dominance. The more fundamentalist religious groups support a strict adherence to gender-differentiated roles. Their influence extends into issues of sexuality, marriage, and reproductive rights. They sometimes have successfully organized politically to control state and federal policies on family and women's affairs. On the other hand, the more liberal religious groups support the marriages of gays and lesbians, the right of a woman to choose abortion, and encourage both males and females to lead their congregations.

When a religious dogma declares that homosexuality is wrong, it is very difficult for its members to recognize homosexuality as normal and of equal status to heterosexuality. Awareness of the community and cultures within which schools are located will be essential as teachers ensure that they don't discriminate, that they support students as appropriate, and that they help all students know their possibilities and develop their potential to reach them.

The Women's Movement

Women have participated in a number of movements since the mid-nineteenth century to fight for gender equality. Some of the early feminists who were participating in the antislavery movements prior to the Civil War raised concerns about women's issues, including the right to divorce, property rights, the right to speak in public, abuse by husbands, work with little or no pay, and suffrage. At the Seneca Falls Convention in 1848, women organized to fight against their oppression. This effort involved some male supporters, including Frederick Douglass and white abolitionists who were fighting against slavery and for human and civil rights for all people. However, most women did not support the women's movement. They did not view their conditions as oppressive and accepted their role as wife and mother.

Later in the century, protective legislation for women and children was enacted. This legislation made some manual jobs inaccessible to women because of the danger involved and limited the number of hours women could work and the time at which they could work. Such legislation did little, however, to extend equal rights to women. Unfortunately, during this period, most feminists segregated their fight for equal rights from the struggles of other oppressed groups and refused to take a stand against Jim Crow laws and other violations of the civil rights of African and Asian Americans. Women's groups, which were predominantly white, also pitted themselves against African American men in the fight for the right to vote.

The most significant advances in the status of women were initiated in the 1960s when feminists were able to gain the support of more women and men than at any previous time in history. As in the previous century, this movement developed out of the struggle for civil rights by African Americans. The 1963 Equal Pay Act required that men and women receive equal pay for the same job, but did not prevent discrimination in who was hired. In an attempt to defeat the Civil Rights Bill in Congress, a Southern congressman added the words "or sex" to Title VII, declaring that discrimination based on "race, color, national origin, or sex" was prohibited. This legislation, which was approved in 1964, was the first time that equal rights had been extended to women. Soon afterwards, President Lyndon Johnson signed an executive order that required businesses with federal contracts to hire women and persons of color, becoming the first affirmative action programs.

By 1983, political leaders were no longer disposed to extend full equal rights to women. Women's groups pushed for an Equal Rights Amendment (ERA) that read "Equality of rights under the law shall not be denied or abridged by the United States or by any state on account of sex." Although Congress passed the one-sentence Equal Rights Amendment, conservative groups concerned about family values lobbied state legislatures to reject the amendment. Although two thirds of the U.S. population supported the ERA, it was not adopted by the required number of states.

The women's movements have traditionally been dominated by middle-class white women. Limited to women's issues, the movement in the early days was not open to broader civil rights for all oppressed groups. This focus prevented the widespread involvement in the movement of both men and women of color. Support from the working class was also limited because the needs of neither these women nor women on welfare were part of the agenda. Lesbians and bisexuals did not feel that the women's movements addressed or highlighted their issues, leading to their establishment of separate groups to meet their needs.

The 1990s ushered in a change toward broader support for civil rights for all groups and greater inclusion of men and women from diverse ethnic groups in the feminist movement. As an example, the nations's largest feminist organization, the National Organization for Women (NOW), has added to its agenda fighting racism and supporting welfare reform, immigrant rights, and affirmative action. A growing number of articles and books on equity by feminists, sociologists, and critical theorists address the interaction of race, gender, and class in the struggle for equity for all groups.

Increasing numbers of men also support the equity agenda, including women's issues. Some men have established their own male liberation groups to promote choices beyond traditional male roles. However, unlike the women's movement, which became a social action, male liberation usually remains a personal, not a political, matter.

Opportunities for Reflection

Why do equal rights for women, gays, and lesbians continue to be contested? People hold different views about the equality of the sexes. Feminists fight for equality in jobs, pay, schooling, responsibilities in the home, and the nation's laws. They believe that women and men should have a choice about working in the home or outside the home, having children, and acknowledging their sexual orientation. They believe that women should not have to be subordinate to men at home, in the workplace, or in society. They fight to eliminate the physical and mental violence that has resulted from such subordination by providing support groups and shelters for abused women and children, as well as by pushing the judicial system to outlaw and severely punish such violence. In addition, they promote shared male and female responsibilities in the home and the availability of child care to all families. *How much of a feminist are you? What feminist issues do you support?*

Some feminists think that there are few differences between males and females and that those differences are not linked to psychological traits or social roles. Differences are socially constructed. Others think that women's psyches and values do differ from those of men—that there are distinct female and male cultures. They believe that the world would be better served if traditional female values, rather than masculine values, guided society. They focus on the special qualities of being a woman and do not accept the adoption of male characteristics and values to succeed.

A vocal group of antifeminists that includes both men and women have fought against the ERA and women's equality. This group is led by political conservatives who believe that the primary responsibilities of a woman are to be a good wife and mother. Employment outside the home is viewed as interfering with these roles. They argue that homemaking and mothering are themselves viable careers that should be pursued. The male is to be the primary breadwinner in the family, and a woman's dependency on the husband or father is expected. They believe that feminism and equal rights will lead to the disintegration of the nuclear family unit. Homosexuality and abortion are rejected. The men and women who support these positions have effectively organized themselves politically to defeat legislation that will provide greater equality of men and women. Opponents to the women's movement fight against gay and lesbian rights. They promote abstinence programs and fight against the dissemination of information on sexuality in schools and health clinics.

Many young women take for granted the rights that have been won by women over the past century. The first feminists set the stage for recognizing women as equal to men, finally gaining the right to vote in 1919. Joining the civil rights movement in the last half of the twentieth century, the women's movement was renewed. These feminists fought for equal pay, equal opportunities for education and jobs, inclusion in medical tests, attention to breast cancer and other diseases affecting women, women's studies, **nonsexist education,** the right to choice, and the recognition of lesbianism. By the end of the century, most women were both working and raising families. The media was highlighting supermoms who held high-power jobs, but also attended PTA meetings, shuffled their children to soccer and baseball, cooked breakfast and dinner, took care of themselves by exercising before their children were up in the morning, and returned to their e-mail after the kids had gone to bed. Of course, most women do not have high-power jobs, but they still have the greater responsibility for household work and childrearing. Some high-powered women are leaving their jobs and returning home to be full-time mothers.

Much has been accomplished over the past 35 years, but other struggles remain. The current movement is more inclusive, addressing the civil rights of women of color, women in poverty, and elderly women. A number of social issues have still not been embraced by political leaders. Thus, feminists continue to lobby for universal child care, safety nets for the nation's children, increasing the minimum wage for men and women workers, health care for women and children, and other laws and practices that support females. They also continue to fight to maintain the rights that have been won. Emphasizing the success of the women's movement, historian and journalist Ruth Rosen (2000) observed that "by the end of the twentieth century, feminist ideas had burrowed too deeply into our culture for any resistance or politics to root them out" (p. xv).

Sexism and Gender Discrimination

Only a century ago, most women could not attend college, had no legal right to either property or their children, could not initiate a divorce, and were forbidden to smoke or drink. Because these inequities no longer exist and laws now protect the rights of women, many people believe that men and women are treated equally in society. However, society's deep-rooted assumptions about how men and women should think, look, and behave can lead to discriminatory behavior based on gender alone.

When physical strength determined who performed certain tasks, men conducted the hunt for food, whereas women raised food close to the home. With industrialization, this pattern of men working away from home and women working close to home was translated into labor market activity for men and nonlabor market activity for women. Men began to work specific hours and to receive pay for that work. By contrast, women worked irregular and unspecified working periods in the home and received no wages for their work. The value of women's work was never

Women still work disproportionately in traditionally female jobs. For example, they make up more than 98% of the preschool and kindergarten teachers in the United States.

rewarded by money paid directly to them. It certainly was not as valued as the work of men, who contributed to labor market production. In our society, individuals who provide services for which they are paid have a higher status than those who are not paid for their work, such as homemakers.

Sexism is the belief that males are superior to females and thus, should dominate them. Often, sexism is practiced by individuals in personal situations of marriage and family life, as well as in their occupational roles as manager, realtor, secretary, or legislator. Socialization patterns within the family may limit the potential of children when they are taught gender-differentiated behaviors. For example, girls are sometimes taught to be more obedient, neat, passive, and dependent, whereas boys are allowed to be more disobedient, aggressive, independent, exploring, and creative. These gender-differentiated behaviors prepare each for gender-specific jobs and roles. Aggressive and independent individuals (usually men) are likely to manage those who are obedient and dependent (usually women).

Many of us discriminate on the basis of gender without realizing it. Because we were raised in a sexist society, we think our behavior is natural and acceptable, even when it is discriminatory. Women often do not realize the extent to which they do not participate equally in society, nor men the privilege that maleness bestows on them—a sign that the distinct roles have been internalized well during the socialization process. Most parents do not directly plan to harm their daughters by teaching them feminine roles. They do not realize that such characteristics may prevent their daughters from achieving societal benefits comparable to those of men. Young women are sometimes encouraged to gain such societal rewards through marriage, rather than by their own achievement and independence.

Many individuals outside the family also practice gender discrimination. The kindergarten teacher who scolds the boy for playing in the girls' corner is discriminating. The personnel director who hires only women for secretarial positions and only men as managers is overtly discriminating on the basis of gender. Educators have the opportunity to help students break out of group stereotypes and provide them opportunities to explore and pursue a wide variety of options in fulfilling their potential as individuals.

Gender discrimination not only is practiced by individuals but also has been institutionalized in policies, laws, rules, and precedents in society. These institutional arrangements benefit one gender over the other as described in the next sections.

JOBS AND WAGES

Regardless of their education, men are expected to work, but women sometimes have a choice about working. The amount of education obtained by women does little to close the gap between the earnings of men and women. The more education received, the greater the expected earnings for both genders. However, women with bachelor's degrees earn less than men with some college, but no degree. Women with bachelor's degrees or beyond have median incomes that are only 63% of the income earned by males with the same degree (U.S. Census Bureau, 2003).

Opportunities for Reflection

The difference in income between men and women generally increases with age. The difference shown in Figure 4.1 is not affected by women who do not work for wages. It reflects the income of male and female full-time workers. *Why do these differences exist and continue to increase throughout life?*

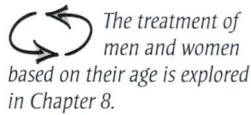 *The treatment of men and women based on their age is explored in Chapter 8.*

Discrepancies in income are, in part, a result of the types of jobs held by the two groups. The stereotypes about the capabilities and roles of women in the domestic setting have been transferred to the labor market. Women first entered the labor market in jobs that were similar to those performed in the home, such as sewing, teaching, nursing, and doing household services. Women workers continue to be

Figure 4.1

Median annual income of year-round, full-time workers by age and gender in 2001.

Source: U.S. Census Bureau. (2003). *Statistical abstract of the United States: 2003* (123rd ed.). Washington, DC: U.S. Government Printing Office.

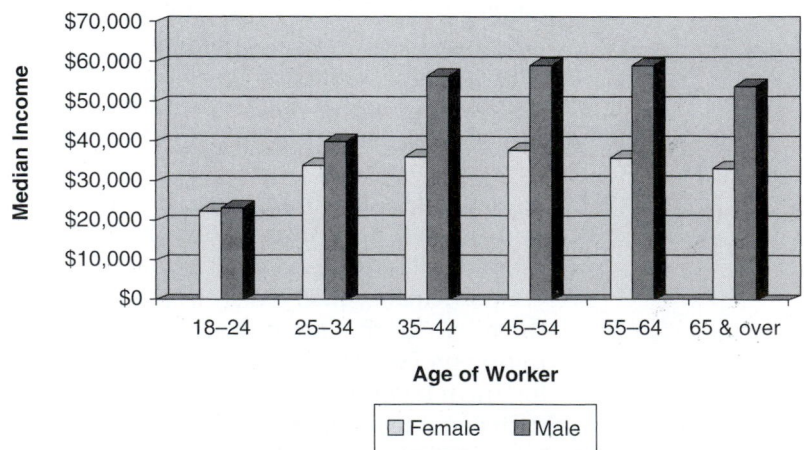

Figure 4.2

Percentage of female and male workers in different occupations in 2002.

Source: U.S. Census Bureau. (2003). *Statistical abstract of the United States: 2003* (123rd ed.). Washington, DC: U.S. Government Printing Office.

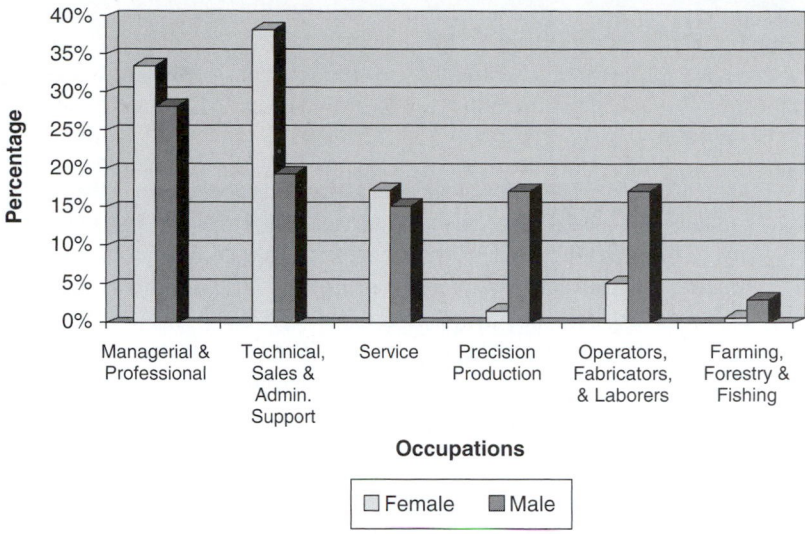

heavily concentrated in a few occupations that are accompanied by neither high prestige nor high income. Women continue to be underrepresented as managers and skilled workers, but are overly represented as professionals, especially as teachers and nurses, and in sales, administrative support and service occupations (see Figure 4.2).

It has been difficult for women to enter administrative and skilled jobs. These jobs have fewer entry-level positions than the less prestigious ones. The available openings are often for jobs that have short or nonexistent promotion ladders, few opportunities for training, low wages, few chances for stability, and poor working conditions. Clerical and sales positions are examples of such jobs, but even professions such as teaching and nursing offer little opportunity for career advancement. To earn the comfortable living that is the American Dream requires women to seek either a traditionally male job or a husband with a good job. Unfortunately, society does not currently value traditional female jobs. Although these jobs are essential to society, the women who hold them do not earn the prestige and salaries they deserve.

When men enter traditionally female fields, they often do not hold the same positions as women in the field. In 2003, men comprised less than 3% of all prekindergarten and kindergarten teachers and 19% of all elementary teachers (U.S. Census Bureau, 2003). However, nearly half of the high school teachers (U.S. Census Bureau, 2003), and 77% of the secondary principals are men (U.S. Department of Education, 2004). Male social workers are more often community organizers, rather than group workers or caseworkers. Although the percentage of men participating in traditionally female jobs has increased over the years, they have become overrepresented in the higher status, administrative levels of these occupations. For example, 75% of all preschool through grade 12 teachers are women as compared with 43% of the college and university faculty (U.S. Census Bureau, 2003).

Gender segregation and wage discrimination also affect women in blue-collar and white-collar jobs. The majority of women enter the labor force at the lowest level of these categories, with unstable employment opportunities and low wages. Much of the discrimination against women in the labor force results from decisions of employers

The Fairer Sex?

Although those fighting for women's rights have made great strides in the past several decades, women still earn only 78 cents for every dollar that men make, and they often pay more for things like consumer goods and medical care. In the video segment, a man and a woman decide to see for themselves whether men and women are treated differently in otherwise identical situations, such as buying a car, getting clothes dry cleaned, setting a tee time at a golf course, and interviewing for a job. Using hidden cameras, they document that women often suffer from a subtle and insidious kind of discrimination, the kind of discrimination that is difficult to quantify and even more difficult to prove.

1. *Have you ever felt as though you suffered from gender bias?*

2. *Share with a group of male and female peers your own stories about how you believe your gender has affected your opportunities and life decisions. Note not only the differences in how men and women respond but also the differences in the way men and women in your group react to those differences.*

3. *What do the stories and responses that you've shared tell you about how entrenched cultural stereotypes about gender are?*

4. *What gendered behaviors do you think are developed through stereotyping, and what might be innate to each sex?*

To answer these questions online, go to the ABC News Video Insight module for this chapter of the Companion Website.

DVD

CW

concerning promotions and wage increases. In addition, many of the occupations in which women are concentrated have not been organized by unions that might help change poor working conditions and low wages.

The interaction of gender and socioeconomic level is discussed in more detail in Chapter 2.

Gradually, more women are entering traditionally male occupations as barriers against their entry are broken. In 1950, only 6.5% of all physicians were women; by 2001, 31% were women. The percentage of lawyers and judges has increased from 4% to 29%, but only 11% of all engineers and 20% of architects are women (U.S. Census Bureau, 2003). The number of women in these professional jobs should rise over time since the percentage receiving degrees in these fields has increased dramatically over the past two decades. Women are now earning more than 40% of the professional degrees being granted in medicine and law. In education, the percentage of female principals has increased from 20% in 1982 to 46% in 2000. Women are earning nearly 40% of the architecture degrees, but they receive only 18% of the bachelor's degrees in engineering and 28% of the computer science degrees (U.S. Census Bureau, 2003).

Although more women are entering the traditionally male-dominated fields, they continue to face discrimination in wages earned. In 1970, women working full-time earned 59 cents for every dollar earned by men; by 2002, they were earning only 78 cents for every dollar earned by men (U.S. Department of Labor, 2004). This disparity is, in part, a result of the lower-status jobs held by many women. Although differences in the salaries of women and men in working-class jobs have decreased, women continue not to earn enough income to be much above the poverty threshold. One of the problems is that wages for these jobs have remained rather stagnant for men as well as women, not increasing at the same rates as jobs at the top end of the labor market (McCall, 2001). Such discrimination greatly affects the quality of life for men and women, particularly those who are single heads of households, and their children.

SEXUAL HARASSMENT

Sexual harassment of women has long existed in the workplace when women are the recipients of unwanted and unwelcome sexual behavior that interferes with their lives. Sometimes the perpetuator is in a position of power over the woman and uses that power to secure favors or to make sexual advances. In other cases, it is a coworker who makes unwanted advances. As in other areas related to gender socialization, schools mirror society in its perpetuation of sexual harassment. In fact, students in high schools probably fare much worse than adults in other settings. Girls report receiving unwanted sexual attention in schools more often than boys (83% vs. 79%). More than half of these students have themselves harassed other students (American Association of University Women [AAUW], 2001).

The study *Hostile Hallways: Bullying, Teasing, and Sexual Harassment in School* (American Association of University Women, 2001) reports that sexual harassment occurs in public places, primarily in the halls and classrooms of our schools. Seventy-six percent of the students had experienced nonphysical harassment; 68% had been physically harassed. Students are most upset when someone

- spreads sexual rumors about them (75%)
- pulls off or down their clothing (74%)
- says they are gay or lesbian (71%)
- forces them to do something sexual other than kissing (72%)
- spies on them as they dress or shower (69%)
- writes sexual messages or graffiti about them on bathroom walls, in locker rooms, etc. (63%). (American Association of University Women, 2001, p. 5)

The most common excuse for sexual harassment is the "its just part of school life, a lot of people do it, or it's no big deal" (AAUW, 2001, p. 41). Some harassers (3 of 10) think that the victim liked it. Others (1 of 4) say their friends encouraged them to do it. Young men may be confused by accusations of sexual harassment, in part because the behavior has long been viewed as typical for male adolescents. Educators and parents alike may explain away sexual harassment as "boys will be boys" and attribute the pushing of other students to the perennial school bullies. It is not only boys who harass others; girls are also guilty, but less often. Teachers and other school personnel are the sexual harassers according to 38% of the students. Although a few of these are the well-publicized physical assaults, most are nonphysical attacks. *Have you been a victim of sexual harassment? Have you observed sexual harassment of others? How could someone have intervened to stop the harassment?*

Many principals and teachers either don't know that harassment is occurring in schools or ignore it. Surveys of young people provide a different picture of school

Opportunities for Reflection

 # CRITICAL INCIDENTS IN TEACHING

Sexual Harassment

Jenny Reid is a middle-school teacher in a suburb of Atlanta. Her sixth-grade students are primarily majority group students from middle-class backgrounds. The children in her class are good students, well motivated, and reasonably well behaved. Her only discipline problem is the excessive teasing that some of the boys in the class impose on the girls.

Near the end of recess, Amy Hotchkiss approaches Ms. Reid, obviously very upset. Amy is one of the more physically mature girls in the class. She is one of a half dozen in the class who has started wearing a bra. Angry and trying to control her temper, she whispers rather loudly that Eric, Darren, Kevin, and Myles have been teasing some of the girls, calling them names and making reference to their physical development. In addition, they have been running up to the girls wearing bras and pulling at the elastic in the back. "What are you going to do to them?" she asks.

Questions for Discussion

1. *Is this incident simply a schoolboy prank, or is this sexual harassment?*
2. *Should the boys involved be punished? If so, what should the punishment be?*
3. *Should this incident be limited to the class, or should the principal and parents be notified?*
4. *Should Ms. Reid turn the incident into a learning situation for the entire class? If she does so, how should she do it? What can the class learn from the incident?*

To answer these questions online, go to the Critical Incidents in Teaching module for this chapter of the Companion Website.

CW

behavior. Most students are not comfortable reporting incidents to teachers or other school personnel. They usually tell a friend, but many, especially boys, tell no one. However, harassment and sex discrimination are social justice issues and are included under civil rights laws. Students who have suffered from such harassment are beginning to fight back through the courts. They argue that although the harassment has been reported to teachers, counselors, or administrators, no action has been taken to stop it.

School officials are no longer allowed to ignore the sexual harassment and abuse of students and may face the payment of damage awards. Teachers, administrators, and staff need to become more alert to sexual harassment among students. In addition, they should monitor their own behaviors to ensure that they are not using their power as an authority figure to harass students. Policies and practices within schools may need to be revised, but discussions should involve the broader community of students and parents.

CD

EXPLORE DIVERSITY Go to the *Exploring Diversity* CD located in the accompanying booklet to hear a teacher discussing the role of teachers in stopping sexual harassment in the case called *One Teacher's Influence.*

School should be a safe haven for children and youth. For many students, schools are not safe, and sometimes they are dangerous. Educators can assist in the elimination of harassment, bullying, and other youth violence. Teachers should model appropriate behavior with their students by avoiding sexual references, innuendoes, and jokes. They cannot be passive bystanders; they must intervene when students are sexually harassing each other. They can also encourage students to form or join school leadership groups that work to educate others about and prevent sexual harassment.

Educational Implications

Education is a key to upward mobility and financial security in adulthood. Therefore, the occupational roles that individuals pursue will influence the way they are able to live in the future. One's chances to pursue postsecondary education are greatly influenced by one's education in elementary and secondary schools. By the time students reach the secondary level, they have chosen, or been helped to choose, a college preparatory program, a general education program, or a specific vocational training program. When college students select a major, disproportionate numbers of males select engineering and computer science, which provide the highest salaries upon graduation. These early choices can make a great difference in later job satisfaction and rewards.

Girls appear to take better advantage of education than their male peers. Although males generally end up with better jobs and higher salaries, not all males are served well in schools. For example, the number of males assigned to special education classes is disproportionately high especially for boys and young men of color and from low-income families (Wehmeyer & Schwartz, 2001). Young women, on the other hand, are more likely to graduate from high school and enroll in college. In 2001, 57.3% of the persons who earned bachelor's degrees were females. They also earn the majority of master's degrees. Males, however earn the majority of doctorates (U.S. Census Bureau, 2003).

Tests and other assessments provide evidence of performance and learning throughout school. The assessments may assist teachers in knowing the gaps in student learning, allowing them to develop strategies that build on the prior experiences of students. Tests are also used to make high-stakes decisions that may dramatically affect a student's future. They are used to determine promotion to the next grade, eligibility for a high school diploma, and admission into college and a profession. Differences between the scores of females and males have narrowed over the past few decades. Girls are slightly ahead in reading and writing; boys in mathematics. Males tend to do better than females on college admission examinations, in part because multiple-choice tests favor boys who take less time to guess when they do not know the answer. If the tests included more essay questions, the gap between the sexes would be reduced even further. The most recent data on test performance shows that

■ At grades 4 and 8, girls outperform males on national assessments of reading (U.S. Department of Education, 2004).

- At grades 4, 8, and 12, girls perform better than boys on national writing assessments (U.S. Department of Education, 2004).

- At grades 4 and 8, boys, on average, score slightly higher than girls on national assessments of mathematics (U.S. Department of Education, 2004).

- More females than males take advanced placement examinations, and there is little difference in their performance on advanced placement examinations on literature and composition (Coley, 2001).

- Males perform better than girls on advanced placement examinations in biology and calculus (Coley, 2001).

- Males score higher than females on the SAT (U.S. Census Bureau, 2003).

- Females score higher on the English and reading sections of the ACT (U.S. Census Bureau, 2003).

Many people believe that if the school experiences of boys and girls are changed, differences in academic achievement will be eliminated, and both will have a chance for more equitable lives as adults. There is not common agreement, however, on how to accomplish this goal. Professional development programs on gender equity focus on changing the behavior of teachers toward students and the content of curriculum. Teachers, counselors, teacher aides, coaches, and principals all have roles in eradicating the inequities that result from sexism.

Women's studies programs in schools and universities allow men and women to study the history, culture, and psychology of women. These programs have promoted research on girls and women that support a gender equity agenda. Nonsexist classrooms in P–12 education incorporate curricula that include females as well as males, and support the learning of both sexes. A number of private schools, including colleges, enroll only female students. Some of the goals for these schools are similar to ethnocentric schools in that they help women develop the self-confidence to achieve at high levels. A number of public school systems have also established single-sex schools for the same purpose. At least one school system (New York City) has a school whose enrollment is limited to gay students. The federal legislation, **Title IX,** makes it illegal for schools to discriminate against girls and women in any educational programs, including athletics. These approaches for providing gender equity in education are discussed in the next sections.

WOMEN'S STUDIES

Women's studies programs are similar to ethnic studies programs in their attempt to record and analyze the historical and contemporary experiences of a group that has traditionally been ignored in the curriculum. Courses in women's studies include concepts of consciousness-raising and views of women as a separate group with unique needs and disadvantages in schools and other institutions. They examine the culture, status, development, and achievement of women as a group.

Women's studies have evolved in high schools, colleges, and universities as units in history, sociology, and literature courses; as separate courses; and as programs from which students can choose a major or minor field of study. Similar to the ethnic studies programs, the experiences and contributions of women and related concepts have been the focus.

Women's studies provide a perspective that is foreign to most students. Historical, economic, and sociological events are viewed from the perspective of a group that has been in a position subordinate to men throughout history. Until students participate in such courses, they usually do not realize that 51% of the population has received so little coverage in most textbooks and courses. These programs allow students to increase both their awareness and their knowledge base about women's history and the contributions of women. Sometimes women are taught skills for competing successfully in a man's world or for managing a career and a family. In addition, many women's studies programs assist in developing a positive female self-image within a society that has historically viewed women as inferior to men. Psychological and career assistance to women is also a part of some programs.

Although the content of women's studies is needed to fill the gaps of current educational programs, it usually is a program set aside from the general academic offerings. Instead of being required, it is usually an elective course. Thus, the majority of students may never integrate the information and concepts of women's studies into their academic work. The treatment of women as a separate entity also subtly suggests that the study of women is secondary to the important study of a world that is controlled by males. All students need to learn about a world in which the contributions of both males and females are valued.

NONSEXIST EDUCATION

When women's studies programs are part of a nonsexist education, they become an integral part of the total education program, rather than a separate luxury. Knowledgeable teachers point out differences that exist between the genders, discuss how and why such inequities are portrayed, and supplement instructional materials with information that provides a more balanced view of the roles and contributions of both men and women. Required readings should include the writings of women, as well as those of men. At a minimum, nonstereotypical male and female examples can appear on bulletin boards and in teacher-prepared materials.

All students should be exposed to the contributions of women as well as men throughout history. History courses that focus primarily on wars and political power will almost totally focus on men; history courses that focus on the family and the arts will more equitably include both genders. Science courses that discuss all of the great scientists often forget to discuss the societal limitations that prevented women from being scientists. (Women scientists and writers of the past often had to use male names or give their work to men for publication.) Students are being cheated of a wealth of information about the majority of the world's population when women are not included as an integral part of the curriculum. Because teachers control the information and concepts taught to students, it is their responsibility to present a view of the world that includes women and men and their wide ranges of perspectives. *Think back on the courses you have taken in college. Which ones covered men and women and their issues at about the same level? Which group received the greatest attention?*

It is also the responsibility of teachers to provide students the opportunity to reach their potential. If boys are stereotypically portrayed as more active, smarter, more aggressive, and exerting more control over their lives than girls, girls

*Opportunities
for Reflection*

become the other with characteristics that may not serve them well in the future. Boys who are always expected to behave in stereotypically masculine ways also suffer. They need to be helped to develop social skills for interacting appropriately with others.

Students are bombarded by subtle influences in schools that reinforce the notion that boys are more important than girls. This unplanned, unofficial learning—the hidden curriculum—has an impact on how students feel about themselves and others. Sexism is often projected in the messages that children receive in the illustrations, language, and content of texts, films, and other instructional materials. Sexism should be eliminated in the interaction of school authorities with male and female students and in the participation of the two sexes in sports and extracurricular activities. A school that is nonsexist is staffed by influential female and male role models who are sensitive to the importance of gender in the classroom and who model nonsexist and nonhomophobic behavior.

EXPLORE DIVERSITY Go to the *Exploring Diversity* CD located in the accompanying booklet to watch a teacher integrate stereotyping into a science lesson in the case called *The Emerging Competence of Youth in 7th Grade.*

One of the goals of nonsexist education is to allow girls and young women to be heard and to understand the legitimacy of their experiences as females. Girls are often silenced as they enter adolescence and take on their more feminine roles, being less assertive and letting boys control discussions in the classroom. Young men are often not encouraged to break out of the expected masculine role with its own rules of what is required to be a man. They may become depressed and have lower self-esteem as they try to conform to the rules (Flood, 2001). Young men should have the opportunity to explore their privileged role in our inequitable society. They should learn to speak on behalf of women. Teachers will not find this an easy task. Many females and males resist discussions of power relations and how they benefit or lose within those relations. However, the value to students and society is worth the discomfort that such discussion may cause students, and perhaps the teacher. The classroom may be the only place in which students can confront these issues and be helped to make sense of them.

EXPLORE DIVERSITY Go to the *Exploring Diversity* CD located in the accompanying booklet to hear a teacher's suggestions for supporting girls' self-esteem in the case called *One Teacher's Influence.*

Participation in Mathematics, Science, and Technology. As indicated at the beginning of this section, girls do not perform as well on mathematics and science assessment as boys. The percentage of female high school students taking science courses has increased during the past decade. Girls are now more likely to complete advanced academic courses in science and mathematics than boys (U.S. Department of Education, 2004). However, advanced placement courses are not available to either girls or boys in a number of low-income schools, limiting their ability to compete with students from other schools. As educators, we may be able to improve participation in these areas by encouraging girls to develop positive attitudes about these subjects, and counseling them not only into advanced mathematics and science courses, but also computer science classes.

Although both girls and boys use computers at home and at school at about the same rate, girls are more likely to be involved with "computer 'tools,' such as databases, page layout programs, graphics, online publishing, and other 'productivity software'" (AAUW, 2000, p. 6). Boys, on the other hand, are more involved in programming and designing. The choices about courses taken in middle school and high school have an influence not only on achievement on standardized tests, but on one's future job options. For instance, technology jobs are among the fastest growing occupations at the beginning of the twenty-first century with some of the highest salaries. Women and African Americans, Latinos, and American Indians are not preparing for jobs in this field at the same rate as white and Asian American men. Therefore, the participation of females in technology and computer science in schools deserves special attention.

Different approaches to schooling and teaching may increase the participation rates of females in mathematics and science. Girls report that computer work is very passive. They do not like the violence and redundancy of many computer games. They perceive programming as an uninteresting job in which their social interactions would primarily be with the computer. Girls need to be encouraged to become fluent in information technology, which requires skills in abstract reasoning,

Although girls and boys use computers at about the same rate, girls are less likely to take courses in computer programming and design. As a result, they are less likely to select computer science as a college major.

problem solving, and the interpretation and analysis of data. Girls are likely to be more interested in the field if they learn to solve real-world problems with technology (AAUW, 2000).

Interactions in the Classroom. An area over which all educators have control is their own interactions with students. Consistently, researchers find that educators treat boys and girls differently in the classroom, on the athletic field, in the hall, and in the counseling office. Most teachers indicate that they do not discriminate in the way they respond to boys and girls. Once they critically examine their interactions, however, most find that they do respond differently. The most important factor in overcoming gender biases in the classroom is recognizing that subtle and unintentional biases exist. Once these are recognized, the teacher can begin to make changes in the classroom and in the lives of the students in that classroom.

One of the goals of a nonsexist education is to eliminate the power relationships based on gender in the classroom. Teachers should monitor the tasks and activities in which students participate in the classroom. Female and male students should share the leadership in classroom activities and discussions. Girls and young women may need to be encouraged to participate actively in hands-on activities, and boys may need encouragement in reading and writing activities. Research suggests that boys and girls provide leadership equally in middle school science activities, but girls begin to lose confidence in their science abilities. The problem observed in a number of science classes is that boys manipulate the equipment, usually delegating the girls in their group to note-taking and providing information (Jovanovic & King, 1998). Teachers need to intervene in these cases to ensure that girls are involved in all levels of the hands-on work.

If left alone, many girls and boys choose to sit with members of the same sex and participate in group activities with members of the same sex. To ensure that they work together in the classroom, the teacher may have to assign seats and groups. Small, heterogeneous, cooperative work groups reduce the emphasis on power relationships that characterize competitive activities. These activities can be designed to provide all students, even those who are often marginalized in the classroom, with the opportunity to participate at a more equitable level.

Nonsexist education does not ignore gender in the classroom. It does not require that boys and girls be treated the same in all cases. Gender may need to be emphasized at times to ensure equity. However, nonsexist education is reflected in the school setting when students are not sorted, grouped, or tracked by gender in any aspect of the school program, including special education. The teacher can develop a curriculum that does not give preferential treatment to boys over girls or girls over boys; that shows both genders in aggressive, nurturing, independent, exciting, and emotional roles; that encourages all students to explore traditional and nontraditional roles; and that assists them in developing positive self-images about their sexuality. One's actions and reactions to students can make a difference.

Educators also should incorporate factual information on homosexuality. The contributions of gays and lesbians to society should not be ignored. Homophobic name-calling by students could be used to provide facts and correct myths about gays and lesbians. If educators ignore homophobic remarks made by students or other adults, children and youth are quick to conclude that something is wrong with gays and that they can be treated disrespectfully.

In addition to helping all students correct the myths they have about gays and lesbians, educators should promote the healthy development of self-identified homosexual youngsters in the school setting. Key to this approach is breaking the silence that surrounds the discussion of homosexuality. The classroom and school should provide a safe and supportive climate for adolescents to discuss their sexual orientation in a nonthreatening way. Finally, teachers and other school personnel need to develop a nonjudgmental posture on this topic.

SINGLE-SEX EDUCATION

Single-sex schools focus on developing the confidence, academic achievement, and leadership skills of young women or men by using their unique learning styles and cultural experiences. Although most single-sex schools are for females, schools in some urban areas have been established for young African American men. These schools often make their African American culture the context for the curriculum with the goal of developing self-esteem, academic achievement, and leadership of students who often confront a hostile environment.

Early in U.S. history, education for girls and boys was segregated, but by 1850, public schools had quietly become coed (Tyack, 2003). Since then, most single-sex schools and colleges were private. Over time, the courts have required public men's colleges to open their doors to women. The most recent example was the Virginia Military Institute, which admitted women for the first time in 1997. Public schools have also not been allowed to segregate schools or classes by sex. However, new federal regulations in 2002 provided greater flexibility to public schools in experimenting with single-sex education to improve the achievement of both girls and boys. A number of public schools and academies have now been established.

Some research shows that girls are more likely to participate in advanced mathematics and science courses when they are in single-sex classes. They may feel less threatened when they are not competing with males in coeducational settings. Teachers are more likely to use strategies such as cooperative teaching, which are well suited to the learning styles of many girls. However, little is known about whether the instruction in single-sex courses and schools differs from that in coed settings. Reviews of the research show that students in single-sex settings do have a higher general self-esteem than their peers in coed settings. However, little or no differences in achievement and attitudes about the academic subject have been found (Campbell & Sanders, 2002; Haag, 2002). A recent study of girls-only courses in mathematics and science found positive differences in performance and persistence in continuing to take mathematics and science courses (Shapka & Keating, 2003). Opponents to single-sex classes argue that teachers should learn to teach both girls and boys effectively and that girls should be encouraged throughout their schooling to enroll in advanced courses.

NONDISCRIMINATION AND TITLE IX

Title IX of the 1972 Education Amendments addresses the differential, stereotypical, and discriminatory treatment of students on the basis of their gender. It protects students and employees in virtually all 16,000 public school systems and 2,700 postsecondary institutions in the United States. The law prevents gender discrimination in: (1) the admission of students, particularly to postsecondary and vocational education institutions, (2) the treatment of students, and (3) the employment of all personnel.

Should Girls Learn Technology in Classes Without Boys?

Only a few girls in your school are signing up for the information technology course that would prepare them with the basic skills for studying computer science in college. Overall, the girls in your school use the computer to write their papers. They use e-mail to communicate with their friends and to conduct research for school projects. They just don't seem interested in a technology career. A school district task force has recommended that your school try an experiment that would segregate boys and girls into separate courses next year. Teachers at your school have been asked to comment on the proposal. The following stances are being taken by your peers.

FOR

■ Girls and boys have different learning styles that could be enhanced in separate classes.

■ The teacher would have more time to spend with girls in a segregated class because he or she would not have to spend time disciplining the boys rather than teaching the content.

■ Efforts to get girls involved in coed technology courses have not been successful.

■ Girls will be less threatened by the technology if they are not competing with boys.

AGAINST

■ Research shows little or no difference in the achievement of girls or their attitudes to the subject when they are in girls-only or coed courses.

■ Single-sex courses reinforce gender stereotypes.

■ This approach just lets the teachers of coed courses off the hook when the school system should be helping all teachers provide an equitable education for boys and girls.

■ When girls go to college or enter the workforce, they most likely will be working with men. To be in a course with girls only does not mirror the real world.

QUESTIONS

1. *What reasons for establishing a girls-only course in technology are the most compelling to you?*

2. *Even though the research on single-sex courses generally does not show significant improvement in the achievement of girls, are there other reasons that the approach may be viable? Why or why not?*

3. *Are you supportive of the task force recommendation? Why or why not?*

4. *What other strategies might encourage more girls to take this technology course?*

To answer these questions online, go to the Focus Your Cultural Lens: Debate module for this chapter of the Companion Website.

CW

Source: Campbell, P. B., & Sanders, J. (2002). Challenging the system: Assumptions and data behind the push for single-sex schooling. In A. Datnow & L. Hubbard (Eds.), *Gender in policy and practice: Perspectives on single-sex and coeducational schooling* (pp. 31–46). New York: Routledge.

What does Title IX require of teachers and other educators in preschool through twelfth-grade settings? The law clearly makes it illegal to treat students differently or separately on the basis of gender. It requires that all programs, activities, and opportunities offered by a school district be equally available to males and females. All courses must be open to all students. Boys must be allowed to enroll in family and consumer science classes, and girls allowed in technology and agriculture courses. Regarding the counseling of students, Title IX prohibits biased course or career guidance; the use of biased achievement, ability, or interest tests; and the use of college and career materials that are biased in content, language, or illustration. Schools cannot assist any business or individual in employing students if the request is for a student of a particular gender. There can be no discrimination in the type or amount of financial assistance or eligibility for such assistance.

Membership in clubs and other activities based on gender alone is prohibited in schools, with the exceptions of YWCA, YMCA, Girl Scouts, Boy Scouts, Boys' State, Girls' State, Key clubs, and other voluntary and tax-exempt youth service organizations that have been traditionally limited to members of one gender who are 19 years of age or younger. Rules of behavior and punishments for violation of those rules must be the same for all students. Honors and awards may not designate the gender of the student as a criterion for the award.

The most controversial program covered by Title IX has been the area of athletics. Provisions for girls to participate in intramural, club, or interscholastic sports must be included in the school's athletic program. The sports offered by a school must be coeducational with two major exceptions: (1) when selection for teams is based on competitive skill and (2) when the activity is a contact sport. In these two situations, separate teams are permitted but are not required. Although the law does not require equal funding for girls' and boys' athletic programs, equal opportunity in athletics must be provided. The courts apply a three-part test to determine equal opportunity. First, the percentage of male and female athletes is substantially proportionate to the percentage of females and males in the student population. Second, the school has a history of expanding opportunities for females to participate in sports. Third, a school fully and effectively meets the interest and abilities of female students even if it may not be meeting the proportionate expectation of the first requirement.

Although providing equal athletic opportunities remains controversial, this part of Title IX has resulted in major changes in schools. When Title IX was passed in 1972, fewer than 295,000 young women participated in high school sports. That number has increased by 847% with nearly 2.8 million females now participating in high school sports. Female athletes now comprise 41.5% of all high school athletes (National Coalition for Women and Girls in Education, 2002). The number of women in intercollegiate athletics has increased from 32,000 to 163,000, and the number of scholarships for female athletes jumped from a few to 10,000 (National Federation of State High School Associations, 2002). At the same time, some groups charge that Title IX has led to the elimination of some men's sports as women's sports are expanded. *In what sports are women in your college participating? How do you and other college students support women's sports? Why are women's sports receiving less or equal student support than men's sports?*

The law alone will not change the basic assumptions and attitudes that people hold about appropriate female and male roles, occupations, and behaviors, but it is

Opportunities for Reflection

The number of women who participate in sports has increased dramatically since Title IX was passed in 1972.

equalizing the rights, opportunities, and treatment of students within the school setting. Experience has shown that once discriminatory practices are eliminated and discriminatory behavior is altered, even unwillingly, changes in prejudiced attitudes often follow. Equal treatment of students from preschool through college will more adequately encourage all students to explore available career options.

Summary

Researchers and theorists disagree about the importance of biology on the differences between males and females. Some argue that the differences are primarily culturally determined. Our culture determines, in large part, how parents and others treat boys and girls. Although girls and boys are members of all other cultural groups, the culture at large has different expectations of them solely on the basis of their gender. Culture establishes the norms of acceptable gender-typical behavior. Children are socialized for their roles as male or female. These roles are usually defined as distinct from one another—a distinction that is reinforced in many families.

Individuals are biologically a female or male, but their gender identity is based on their feminine or masculine characteristics. The degree to which an individual adheres to a traditional gender identity varies as a result of past socialization patterns and is influenced by the family's ethnicity, race, or religion.

Gender discrimination has kept women in less prestigious and lower-paying jobs than men. Even the amount of education obtained by a woman does little to close the gap between the earnings of men and women—now at 78 cents earned by a woman for every dollar earned by a man. Such discrimination greatly affects the quality of life for families, single mothers, and children.

Women's studies, nonsexist education, and single-sex education represent educational approaches to combating sexism in schools and society. Women's studies programs attempt to record and analyze the historical and contemporary experiences of women and are usually offered as separate courses. Nonsexist education attempts to eradicate sexism in the school curriculum by incorporating content that reflects female as well as male perspectives. Single-sex education segregates boys from girls to help develop the self-esteem of the members of each group, improve their achievement in subjects in which they traditionally do not perform as well as the other sex, and help them develop positive attitudes about the academic subjects. The federal government provides support for eliminating sexism in education through Title IX of the 1972 Education Amendments. This law protects against the differential, stereotypical, and discriminatory treatment of students on the basis of their sex.

QUESTIONS FOR DISCUSSION

1. In what ways are differences between the sexes culturally, rather that biologically, determined?

2. How does socialization into stereotypical roles harm females and males in our changing society?

3. Explain how gender discrimination has disproportionately affected women.

4. In what ways do men have power over women? Why is it difficult for men to see they have a privileged position in society?

5. Contrast women's studies and nonsexist education and explain the advantages of both.

6. How can teachers learn whether they are discriminating against students on the basis of gender?

7. How does homophobia manifest itself in schools? What can educators do toward eliminating the prejudice and discrimination against gays and lesbians that occur?

8. What are signs of sexual harassment in schools?

9. How can you as an educator help increase the participation of females and other underrepresented groups in computer science, mathematics, and science careers?

10. What impact has Title IX had on schooling during the past 30 years?

 ONLINE ACTIVITIES For additional questions and activities linked to the Exploring Diversity CD, and additional chapter exercises, visit this text's Companion Website at **http://www.prenhall.com/gollnick**.

PORTFOLIO ACTIVITIES

1. Collect data on the number of boys and girls in mathematics, science, or technology courses in the schools you are observing. Describe the course-taking patterns by the level of the course (for example, general education and advanced placement). What, if any, differences exist between the course-taking of girls and boys? (INTASC Standards 2, 3, and 10)

2. Observe the differences between how boys and girls act in classrooms and interact with teachers. Analyze the differences and discuss how the teacher may reinforce stereotypical gender behavior. Discuss the teacher responses to students that are most supportive of learning. Discuss how these responses differ for boys and girls. (INSTASC Standards 3 and 6)

3. Observe classes using cooperative learning and other instructional strategies. Record the engagement of boys and girls in the different instructional approaches. Analyze your findings based on gender. Discuss whether the differences could be generalized to a sex or whether differences existed within the same sex. (INTASC Standards 1, 3, 4, 5, 6, and 7)

SUGGESTED READINGS

American Association of University Women Educational Foundation. (2000). *Tech-savvy: Educating girls in the new computer age*. Washington, DC: Author.

This report explores why girls are not using computers in the same way as boys and makes recommendations for increasing girls' participation in today's computer age.

Kekelis, L., & Heber, E. (2001). *Girls first: A guide to starting science clubs for girls*. Oakland, CA: Chabot Space & Science Center.

The Female Involvement in Real Science and Technology (FIRST), which was supported by the National Science Foundation, shares in this book how to involve girls in science clubs and projects. Additional sources for involving girls in science are also included.

Kindlon, D., & Thompson, M. (1999). *Raising Cain: Protecting the emotional life of boys*. New York: Ballantine.

Two child psychologists discuss what boys need to overcome societal pressures for becoming the stereotypical man. They urge parents and teachers to help boys and young men to develop empathy and emotional literacy that they need to navigate the social pressures of youth.

Lopez, N. (2003). *Hopeful girls, troubled boys: Race and gender disparity in urban education*. New York: Routledge.

Based on interviews with young adults from Dominican, West Indian, and Haitian families, the author explores their school experiences in New York City. The author learns that the females are optimistic about the promises of education while the males are ambivalent.

Marcus, Eric. (2002). *Making gay history: The half-century fight for lesbian and gay equal rights*. New York: Perennial.

This history walks through the past 50 years of the battle for gay and lesbian rights. The story is told in the words of the people who participated at different stages of the struggle by teenagers and grandparents, journalists and housewives.

Orenstin, P. (2002). Anita Hill is a boy: Tales for a gender-free classroom. In *The Jossey-Bass reader on gender in education* (pp. 734–755). San Francisco: Jossey-Bass.

This chapter describes how one middle-school teacher has developed a gender-free classroom. Boys and girls in the class talk about what it means to study women as well as men and be involved in girls' as well as boys' projects throughout the school year.

Ward, J. (2002). School rules. In *The Jossey-Bass reader on gender in education* (pp. 510–542). San Francisco: Jossey-Bass.

The experiences of African American girls in today's schools are explored in this chapter. The struggles they endure to maintain high self-esteem and high expectations for their academic performance are described with reflections from students and their parents. The accounts show how educators can limit and encourage learning.

REFERENCES

American Association of University Women Educational Foundation, (2000). *Tech-savvy: Educating girls in the new computer age.* Washington, DC: Author.

American Association of University Women Educational Foundation, (2001). *Hostile hallways: Bullying, teasing, and sexual harassment in school.* Washington, DC: Author.

Cambell, P. B., & Sanders, J. (2002). Challenging the system: Assumptions and data behind the push for single-sex schooling. In A. Datnow & L. Hubbard (Eds.), *Gender in policy and practice: Perspectives on single-sex and coeducational schooling* (pp. 31–46). New York: Routledge.

Coley, R. J. (2001). *Differences in the gender gap: Comparisons across racial/ethnic groups in education and work.* Princeton, NJ: Educational Testing Service.

de Beauvoir, S. (2003). The second sex, Introduction. In C. R. McCann & S. Kim (Eds.), *Feminist theory reader: Local and global perspectives.* New York: Routledge.

Flood, C. (2001). Schools fail boys too: Exposing the con of traditional masculinity. In H. Rousso & M. L. Wehmeyer (Eds.), *Double jeopardy: Addressing gender equity in special education* (pp. 207–236). Albany, NY: State University of New York Press.

Gay, Lesbian, and Straight Education Network. (2003). *The 2003 national school climate survey: The school related experiences of our nation's lesbian, gay, bisexual and transgender youth.* New York: Author.

Gurian, M. (2001). *Boys and girls learn differently!: A guide for teachers and parents.* San Francisco: Jossey-Bass.

Haag, P. (2002). Single-sex education in grades K–12: What does the research tell us? In *The Jossey-Bass reader on gender in education* (pp. 647–676). San Francisco: Jossey-Bass.

Jovanovic, J., & King, S. S. (1998, Fall). Boys and girls in the performance-based science classroom: Who's doing the performing? *American Educational Research Journal, 35*(3), 477–496.

Kindlon, D., & Thompson, M. (2000). *Raising Cain: Protecting the emotional life of boys.* New York: Ballantine.

McCall, L. (2001). *Complex inequality: Gender, class and race in the new economy.* New York: Routledge.

National Coalition for Women and Girls in Education. (2002, June). *Title IX at 30: Report card on gender equity.* Washington, DC: Author.

National Federation of State High School Associations. (2002). *2002 High School Athletics Participation Survey.* Indianapolis, IN: Author.

National Gay and Lesbian Task Force. (2004a). *Hate crimes.* Retrieved September 24, 2004, from http://www.thetaskforce.org/theissues/issue.cfm?issueID=12

National Gay and Lesbian Task Force. (2004b): *Sodomy.* Retrieved September 24, 2004, from http://www.thetaskforce.org/theissues/issue.cfm?issueID=11

National Gay and Lesbian Task Force. (2004c). *Youth.* Retrieved September 24, 2004, from http://www.thetaskforce.org/theissues/issue.cfm?issueID=13

Ortner, S. B. (1996). *Making gender: The politics and erotics of culture.* Boston: Beacon.

Rosen, R. (2000). *The world split open: How the modern women's movement changed America.* New York: Viking.

Sears, J. T. (1992). Educators, homosexuality, and homosexual students: Are personal feelings related to professional beliefs? In K. M. Harbeck (Ed.), *Coming out of the classroom closet: Gay and lesbian students, teachers, and curricula* (pp. 29–79). Binghamton, NY: Harrington Park Press.

Shapka, J. D., & Keating, D. P. (2003, Winter). Effects of a girls-only curriculum during adolescence: Performance, persistence, and engagement in mathematics and science. *American Educational Research Journal, 40*(4), 929–960.

Tyack, D. (2003). *Seeking common ground: Public schools in a diverse society.* Cambridge, MA: Harvard University Press.

U.S. Census Bureau. (2003). *Statistical abstract of the United States: 2003* (123rd ed.). Washington, DC: U.S. Government Printing Office.

U.S. Department of Education, National Center for Education Statistics. (2004). *The condition of education 2004.* Washington, DC: Author.

U.S. Department of Labor, Bureau of Labor Statistics. (2004, February). *Women in the labor force: A databook.* Washington, DC: Author.

Wehmeyer, M. L., & Schwartz, M. (2001). Research on gender bias in special education services. In H. Rousso & M. L. Wehmeyer (Eds.) *Double jeopardy: Addressing gender equity in special education* (pp. 271–287). Albany, NY: State University of New York Press.

No otherwise qualified handicapped individual in the United States . . . shall, solely by reason of his [or her] handicap, be excluded from the participation in, be denied benefits of, or be subjected to discrimination under any program or activity receiving federal financial assistance.

SECTION 504, PL 93-112 (VOCATIONAL REHABILITATION ACT, 1993)

Chapter 5

Exceptionality

R iley Behler, a third-grade teacher at the Martin Luther King Elementary School, has been asked to see the principal, Erin Wilkerson, after the students leave. Dr. Wilkerson explains that the school is implementing a **full inclusion** program in which children with severe disabilities will be fully integrated into general education classrooms. Because Behler had been a nominee for the district's teacher of the year award two years ago and singled out for his outstanding classroom skills, Wilkerson had decided that Behler would be a likely choice to be a part of the school's first attempt at full inclusion. "What this will involve, Riley, is two students with severe disabilities. One is a child with Down syndrome who has **developmental disabilities** (characterized by severe delays in the acquisition of cognitive, language, motor, and social skills). He has some severe learning problems. The other child has normal intelligence but is nonambulatory, with limited speech and severe cerebral palsy." Dr. Wilkerson advises Behler that while the district had mandated the implementation of full inclusion, she is asking for teachers to volunteer in her school.

"If you are willing to be a part of this program, you will have a full-time aide with a special education background. In addition, Bill Gregg, the inclusion specialist, will assist you with instructional plans and strategies. What is important is that you prepare the students in your class and the parents so that a smooth transition can be made when these students come into your class in January, in just two and a half months. If you agree to do this, I'd like you and Bill to map out a plan of action and give it to me in two weeks."

This scenario has been played out in schools across the country in recent years.

Opportunities for Reflection

1. *What should Behler and Gregg's plan of action include?*
2. *What are some critical elements in a successful plan to move into full inclusion?*
3. *When students with severe disabilities are integrated into general education classrooms, do they detract from the programming of nondisabled students?*
4. *Are the students with disabilities potentially a disrupting influence in the classroom?*
5. *Do general education teachers like Riley Behler have adequate training and background to accommodate students with disabilities in their classrooms?*
6. *Should all children with disabilities be integrated into general education classes?*
7. *Should they be integrated, regardless of the type of disability?*
8. *Should they be integrated, regardless of the degree of disability?*

To answer these questions online, go to this chapter's Opening Scenario module of the Companion Website.

Students with Disabilities and Those Who Are Gifted and Talented

A significant segment of the population in the United States is made up of exceptional individuals. Twenty-five million or more individuals from every ethnic and socioeconomic group fall into one or more of the categories of exceptionality. Nearly every day, educators come into contact with exceptional children and adults. They may be students in our classes, our professional colleagues, our friends and neighbors, or people we meet in our everyday experiences.

Exceptional people include both individuals with disabilities and gifted individuals. Some, particularly persons with disabilities, have been rejected by society. Because of their unique social and personal needs and special interests, many exceptional people become part of a cultural group composed of individuals with similar exceptionalities. For some, this cultural identity is by ascription; they have been labeled and forced into enclaves by virtue of the residential institutions where they live. Others may live in the same communities or even neighborhood by their own choosing. This chapter will examine the exceptional individual's relationship to society. It will address the struggle for equal rights and the ways the treatment of individuals with disabilities often parallels that of oppressed ethnic minorities.

Definitions for exceptional children vary slightly from one writer to another, but Heward's (2003) is typical of most:

Exceptional children differ from the norm (either below or above) to such an extent that an individualized program of adapted specialized education is required to meet their needs. The term exceptional children includes children who experience difficulties in learning and children whose performance is so superior that modifications in curriculum and instruction are necessary to help them fulfill their potential. Thus, exceptional children is an inclusive term that refers to children with learning and/or behavior problems, children with physical disabilities or sensory impairments, and children who are intellectually gifted or have a special talent. (p. 9)

Opportunities for Reflection

If you completed a public school education within the past ten years, there is a high likelihood that you experienced having a person with a disability in one or more of your classes. *Did your teachers do anything to enhance your understanding or acceptance of these fellow students? How did you feel about them being in your classes? Did you make an effort to get to know them? What were they like? Were their needs and hopes for the future any different from your own?*

This definition is specific to school-age children who are usually referred, tested to determine eligibility, and then placed in special education programs. Included in the process is the labeling of the child. At one end of the continuum are the **gifted and talented** children, who have extraordinary abilities in one or more areas. At the other end are children with disabilities (some of whom may also be gifted). Students with disabilities are categorized with labels such as having mental retardation, learning disabilities, speech impairment, visual impairment, hearing impairment, emotional disturbance (or behavioral disorders), or physical and health impairments.

LABELING

The categorizing and labeling process has its share of critics. Opponents characterize the practice as demeaning and stigmatizing to people with disabilities, with the effects often carried through adulthood. Earlier classifications and labels, such as moron, imbecile, and idiot, have become so derogatory that they are no longer used in a professional context. Some individuals, including many with learning disabilities and **mild mental retardation (MMR),** were never considered to have disabilities prior to entering school. The MMR individuals often have significant problems in intellectual functioning and in socially appropriate behaviors for their age group. The school setting, however, intensifies their academic and cognitive deficits. Many, when they return to their homes and communities, do not seem to function as individuals with disabilities. Instead, they participate in activities with their neighborhood peers until they return to school the following day, where they may attend special classes (sometimes segregated) and resume their role in the academic and social structure of the school as children with disabilities. The problem is so pervasive that it has led to the designation of "the 6-hour retarded child." These are children who spend 6 hours a day as children with mental retardation in our nation's schools. During the remaining 18 hours a day away from the school setting, they are not considered retarded by the people with whom they interact (President's Committee on Mental Retardation, 1969). Heward (2003) suggests that the demands of the school seem to "cause" the mental retardation.

The labels carry with them connotations and stigmas of varying degrees. Some disabilities are socially more acceptable than others. Visual impairment carries with it public empathy and sometimes sympathy. The public has for years given generously to causes for the blind, as evidenced by the financially well-endowed Seeing Eye Institute, which produces the well-known guide dogs. The blind are the only group with a disability who are permitted to claim an additional personal income tax deduction by reason of their disability. Yet, the general public perceives blindness to be one of the worst afflictions imposed on humankind.

In contrast, mental retardation, and to some extent emotional disturbance, is often linked to lower socioeconomic status. Both labels are among the lowest socially acceptable disabilities and perhaps the most stigmatizing. This is, in part, because of the general public's lack of understanding of these disabilities and the sometimes debilitating impact they can bring to the family structure.

Learning disabilities, one of the newest categories of exceptionality, is one of the more socially acceptable disability conditions. Whereas mental retardation is often identified with lower socioeconomic groups, those with learning disabilities often have middle-class backgrounds. Whether these perceptions are accurate or not, middle-class parents more readily accept learning disabilities than mental retardation as a cause of their child's learning deficits. What has been observed is a reclassification of many children from having mental retardation to being learning disabled. It has sometimes been said that one person's mental retardation is another's learning disability and still another's emotional disturbance. The sometimes fine line that distinguishes one of these disabilities from another is at times so difficult to distinguish that an individual could be identified as a student with emotional disturbance by one school psychologist and as a student with learning disabilities by another.

Although the labeling controversy persists, even its critics often concede its necessity. Federal funding for special education is predicated on the identification of individuals in specific disabling conditions. These funds, which totaled nearly $9 billion in 2003, are so significant that many special education programs would all but collapse without them, leaving school districts in severe financial distress. Consequently, the labeling process continues, sometimes even into adulthood, where university students may have to be identified with a disability in order to receive necessary accommodations to their learning needs. Vocational rehabilitation counselors often use labels more indicative of their clients' learning problems than their work skills. If the labels become known to their work peers, it could stigmatize them and lead to social isolation.

HISTORICAL ANTECEDENTS

The plight of persons with disabilities has, in many instances, closely paralleled that of oppressed ethnic groups. The history of the treatment of those with disabilities has not shown a society eager to meet its responsibilities. Prior to 1800, with a few exceptions, those with mental retardation, for example, were not considered a major social problem in any society. Those with more severe retardation were killed, or they died early of natural causes (Drew & Hardman, 2004).

The treatment and care of people with mental and physical disabilities have typically been a function of the socioeconomic conditions of the times. In addition to attitudes of fear and disgrace brought on by superstition, early nomadic tribes viewed individuals with disabilities as nonproductive and as a burden, draining available resources. As civilization progressed from a less nomadic existence, individuals with disabilities were still often viewed as nonproductive and expendable (Drew & Hardman, 2004).

They were frequently shunted away to institutions designated as hospitals, asylums, and colonies. Many institutions were deliberately built great distances from the population centers, where the residents could be segregated and more easily contained. For decades, American society did not have to deal with its conscience with respect to its citizens with severe disabilities. Society simply sent them far away and forgot about them. Most Americans did not know of the cruel and inhumane treatment that existed in many facilities, and they did not really want to know. Today, due to urban sprawl, many of these institutions are now close to population centers.

Individuals with mild disabilities were generally able to be absorbed into society, sometimes seeming to disappear, sometimes contributing meaningfully to an agrarian society, often not even being identified as having a disability. As society became more industrialized and educational reforms required school attendance, the academic problems of students with disabilities became increasingly more visible. Special schools and special classes were designated to meet the needs of these children. Thus, society segregated these individuals, often in the guise of acting in their best interests.

Opportunities for Reflection

Society's treatment of some groups with disabilities, such as those with mental retardation, has frequently been questionable with respect to their civil rights. Although many Americans find the old miscegenation laws prohibiting intermarriage between different ethnic groups abhorrent, few realize that as recently as the latter part of the twentieth century, nearly half of the states had miscegenation laws that prohibited marriage between individuals with mental retardation. *Do you feel that individuals with known genetic disorders should be allowed to marry and have children if there is a liklihood that their child would also share the same disability?*

In some instances, individuals with mild mental retardation were released from state institutions into society under the condition that they submit themselves to eugenic sterilization (Edgerton, 1967). The issue of marriage prohibitions and eugenic sterilization for persons with mental retardation raises serious social and ethical issues. The nondisabled segment of society, charged with the care and education of individuals with disabilities, apparently views as its right and responsibility those matters dealing with sexual behavior, marriage, and procreation. In a similar way, educators determine the means of communication for the deaf individual, either an oral/aural approach or a manual/total communication approach. Such decisions have profound implications because they determine not only how these individuals will communicate but also, to a great extent, with whom they will be able to communicate. Too often, society seeks to dehumanize people with disabilities by ignoring their personal wishes, making critical decisions for them, and treating them as children throughout their lives.

Litigation

Educational rights of individuals with disabilities were not easily gained. In many respects, the struggle for these rights paralleled the struggles of ethnic minorities for their rights to education. These rights were not handed to children with disabilities out of the goodness in the hearts of educators. Many educators were reluctant to extend educational rights to children with disabilities and when they finally did so, it was because their rights had been won in the courts and the education community was ordered by the courts to admit these students.

Some of the same court decisions, and many of the arguments that advanced the rights of African Americans and other oppressed groups, were used by the advocates of children with disabilities. However, in reality, the battles and the rights gained by the disability rights advocates followed years after similar rights were won by ethnic minority groups.

CASE LAW

Attorneys for the children with disabilities and their parents utilized case law to fight their court battles. Case law is the published opinions of judges, which interpret statutes, regulations, and Constitutional provisions. The U.S. legal system relies on the value of these decisions and the legal precedents they established. Few cases result in published opinions and those that are published take on great importance.

BROWN V. BOARD OF EDUCATION

As was with African American students, the initial struggles for children with disabilities involved the right to, or the access to, a public education. One of the most famous and important court decisions was the Supreme Court decision on *Brown v. Board of Education of Topeka* (1954). Historically, the Supreme Court of the United States had sided with the Louisiana District Court in *Plessy v. Ferguson* in 1896, which upheld the Constitutionality of Louisiana's Separate Car Act, that provided for separate but equal transportation facilities for African Americans. The *Plessy* verdict became a part of case law, and set a precedent segregating blacks from transportation, public facilities, schools, restaurants, and so on. This decision "legitimized" the establishment and maintenance of racially segregated "Jim Crow" schools, which were supposed to be separate but equal. As history clearly showed us, these schools were inherently unequal. This was the setting for the *Brown* case.

In 1950, Topeka student Linda Brown had to ride the bus to school five miles when a school was located just four blocks from her home. Linda met all of the requirements to attend the nearby school, but was prohibited from doing so because she was African American. Linda Brown's parents and 13 other black families filed suit against the Topeka Board of Education because of the district's refusal to admit their children in all-white schools. Linda Brown's name was the first name listed on the suit and the case became known as *Brown v. Board of Education.* The case eventually found its way to the United States Supreme Court. The rest became a major part of U.S. history.

The U.S. Constitution mandates that all citizens have a right to life, liberty, and property. They cannot be denied these without due process. *Brown* determined that education was a property right. Although there is no Constitutional guarantee of a free public education, in *Brown* the U.S. Supreme Court found that if a state undertakes the provision of free education for its citizenry, a property right of an education is established. The property (education) rights of Linda Brown and the other African American children had been taken without due process, a clear violation of the Fourteenth Amendment to the U.S. Constitution. The *Brown* decision overturned *Plessy* with regard to education (some of the other rights were not clearly gained until the Civil Rights Act of 1964), and began the integration of all children of color into American schools.

Brown vs. Board of Education and other related cases are discussed in Chapter 3.

Brown did not involve children with disabilities, but as the precedent was set to guarantee equal educational opportunity for ethnic minority children, it too, set a precedent in the argument of guaranteeing the rights of students with disabilities. The Court had essentially ruled that what the Topeka School District had provided Linda Brown and the other African American children was not appropriate. Not only have the courts supported rights of students with disabilities to have a free education, but legislation has also sought to bring them the right to an appropriate education (Chinn, 2004).

The *Brown* decision found "separate but equal" education to be unequal. Separate education denied African American students an equal education. It mandated a fully integrated education, free from the stigma of segregation. Chief Justice Warren stated that segregation "generates a feeling of inferiority as to their (children) status in the community that may affect their hearts and minds in a way unlikely ever to be undone."

Throughout the history of special education in the United States, children with disabilities have faced a continuous uphill struggle to gain their right to attend public schools. Eventually some programs were instituted, but until the mid-1970s some children, particularly those with moderate to severe disabilities, were routinely excluded from public education. One of the arguments to deny admission to children with moderate and severe mental retardation was that they could not learn to read, write, and do arithmetic in the same manner that nondisabled students learned. Learning these academic skills is education, it was argued. Since they were not educable, they did not belong in schools.

Parents and supporters of these children countered by arguing that learning self-help skills and other important life skills was indeed learning, and this was education. These children, along with children with severe physical disabilities could learn, particularly if support services were provided.

PARC V. THE COMMONWEALTH OF PENNSYLVANIA

In 1971, the Pennsylvania Association for Retarded Children (PARC) brought a class action suit against the Commonwealth of Pennsylvania for the failure to provide a public supported education to students with mental retardation. The attorneys for the plaintiffs argued the following:

- Education cannot be defined as only the provision of academic experiences for children.

- All students with mental retardation were capable of benefiting from programs of education and training.

- Having undertaken a free public education for the children of Pennsylvania, the state could not deny children with mental retardation the same opportunities.

- The earlier the students with mental retardation were provided education, the greater the amount of learning could be predicted.

The Federal District Court ruled in favor of the plaintiffs, and all children ages 6 to 21 were to be provided a free public education. The court stipulated that it was most

Opportunities for Reflection

desirable to educate children with mental retardation in programs most like those provided to their peers without disabilities (Murdick, Gartin, & Crabtree, 2002; Yell, 1998). *Do you think we should equate the educational property right of black children with that of severely mentally retarded children, when black children are of normal intelligence and the children with retardation are not? Is this really a comparable issue?*

MILLS V. BOARD OF EDUCATION

Following the *PARC* decision, another class action suit, *Mills v. Board of Education,* was brought before the Federal District Court in the District of Columbia, on behalf of 18,000 out-of-school children with behavior problems, hyperactivity, epilepsy, mental retardation, and physical problems. The court again ruled in favor of the plaintiffs and mandated the District of Columbia schools to provide a public supported education to all children with disabilities. In addition, the court ordered the following:

- The district to provide due process procedural safeguards.
- Clearly outlined due process procedures for labeling, placement, and exclusion.
- Procedural safeguards to include right to appeal, right to access records, and written notice of all stages of the process (Murdick, Gartin, & Crabtree, 2002; Yell, 1998).

While these two high-profile cases were being played out in their respective communities, other states were finding similar challenges. The PARC was a state chapter of the National Association for Retarded Children (NARC, now the Association for Retarded Citizens). The NARC and other national organizations, such as the Council for Exceptional Children, actively supported disability advocates throughout the country in preparing court briefs and in offering other means of support. Armed with their victories and case law favorable to their cause, parent groups in other states began taking on their legislatures and school districts and winning. Fresh with many court victories, disability advocates in the early 1970s were busy preparing for their next battleground, the U.S. Congress.

Legislation

SECTION 504 OF PUBLIC LAW 93-112

In 1973, Congress enacted **Section 504 of Public Law 93-112** as part of the Vocational Rehabilitation Act. Section 504 was the counterpart of Title VI of the Civil Rights Act of 1964. The language was brief, but its implications are far reaching:

> No otherwise qualified handicapped individual in the United States . . . Shall, solely by reason of his (or her) handicap, be excluded from the participation in, be denied the benefits of, or be subjected to discrimination under any program or activity receiving federal financial assistance.

Section 504 prohibits the exclusion from programs solely on the basis of an individual's disability. A football coach, marching band director, or a university admissions officer cannot deny participation solely on the basis of a disability. However, if

 **CRITICAL INCIDENTS IN TEACHING**

Meeting the Mandates and Challenges of Section 504

Larry Gladden is a junior high school social studies teacher and the head football coach for the eighth-grade team. With a poor turnout for his initial recruitment effort, Gladden has received permission from the principal to make another recruitment pitch over the school's public address system. Making a strong appeal for all interested able-bodied boys to come out, Coach Gladden sets a meeting time immediately after school. As the new prospects arrive, the coach is shocked to see Massey Brunson walk into the room. Recognizing Massey from the special education classroom adjacent to his own, the coach knows that Massey is a student with mild mental retardation. The others in the room know this, too. "Hi, Coach," says Massey. "You said you need strong, healthy players. That's me! I work out every day at the Nautilus Fitness Center, and I'm in great shape."

Massey is indeed a great physical specimen. He is among the tallest of the new recruits and very muscular. When the coach saw the other team prospects shaking their heads as Massey entered, he had serious doubts about how Massey might fit on the team. Would he be accepted by his teammates? Could he learn the plays and follow instructions?

Questions for Discussion

1. *Is the coach obligated to allow Massey to try out? Why? Why not?*
2. *Should he discourage Massey from trying to play?*
3. *Should he treat Massey differently from other players?*
4. *Should he make special allowances for Massey?*
5. *If Massey is good enough to play, how should the coach foster his acceptance by other team members?*

To answer these questions online, go to the Critical Incidents in Teaching module for this chapter of the Companion Website.

a learning disability prevents a student from learning marching band formations even with accommodations, if test scores are clearly below the university admissions standards and indicative of likely failure, and if mental retardation inhibits a student's ability to learn football rules and plays, then exclusion can be justified. If denial of participation is unjustified, the school or agency risks the loss of all federal funds even in other programs in the institution that are not involved in the discriminatory practice (Murdick, Gartin, & Crabtree, 2002; Yell, 1998).

PUBLIC LAW 94-142

In 1975, **Public Law 94-142, the Education for All Handicapped Children Act,** was signed into law. This comprehensive legislation provided individuals, ages 3 to 21, with the following:

- A free and appropriate education for all children with disabilities
- Procedural safeguards to protect the rights of students and their parents
- Education in the least restrictive environment

- Individualized Educational Programs
- Parental involvement in educational decisions related to their children with disabilities
- Fair, accurate, and nonbiased evaluations

These provisions forever changed the face of American education. Every child with a disability was entitled to a free public education, which is to be appropriate to his or her needs. The education is to be provided in the least restrictive environment, which means that the student is to be educated in a setting as close to a general or regular education class as is feasible. Parents are now to have an integral role in their child's education, and are to be involved in the development of the education program for their child and to share in other decisions relating to their child. When appropriate, the student is also to be involved. There are to be procedural safeguards, which the schools must follow to ensure that the rights of the students and parents are observed by the schools. Each student must have an **Individualized Education Program (IEP),** which is designed to meet the student's unique needs. The identification and evaluation process is to be nondiscriminatory and unbiased, and multifactored methods used to determine eligibility and placement (Murdick, Gartin, & Crabtree, 2002; Yell, 1998).

Prior to the passage of P.L. 94-142, nearly half of the nation's 4 million children with disabilities were not receiving a public supported education. Many of the students who were in special education were often isolated in the least desirable locations within the schools (Losen and Orfield, 2002). In the first two special education teaching assignments (both prior to P.L. 94-142), which one of the authors of this text experienced, this was very much the case. In the first school, all three special education classes were located in the basement of the junior high school, isolated from the other students. In the second school, there were two lunch periods to accommodate the large student body. The special education students were required to eat

Parents in an IEP meeting with school staff. Parents now have by law, a significant voice in their special education child's education.

in the school cafeteria between the two lunch periods, and were expected to leave the facility before any other students entered. When a new school building was completed next to the old, outdated facility, the special education class remained in the old facility, while the rest of the school moved.

AMERICANS WITH DISABILITIES ACT

President George H. W. Bush signed Public Law 101-336, the **Americans with Disabilities Act (ADA),** into law on January 26, 1990. ADA was the most significant civil rights legislation in the United States since the Civil Rights Act of 1964. ADA was designed to end discrimination against individuals with disabilities in private-sector employment, public services, public accommodations, transportation, and telecommunications.

Among the many components of this legislation, the following are a sampling of the efforts to break down barriers for individuals with disabilities:

- Employers cannot discriminate against individuals with disabilities in hiring or promotion if they are otherwise qualified for the job.

- Employers must provide reasonable accommodations for individuals with disabilities, such as attaching an amplifier to the individual's telephone.

- New buses, bus and train stations, and rail systems must be accessible to persons with disabilities.

- Physical barriers in restaurants, hotels, retail stores, and stadiums must be removed; if not readily achievable, alternative means of offering services must be implemented.

- Companies offering telephone services to the general public must offer telephone relay services to those using telecommunication devices for the deaf (Murdick, Gartin, & Crabtree, 2002; Yell, 1998).

INDIVIDUALS WITH DISABILITIES EDUCATION ACT (IDEA)

Congress passed Public Law 101-476, the **Individuals with Disabilities Education Act (IDEA),** in 1990 as amendments to Public Law 94-142. Key components of this amendment act included the addition of students with autism and traumatic brain injury as a separate class entitled to services. A **transition plan** was an added requirement to be included in every student's IEP by age 16. The transition plan includes a needs assessment and individual planning to transition the student with a disability successfully into adulthood. A far-reaching change in the new legislation included the change in language to emphasize the person first and the disability second. The title of the legislation included "Individuals with Disabilities," and not "disabled individuals." In nearly all of the newer literature you will now see "children with mental retardation, students with learning disabilities, individuals with cerebral palsy, and people with hearing impairments." Individuals with disabilities are people or individuals first. Their disability is secondary and at times inconsequential in their ability to perform the tasks they undertake. Referring to a person as a spina bifida student calls immediate attention to his or her disability rather than the student's many assets or abilities (Murdick, Gartin, & Crabtree, 2002; Yell, 1998).

IDEA Amendments. In 1997, Congress passed **Public Law 105-17, IDEA Amendments.** The 1997 Amendments reauthorized and made improvements to the earlier law. It consolidated the law from eight to four parts and made significant additions, including the following:

- Strengthened the role of parents, ensured access to the general education curriculum, emphasized student progress by changing the IEP process
- Encouraged parents and educators to resolve their differences through non-adversarial mediation
- Gave school officials greater latitude in disciplining students by altering some procedural safeguards
- Set funding formulas (Murdick, Gartin, & Crabtree, 2002; Yell, 1998).

Post P.L. 94-142 Litigation

Even with 30 years of legislation, amendments, and refinements, there are many aspects of special education law that remain unclear to the children, their parents and advocates, or to school district personnel. The laws are extremely precise in some areas, and deliberately vague in others. In addition, there are many other variables, which exacerbate the problem of interpreting and implementing the various laws and regulations.

Congress itself is part of the problem. It has mandated specific provisions for children with disabilities. Some of these are time and staff intensive, and expensive to implement. Congress, however, has not come close to funding IDEA as it had obligated itself to do. For example, in fiscal year 2002, the State of Vermont received $13.2 million under IDEA. Had Vermont received the federal government's full 40% funding commitment, it would have received $32.6 million. In 2003, the government funded the states 18.2% of its special education costs, less than half of funding it had committed in IDEA (IDEA Funding Coalition, 2003; Jeffers, 2002). *Should school districts be required to meet the mandates of IDEA when the federal government has failed to live up to its promises of full funding at the 40% level?*

Opportunities for Reflection

Yet, school districts are required to implement expensive mandates without the promised fiscal support. Thus when many states and school districts are experiencing budget shortfalls, special education can be a challenge for educators to find the necessary resources. Staffing is another serious problem facing most states. Even when school districts are committed to full compliance of the laws, the acute national shortage of qualified special education and related services personnel may preclude their ability to do so. In their attempt to meet the staffing needs, districts often hire individuals with emergency certification or credentials. Some of these individuals have no special education preparation. In other instances, school districts seek special waivers to allow them to place more students in classes than is appropriate. Parents who are aware of the law's requirement of an appropriate education, are often angry and may feel that the schools have betrayed the best interests of their children.

Because IDEA does not provide a substantive definition for a "free and appropriate education," the issue has often been resolved in the courts. Parents, as might be expected, often view an appropriate education as the best possible education for their child. In 1982, *Hendrick Hudson School District v. Rowley* became the first case related to "an appropriate education" for a student with a disability to reach the U.S.

Supreme Court. Amy Rowley was a student with a hearing impairment who was placed in a regular education kindergarten class. Several school personnel learned sign language to enable them to communicate with Amy. A Teletype machine was placed in the school office to facilitate communication with Amy's parents who were also deaf. Amy was provided with a hearing aid by the school, and a sign language interpreter was assigned to her class. Amy completed kindergarten successfully and was found to be well adjusted and making better than average progress.

Following the kindergarten year, as was required by P.L. 94-142, an IEP was developed for the upcoming school year. The plan specified that Amy was to continue her education in a regular classroom. She was to continue the use of the hearing aid, and would receive speech and language therapy three hours a week. In addition she was to receive instruction an hour daily from a tutor who specialized in working with children with hearing impairments.

The parents disagreed with the IEP, as they believed that Amy should have a qualified sign language interpreter for all academic classes. The school district, however, concluded that a full-time interpreter was unnecessary and denied the request. As was their right under P.L. 94-142, the parents requested and were granted a due process hearing. The parents prevailed, and the case found its way through lower courts until it finally reached the U.S. Supreme Court.

The Court, noting that the absence in the law of any substantive standard for "appropriate," ruled that Congress' objective was to make a public education available to students with disabilities. The intent was to guarantee access on appropriate terms, but not to guarantee a particular level of education. The Court ruled that schools were not obligated to provide the best possible education, but a "basic floor of opportunity." It found that a free and appropriate public education (FAPE) standard could only be determined by a multifactorial evaluation on a case-by-case basis. This case essentially assured continued litigation to resolve "appropriate education" disputes (Murdick, Gartin, & Crabtree, 2002; Yell, 1998).

This case was significant in that it was the first case related to P.L. 94-142 to reach the Supreme Court. It set a standard for "appropriate education" to be more than simple access to education but less than the best possible educational program. It became part of case law, setting a precedent for similar cases that would follow (Murdick, Gartin, & Crabtree, 2002; Yell, 1998). Consequently, when a school can demonstrate that a student is making satisfactory progress (this too is open for debate), the district's position tends to prevail.

The courts have had to rule on other provisions of the law. For example, the courts have also ruled in favor of the child when parents have sought nonphysician support services necessary to sustain the student's ability to function in school (e.g., *Irving Independent School District v. Tatro*). Through the years there is a developing body of case law that provides both parents and advocates and school personnel with a better understanding of how the law should be implemented.

Public Law 94-142 provided students with disabilities their legal educational rights. However, some school districts too often have been found out of compliance, either deliberately, or due to the negligence of personnel. Over the past 30 years there have been numerous court decisions (e.g., Chandra Smith Consent Decree, Los Angeles Unified School District and Felix Consent Decree, Hawaii Department of Education) resulting in massive judgments costing districts far more in legal fees and staff time than if they had initially complied with the law.

VIDEO INSIGHT

Jessica Parks Surmounts Her Obstacles

In this video, we have the opportunity to see the accomplishments of a truly remarkable young woman, Jessica Parks. Born without arms, she has accomplished more than many individuals without disabilities, and far more than her parents, physicians, and educators could have imagined. Educators (including special educators) often predetermine in their minds what children with disabilities will or will not be able to accomplish, and limit their access to educational programs. This is often a mistake, which can even lead to lawsuits. In a well-known case, *Sacramento City School District v. Rachel Holland,* 1994, school district personnel denied general education placement to a student with mental retardation. They had determined that she could not benefit from such an educational placement. It was clearly demonstrated in court that the school district was very wrong in their assessment of the student's capabilities. In this video, we can see why the courts will almost always side with the student and his or her parents if the schools refuse to allow the student the opportunity to demonstrate the ability to perform in a general education class.

1. Are educators often biased against students with disabilities?

2. Do educators have preconceived notions of the limits of children's abilities?

3. What is the variable which educators often fail to fully consider. Answer: motivation!

To answer these questions online, go to the ABC News Video Insight module for this chapter of the Companion Website.

Pause to Reflect 5.1

Many of us take for granted our ability to come and go as we please. With the exception of a few buildings, which are off-limits to the general public, we are free to enter any building we wish, whenever we wish. During the next week, keep track of the buildings you enter, the streets you cross, and the activities in which you participate.

- *How accessible are these to persons who are in wheelchairs, blind, or hearing impaired?*

- *Are the room numbers in your building labeled in Braille?*

- *Are the steps ramped or is there an accessible lift or an elevator?*

- *What areas have not been made accessible to these individuals?*

- *How does accessibility limit their participation in the activities in which you regularly participate?*

- *How could these areas be made more accessible to individuals with disabilities?*

To answer these questions online, go to the Pause to Reflect module for this chapter of the Companion Website.

More than ever, children and adults with disabilities are becoming an integral part of the nation's educational system and are finding their rightful place in society. Although the progress that has been made in recent years is indeed encouraging, society's attitudes toward individuals with disabilities have not always kept pace with their legal rights. As long as people are motivated more by fear of litigation than by a moral ethical response, we cannot consider our efforts in this arena a complete success.

Exceptional Individuals and Society

Even in modern times, the treatment and understanding of any type of deviance has been limited. Society has begun to accept its basic responsibilities for people with disabilities by providing for their education and care, but social equality has yet to become a reality.

Society's view of people with disabilities can perhaps be illustrated by the way the media portray our population with disabilities. In general, when the media wishes to focus on persons with disabilities, they are portrayed as (a) children, usually with severe mental retardation with obvious physical stigmata, or (b) persons with crippling conditions either in a wheelchair or on crutches. Thus, society has a mind-set about who the people with disabilities are. They are children or childlike, and they have severe disabilities-mentally, physically, or both.

Because society often views those with disabilities as children, they are denied the right to feel and want like nondisabled individuals. Teachers and other professional workers can often be observed talking about individuals with disabilities in their presence, as if the individuals are unable to feel any embarrassment. Their desire to love and be loved is often ignored, and they are often viewed as asexual, without the right to the same sexual desires as the nondisabled.

Contemporary American society places great emphasis on physical beauty and attractiveness. Individuals who deviate significantly from physical norms are subject to possible rejection, even if their physical deviations do not interfere with their day-to-day functioning.

Gliedman and Roth (1980) suggest that nondisabled individuals perceive those with disabilities as individuals who seldom hold good jobs, seldom become heroes in our culture, and are seldom visible members of the community. They further suggest that society systematically discriminates against many capable individuals with disabilities. They indicate that the attitudes of society parallel that of racism, which views disability as incompatible with adult roles. They state that society perceives a "handicapped person as mentally or spiritually inferior because he is physically different or that 'people like that' have no business being out on the streets with 'us regular folks'" (p. 23).

Gliedman and Roth (1980) suggest that, with respect to discrimination, individuals with disabilities are in some ways better off than African Americans in that there is no overt discrimination, no organized brutality, no lynch mob "justice," and no rallies by supremacist groups. In some ways, however, people with disabilities are worse off. African Americans and other groups have developed ethnic pride. It is unlikely that one has ever heard a "cerebral palsy is beautiful" cry. Society opposes racism with the view that blacks are not self-evidently inferior, but at the same time it takes for granted the self-evidently inferior status of those who have disabilities.

As we stereotype individuals with disabilities, we deny them a rightful place in society. The disability dominates society's perception of the person's social value, and creates a mind-set of deviance. Individuals with disabilities are viewed as vocationally limited and socially inept.

Persons with disabilities are too often tolerated and even accepted as long as they maintain the roles ascribed to them. They are often denied basic rights and dignity as human beings. They are placed under the perpetual tutelage of those more knowledgeable and more capable than they. They are expected to subordinate their own interests and desires to the goals of a program decreed for them by the professionals who provide services to them.

The general public may be required by law to provide educational and other services for individuals with disabilities. The public is prohibited by law against certain aspects of discrimination against our citizens with disabilities. No one, however, can require the person on the street to like persons with disabilities and to accept them as social equals. Many do not accept a person with a disability. Just as racism leads to discrimination or prejudice against other races because of the belief in one's racial superiority, handicapism leads to stereotyping of, and discrimination against, individuals with disabilities because of attitudes of superiority held by some nondisabled individuals.

Society tends to place behavioral expectations on both men and women. Males have specific masculine roles they are expected to fulfill. Boys are usually expected to be athletic. Physical impairments, however, may preclude athletic involvement. Unable to fulfill this role, the young paraplegic male may develop devalued feelings of self-worth or a feeling that he is less than a man. Feminine roles are also assigned, and women with physical disabilities who are unable to assume these roles may suffer from feelings of inadequacy. With increased participation of women in athletics, and the success of the American women in the 2004 Olympics, some females may also suffer the frustration of being unable to participate in athletic or other physical programs.

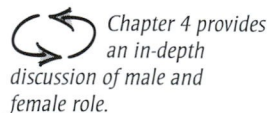 *Chapter 4 provides an in-depth discussion of male and female role.*

EXCEPTIONAL CULTURAL GROUPS

Because of insensitivity, apathy, or prejudice, many of those responsible for implementing and upholding the laws that protect individuals with disabilities fail to do so. The failure to provide adequate educational and vocational opportunities for individuals with disabilities may preclude the possibility of social and economic equality. These social and economic limitations are often translated into rejection by nondisabled peers and ultimately into social isolation.

Not unlike many ethnic minority groups who are rejected by mainstream society, individuals with disabilities often find comfort and security with each other, and in some instances they may form their own enclaves and social organizational structures. Throughout the country, one can find groups of individuals, such as those who have visual or hearing impairments and those who have mental retardation. In some instances, they congregate in similar jobs, in the same neighborhoods, and at various social settings and activities.

 **VIDEO INSIGHT**

Against the Odds: Three Children with Autism

Autism is one of the fastest growing disorders among children. Among the behaviors seen in autistic children are apparent sensory deficits, severe affect isolation, self-multilatory behaviors, and behavior deficiencies. In this film we will see a family with three children with autism. The family has found a highly specialized treatment program, which has had a profoundly positive impact on these children. However, the program requires tuition of more than $170,000 a year for the three children. The family has exhausted their life savings on tuition. The Individuals with Disabilities Education Act (IDEA) requires schools to provide for the educational needs of children with disabilities. The U.S. Supreme Court has ruled that the schools are required to provide a basic floor of opportunity for children with disabilities, but are not required to provide them with the best possible education. With the private schooling, these three children seem to be thriving. The public schools are reluctant to pay the tuition to the private clinic.

1. *Whose responsibility is the education of these children?*

2. *Should the taxpayers be responsible for making certain that these children receive the best possible education?*

3. *School districts have limited funds to spend on special education programming. If the parents prevail in due process and the district has to provide $170,000 for these children, there will be that much less to spend on other children with disabilities. Should the federal government be concerned with this?*

4. *Should the federal government which has never met its financial obligations under IDEA be forced to do so?*

To answer these questions online, go to the ABC News Video Insight module for this chapter of the Companion Website.

DVD

CW

Near Frankfort Avenue in Louisville, Kentucky, three major institutions provide services for individuals who have visual impairments. The American Printing House for the Blind, the Kentucky School for the Blind, and the Kentucky Industries for the Blind are all within close proximity of each other. The American Printing House for the Blind, the leading publisher of materials for individuals with visual impairments, employs a number of individuals who are blind. The Kentucky School for the Blind is a residential school for students with visual impairments, and it also employs a small number of individuals with visual impairments, including teachers. Finally, the Kentucky Industries for the Blind operates as a sheltered workshop for individuals who are blind. With the relatively large number of persons who are blind employed by these three institutions, it is understandable that many individuals with visual impairments live in the surrounding residential area. Living in this area allows them to live close enough to their work to minimize the many transportation problems related to their visual limitations. It also provides a sense of emotional security for the many who, in earlier years, attended the Kentucky School for the Blind and lived on its campus and thus became part of the neighborhood. The neighborhood community can also provide social and emotional security and feelings of acceptance. A few years ago, a mailing was sent from the Kentucky School for the Blind to its alumni; 90% of the mailings had the same zip code as the school.

Many religious groups now provide interpreters for individuals with deafness and other services for individuals with disabilities.

Individuals with visual impairments and hearing impairments are among the most likely to form their own cultural groups. Both have overriding factors that contribute to the need for individuals in these groups to seek out one another and to form cultural groups. Some of the blind have limited mobility. Living in cultural enclaves allows them easier access to one another. They share the same forms of communication—oral language, Braille, and talking books. Social and cultural interests created partly by their physical limitations can often be shared. The hearing impaired may have communication limitations within the hearing world. Their unique means of communication provides them with an emotional as well as a functional bond. Religious programs and churches for individuals with hearing impairments have been formed to provide services in total communication and social activities.

Individuals with physical disabilities may or may not become a part of a cultural group related to the disability. Some function vocationally and socially as part of the mainstream society. With adequate cognitive functioning and adequate communication patterns, normal social interaction is possible. Socialization, however, may depend on the degree of impairment and the individual's emotional adjustment to the disability. Some individuals with physical disabilities may function in the mainstream world and also maintain social contacts with others with similar disabilities. Social clubs for individuals with physical disabilities have been formed to provide experiences commensurate with functional abilities, as well as a social climate that provides acceptance and security. Athletic leagues for competition in sports, such as wheelchair basketball and tennis, have been formed. Many racing events (e.g., the Boston marathon) now include competition for wheelchair entries.

Many of the individuals with mild retardation live independently or in community-based and community-supported group homes. The group homes provide a family-like atmosphere, and house parents supervise the homes. Most of the individuals with moderate retardation who do not live in institutions tend to live at home. Many individuals with severe and profound retardation, and some with moderate retardation, are institutionalized and are thus forced into their own cultural group or enclave, isolated from the rest of society.

The gifted and talented usually do not experience the same type of discrimination and social rejection that many individuals with disabilities experience. Yet, like individuals with disabilities, they may suffer isolation from mainstream society and seek others with comparable abilities that may provide a feeling of acceptance as well as intellectual or emotional stimulation. The existence of Mensa, an organization whose only membership prerequisite is a high score on an intelligence test, attests to the apparent need of some gifted individuals to be with others of their own kind.

Rejection of the gifted and talented may differ from that of individuals with disabilities because the roots may stem from a lack of understanding or jealousy, rather than from the stigma that may relate to certain disabilities.

Disproportionate Placements in Special Education

The overrepresentation of students of color in special education classes has been one of the most problematic issues facing educators in recent years. Dunn (1968) reported that one third of the students in special education had been placed in classes for students with mild mental retardation. Dunn stated, "In my judgment, about 60 to 80 percent of the pupils taught by these teachers are children from low status backgrounds—including Afro-Americans, American Indians, Mexicans, and Puerto Rican Americans; those from nonstandard English speaking, broken, disorganized, and inadequate homes; and children from other non-middle class environments." Dunn has frequently been misquoted as stating that 60 to 80% of students in classes for the mild mentally retarded were students of color. Dunn stated that 60 to 80% of the students in these special education classes included (but were not limited to) students of color. As we do now know, some special education classes then and to some extent today had become a dumping ground for many culturally and linguistically diverse children.

Artiles and Harry (2004) suggest that overrepresentation in special education placement is a problem when children are placed in special education classes when they do not have a disability. They also state that it is a problem if the placement in special education limits their opportunities for positive experiences (e.g., access to the general education curriculum, access to quality programs, obtaining a high school diploma). Similarly, Patton (1998) states that the misplacement of students in special education is problematic in that it is often stigmatizing to the individual and it can deny the student the high quality and life enhancing education to which he or she is entitled.

Overrepresentation in special education is a major problem in education. While overrepresentation in special education does not necessarily translate into inappropriate placement, it is indicative of either problems in the educational system, or society in general. It is possible that in some instances there may actually be more

Placement of a Student with Epilepsy

Max Laird is a sixth-grade teacher in a middle-class suburban school. After school, Mr. Laird finds a note in his in-box, indicating that the principal and the special education resource room teacher want to meet with him the next day before the students arrive. At the meeting the next day, his principal, Dr. Gattelaro, explains to him that a new student, Chris Erickson, will be placed in his class the following Monday morning. He is informed that Chris is slightly above average in academics and a personable young man. However, Dr. Gattelaro wants Mr. Laird to know that Chris has epilepsy and occasionally has generalized tonic-clonic (previously called grand mal) seizures. Although the seizures are generally under control through medication, there is a good possibility that sometime during the school year Chris will have a seizure in the classroom.

At this time, Ms. Chong, the special education resource room teacher, describes generalized tonic-clonic seizures. She explains that they are the most evident and serious type of epileptic seizure. They can be disturbing and frightening to anyone who has never seen one. Chris would have little or no warning that a seizure was about to occur. During a seizure, Chris' muscles will stiffen, and he will lose consciousness and fall to the floor. His whole body will shake violently, as his muscles alternately contract and relax. Saliva may be forced from his mouth, his legs and arms may jerk, and his bladder and bowels may empty. After a few minutes, the contractions will diminish, and Chris will either go to sleep or regain consciousness in a confused and drowsy state (Heward, 2003).

Stunned at this information, Mr. Laird sits in silence as Ms. Chong briefs him about the procedures to take if a seizure occurs in the classroom. She also explains to him that he should inform the other students that the seizure is painless to Chris and that it is not contagious.

Max Laird is aware that he has no option as to whether Chris will be in his class. He is determined to do the right thing and to make Chris' transition into his class as smooth as possible. He is also determined that he will help his class adjust and prepare for the likely seizure. Mr. Laird begins to map out a plan of action.

Questions for Discussion

1. *What can Mr. Laird do with regard to his class?*
2. *What should be his plan of action?*
3. *Should he discuss Chris with his class?*
4. *Should he explain what epilepsy is?*
5. *Should he meet with the parents of his students? Why?*
6. *What should he say to Chris? What other actions can he take?*
7. *Who can teachers contact for help and guidance in these situations?*

To answer these questions online, go to the Critical Incidents in Teaching module for this chapter of the Companion Website.

children of color in need of special education than their numbers or percentages in the general school population might suggest. If the child legitimately qualifies for special education services and is in need of such, it would be a disservice to him or her to not provide special education services because the numbers and percentages do not match. We are addressing the lives and education of children, and wrong decisions can have a lasting impact on their future. There are no doubts that there are inappropriate placements, which result in overrepresentation.

Mercer's research (1973) supported Dunn's earlier contentions. She found that Mexican American students in Riverside, California, were placed in classes for students with mild mental retardation at a rate four times that of the general school population. African American students were placed in the same special education classes at a rate three times what should have been expected given their numbers in the general school population. She stated that Mexican American students were ten times more likely to be placed in these classes than white students, while the likelihood of blacks was seven times greater.

In 1968, the Office of Civil Rights (OCR) began their biannual survey of student placement in special education classes. The data also provided racial backgrounds of the students in the broad categories of white, black, Asian/Pacific American, American Indian, and Latino. While the actual percentages have varied from survey to survey, one fact has remained consistent. African American students, particularly males, have been greatly overrepresented in classes for students with mental retardation and serious emotional disturbance. In some states, Latino students are over-represented in classes for students with mild mental retardation. Another consistent finding is that African American, American Indian, and Latino students are greatly underrepresented in classes for the gifted and talented.

REPORTING BY COMPOSITION AND INDIVIDUAL RISK

There are two valid means of reporting data related to the placement of students of color in special education classes: composition and individual risk (Artiles, Harry,

The overrepresentation of students of color in special education classes is a major problem in education.

Reschly, & Chinn, 2002). Composition gives us the percent of a program by group. It gives us the answer to a question: What is the percentage of African American students in classes for students with mental retardation? Of all of the students in classes for students with mental retardation, 33.16% are African Americans (OCR, 1999). The Office of Civil Rights reports special education enrollments by composition.

Individual risk gives us the percent of a group in a program. It provides us the answer to the question: What percent of African American students are in classes for students with mental retardation? In the entire United States, 2.54% of all African American students were placed in classes for students with mental retardation (OCR, 1999).

With 2.54% of black students having been placed in these classes, the figures may appear to be small. However, it is problematic when we realize that the percentage of African Americans who are in classes of students with mental retardation is five times greater than that of Asian/Pacific American students and twice that of white students. Also important is the fact that one third of African American students are not mentally retarded, as one might mistakenly assume from the OCR composition data. Rather, a little less than one third of those in classes for students with mental retardation are African American. This is a very important concept for the reader to understand.

CONTRIBUTING VARIABLES

While the majority of students in special education have most likely been carefully diagnosed and placed, educators and child advocates have raised concerns that it is also highly likely that many children are inappropriately placed in special education. The variables that contribute to the disproportionate special education placement are multifaceted. Some of the problems that contribute to the placement of these students are rooted in the social structure of the country. Other problems may be related to medical and genetic causes, particularly moderate and severe forms of disability, and may be beyond the ability of educators to remediate.

Poverty. Dunn's 1968 findings that large percentages of students in classes for individuals with mental retardation were from backgrounds of poverty persist to this day. Poverty contributes to a significant number of problems. Pregnant women in poverty are provided less than optimal care during the prenatal period, as well as the period during and after birth. Physicians who provide medical care through government clinics are often burdened with excessive case loads and are unable to provide the quality of care that women are afforded from private physicians and managed care medical facilities. Appropriate nutrition and dietary supplements may be less available both to expectant mothers and to their children. Poverty may necessitate working late into term, even if it would be advisable to stop working and rest.

Children born preterm (those under normal gestation and less than 5 lbs 8 oz [2,500 grams]) may be at risk to develop cognitive and sensory disabilities (Drew & Hardman, 2004; Widerstrom, Mowder, & Sandall, 1991). Though more closely aligned with socioeconomic factors, preterm births have been associated with ethnicity. Younger women having children are more likely to have preterm babies, crack babies, and fetal alcohol syndrome children (Drew & Hardman, 2004), and teen births are disproportionately higher among the poor. Gelfand and Drew (2003) report that 51% of nonwhite births have complications as opposed to 5% of white upper-class births.

Lead Poisoning. Nationally, about 434,000 children between the ages of 1 and 5 have elevated lead levels in their blood, according to the Centers for Disease Control and Prevention (Erickson, 2003). Lead poisoning can create problems for children such as reading and learning disabilities, speech and language disabilities, lowered IQ, neurological deficits, anemia, hearing loss, behavior problems, mental retardation, kidney disease, heart disease, stroke, coma, seizures, and even death (Carolina Environment, Inc., 1999; Erickson, 2003).

The primary sources of lead exposure to children in the United States are house dust contaminated by leaded paint and soil contamination. Both the residue of the leaded paint and decades of industrial and vehicle emissions have contaminated the soil. Leaded paint was in wide use in the 1940s, declined in use in the 1950s and 1960s, and was banned from residential use since 1978. However, older homes built before the ban are potentially a hazard to children. CDC reports that in a study, the children at greatest risk of lead poisoning are those living in pre-1946 homes with a prevalence of 8.6% with elevated lead levels. The high lead prevalence rate for children living in homes built between 1946 to 1973 was 4.6%, and dropped to 1.6% for children in homes built after 1973. The study found that the prevalence among low-income children was 16.4% as compared to children from middle-income (4.1%) and high-income families (0.9%) (Meyer et al., 2003). The latter finding is plausible given the fact that many of America's poor live in older homes.

Overreferrals. The individuals who are placed in classes for students with mild mental retardation and severe emotional disturbance are disproportionately male, African American, and from lower socioeconomic backgrounds. The first step in special education placement is referrals. Anyone (parents, doctors, educators) can make referrals. Most referrals are made by teachers in the elementary school years. These teachers are overwhelmingly female, white, and middle class. There is often incongruence between educators and culturally diverse students with respect to cultural values, acceptable behaviors in the school, and educational expectations. This may result in **overreferrals** to classes for students with disabilities and **underreferrals** to classes for the gifted and talented. In overreferrals, teachers tend to make excessive referrals of students of color for placement in special education classes for students with disabilities. In underreferrals educators fail to recognize potential giftedness and do not make referrals for placement in classes for gifted students. Ysseldyke, Thurlow, Graden, Wesson, Algozzine, and Deno (1983) suggest that a very large percentage of students who are referred to special education are eventually placed in special education programs.

Racial Bias. Losen and Orfield (2002) suggest that undeniable intentional racial discrimination has been replaced by the soft bigotry of low expectations. There are numerous stories that can be told of students of color automatically placed in low academic tracks or in special education, particularly prior to the advent of IDEA. One such example involved a special education student athlete. At a football game many years ago, a high school principal recognized the backup quarterback, who had been called off the bench and who led the team to a come-from-behind victory. The quarterback was a special education student from an ethnic minority background who had been labeled as mentally retarded throughout his entire school years. The principal realized that the diagnosis and label had to be incorrect with the student's calling of complex plays and his clear gift for the game. The principal moved him out of special education and into regular classes where he was provided with extra help to adjust to the transition. He went on to earn a Ph.D., and is currently an associate dean in a Michigan University (Losen and Orfield, 2002).

Both ethnicity and gender are among the most consistent predictors of mental retardation and serious emotional disturbance identification by the schools. The Office of Civil Rights surveys have revealed persistent overrepresentation of students of color in certain disability categories (and underrepresentation in gifted and talented). Losen and Orfield (2002) indicate that the most pronounced disparities have been among African American students. Today, African Americans comprise approximately 17% of the general school population and 33% of those labeled mentally retarded. The U.S. Department of Education reported that in the 2000 to 2001 school year, in at least 13 states, more than 2.75% of all African American students were placed in classes for students with mental retardation. This compares with .75% of white students placed in these same classes (Losen and Orfield, 2002).

Assessment Issues. Assessment of students of color is also a major concern as a contributing variable to the overrepresentation of these students in special education classes. Litigation such as *Diana v. State Board of Education* (1970), involving language minority Latino students, and *Larry P. v. Riles* (1979), involving culturally diverse African American students, demonstrated the dangers of **biased assessment** instruments and procedures. Assessments, which favor certain cultural groups and discriminate in content, are considered biased. It is clear that some students in special education have central nervous system damage and that others have visual, auditory, orthopedic, and speech disabilities. There is no dispute regarding the appropriateness of the special education placement of these individuals. However, the sometimes inappropriate placement of the students of color in the judgmental categories of mild mental retardation and severe emotional disturbance must be addressed if we are to have true equity in our educational system.

Unexplained Issues. Losen and Orfield (2002) suggest that the differences in special education placement between Latino and African American students and between male and female African American students cannot be readily explained by either social background or in terms of measured ability. The poverty rates among Latinos and African Americans have been similar for a number of years. As previously stated, poverty is often listed as a variable that contributes to disability. However, we lack a clear explanation as to why placement rates in disability special education classes for Latinos are relatively low as compared to African American students. We also lack a clear understanding as to why black males and females have such disparate placement percentages when they come from the same socioeconomic backgrounds.

Perhaps one possibility is the fact that males and females are socialized differently regardless of the racial or ethnic backgrounds. Perhaps the socialized behaviors of African American males have a higher level of incongruence with educators' values than that of African American females, and elicit more negative attention.

When observing the placement differences between African Americans and Latinos, it might be noticed that some Latino students have more educational options open to them, including **bilingual education** and **English as a Second Language (ESL)** programs. Bilingual education, which utilizes both the home language and English in the instructional process, is designed to meet the needs of language minority students. ESL programs utilize only English with these students with a primary intent to teach them English. In addition Losen and Orfield (2002) suggest that racial, ethnic, and gender inequities could be a function of unconscious racial and class bias by school authorities. Unjustifiable reliance on IQ and other evaluation tools, high-stakes testing, and power differentials between minority parents and school officials may also be contributing variables.

NEED FOR DISAGGREGATED DATA

While national data show trends for the various racial/ethnic groups, the data are often confusing because of the failure to disaggregate the various groups. For example, Asians and Pacific Americans are consistently shown to be underrepresented in disability categories and overrepresented in gifted and talented classes. There is considerable diversity within this category as it includes Asian groups such as the Chinese, Japanese, Koreans, Indians, and Vietnamese, while also including Pacific Americans such as Hawaiians, Samoans, and Tongans. There are considerable cultural differences between Asian groups and even greater differences between the Asians and Pacific Americans. Japanese Americans and Tongan Americans have little in common culturally. Yet they are grouped together for U.S. government reporting purposes. The same is true among Latinos. There are considerable cultural differences between Cuban Americans living in Miami and Central American immigrants living in East Los Angeles. They are also reported as one group.

When disaggregating data by states, or by ethnic groups, we often find considerable differences when compared to national data. For example, data from the Hawaii State Department of Education, show that Hawaiian students are overrepresented in some categories of special education such as mental retardation. Yet, this cannot be determined from analyzing national data. Latinos or Hispanics are underrepresented in classes for students with mental retardation and emotional disturbance in the OCR national data. Yet in some states they are overrepresented, and Artiles, Rueda, Salazar, and Higareda (2002) found sixth- through twelfth-grade English language learners in 11 predominantly Latino urban school districts to be overrepresented in special education.

To explore the political and legal issues related to English language learners, see Chapter 7.

The inequities in special education raise concerns about the inequities in other areas of education and raise the prospect that there may be a relationship in these problematic issues. Special education overrepresentation often mirrors the overrepresentation seen in other categories and viewed by some as problematic: dropouts, low-track placements, corporal punishment, suspensions, and involvement in the juvenile justice system (Losen and Orfield, 2002).

The problem has persisted for decades and will not be easily ameliorated. It will take a concerted effort to eliminate all bias from the assessment process, a restructuring of teacher education curricula, and a commitment of the wealthiest nation to eliminate the insidious effects of poverty on our children.

California Proposition 227 and Special Education

California's voters passed **Proposition 227** in 1998. This proposition, now a California law, requires all language minority students to be educated in **sheltered English immersion** programs, not normally intended to exceed one year. Sheltered English immersion is an instructional process in which English language acquisition for young children is structured so that all or nearly all classroom instruction is in English. However, one aspect will be addressed in this chapter. The proposition, which intended to dismantle bilingual education, sent waves of panic through California's bilingual education community. Those working with special needs students had even greater concerns because many believed that they were prohibited from using the home language with limited and non-English-speaking students (Baca and Cervantes, 2004). They were also concerned that the new law would require them to transition the students into general education classrooms after one year. Proposition 227 is a state law, as is a similar proposition in Arizona, and a similar law in Massachusetts. The federal law, IDEA, always takes precedence over a state law. Therefore, if the student's IEP requires bilingual education, it must be provided for as long as it is written.

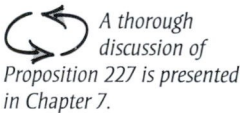 *A thorough discussion of Proposition 227 is presented in Chapter 7.*

Educational Implications

The educational implications for working with exceptional individuals are numerous and entire chapters could be devoted to each exceptionality. Educators should remember that exceptional children, those with disabilities and those who are gifted, are more like than unlike normal children. Their basic needs are the same as all children's. Abraham Maslow's theory on self-actualization is familiar to most students in education. To be self-actualized or to meet one's full potential, Maslow (1954) theorized, one's basic needs must be fulfilled: That is, to reach self-actualization, one's physiological needs, safety needs, belongingness or love needs, and esteem needs must first be met. Although many individuals with disabilities may never match the accomplishments of their nondisabled peers, they can become proficient at whatever they are capable of doing. Educators can assist them by helping to ensure that their basic needs are met, allowing them to strive toward self-actualization.

Teachers must be constantly cognizant of the unique needs of their exceptional children. The exceptional adult may choose, or may be forced by society, to become part of a cultural group. The interactions between educators and the exceptional child may not change what will eventually take place. Even if exceptional adults are part of a cultural group, they also will interact with the mainstream society on a regular basis. Efforts on the part of the educator to meet the needs of the child may ultimately affect the exceptional adult's interaction with society.

Teachers of children with physical and other health impairments may find it advantageous to check the student records carefully to determine potential problem situations with these students in the classroom. If a child has particular health problems that may surface in the classroom, the child's teachers need to be prepared so that they will know precisely what to do should the child have, for example, an epileptic seizure. The parents will most likely be able to provide precise instructions, and the school nurse could also provide additional recommendations. If the children are old enough to understand, they too can be a valuable source of information. Ask them what kinds of adaptations, special equipment, or teaching procedures work best for them. Teachers should not be afraid of their own uncertainties. They should feel free to ask the students when they won't or don't want help. Teachers should treat their students with disabilities as normally as feasible, neither overprotecting them nor giving or doing more for them than is needed or deserved. Allowing them to assume responsibility for themselves will do much to facilitate their personal growth.

Many variables affect the learning, cognition, and adjustment of individuals with disabilities. This is particularly evident for culturally and linguistically diverse learners who must cope with issues of language, culture, and values. Harry, Kalyanpur, and Day (1999) implore professionals who work with students with disabilities to take special note of the cultural values that may be embedded in their interpretation of a particular student's difficulties. They suggest that developing a sense of cultural self-awareness is crucial to effective interactions with students and families and that it will enable them to make appropriate decisions regarding services.

The range and variety of experiences imposed on, or withheld from, persons with disabilities may result in undue limitations. Too often, parents and teachers assume that a child's visual limitation precludes the ability to appreciate the typical everyday experiences of sighted children. Children who are blind may not be able to see the animals in a zoo, but they can smell and hear them. They may not be able to enjoy the scenes along a bus route, but they can feel the stop-and-go movements, hear the traffic and people, and smell their fellow travelers. The child who is deaf may not be able to hear the sounds at the symphony or the crowd's roar at a football game. Both events, however, offer the possibility of extraordinary sensory experiences to which the child needs exposure. The child with cerebral palsy needs experiences such as going to restaurants, even if there is difficulty using eating utensils in a socially acceptable manner.

Well-adjusted individuals with a sensory disability usually attain a balance of control with their environment. Individuals who depend completely on other members of the family and on friends may develop an attitude of helplessness and a loss of self-identity. Individuals with disabilities who completely dominate and control their environment with unreasonable demands sometimes fail to make an acceptable adjustment and could become selfish and self-centered.

It is critical to remember that children who are exceptional are, first and foremost, children. Their exceptionality, though influencing their lives, is secondary to their needs as children. They are more like than unlike nondisabled children. They therefore have the same basic needs as those children. Chinn, Winn, and Walters (1978) identify three of those needs: communication, acceptance, and the freedom to grow.

COMMUNICATION NEEDS

Exceptional children are far more perceptive than many adults give them credit for being. They are sensitive to nonverbal communication and hidden messages that may be concealed in half-truths. They, more than anyone else, need to deal with their exceptionality, whether it is a disability or giftedness. They need to know what their exceptionality is all about so that they can deal with it. They need to know how it will affect their lives in order to adjust appropriately, to make the best of their lives, and to reach their full potential. They need straight, honest communication tempered with sensitivity.

ACCEPTANCE NEEDS

The society in which we live often fails to provide the exceptional child with a positive and receptive environment. Even the educational setting can be hostile and lacking in acceptance. The teacher can facilitate the acceptance of a child in a classroom by exhibiting an open and positive attitude. Students tend to reflect the attitude of the teacher. If the teacher is hostile, the students will quickly pick up these cues. If the attitude is positive, the students are likely to respond and provide a receptive environment for their classmates with disabilities.

Jeff, a first-grade student who suffered from a hearing loss, was fitted with a hearing aid. When he came to school with the hearing aid, the students in the class immediately began whispering about the "thing" Jeff had in his ear. After observing the class behavior, the teacher assisted Jeff in a "show and tell" preparation for the next day. With the teacher's assistance and assurances, Jeff proudly demonstrated his hearing aid to the class. By the end of the demonstration, Jeff was the envy of the class, and any further discussion of the hearing aid was of a positive nature.

FREEDOM TO GROW

Students with disabilities need acceptance and understanding. Acceptance implies a freedom for the exceptional child to grow. At times, it may seem easier to do things for a child, rather than to take the time to teach the child.

> Sarah was a nine-year-old girl who was blind and who had an orthopedic disability. She attended a state residential school for the blind. She wore leg braces but had a reasonable amount of mobility with crutches. To save time and effort, fellow students or staff members transported her between the cottage where she lived and the classroom building in a wagon. One day her teacher decided she needed to be more independent in her travel to and from her cottage. To Sarah's surprise, the teacher informed her after school that she would not ride back in the wagon but that he was walking her back. Angered, she denounced him as cruel and hateful in front of the entire class. She complained bitterly the full thirty minutes of their walk back to the cottage. After a few days the complaining subsided and the travel time was curtailed. Within a few weeks Sarah was traveling on her own in ten minutes or less with newfound self-respect. (Chinn et al., 1978, p. 36)

At other times, it may be tempting for teachers and parents to make extra concessions for the exceptional child. Often, these exceptions preclude the emotional growth of the child and may later cause serious interpersonal problems.

> Jimmy was a seven-year-old boy who was blind at the same state institution attended by Sarah. He was a favorite of the staff members because of his pleasant personality and overall adjustment. On a Sunday afternoon in the fall, he was assisting a staff member in making block prints for Christmas. The conversation turned to Christmas and Jimmy's wish for a transistor radio. This incident took place in 1960 when transistor radios were new on the market and very expensive. Since Jimmy had already made his request to his parents, the staff member was confident that the parents would not deny this child his wish. To the surprise of the staff, Jimmy returned after the holidays without a radio. He very philosophically explained to the staff that the radios were so expensive that had his parents granted his wish it would be at the expense of the other children in the family. Weeks later, when Jimmy returned from his birthday weekend at home, he entered his cottage with a transistor radio in hand, but in tears. He informed the staff that he and his younger brother Ralph had been fighting in the car on the way to the school and both had received a spanking. When a staff member went out to greet Jimmy's parents, his younger brother Ralph was also crying from the insult to his rear end. (Chinn et al., 1978, p. 36)

Jimmy's father was a laborer with a modest income. Although their child's disability created adjustment problems for everyone, they had resolved to treat him as an equal in the family. As such, he shared all of the family privileges. He also suffered the same consequences for inappropriate behavior. This attitude on the part of the parents was probably a primary factor in Jimmy's excellent adjustment to his disability.

Normalization and Inclusion

Much effort is directed today toward the concept of normalization. **Normalization** means "making available to all persons with disabilities or other handicaps, patterns of life and conditions of everyday living which are as close as possible to or indeed the same as the regular circumstances and ways of life of society" (Nirje, 1985, p. 67). Normalization was expanded and advocated in the United States by Wolfensberger (1972). He has subsequently suggested a rethinking of the term normalization and introduced the concept of "**social role valorization**"—giving value to individuals with mental retardation (Wolfensberger, 1983, 2000). He suggests that the "most explicit and highest goal of normalization must be the creation, support, and defense of valued social roles for people who are at risk of social devaluation" (Wolfensberger, 1983, p. 234).

Drew and Hardman (2004) suggest that normalization and social valorization have brought about an emphasis on deinstitutionalization, whereby individuals from large residential facilities for people with retardation are returned to the community and home environments. They add that the concept is not limited to movement away from institutions to a less restrictive environment; it also pertains to those individuals living in the community for whom a more "normal" lifestyle may be an appropriate goal.

The principles of normalization as they were first introduced were developed with individuals with mental retardation as the target group. In more recent years, the concept has broadened so that all categories of individuals with disabilities are now targeted. The term "mainstreaming" now giving way to "**inclusion,**" seemed to undergo a natural evolutionary process from the concept of normalization. Turnbull, Turnbull, Shank, and Smith define inclusion as students with disabilities learning in general education and having a sense of belonging in the class (2004, p. 65). Tiegerman-Farber and Radziewicz (1998) further assert that in its "purest" form inclusion means that students with disabilities have a right to be integrated into general education classes regardless of their ability to meet "traditional" academic standards. Mastropieri and Scruggs (2004) differentiate between *inclusion* and *full inclusion* with the latter serving students with disabilities and other special needs *entirely within the general classroom.* This is an important difference, as students in full inclusion do not receive any of their education in segregated settings.

Initially inclusion was intended for students with mild disabilities. A more current movement, full inclusion, seeks to provide children with moderate to severe disabilities with similar opportunities. Although resistance to inclusion of students with mild retardation is far less intense than it once was, resistance from some educators still remains. The arguments against integrating children with severe disabilities have often been centered on the presumed inability of nondisabled children to accept their peers with disabilities. In reality, some of the reservations may be more a reflection of educators who themselves are unable or unwilling to accept the dignity and worth of individuals with severe disabilities.

Historically special education in the United States has offered a full continuum of placements for students with disabilities. These services have included the most restrictive placements such as residential schools and special schools, to the least restrictive settings, such as full inclusion into the general education classroom.

Federal special education law (IDEA) does not require inclusion. The law does require the least restrictive environment for students with disabilities. Herein lies the basis for considerable controversy in special education. The controversy is often fueled within special education itself, as special educators themselves are not in complete agreement regarding what is the least restrictive environment. "**Least restrictive environment**" means that children with disabilities are to be educated with nondisabled children whenever possible, in as normal an environment as possible. Few special educators would argue against the concept of inclusion. However, disagreement is centered on whether full inclusion is appropriate for every child regardless of the type of disability or the severity of the disability.

To some, and perhaps many of the advocates of full inclusion, the issue is not one of the efficacies of general education placement. Rather, it is a moral and ethical issue. Opponents of inclusion use many of the same arguments that segregationists used more than 50 years ago. Most Americans today would consider it unconsicionable to segregate children in schools on the basis of race or ethnicity. This, we can agree, is morally and ethically wrong. Advocates for full inclusion find it equally repugnant to segregate children on the basis of a disability. *How would you feel if you had no preparation for special education other than an undergraduate survey class on exceptional children, and your principal advised you that two children with severe disabilities are to be fully included in your class?*

In reality, most (if not all) children with disabilities could be served in a general education classroom if adequate resources and supports were made available. Therein lies a primary problem. Special education resources are too often inadequate. There is seldom an adequate supply of certified or credentialed personnel in

Opportunities for Reflection

An increasingly larger number of students with disabilities are now being fully included in general education classrooms.

special education and in related services (e.g., school psychologists). General educators have many issues and concerns to address in inclusion. They may be concerned

- that the special needs student will detract from the attention normally provided other students.
- about the reception the nondisabled students will give to the students with disabilities.
- that if they are not provided with appropriate training to accommodate the students with disabilities, they will not be able to provide appropriate instructional services.
- that the younger students and those with more severe disabilities will require greater attention.
- that the promises of support in classroom personnel and other resources may not be kept.

A pragmatist would argue that there are not enough fiscal resources to provide the supports necessary for successful full inclusion for all children. We know that the courts will not accept, "we don't do it because there are inadequate resources." The courts may accept an argument that a particular program or service is not in the best interests of the student, but it must be clearly supported and documented. However, if full inclusion is warranted, the courts will order the schools (and they have consistently done so) to "get the resources and to do it."

Some who may question aspects of full inclusion may argue that some children are too disruptive and dangerous to themselves and to other students that they cannot be provided for in general education. Supporters of full inclusion can argue that given adequate resources, the student can be taught to stop disruptive and dangerous behaviors.

FOCUS YOUR CULTURAL LENS: DEBATE

Is Full Inclusion Feasible for All Children with Disabilities?

The Individuals with Disabilities Education Act is a federal law that requires the placement of students with disabilities in the least restrictive environment. This means that these students should be placed in settings in or as close to a general education setting as is feasible for them. What is the least restrictive setting for a child with a disability? Is it feasible to place every child with a disability in a general education setting? Are there realistically adequate resources to do this? Do we have the skill and the will to make it work?

FOR

- Full inclusion for all children with disabilities is a moral and ethical issue. It is as immoral to segregate a child because of his or her disability as it is to segregate children because of the color of their skin.

- The least restrictive environment that is feasible for every child is a general education classroom. We have the know-how to deliver quality educational services for every child in an inclusive general education classroom.

- The fact that we do not have adequate fiscal resources is not the fault of the child with a disability. If we don't have the resources, then we need to find ways to get them.

AGAINST

- Full inclusion may work for some students with disabilities, but it makes no sense to insist on it for every student regardless of the disability or the degree of impairment.

- Some students with disabilities lack the maturity, the cognitive ability, the social skills, or adequate behaviors to function in general education.

- Until the Federal Government makes good on its commitment to fully fund IDEA, there will never be adequate resources to successfully Implement full inclusion for all children with disabilities.

- Even if there were the fiscal resources, there simply are not enough professionally prepared personnel to provide the type of services needed for successful inclusion of every child.

QUESTIONS

1. *Are there some students who should never be considered for general education placement?*
2. *If the Federal Government mandates special education for all children, commits itself to funding 40% of the cost, and continues to renege on the full funding, should school districts be forced to fully implement IDEA?*
3. *Is excluding children with disabilities from being fully included in general education morally and ethically comparable to excluding children because of race?*

To answer these questions online, go to the Focus Your Cultural Lens: Debate module for this chapter of the Companion Website.

Source: VIDEO: Special Education Inclusion, Wisconsin Education Association Council, undated. Retrieved from http://www.weac.org/resource/june96/speced.htm

Turnbull and his associates do suggest that there has been a progressive trend toward greater inclusion in the nation's schools. They indicate that prior to the 1984–1985 school year, only about a fourth of the students with disabilities spent a significant part of their day in general education classrooms. By the 1998–1999 school year, nearly half of the students were involved in general education most of the school day. There are some general conclusions, which we could draw from the issues raised:

- As long as Congress fails to meet its financial obligations in fully funding IDEA, school districts will continue to have difficulty in providing adequate resources for special education.
- Segregating students with disabilities from general education classes without justification is morally and ethically wrong.
- The debate over inclusion and full inclusion continues and is not likely to be fully resolved in the immediate future.

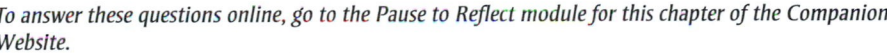

Pause to Reflect 5.2

Students with disabilities are sometimes forced into segregated settings for reasons beyond their control. For example, Kevin was a student who lived with his family on the side of a mountain in Appalachia. Kevin was blind, with no travel vision. It was a three-quarter-mile hike down the side of the mountain to the school bus stop. Kevin had good mobility skills and could negotiate the trail to and from the bus stop when weather conditions were good. The school was able to provide appropriate special education and general education services for him. During the winter, however, when snow covered the ground for the entire season, he could not get his bearings with his long cane and could not negotiate the trail. There was no one who could help him get to and from the bus stop, so during the winter he stopped going to school. The only school that could apparently meet his needs was the state school for the blind, which could provide him with residential services. The state residential school, however, is the most extreme form of a segregated setting for students with disabilities.

- *Is segregating Kevin from his nondisabled peers inappropriate? Immoral? Unethical?*
- *Is the issue of full inclusion for students with disabilities similar to the issue of desegregation for all students of color into integrated classroom settings?*
- *When educators say they want a full continuum of services for students with disabilities that would permit inclusion for some and segregated classrooms for others or even institutionalization, is this a moral and ethical way to educate America's students? Is this an excuse for educators to discriminate against some?*

To answer these questions online, go to the Pause to Reflect module for this chapter of the Companion Website.

It is important for us as educators to see the parallels and differences that exist between the current debate regarding this group of students and the issues that *Brown* addressed more than 50 years ago. The two situations have similarities, but the groups are different. It is important that, as educators, we maintain an open mind so that perhaps we ourselves can be educated.

The legal mandates do not eliminate special schools or classes, but they do offer a new philosophical view. Instead of the physical isolation of individuals with disabilities, an effort to enable students with disabilities to assume a more appropriate place in the educational setting is being promoted. Still, many children with disabilities apparently may not benefit appreciably from an inclusive setting and may be better educated in a special setting. As attitudes become more congruent with the laws, people with disabilities may have more options in the decision to be a part of the mainstream or to segregate themselves into their own cultural groups.

Summary

The concerns related to the disproportionate placement of ethnic minorities, males, and students from low-income families in special education programs have been addressed to focus on a long-standing educational problem. The issues raised are not intended to negate the fact that there are students with retardation, serious emotional disturbance, and other disabilities in both majority and minority groups. Rather, they are raised to call attention to problems in referral and assessment, as well as to the problems associated with poverty.

Adults with disabilities often become part of a cultural group for individuals with disabilities by ascription or by individual choice. They do not choose to have a disability, and their situation often precludes full acceptance or integration into the world of those who are perceived to be physically, socially, or mentally normal. Their adjustment to their environment may be, in part, a function of the way they are perceived, treated, and accepted by educators. Consequently, teachers and other educators may have a greater influence on children with disabilities than they realize.

The Education for All Handicapped Children Act (EHA; P.L. 94-142), the Individuals with Disabilities Education Act (IDEA; P.L. 101-476), Section 504 of the Vocational Rehabilitation Act Amendments of 1973 (P.L. 93-112), and the Americans with Disabilities Act (ADA; P.L. 101-336) guarantee all exceptional children the right to a free and appropriate education and freedom from discrimination resulting from their disability. While thousands of children with disabilities are experiencing inclusive education in general education classes, many others are excluded because of bias, prejudice, or lack of understanding. Despite these mandates, equality still eludes millions of individuals with disabilities in this country. Until and unless the Federal Government fulfills its fiscal commitment to fully fund IDEA, full inclusion will continue to be a problematic and controversial issue for educators.

Insensitivity, apathy, and prejudice contribute to the problems of those with disabilities. Because of prejudice, institutionalization, or a desire to meet their own needs, some exceptional individuals form their own cultural groups and some their own enclaves, where they live and socialize with one another. The laws can force services for individuals with disabilities, but only time and effort can change public attitudes.

QUESTIONS FOR DISCUSSION

1. What are some of the objections to labeling children with disabilities?

2. Why was *Brown v. Board of Education* (1954) important to special education?

3. What are the major implications for P.L. 94-142, IDEA, Section 504 of P.L. 93-112, and the Americans with Disabilities Act?

4. In what ways has the treatment of individuals with disabilities paralleled that of oppressed minority groups?

5. How do individuals with disabilities sometime become a part of an exceptional cultural group?

6. In what ways are ethnic minority children disproportionately placed in special education classes?

7. Explain the difference of reporting placement in special education classes by composition and by risk.

8. What are some of the variables that contribute to the overrepresentation of students of color in special education classes?

9. What are the educational implications of California's Proposition 227 for students with disabilities?

10. What are some of the needs of exceptional children?

11. Explain the concepts of normalization and social role valorization.

12. Explain the differences between the terms *inclusion* and *full inclusion*.

13. What are the problems with providing full inclusion to all children with disabilities?

ONLINE ACTIVITIES For additional chapter questions and activities, visit this text's Companion Website at http://www.prenhall.com/gollnick.

PORTFOLIO ACTIVITIES

1. Examine an entire building on your campus to determine its accessibility to individuals with wheelchair mobility. Make a notation of the following:
   a. Do curbs leading to the building allow wheelchair access?
   b. Is the entrance into the building accessible by wheelchair? Is it ramped?
   c. Are restrooms accessible with larger stalls to accommodate wheelchairs?
   d. Is the building multilevel, and if so, how does the student access the different floors?
   e. Are there Braille signs in appropriate places? (INTASC Standards 3 and 10)

2. Examine your campus to determine if it is accessible to visually impaired individuals. Determine if there are hazards on the campus, which endanger individuals who are blind (e.g., holes in the ground, posted metal sign at face height). (INTASC Standards 3 and 10)

3. Determine the percentage of students of color in the school in which you are working or student teaching. Determine the percentage of students of color in this same school who have placement in special education classes and determine if there is some degree of overrepresentation. This information is for your own use and possibly university classroom discussion. If you are a student teacher in the school, it may not be in your best interest to make an issue of overrepresentation with the school administration. (INTASC Standards 3 and 10)

SUGGESTED READINGS

Drew, C. J., & Hardman, M. L. (2004). *Mental retardation: A life cycle approach* (8th ed.). Upper Saddle River, NJ: Merrill/Prentice Hall.

This is an excellent developmental approach to mental retardation. It includes a sensitive view of mental retardation and its impact on the family. It examines some of the early treatments of individuals with mental retardation. A chapter on legislative and legal issues related to individuals with mental retardation is also included.

Heward, W. L. (2003). *Exceptional children* (7th ed.). Upper Saddle River, NJ: Merrill/Prentice Hall.

This survey text is an overview of all exceptionalities that will provide a good basic understanding of the gifted and talented, as well as the various disabling conditions. It includes a chapter on culturally diverse exceptional students.

Losen, D. J., & Orfield, G. (2002). *Racial inequality in special education.* Cambridge, MA: Harvard Education Press.

This text is an excellent treatment in helping the reader to understand the problems of overreferral, overidentification, and overrepresentation of students of color (particularly African American) in special education classes. A thorough treatment of variables that contribute to the problems including bias, discrimination, poverty, and assessment issues is presented.

Turnbull, R., Turnbull, A., Shank, M., & Smith, S. (2004). *Exceptional lives: Special education in today's schools.* Upper Saddle River, NJ: Merrill/Prentice Hall.

This is an excellent introductory text on exceptional children, which includes a very good treatment on inclusion.

Yell, M. L. (1998). *The law and special education.* Upper Saddle River, NJ: Merrill/Prentice Hall.

This text provides an excellent overview of litigation and legislation in special education. It provides excellent insights into how litigation is developed and how it influences legislation, and also provides an explanation of legal terminology.

REFERENCES

Americans with Disabilities Act of 1990, 42 U.S.C. 12101 *et seq.* (P.L. 101-336).

Artiles, A. J., & Harry, B. (2004). *Addressing culturally and linguistically diverse student overrepresentation in special education: Guidelines for parents.* Denver, CO: National Center for Culturally Responsive Educational Systems.

Artiles, A. J., Harry, B., Reschly, D. J., & Chinn, P.C. (2002). Over-identification of students of color in special education: A critical overview. *Multicultural Perspectives.* (4), 1, p. 3–10.

Artiles, A. J., Rueda, R., Salazar, J. J., & Higareda, I. (2002). English-language learner representation in special education in California urban school districts. In D. J.

Losen & G. Orfield (Eds.), *Racial inequality in special education.* Cambridge, MA: Harvard Education Press.

Baca, L. M., & Cervantes, H. (2004). *The bilingual special education interface* (4th ed.). Upper Saddle River, NJ: Merrill/Prentice Hall.

Board of Education of the Hendrick Hudson School District v. Rowley, 458 U.S. 176 (1982).

Brown v. Board of Education of Topeka, 347 U.S. 483, 74 S.Ct. 686, 91, L.Ed. 873 (1954).

Carolina Environment, Inc. (1999). *How lead affects your child's health.* Retrieved August 2, 2004, from http://www.knowlead.com/affect.htm

Chinn, P. C. (2004). Brown's far reaching impact. *Multicultural Perspectives, 6* (4), 9–11.

Chinn, P. C., Winn, J., & Walters, R. H. (1978). *Two-way talking with parents of exceptional children: A process of positive communication.* St. Louis: Mosby.

Diana v. State Board of Education, Civil Action No. C-7037RFP (N.D. Cal. Jan. 7, 1970 & June 18, 1973).

Drew, C. J., & Hardman, M. L. (2004). *Mental retardation: A lifespan approach to people with intellectual disabilities* (8th ed.). Upper Saddle River, NJ: Merrill/Prentice Hall.

Dunn, L. (1968). Special education for the mildly retarded: Is much of it justifiable? *Exceptional Children, 7,* 5–24.

Edgerton, R. B. (1967). *The cloak of competence.* Berkeley: The University of California Press.

Education for All Handicapped Children's Act of 1975, 20 U.S.C. 1401 *et seq.* (P.L. 94-142).

Erickson, S. (2003, April 17). Florida officials reach out to save children from lead poisoning. *Orlando Sentinel,* FL, pITEM03207051.

Gelfand, D. M., & Drew, C. J. (2003). *Understanding child behavior disorders* (4th ed.). Ft. Worth, TX: Harcourt Brace.

Gliedman, J., & Roth, W. (1980). *The unexpected minority.* New York: Harcourt Brace Jovanovich.

Harry, B., Kalyanpur, M., & Day, M. (1999). *Building cultural reciprocity with families: Case studies in special education.* Baltimore: Paul H. Brookes.

Heward, W. L. (2003). *Exceptional children* (7th ed.). Upper Saddle River, NJ: Merrill/Prentice Hall.

IDEA Funding Coalition. (2003). *IDEA funding: Time for a new approach.* Mandatory Funding Proposal, March 2003. Retrieved August 2, 2004, from http://www.aasa.org/government_relations/idea/Mandatory_2003_Proposal.pdf

Individuals with Disabilities Education Act of 1990, 20 U.S.C. 1401 *et seq.* (P.L. 101-476).

Individuals with Disabilities Education Act Amendments of 1997, (P.L. 105-17), 105th Congress.

Individuals with Disabilities Education Act Regulations, 34 C.F.R. 300. 1 *et seq.*

Irving Independent School District v. Tatro, 468 U.S. 883 (1984).

Jeffers, J. M. (2002). Forward. In D. J. Losen & G. Orfield (Eds.), *Racial inequality in special education.* Cambridge, MA: Harvard Education Press.

Larry P. v. Riles, C-71-2270, FRP. Dis. Ct. (1979).

Losen, D. J., & Orfield, G. (2002). *Racial inequality in special education.* Cambridge, MA: Harvard Education Press.

Maslow, A. (1954). *Motivation and personality.* New York: Harper.

Mastropieri, M. A., & Scruggs, T. E. (2004). *The inclusive classroom: Strategies for effective instruction* (2nd ed.). Upper Saddle River, NJ: Merrill/Prentice Hall.

Mercer, J. (1973). *Labeling the mentally retarded.* Los Angeles: University of California Press.

Meyer, P. A., Privetz, T., Dignam, T. A., Homa, D. M., Schoonover, J., & Brody, D. (2003). Surveillance for elevated blood lead levels among children—United States, 1997–2001. *Morbidity and Mortality Weekly Report,* September 12, 2003/52 (SS10), 1–21. Atlanta, GA: Centers for Disease Control and Prevention.

Mills v. Board of Education, 348 F. Supp. 866 (D.D.C 1972).

Murdick, N., Gartin, B., & Crabtree, T. (2002). *Special education law.* Upper Saddle River, NJ: Merrill/Prentice Hall.

Nirje, B. (1985). The basis and logic of the normalization principle. *Australia and New Zealand Journal of Developmental Disabilities, 11,* 65–68.

Patton, J. M. (1998). The disproportionate representation of African Americans in special education: Looking behind the curtain for understanding and solutions. *The Journal of Special Education, 32* (1), 25–31.

Pennsylvania Association for Retarded Citizens v. Commonwealth of Pennsylvania, 343 F. Supp. 279 (E.D. Pa. 1972).

Plessy v. Ferguson, 163 U.S. 537 (1896) U.S. Supreme Court, http://caselaw.1p.findlaw.com/scripts/printer_friendly.pl?page=us/163/537.html

President's Committee on Mental Retardation. (1969). *The six-hour retarded child.* Washington, DC: U.S. Department of Health, Education & Welfare.

Rehabilitation Act of 1973, Section 504, 29 U.S.C. 794.

Tiegerman-Farber, E., & Radziewicz, C. (1998). *Collaborative decision making: The pathway to inclusion.* Upper Saddle River, NJ: Merrill/Prentice Hall.

Turnbull, R., Turnbull, A., Shank, M., & Smith, S. J. (2004). *Exceptional lives* (4th ed.). Upper Saddle River, NJ: Merrill/Prentice Hall.

U.S. Office of Civil Rights (OCR). (1999). *1997 Elementary and Secondary Schools Civil Rights Survey.* Washington, DC: U.S. Department of Education.

Widerstrom, A. H., Mowder, B. A., & Sandall, S. R. (1991). *At-risk and handicapped newborns and infants.* Englewood Cliffs, NJ: Prentice Hall.

Wolfensberger, W. (1972). *Normalization: The principle of normalization in human services.* Toronto: National Institute on Mental Retardation.

Wolfensberger, W. (1983). Social role valorization: Proposed new form for the principle of normalization. *Mental Retardation, 21* (6), 234–239.

Wolfensberger, W. (2000). A brief overview of social role valorization. *Mental Retardation, 38* (2), 105–123.

Yell, M. L. (1998). *The law and special education.* Upper Saddle River, NJ: Merrill/Prentice Hall.

Ysseldyke, J. E., Thurlow, M., Graden, J., Wesson, C., Algozzine, B., & Deno, S. (1983). Generalizations from five years of research on assessment and decision-making: The University of Minnesota Institute. *Exceptional Education Quarterly, 4,* 75–93.

"Congress shall make no law respecting an establishment of religion, or prohibiting the free exercise thereof; or abridging the freedom of speech, or of the press; or the right of the people peaceably to assemble, and to petition the Government for a redress of grievances."

FIRST AMENDMENT TO THE UNITED STATES CONSTITUTION, 1791

Chapter 6

Religion

*I*n a suburb of San Francisco, the teachers and administrators of the Edison Onizuka middle school have put the finishing touches on their plans for the school's honors convocation. The principal, Dr. Alan Hovestadt, had suggested that the event should recognize the school's high academic achievers in each grade. This effort to stimulate and reinforce student academic efforts was enthusiastically endorsed by the faculty. Ramakrishnan Gupta and Rebecca Rose were tied with the highest grades in the eighth grade and were to be recognized in a convocation ceremony and asked to make a 7- to 10-minute speech on the value of an education. Because the faculty and Dr. Hovestadt wanted the district superintendent to be part of the ceremony, they had agreed to schedule the event at 3:00 P.M. on the fourth Saturday in May. This was the superintendent's only available time because she was participating in high school commencement ceremonies at all the other times that were proposed.

Dr. Hovestadt called the Gupta and Rose families to inform them of their children's selection as convocation speakers. As expected, both sets of parents were delighted at the news of their son and their daughter's accomplishments and selection. Mr. Rose indicated, however, that Saturday was quite impossible because it was the **Sabbath** for their family, who were **Orthodox Jews.** The Sabbath, a day of religious observance and rest among Jews is from sundown on Friday until sundown on Saturday. Orthodox Jews are a conservative branch of Judaism, which strictly observes religious law. The event had to be rescheduled to any other day but the Sabbath. It was impossible, Dr. Hovestadt pleaded. All the plans were made, and no satisfactory alternate dates were available. "Would you plan the event on a Sunday?" Mr. Rose exclaimed. "I would not ask you to. Then why do you schedule it on our Sabbath? You must change the day." At an impasse, Dr. Hovestadt knew he had to come up with an alternative plan in a hurry.

Opportunities for Reflection

1. *Is Mr. Rose being unreasonable?*
2. *What if the event in question took place in a homogenous community that was primarily Christian and the Rose family was one of only two Jewish families in the community? In a democracy, does the majority always rule?*
3. *Does the thought that one family can create such chaos in the careful planning of a school event irritate you?*
4. *How would you feel if you were a Christian living in a non-Christian community, and a major event that you were expected to attend was scheduled on Christmas Day?*
5. *Should the majority always rule?*
6. *Do the rights of every individual have to be considered?*

To answer these questions online, go to this chapter's Opening Scenario module of the Companion Website.

Religion and Culture

In November 2003, Alabama's chief Supreme Court Justice, Roy Moore, was removed from office. A nine-member panel ousted him for his defiance of a federal district court order to remove a 5,300-pound granite monument of the Ten Commandments. After his election to the high court, Moore had the monument installed in the rotunda of the Alabama Judicial Building. After a 10-day trial in 2002, a U.S. District Court judge found Moore's actions to be a violation of the doctrine of separation of church and state and ordered the monument removed. This resulted in the standoff, which eventually led to Moore's removal (Johnson, 2003).

Moore had indicated that it was not only his right, but also his obligation to acknowledge God in his courtroom. When Moore campaigned to become his state's ranking judicial officer, he vowed to restore the moral underpinnings of the law (Johnson, 2003).

Moore's defiance was hugely popular among his fellow citizens. Seventy-five percent of those in Alabama supported his position. He also received support from others outside the state. Moore indicated that the U.S. Government stamps "In God We Trust" on our coins and imprints the same on our currency. Yet, he was denied the right to put

Opportunities for Reflection

"God's Commandments" on display. This, he indicated, is an inconsistency at best. Moore's right to his beliefs or his desire to enhance morality was never in question. *Was Justice Moore correct in stating that our government is inconsistent in the way we enforce the doctrine of separation of church and state? If the majority of people want the Ten Commandments, why should the courts interfere?* What was in question was the use of his public office to foster religious concepts in a public area. Even though he was supported by a vast majority, the Court and the judicial panel ruled that the minority, no matter how small, had a right not to be subjected to his (and that of others) beliefs.

Justice Moore was likely fully aware of the consequences of his actions, however he was apparently willing to give up the highest judicial position in his state to adhere to his religious convictions (Johnson, 2003). Some see this as admirable. As educators, we need to reflect on what our responsibilities are to students. We have the right to have our own religious convictions. Educators who feel strongly about including their religious beliefs in the instructional process should consider teaching opportunities in private church-related schools. Every student should have the security in knowing that they will not have anyone else's religious dogma imposed on them.

At almost the same time that Justice Moore was taking his action in Alabama, halfway across the world in Istanbul two nearly simultaneous suicide car bombings tore into two crowded synagogues during Shabbat prayers killing at least 20 people, injuring more than 300, and laying waste to neighborhoods where Jews had lived for generations among Turkey's Muslims. Muslims, or adherents of Islam, represent the majority religious group in Turkey. This was believed to be the work of Muslim terrorists who were willing to kill and give up their lives for their religious and political convictions.

INFLUENCE OF RELIGION ON EDUCATION

In the United States, 190 million people claim affiliation with a religious group. As can be seen in Table 6.1, in an average week 41% of adults attend a church, synagogue, mosque, or temple (Carroll, 2004). Religion is clearly an important aspect of the lives of many people. Although it may have little impact on the lives of some people, it influences the way many other people think, perceive, and behave. The forces of religious groups are far from dormant. They can influence the election of school board members as well as the curriculum and textbooks used in schools. Principals, teachers, and superintendents have been hired and fired through the influence of religious groups. This chapter provides an overview of religion in the United States and its influence on the individual and on the educational system.

The religious pluralism of the school in which one teaches will be determined, in great part, by the geographic region of the United States. Because of various immigration and migration patterns throughout history, different ethnic and religious groups have settled in different parts of the country. Although a few areas remain totally homogeneous, families that strongly identify with a particular ethnic group may dominate a school community. More often, families identify strongly with the religious orientation of one or more denominations in the community. The perspective of a particular religious doctrine often influences what a family expects from the school and, therefore, from the teacher. In an area where the religious perspectives and school expectations differ greatly, educators face numerous challenges. A look at the religious composition of schools in various sections of the country will provide a sense of the diversity one might face throughout a career in education.

Table 6.1 Average Weekly Attendance at Worship Services Among U.S. Adults

2003	41%
2002	44%
2001	41%
2000	44%
1998	40%
1995	43%
1990	40%
1985	42%
1980	40%
1975	40%
1970	42%
1965	44%
1960	47%
1955	49% (a) High point tied with 49% in 1958
1950	39%
1940	37% (b) Low point

Source: Adapted from Carroll, J. (2004, March 2). American Public Opinion About Religion. *Gallup Tuesday Morning Briefing*; Gallup, G., Jr., and Lindsay, D. M. (1999). *Surveying the Religious Landscape.* Harrisburg, PA: Morehouse Publishing.

For example, a consolidated rural high school in the South may be primarily comprised of students whose families are conservative Southern Baptist, Church of Christ, or Pentecostal. The United Methodist students may be less conservative than the others. The church serves as the center of most community activities, and many families spend several nights a week at church or serving the church. Sex education is not allowed in the public school curriculum. Teachers may face harsh criticism if they teach about evolution or lifestyles that conflict with those acceptable in that community. Textbooks and assigned readings are often scrutinized to ensure that the content does not stray far from the beliefs of this conservative community.

At a middle school in northeastern Indiana, most students are from the same European background, but they dress and behave differently. Some students are from a local **Old Order Amish** community with strict codes for the behavior and dress of its members, whereas the majority of other students are **Mennonites.** Both the Amish and the Mennonites are part of conservative Christian groups. The former are very respectful and well behaved, but some may experience ridicule by their non-Amish peers. After completing the eighth grade, the Amish students are no longer part of the school system because their families withdraw them to work full-time on their farms, which utilize neither electricity nor motorized vehicles. The Mennonites, though not as conservative as the Amish, share some of the same origins as the Amish. The early Amish were a group that separated from the Mennonites.

Students from Catholic, Jewish, Protestant, Muslim, Hindu, Sikh, and Buddhist (these religious groups are described in this chapter within the section on religious pluralism in the United States) families attend a suburban school on the West Coast. Some students are from families with no religious affiliation. Although the religious backgrounds of the students differ, they seem to share many of the same values. The school projects a generally liberal curriculum that includes sex education, ethnic studies, and religion courses. Except for the students' observance of various religious holidays, religion seems to have little impact on the students or the school.

At an inner-city school in an East Coast city, the religious backgrounds of students vary greatly. Some students attend Catholic services; others attend Baptist churches or storefront Pentecostal churches; some belong to a New Age group that has organized in the community; and others have no religious affiliation. There are a few atheists and agnostics in this community as there are in others throughout the country. The **atheists** believe that there is no God, while the **agnostics** argue that we do not and cannot know God or gods exist. Some students are involved in religious activities during their nonschool time. The school reflects little of these diverse religious perspectives in the curriculum or school environment.

In Utah, the educator will find a school in a moderate-size community dominated by members of the Church of Jesus Christ of Latter-Day Saints (LDS, or Mormons, are described in this chapter within the section on religious pluralism). Many Mormon families participate in their ward activities several nights every week, and socialize almost exclusively with other Mormon families. LDS beliefs do not permit smoking or the drinking of alcohol, coffee, or tea. In that Utah community, this religious group controls most major institutions and businesses. Religion itself is not and cannot lawfully be taught as part of the school curriculum, but the perspective of the dominant religious group in this community is reflected in school and curriculum practices (e.g., what is and is not lawfully taught in the schools). The vast majority of teachers and school administrators are LDS Church members. Their daily behaviors, their orientation toward life, morality, politics, and social issues reflect their religious beliefs. This in turn either directly or indirectly influences the topics they select for classroom discussions, and the treatment of the discussions.

Opportunities for Reflection

Many students leave during school hours to receive religious instruction at a Mormon seminary adjacent to the school. Many will leave home following high school or shortly after to serve on a church mission for two years. Most of the elected officials are members of the Mormon Church; therefore state and local laws affecting education reflect a Mormon influence. *Should students be allowed to leave public schools during the school day to attend off campus religious instruction?*

People differ greatly in their beliefs about the role that religious perspective should play in determining school curriculum and environment. Like all other institutions in the United States, schools have a historical background of rural, white, Protestant domination. Such influence has determined the holidays, usually Christian holidays such as Christmas, which are celebrated by most public schools. Moreover, the Protestant majority has determined the moral teachings that have been integrated into the public schools.

THE FIRST AMENDMENT AND THE SEPARATION OF CHURCH AND STATE

Although the First Amendment affirms the principles of separation of church and state, it is one of the most controversial parts of the Constitution because various individuals and groups tend to interpret it to meet their own needs and interests. For some people, religious emphasis is appropriate in the public schools as long as it is congruent with their own religious persuasion. These same people, however, may be quick to cite the constitutional safeguards for separation of church and state if other groups attempt the infusion of their religious dogmas. Equity and propriety are often in the eye of the beholder, and one's religious orientation may strongly influence one's perception of what constitutes objectivity, fairness, and legality.

Since the removal of prayer from the schools by a 1963 Supreme Court decision, parent groups have continued to fight to restore prayer in the schools through state and federal legislation. Parent groups have fought on religious grounds to prevent the teaching of sex education and evolution. Coming from different religious backgrounds, parents have fought verbally and physically over what books their children should read in literature courses and what curriculum should be used in social studies and science classes. Members of more liberal Protestant, Catholic, and Jewish denominations often argue that they want their children exposed to the perspectives of different religious and ethnic groups. Members of the more conservative, especially **fundamentalist,** groups argue that they do not want their children exposed to what they consider immoral perspectives and language inherent in such instructional materials. They object to what they consider **secular humanism** in the curriculum, which emphasizes respect for human beings and de-emphasizes or ignores God. Community resistance to cultural pluralism and multicultural education has, at times, been led by some individuals associated with conservative religious groups. Because cultural pluralism inevitably involves religious diversity, multicultural education is sometimes viewed as an impediment to efforts to maintain the status quo or to return to the religious values of the past.

Multicultural education is sometimes maligned as a bedfellow of the secular humanist movement, which emphasizes the dignity and worth of the human being rather than the belief in the supernatural (discussed in the section on censorship in this chapter). Multicultural education is erroneously accused of supporting movements that detract from basic moral values. Multicultural education, however, provides a basis for understanding and appreciating diversity and minimizes the problems inherent in people being different from one another.

Of all the cultural groups examined in this book, religion may be the most problematic for educators. In one school, the religious beliefs of students appear to have little influence on what is taught in a classroom; in fact, the teacher is expected to expose students to many different perspectives. In another school, the teacher may be attacked for asking students to read *The Catcher in the Rye.*

Educators themselves vary in their beliefs about the role of religious perspective in education. If one shares the same religion or religious perspectives as the community, there will probably be little conflict between one's own beliefs and the beliefs reflected in the school. If the educator is from a religious background that is different from that prevalent in the community or has a perspective about the role of religion that differs from that of the community, misunderstanding and conflicts may arise that prevent effective instruction. If an educator does not understand the role of religion in the lives of students, it may be difficult to develop appropriate instructional strategies. In some cases, it would be difficult to retain one's job.

On the following pages, we examine religion's impact on a student's life, some of the more prevalent religions in the United States, the degree to which individuals identify with a particular religious doctrine, and the educational implications of religion.

Religion as a Way of Life

Although the separation of church and state is an integral part of our heritage, the two usually support each other. In many churches, the American flag stands next to the church flag, and patriotism is an important part of religious loyalty. God has been mentioned in all presidential inaugural addresses except Washington's second address, and it is not uncommon for politicians and preachers to refer to the United States as the "promised land." The secular ideas of the American dream also pervade many religions in this country. In fact, many religions reflect the dominant values of our society.

Many Western religions emphasize individual control over life—an emphasis that prompts believers to blame the disadvantaged for their problems. Many religions are particularistic in that members believe that their own religion is uniquely true and legitimate and all others are false. Some religious groups accept the validity of various religions that have grown out of different historical experiences. The values and lifestyles of families are affected by their religious beliefs.

As seen in Table 6.2, 60% of Americans in 2004 regard their religious beliefs to be very important to them (Carroll, 2004). Two out of three adults indicate that religion provides all or most of the answers to today's problems (Gallup & Lindsay,

Table 6.2 The Importance of Religion to Americans

Very Important	60%
Fairly Important	24%
Not Very Important	15%
In last decade, high of 61% in 1998, low of 57% in 1998	
Very Important by Age	
65 and older	73%
50 to 64	65%
30 to 49	59%
18 to 29	48%
Very Important by Gender	
Men	51%
Women	69%
Very Important by Political Affiliation	
Republicans	66%
Democrats	63%
Independents	54%

Source: Adapted from Carroll, J. (March 2, 2004). American Public Opinion About Religion. *Gallup Tuesday Morning Briefing.*

1999). Although less than half of the population attends church weekly, most people identify with a religious perspective that is reflected in their daily living. Religion appears to influence patterns of sex roles, marriage, divorce, birthrates, child training, sexual activity, friendships, and political attitudes. It may affect one's dress, social activities, and dietary habits, including alcohol consumption and smoking.

If the religious group is tightly knit, a member may have little chance to interact on a personal level with anyone other than another member of the same religion, especially if attendance at a religious school is involved. Tight control over criteria for membership in the group and little contact with those who are not group members are often key factors in maintaining the integrity of religious sects. The Hutterites and, to a great extent, the Amish have been able to survive in this way. Mormons, a much larger group, were able to grow with little outside interference once they were established in Salt Lake City. Even in suburban areas, friendship patterns are largely based on religious preference.

Churches and their religious programs serve as a strong socialization mechanism in the transmission of values from one generation to another. Rituals, parables, and stories reinforce these values, and Sunday schools serve as primary agents for transmitting these values. Religious institutions are also responsible for reinterpreting social failure in spiritual terms, compensating for the lack of value realization, and functioning as an agent of social control by reward and punishment.

Religious behavior is learned as a normal part of the socialization pattern. The church or religious center is not only a place of worship but also a social center. Religion and religious differences are important in our study of this pluralistic nation because it is a way of life for many people. In many areas of the United States, going to church is a primary family function. Following church services, families may go out to restaurants or enjoy their main meal of the week in their home. This is particularly true in the South, where church attendance is highest.

Religiosity appears to be a function of culture. Age, gender, geographical background, and political affiliation appear to influence the religious nature of a person. As seen in Figure 6.1 and Table 6.3, in 2003, the Gallup Organization found that older Americans (50 plus) were more likely to be church members and attend religious services than their younger counterparts. Women attended more regularly than men. Those with higher incomes attended more regularly than those with

Figure 6.1

Church membership in the United States: national average = 65%.

Source: Adapted from Lyons, L. (2003, March 11). Age, Religiosity, and Rural America. *Gallup Tuesday Morning Briefing.*

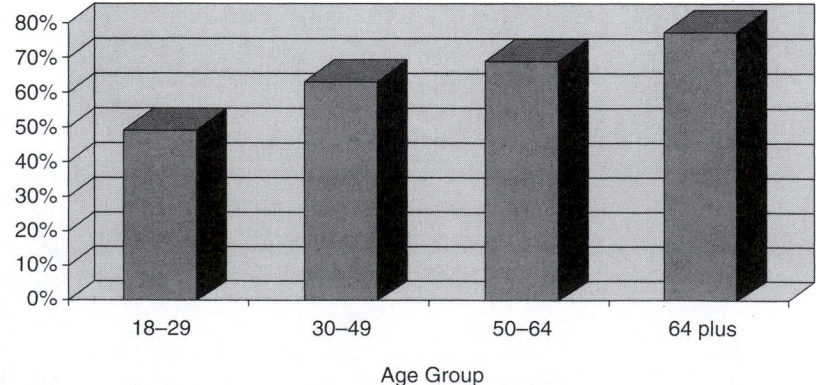

Age Group

Table 6.3 Church Attendance in the United States (within the past seven days)

Age Group *

National Average	43%
18–29	30%
30–49	40%
50 plus	46%

Gender *

Women	44%
Men	36%

Political Affiliation *

Republicans	49%
Democrats	40%
Independents	34%

Geographical Background *

Southerners	49%
Midwesterners	39%
Easterners	36%
Westerners	33%

Income *

$20,000 or less	37%
$75,000 or more	42%

Religious Group

Catholics	45%**
Protestants	48%
Jews	27%***

*Adapted from Carroll (2004, March 2). American Public Opinion About Religion. *Gallup Tuesday Morning Briefing.*

**Adapted from Gallup (2003, December 16). Catholics Trail Protestants in Church Attendance. *Gallup Tuesday Morning Briefing.*

***Adapted from Gallup and Lindsay (1999). *Surveying the Religious Landscape.*

lower incomes. Additionally, Republicans attend church more regularly than either Democrats or Independents. Southerners are more likely to report religious attendance more regularly than those in other parts of the United States. Gallup (2003) found that Protestants attended religious services more regularly than Catholics or Jews. However, Jewish attendance during their High Holy Days tends to increase. Catholic attendance exceeded that of Protestants at the end of the previous decade (Gallup & Lindsay, 1999), but dropped precipitously beginning in 2002, in the wake of the abuse problems. However, as seen in Table 6.3, Catholic attendance has since started to rebound.

Religious Pluralism in the United States

Four decades ago, few Americans would have envisioned their country led by a Catholic President or foreseen William H. Gray, an African American minister, being elected as the majority whip in the U.S. House of Representatives. In 1988, Pat Robertson, a popular televangelist, was a serious candidate for the Republican Party's presidential nomination and received strong support financially and otherwise. In recent years, Jesse Jackson, an African American minister, twice made bids for the Democratic Party's presidential nomination. The Reverend Al Sharpton, another African American, made a bid for the 2004 Democratic nomination.

Religion in the United States is dynamic, as it is constantly changing. A Korean minister and leader of the **Unification Church** (considered a cult and an adaptation of Christianity, which believes in a cosmic struggle between the forces of good and evil) has led thousands of young people, many who are white, into his church's membership. African Americans have left traditional African American Protestant churches and joined the ranks of the Black Muslims. Tens of thousands of Latinos have left the Roman Catholic Church for Pentecostal churches, and some college students have embraced Buddhism (Black Muslims and Buddhism are described later in this chapter).

Today, televangelism reaches the homes of millions of Americans, influences their lives and their voting patterns, and has helped elect or defeat politicians that will change the face of America for years to come.

Americans tend to identify not only with major groups, such as Protestants, Catholics, or Jews, but also with smaller groups or denominations within these major religious groups. For example, former President Jimmy Carter, a Southern Baptist, identifies himself as a "born again" Christian. Others may identify themselves as charismatic Catholics. It is important to note that within each major group is considerable heterogeneity.

Religious demographic data is often problematic. The U.S. Census Bureau does not gather information on religious membership or preferences. The data that is available is often self-reported by each religious group. The groups that do report do not always do so regularly. Of the U.S. population, 80% identify themselves as belonging to one of the six largest faiths (see Figure 6.2): Protestant, Catholic, Jewish, Islam, Eastern Orthodox, or Latter-Day Saints (Carroll, 2004). Until early in the twentieth century, however, Protestantism was by far the dominant religious force in the country. Most U.S. institutions continue to bear the mark of the white Protestants who established them. After the great immigrations from Southern and Eastern Europe, Catholic Ireland, and Asia, however, pluralism described the religious diversity of the nation. Protestants as a group are still in the majority, with 49% of the population; 24% of the population identify themselves as Catholic, 10% indicate no religious affiliation (Carroll, 2004), 2% are Muslim (Corduan, 1998), 2% are Jewish (Singer & Grossman, 2002), 2% are Latter-Day Saints or Mormon (*National Catholic Reporter,* 2004), and 1% are Orthodox. Less than 1% claim Buddhist or Hindu affiliation (Gallup & Lindsay, 1999).

While Islam, in recent years, has grown rapidly in the United States, and may by now have become the third largest religious group, much of the literature still lists

Figure 6.2

Religious preference among Americans 2003.

Source: Adapted from Carroll, J. (2004, March 2). American Public Opinion About Religion. *Gallup Tuesday Morning Briefing.*

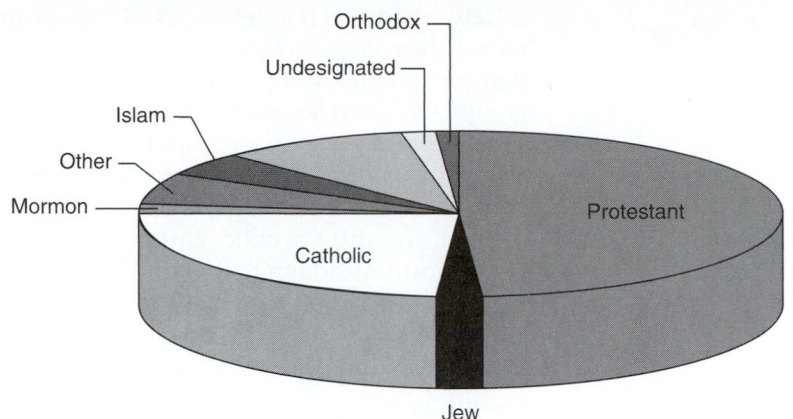

Judaism as one of the three major religious groups. This is likely due to the fact that Judaism has been a driving force in the country for such a long period of U.S. history, and because Jewish individuals have provided so much leadership in the cultural, economic, and political landscape of the country.

The fact that most Americans place themselves in one of the major faiths (Catholic, Protestant, Jewish, or Muslim) is misleading in understanding the great diversity of religious beliefs in this country. Judaism, Catholicism, and Protestantism share the same Old Testament heritage, but they do not share in all of the diverse beliefs and interpretations of the Bible. Islam has some of its roots in the Old Testament and views Jesus and others such as John the Baptist among its prophets.

Some denominational differences have their origin in ethnic differences. The English established the Anglican (Episcopalian) and Puritan (later Congregational) churches here; the Germans established some of the Lutheran, Anabaptist, and Evangelical churches; the Dutch, the Reformed churches; the Spanish, French, Italians, Poles, and others, the Roman Catholic churches; and the Ukrainians, Armenians, Greeks, and others, the Eastern Orthodox churches. Over time, many of these separate ethnic denominations have united or expanded their membership to include other ethnic groups.

Most denominations have remained in their traditional regional strongholds, with Catholics in the Northeast, liberal and moderate Protestants in the Northeast and Midwest, and conservative Protestants in the South. Some groups, however, have expanded their base considerably. Episcopalians, Presbyterians, and members of the United Church of Christ are no longer as concentrated in the Northeast as they once were; some numerical base shifts have been made into the Sun Belt, which is the region south of the 37th parallel, primarily the southern and southwestern regions. Conservative Protestants, such as the Southern Baptists, are growing in all regions, including the Northeast and the West. Mormons have extended their influence far beyond the borders of Utah, Idaho, and Nevada. Their presence is felt in every state, as well as in many other countries. The Jewish population tends to be located in metropolitan areas throughout the country, with large concentrations in the mid-Atlantic region.

Although religious pluralism has fostered the rapid accommodation of many American religious movements toward a mainstream of acceptability and respectability by society, groups such as Jehovah's Witnesses and Seventh-Day Adventists have maintained their independence. The smaller groups that maintain their distinctiveness have historically been victims of harassment by members of mainstream religious groups. Christian Scientists, Jehovah's Witnesses, Children of God, and the Unification Church are minority groups that have been subjected to such treatment.

Conflict among the four major faiths (Protestantism, Catholicism, Judaism, and Islam) has also been intense at different periods in history. Anti-Semitic, anti-Muslim, and anti-Catholic sentiments are still perpetuated in some households and institutions. Although religious pluralism in our past has often led to conflict, the hope of the future is that it will lead to a better understanding and respect for religious differences. In the following sections, we examine in greater detail the four major faiths and a few other faiths that the educator may find in various U.S. communities.

The purpose of this chapter is to assist you in understanding how religion can be an important part of the cultural makeup of an individual, rather than to provide a comparative review of all religions. We will briefly examine the larger religious groups and a few smaller groups. It is impossible to address every religious group or sect in a single chapter. Our decision to limit the groups or denominations discussed is not to suggest that they are not important. All religions and religious groups are important, especially to those who belong to them.

PROTESTANTISM

Many sects that separated from the Catholic Church after the **Reformation** (the religious movement that sought to bring reform to the Catholic Church in the 1500s) are now recognized as established Protestant denominations. The Western Europeans who immigrated into this country in large numbers brought with them their various forms of Protestantism. Still claiming 49% of the population (Carroll, 2004), Protestants in the United States are not as numerically dominant as they once were.

Similarities Among Diversity.   As one visits various Protestant services and listens to the different doctrines espoused by members, one may wonder how such a diverse conglomeration can be classified into one faith. No one doctrine or one church is representative of Protestantism. Traditionally, **Protestantism** has stressed individualism, activism, and pragmatism for its members. Other similarities have little to do with religious doctrine but are based instead on a shared American experience and its accompanying values.

To understand the differences that exist in Protestantism and that are often reflected in the classroom, the faith can be divided into two broad categories—liberal and conservative. Liberal Protestants attempt to rethink Christianity in forms that are meaningful for a world dominated by science and rapid change. They stress the right of individuals to determine for themselves what is true in religion. They believe in the authority of Christian experience and religious life, rather than in dogmatic church pronouncements of the Bible. They are likely to support and participate in social action programs because of their belief that what individuals become depends greatly on an environment over which they have little control. They may or may not believe in the virgin birth of Jesus, and may not believe the Bible to be inerrant, as do their conservative counterparts. Some may not accept the miracles cited in the Bible to be factual. The mainline, traditional denominations are included in this group. The United Church of Christ and Episcopalian churches are examples, although the degree of liberalism depends on the individual congregation. Methodists and Disciples of Christ represent more moderate denominations within this category.

Conservative Protestants generally believe that the Bible is inerrant, that the supernatural is distinct from the natural, salvation is essential, and that Jesus will return in bodily form during the Second Coming. They emphasize personal morality, rather than social ethics. The conservative branch can be divided further into the Fundamentalists, who are literalistic and typically inflexible biblically, and the Evangelicals, who are less so. Billy Graham's ministry, for example, would fit more appropriately into the second category.

Conservative churches include the Church of Christ, Southern Baptist, Assembly of God, other Pentecostal groups, and Church of the Nazarene. Some sects of the more liberal denominations have reacted to liberalism and established themselves as conservative groups, such as Wesleyan Methodist and Orthodox Presbyterian.

Although the Fundamentalist groups strictly and literally interpret the Bible, the different groups do not necessarily interpret it or practice their faith in the same way. The various sects and denominations are unrelenting in their belief that they are the one true church. Some groups, such as the Pentecostals, charismatic Catholics, and charismatic Episcopalians believe that their lives have been dramatically changed by infusion of the Holy Spirit in a spiritual baptism that results in the individual being able to speak in other tongues.

Some Fundamentalist groups, such as the Mormons and Jehovah's Witnesses, do not classify themselves as Protestants, although they are often classified as such by some nonmembers. These two groups and the Seventh-Day Adventists tend to stand out from some other religious groups because their religious practices thoroughly pervade their way of life. Members of both the Mormon and Jehovah's Witness groups proselytize as a part of their commitment to their beliefs. Jehovah's Witnesses distribute the publication *Watchtower* widely in communities, and Mormon missionaries often work door-to-door. Members are unrelenting in their beliefs and in their commitment to prepare themselves for future fulfillment in the establishment of a latter-day sainthood and a life in heaven (Mormons), in life after the Armageddon (Jehovah's Witnesses), or in the millennium after Christ's Second Coming (Adventists).

Effect on Education. Differences in beliefs among Protestants themselves have resulted in many court cases to determine what can or cannot be taught to or asked of students in the public schools. Fundamentalism versus liberalism came to the forefront in the 1925 Scopes trial, in which a biology teacher was convicted for teaching Darwin's theory of evolution. Although the teacher's conviction was later reversed, the argument continues today as Fundamentalists push for state legislation instituting the teaching of creationism. Jehovah's Witnesses have been taken to court because their children have refused to salute the flag. The Amish have fought in courts to remove their children from public schools after they have completed the eighth grade. Some religious groups continue to fight against the 1963 Supreme Court decision that disallowed prayer in school. Protestants have had a long history of involvement in both public and private educational programs.

Some of their influence in the public schools is discussed in the section on the Religious Right. Historically, Protestant involvement in private institutions can be found from the Eastern United States to Hawaii both in K–12 and higher education.

Ten Connecticut clergymen founded Yale, the nation's third oldest university, in 1701. Now considered as a nonsectarian institution, Yale still maintains some religious influence with its prestigious Yale Divinity School. Baylor University (Southern Baptist), Southern Methodist University (United Methodist), Goshen College (Mennonite), and Centre College (Presbyterian) are a few examples of the hundreds of Protestant institutions of higher education in the United States that have educated and influenced the lives of millions of American and international students.

Political Influence. The political leadership in the country often reflects the influence of various religious groups. Table 6.4 shows the trends in the U.S. Senate, while Table 6.5 shows the religious representation in the U.S. House of Representatives by denomination. In 2004, as in the past, Protestants led in Congress with 54.8%, as compared to the 49% of the general population who indicated they were Protestants that year. Roman Catholics followed with 26.8%, which is slightly higher than the Gallup findings of 24% for the general population. Jewish congressional members made up 5.74% of congressional seats, which is

Table 6.4 2004 Religious Affiliation of Members of the U.S. Senate

	Democrats	Republicans
Catholic	15	8
Jewish	9	2
Protestant*	1	3
Presbyterian	4	8
Baptist	1	6
Methodist	7	7
Episcopalian	2	6
Lutheran	3	1
Christian**	2	
Congregationalist	1	
United Church of Christ	2	
Church of Christ	1	
Mormon	1	4
Greek Orthodox	1	1
Unitarian	1	
None		2

*Did not indicate which Protestant denomination

**Did not indicate which Christian group or denomination

Source: Data extracted from Claflin, E. J. (2004, Spring). *Congressional Yellow Book.* New York: Leadership Directories, Inc.

Table 6.5 Religious Affiliation of Members of the U.S. House of Representatives in 2004

	Democrats	Republicans	Independent
Catholic	69	50	
Jewish	23	1	1
Protestant	9	13	
Presbyterian	13	22	
Baptist	33	30	
Methodist	20	30	
Episcopalian	11	22	
Lutheran	8	7	
Congregationalist		3	
Christian Scientist		3	
African Methodist Episcopal	2		
Assembly of God		2	
Church of Christ		2	
Seventh-Day Adventist	1	1	
Mormon	2	9	
Christian	6	12	
Unitarian	1	1	
Antioch Christian Church		1	
Christian Church	1		
Christian Reformed		1	
Disciples of Christ	1		
United Brethren in Christ		1	
None	13	5	

Source: Data extracted from Claflin, E. J. (2004, Spring). *Congressional Yellow Book.* New York: Leadership Directories, Inc.

considerably higher than the 2% of the general population. Mormon presence in Congress was 2.59%, slightly higher than their presence in the overall population (Carroll, 2004; Claflin, 2004).

Members of more liberal churches (e.g., Episcopalians, Presbyterians) and Jews may be disproportionately overrepresented because, historically, they have felt a responsibility for social issues. Another factor is probably related to the social class of members of these various denominations. Because seeking political office can be quite costly, religious groups whose members are typically upper middle class tend to be overrepresented in political offices. For example, a survey by the Princeton Religion Research Center (1995) revealed that the income and education level of Presbyterians (who have high political representation) was significantly higher than that of Baptists, Methodists, and Lutherans. Support for this is documented in a report indicating differential per capita contributions of various denominations. For example, the per capita contribution for Southern Baptists was $582; Methodists, $611; Episcopalians, $1,091.05; and Presbyterians, $1,183 (Lindner, 2004). While some could argue that each group may have its own culture toward giving, this logic does not explain the differences in these particular groups. Southern Baptists, who ranked lowest, place a very high emphasis on tithes (giving at least 10% of their income) and offerings in their churches.

Gallup Organization researchers found that white born-again Protestants are likely to be Republicans and supporters of Republican politicians such as George W. Bush. They viewed President Bush as a deeply religious individual whom they could trust. These individuals have tended to give Bush high approval ratings (Newport & Carroll, 2003). Gallup researchers also found a high level of support for the war in Iraq among the country's more religious citizens. The Religious Right (70%) in particular, strongly supported the war (Newport, 2003).

Protestantism maintains not only the major religious influence on society but also on political leadership. Because Protestants continue to represent such a large segment of the population, such influence is to be expected. Pluralism increasingly forces the sharing of power and resources, however, among diverse groups of people in society.

CATHOLICISM

Although the doctrine and pattern of worship within the Catholic Church are uniform, individual parishes continue to differ to some extent according to the race, ethnic background, and social class of their members. Individual dioceses also may differ with the more conservative or liberal (progressive) views of the presiding bishop. Unlike the Protestant faith, however, which includes denominational pluralism, the **Catholic** faith is one denomination under papal authority.

In 1930, the United States had 20 million Roman Catholics. With approximately 24% of the U.S. population identifying with the Roman Catholic Church (Carroll, 2004), in 2004, the National Council of Churches reported Catholic Church membership to be 66.4 million (*National Catholic Reporter,* 2004).

Today, the Catholic Church in the United States is the wealthiest national church in the Roman Catholic world and contributes approximately half of its income to the Church in Rome. The increasing number of American cardinals and American priests appointed to important posts in Rome attests to the growing importance of the Catholic Church in the United States (Corrigan & Hudson, 2004).

Similarities Among Diversity. The movement toward conservatism has not been limited to Protestants. Some Catholics have objected to changes in liturgy and other areas of modernization instituted by Vatican II. In many instances, conservative Catholics have joined forces with conservative Protestants on such issues as abortion and sexual morality. Some Catholics have even abandoned their traditional support of the Democratic Party to support conservative Republican candidates. On the other end of the continuum, some Catholics have protested the conservative position of their church regarding the limited participation of women in leadership roles and some support the pro-choice movement. In the 1960s, Roman Catholics, including some priests, engaged in political activism and joined radical elements in opposing the Vietnam War.

Membership in U.S. Catholic churches involves many different ethnic groups. Some parishes are predominantly Irish, while others are predominantly Italian, Polish, Mexican, Puerto Rican, and so on. A parish may choose to conduct services in the predominant language group of its parishioners or may have individual masses for different language groups. Cultural events of the ethnic groups may be incorporated into the daily activities of the particular parish (for example, Quinceniera for Latino females reaching the age of 15, as seen in the photo on p. 232).

Effect on Education.   In addition to its phenomenal numerical growth, the Roman Catholic Church in the United States has developed the largest private educational system in the world. In many communities, Catholic parochial schools often offer quality educational options to both Catholic and non-Catholic students at a relative lower cost than most other private institutions.

With thousands of elementary and secondary schools from Vermont to Hawaii and such internationally recognized universities as Notre Dame, Creighton, and Loyola, Roman Catholic schools and universities have educated millions of Americans and greatly influenced the culture of the country.

Political Influence.   In 1928, Alfred Smith, the Democratic nominee, was the first Roman Catholic to run for the office of President. There were two major issues in that campaign—prohibition and religion. Attacks were made against Smith, claiming that if elected he would make Catholicism the national religion. In the 1960 Presidential election, similar attacks were made against John F. Kennedy and his Catholic background. However, Kennedy was elected. In 2004, Roman Catholics were very well represented in Congress. There were 23 Catholic Senators and 119 Congressional delegates. Catholic representation was equal to or slightly higher than the numbers in the general U.S. population. Also in 2004, John Kerry, a Catholic, was the Democratic candidate for the office of President. During the 2004 campaign, however, some conservative Catholics voiced objections to Kerry because of his pro-choice position on abortions.

By becoming a uniquely American church, members of the Catholic Church have not rejected the belief that they belong to the one universal church. Instead, they have accepted the fact that U.S. society is intrinsically pluralistic and that their religion is one of the four major faiths that exists together with Protestantism, Judaism, and Islam.

JUDAISM

Judaism is one of the oldest religions known to humanity and provides the historical roots of both Catholicism and Protestantism. Primarily as a result of Jews from many countries amalgamating under the identification of Jewish American, Judaism has become one of the four major faiths in this country. While Judaism represents only about 2% of the population, the contributions of Jewish Americans to the fields of medicine, science, academia, business, economics, entertainment, and politics in the United States has been profound.

In the nineteenth century, large numbers of Jews emigrated from Germany and many began moving from Jewish enclaves along the East Coast to other parts of the

A thirteen-year-old Jewish female observes her Bat mitzvah by reading from the Torah in Hebrew. The event marks her entry into religious adulthood. In a Los Angeles area church a fifteen-year-old Mexican American female observes mass in celebrating her entry into womanhood.

country. By the 1920s, Eastern Europeans were immigrating in larger numbers, increasing the Jewish population to more than 2.5 million.

Current estimates of the U.S. Jewish population are approximately 6,155,000 (Singer & Grossman, 2002). Compared with the Protestant and Catholic populations, the Jewish population has declined, partly as a result of intermarriage and low birthrates. Yet, as a group, they remain a distinctive, identifiable religious minority whose social standing and influence are disproportionate to their numbers.

Later generations changed the entire picture of American Jewry and Judaism in America; ethnic and an American religious identity emerged. The lifestyle evolved into a microculture of the American middle class. Education, including higher education, played an important role in the Jewish community by advancing young people from the working class into white-collar and professional positions.

Similarities Among Diversity. Judaism's long and varied history makes it difficult to define a Jew. There is no Jewish race. Jewish identity is blended in a blending of historical, religious, and ethnic variables. Early Jewish settlers in the United States found it difficult, if not impossible, to practice Judaism in the traditional ways that they had experienced in Europe. Jewish religious practices and patterns were modified to meet the needs of the immigrants and in ways that made them characteristically American.

While some Jewish families have maintained their ties to Orthodox and Conservative Judaism, the majority of American Jews affiliated with Reformed Synagogues. Reformed Jews represent the more liberal end of the continuum. For example, according to Jewish law, one who is born to a Jewish mother, or who converts to Judaism is considered a Jew. Reformed Jews also accept children born to non-Jewish mothers as Jews. At the other end of the continuum from the reformed Jews are the conservative and the Orthodox Jews. They tend to hold firm to Jewish law, including diet and dress.

In addition to differences in religious adherence to traditional Jewish law, American Jews come from diverse backgrounds. There are two major groups of Jews who immigrated into the United States. The Ashkenazim came from Jewish communities of central and Eastern Europe. The Sephardim were Jews from Spain, Portugal, or other Mediterranean countries and the Middle East. Other groups of Jews include those from Jewish communities of Ethiopia and India. These different groups brought much of the culture of their countries of origin when they immigrated to the United States. Some of the Sephardic Jews from Spain settled in Hispanic communities in areas such as New Mexico. Many blended in with their Hispanic neighbors and became an integral part of their communities.

Although most Jews strongly identify with their religion, the Jewish practice of religion is relatively low regarding synagogue attendance and home religious observance. Nevertheless, the U.S. synagogue is the strongest agency in the Jewish community. Although they may not attend services as regularly as their Catholic and Protestant counterparts, a large percentage of Jews retain some affiliation with a synagogue. Some believe that Jewish identity does not require regular attendance at the synagogue. Attending religious services and studying Jewish texts hold little interest for much of the Jewish population. Attendance on High Holidays such as Rosh Hashanah, Yom Kippur, and Passover, however, is always high. The synagogue in the United States serves not only as a place of religious worship but also as a primary base for Jewish identity and survival.

Effect on Education.   Many of the Jewish temples or synagogues throughout the country operate private schools. Some schools operate only at the elementary grades, while others are more comprehensive. In some of the larger Jewish communities, particularly among the Orthodox groups, yeshivas, or private religious schools, have been established to provide high-quality instruction in both academics and in-depth religious studies. Jewish universities such as Yeshiva University in New York, and Brandeis University in Massachusetts have made significant contributions to higher education in the United States.

Political Influence.   While the Jewish population in the United States is relatively small (about 2%), the group's political influence is significant (see Tables 6.4 and 6.5). Jewish representation in political office is disproportionately high. There are a total of 11 U.S. Senators of Jewish background, and 25 members of the House of Representatives.

Anti-Semitism.   Jews in the United States and throughout the world have been the targets of prejudice and discrimination, sometimes leading to attempted annihilation of the population. During World War II, the Jewish Holocaust, which resulted in the deaths of millions of European Jews, was systematically conducted by one of the most economically and technically advanced nations of the period. The civilized world cannot ignore the fact that despite overwhelming evidence of what was being done by the Nazis, nothing was done to stop one of the greatest atrocities ever committed against humankind. Now in the twenty-first century, other attempts at genocide persist. It is the responsibility of educators to help their students understand that, even today, other holocausts have taken place in places such as Europe and Africa.

Anti-Semitism is rooted in Jewish-Gentile conflicts that have existed for centuries. In the United States, Jews and Catholics were also targets of the Ku Klux Klan especially in the 1920s and 1930s when anti-Semitic newspapers and radio commentators proliferated (Johnstone, 2001; Williams, 1990). Discrimination has occurred in both occupational and social life. In some instances, Jews have often been denied high-level corporate management positions and have been barred from membership in social clubs. The form and degree of anti-Semitism vary with world and national events; when non-Jews believe that events are the result of Jewish action, prejudices resurface in work and deed. Events in the Middle East that involve Israel often initiate these reactions. Examples of continued anti-Semitic hate crimes persist with the burning of synagogues and the attack on a Jewish day care center in Los Angeles in recent years. In June of 2004, two teenagers were found guilty of spray painting swastikas and "kill Jews" in New York.

ISLAM

Islam is one of the major religions of the world, with 1.3 billion or more adherents worldwide. Islam is also one of the fastest growing religions in the United States, with as many as 7 million followers (**http://www.islamfaq.org**) and 1,209 mosques located throughout the country (U.S. State Department, 2004). While many Ameri-

Educators will continue to see increasing numbers of religious minority group students in their classrooms reflecting the religious diversity of the United States.

cans think Islam is primarily a Middle Eastern religion, only 20% of the world's Muslims are Arabs. India and Indonesia have the largest Muslim populations with about 175 million each (**http://www.islamfaq.org**).

More than a hundred years ago, a group of immigrants from the Middle East settled in Cedar Falls, Iowa. They were among the first Muslims to settle in this country. The descendants of these immigrants have maintained the religion of their ancestors, built a new mosque, and have become an integral part of their community. As everyday citizens, businesspeople, and professionals, they dress, talk, and act like any other American. Only their religion distinguishes them from their Christian and Jewish neighbors.

Islamic Beliefs. As a religious term, *Islam* means to surrender to the will or law of God. Those who practice Islam are **Muslims.** Islam is both a belief system and a way of life for individuals and entire societies. Islam is based on the holy writings of the Qur'an, or Koran. Muslims believe that the Qur'an consists of the exact words that were revealed by God through the Angel Gabriel to the prophet Muhammad (A.D. 570–632). The Qur'an's basic theme is the relationship between God and His creatures. It provides guidelines for a society that is just with proper human conduct, and an economic system that is equitable. Muslims believe that Islam began with Adam and continued through the line of prophets including Abraham, Moses, Jesus, and Mohammad. The basic tenets of Islam include: (1) *Faith:* belief in one God and Mohammad as his last messenger. (2) *Prayer:* five times daily, facing Mecca. (3) *Charity:* contributing to the poor. (4) *Fasting:* without food or water from sunrise to sunset during Ramadan (9th month of the Islamic year). (5) *Pilgrimage:* a visit to Mecca once in a lifetime, performing the Hajj (Ellwood & McGraw, 2005).

The pilgrimage to Mecca is an obligation to those who are physically and financially able. The rites of the Hajj (pilgrimage) begin in the 12th month of the Islamic lunar year. They include circling the Ka'ba seven times and joining in prayer for God's forgiveness. Muslims believe that the Ka'ba is the place of worship that **Allah,** the Arabic word for God, commanded Abraham and Ishmael to build. Muslims worship the same God as Christians and Jews. Christian Arabs also refer to God as Allah (Ellwood & McGraw, 2005).

Among Westerners, **jihad** is one of the most misinterpreted concepts in Islam. It is often mistakenly translated as "holy war," evoking images of terrorists and Osama bin Laden. The correct meaning of jihad is "struggle in the path of God." It can mean a physical struggle in building or cleaning of a mosque, a struggle to avoid religious persecution, or even the struggle against human passions and instincts, which inhibit one from doing the work of God. It can also mean an armed struggle against forces of injustice. Muslim scholars teach that only defensive wars are truly jihad (Hopfe & Woodward, 2004).

The tragic destruction of the World Trade Center on September 11, 2001, the airliner crash in Pennsylvania, and the damage to the U.S. Pentagon resulted in the loss of thousands of lives and focused world attention on Muslim extremists. Since then, the United States has been in almost continuous conflict with Muslim extremists in Afghanistan and Iraq. Around the world, in countries such as Spain and the Philippines, hundreds of lives have been lost at the hands of Islamic militants. At times it is difficult to separate the actions that are politically motivated from those actually motivated by an individual's religion. Educators, however, should be mindful of the fact that there are extremists in almost every religious group, and the vast majority of Muslims in the United States and throughout the world are peace-loving individuals who abhor violence.

When acts of terrorism occur, such as the Oklahoma City bombing in 1995, Muslim Americans often are blamed and become the targets of hate crimes. As feared, local and national news media incorrectly speculated that Muslim terrorists perpetrated the Oklahoma City bombing. As educators, it is our responsibility to assist our students in understanding that their Muslim classmates and their families are no more responsible for these acts than were German Americans responsible for the Holocaust.

Similarities Among Diversity. Believers are of two major groups. Sunni Muslims, who comprise 85% of Islam, believe that the rightful leadership began with Abu Bakr and that the succession has passed to *caliphs,* or political leaders. Shi'i or Shi'ite Muslims are a smaller but highly visible group. Shi'ite Muslims believe that Muhammad intended the succession of leadership to pass through the bloodline of his cousin and son-in-law, 'Ali. Shi'ite Muslims have attracted considerable world attention in recent years because of their insistence of adherence to Islamic law by their countries' governments (Hopfe & Woodward, 2004; Oxtoby, 1996; Robinson, 1996).

 # CRITICAL INCIDENTS IN TEACHING

Who Is an American?

Nadar Hoseini is a third grader in a suburban community in northern Virginia. Nadar's parents emigrated from Iran in the mid-1970s and are now naturalized citizens. Nadar was born in Virginia, where his father is a chemist for a large manufacturer. During recess, Ms. Nash, Nadar's teacher, notices that Nadar is sitting alone and is visibly upset. After some probing into an apparent problem, she learns that Nadar's friends have shunned him. Michael, he tells Ms. Nash, told the group that his father says the World Trade Center was destroyed by Muslims who are all fanatics trying to blow up America and kill innocent Americans. "Your friend Nadar is one of them Muslims, and you had better not let me catch you playing with him again. We ought to ship all of them Muslims back where they came from!" Michael quotes his father.

Protesting, Nadar insists that he was born in the United States and that he and his family are American. The protest falls on deaf ears as Nadar's classmates join Michael in ostracizing him. Ms. Nash is determined to help Nadar's situation but at the moment is at a loss as to how she will approach the problem.

Questions for Discussion

1. *What should Ms. Nash say to Nadar?*
2. *Should Ms. Nash go directly to Michael and the other boys involved?*
3. *How can she change the perceptions of the boys without seeming to attack Michael's father?*
4. *What sensitivity activities can she conduct in the class?*

To answer these questions online, go to the Critical Incidents in Teaching module for this chapter of the Companion Website.

A group of Shi'ite Muslims, followers of the Ayatollah Kohmeni, overthrew Shah Reza Pahlavi of Iran and later gained international attention by seizing American hostages. Some of the religious/political Shi'ite leaders view Western culture as antithetical to Islam and have strongly resisted U.S. and other Western influences on their countries. This has often led to fierce political battles between the two groups and has occasionally resulted in acts of terrorism against Western countries. Saddam Hussein who led Iraq for many years was a Sunni Muslim. He and his followers were in continuous conflict with the Shi'ites in his country and at one time waged war with the Shi'ite government in Iran.

Black Muslims. While U.S. **Black Muslims** have primarily aligned themselves with the Sunni form of Islam, they form a unique identity of their own. Although a few black slaves may have been Muslims, the origins of the Black Muslims in the United States likely began with Timothy Drew or Noble Drew Ali (1886–1927), who taught that blacks were from Asia and, therefore, Moors or Muslims.

Elijah Poole (1875–1975), who became known as Elijah Muhammad, led the Nation of Islam into national visibility. In the early 1960s, Malcolm X (1925–1965) became the most articulate spokesperson for the Nation of Islam. Born Malcolm Little, he renounced his "slave" name *Little* and adopted *X,* which symbolized identity lost when his ancestors were forcibly taken from their homeland as slaves (Ellwood & McGraw, 2005; Fisher 2002).

Malcolm X and other Black Muslims sought to use the Nation of Islam to engage African Americans in economic nationalism and to instill in them a sense of pride and achievement. This was accomplished through the rejection of Christianity, which they taught to be a symbol of white oppression in America.

In 1964, following a rift with Elijah Muhammad, Malcolm X broke with the Nation of Islam and formed the Organization of Afro-American Unity (OAAU). In that same year, he made a pilgrimage to Mecca and embraced traditional Sunni Islam, which he believed offered a superior religious path based on inclusiveness, rather than divisiveness and antagonism (Lincoln, 1994). In 1965, Malcolm X was assassinated.

Wallace Deen Muhammad became the leader of the Nation of Islam after the death of his father, Elijah Muhammad, in 1975. Under his leadership, the Nation of Islam embraced traditional Sunni Islam and changed its name to the American Muslim Mission. "During the 1970s and 1980s, W. D. Muhammad, as he is known, slowly dispensed with the racist rhetoric of his sect's past and led his followers toward orthodox Koranic Islam" (Kosmin & Lachman, 1993, p. 136). As a result, the group often supports conservative causes such as the free market. Hard work, personal responsibility, and family values are expected of members (Fisher, 2002; Kosmin & Lachman, 1993).

The well-known leader of Black Muslims, Louis Farrakhan, led a splinter movement in the 1980s that resumed the use of the original name, Nation of Islam, and the black separatist position. He continues to receive considerable attention from the press and political leaders because of his sometimes inflammatory rhetoric as well as appeal to many African Americans who are not Muslims. This influence was demonstrated in his ability to mobilize an interfaith coalition that drew nearly 1 million African American men together for the One Million Man March in Washington, DC, in 1996. Members have become role models in many inner cities as they establish businesses. They often serve as visible neighborhood guardians against crime and drug abuse, and have assumed an important role in the rehabilitation of individuals released from prison (Corduan, 1998; Fisher, 2002; Johnstone, 2004; Kosmin & Lachman, 1993).

Effect on Education.   The vast majority of Muslim students in the United States and Canada attend public schools. However, about 15,000 students attend Islamic schools, which provide full-time educational programs "to help a child grow into an Islamic personality with the ideals and images which can help him and her achieve the best in this world and the best in the Hereafter" (SoundVision, 2004). Many of these schools are located in Islamic Centers throughout the country. In addition, another half million Muslim students attend weekend religious training in weekend Islamic schools (SoundVision, 2004).

BUDDHISM

Buddhism is one of the world's major religions with estimates ranging from a quarter of a billion to a third of a billion members worldwide. Immigration of Asians each year from countries such as China, Taiwan, Korea, Thailand, Japan, and Tibet brings thousands of additional Buddhists into the United States, changing further the religious landscape of the country. Estimates of more than 1 million Buddhists in the United States appears to be conservative given the fact that there are now approximately 12 million Asians in the country, with over half having immigrated from predominantly Buddhist countries.

Similarities Among Diversity.   With the Buddhists coming from so many regions of the world, there are invariably different forms of Buddhism practiced. Consequently there is tremendous diversity in both beliefs and in practice, just as there is diversity among the various Christian faiths we have discussed. Buddhist schools of thought or belief are united in a twofold orientation toward existence: a fundamental negative attitude toward life and a pessimistic approach to ordinary existence. Buddhists view existence itself as the problem with life. As long as there is existence, there is suffering. The second common orientation of all Buddhists is that Buddha provides a solution to the frustrations of life. Each school of Buddhism provides a pathway to overcome the meaninglessness of life. Buddha is the solution to life's dilemma (Corduan, 1998; Fisher, 2002).

Buddha was believed to be a prince of India, Siddhartha Gautama. On an outing, Siddhartha saw successively an old man on the verge of death, a diseased man, a funeral procession, and a holy monk. This experience led him to see his life of luxury leading him to an end of death and decay. With this, he left his wife and child, cut his hair, and sought spiritual enlightenment through austerity (Corduan, 1998; Hopfe & Woodward, 2004).

After 7 years as an ascetic, he decided to let his experience end in enlightenment or death. In spite of temptations by Mara, the god of desire, Siddhartha prevailed and finally found enlightenment as he sat under a fig tree known now as the "bodhi tree." He had now become a Buddha, an "awakened one." Buddha then set forth on a life of teaching (Corduan, 1998; Hopfe & Woodward, 2004).

The Fo Kuang Shan Hsi Lai Temple opened in Hacienda Heights, California, in 1988. This Los Angeles temple is the largest Buddhist temple in the Western Hemisphere.

Buddha's secret to enlightenment was neither through a life of luxury nor through self-deprivation, but through the middle way, away from the extremes. The key to salvation, he taught, was to let go of everything. Salvation and enlightenment occurs when one realizes his or her place of non-self in the world. Nonexistence is the reality and self-extinction is the reality. With enlightenment comes the state of nirvana, meaning "blown out" (Corduan, 1998; Hopfe & Woodward, 2004).

Teachings of Buddha.   Buddha taught four noble truths:

- To live is to suffer
- Suffering is caused by desire
- One can eliminate suffering by eliminating desire
- Desire is eliminated by an eightfold path

The eightfold path to eliminating desire consists of the following:

1. The right view (understanding the truths of existence)
2. The right intention (willing to achieve enlightenment)
3. The right speech
4. The right action
5. The right livelihood (being a monk)
6. The right effort
7. The right mindfulness (meditating properly)
8. The right concentration (Corduan, 1998)

To know that your student is from a Buddhist family may or may not tell you much about the family belief structure or religious practices. While one might expect belief in the four noble truths and practice of the eightfold path from a Buddhist priest or monk, the layperson may take bits and pieces of the religion into his or her everyday life. Chinese, Japanese, Korean, and Vietnamese individuals are often influenced by Confucian philosophy, which directs daily behaviors in much the same way that a religion can. Thus some individuals may be Buddhist with a strong philosophical overlay of Confucianism. It may be somewhat difficult to clearly separate the religious from the cultural and philosophical backgrounds of a Buddhist layperson from Taiwan, one from Tibet, and another from Japan.

HINDUISM

Hinduism is the major religion of India and the world's third largest religion after Christianity and Islam. There are approximately 762,000,000 adherents in the world, representing 13% of the world's population. The number of Hindus in the United States ranges from between 766,000 to 1,100,000. Generally regarded as the world's oldest organized religion, it differs from Christianity and other Western religions in that it does not have a single founder (Robinson, 2003a). Its roots date back to prehistoric times in India. Neither does it have a single system of morality or a central organization. Robinson (2003a) suggests that it consists of thousands of different religious groups that evolved out of India since 1500 B.C.E. Hinduism is credited with influencing the development of both Buddhism and Jainism.

As with most other religions, Hinduism has basic beliefs about divinities, life after death, and how followers should conduct their lives. Unlike Judaism, Christianity, and Islam, Hinduism does not limit itself to a single book or writing. Hinduism has several sacred writings, which contribute to the basic beliefs of Hinduism. The most important writings are known as the Vedas, the Puranas, the Ramayana, the Mahabharata, the Bhagavad-Gita, and the Manu Smriti. These sacred writings include prayers, hymns, philosophy, myths, epics, discussions of the meaning of nature and existence, and Hindu religious and social law. Part of the latter includes the basis of the caste system. The caste system was legally abolished in 1949, but its influence remains to this day. Each follower of Hinduism belonged to one of the communities, which were grouped into one of four social castes that included the following:

- Brahmins, the priests and academics
- Kshatriyas, the rulers and military
- Vishyas, the farmers, landlords, and merchants
- Sudras, the peasants, servants, and workers in nonpolluting jobs

The Dalit represented a fifth group, who were considered outcasts and not a part of one of the castes. They worked in what was considered polluting tasks (e.g., tanning hides) and are, therefore, untouchable by members of the other four castes. Even their shadow could not fall on one of the caste members. Although the caste system is now illegal in India, and has lost much of its influence in the cities, it remains a way of life in some of the rural areas. Consequently, some of the Dalit have left Hinduism and have converted to Buddhism and Christianity (Ellwood & McGraw, 2005; Robinson, 2003a).

There are many deities in Hinduism. However, there are three gods that are generally considered the most important. They include Brahma, the creator of the universe; Vishnu, its preserver; and Shiva, the destroyer.

Hinduism teaches that the soul never dies. When the body dies, the soul is reincarnated. The soul may be born into an animal or another human being. The law of karma states that every action taken by an individual influences how he or she will be reincarnated. Those who live a good life will be reincarnated into a higher state. Those who do evil will be reincarnated in lower forms such as a worm. Reincarnation continues until a person reaches spiritual perfection. The soul then enters a new level of existence referred to as moksha, from which it never returns (Ellwood & McGraw, 2002).

OTHER DENOMINATIONS AND RELIGIOUS GROUPS

In addition to the four major faiths in the United States, what other religions might an educator encounter in a community? They include Christian religions that do not fall into the discrete categories of Protestantism or Catholicism, Islam, Eastern religions, and religions based on current psychological thinking.

Latter-Day Saints. The Church of Jesus Christ of Latter-Day Saints (LDS or Mormon) is a rapidly growing group that is neither Catholic nor Protestant. In the early 1830s, Joseph Smith founded the LDS Church in western New York State. By his own account, Smith was instructed to translate a history of ancient inhabitants of North America written on tablets of gold, which had been stored in a nearby hillside. The translations were published in 1830 as the Book of Mormon, which together with the Old and New Testaments and some of Smith's later revelations became the sacred scripture of Mormonism.

Smith and his followers met strong opposition from established Protestant groups, and he and his followers were harassed and violently driven out of various communities. The Mormon practice of polygamy (the Church discontinued the practice of plural marriage in 1890) exacerbated their rejection by other groups, and in 1844, Smith and his brother were killed by a mob in Carthage, Illinois. With the death of Smith, Brigham Young became the new leader of the group and led them to Utah, now the religious center of the Mormons. The Mormons aggressively proselytize, and as a result have grown to a membership of 5.41 million in the United States (History of the Church, 2004; *National Catholic Reporter,* 2004).

Eastern Orthodoxy. The Eastern Orthodox Church is another Christian religion that does not fall into the two major groupings of Protestant or Roman Catholic. Eastern Orthodoxy probably claims about one fourth of all Christians worldwide. One reason that the Eastern Orthodox Church is less well known in this country may be that its members, from Syria, Greece; Armenia, Russia, and the Ukraine, only immigrated during the last century. Although they split with the Roman Catholic Church in 1054 over theological, practical, jurisdictional, cultural, and political differences, to many outsiders they appear very similar to the pre-Vatican II Catholic church.

The actual and reported memberships in Eastern Orthodox churches vary considerably. The churches themselves have in recent years reported membership of approximately 4,000,000. The Hartford Research Institute suggests that the actual number of adherents is approximately 1,200,000 (Hartford Research Institute, 2002). The Institute suggests that the discrepancy is due to the common practice of equating the number of members to the number of members of the corresponding ethnic groups. This practice does not take into consideration the second- and third-generation descendants of the original immigrant church members who are not currently involved with the respective churches.

Christian Science and Unitarian Universalists. At least two other religions have a Christian heritage but seem to fall through the cracks of discrete categorization because of their precepts—the Christian Scientists and Unitarian Universalists. The Christian Scientists are one of these groups, with probably fewer than a half million members. Like some Fundamentalist Protestant groups and others described in this section, their beliefs are so different from conventional religious beliefs that they attract public attention. They exist "to dispel illusion and bring people into harmony with mind, with God as All—away from what others call disease, sin, evil, matter, and death" (Marty, 1975, p. 205). Although they do not proselytize, they maintain reading rooms in business and shopping centers of many communities. Their newspaper, *Christian Science Monitor,* is a highly respected general newspaper (Corrigan & Hudson, 2004).

The second group that defies categorization is the Unitarian Universalists—a church that connotes liberalism to most people. Their membership has included several U.S. presidents (William Howard Taft, Thomas Jefferson, John Adams, and John Quincy Adams) and several New England writers (Henry Wadsworth Longfellow, James Russell Lowell, and William Cullen Bryant), helping make the church an influence beyond that expected of a relatively small group. Unitarians are often found in suburbs, small towns, and college communities; many members could be described as political liberals. Although many members have the highest respect for Jesus Christ, the church is "most open to the wisdom of non-Christian religions and may draw many of its readings from scriptures of Buddhism, Hinduism and religious philosophies" (Marty, 1975, p. 217). As an expression of this openness, Unitarianism houses both Christian and non-Christian wings. The denomination follows no imposing standards of dogma or membership. Thus, their worship services appear extremely simple and are often experimental (Corrigan & Hudson, 2004; Marty, 1975).

Native American Religions. Native Indian religions are among the most difficult to describe or characterize, as there are 314 federally recognized tribes or groups and each is likely to have its own distinctive views on religion. Corduan (1998) estimates that there are only about 47,000 practitioners of Native American religion. Many of these individuals are likely to live on reservations and some of the children attend Bureau of Indian Affairs schools. There are a few general characteristics that are universal or tend to transcend across tribal boundaries. Traditional Native American religions recognize three levels of spiritual beings—a supreme god, nature spirits, and ancestor spirits. Superior spirits with god-like characteristics also factor into the religious equation. Tribes differ in their emphasis of the different spirits. *Wakan* or *orenda* apply to the spiritual power found in all entities. They are found in grass, rocks, animals, and spiritual beings. Each plant, rock, or even body of water may be sacred. Some may even inform a deer of its impending fate before killing it in a hunt in order to maintain harmony with the natural world (Corduan, 1998).

Shamans are men and women who heal through their contact with spirits. Individuals become shamans through supernatural calling. Frequently this happens when one vows to become a shaman if they are healed from an illness (Corduan, 1998). Among some tribes, much importance is placed on receiving and implementing visions. Visions are attained in different ways. Sometimes they may come after a tranquil moment or after great stress. Fasting, self-imposed exposure to climatic extremes, or injury may induce a vision. Individuals from some tribes may experience a vision where an animal enters the body. A person or a group of individuals may come to an individual in order to deliver a message. The recipient of a vision can anticipate success because of it (Corduan, 1998).

Jainism. Jainism evolved out of India in the sixth century B.C.E. Vardhamana Jnatiputra (aka Nataputta Mahariva) was the founder of this religion and a contemporary of Buddha. Both Jainism and Buddhism grew out of Hindu traditions. Jains reject karma and rebirth, observing the "three jewels" of right faith, right knowledge, and right conduct. They emphasize peacefulness and moderation, and refuse to injure animals. Their philosophy of nonviolence had a profound influence on Gandhi. There are an estimated 4,000 Jains in North America (Corduan, 1998; Ellwood & McGraw, 2005).

Sikhism. Sikhism was founded by Guru Nanak during the fifteenth or sixteenth century B.C.E. in India. Nanak, who lived in India, was influenced by Kahir, a Muslim. He drew from the elements of Hinduism and Islam, and stressed a universal single God. Union with God, he said, is accomplished through meditation and surrender to divine will. He believed in reincarnation, karma, and the destruction and rebuilding of the universe, but he rejected the Hindu belief in the caste system. Devoted to divine incarnations, priesthood, and idol worship, Nanak was the first of 10 gurus or teachers. Male Sikhs are initiated into a religious brotherhood called the Khalsa, vowing to never cut their hair or beard, to wear special pants, an iron bangle, a steel dagger, and a comb. There are an estimated 490,000 Sikhs in North America (Corduan, 1998; Ellwood & McGraw, 2005).

Baha'ism. Baha'ism was founded in Persia (Iran) in the late nineteenth century by Mirzu Hussein Ali Nuri (aka Baha'ullah, glory to God in Arabic). Baha'ullah claimed to be the divine manifestation of God and the last of a line of divine figures including **Zoroaster,** Buddha, Christ, and Muhammad. His son Abd al-Baha spread his father's teaching to the West emphasizing the principles of equality of sexes, races, and religious adherence. Bahai believers advocate for peace, justice, racial unity, economic development, and education. There are an estimated 300,000 or more members in the United States (Corduan, 1998; Ellwood & McGraw, 2005).

New Age Spirituality. The New Age movement began around the early 1980s. New Age has roots in nineteenth-century spiritualism and in the counterculture movement of the 1960s, rejecting materialism and favoring spiritual experience to organized religion. The movement emphasizes, among many of its followers, reincarnation, biofeedback, shamanism, the occult, psychic healing, and extraterrestrial life. It is a movement that is difficult to define as evidenced by the multitude of the movement's publications on a wide range of topics, viewpoints, and paraphernalia, from crystals to tarot. Much of the emphasis of the various groups is on the paranormal or parapsychology. It involves such experiences as meditation, visualization, dream interpretation, self-improvement, extrasensory perception, telepathy, clairvoyance, divination, precognition, out-of-body experiences, channeling spirit guides, angels, regression analysis of past lives, and so forth. It has influences from Eastern religions such as Buddhism, Sufism, Taoism, and Hinduism (Brown, 2000; Chryssides, 1999).

The term **New Age** refers to the 2000 zodiacal period Age of Aquarius. Since the Age of Aquarius is the successor to the Age of Pisces represented by the 2,000-year period of Christianity, some New Agers believe Christianity to be a thing of the past. New Agers tend to reject highly structured institutionalized religion, such as the organized Christian religious authority of the Roman Catholic Church. There is no formal institutional structure for the New Age movement, nor is there any agreed upon creed. There is no authoritative hierarchy, and it is unclear precisely what the New Age groups are and what they are not. They are treated with suspicion by some evangelical Christians who see them as a threat to Christianity with the claim of being post-Christian (Brown, 2000; Chryssides, 1999).

Some New Agers place a lot of emphasis on healing, which often takes unconventional routes such as homeopathic and herbal remedies. Spiritual healing is often emphasized and the practice of *Reiki,* which is a ritualistic laying on of hands with a Japanese origin, is widely practiced by some groups (Chryssides, 1999).

CULTS

The term *cult* evokes a wide variety of reactions from positive to contempt on the part of members of mainline religious groups. Ellwood and McGraw (2005) define cults as "Minority religions characteristically centered on a charismatic leader, who requires strict adherence to beliefs and practices of the group. Generally, the cult contains teachings and practices from several sources and often requires adherents to sever ties with people who are not a part of the cult" (p. 494). Johnstone (2004) further suggests that cults tend to be transitory and short lived. When the cult's charismatic leader dies, leaves, or is discredited, the cult usually disbands or disappears, as in the case of People's Church and its leader, Jim Jones. At times the cult grows, develops a structure, and develops a leadership succession. The cult may then develop into a denominational status. In this sense, during its early years, Christianity might have been characterized as a cult. Likewise, the Mormon Church could have been considered a cult in its early years, prior to becoming a sizable denomination with over 10 million members worldwide.

Young people in many communities practice religions based on an Eastern religious tradition. This grouping includes the Hare Krishna, the Divine Light Mission, and the Unification Church. Members of some of these groups are very visible to the public. The Hare Krishna can sometimes be seen dancing with tambourines on sidewalks in larger cities.

These various religions are practiced by a small minority of the population, but their presence in a community is often exaggerated beyond that warranted by their numbers. This notoriety often stems from the fact that their doctrine and practices are viewed as heretical by members of the major faiths, especially fundamentalist Christians. In addition, members of the majority faiths, especially parents, fear the attraction of some of these groups, some of which are considered cults, because they allegedly practice some degree of mind control.

As mentioned above, the term *cult* will generally evoke negative reactions that may range from fear, to contempt, to disgust on the part of many individuals. The term may kindle thoughts of brainwashing or that which is most feared by families—suicide. During the past 20 or so years, there have been a number of highly publicized mass suicides among the so-called "Suicide Cults." Among those most publicized involving Americans were the People's Temple, the Branch Davidians, and the Heaven's Gate groups.

Jim Jones was the charismatic leader of the People's Temple based in California. Jones moved the majority of his membership to his complex in Jonestown, Guyana. U.S. Congressman Leo Ryan arrived in November 1978 to investigate alleged abuses and individuals held against their will. Sixteen of Jones's followers chose to leave with Ryan. At the airfield, Ryan and four others including three members of the press were shot to death by People's Temple security guards. At that point, 919 individuals, including Jones, died through mass suicide or murder with poison, lethal injections, or gunshot wounds (Chryssides, 1999; Johnstone, 2004; Robinson, 2003b).

The Branch Davidians and their leader, David Koresh, evolved from fundamentalist Seventh-Day Adventist roots. Koresh and his Davidians settled in Waco, Texas, where he taught that all of the Davidian women belonged to him and only he was permitted to have children. Authorities were alerted to allegations of child abuse and statutory rape, as well as the storage of illegal weapons. In 1993, four Federal agents were killed while attempting to serve a search warrant and, after days in a standoff, 93 Davidians including children died in a fire. The cause of the fire is still debated to this day. The federal government stands firm in their claim that Koresh and his followers started the fire, while others believe that the government agents were responsible (Chryssides, 1999; Johnstone, 2004).

In spring 1997, 39 bodies of Heaven's Gate members were found in a suburb of San Diego, California, resulting from mass suicide. Led by Marshall Applewhite in a blend of Christianity and UFOlogy, members were taught that a spacecraft trailed the Hale-Bopp Comet. This spacecraft would take Heaven's Gate members beyond the human level, on to the next evolutionary level. However, they had to leave their earthly bodies behind, requiring their suicide (Brown, 2000; Chryssides, 1999).

The three suicide groups described above contained some components of Christianity. While these groups had substantial differences, there are two common elements that are found in all of the groups. All were isolated from the rest of the community, operating on their own, remote, and separated from others. All of these groups tended to believe in the impending end of the world or humanity. The belief structure of groups of this nature tends to tie the cataclysmic end of the world to the end of the millennium (Corduan, 1998).

Interaction of Religion with Gender, Homosexuality, and Race

RELIGION AND GENDER

Opportunities for Reflection

In many of the more conservative religious bodies, the role of women is clearly defined and limited. There are no female priests in the Roman Catholic Church, no women can attain the priesthood in the Mormon Church, and very few fundamentalist churches or denominations have or are willing to ordain women ministers. The same can be said about many other religious groups. At the 2000 annual convention of the Southern Baptist Convention, the 16,000 delegates voted on an explicit ban on women pastors. This action followed an earlier action by the Baptists to support the submission of women to their husbands. *Church groups represent private religious bodies. No one is forced to join or believe and share in the church's doctrines. Is it anyone's business or concern other than their members what limits they place on women in their church?*

Although Gomes (1996) indicates that Lydia, Phoebe, and Priscilla were women mentioned in the New Testament as having prominent roles in the formative days of early Christianity, other biblical passages are used to delimit the participation of women in leadership roles in religious activity. In supporting the ban or limitations of female leadership and wifely submission, these groups cite the fact that Jesus did not call on women to serve as his disciples. Biblical verses (e.g., I Corinthians 14:34–35) admonish women to submit themselves to their husbands and indicate that the husband is the head of the wife.

Van Leeuwen (1990) suggests that some biblical interpreters believe that God gave men, through Adam (Genesis 1:26–27), dominion over Eve and, therefore, over women. At the same time, some biblical scholars argue that such an interpretation is incorrect and that both Adam and Eve (man and woman) were given dominion over every other living thing. Groothuis (1997) indicates that in addition to the examples provided by Gomes (1996), there are numerous other biblical examples of women who were leaders or prophets (e.g., Deborah, Judges 4–5). Groothuis indicates that Deborah was a prime example of a woman called to lead by God and questions how her female leadership could be considered a violation of moral principles if ordained by God. Traditionalists counter that Deborah was an extreme exception to the long-standing precedent of male authority. Other traditionalists counter that Deborah's position of leadership was less authoritative than that of male prophets. The participation of women in leadership roles in both Protestantism and Judaism is a function of where the particular denomination is on the liberal to conservative continuum. Liberal Protestants (e.g., Episcopalians) ordain women as priests. Likewise the Reformed Jewish movement has ordained women as rabbis for more than 30 years. The Conservative Jewish seminaries are also training women to be rabbis, but the Orthodox Jewish movement does not.

Limitations on participation of females in religious activities are by no means the sole province of Judeo-Christian groups. Islam and other religions either limit the participation of females or typically rest leadership in the hands of men. Islam views women as equal but different from men. They do not worship alongside the men in their mosques, but in separate areas. They are expected to observe all pillars of Islam including the five daily prayers and fasts during Ramadan. They are, however, exempted from five daily prayers and fasts of Ramadan during their menses and in pregnancy. Women in some Middle Eastern countries have severe limitations placed on them. These limitations are more a function of the culture of the country or region than the mandates of Islam.

Due to the diversity of the backgrounds of its adherents as well as the society in which they live, many Islamic women in the United States function differently than Islamic women in some other parts of the world. This includes the extent to which they are allowed to work outside the home, assume active roles in Islamic centers and community life, and interact with the non-Muslim community (Peach, 2002).

Not only is religion used to define the parameters of religious participation of males and females, but religion may also be used to prescribe male and female roles outside the religious context. Such prescriptions may be done either directly or indirectly. In religious groups in which women are given a less prominent status, this may carry over into general family life and other aspects of society as a natural course. In other instances, the pronouncements may be more direct. Religious writings with great importance, such as the Bible, are continuously interpreted, studied, and analyzed. In the United States, the Bible (or at least the Old Testament) is viewed as very sacred by most of its citizens who claim church membership. Consequently, the Bible and other religious writings, such as the Koran, have a profound influence on many Americans.

The importance of religion in determining male and female roles is also discussed in Chapter 4.

Pause to Reflect 6.1

Historically, and to this day, many religions have treated men and women differently. Today, there are still many religions that do not allow women to assume their highest religious and spiritual leadership positions. This often carries into society in general. It is the right of every American to believe what they choose in terms of gender roles in the home, in society, and in the place of worship.

- *If you teach in a public school setting what is your responsibility to your male and female students?*
- *Are there any differences in the way you can or should treat gender bias in private, church related schools?*
- *What should you do if a student makes inappropriate gender biased statements in your class?*

To answer these questions online, go to the Pause to Reflect module for this chapter of the Companion Website.

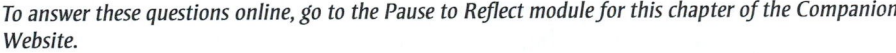

RELIGION AND HOMOSEXUALITY

Homosexuality is one of the most controversial issues in religious institutions today. Attacks on homosexuality in the religious context are often justified through biblical interpretation or other religious writings. Some argue that the textual interpretation and, in some cases, translation of biblical passages regarding homosexuality are not clear and may be subject to misinterpretation and misguided beliefs. Others argue that the Bible is clear on the issue of homosexuality, as in the book of Genesis where God destroyed Sodom and Gomorrah because of the sinful behaviors, including homosexuality, of the inhabitants. The debate is serious, as are the consequences. Conservative Christians and other conservative religious groups tend to view homosexuality as a matter of choice, a sin, and an abomination. More liberal religious groups tend to believe that the only choice is in whether or not the individual engages in homosexual behavior. They contend that the individual is born homosexual or predisposed to that life.

Because some conservative Christians, as well as members of other religious bodies, view homosexuality as a sin, they believe the AIDS epidemic is God's retribution for the gay life. Other Christian groups have willingly accepted gays and lesbians into their congregations, and some have even been ordained into leadership positions, often creating controversy within the respective churches or denominations.

Views toward homosexuality vary considerably in other religious groups. There are often intergroup as well as intragroup differences. The Roman Catholic position on homosexuality is congruent with that of many other conservative groups. These groups view homosexuality as *"objectively disordered"* and view homosexual practices as very serious *"sins gravely contrary to chastity"* (Religious Tolerance, 2004).

The Catholic Church, however, has had to address the issues related to homosexuality among its own clergy. The unfortunate clergy abuse scandals, which have surfaced in recent years, have caused great spiritual and economic concerns in various dioceses. Even though the abuses have been linked to a minority of priests, the scandal has caused immense problems for the Church.

The views toward homosexuality among Jewish groups tend to mirror those of Christians and are typically a function of where the group lies on the continuum of liberal to conservative. Reformed Judaism tends to view homosexuality as the normal behavior of a minority of adults. Orthodox Judaism views it as abnormal and condemned by God (Religious Tolerance, 2004).

Homosexuality in Islam is viewed as lewd and sinful. There are two primary references to homosexuality in the Qur'an (Qur'an 7:80–81 and Qur'an 26:165). Both address homosexuality negatively. In Southern and Eastern Asian Islamic countries, no physical punishment for homosexuality is considered warranted. However, Arabic Islamic countries tend to deal with it more harshly, especially in Iran and in Afghanistan when under the rule of the Taliban (Religious Tolerance, 2004).

It is important to understand that clergy and other church and religious authorities have considerable influence on the people they lead. They, the writers and theologians who influence others, often get their inspiration or their justification for their positions through religious scriptures. These writings are then interpreted for laypersons and may be used to shape their perceptions of self and others. Children growing up in a religious environment may learn to condemn or to practice tolerance. They may learn that homosexuality is an abomination, or they may learn that homosexuality is an innate and natural sexual orientation for some. Hopefully they will learn to respect all individuals as valued members of society. For more information, visit the Religious Tolerance website (**http://www.religioustolerance.org**), which provides the views toward homosexuality of the various Christian groups or denominations, Jewish groups, and other religious groups. *As a teacher, you know that it is your obligation to be supportive of all students, but how would you feel if a gay couple came to a school prom and danced with each other?*

Opportunities for Reflection

↪ *For a more in-depth discussion of sexual orientation and homosexuality, see Chapter 4.*

Pause to Reflect 6.2

Homosexuality is one of the most controversial issues in today's society. Most individuals have an opinion about it, and very often it is a strong opinion. Conservative religious groups do tend to view homosexuality as a matter of choice and as extremely deviant behavior. Others view homosexuality as an orientation that one is born into, and normal behavior for a small segment of the population. Neither side is likely to be able to convince the other of the validity of their beliefs. Understand that there is a disproportionate number of children and youth who commit suicide because of their sexual orientation and their rejection by their families, peers, and even educators.

 A discussion on adolescent suicide is presented in Chapter 8.

- *How would you feel if you were in a situation in which your parents have rejected you because of your sexual orientation (whatever it may be, even heterosexual)?*

- *How would you feel if in your school, your peers and some of your teachers rejected you because of your sexual orientation?*

- *What if you were ridiculed, called names, and physically bullied?*

- *How would you feel as a teacher if you had done nothing to help provide a safe and accepting environment in the school for a gay student who was ridiculed and bullied?*

- *What if you heard on the news on the way to school that this student committed suicide?*

To answer these questions online, go to the Pause to Reflect module for this chapter of the Companion Website.

CW

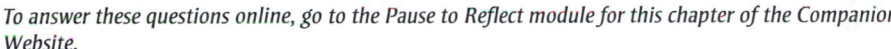

RELIGION AND RACE

As with gender issues, religion has had a profound impact on race and ethnic diversity issues. Gomes (1996) notes that Christians seek to establish the kingdom of God on the earth. In doing so, they seek guidance from the Bible on how to conduct themselves in society. When individuals misinterpret biblical scriptures or interpret them to justify aberrant behavior, the consequences can be severe. Gomes points out that at their 1995 meeting, the Southern Baptist Convention, which is the country's largest Protestant denomination, in an unprecedented act of contrition apologized for the role it had played in the justification of slavery and in the maintenance of a culture of racism in the United States.

Slavery and Racism. Historically, many religious groups had found justification for the practice of slavery in the Bible. The Bible does not condemn slavery, and its practice can be found throughout both the Old and New Testaments. Therefore, proponents of slavery believed that this institution was built on a solid biblical foundation.

Gomes (1996) suggests that the Catholic king of Spain and his ministers viewed it as their divine right and obligation to enslave and Christianize or slaughter the natives of Latin America. Both Cortés and Pizarro operated under papal and governmental authority as they enslaved and killed thousands of natives and justified their behavior by biblical texts.

Anti-Semitism can also find many of its historical roots in the Bible and other religious works. Gomes (1996) further suggests that Bach's *Passion of St. John,* though musically beautiful and inspiring, is filled with strong anti-Semitic German lyrics.

Biblical passages are often used to justify anti-Semitic behaviors (e.g., Matthew 27: 25–26, Romans 3:1). It is ironic that those who justify their anti-Semitic behaviors through religious doctrines and sacred writings may have failed to recognize that Jesus and his earliest followers were themselves Jews.

Important Role of Black Religious Groups.   Historically, African Americans often organized their own religious institutions due to racism, which either prohibited or limited their membership, participation, or attendance. Black churches and religious institutions have served their people in different ways. Some provide food, shelter, and occasional employment opportunities. Others, such as the Black Muslims, have provided a sense of Black Nationalism, pride, and a self-help philosophy. They have encouraged education and black entrepreneurship. Other black religious leaders have solicited help from philanthropy from the white community (Johnstone, 2004).

Civil Rights Movement and Black Churches.   The modern civil rights movement was centered in Southern African American churches. Many of the civil rights leaders were or are ministers or church leaders (e.g., Martin Luther King, Jr., Ralph Abernathy, Andrew Young, and Jesse Jackson). From their pulpits, these religious leaders were able to direct boycotts and organize civil disobedience and nonviolent confrontations.

In earlier times, spirituals provided comfort, hope, or a promise of a better life after death. Today, many of these spirituals are still sung in the churches, but the people who sing them and the people who listen to them seek a more immediate response to the demands for equity. Clearly, African American churches deserve much credit for bringing about many of the civil rights gained in the last three or four decades. Alienated and disillusioned by mainstream politics, few African Americans registered to vote in the past. Recent data suggest that well over 90% of African American clergy nationwide advocate church involvement in social and political issues. In recent years, black churches have been extremely successful in registering well over a million voters and in becoming an important voice in the electoral process (Lincoln & Mamiya, 1990).

Disenchantment Among Younger Generations.   Johnstone (2004) suggests that some young blacks have become increasingly disenchanted with their black churches. They have turned to secular organizations, which deal more directly with their life situations and with the social problems they face. Johnstone emphasizes that this situation does not mean the demise of the black church. While some will remain because of habit, others would be unwilling to give up the important associations and relationships available to them in their respective churches. The historical nature of the black church as the center of the black community life, makes it unlikely that the masses will abandon it.

In some religious groups, African Americans were permitted membership but prohibited from attaining the higher positions of church leadership. These prohibitions were justified through biblical interpretations or through divine revelations received by church leaders. Although nearly all such racial limitations on membership and church leadership have been removed in recent years, the effects of these religious prohibitions remain to be seen. Many individuals who read or listened to leaders justifying segregation or bans against leadership positions cannot readily dismiss some of the attitudes developed through years of prolonged exposure to negative points of view.

Changing Attitudes.   Like the gender issues that have become a center of religious debate, racial issues have been debated for decades. As the courts and society as a whole have turned their backs on segregation and racially limiting practices, so too have most religious bodies taken an official position of openness. Although the official position and the actual positions may differ somewhat, at least in churches that express brotherly love the two may be moving to a higher level of congruence.

It is important to note that society in general often reflects the positions of religious institutions. We are still experiencing the lingering effects of the proslavery and prosegregationist view of religious groups. Women who are not permitted leadership roles in their churches find the same attitudes in other areas of society where few are encouraged to seek leadership roles in school, work, or politics. The influence of religious beliefs on the everyday behavior of individuals can be considerable. Religion has often inspired goodness and charity. Unfortunately, in some instances, some people have used it to justify inflicting pain and suffering on others.

Individual Religious Identity

Most Americans are born into the religion of their parents, later joining that same body. Within the context of the religious freedom espoused in the United States, however, individuals are always free to change their religion or to choose no religion. The greatest pressure to retain membership in the religious group in which one was born usually comes from the family and from other members of that same religious group. Often, it is more difficult for individuals to break away from their religious origins than to make breaks from any of the other cultural groups of which they are members.

See Chapter 3 for further details on the interaction of race with other microcultures.

Although a person's ethnicity, class, or gender may have a considerable influence on behavior or values, religion may well be the primary microculture with which many individuals identify. When ethnic identity is very important to an individual, it is often combined with a religious identification such as Irish Catholic, Russian Jew, or Norwegian Lutheran. Understanding the individual's relationship to both ethnic and religious microcultures is important in understanding the individual.

The region of the United States in which one lives also affects the strength of identification with a specific religious group. For example, in parts of Alabama, many people will have the same or similar views; religious diversity may be limited. In many areas of the country, any deviation from the common religious beliefs and practices is considered heretical, making it very difficult for the nonadherent to be accepted by most members of the community. In other areas, the traditionally religious individual may not be accepted as a part of a community that is religiously liberal. Educators, as well as students, are usually expected to believe and behave according to the mores of the community—mores that are often determined by the prevailing religious doctrine and the degree of religious diversity.

Most communities have some degree of religious diversity, although the degree of difference may vary greatly, depending on the community. Often, students whose beliefs are different from those of the majority in the community are ostracized in school and social settings. For instance, Jews, atheists, Jehovah's Witnesses, and Pentecostals are among those groups whose members are sometimes shunned and suffer discrimination for their beliefs. Educators must be careful that their own religious beliefs and memberships do not interfere with their ability to provide equal educational opportunity to all students, regardless of their religious identification.

INFLUENCE OF THE RELIGIOUS RIGHT

Court cases involving religion, particularly the principle of separation of church and state, have often become contentious and strongly debated in the public school arena. An example includes *McCollum v. Board of Education,* 333 U.S. 203 (1947) [Illinois], a plan that called for religious teachers to come into the school to provide religious instruction. This was found to be unconstitutional. Numerous laws that reinforced Protestant morality have been challenged, some have been upheld, while some have been repealed. Attempts to legislate the public's morality (e.g., state laws, which once required teachers to attend church on Sundays), however, date back several decades. In the 1920s, Prohibition laws were passed in an attempt to address the welfare of the American people. After 13 years, however, this law was repealed and the courts began to protect the rights of those outside the Protestant mainstream. Laws restricting behaviors on moral grounds such as divorce and sexual practices were repealed, and the courts began to reinforce the principle of separation of church and state. One dramatic example of the courts' new attitude was the 1973 decision rendered by the U.S. Supreme Court in *Roe v. Wade,* which protected a woman's right to an abortion in early stages of pregnancy (Corrigan & Hudson, 2004).

By the late 1970s, the ideologies of a conservative and increasingly influential group referred to as the Religious Right were clashing head-on with the ideologies of secular humanism. The battle was waged on two fronts: the family and the school. Controversies centered on the family, gender roles, and issues such as abortion, the Equal Rights Amendment, and gay rights. Conservatives supported a return to traditional roles for men and women and opposed equal opportunity for women and homosexuals, such as the hiring of gays and lesbians as public school educators (Roof & McKinney, 1985).

See Chapter 4 regarding issues related to sexual orientation and rights.

The New Christian Right, or the Religious Right, became a potent force in the 1970s and 1980s partly because of the effective television ministries of individuals such as Jerry Falwell and Pat Robertson. With their ability to reach millions in their own homes, these religious leaders encouraged political involvement and mounted efforts on issues such as school prayer, abortion, pornography, and national defense. They believe that the Bible is inspired by God and is inerrant. They believe that the Bible is literally the word of God, and that it is consistent and free of error.

The Religious Right has provided strong support or opposition for political candidates on the basis of their voting records or positions on issues (Roof & McKinney, 1985). In 1980 and 1984, they were a strong factor in the election of Ronald Reagan. The American electorate is often inconsistent in its concerns. The Protestant majority, particularly those aligned with the religious right, support candidates who can provide assurances that they will bring their religious values into public office. However, concerns are sometimes articulated about non-Protestant candidates. As previously mentioned, in 1960 John F. Kennedy assured the American electorate that he

 **CRITICAL INCIDENTS IN TEACHING**

Educators and Issues of Choice in the Classroom

Charlotte Silva is a fifth-grade teacher in a suburban school near a major city in Texas. "Ms. Silva," Terry Smith blurts out, "Holly Segal's sister is getting an abortion next week. That's a sin."

"It's not," protests Holly. "My parents said it is a woman's right to do as she pleases with her body."

"She's going to have an unborn child killed. She's only 17 and she's pregnant. She's not even married. That's a sin, too. My mother and daddy told me that those things are sins. They are, aren't they? Our preacher says that you can rot in hell for sins like that, and he doesn't lie. That's true, isn't it, Ms. Silva? Will you please tell Holly?"

The entire class has heard this outburst, and they are all staring at the teacher, waiting for her response.

Questions for Discussion

1. *Although the teacher must provide some response, should she allow a discussion on religious ethics in the classroom?*
2. *If she decides not to discuss the issue, how should she acknowledge the question and avoid a judgmental response to the ethics question?*
3. *If the teacher decides to allow a discussion of the issues, how should she proceed?*
4. *What can she allow in the discussion? What must be avoided?*

To answer these questions online, go to the Critical Incidents in Teaching module for this chapter of the Companion Website.

CW

would not allow American politics to be influenced by his Catholic faith. In 1980 and again in 1984, Ronald Reagan experienced the exact opposite, assuring Fundamentalist groups that he was a creationist and that he would seek to bring prayer back into the public schools. Following the 1992 and 1996 election and re-election of Bill Clinton, religious conservatives organized their forces, providing strong support for George W. Bush. Their support helped elect him in 2000 and again in 2004.

TESTING THE FIRST AMENDMENT

School districts and various state legislators who seek to circumvent the principle of Separation of Church and State continually test the First Amendment. It would be difficult to believe that state legislators, many of whom are attorneys, are not aware that laws requiring a form of religion are not intended to create a government sponsored religious activity. It is likely that these legislators or school officials believe it their responsibility to infuse morality and ethics into school activity or curriculum. The Supreme Court, however, has the responsibility to rule on the constitutionality of such directives. The following are examples of Supreme Court rulings related to education, the First Amendment, and the principle of the Separation of Church and State:

- *Engel v. Vitale,* 82 S. Ct. 1261 (1962) [New York]. The Court ruled that any type of prayer, even that which is nondenominational is unconstitutional government sponsorship of religion.
- *Abington School District v. Schempp,* 374 U.S. 203 (1963) [Pennsylvania]. The Court found that Bible reading over the school intercom was unconstitutional

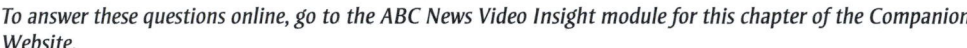
God and Evolution in Kansas Classrooms

Proponents of creationism say it should be taught in schools because it is a more scientifically valid theory than evolution. To these people, it is not an issue of religious fundamentalism versus science; it's an issue of science versus science.

This video segment shows how and why the State Board of Education in Kansas, decided in the late 1990s to side with creationists and not require the teaching of evolution in their schools. To the opponents of creationism, this seemed an irresponsible move in the education of Kansas' children. Will these students have the education necessary to compete? Will they be able to pass standardized tests?

1. *Should teachers be allowed to teach the book of Genesis in a public school science class? Why or why not?*

2. *Do you think the decision of the Kansas Board of Education infringed on the separation of church and state?*

3. *Or, as its proponents argue, is creationism a valid scientific theory that should be taught in the schools? Defend your opinions.*

To answer these questions online, go to the ABC News Video Insight module for this chapter of the Companion Website.

DVD

CW

and in *Murray v. Curlett,* 374 U.S. 203 (1963), the Court found that forcing a child to participate in Bible reading and prayer was unconstitutional.

- *Epperson v. Arkansas,* 89 S. Ct. 266 (1968). The Court ruled that a State statute banning teaching of evolution was unconstitutional. A state cannot set a course of study in order to promote a religious point of view.

- *Stone v. Graham,* 449 U.S. 39 (1980) [Kentucky]. The Court ruled that the posting of the Ten Commandments in schools was unconstitutional.

- *Wallace v. Jaffree,* 105 S. Ct. 2479 (1985) [Alabama]. The Court ruled that the State's moment of silence in a public school statute was unconstitutional as a legislative record revealed that motivation for the statute was the encouragement of prayer.

- *Edwards v. Aquillard,* 107 S. Ct. 2573 (1987) [Louisiana]. The Court found it was unconstitutional for the state to require teaching of "creation science" in all instances in which evolution is taught. The statute had a clear religious motivation.

- *Lee v. Weisman,* 112 S. Ct. 2649 (1992) [Rhode Island]. The Court ruled it to be unconstitutional for a school district to provide any clergy to perform nondenominational prayer at elementary or secondary school graduation. It involves government sponsorship of worship.

The Religious Right is a very conservative and politically active group of Christians. It is difficult to identify precisely who comprises the group and how many individuals are included in their ranks. Groups identified as part of the Religious Right include the American Family Association, Christian Coalition, Concerned Women for America, Family Research Council, and Focus. They are actively involved in reducing choice in abortion access, homosexual rights, same-sex marriage, physician assisted suicide, and prayer in the public schools (Ontario Consultants on Religious Tolerance, 2003).

In the late 1980s and early 1990s, as the remaining liberal U.S. Supreme Court justices were advancing in age, President Bush appointed conservative replacements. Thus, by the time Bill Clinton assumed office, Ronald Reagan and George Bush had been successful in placing conservative judges on the federal benches and on the U.S. Supreme Court (Corrigan & Hudson, 2004). The efforts of religious conservatives have altered the course of American history and will affect the judicial system in the United States for decades. However, with Bill Clinton, a more liberal president elected in 1992 and reelected in 1996, the balance of power in the Supreme Court was affected as new appointments were made. With a conservative Republican President in the White House in 2000 and again in 2004, nominations for judicial appointments in the various levels of Federal court appointments were once again made with a conservative orientation (West, 2004). Thus, the laws and the interpretation of laws, which have a direct bearing on religion and the lives of U.S. residents, are often a function of whom we elect to public office.

Large numbers of Americans believe that religion is losing its influence on American life and education. This, along with increasing frustration with drugs in the schools, gang violence, and declining achievement scores, has religious conservatives placing considerable pressure on the U.S. educational system. They want schools to support the values of the conservative Right as they once did. Religious conservatives have allied themselves with political conservatives and have worked diligently to elect their members to school boards. In some communities, they have established their own private schools to ensure that their convictions and values are reflected in all aspects of schooling. Today's educators should recognize the influence of these groups and that in some communities, they enjoy considerable support.

Pause to Reflect 6.3

It has already been stated that it is important for you to be aware of your religious beliefs and that of your community. It is also important that you reflect on where you lie on the religious continuum with respect to being religiously liberal or religiously conservative. As stated before, it is your right to believe as you wish. However, it is not your right to impose your religious orientation to your students in a public school setting. The nation is unfortunately polarized in some of the issues related to religion and the public schools. The sides typically feel passionately about their perspectives. Again, this is their right to do so. It is neither their right nor your right to bring it into the classroom. It is your responsibility as an educator to make every child feel welcome and safe in your classroom and in your school.

■ *What are the religious affiliations of people in the community in which you now reside?*

■ *How does the religious diversity differ from where you grew up?*

■ *How would you classify the majority groups on a scale of conservative to liberal?*

■ *What influence might these religions have on what you teach in the classroom?*

To answer these questions online, go to the Pause to Reflect module for this chapter of the Companion Website.

Nationally, adherence to the principle of separation of church and state has been schizophrenic, at best. Oaths are typically made on Bibles and often end with the phrase "so help me God." U.S. coins and currency state "In God We Trust." We have military chaplains and congressional chaplains, and we hold congressional prayer breakfasts. The Pledge of Allegiance includes the words, "under God." This has been interpreted by some to mean that the separation of church and state simply means that there will be no state church.

Complete separation of church and state, as defined by strict constitutionalists, would have a profound effect on social-religious life. It is likely that the American public wants some degree of separation of these two institutions, but it is equally likely that the public would be outraged if total separation were imposed. Total separation would mean no direct or indirect aid to religious groups, no tax-free status, no tax deductions for contributions to religious groups, no national Christmas tree, no government-paid chaplains, no religious holidays, no blue laws, and so on. The list of religious activities, rights, and privileges that could be eliminated seems almost endless.

Educational Implications

Religious groups place different emphases on the need for education and have different expectations of what children should be taught. For instance, the Amish usually want to remove their children from formal schooling after they complete the eighth grade in order to work with their families. The Hutterites often do not want their children to attend school with non-Hutterite students. Catholics, Lutherans, Episcopalians, Hutterites, Seventh-Day Adventists, and some Fundamentalist Christian groups have established their own schools to provide both a common education (the general, nonreligious skills and knowledge) and a religious education.

Public schools are supposed to be free of religious doctrine and perspective, but many people believe that schools without such a perspective do not provide a desirable values orientation for students. Debate about the public school's responsibility in fostering student morality and social responsibility is constant. A major point of disagreement focuses on who should determine the morals that will provide the context of the educational program in a school. Because religious diversity is so great in this country, that task is nearly impossible. Therefore, most public schools incorporate commonly accepted American values that transcend most religions. In response, some students are sent to schools operated by a religious body; other students attend religion classes after school or on Saturdays; and many students receive their religious training at Sunday School.

Although the U.S. Constitution requires the separation of state and church as previously stated, this does not mean that public schools and religion have always been completely separated. Until 1962 and 1963, when Supreme Court decisions [i.e., *Engel v. Vitale,* 82 S. Ct. 1261 (1962) and *Abington School District v. Schempp,* 374 U.S. 203 (1963)] determined that these practices were unconstitutional, some schools included religious worship and prayer in their daily educational practices. Although schools should be secular, they are greatly influenced by the predominant values of the community. Whether evolution, sex education, and values clarification are taught in school is determined, in great part, by the religious beliefs of a community. Educators must be cognizant of this influence before introducing certain readings and ideas that stray far from what the community is willing to accept within their belief and value structure.

CONTROVERSIAL ISSUES

School Prayer. Among the controversial issues that surround the efforts of the New Right and Fundamentalist religious groups are school prayer, school vouchers, and censorship. Despite the 1962 and 1963 Supreme Court decisions regarding school prayer, conservative groups have persisted in their efforts to revive school prayer in the schools. The law now is, in essence, a voluntary prayer law. The law in no way precludes private prayer in school. The Supreme Court decisions do not prevent teachers or students from praying privately in school. Any teacher or student can offer his or her own private prayer of thanks before the noon meal or meditate or pray between classes and before and after school. The law forbids public group prayer. Advocates of school prayer sometime advance their efforts under the term *voluntary* prayer. The interpretation of what constitutes voluntary school prayer has become a main issue in the prayer controversy. Some proponents of school prayer advocate mandated school prayer, with individuals voluntarily choosing to participate or not participate. It is likely that if such laws were ever enacted, the considerable social pressure to participate would be particularly difficult for younger children to resist.

In 2000, the Supreme Court ruled against a Texas school district, which had permitted prayer at a football game over the public address system. The district maintained that the football games were extracurricular, and students were not required to attend and be a part of the prayer (*Santa Fe Independent School District v. DOE,* 2000). Prayers and invocations have been a long-standing tradition at many high school games to invoke the protection against harm for all of the football players and typically ask for good sportsmanship. Seldom has the practice been challenged in the past because it had the support of the vast majority of students and parents. However, the Court has ruled that this is a violation of the separation of church and state. Lyons (2002) reports Americans continue to provide support for public school prayer and other religious activities. Lyons suggests that in the last few decades consensus appears to have shifted away from the view that government should be able to require such expressions. Furthermore, a majority of Americans indicate that they would oppose public school prayer if it offended a large proportion of parents (Lyons, 2002).

Since 1962, the Supreme Court has ruled several times against school prayer, and other state sponsored religious activities (Lyons, 2002). With public sentiment favoring prayer in the schools, it is understandable why continued attempts are made to change or to circumvent the Supreme Court's decision.

School Vouchers. Various groups raise school voucher initiatives periodically. Vouchers are intended to provide parents with a choice of schools for their children, public, or private. Secretary of Education Rod Paige in the first George W. Bush administration supported voucher programs in what he said would help low-income parents and children to escape low performing schools (Gordon, 2002). The funds for vouchers come from tax monies and usually range between $2,500 and $5,000, with around $3,000 typical. Voucher initiatives are often strongly supported by religious factions, particularly those who send their children to private religious schools. Parents and others who support these initiatives point to the failure of the public schools to educate their children adequately. They point to the states' low national rankings in student math proficiency, reading proficiency, SAT scores, class size, teacher/student ratios, computer availability, and per pupil spending (38 YES-School Vouchers, 2000). They also point to falling system-wide test scores and to the moral decline in schools as evidenced by school violence, drugs, and teen pregnancies. They believe that school vouchers will make it possible to send their children to the schools of their choice.

Proponents of voucher programs argue that vouchers will not require any further appropriations since school districts can provide vouchers to students who are not using their services, thereby decreasing their expenses. They argue that when parents redeem a school voucher, part of the expense that would otherwise cost the school to educate the student can remain in the public schools. The voucher program will enable all parents to ensure the quality education that they wish for their children.

 ## VIDEO INSIGHT

Standing Alone

Although the Supreme Court voted in 1963 to remove prayer from schools, the issue is still not settled. In some areas of the country, where religious diversity is minimal, this ruling is effectively ignored. Other districts have agreed to a "moment of silence" for the purpose of moral reflection. Still others are locked in battle over this issue, like the high school choir in Utah, an area with a large Mormon population, that refused to honor the wishes of Rachel, its single Jewish member, to sing fewer religious songs.

Rachel's parents accused the choir director of insensitivity to their concerns, offering a "Jewish song" to appease them. Rachel's father encouraged the protests, and wrote letters to add to the protest.

1. *Consider how you would have reacted to Rachel's request if you were the choir director.*

2. *As an educator, is it your responsibility to represent various religious viewpoints, even if the majority of your students share the same religious beliefs?*

3. *Did Rachel's father act in her best interest by his involvement and by encouraging her to take issue with a popular school position? Should an individual (and parents) stand up for a principle even if it will lead to rejection, social isolation, and harassment?*

4. *How will you handle similar issues in your own classroom?*

DVD

CW

To answer these questions online, go to the ABC News Video Insight module for this chapter of the Companion Website.

Opponents to voucher initiatives maintain that vouchers will indeed take away needed funds from the public schools. School districts have many fixed costs and already are suffering from inadequate funding. Opponents also suggest that voucher systems will indeed create a fiscal crisis in the public school system, and there will be a need for additional state support to even maintain the status quo. They further state that the $3,000 or $4,000 provided by the vouchers will not enable any child to go to any school of choice. Many private schools have annual tuitions of $12,000 to $14,000, or more, and the $3,000 or $4,000 vouchers will not even begin to cover the cost of the full tuition. While some schools may grant partial scholarships to deserving students with financial need, it will not be possible to provide support to all. Private schools tend to be located in the more affluent areas of the community. Transportation will be a major problem for students who live in areas distant from the preferred schools. Opponents also contend that the primary beneficiaries of the school voucher programs will be the wealthy who can afford the private schools and already enroll their children in them, and the few borderline families who can send their children to private schools only with the help of vouchers. The American public (43% to 54%) tends to be against spending public funds to assist low-income children to attend religious schools (Gordon, 2002).

CENSORSHIP

The discussion of censorship is included in this section because the censorship movement tends to be heavily influenced by many individuals from fundamentalist and conservative religious groups. In most cases, a censor is a concerned citizen who sincerely seeks to improve society or protect children. At other times censorship may take place to forward one's own religious or political agenda (American Library Association, 2004).

Individuals or groups may be self-appointed and pressure school districts or libraries, video stores, publishers, art galleries, and so forth not to stock or show, publish, or distribute the targeted materials. Censorship may also take place with committees appointed by a state or school district as textbook selection committees. Censorship of textbooks, library books, and other learning materials in education has become another major battleground in education for the Religious Right and other fundamentalist groups.

The impact of censorship in the public schools cannot be underestimated. It is a serious matter. Censorship or attempts at censorship have resulted in the dismissal or resignation of administrators and teachers. It has split communities and has the potential of creating as much controversy as did the desegregation of schools. Few can doubt the sincerity of censors and their proponents. They feel passionately that the cause they support is just and morally right. Censors believe that they are obligated to continue their fight to rid schools of objectionable materials that contaminate supple minds and that contribute to the moral decay of society.

At the other end of the continuum, opponents to the censors also tend to share a conviction that they are the ones in the right and that censors infringe on academic freedom, seeking to destroy meaningful education. Opponents to the censors believe that their antagonists thrive on hard times, such as when schools come under fire because of declining Scholastic Aptitude Test (SAT) scores, rising illiteracy rates,

FOCUS YOUR CULTURAL LENS: DEBATE

School Vouchers

With every report of declining achievement test scores or school violence, we can expect to hear the cry for school vouchers. Some view vouchers as the answer to ineffective schools. Typically in the range of $3,000 to $4,000, parents can use the vouchers to choose and offset the cost of private schools. Presumably, the districts would save the cost of educating students who opt for private schools, and these savings can be used by the districts to pay for the vouchers. Opponents see vouchers as damaging to the public school system as well as a way to finance the education of students in church operated schools.

FOR

- School districts spend $7,000 or more a year to educate each student.

- With the typical voucher in the $3,000 range, this will save the school districts $4,000 or more a year for each student who withdraws from a public school utilizing the voucher.

- Vouchers will improve the quality of education in public schools.

- They will create a healthy competition and force the schools to improve or close.

- Most important is the fact that parents and students would then have an opportunity to select a school that will provide a quality education.

AGAINST

- Voucher programs will require taxpayers to support religious education or to support students to attend private racially segregated schools.

- Students already attending private schools will seek vouchers.

- When students leave the public schools with their vouchers, most of the schools' fixed costs would remain.

- Vouchers will drain the resources of school districts and exacerbate the fiscal problems most schools already face.

- Many inner-city students will not be able meet the entrance requirement of the better private schools.

- Even if they can, they may have difficulty with transportation or in paying the balance of the tuition beyond the value of the voucher.

- Vouchers are likely to benefit primarily the wealthy and those whose children already attend church related schools.

Questions

1. *If the parents are paying taxes, why shouldn't they get some support to send their children to the school of their choice even if it is a church related school or one that is segregated?*
2. *If the public schools can't compete adequately with private schools, shouldn't they be closed?*

To answer these questions online, go to the Focus Your Cultural Lens: Debate module for this chapter of the Companion Website.

Sources: Citizens for Educational Freedom, *Frequently Asked Questions,* **http://www.educational-freedom.org/faq.html**; *Myth Conceptions about School Choice,* **http://www.schoolchoices.org/roo/myths.htm**; National Education Association, *Vouchers,* **http://www.nea.org/issues/vouchers/**; Anti-Defamation League (ADL), *School Vouchers: The Wrong Choice for Public Education,* **http://www.adl.org/vouchers/vouchers_main.asp**

escalating costs of education, and increasing concern about violence and vandalism in the schools. Other factors that prompt the activities of censors are the removal of school prayer; teaching methods that are branded as secular humanism; and programs such as values clarification, drug education, and sex education. Books written specifically for teenagers about subjects that are objectionable to some parents and in language that others consider too realistic are often a source of concern. The emergence of African American literature, sometimes written in the black vernacular, is sometimes the source of irritation or concern.

Censorship occurs when expressive materials such as books, magazines, films, videos, or works of art are removed or kept from public access, including the removal of materials from textbook adoption lists. Censorship may be based on the age of or other characteristics of the potential user. Targets for the censors are books and materials that are identified as disrespectful of authority and religion, destructive of social and cultural values, obscene, pornographic, unpatriotic, or in violation of individual and familial rights of privacy. Books written by gays and lesbians are frequently attacked. Other materials attacked by censors may be those that are considered nonracist or nonsexist. In a conservative community, teachers may be surprised to find that magazines such as *Time, Newsweek,* and *U.S. News and World Report* are sometimes attacked because they publish stories about war, crime, death, violence, and sex. In this same community, a teacher can anticipate a negative reaction to the teaching of evolution without presenting the views on creationism. In addition, certain dictionaries with words and definitions described as offensive have been forced off book adoption lists. *How would you feel as a biology teacher if you were informed that you would be required to teach creation science along with lessons on evolution?*

Opportunities for Reflection

One can understand the concern of parents who are often influenced by censors. These parents believe that unless they choose sides and act, their children will be taught with materials that are anti-God, anti-family, anti-authority, anti-country, anti-morality, and anti-law and order. The failure to communicate effectively with parents is a contributing source of alienation between educators and parents. Failure to communicate the objectives of new curricula and to explain how these programs enrich the educational experience may cause suspicion and distrust. Many administrators and librarians indicate that communication with parents is more crises oriented than continuous. Information about programs, policies, and procedures tends to be offered in response to inquiries or challenges, rather than as part of an ongoing public relations effort.

Often controversy develops when parents do not understand what educators are including in their children's curriculum. Controversy can be avoided or minimized when time and care is devoted to clearly explaining curricular content and its purpose before the instructional process is undertaken. Showing parents how the curriculum will support rather than conflict with basic family values can avoid potential conflict.

Secular Humanism. Secular humanism has been one direct target of the censors, particularly those affiliated with Fundamentalist religious groups. The emphasis in secular humanism is a respect for human beings, rather than a belief in the supernatural. Its objectives include the full development of every human being, the universal use of the scientific method, affirmation of the preciousness and dignity of the individual person, personal freedom combined with social responsibility, and fulfillment through the development of ethical and creative living (Robinson, 2004).

Because many Secular Humanists feel that the role of religion throughout history has been profoundly negative, and because some humanists regard God as a creation of mankind rather than the reverse, they are often targets of Conservative Christians. Secular humanism is not an organized religion like Roman Catholicism, Protestantism, and Judaism. It does not have rituals, a church, or professed doctrines. Its existence is in the minds of individuals who align themselves with these perspectives. The specific beliefs and manifestations of beliefs vary from one believer to another.

Conservative Christians tend to view Secular Humanism as a religion, and one that has taken over the public school systems. This may be unlikely since the majority of teachers in the public schools are from Christian backgrounds. The principle of separation of church and state requires public schools to base their curriculum on secular or nonreligious foundations. In mathematics, reading, writing, chemistry, and physics there is no conflict. However in subjects such as human sex education, biology, sociology, and history, the secular approach often comes into conflict with conservative Christian theology. Consequently, books and materials viewed as Secular Humanist in orientation are often targets for censorship (Robinson, 2004). Materials and topics infused into the curriculum that address issues such as abortion, corporal punishment of children, death penalty, enforced prayer in schools, homosexuality, and physician-assisted suicide will typically draw the attention of censors who view them as secular humanist objectionable material. Writings by individuals such as B. F. Skinner, Abraham Maslow, Carl Rogers, and Mary Calderone would likely be targets of some censors who identify them with secular humanists.

Teachers new to the profession or new to a community should never underestimate the determination of those involved in the censorship movement. Teachers would be well advised to make certain that they are fully aware of the climate within the community before introducing new, innovative, or controversial materials, teaching strategies, and books. Experienced colleagues and supervisors can usually serve as barometers as to how students, parents, and the community will react to the new materials or teaching techniques. With this type of information, the new teacher can proceed with a more realistic anticipation of the reception that can be expected.

CLASSROOM IMPLICATIONS

Although religion and public schooling are to remain separate, religion can be taught in schools as a legitimate discipline for objective study. A comparative religion course is part of the curriculum offered in many secondary schools. In this approach, the students are not forced to practice a religion as part of their educational program. They can, however, study one or more religions.

GUIDELINES FOR TEACHING ABOUT RELIGIONS

The Fairfax County Schools in Virginia have provided teachers with a handout titled *Religion and Public Schools: The Path Between Too Much and Too Little.* In the handout are guidelines for teaching about religions. This important advice will assist teachers in understanding how religion can be taught while maintaining the all-important separation of church and state:

- The school may sponsor the study of religion, but may not sponsor the practice of religion.
- The school may expose students to all religious views, but may not impose any particular view.
- The school's approach to religion is one of instruction, not one of indoctrination.
- The function of the school is to educate about all religions, not to convert to any one religion.
- The school should study what all people believe, but should not teach a student what to believe.
- The school should strive for student awareness of all religions, but should not press for student acceptance of any one religion.
- The school should seek to inform the student about various beliefs, but should not seek to conform him or her to any one belief. (Becker, undated)

As part of the curriculum, students should learn that the United States (and indeed the world) is rich in religious diversity. Educators show their respect for religious differences by their interactions with students from different religious backgrounds. Understanding the importance of religion to students and their families is an advantage in developing effective teaching strategies for individual students. Instructional activities can build on students' religious experiences to help them learn concepts. This technique helps students recognize that their religious identity is valued in the classroom and encourages them to respect the religious diversity that exists.

At the same time, educators should avoid stereotyping all students from one denomination or church. Diversity is found within every religious group and denomination as mentioned earlier in this chapter. Within each group are differences in attitudes and beliefs. For example, Southern Baptists may appear to be conservative to outsiders. Among Southern Baptists, however, some would be considered part of a liberal or moderate group, whereas others would be identified as conservative. Some Southern Baptist churches may hold services so formal in nature that they might even be described as resembling an Episcopalian service.

It is the responsibility of educators to be aware of the religious diversity and the influence of religion in the community in which they work. They must also understand the influence of religion on the school's curriculum and climate in order to teach effectively. Finally, educators must periodically reexamine their own interactions with students to ensure that they are not discriminating against students because of differences in religious beliefs. It is imperative that educators recognize how influential membership in a religious microculture is in order to help students develop their potential.

Summary

Educators should never understimate the importance that Americans place on religion. For some individuals, their religion takes precedent over all other microcultures. People have been willing to die for their religion; some have been willing to inflict great pain on others because of their beliefs. We live in a society that has become increasingly diverse. Along with increasing ethnic diversity has come increasing religious diversity. The United States has operated under Judeo-Christian principles for more than two centuries. When new religions threaten established religions, however, controversies and challenges arise.

Educators would do well to inform themselves of the religious groups in their community and in their school. In doing so, they greatly enhance their ability to function in the classroom, mindful and respectful of the religious rights of all students.

One's religion has considerable impact on how one functions on a day-to-day basis. For example, an individual's education may be greatly influenced by religious groups. Some private schools are established on religious principles and, in those schools, religion is an integral part of the curriculum. Even in public schools, attempts by religious groups to influence the system are made regularly. The degree of religious influence in the schools varies from one community to another. Educators should not underestimate the influence and strategies of both conservative and liberal religious groups and would be well advised to know their community before introducing controversial materials.

QUESTIONS FOR DISCUSSION

1. Discuss how the religious majority in a community can influence curriculum and instructional methodology. Does the majority rule? Can and should the majority religious group in a community be able to mandate what is taught in the schools?

2. To what extent does religion influence American life with respect to its importance to the individual and church or synagogue attendance?

3. What is the relationship of religion to public office? Why are some groups disproportionately represented in Congress?

4. What are the current trends with respect to membership in conservative, moderate, and liberal religious groups? What are the implications of these trends for the political and legal directions of the country?

5. How have Protestantism, Catholicism, and Judaism influenced American culture?

6. In what ways does gender affect religion and religion affect gender issues?

7. How do the perceptions about gay and homosexual individuals differ between religious conservatives and liberals? What are the responsibilities of the schools toward gay and lesbian students?

8. What is the relationship of religion to race?

9. What is the First Amendment to the Constitution? Explain the concept of Separation of Church and State. Does it mean that no religion can be taught in public schools?

10. What do laws permit with respect to school prayer? How and why does the Religious Right want to change these laws? Do religious conservatives have valid concerns about our public schools?

11. What are the issues surrounding school vouchers?

12. What is secular humanism? What objections does the Religious Right have against secular humanism in the schools?

ONLINE ACTIVITIES For additional chapter questions and activities, visit this text's Companion Website at **http://www.prenhall.com/gollnick**.

PORTFOLIO ACTIVITIES

1. Form a group to work on a project to determine religious or theological implications of parents having a child born with a disability. Divide your assignments so that the group can interview (if your community is large enough) at least two or three Catholic priests, Protestant ministers (from different denominations), Jewish rabbis, Mormon bishops, and Islamic center directors. Ask them what information they would provide parents of a newborn child with a disability when they ask what God's reason was for bringing a child with a disability into the world. As a group formulate a report looking at the similarities and differences of each religious group or denomination. (INTASC Standards 3, 8, and 10)

2. Utilizing various sources including legal documents and search engines, find and summarize the court cases in your state in the last 25 years involving challenges to the First Amendment and public schools. (INTASC Standard 10)

3. Write a plan of action for meeting with parents and explaining to them how you will be addressing evolution in your class. Show what steps will be taken to avoid conflict with parental religious views. (INTASC Standards 3 and 10)

SUGGESTED READINGS

Chryssides, G. D. (1999). *Exploring new religions.* London: Cassell.

This book provides an excellent overview of some of the nontraditional religions in the world. Included are religious groups such as suicide cults, new Christian movements, new forms of Buddhism, New Age, witchcraft, and paganism.

Corduan, W. (1998). *Neighboring faiths.* Downers Grove, IL: InterVarsity Press.

Written from a Christian perspective, the text covers the major non-Christian religions in the United States with a historical background of the religion and the basic belief structure of the particular group.

Corrigan, J., & Hudson, W. S. (2004). *Religion in America* (7th ed.). Upper Saddle River, NJ: Prentice Hall.

A look at the history of religion in this country and its profound influence on the formation of culture in America. It includes a discussion of the pluralistic nature of religion today.

Ellwood, R. S., & McGraw, B. A. (2002). *Many people, many faiths.* Upper Saddle River, NJ: Prentice Hall.

This text provides the conceptual, sacred, and social elements of the various religions. It also provides an examination of the role of women in the world's religions.

Gallup Poll, *Tuesday Morning Briefing.*

The Gallup Organization provides a weekly Internet reporting each Tuesday of the results of their research. The service provides a look at the Nation's pulse, so that you can see what Americans think, feel, and what they are doing. There is always information on politics, the economy, and religion. This is a subscription service, which has an annual $95 fee.

Hopfe, L. M., & Woodward, M. R. (2004). *Religions of the world* (9th ed.). Upper Saddle River, NJ: Prentice Hall.

This work provides comprehensive and concise descriptions of the world's great religions as well as the smaller and less well-known religions. It explores the historical and cultural factors related to religions as well as their teachings and current status in the world.

Johnstone, R. L. (2001). *Religion in society* (6th ed.). Upper Saddle River, NJ: Prentice Hall.

This text provides an examination of religions from a sociological perspective. It includes but is not limited to chapters on religious politics, religion and economy, and women and religion.

Lincoln, C. E., & Mamiya, L. H. (1990). *The black church in the African American experience.* Durham, NC: Duke University.

This work is, unfortunately, slightly dated. It is considered by some religious scholars as a seminal work, which provides a definitive examination of the history and role of the black church in American society.

Van Leeuwen, M. S. (1990). *Gender and grace.* Downers Grove, IL: InterVarsity Press.

This volume is an excellent examination of gender issues in a Christian biblical context. It was written several years ago, but it is still relevant.

REFERENCES

American Library Association. (2004). *Intellectual freedom and censorship Q & A.* Chicago: American Library Association, http://www.ala.org/ala/oif/basics/intellectual.htm#ifpoint3

Becker, B. (undated). *Religion and public schools: The path between too much and too little.* Springfield, VA: Fairfax County Schools.

Brown, M. F. (2000). The New Age and related forms of contemporary spirituality. In R. Scupin (Ed.), *Religion and culture.* Upper Saddle River, NJ: Prentice Hall.

Carroll, J. (2004, March 2). American public opinion about religion. *Gallup Tuesday Morning Briefing.*

Chryssides, G. D. (1999). *Exploring new religions.* London: Cassell.

Claflin, E. J. (2004, Spring). *Congressional Yellow Book.* New York: Leadership Directories, Inc.

Corduan, W. (1998). *Neighboring faiths.* Downers Grove, IL: InterVarsity Press.

Corrigan, J., & Hudson, W. S. (2004). *Religion in America* (7th ed.). Upper Saddle River, NJ: Prentice Hall.

Ellwood, R. S., & McGraw, B. A. (2005). *Many people, many faiths.* Upper Saddle River, NJ: Prentice Hall.

Fisher, M. P. (2002). *Living religions* (5th ed.). Upper Saddle River, NJ: Prentice Hall.

Gallup, G. H., Jr. (2003). December 16, 2003. Catholics Trail Protestants in Church Attendance, Gallup Tuesday Morning Briefing.

Gallup, G. H., Jr., & Lindsay, D. M. (1999). *Surveying the religious landscape.* Harrisburg, PA: Morehouse Publishing.

Gomes, P. (1996). *The good book.* New York: Morrow.

Gordon, G. (2002, July 9). Beyond vouchers: Fixing public schools. *Gallup Tuesday Morning Briefing.*

Groothuis, R. M. (1997). *Good news for women: A biblical picture of gender equality.* Grand Rapids, MI: Baker Books.

Hartford Research Institute. (2002). *A quick question: How many Eastern Orthodox are there in the USA?* Retrieved on July 15, 2004, from http://hirr.hartsem.edu/research/quick_question17.html

History of the Church. (2004). *The history of the LDS Church.* Retrieved on July 15, 2004, from http://www.lds.org/churchhistory/history

Hopfe, L. M., & Woodward, M. R. (2004). *Religions of the world* (9th ed.). Upper Saddle River, NJ: Prentice Hall.

The Islam FAQ: Answers to frequently asked questions about Islam. Retrieved on July 15, 2004, from http://www.islamfaq.org

Johnson, J. (2003, November 14). Panel removes Alabama's "Ten Commandments judge" *Los Angeles Times,* pp. A1, A34.

Johnstone, R. L. (2004). *Religion in society:* a sociology of Religion, (7th ed.). Upper Saddle River, NJ: Prentice Hall.

Kosmin, B. A., & Lachman, S. P. (1993). *One nation under God: Religion in contemporary American society.* New York: Harmony.

Lincoln, C. E. (1994). The Black Muslims in America (3rd ed.). Grand Rapids, MI: Eerdmans.

Lincoln, C. E., & Mamiya, L. H. (1990). *The black church in the African American experience.* Durham, NC: Duke University.

Lindner, E. W. (2004). *2004 yearbook of American and Canadian churches.* Nashville: Abingdon Press.

Lyons, L. (2002, December 10). The Gallup brain: Prayer in public schools. *Gallup Tuesday Morning Briefing.*

Marty, M. E. (Ed.). (1975). *Our faiths.* Royal Oak, MI: Cathedral Publications.

National Catholic Reporter. (2004, March 26). Membership figures reported—USA—the 10 largest churches in the United States. According to the National Council of Churches.

Newport, F. (2003, February 27). Support for war modestly higher among more religious Americans. *Gallup Tuesday Morning Briefing.*

Newport, F., & Carroll, J. (2003, March 6). Support for Bush significantly higher among more religious Americans. *Gallup Tuesday Morning Briefing.*

Ontario Consultants on Religious Tolerance. (2003). *Definition for the Religious Right.* Retrieved on July 15, 2004, from http://www.religioustolerance.org/gl_r.htm

Oxtoby, W. G. (Ed.). (1996). *World religions.* Oxford, UK: Oxford University Press.

Peach, L. J. (2002). *Women and world religions.* Upper Saddle River, NJ: Prentice Hall.

Princeton Religion Research Center. (1995). *Religion in America.* [Supplement]. Princeton, NJ: Princeton Religion Research Center.

Religious Tolerance. (2004). *Religious group's policy toward homosexuality.* Retrieved on July 15, 2004, from http://www.religioustolerance.org/hom_chur.htm

Robinson, B. A. (2003a). *Hinduism, the world's third largest religion.* Ontario Consultants on Religious Tolerance. Retrieved on July 15, 2004, from http://www.religioustolerance.org/hinduism.htm

Robinson, B. A. (2003b). *The People's Temple, led by James Warren (Jim) Jones.* Ontario Consultants on Religious Tolerance. Retrieved on July 15, 2004, from http://www.religioustolerance.org/dc_jones.htm

Robinson, B. A. (2004). *Humanism and the humanist manifestos.* Ontario Consultants on Religious Tolerance. Retrieved on July 15, 2004, from http://www.religioustolerance.org/humanism.htm

Robinson, F. (Ed.). (1996). *Islamic world.* Cambridge, UK: Cambridge University Press.

Roof, W. C., & McKinney, W. (1985, July). Denominational America and the new religious pluralism. *Annals of the American Academy of Political and Social Science, 480,* 24–38.

Santa Fe Independent School District v. DOE (99–62) 168 F. 3d 806 (June 19, 2000).

Singer, D., & Grossman, L. (2002). *American Jewish yearbook.* New York: American Jewish Committee.

SoundVision. (2004). *Education, educating our future!* Retrieved on July 15, 2004, from http://www.soundvision.com/info/education/

38 YES-School Vouchers 2000. Retrieved on July 15, 2004, from http://www.vouchers2000.com

U.S. State Department. (2004). *Muslim life in America.* International Information Programs. Retrieved on July 15, 2004, from http://usinfo.state.gov/products/pubs/muslimlife/

Van Leeuwen, M. S. (1990). *Gender and grace.* Downers Grove, IL: InterVarsity Press.

West, P. (2004). FreeRepublic.com. A conservative news forum. *Bush's pro-life record as of May 18, 2004.* Retrieved on July 15, 2004, from http://www.freerepublic.com/focus/f-news/1140835/posts

Williams, P. W. (1990). *America's religions: Traditions and cultures.* New York: Macmillan.

To devalue his [her] language or to presume Standard English is a better system is to devalue the child and his [her] culture and to reveal a naiveté concerning language.

JOAN BARATZ, 1968

Chapter 7

Language

Theresa Roberts, a kindergarten teacher at Kaahumanu Elementary School in Honolulu, had just finished welcoming her new kindergarten class and introducing herself. As she wrote her name and the school's on the chalkboard, she felt a slight tug on the back of her skirt and heard a faint voice just above a whisper say, "Teacha, I like go pee pee." Turning around, she saw the pleading face of Nohea Kealoha. "What did you say?" Ms. Roberts said disgustedly. In a slightly louder voice, Nohea repeated herself, "I like go pee pee." With classmates beginning to giggle, Ms. Roberts exclaimed, "You will go nowhere, young lady, until you ask me in proper English. Now say it properly." "I no can," pleaded Nohea. "Then you can just stand there until you do." With the students still giggling and Nohea standing as ordered, Ms. Roberts proceeded with her lesson.

A few minutes later, the occasional giggle exploded in a chorus of laughter. As Ms. Roberts turned to Nohea, the child was sobbing as she stood in the middle of a large puddle of urine on the classroom floor.

Opportunities for Reflection

CW

1. *Do teachers have the right to expect and demand Standard English from their students?*
2. *How important is it for students to be able to speak Standard English?*
3. *If a student is able to communicate well enough in his or her nonstandard English for others to understand, why should educators be concerned about nonstandard English usage?*

To answer these questions online, go to this chapter's Opening Scenario module of the Companion Website.

Language and Culture

The above incident took place in a school in Hawaii many years ago. Nohea (not her real name) is now a great-grandmother and describes the incident as one of the most painful and humiliating in her life. When she entered school, she was unable to speak **Standard English** (language considered proper in a community); she could speak only Pidgin English (a Creole of English with words and phrases from Hawaiian, Chinese, Japanese, etc.). The teacher knew precisely what the child was trying to say. The teacher's insensitivity, however, resulted in lasting emotional scars on a child, and now as an adult. This type of insensitivity, unfortunately, is not an isolated incident. Individuals in southeastern New Mexico have described similar incidents involving non-English-speaking Latino students entering school for the first time.

Language is a system of vocal sounds and/or nonverbal systems by which group members communicate with one another. It is a critical tool in the development of an individual's identity, self-awareness, and intellectual and psychological growth (Jay, 2003). It makes our behavior human. It can incite anger, elicit love, inspire bravery, and arouse fear. It binds groups of people together. Language and dialect serve as a focal point for cultural identity. Language has a role in connecting individuals to each other and shapes personal identity. People who share the same language or dialect often share the same feelings, beliefs, and behaviors. It provides a common bond for individuals with the same linguistic and same common heritage. It may also be the means by which one group of people stereotypes another. Language and accents can usually be altered, whereas racial and physical appearance generally cannot. Thus, through changing the style of one's language or even the language itself, an individual can express relationships to those with whom he or she interacts (Dicker, 2003).

Most students enter school speaking Standard English. Some students, however, come to school barely speaking English. Some are bilingual, some speak a **nonstandard dialect** (the same language by a different dialect than that which is considered standard—for example Black English), and a few students with hearing impairments may use sign language to communicate. As the scene changes from school to school, the languages and **dialects** (variations of a language usually determined by region or social class) spoken also change. The scene, however, is indicative of the multilingual nature of the United States, a result of its multicultural heritage. Students exhibit cultural similarities and differences related to language, as well as to gender, class, ethnicity, religion, exceptionalities, and age. Because they speak one or more languages, as well as dialects of these languages, they are part of another cultural group. Of course, not all African American children speak **Black English** (a vernacular or dialect of the majority of Black Americans), nor do all Latinos speak Spanish. Within most cultures, members will vary greatly in language or dialect usage.

Eurocentrism and Eurocentric curricula place Europeans and European Americans as the focus of the world with respect to culture, history, economics, values, lifestyles, worldviews, and so forth (Nieto, 2004; Smith, 2004). Because U.S. society has such strong Eurocentric roots, European languages and accents may be given higher status than those from non-European countries. French and German languages may be viewed as more academic, more sophisticated, and more prestigious in some segments of society. Children from these linguistic backgrounds may be viewed with greater esteem than immigrant children from Third World countries. Society and educators may stigmatize bilingual students or those from limited English backgrounds if they are from backgrounds of poverty. They may perceive them to be low status and educationally at risk. Over the years, numerous individuals with doctoral degrees from immigrant and language minority backgrounds have shared with the authors their experiences of being discouraged by their teachers from seeking a college education. Rather than value and promote the use of two or more languages, some educators expect students to replace their native languages with English as soon as possible. Movements to establish English-only policies and practices may further devalue the immigrant student's home language.

Individuals who have limited English proficiency frequently suffer institutional discrimination as a result of the limited acceptance of languages other than English. Wolfram, Adger, and Christian (1999) assert that students in this group are frequently at great risk for school failure, despite the fact that they may not necessarily be categorized as disadvantaged. Garcia (1999) suggests that there may be adverse effects on students' cognitive development if their culture and native language are ignored or denigrated.

LANGUAGE AS A SOCIALIZING AGENT

Language is much more than just a means of communication. It is used to socialize children into their linguistic and cultural communities, developing patterns that distinguish one community from another. Thus, the interaction of language and culture is complex but central to the socialization of children into acceptable cultural patterns. Although there are many theories regarding the development of language, exactly how a language is learned is not completely understood. Almost all children have the ability to learn one or more native languages. In part through imitating older persons, children gradually learn. They learn to select almost instinctively the right word, the right response, and the right gesture to fit the situation. By age 5, children have learned the syntax of their native language, and they know that words in different arrangements mean different things. This suggests that within their own communities, children develop impressive language skills, although these skills may vary greatly from school requirements (Wolfram, Adger, & Christian, 1999). At an early age, children acquire the delicate muscle controls necessary for pronouncing the words of the native language or for signing naturally if the child is deaf. As the child grows older, it becomes increasingly more difficult to make the vocal muscles behave in new, unaccustomed ways necessary to master a foreign language. For example, some individuals from the Philippine Islands are unaccustomed to the sounds associated with the letter *f*, which makes it difficult, if not impossible, for some to pronounce the word *four* as an American does. All this tends to inhibit people from learning new languages and encourages them to maintain the one into which they were born.

Native speakers of a language unconsciously know and obey the rules and customs of their language community. Society and language interact constantly. A wrong choice in word selection may come across as rude, crude, or ignorant. Individuals who are learning a new language or who are unfamiliar with **colloquialisms,** the informal or conversational speech in a community, may make wrong choices or even be surprised at the use of certain words when such use is incongruent with their perceptions of what is proper. For instance, an Australian student in a Southwestern U.S. university was shocked when a woman in his class responded to his query of what she had been doing during the summer: "Oh, just piddling around." Her response was meant to convey the message that she had been passing her time in idle activities. From his frame of reference, however, the Australian student understood her to say that she had been urinating. It is important for classroom teachers to recognize that students who are new to a language may not always be able to make appropriate word selections or to comprehend the meaning of particular dialects or colloquialisms. Although the United States is primarily an English-speaking country, many other languages are spoken here. Spanish, Chinese, French, German, Tagalog, Vietnamese, and Italian are the most commonly used languages other than English (U.S. Census Bureau, 2003).

In the 1930s, Fiorello La Guardia was the mayor of New York City. La Guardia, of Jewish and Italian ancestry, was fluent in Yiddish, Italian, German, and French as well as the New York dialect of English (NYC Mayors, 2004). La Guardia was known to vary not only the language, but his speech styles with each ethnic group. For example, when speaking to Italian audiences, he used broad, sweeping gestures, characteristic of the people of southern Italy. When speaking to Jewish audiences, he used the forearm chop identified with many of the Eastern European Jews. The example of La Guardia suggests not only that different ethnic groups have different communication styles but also that individuals adjust their communication style, whenever possible, to suit the needs of the intended audience.

LANGUAGE DIVERSITY

Among English-speaking individuals are numerous dialects—from the Southern drawl of Atlanta, to the Appalachian white dialect, to the Brooklyn dialect of New York. Each is distinctive, and each is an effective means of communication for those who share its linguistic style. The U.S. Census Bureau (2003) estimated that there were approximately 47 million non-English speaking individuals living in the country in 2000. This represents a 14% increase from the 1990 numbers. Although the population grew by more than one fourth from 1980 to 2000, the number of individuals speaking a language other than English at home more than doubled. This figure does not include the millions of English-speaking individuals whose dialects are sometimes labeled as nonstandard. The U.S. Census Bureau (2003) also identified 329 languages spoken in the United States in 2000. Language diversity in the schools is addressed in the "Educational Implications" section on page 294.

The multilingual nature of U.S. society reflects the rich cultural heritage of the people. Such language diversity is an asset to the nation, especially in its interaction with other nations in the areas of commerce, defense, education, science, and technology. The advantage to being bilingual or multilingual is often overlooked because of our ethnocentrism, or belief in the superiority of our own ethnicity or culture. In many other nations, children are expected to become fluent in two or more languages and numerous dialects, enabling them to communicate with other groups and to appreciate language diversity.

Pause to Reflect 7.1

In many countries other than the United States, individuals learn to speak two, three, or more languages. Schools in these areas promote the use of both the native language and other local and regional languages. Two or more languages are taught from the early grades.

- *Why do you think bilingualism and multilingualism do not receive the same support in the United States?*

- *Are there advantages to being fluent in more than one language in the United States? If yes, what are they? Are there any disadvantages? If yes, what are they?*

To answer these questions online, go to the Pause to Reflect module for this chapter of the Companion Website.

The Nature of Language

As humans, we communicate to share ourselves with others. Language is our medium of exchange for sharing our internal states of being with one another. Through language, we reach out and make contact with our surrounding realities. Through language, we share with others our experiences with that reality (Samovar & Porter, 2004).

Samovar and Porter (2004) suggest that language is not simply a means of reporting experience, but rather a way of defining experience. Different languages represent different social realities. Thus, to understand what is being said, we must also understand the social context of the language itself. Language goes beyond the simple understanding of one another. It helps us understand culture itself; it represents culture. Each language provides us with a means to perceive the world and a means to interpret experiences.

There is no such thing as a good language or a bad language from a linguistic point of view. All languages have developed to express the needs of their users. In that sense, all languages are equal. It is true that languages do not all have the same amounts of grammar, phonology, or semantic structure. It is also true that society places different levels of social status on the different language groups. These judgments are based not on linguistic acceptability, but on social grounds (Owens, 2005; Wolfram, Adger, & Christian, 1999). Languages are equal, however, in the sense that there is nothing limiting, demeaning, or handicapping about any of them. All languages meet the social and psychological needs of their speakers and, as such, are arguably equal (Crystal, 1997).

CULTURAL INFLUENCES

Language usage is culturally determined. In addition to influencing the order of words to form phrases, language influences thinking patterns. "Time" is described differently from culture to culture. Western societies view time as something that can be saved, lost, or wasted; punctuality is highly valued. In other societies, time assumes different values and is reflected in the language of the group. The language of the Lakota Sioux American Indians, for example, has no words to convey "late" or "waiting" (Samovar & Porter, 2004).

Individuals from the Southern United States may be accustomed to exchanging pleasantries and what they may consider "small talk," prior to substantive or business conversation. To do otherwise, might be considered rude by some individuals. Some Asians tend to be circular in their speaking patterns. They may not speak directly to the point, but provide broad background information on what they are trying to convey. One reason for this manner of speaking is the feeling that, for one to understand and appreciate the point to be made, a foundation or background must be fully laid out. In this manner, the point of the discussion is clearly in proper context. For those Westerners and others who are more accustomed to getting directly to the issue at hand, the point could be lost in the circular presentation of the concept.

For effective communication to take place, it is important that there are enough cultural similarities between the sender and the receiver for the latter to decode the message adequately. Even when one is familiar with a word or phrase, comprehension of the intended meaning may not be possible unless there is similarity in cultural backgrounds.

In certain cultural groups, *bad* takes on an opposite meaning and may denote the "best." A *candy man* is not one who sells sweets, but one who sells drugs. *Bad* and *candy man* are examples of **argot,** a more or less secretive vocabulary of a co-culture group. Here, a word sounds the same but the meaning is different (for example, *bad* meaning best, and *bad* meaning the opposite of good). **Co-cultures** are groups of people who exist and function apart from the dominant culture. Users of argot include prisoners, homosexuals, gang members, and prostitutes (Samovar & Porter, 2004).

Language is very much cultural. It, together with dialects, is usually related to one's ethnic, geographic, gender, or class origins. Speakers from a particular background often downgrade the linguistic styles of others. For example, Easterners may be critical of the speech of Southerners, citing the use of slow, extended vowels and the expression "y' all." A graduate student from the eastern United States, who attended a Dallas, Texas area university, admitted to a friend that he initially thought that Texans with a drawl were ignorant individuals. Southerners, on the other hand, may be critical of the speech and language patterns of people from Brooklyn, who seem to some to speak through their noses and to use such phrases as "youse guys." The Eastern dialect of English is appropriate in the East, the Southern dialect appropriate in the South, and Black English, or **Ebonics,** the dialect of the majority of Black Americans, is appropriate in many African American communities.

Language systems are dynamic like most other cultural groups. They change constantly as society changes. Language change is inevitable and rarely predictable. For example, an elderly third-generation Japanese American born and raised in Maryland learned Japanese from both his grandparents and parents. On his first trip to Japan many years ago, he had no difficulty in conversing with the people, but he noticed smiles, grins, and giggles when he spoke. When he asked whether he had said anything humorous, the people politely explained that he was speaking as if he were someone out of the 1800s. His grandparents had immigrated to the United States in the 1800s and his

For more information on identity with cultural groups, see Chapter 1.

family, insulated from modern-day Japanese, had maintained the language systems used more than 100 years ago. The language in Japan, however, had changed sufficiently to make his language patterns stand out as archaic.

In some areas, language changes are so gradual that they go unnoticed. In other circumstances, changes are more easily noted. Expressions and words tend to be identified with a particular period. Sometimes the language is related to particular cultures for certain periods. For example, slang words and phrases such as *he got game, airhead,* and *411,* may be a part of our language for a time, only to be replaced by other expressions.

Language Differences

Literally thousands of languages are known in the world today. Most reference books suggest 4,000 to 5,000, but estimates are as high as 10,000 languages (Crystal, 1997). Professor Vyacheslav Ivanov of the University of California, Los Angeles, indicates that there are at least 324 identified languages in Los Angeles County. In addition, many of these languages have different dialects (for example, Chinese Mandarin, Cantonese, Taiwanese, etc.). Professor Ivanov estimates that publications are locally produced in about 180 languages. There are 92 languages that have been specifically identified among students in the Los Angeles Unified School District (*Los Angeles Almanac,* 2004).

Social variables also contribute to language differences. Both class and ethnicity reflect differences in language. The greater the social distance between groups, the greater the tendency toward language differences. Upwardly mobile individuals often adopt the language patterns of the dominant society because it may, at times, facilitate social acceptance.

BILINGUALISM

Language diversity in the United States has been maintained primarily because of continuing immigration from non-English-speaking countries. In its short history, the United States has probably been host to more bilingual people than any other country. As new immigrants enter the country, they bring with them their own culture, values, and languages. As their children and grandchildren are born in this country, these immigrants witness with ambivalence, the loss of their home language in favor of English.

One aspect of **bilingualism,** the ability to speak two languages, in the United States is its extreme instability, for it is a transitional stage toward **monolingualism** (ability to speak only one language) in English. As defined above, bilingualism is the ability to use two languages, and many children who are bilingual in their homes eventually lose the ability to utilize the home language in favor of the dominant language. In this, they become monolingual, with the ability to function in just one language. Schools have assisted in this process. Prior to World War I, native languages were used in many schools where a large number of ethnic group members were trying to preserve their language. In this country, the maintenance and

The United States has become increasingly diverse linguistically, as evidenced by the various business signs we see in our communities.

use of native languages other than English now depend on the efforts of members of the language group through churches and other community activities. Now, even our bilingual education programs are designed to move students quickly into English-only instruction. However, a review of the research suggests that bilingual education in the United States is far more effective than a strictly monolingual approach (Corson, 1999).

Early language policies throughout this country were extremely narrow in focus, and failed to take into account the social-cultural problems inherent in language and learning (Corson, 1999). The acquisition of a second language is important when it serves one's own social and economic needs. Without English language skills, immigrants are often relegated to the most menial, lowest paying, and sometimes dangerous jobs in society.

During the civil rights movement of the 1960s, language-minority groups, especially Latinos, began to celebrate their native language traditions. Other ethnic groups decried the loss of their native languages over a few generations and blamed the school's Americanization process for the loss. The passage of federal legislation for bilingual education resulted. Many of those early advocates, however, hoped that the bilingual programs would help maintain and promote the native language while teaching English skills.

People hold different opinions about the degree of fluency required to be considered bilingual. Whereas some maintain that a bilingual individual must have native-like fluency in both languages, others suggest that measured competency in two languages constitutes bilingualism (Baca & Cervantes, 2004). Baca and Cervantes (2004) suggest that there are two types of bilingualism: **subtractive bilingualism** and

additive bilingualism. Subtractive bilingualism occurs when a second language replaces the first. Additive bilingualism is the development of a second language without detriment to the first. The latter has the more positive effect on academic achievement, as the learner is able to acquire a high level of proficiency in both languages.

ACCENTS

An **accent** generally refers to how an individual pronounces words. Because many monolingual Japanese speakers do not have the sound of an "*l*" in their language, many tend to pronounce English words that begin with the letter "*l*" as if they began with the letter "*r*." Thus, the word *light* may be pronounced as if it were *right,* and *long* as if it were *wrong.* Note that an accent differs from the standard language only in pronunciation. A dialect, however, may contain changes both in pronunciation and in grammatical patterns of the language system. Teachers should be aware that persons who speak with an accent often speak Standard English but, at this level of their linguistic development, are unable to speak without an accent.

DIALECTS

In the United States, English is the primary language. Numerous English dialects are used throughout the country, however. There is no agreement on the number of dialects of English spoken in the United States. There are at least 11 regional dialects: Eastern New England, New York City, Western Pennsylvania, Middle Atlantic, Appalachian, Southern, Central, Midland, North Central, Southwest, and Northwest (Owens, 2005). Social, ethnic, age, and gender considerations, however, complicate any attempt to isolate areas completely. Dialects are language rule systems used by

 VIDEO INSIGHT

American Spoken Here

In this information age where everyone is a phone call, an e-mail, or a flight away from another, it would seem logical that the different accents and dialects around the country might merge into one, but research from the University of Pennsylvania tells a different story. In this video segment you will see how American accents are becoming more and more distinct from one another.

1. *Sit down with a group of your peers.*
2. *Does anyone have a noticeable accent?*
3. *How would you characterize it?*
4. *Have you ever judged others on the basis of a dialect or an accent? If yes, when and how? Where was the person from?*
5. *What kind of dialect do the people of your hometown have?*

To answer these questions online, go to the ABC News Video Insight module for this chapter of the Companion Website.

DVD

CW

identifiable groups that vary in some manner from a language standard considered ideal. Each dialect shares a common set of grammatical rules with the standard language and should be considered structurally equal (Wolfram, Adger, & Christian, 1999). Theoretically, dialects of a language are mutually intelligible to all speakers of the language; however, some dialects enjoy greater social acceptance and prestige. No dialect is better than any other, nor should a dialect be characterized as substandard, deviant, or inferior (Owens, 2005).

Certain languages are sometimes improperly referred to as dialects. Examples are the labeling of African languages as African dialects or the languages of the American Indians as Indian dialects. This improper practice would be synonymous with labeling French and German as dialects spoken in the different countries in Europe.

Regional Dialects.   Dialects differ from one another in a variety of ways. Differences in vowels are a primary means of distinguishing regional differences, whereas consonant differences tend to distinguish social dialects. Regional and social dialects cannot be divorced from one another, however, because an individual's dialect may be a blend of both. In Northern dialects, for example, the *i* in words such as *time, pie,* and *side* is pronounced with a long-i sound that Wolfram and Christian (1989) describe as a rapid production of two vowel sounds, one sounding more like *ah* and the other like *ee.* The second sound glides off the first so that *time* becomes *taem, pie* becomes *pae,* and *side* becomes *saed.* Southern and Southern-related dialects may eliminate the gliding *e,* resulting in *tam* for *time, pa* for *pie,* and *sad* for *side.*

Social Dialects.   In social dialects, consonants tend to distinguish one dialect from another. Common examples of consonant pronunciation differences are in the "*th*" sound and in the consonants "*r*" and "*l.*" In words such as *these, them,* and *those,* the beginning "*th*" sound may be replaced with a "*d,*" resulting in *dese, dem,* and *dose.* In words such as *think, thank,* and *throw,* the "*th*" may be replaced with a "*t,*" resulting in *tink, tank,* and *trow.* Wolfram, Adger, and Christian (1999) suggest that middle-class groups may substitute the "*d*" for "*th*" to some extent in casual speech, whereas working-class groups make the substitution more often.

In some groups, particularly the African American working class, the "*th*" in the middle or end of the word is not spoken. The "*th*" in author or tooth may be replaced with an "*f,*" as in *aufor* and *toof.* In words such as *smooth,* a "*v*" may be substituted for the "*th,*" resulting in *smoov.* In regional and socially related dialects, "*r*" and "*l*" may be lost, as in *ca* for *car* and *sef* for *self. If social dialects such as Black English, is stigmatized and interferes with some vocational opportunities, why don't Americans just learn to speak standard English?*

Opportunities for Reflection

Grammatical Differences.   Among dialects, differences in various aspects of grammatical usage can also be found. Wolfram, Adger, and Christian (1999) suggest that nonstandard grammar tends to carry with it a greater social stigma than nonstandard pronunciation.

A common example of grammatical differences in dialect is in the absence of suffixes from verbs where they are usually present in standard dialects. For example, the *-ed* suffix to denote past tense is sometimes omitted, as in, "Yesterday we play a long time." Other examples of grammatical differences are the omission of the *s* used in the present tense to denote agreement with certain subjects. "She have a car" may be used instead of "She has a car." The omission of the suffix has been observed in certain Native Indian communities, as well as among members of the African American working class. In the dialect of some African American working-class groups, the omission of the *s* in the plural form of certain words and phrases, as in "two boy" rather than "two boys," has been observed. *Two* is plural, and an *s* to show possession after boy is viewed as redundant. Also often omitted in these dialect groups is the possessive *'s,* as in "my friend car" instead of "my friend's car."

Other Differences.   Variations in language patterns among groups are significant when compared by age, socioeconomic status, gender, ethnic group, and geographic region (Wolfram, Adger, & Christian, 1999). For example, individuals in the 40- to 60-year-old age group tend to use language patterns different from those of teenage groups. Teenagers tend to adopt certain language patterns that are characteristic of their age group. Slang words, particular pronunciation of some words, and certain grammatical contractions are often related to the teenage and younger groups.

Social factors play a role in the choice of language patterns. The more formal the situations are, the greater the likelihood to use more formal speech patterns. The selection of appropriate speech patterns appears to come naturally and spontaneously. Individuals are usually able to "read their environment" and to select, from their large repertoire, the language or speech pattern that is appropriate for the situation.

Wolfram, Adger, and Christian (1999) also indicate that although the evidence is not conclusive, the range between high and low pitch used in African American communities is greater than that found in white communities. Such differences would, of course, be the result of learned behavior. African American males may tend to speak with raspiness in their voices. American women, it has been suggested, may typically have a greater pitch distribution over a sentence than do men.

Other differences in dialects exist as well. Because educators are likely to find dialect differences in the classroom, additional reading in this area may be appropriate. The "Suggested Readings" section at the end of this chapter includes some helpful resources.

BI-DIALECTICISM

Certain situations, both social and professional, may dictate adjustments in dialect. Some individuals may have the ability to speak in two or more dialects, making them **bi-dialectal.** In possessing the skills to speak in more than one dialect, an individual may have some distinct advantages and may be able to function and gain acceptance in more cultural contexts. For example, a large-city executive with a rural farm background may quickly abandon his Armani suit and put on his jeans and boots when visiting his parents' home. When speaking with the hometown folks, he may put aside the Standard English necessary in his business dealings and return to the hometown dialect, which validates him as the local town person they have always known.

Likewise, an African American school psychologist who speaks Standard English both at home and at work may elect to include some degree of Black English in her conference with African American parents at the school. The **vernacular,** or native language, dialect, or speech, may be used to develop rapport and credibility with the parents. This strategy may allow the psychologist to show the parents that she is African American more than just in appearance and that she understands the problems of black children and parents. However, she may choose to use little if any of the parents' dialect in order to maintain her credibility as a professional. In a

Opportunities for Reflection

conference with white parents, the same psychologist may choose to be scrupulously careful to speak only Standard English, believing this to be necessary for effective communication and to maintain professional credibility. *Why don't more teachers realize that the ability to speak in two or more languages and two or more dialects has advantages of being able to function in just one?*

Children tend to learn adaptive behaviors rapidly, a fact that is often demonstrated in the school. Children who fear peer rejection as a result of speaking Standard English may choose to use their dialect even at the expense of criticism by the teacher. Others may choose to speak with the best Standard English they possess in dealing with the teacher but use the dialect or language of the group when outside the classroom.

Educators must be aware of children's need for peer acceptance, and balance this need with realistic educational expectations. Pressuring a child to speak Standard English at all times and punishing him or her for any use of dialects may be detrimental to the overall well-being of the child, as indicated in the scenario involving Nohea and Ms. Roberts at the beginning of the chapter.

PERSPECTIVES ON STANDARD ENGLISH

With the wide variations of dialects, there are actually several dialects of Standard American English (Wolfram, Adger, & Christian, 1999). Although Standard English is often referred to in the literature, no single dialect can be identified as such. In reality, however, the speech of a certain group of people in each community tends to be identified as standard. Norms vary with communities, and there are actually two norms: informal standard and formal standard. The language considered proper in a community is the **informal standard.** Its norms tend to vary from community to community. **Formal standard** is the acceptable written language that is typically found in grammar books. Few individuals speak formal Standard English.

Because no particular dialect is inherently and universally standard, the determination of what is and what is not standard is usually made by people or groups of people in positions of power and status to make such a judgment. Teachers and employers are among those in such a position. These are the individuals who decide what is and what is not acceptable in the school and in the workplace. Thus, people seeking success in school and in the job market often tend to use the standard language as identified and used by individuals in positions of power. Moreover, certain individuals may be highly respected in the community. Just as people who are respected and admired often influence hairstyles, the language of those who are admired also serves as a model. Generally speaking, Standard American English is a composite of the language spoken by the educated professional middle class.

PERSPECTIVES ON BLACK ENGLISH

Black English, sometimes referred to as Vernacular Black English, African American Vernacular English (AAVE), or Ebonics, is one of the best-known dialects spoken in the United States. It becomes controversial when schools consider using it for instruction. Its use is widespread and it is a form of communication for the majority of African Americans. It is a linguistic system used primarily by working-class African Americans within their speech community (Owens, 2005; Wolfram, Adger, & Christian, 1999).

Although there has been much debate regarding its nature and history, Black English is considered by most linguists and African Americans to be a legitimate system of communication. It is a systematic language rule system of its own and not a substandard, deviant, or improper form of English. Although differences are found between Black English and Standard English, they both operate with the same type of structural rules as any other type of language or dialect. Wolfram, Adger, and Christian (1999) assert that when comparing the linguistic characteristics of Black English and Standard English, we find far more common language features than distinctive ones. They dispute the theory by some linguists that Black English is increasingly evolving in a divergent path from other vernacular English dialects. In fact, there is considerable overlap among Black English, Southern English, and Southern white nonstandard English. Much of the distinctiveness of the dialect is in its intonational patterns, speaking rate, and distinctive lexicons (Owens, 2005). Jay (2003) contends that some individuals have used these differences to reinforce prejudice toward African Americans and their dialects.

Teacher bias against Black English is common among majority-group educators and among some African American educators as well. Although Black English is an ethnically related dialect, it is also a dialect related to social class. Dialects related to lower social classes, such as Appalachian English and Black English, are typically stigmatized in our multidialectal society. Unfortunately, many people attach relative values to certain dialects and to the speakers of those dialects. Assumptions are made regarding the intelligence, ability, and moral character of the speakers, and this can have a significant negative impact (Wolfram, Adger, & Christian, 1999). As such, the use of these dialects without the ability to speak Standard American English leaves the speaker with a distinct social, educational, and sometimes occupational disadvantage. The refusal to acknowledge Black English as a legitimate form of communication could be considered as another example of Eurocentric behavior. Insofar as teachers endorse this rejection, they are sending a message to many of their African American students that the dialect of their parents, grandparents, and significant others in their lives is substandard and unacceptable. The rejection of Black English as a legitimate form of communication has been detrimental to the academic development and achievement of students (Hecht, Jackson, & Ribeau, 2003).

DIALECTS AND EDUCATION

In 1996, the Oakland (California) Unified School District moved into the center of controversy with their adopted policy on Black English, or Ebonics. At that time, African American students comprised 53% of Oakland's 52,300-student district. Of all the ethnic groups in the district, they had, on average, the lowest grade point average (1.8), and they comprised 71% of the students enrolled in special education programs. In an attempt to remediate some academic problems of black students in the district, the school board voted unanimously to recognize Black English, or Ebonics, as a second language and the primary language of its African American students.

The school board's December 18, 1996, resolution stated, "African language systems are genetically based and not a dialect of English, and. . . the interests of the Oakland Unified School District in providing equal opportunities for all of its students dictate limited-English proficient education programs recognizing the English-language acquisition and improvement skills of African-American students are as fundamental as is application for bilingual principles for others whose primary languages are other than English" (*Education Week,* 1997, pp. 1–2).

Attitudes Toward Black English

Israel Martinez is the principal of Jackie Robinson Middle School. An appointment was made for him with Ms. Kermit Norton, the mother of a sixth grader. She declined to give Martinez's secretary any information on why she was coming. Martinez exchanges the customary greeting and then asks Ms. Norton what he can do for her. At this point, she calmly tells Mr. Martinez that his teachers need to stop being racist and to start respecting the culture of African American students.

Mr. Martinez is feeling defensive and tries to maintain his composure as he inquires about the nature of the complaint. "This white teacher of Trayson's says to my son to stop talking this Black English stuff because it is bad English and he won't allow it in his classroom. He says it's a low-class dialect, and if Trayson keeps talking like that, he ain't never going to amount to nothing, will never get into college, and won't never get a good job. That's just plain racist. That's an attack against all black folk. His granddaddy and grandmother talk that way. All my kinfolk talk that way. I talk that way. You mean to tell me that this school thinks we're all low-class trash? Is that what your teachers think of black folk?"

Questions for Discussion

1. *How should Mr. Martinez respond to Ms. Norton?*
2. *Should he arrange a meeting between Ms. Norton and Aaron Goodman, Trayson's teacher?*
3. *What should be the school's position on Ebonics, or vernacular Black English?*
4. *Is this a school district or individual school issue?*
5. *Is Mr. Goodman wrong to tell Trayson that his speech is a low-class dialect?*
6. *Is Mr. Goodman wrong to tell Trayson that if he speaks only Black English it will have negative educational and vocational consequences?*

To answer these questions online, go to the Critical Incidents in Teaching module for this chapter of the Companion Website.

The resolution was seen by some as the school district's attempt to obtain more funding from both state and federal sources for bilingual education. It was praised by some and attacked by others. Prominent African Americans such as Maya Angelou and Jesse Jackson were among the early critics. Jackson, who met with school officials, later moderated his position. Richard Riley, who was Secretary of Education at the time, stated, "Elevating 'black English' to the status of a language is not the way to raise standards of achievement in our schools and for our students. The use of federal bilingual-education funds for what has been called 'black English' or 'Ebonics' is not permitted. The administration's policy is that 'Ebonics' is a nonstandard form of English and not a foreign language" (Schnaiberg, 1997, p. 3).

Lost in the Oakland School Board controversy was the fact that education literature suggested that the original decision had considerable scientific support (Wheeler, 1999). This was clearly demonstrated by the support of the Linguistic Society of America (Wolfram, Adger, & Christian, 1999) and the success of the 1977 Bridge program (Wheeler, 1999). The Bridge program consisted of a series of readings and cassette recordings using Black English in an attempt to help children learn to read. After four months of testing, the Bridge program students made better progress with their dialect readers than other African American students utilizing Standard English materials (Wheeler, 1999). Although public outcry forced the cancellation of the Bridge readers, the success of the program was undeniable. Learning to read and dialect acquisition are two distinct tasks. Attempts to merge the two may contribute to children's failure in school (Wheeler, 1999).

The issue of requiring a standard American English dialect in the schools is both sensitive and controversial. Because of the close relationship between ethnic minority groups and dialects that are often considered nonstandard, this issue also has civil rights implications.

To require that Standard English be spoken in the schools is considered discriminatory by some who think that such a requirement places an additional educational burden on the nonstandard-English-speaking students. The insistence on Standard English could hinder the acquisition of other educational skills, making it difficult for these students to succeed.

Others argue that the school has the responsibility to teach each student Standard English to better cope with the demands of society. There is little doubt that the inability to speak Standard English can be a decided disadvantage to an individual in certain situations, such as seeking employment.

Dialect differences in the school may cause problems beyond the interference with the acquisition of skills. A second problem tends to be subtler and involves the attitude of teachers and other school personnel toward students with nonstandard dialects. Too often, educators and other individuals make erroneous assumptions about nonstandard dialects, believing at times that the inability to speak a standard dialect reflects lower intelligence. Wolfram, Adger, and Christian (1999) suggest that unlike prejudice based on gender or ethnicity, which may often result in litigation and positive change, language prejudices are rarely challenged and, therefore, are much less likely to change.

Many individuals have distinct preconceived notions about nonstandard-English-speaking individuals. If teachers and other school personnel react in this manner to students, the consequences could be serious. Students may be treated as if they are less intelligent than they are, and they may respond in a self-fulfilling prophecy in which they function at a level lower than they are capable of reaching. In cases where children are tracked in schools, they may be placed in groups below their actual ability level. This problem surfaces in the form of disproportionately low numbers of African American and Latino children being placed in classes for the gifted and talented (Office of Civil Rights, 1999). School administrators cite the inability to appropriately identify these gifted and talented ethnic minority children as one of their biggest challenges. Teachers who have negative attitudes toward children with nonstandard dialects may be less prone to recognize potential giftedness and may be less inclined to refer these children for possible assessment and placement. *Does a person who speaks in a Brooklyn, New York accent, a Southern drawl, or Hawaiian Pidgin English seem less intelligent to you than a person who speaks standard English?*

Opportunities for Reflection

Educators have several alternatives for handling dialect in the educational setting. The first is to accommodate all dialects on the basis that they are all equal.

Teacher expectations and tracking are discussed in more detail in Chapter 2.

The second is to insist that only a standard dialect be allowed in the schools. This second alternative would allow for the position that functional ability in such a dialect is necessary for success in personal, as well as vocational, pursuits. The third alternative is a position between the two extremes, and it is the alternative most often followed. Native dialects are accepted for certain uses, but Standard English is encouraged and insisted on in other circumstances. Students in such a school setting may be required to read and write in Standard English because this is the primary written language they will encounter in this country. They would not be required to eliminate their natural dialect in speaking. Such a compromise allows students to use two or more dialects in the school. It tends to acknowledge the legitimacy of all dialects while recognizing the social and vocational implications of being able to function in Standard English.

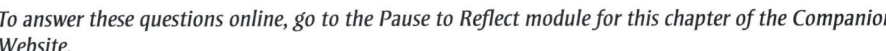

Pause to Reflect 7.2

Some activists have suggested that the language of instruction should be in the dialect of students' cultures. Others argue that Standard English should be the only acceptable language within the classroom.

- *What are the advantages and disadvantages of each approach?*
- *Do you think teachers should at least be familiar with the dialects used by students in the classroom? Why or why not?*
- *How do you plan to respond to different dialects in your classroom?*

To answer these questions online, go to the Pause to Reflect module for this chapter of the Companion Website.

The issue that seems to be at stake with some supporters of the right to use nonstandard dialects is the recognition of the legitimacy of the particular dialect. Few, if any, will deny the social and vocational implications of dialects. Some parents may prefer to develop, or have their children develop, a standard dialect. However, the arrogant posture of some school officials in recognizing standard dialects as the only legitimate form of communication is offensive to many and may preclude rational solutions to this sensitive issue.

SIGN LANGUAGE

Some languages do not have a written system. Individuals who are deaf are not able to hear the sounds that make up oral languages and have developed their own language for communication. **American Sign Language (ASL)** is a natural language that has been developed and used by persons who are deaf. Just in the past 30 years, linguists have come to recognize ASL as a language with complex grammar and well-regulated syntax. A growing number of colleges and universities will accept fluency in ASL to meet a second-language requirement. The majority of adults who are deaf in Canada and the United States use ASL. Individuals who are deaf use it to communicate with each other. Like oral languages, different sign languages have developed in different countries.

Children who are deaf are able to pick up the syntax and rhythms of signing as spontaneously as hearing children pick up their oral languages. Both children who hear and children who are deaf who are born into deaf families usually learn ASL from birth. Most children who are deaf, however, have hearing parents and do not have the opportunity to learn ASL until they attend a school program for the deaf, where they learn from both their teachers and peers.

ASL is the only sign language recognized as a language in its own right, rather than a variation of spoken English. With its own vocabulary, syntax, and grammatical rules, ASL does not correspond completely to spoken or written English (Heward, 2003; Smith 2004). To communicate with the hearing, those who are deaf often use signed English. It is a system of signing that parallels the English language. Rather than have its own language patterns like ASL, **signed English** is a system that translates the English oral or written word into a sign. Few hearing individuals know ASL because they rarely observe it. When one sees an interpreter on television or at a meeting, it is usually signed English that is being observed.

Sign language is one component of the deaf culture that sets its users apart from the hearing world. Because of the residential school experiences of many individuals who are deaf, a distinct cultural community has developed. As a cultural community, they are highly endogamous, with in-group marriages estimated at between 85% of all marriages involving individuals who are deaf (News-Medical.Net, 2004). Although ASL is the major language of the deaf community, many individuals are bilingual in English and ASL.

Nonverbal Communication

Although most people think of communication as being verbal in nature, nonverbal communication can be just as important in the total communication process. Because it is so clearly interwoven into the overall fabric of verbal communication, nonverbal communication often appears to be inseparable from it.

Nonverbal communication can serve several functions. It conveys messages through one's attitude, personality, manner, or even dress. It augments verbal communication by reinforcing what one says: A smile or a pat on the back reinforces the positive statement made to a student. It contradicts verbal communication: A frown accompanying a positive statement to a student sends a mixed or contradictory message. Nonverbal communication can replace a verbal message: A finger to the lips or a teacher's hand held in the air may communicate "Silence" to a class.

The total meaning of communication includes not only the surface message as stated (content) but also the undercurrent (emotions or feelings associated with that content). The listener should watch for congruence between the verbal message and the message being sent nonverbally.

How we appear to others is a form of nonverbal communication and can, therefore, be considered as a part of our communication or language. Research has supported the contention that definite prejudices are based on physical characteristics.

There is often as much or more communicated nonverbally as there is verbally.

Opportunities for Reflection

For example, physical attractiveness plays a part in the way we perceive other people. If one has a bias against a particular group, individuals from that group could be perceived as unattractive, and can suffer from social rejection based on the perceptions and bias in the work situation (Hosoda, Stone-Romero, & Coats, 2003; McDonald, 2003; Seifert, 2001). *Does a person's physical appearance create a biased perception about the individual for you? What are your initial impressions of a person who is extremely obese, weighing 400 pounds or more?*

Cultural differences have profound implications on how individuals interact nonverbally with one another. Some cultural groups are more prone toward physical contact than others. Latinos and Native Hawaiians, for example, tend to be among the contact cultures. Consequently, one can often observe Latinos or Hawaiians greeting each other with a warm embrace. This is true among the men from these groups. As they meet their friends, it is certainly not uncommon to see these men embracing one another. On the other hand, however, it might be surprising to see Asian men embracing one another. Of course, the more acculturated Asian American men are likely to observe behaviors typical in the general society.

The usual conversational distance between Americans is about 20 to 36 inches (Haynes, 2004). A distance much greater than this may make the individuals feel too far apart for normal conversation and a normal voice level. Individuals of other cultural groups, such as Arabs, Latin Americans, and Southern Europeans are accustomed to standing considerably closer when they talk. In contrast with these contact cultures, Asians and Northern Europeans have been identified as noncontact cultures and may maintain a greater distance in conversation. Students maintain differential distances in cross-cultural relationships. White Americans tend to maintain a greater distance when conversing with blacks than when conversing among themselves. Women tend to allow a closer conversational space than do men. Straight individuals distance themselves more from conversational partners they perceive to be gay (Samovar & Porter, 2004).

Educators need to be aware that different cultural groups have different expectations when it involves contact with a teacher. The differences may have implications for educators. Some groups may view a pat on the head of a child to be a supportive gesture. However, some Southeast Asians believe that the individual's spirit resides in the head, and a pat on the head of a child may very well be viewed as offensive by both the parents and child.

Other nonverbal issues may involve the facial expressions or behaviors of the student. American teachers typically expect a child to look at them while they are having a conversation. However, some groups consider it disrespectful for the child to look directly into the eyes of the teacher. Consequently, as a sign of respect, the child may look at the floor while either speaking to the teacher or being spoken to. The teacher, however, may view the behavior in an opposite manner than intended, and demand that the child look her or him in the eye.

Any discussion of nonverbal behavior has inherent dangers. As examples are given, you must realize that these are generalizations and not assume that any given behavior can immediately be interpreted in a certain way. Nonverbal communications are often a prominent part of the context in which verbal messages are sent. Although context never has a specific meaning, communication is always dependent on context.

Second Language Acquisition

With the arrival of new immigrants annually into the United States, the resulting effect is the addition of more language minority students in our schools. Most of these students are able to move from bilingual education programs to English-only instruction. Motivation is usually high. The acquisition of English skills serves both social and economic needs. Without linguistic acculturation, assimilation into mainstream society may be impossible. This, in turn, effectively keeps non-English speakers or **English language learners (ELL),** previously referred to as limited English proficient (LEP), out of many job markets. In the future teachers can anticipate increasing numbers of ELL students whose primary language is other than English.

We should clarify here that different terms are used to identify students from minority language groups. For our purposes, we will primarily use English language learners (ELL). Some writers use English learners (EL). ELL is the term now used in most of the professional literature and is taking the place of limited English proficient (LEP) used in most of the professional literature through the late 1990s. It is still used by the Federal Government today, particularly within the U.S. Office of English Language Acquisition, Language Enhancement, and Academic

Achievement for Limited English Proficient Students (OELA). This office, within the U.S. Department of Education, was formerly the Office of Bilingual Education and Minority Language Affairs (OBEMLA). It was renamed with the George W. Bush administration, perhaps indicating a shift in the administration's emphasis in bilingual education programs. OELA's National Clearinghouse for English Language Acquisition & Language Instruction Educational Programs (NCELA), formerly the Bilingual Clearinghouse, was also renamed with the Bush administration.

THE ROLE OF FIRST LANGUAGE IN SECOND LANGUAGE ACQUISITION

Most children acquire their first language naturally through constant interaction with their parents or significant others. Knowledge of their first language plays an important role in the process of acquiring and learning a second language. Some concepts acquired through their first language (for example, Spanish) can be transferred to a second language (for example, English) when a comparable concept in the second language exists. However, English speakers should not think of Spanish, French, Chinese, or any other language as essentially English with Spanish, French, or Chinese words that, if translated, is basically the same language. There are words and concepts in all of these languages for which there is no English equivalent. There may be no exact English translation to convey the exact same meaning. For example, *"heung"* in the Chinese Cantonese dialect is translated into English as *"fragrant."* However, *"heung"* has no exact English translation. The Chinese have a very distinctive meaning, which not only conveys fragrance, but a multisensory experience. When Cantonese speakers say that food that they have placed in their mouths is *"heung,"* it may imply that it tastes, smells, and feels very special.

Corson (1999) suggests that early brain development of young children is shaped by the signs and symbols involved in first language acquisition. The failure of schools to build on a child's first language during these early years may have serious consequences in the learning process. The implications of these observed language behaviors suggest that ELL children should be allowed to develop a firm grasp of basic concepts in their home language prior to instruction of academic concepts in an English-only environment. Garcia (1999) advocates for a new pedagogy that is responsive and demonstrates respect for the skills and knowledge students bring to the classroom. Cummins (1996) maintains that we learn "by integrating new input into our existing cognitive structure or schemata" (p. 85). Consequently, a student's prior experience is the foundation for acquiring and interpreting new knowledge.

Language Proficiency. Cummins (1996) found that many ELL students failed academically after completing English as a second language (ESL) training and being placed in monolingual English class settings. Many of these students were subsequently referred and placed in special education classes. In carefully studying the language characteristics of these students, Cummins found that in two years these students were able to acquire adequate English communication skills to suggest to their teacher that they were prepared to function in a monolingual English class placement. Cummins also found, however, that the basic language skills, which he labeled **"basic interpersonal communicative skills" (BICS),** are adequate everyday conversational skills, but are inadequate to function in high-level academic situations. Crawford (2004) suggests that a good example of BICS is "playground English," which relies on nonlinguistic cues and context, used to facilitate communication (for example gestures, and other nonverbal cues). BICS, he indicates, is primarily social rather than intellectual. It requires less knowledge of the language, and utilizes simpler syntax, and a more limited vocabulary than is needed in academic settings.

Although two years is adequate for everyday conversational usage, an additional five to seven years of school training was essential to develop the higher levels of proficiency required in highly structured academic situations. Cummins (1984) labeled this higher level of proficiency **"cognitive academic language proficiency" (CALP).** Crawford (2004) suggests that CALP is a level of linguistic proficiency that is required for abstract and analytical thinking and expressions with complex meaning. He further indicates that children need this level of proficiency, for example, in writing a journal entry, which describes what they have learned, or in making a persuasive oral presentation.

Professors, who were themselves ELL students in their earlier years, have shared with the authors their experiences in making professional presentations in foreign countries. For example, a Chinese American professor who was born in China and whose first language was Chinese, can carry on fluent conversations in both Mandarin and Cantonese. However, this professor insists on translators for her presentations in China because she does not consider herself proficient in academic Chinese. Additionally, other colleagues from non-English-speaking backgrounds have shared similar experiences. This may have some similarities to BICS-level students who have not yet developed academic-level English competence and who are thrust into English-only academic situations. Unfortunately, these students are not in a position to insist on translators.

Cummins' framework for conceptualizing language proficiency has been widely adopted by many ESL and bilingual special education programs and has profound implications for language minorities. Cummins (2000) suggests that there are two reasons why it takes much longer for ELL students to learn academic language than it does to learn basic conversational language. First, academic language is the language of subject matter (for example, science, math), literature, magazines, and so forth. It is very different from conversational language. As students progress through successive grades, they encounter words that Cummins characterizes as "low frequency" words. These are words with Greek and Latin derivations. In addition, they are exposed to more complex syntax (for example, passive) and abstract expressions that are seldom if ever heard in everyday conversation. Secondly, academic language is what educators develop among native English speakers who are already fluent in conversational English when they enter school. Therefore, the ELL student is learning conversational English while classmates are at a higher level, learning academic English.

In discussing Cummins' theories, Crawford (2004) suggests that the language of instruction is not the most significant variable for ELL students. Cummins believes that sociocultural determinants of school failure for these students are more significant than linguistic factors. Schools must counteract the power relations, which exist in society, removing the racial and linguistic stigmas of being a minority group child. Cummins suggests that power and status relationships between majority and minority groups exert influence on the school performance of these students. He states that the lower the status of a group that is dominated, the lower the academic achievement (Cummins, 1996).

Hakuta, Butler, and Witt (2000) suggest that one of the most commonly asked questions regarding the education of language minority students is how long will they need specialized services such as bilingual education or English as a second language (ESL). Putting together the findings of studies of four different school districts in the San Francisco Bay area and from summary data from Canadian researchers, Hakuta and his associates came to conclusions that supported Cummins' earlier findings. The research findings suggest that oral proficiency takes three to five years to develop, and academic proficiency four to seven years.

OFFICIAL ENGLISH (ENGLISH ONLY) CONTROVERSY

In 1981, U.S. Senator S.I. Hayakawa, a strong and harsh critic of bilingual education and bilingual voting rights, introduced a constitutional amendment to make English the official language of the United States. The measure sought to prohibit federal and state laws, ordinances, regulations, orders, programs, and policies from requiring the use of other languages. Hayakawa's efforts were made not only in support of English but also against bilingualism. Had the amendment been adopted, Hayakawa's proposal would have reversed the efforts that began in the 1960s to accommodate linguistic minorities in this country. The English Language Amendment died without a hearing in the 97th Congress (Crawford, 1992).

In 1983, Hayakawa helped found the organization called "U.S. English" and began lobbying efforts that resulted in a reported 1.8 million-member organization and an annual budget in the millions of dollars (U.S. English, 2004). The movement, also referred to as **"Official English"** or "English Only," supports only the limited use of bilingual education, and has mounted a major effort to lobby the U.S. Congress to pass legislation to make English the official language of the United States. By 2004, English as the official language has been adopted as statutes or state constitutional amendments in 27 states (Crawford, 1992; U.S. English, 2004). The organization favors sheltered English immersion, and it maintains its position that ELL students should be transitioned completely out of bilingual education and into mainstream English usage within a maximum of one or two years.

Official English has become a polarizing issue. For supporters of the English Only movement, English has always been the common language in the United States. It is a means to resolve conflict in a nation that is diverse in ethnic, linguistic, and religious groups. English is an essential tool of social mobility and economic advancement (Crawford, 1992).

William Bennett (1992), Secretary of Education during the Reagan administration, leveled an attack on the Bilingual Education Act as a failure and a waste of tax dollars. Bennett indicated that he received a considerable amount of mail supporting his position. An examination of these letters by Crawford (1992), however, found that they contained little evidence or support with respect to the education of non-English-speaking students. Instead, the letter writers used the opportunity to vent their frustrations about illegal immigrants on welfare, Asians and Latinos overrunning communities, and other issues such as the out-of-control birthrates of linguistic minorities. They were offended by the use of tax dollars to support what they viewed as the perpetuation of a foreign language.

California's Proposition 227. U.S. English members have vigorously supported California **Proposition 227,** a state ballot initiative, which passed in 1998 by a margin of 61 to 39%. This law was intended by its supporters to put an end to bilingual education in the state. This proposition is often referred to as the Unz initiative after its coauthor, Ron Unz. Operating under the organization, One Nation, Unz and his supporters cite numerous examples of bilingual education failures. The proposition requires all language minority students to be educated in sheltered English immersion programs, not normally intended to exceed one year. Sheltered English immersion or structured English immersion involves a classroom where English language acquisition is accomplished with nearly all instruction in English, but with the curriculum and presentation designed for children who are learning the language. During this time, ELL students are temporarily sheltered from competing academically with native English-speaking students in mainstream classes. At the completion of the year, the students are transferred to English language mainstream classrooms (Education Commission for the States, 2004; Unz & Tuchman, 1998). The law allows parents to seek waivers and, if granted, the child's education may continue in a bilingual classroom. If schools or teachers fail to implement a child's education as prescribed by the law, they may be sued.

As might be expected, supporters of bilingual education have vigorously attacked the proposition with concerns that the Unz initiative will spread to other states. Proposition 227 opponents argue that the Unz initiative was not backed by research or scientific data. Rather, they argue, it was based on observations of the high failure and dropout rate of ELL students, primarily Latino. It was also based on observations that most ELL students are able to grasp the fundamentals of speaking English in a year. They support their arguments against the proposition by citing research (for example, Cummins, 1984), which suggests that only basic conversational skills can be acquired in such a limited time and not the necessary academic language skills, which take years to develop adequately. Opponents of Proposition 227 contend that the law is a "one size fits all" approach to educating students and that it cannot have lasting benefits. Further, they argue, that during K–4 years in school, it is extremely difficult for parents to obtain waivers to keep their children in bilingual education. Parents, they contend, have no appeal rights, and the law intimidates teachers and administrators and inhibits them from doing what they know is educationally appropriate for students (National Association for Bilingual Education [NABE], 2000). *If California voters were provided the ballot initiative, Proposition 227, with such educational significance but no research or scientific basis, why would they support such an initiative in such overwhelming numbers?*

Opportunities for Reflection

After its passage, both supporters and opponents of Proposition 227 were eager to see the state achievement test results, which would either provide evidence of its efficacy or its failure. In 1999, the results of California SAT-9 test scores for the 1998–1999 academic year were released. These achievement test scores included the results of the first ELL students to be tested after the implementation of Proposition 227. Hakuta and his bilingual education research colleagues at Stanford University examined the test results for the first three years after implementation (Hakuta, Butler, & Bousquet, 1999; Hakuta, 2001a; 2001b; Orr, Butler, Bousquet, & Hakuta, 2000). In the first two academic years (1998–1999 and 1999–2000), SAT-9 test scores for ELL students increased somewhat across the board, particularly in grades 2 and 3. Proposition 227 proponents quickly called attention to the success in test scores in California's Oceanside City Unified School District, which had faithfully implemented the mandates of the proposition. They pointed to the scores for second-grade ELL students in that district in 1998–1999, which had increased 11 percentile points from the previous year. The results in the second year were also positive, adding to the Proposition 227 supporters' claims of victory and validation. As was previously noted, increases occurred across the board in the state for all students, including ELL and monolingual English-speaking students. Scores rose for ELL students in English-only programs as well as students in bilingual programs (Hakuta et al., 1999; Orr et al., 2000).

Hakuta and his Stanford associates point out that other districts, which had maintained various forms of bilingual education (for example, Vista Unified, Santa Ana Unified, and Ocean View Unified) also had similar increases among their ELL students in the second grade. They further suggested that because the Oceanside students started at a lower baseline (12th percentile) as compared to districts such as Vista Unified (18th percentile), Santa Ana Unified (17th percentile), and Ocean View Unified (17th percentile), a statistical phenomenon known as **"regression to the mean"** had been operating. Regression to the mean implies that scores at the extreme ends of the statistical distribution move toward the population average (mean), with low scores moving higher and high scores moving lower. Hakuta and his associates suggest that the schools and school districts had become used to the tests and were taking them more seriously. They also point to class size reduction, which had just taken place in California schools, as contributing to the improved scores. While the test scores for ELL students had improved, they point to the fact that they were still low. Educators are very much aware that their students are being tested, and in a statewide "experiment" of English immersion versus bilingual education, educators may be motivated to do their best to improve learning and enhance test scores. Since test scores have improved for all groups of children, utilizing test scores as a sole criteria for determining the effectiveness of bilingual education or English immersion programs may not be the most efficacious method of making a determination. The researchers further point to the benefits of increased attention and concern about the achievement level of these students and the increasing attention given by the public and policymakers (Hakuta et al., 1999; Orr et al., 2000; UCLMRI Newsletter, 2003).

In 2001, however, the ELL test scores in the Oceanside Unified School District were disappointing to Unz and his supporters. The percentile scores in that district had stalled and in some instances had dropped. The ELL third-grade reading scores were one percentile point below the California State ELL percentile score. In more than half the schools, the percentile scores for ELL students had dropped that year in comparison to the previous school year. This was contrary to the state ELL trend of rising ELL SAT-9 scores. Hakuta pointed to what was previously stated, that the district had started out at a low baseline and regression to the mean had taken place. Now it was apparently leveling off (Hakuta, 2001a). The 2002 California achievement test results for ELL students offered no additional new information (Hakuta, 2002).

The American Institutes of Research (AIR) was commissioned by the California Department of Education in 2000 to conduct a five-year study on the effects of Proposition 227 on the education of ELL. The third-year report released in late 2003 indicated that since the passage of 227, almost all students across all language groups had experienced gains in math, reading, and language as measured by the SAT-9 achievement test. Student performance can be a function of a number of variables, which can vary from school site to school site, and are probably difficult to control for research purposes. These may include factors such as (1) leadership, (2) a clear instructional plan, (3) accountability and assessment, (4) schoolwide climate, (5) instructional strategies, (6) staff development, and (7) family involvement (AIR & WestEd, 2003).

While the supporters of Proposition 227 set out to dismantle bilingual education in California, so far they have only partially succeeded in doing so. In the school year prior to Proposition 227, there were 408,879 students enrolled in bilingual education programs. By the following academic year, 1998–1999, the bilingual education enrollment had dropped to 169,440. This represented a drop in the bilingual education student enrollment of 29% of the ELL enrollment to 12%. The most recent data in Table 7.1 suggests that the drop has stabilized at fewer than 170,000 students and about 11% of ELL population.

In Los Angeles Unified, the largest district in the state, the decline in 1998–1999 was precipitous, and remained low the following two years. However, in two of the larger school districts, San Diego Unified and San Francisco Unified, the declines after the passage of Proposition 227 were temporary. The number of ELL students enrolled in bilingual programs in 2000–2001 almost equaled the percentages prior to Proposition 227. In San Francisco Unified, the percentage dropped from 54% in 1997–1998 to 52% the following year, and 47% and 46% the two subsequent years. In 2002, the State Board of Education in California allowed principals and educational staff, as well as parents, to make the decision on whether children should be placed into bilingual education programs. This significantly weakened the mandates of Proposition 227 (Rossell, 2003).

Other Efforts to Dismantle Bilingual Education.   English language learners are often caught in the middle of politics. Both sides of the English Only movement believe strongly that their positions are best for language minority immigrant students. Ron Unz and his supporters continue their efforts to bring what they consider a success in California (both the passage of Proposition 227 and the educational results) to

Table 7.1 Effects of Proposition 227 on California's Bilingual Education Student Enrollment

Academic Year	Numbers Enrolled	Percent Enrolled
1997–1998	408,879	29%
1998–1999	169,440	12%
1999–2000	169,929	11%
2000–2001	167,163	11%

Source: Adapted from Rossell, C. (July 20, 2002). *Dismantling Bilingual Education Implementing English Immersion: The California Initiative.* University of California Minority Research Institute. Retrieved from http://lmri.ucsb.edu/resdiss/prop227.htm

other parts of the country. They were successful in bringing about a similar measure (Proposition 203) in Arizona in 2000 (Crawford, 2001), and in Massachusetts in 2002, but were unsuccessful in Colorado. States such as California and Arizona allow referendums on their ballots and are apparently less difficult for Unz and his supporters to gain inroads than states in which they must go through the legislative process. Legislators in Massachusetts have worked toward legislation to weaken the new English immersion law (*Boston Globe,* 2003).

Opponents of the English Only movement readily agree on the importance of learning English. However, they view their adversaries as individuals trying to force Anglo conformity by ending essential services in foreign languages. They view the attacks on bilingual education as unjustified because good bilingual education has been shown to be effective. Bad bilingual education, they concede, is ineffective and is seldom bilingual education, except in name. Opponents of bilingual education, they argue, have seen to it that these programs fail by giving inadequate support or resources, by staffing programs with unqualified personnel, by obtaining faulty test results on bilingual education students, by testing them in English, and by other means that cast negative outcomes on bilingual education (Fillmore, 1992).

It is true that many earlier immigrants did not have the benefit of bilingual education programs. Thrust into sink-or-swim situations, they ended up swimming, succeeding in school, and finding their niche in society. It is also true, however, that many students were unable to swim and sank in their efforts to acculturate in school. Since the number of language minority students today has increased dramatically, we can ill afford a sink-or-swim system, which could result in an education breakdown for massive numbers of students who are unable to succeed.

In spite of their differences, the majority of the individuals who support bilingual education, as well as those who are opposed to it, are well-intentioned individuals who want to enhance the educational opportunities for immigrant children. If all interested parties would be less concerned with the politics of the issue and would base their programmatic preferences on sound, well-documented research, the students would be the ultimate winners.

Educational Implications

Language is an integral part of life and an integral part of our social system. The diversity and richness of the language systems in this country are a reflection of the richness and diversity of American culture. The ability of U.S. educators to recognize and appreciate the value of different language groups will, to some extent, determine the effectiveness of our educational system.

By the year 2026, it is estimated that there will be approximately 15 million students with limited proficiency in English enrolled in our schools. In California, 70% of the students will be nonwhite and Hispanic, and 50% of those will speak a

Table 7.2 Elementary and Secondary Enrollment of ELL Students in U.S. 1992–93 to 2002–2003

School Year	Total Enrollment	Growth from 1992–93	ELL Enrollment	Growth from 1992–93
1992–1993	44,444,939	—	2,735,952	—
1993–1994	45,443,389	2.25%	3,037,922	11.04%
1994–1995	47,745,835	7.43%	3,184,696	16.40%
1995–1996	47,582,665	7.06%	3,228,799	18.01%
1996–1997	46,375,422	5.11%	3,452,073	26.17%
1997–1998	46,023,969	3.55%	3,470,268	26.84%
1998–1999	46,153,266	3.84%	3,540,673	29.41%
1999–2000	47,356,089	6.55%	4,416,580	61.43%
2000–2001	47,665,483	7.25%	4,584,946	67.58%
2001–2002	48,296,777	8.67%	4,747,763	73.53%
2002–2003	**49,509,923**	**11.40**%	**5,044,361**	**84.37**%

Source: U.S. Department of Education's survey of the states' limited English proficient students and available educational programs and services, 1991–92 through 2001–2002 summary reports. Supplemented by state publications (1998–99 data), and enrollment totals from the National Center for Education Statistics (NCES).

language other than English when first entering the school system (Garcia, 1999). The U.S. Office of English Language Acquisition, Language Enhancement, and Academic Achievement for Limited English Proficient Students (OELA) reported that in the 2001–2002 school year, there were a total of 4,747,763 English language learners in U.S. schools. That number represents 9.84% of the 48,296,777 students reported by OELA in the general school population that year. This increase in ELL students also represented a growth rate of 95% from the 1991–1992 school year. The estimated increase in the number of enrolled ELL students by school year is shown in Table 7.2.

All children bring to school the language systems of their cultures. It is the obligation of each educator to ensure the right of each child to learn in the language of the home until the child is able to function well enough in English. This may imply the use of English as a second language (ESL) or bilingual programs for ELL children. Research overwhelmingly demonstrates that encouraging the development of students' native language does not negatively impact the development of academic skills in English (Schechter & Cummins, 2003). Equally important, especially for educators, is the responsibility to understand cultural and linguistic differences and to recognize the value of these differences while working toward enhancing the student's linguistic skills in the dominant language. Although it is important to appreciate and respect a child's native language or dialect, it is also important that the teacher communicate the importance and advantages of being able to speak and understand Standard English in certain educational, vocational, and social situations.

LANGUAGE AND EDUCATIONAL ASSESSMENT

Few issues in education are as controversial as the assessment of culturally diverse children. The problem of disproportionate numbers of ethnic minority children in special education classes for children with disabilities has resulted from such assessment (Artiles, Harry, Reschly, & Chinn, 2002). The characteristics of language are directly related to the assessment of linguistically different children. Despite genuine attempts to accommodate the diverse backgrounds of students, many of the educational and intelligence tests used to assess ethnic and linguistic minority children are normed primarily on children from white, middle-class backgrounds. There is an expectation of cultural and linguistic uniformity in the development of assessment tests (Wolfram, Adger, & Christian, 1999). Therefore, such tests are often considered biased against the student who is not proficient in English or who speaks a dialect. Nieto (2002) estimates that approximately 100 million standardized tests are given every year with an average of 2.5 tests per student, per year. It is unlikely that there are any completely unbiased assessment instruments being used to test achievement or intelligence.

Most intelligence tests rely heavily on language. Yet, little attempt may be made to determine a child's level of proficiency in the language or dialect in which a test is administered. For example, a Latino child may be able to perform a task that is called for in an intelligence test, but may not be able to understand the directions given in English. Even if a Spanish translation was available, it might not be in a dialect with which the child is familiar. Using an unfamiliar Spanish dialect may place a student at an extreme disadvantage and may yield test results that are not a true indication of the student's abilities. The same may be true for Asians, African Americans, or Native Americans who are being tested. Rather than accurately testing specific knowledge or aptitude, all too often intelligence tests measure a student's competence in standard forms of the language (Wolfram, Adger, & Christian, 1999). Corson (1999) warns that one of the dangers of assessment tests is that they measure intelligence by those things that are valued within the dominant group and tend to exclude things that are culturally specific to minority children. Garcia (1999) contends that this bias calls into question the conclusions drawn from such tests regarding intelligence and ethnic background. Refusal to acknowledge the value of linguistic differences has resulted in inadequate services and the inappropriate placement of children through highly questionable assessment procedures.

Several successful class-action lawsuits have been brought against school boards or school districts on behalf of children placed in special education classes on the basis of low scores on IQ tests. Typically the suits argue that biased and inappropriate test instruments were used on language minority students, which resulted in inappropriate special education placement. Among the cases often cited is *Guadalupe Organization, Inc. v. Tempe Elementary School District No. 3,* 587 F.2d 1022, 1030 (9th Cir. 1978), which was a suit filed in Arizona that resulted from the disproportionately high placement of Yaqui Indian and Mexican American children in classes for students with mental retardation. *Diana v. State Board of Education* was a suit brought on behalf of children of Mexican immigrants placed in classrooms for students with mental retardation on the basis of low IQ scores on tests argued to be discriminatory.

BILINGUAL EDUCATION

The definition of **bilingual education** that is generally agreed on is "the use of two languages as media of instruction" (Baca & Cervantes, 2004). Bilingual education has been supported, in part, by federal funds provided by the Bilingual Education Act of 1968, reauthorized in 1974, 1978, and 1984. The federal legislation views bilingual education more broadly than do Baca and Cervantes (2004), allowing and even encouraging methods other than the use of two languages.

Children who speak little or no English cannot understand English-speaking children or lessons that are presented in English. Not only are these children faced with having to learn new subject matter, but they must also learn a new language and often a new culture. It is likely that many of these children will not be able to keep up with the schoolwork and will drop out of school unless there is appropriate intervention. The school dropout rate for Latino students is disproportionately high. The high school dropout rate for Latino immigrants was 44.2% in 2001, versus 7.4% for all non-Latinos. The dropout rate for second-generation (children of immigrants) Latinos drops to 14.6% but holds at 15.9% for the third generation, almost double the non-Latino rate (Mehring, 2004). Most of the first-generation dropouts, however, had left school prior to immigrating to the United States (Rubin, 2003). Jeffries, Nix, and Singer (2002) indicate that the dropout rates for Native American students are also high. They cite a 1994 U.S. Department of Education report indicating a 25.4% dropout rate for Native American students. Although language differences may not be the sole contributor to the academic problems of these children, they are considered by many to be a major factor.

Lau v. Nichols. In 1974, a class-action suit, *Lau v. Nichols* (1974), on behalf of 1,800 Chinese children was brought before the U.S. Supreme Court. The plaintiffs claimed that the San Francisco Board of Education failed to provide programs designed to meet the linguistic needs of those non-English-speaking children. The failure, they claimed, was in violation of Title VI of the Civil Rights Act of 1964 and the equal protection clause of the Fourteenth Amendment. They argued that if the children could not understand the language used for instruction, they were deprived of an education equal to that of other children and were, in essence, doomed to failure.

Opportunities for Reflection

The school board defended its policy by stating that the children received the same education afforded other children in the district. The position of the board was that a child's ability to comprehend English when entering school was not the responsibility of the school, but rather the responsibility of the child and the family. *If no one in the family could speak English, how did the school district expect the children to learn the language?* In a unanimous decision, the Supreme Court stated: "Under state imposed standards, there was no equality of treatment merely by providing students with the same facilities, textbooks, teachers, and curriculum; for students who do not understand English are effectively foreclosed from any meaningful education" (*Lau v. Nichols,* 1974). The Court did not mandate bilingual education for non-English-speaking or limited-English-speaking students. It did stipulate that special language programs were necessary if schools were to provide an equal educational opportunity for such students. Hence, the *Lau* decision gave considerable impetus to the development of bilingual education as well as ESL programs.

There are a million new immigrants entering the United States annually. Many will be students in our schools who will need specialized instruction to help them acquire English.

In 1975, the Education for All Handicapped Children Act (amended in 1990 as the Individuals with Disabilities Education Act [IDEA]) required each state to avoid the use of racially or culturally discriminating testing and evaluation procedures in the placement of children with disabilities. It also required that placement tests be administered in the child's native language. In addition, communication with parents regarding such matters as permission to test the child, development of individualized education programs (IEPs), and hearings and appeals must be in their native language. The IEP specifies the programming and services children with disabilities will receive and requires the participation of the parents in its development.

Throughout the 1970s, the federal government and the state courts sought to shape the direction of bilingual education programs and mandate appropriate testing procedures for students with limited English proficiency. The *Lau* remedies were developed by the U.S. Office of Education to help schools implement bilingual education programs. These guidelines prescribed transitional bilingual education and rejected ESL as an appropriate methodology for elementary students. With a change of the federal administration in 1981, a shift to local policy decisions began to lessen federal controls. Emphasis was placed on making the transition from the native language to English as fast as possible. The methodology for accomplishing the transition became the choice of the local school district. Thus, ESL programs began to operate alongside bilingual programs in many areas. Although the future level of federal involvement in bilingual education is uncertain, there is little doubt among educators that some form of bilingual education is needed.

The primary goal of bilingual education is not to teach English or a second language per se, but to teach children concepts, knowledge, and skills in the language they know best and to reinforce this information through the use of English (Baca & Cervantes, 2004). Two philosophies currently shape programs in bilingual education: the transitional approach and the maintenance approach.

Transitional programs emphasize bilingual education as a means of moving from the culture and language most commonly used for communication in the home to the mainstream of U.S. language and culture. It is an assimilationist approach in which the ELL student is expected to learn to function effectively in English as soon as possible. The native language of the home is used only to help the student make the transition to the English language. The native language is gradually phased out as the student becomes more proficient in English.

In contrast, **maintenance programs** provide a pluralistic orientation. The goal is for the ELL student to function effectively in both the native language and English. The student actually becomes bilingual and bicultural in the process, with neither language surfacing as the dominant one. The student's native language and culture are taught concurrently with English and the dominant culture. By using both languages for instruction, students develop fluency in both.

Bilingual education can be justified as: (a) the best way to attain maximum cognitive development for ELL students, (b) a means for achieving equal educational opportunity and/or results, (c) a means of easing the transition into the dominant language and culture, (d) an approach to educational reform, (e) a means of promoting positive interethnic relations, and (f) a wise economic investment to help linguistic minority students become maximally productive in adult life for the benefit of society and themselves (Baca & Cervantes, 2004).

Whereas many bilingual educators favor maintenance programs, the majority of the programs in existence are transitional. The acute shortage of trained personnel and the cost of maintenance programs are frequently cited as reasons for the predominance of transitional programs. Bilingual educators, however, strongly support the use of bicultural programs even within the transitional framework. A bicultural emphasis provides students with recognition of the value and worth of their families' cultures and enhances the development or maintenance of a positive self-image.

A comprehensive study from 1982 to 1996 of 700,000 language minority students from a number of large school districts found that in all content areas students receiving bilingual education completed their schooling with average scores exceeding the 50th national percentile. In contrast, those language minority students who received only ESL-pullout instruction, typically completed school "with average scores between the 10th and 18th national percentile" (Nieto, 2002).

Advocates of bilingual education see the advantages in being bilingual. Although bilingual education programs have primarily been established to develop English skills for ELL students, some offer opportunities for English-speaking students to develop proficiency in other languages. In addition, bilingualism provides an individual with job market advantages. As the United States becomes less parochial, the opportunity for business and other contacts with individuals from other countries increases, providing decided advantages to bilingual individuals.

Bilingual education as it currently exists has many problems and many critics. Research has provided evidence that well-developed and well-delivered bilingual education programming can deliver positive results. Critics have also provided ample evidence that some children in bilingual education programs have fared poorly and many have dropped out of school. What should be recognized is that there is an acute national shortage of qualified bilingual educators. Being bilingual does not necessarily qualify an individual as a bilingual educator. Many who fill bilingual education positions are not fully qualified in their preparation and training. When these individuals fail to deliver desired results, bilingual education is often unfairly characterized as being programmatically unsound.

ENGLISH AS A SECOND LANGUAGE

English as a second language (ESL) is a program often confused with bilingual education. In the United States, learning English is an integral part of every bilingual program. But teaching English as a second language in and by itself does not constitute a bilingual program. Both bilingual education and ESL programs promote English proficiency for ELL students. The approach to instruction distinguishes the two programs. Bilingual education accepts and develops native language and culture in the instructional process. Bilingual education may use the native language, as well as English, as the medium of instruction. ESL instruction, however, relies exclusively on English for teaching and learning. ESL programs are used extensively in this country as a primary medium to assimilate ELL children into the linguistic mainstream as quickly as possible. Hence, some educators place less emphasis on the maintenance of home language and culture than on English language acquisition, and they view ESL programs as a viable means for achieving their goals.

NONVERBAL COMMUNICATIONS IN THE CLASSROOM

As discussed earlier in this chapter, cultural differences in nonverbal communications between students and teachers can be very frustrating to both. To begin to overcome such differences, a teacher must try to analyze particular nonverbal communications when students, especially those from a different cultural background, are not responding as the teacher expects. What the teacher perceives as inattention on the part of the students, interruptions by the students at times considered inappropriate by the teacher, or even a tendency on the part of the students to look away from the teacher while being addressed may, in fact, be due to cultural differences.

In most school settings, students from subordinate groups are expected to become bicultural and adopt the nonverbal communication patterns of the dominant group while in school. A more sensitive approach is for teachers also to learn to operate biculturally in the classroom.

Teachers should reflect on what is occurring in the classroom when communications are not as expected. The first step is to become more aware of the nature of the difficulty. In the school setting, students should sometimes have access to teachers, counselors, or administrators who are from a culturally similar background. Teachers can make an effort to learn what the cultural cues of students mean and to react appropriately. A more effective approach, however, is to be able to analyze what is happening in the classroom and to respond on the basis of what is known about the student and his or her cultural background.

FOCUS YOUR CULTURAL LENS: DEBATE

Curtailing Bilingual Education

With the Supreme Court decision in the *Lau v. Nichols* case in 1974, bilingual education came to the forefront in American education and was given a greater sense of legitimacy. While *Lau v. Nichols* did not mandate bilingual education, it required schools to address the linguistic needs of their students from diverse backgrounds.

Over the past 30 years, the road for bilingual education has often been bumpy. Critics have attacked it as a colossal failure, and advocate for English immersion classes and the discontinuation of bilingual education. Even the federal government in the George W. Bush Administration appears to be de-emphasizing bilingual programs. The name of the U.S. Office of Bilingual Education and Minority Language Affairs has been renamed as the Office of English Language Acquisition, Language Enhancement, and Academic Achievement for Limited English Proficient Students (OELA).

FOR

- Opponents of bilingual education advocate sheltered English immersion limited to one year, while they have no research to back the efficacy of what they propose.

- Research by Cummins and Hakuta has clearly shown that ELL students cannot become proficient in English for academic purposes in one year's time.

- The problems in bilingual education have been rooted in the lack of qualified personnel trained in bilingual education techniques, lack of adequate resources, and the lack of commitment both at the federal and state levels.

- Research has clearly demonstrated that bilingual education, properly implemented, is highly effective.

AGAINST

- Over 400,000 California students began the school year as non-English proficient, and prior to Proposition 227, at the end of the school year, only 5% had learned English.

- Prior to California's Proposition 227, English language learners studied grammar, reading, writing, and all other academic subjects in their own native language—almost always in Spanish—while receiving only small amounts of English instruction.

- Achievement test scores for immigrant children are low and dropout rates are high.

- Bilingual education in California, Arizona, and Massachusetts has been reduced to a fraction of what it used to be. The same should happen throughout the United States.

Questions

1. *What should programmatic decisions (for example, what type of program should be offered for ELL?) be based on?*
2. *Are the attacks on bilingual education justified?*
3. *What has the research shown with respect to language acquisition and ELL?*

To answer these questions online, go to the Focus Your Cultural Lens: Debate module for this chapter of the Companion Website.

Sources: http://onenation.org/unz101997.html and http://www.stanford.edu/~hakuta/Docs/HowLong.pdf

Summary

The *Lau* decision of 1974 ensures non-English-speaking children the right to an appropriate education that meets their linguistic needs. Even with a legal mandate, appropriate services may not always be delivered because of lack of tolerance or insensitivity to language or dialects that are not considered Standard English. Because nonstandard dialects tend to have a negative stigma attached to them, some educators may refuse to view them as legitimate forms of communication. Although they may indeed be legitimate forms of communication and may serve the speaker well in certain contexts, nonstandard English dialects may preclude certain social and vocational opportunities.

Bilingual education has both its supporters and its detractors. Through proper educational programming, however, children with limited English proficiency can have the education to which they are entitled. Our responsibility as educators is to recognize the linguistic diversity of our nation's students, and to recognize the value of the family's unique cultural and linguistic background. As students become bilingual and bi-dialectal, they will find themselves in the position of being able to navigate through a greater variety of social, academic, and vocational settings.

QUESTIONS FOR DISCUSSION

1. How is language a function of culture?

2. Why is there no such thing as a good or a bad language?

3. What are the advantages of being bilingual in the United States?

4. How is bilingualism encouraged and discouraged within educational settings?

5. What is the difference between an accent and a dialect?

6. What are dialects? What factors generally determine whether an individual becomes bi-dialectal?

7. Why is Black English a controversial issue in education? How should it be handled in the classroom?

8. Why is it important to be sensitive to nonverbal communications between teacher and student and among students?

9. Why might it be unwise to assume that a student is ready for academic instruction in English as soon as he or she has some basic English conversational skills?

10. What is cognitive academic language proficiency?

11. What was California's Proposition 227, and how does it impact English language learners?

12. What has the research on the effects of Proposition 227 yielded thus far?

13. What is the relationship between language and educational assessment?

14. What was *Lau v. Nichols,* and how was it important to English language learners?

15. Contrast maintenance and transitional bilingual education. Which do you think is more appropriate? Why?

16. When might an ESL approach be the most appropriate strategy to use in a classroom?

ONLINE ACTIVITIES For additional chapter questions and activities, visit this text's Companion Website at http://www.prenhall.com/gollnick.

PORTFOLIO ACTIVITIES

1. Survey your students (where you teach, student teach, or are involved in a practicum) to find out how many different languages or dialects they speak. Ask them when and where they feel comfortable speaking a different dialect or language other than Standard English. (INTASC Standard 3)

2. Check with your local school district office and find out how many different language groups are served in the district. (INTASC Standard 3)

3. Find out what type of programs are used in your district to facilitate English language acquisition of English language learners in the schools. (INTASC Standard 3)

4. Survey the teachers who have language minority students in their classes and find out what type of programming they favor for their students and why. (INTASC Standard 3)

SUGGESTED READINGS

Baca, L. M., & Cervantes, H. (2004). *The bilingual special education interface* (4th ed.). Upper Saddle River, NJ: Merrill/Prentice Hall.

   An excellent overview of bilingual special education, this book contains basic but important information on general bilingual education, including litigation and legislation related to the rights of children with limited English proficiency.

Crawford, J. (2004). *Education of English learners: Language diversity in the classroom* (5th ed.). Los Angeles: Bilingual Educational Services.

   Written by the former Washington Editor of *Education Week,* and current Executive Director of the National Association for Bilingual Education, the text provides an excellent overview of bilingual education. Among several issues addressed are language policies in the United States, the politics surrounding bilingual education, and an overview of research on language acquisition.

Samovar, L. A., & Porter, R. E. (2004). *Communication between cultures* (5th ed.). Belmont, CA: Wadsworth.

   An excellent treatment of language and culture, this book includes chapters on intercultural communication and the communication of a nonmainstream group.

Wolfram, W., Adger, C., & Christian, D. (1999). *Dialects in schools and communities.* Mahwah, NJ: Lawrence Erlbaum Associates.

   This is an excellent overview of dialects by well-recognized authorities in the field of dialects. The text addresses language variations in the United States, and defines and explains dialects and the sources of language differences. It also addresses communicative interactions and cultural styles in the classroom, and explains why language differences do not mean language deficits.

REFERENCES

American Institutes of Research (AIR) & WestEd. (2003). Effects of the implementation of Proposition 227 on the education of English learners, K–12, Year 3 Report. Submitted to the California Department of Education, October 29, 2003.

Artiles, A. J., Harry, B., Reschly, D. J., & Chinn, P. C. (2002). Over-identification of students of color in special education: A critical overview. *Multicultural Perspectives* (4), 1.

Baca, L. M., & Cervantes, H. (2004). *The bilingual special education interface* (4th ed.). Upper Saddle River, NJ: Merrill/Prentice Hall.

Bennett, W. (1992). Bilingual education: A failed path. In J. Crawford (Ed.), *Language loyalties.* Chicago: University of Chicago Press.

The Boston Globe (via Knight Ridder Tribune Business News). (2003, April 27). Second bilingual education battle gears up in Massachusetts.

Corson, D. (1999). *Language policy in schools: A resource for teachers and administrators.* Mahwah, NJ: Lawrence Erlbaum Associates.

Crawford, J. (Ed.). (1992). *Language loyalties.* Chicago: University of Chicago Press.

Crawford, J. (2001). Bilingual education: Strike two, Arizona voters follow California's lead and mandate English-only programs. *Rethinking Schools, 15* (2).

Crawford, J. (2004). *Education of English learners: Language diversity in the classroom* (5th ed.). Los Angeles: Bilingual Educational Services.

Crystal, D. (1997). *The Cambridge encyclopedia of language* (2nd ed.). Cambridge, UK: Cambridge University Press.

Cummins, J. (1984). *Bilingualism and special education: Issues in assessment and pedagogy.* San Diego: College-Hill Press.

Cummins, J. (1996). *Negotiating identities: Education of empowerment in a diverse society.* Los Angeles: California Association for Bilingual Education.

Cummins, J. (2000). *Language, power and pedagogy: Bilingual children in the crossfire.* Clevedon, England: Multicultural Matters.

Diana v. State Board of Education, Civil Action No. C-7037 RFP (N. D.Cal. Jan. 7, 1970 and June 18, 1973).

Dicker, S. J. (2003). *Languages in America: A pluralistic view* (2nd ed.). Bristol, PA: Multilingual Matters.

Education Commission for the States. (2004). *Bilingual/ESL.* Retrieved August 5, 2004, from http://www.ecs.org/ecsmain.asp?page=/html/issues.asp

Education Week. (1997, January 15). Full text of the "Ebonics" Resolution adopted by Oakland School Board.

Fillmore, L. W. (1992). Against our best interest: The attempt to sabotage bilingual education. In J. Crawford (Ed.), *Language loyalties.* Chicago: University of Chicago Press.

Garcia, E. (1999). *Student cultural diversity: Understanding and meeting the challenge* (2nd ed.). Boston: Houghton Mifflin.

Hakuta, K. (2001a). *Silence from Oceanside and the future of bilingual education.* Retrieved August 5, 2004, from http://www.stanford.edu/%7Ehakuta/SAT9Silence%20from%20Oceanside.htm

Hakuta, K. (2001b). *Follow-up on Oceanside: Communications with Ron Unz.* Retrieved August 5, 2004, from http://www.stanford.edu/%7Ehakuta/SAT9Silence%20from%20Oceanside%202.htm

Hakuta, K. (2002). *What can we learn about the impact of Proposition 227 from SAT-9 scores?* Retrieved August 5, 2004, from http://www.stanford.edu/%7Ehakuta/SAT9/index.htm

Hakuta, K., Butler, Y. G., & Bousquet, M. (1999). *What legitimate inferences can be made from the 1999 release of SAT-9 scores with respect to the impact of California's Proposition 227 on the performance of LEP students.* Retrieved August 5, 2004, from http://www.stanford.edu/%7Ehakuta/SAT9/NABE

Hakuta, K., Butler, Y. G., & Witt, D. (2000). *How long does it take English language learners to attain proficiency?* Santa Barbara, CA: University of California Linguistic Minority Research Institute Policy Report 2000–1.

Haynes, J. (2004). *Proxemics and U.S. culture.* Retrieved August 5, 2004, from http://www.everythingesl.net/inservices/proxemics_elevator.php

Hecht, M., Jackson, R., II, & Ribeau, S. (2003). *African American communication: Exploring identity and culture* (2nd ed.). Mahwah, NJ: Lawrence Erlbaum Associates.

Heward, W. L. (2003). *Exceptional children* (7th ed.). Upper Saddle River, NJ: Merrill/Prentice Hall.

Hosoda, M., Stone-Romero, E. F., & Coats, G. (2003, Summer). The effects of physical attractiveness on job-related outcomes: A meta-analysis of experimental studies. *Personnel Psychology, 56* (2), 431–432.

Jay, T. (2003). *The psychology of language.* Upper Saddle River, NJ: Prentice Hall.

Jeffries, R., Nix, M., & Singer, C. (2002, February–March). Urban American Indians "dropping" out of traditional high schools: Barriers and bridges to success. *High School Journal, 85* (3), 38–39.

Lau v. Nichols, 414 U.S., 563–572 (Jan. 21, 1974).

Los Angeles Almanac. (2004). Retrieved August 5, 2004, from http://www.losangelesalmanac.com/LA/la10b.htm

McDonald, J. J., Jr. (2003, Fall). Civil rights for the aesthetically-challenged. *Employee Relations Law Journal, 29* (2), 118.

Mehring, J. (2004, August 2). Latinos' education gap; High-school dropout rates remain high. *Business Week, i3894,* 28.

National Association for Bilingual Education (NABE). (2000). *The Unz intiative: Extreme, irresponsible, and hazardous to California's future.* Washington, DC: Author.

News-Medical.Net. (2004, April 27). *A high rate of marriage among deaf individuals can explain the increased frequency of connexin deafness in the United States.* Retrieved August 5, 2004, from http://www.news-medical.net/print_article.asp?print=yes&id=911

Nieto, S. (2002). *Language, culture, and teaching: Critical perspectives for a new century.* Mahwah, NJ: Lawrence Erlbaum Associates.

NYC Mayors. (2004). *Fiorello Henry LaGuardia.* Retrieved August 5, 2004, from http://www.nyc.gov/html/nyc100/html/classroom/hist_info/mayors.html#laguardia

Office of Civil Rights. (1999). *1997 elementary and secondary civil rights survey.* Washington, DC: U.S. Government Printing Office.

Orr, J. E., Butler, Y. G., Bousquet, M., & Hakuta, K. (2000). What can we learn about the impact of Proposition 227 from SAT-9 scores? *An Analysis of Results from 2000.* Retrieved August 5, 2004, from http://www.stanford.edu/%7Ehakuta/SAT9/SAT9_2000/analysis2000.htm

Owens, R. E., Jr. (2005). *Language development* (6th ed.). Needham Heights, MA: Allyn & Bacon.

Rossell, C. H. (2003). *Dismantling bilingual education, implementing English immersion: The California initiative.* San Francisco: Public Policy Institute of California, August 20, 2002.

Rubin, H. G. (2003, June 19). Hispanic dropout rates lower than feared. *Education Daily, 36* (116), 4.

Samovar, L. A., & Porter, R. E. (2004). *Communication between cultures* (5th ed.). Belmont, CA: Wadsworth.

Schechter, S., & Cummins, J. (Eds.). (2003). *Multilingual education in practice: Using diversity as a resource.* Portsmouth, NH: Heinemann.

Schnaiberg, L. (1997, January 15). "Ebonics" vote puts Oakland in maelstrom. *Education Week on the Web.* Retrieved August 5, 2004, from http://www.edweek.org/ew/vol-16/16oak.h16

Seifert, M. W. (2001, July 20). Appearances count to the point of bias? *Austin Business Journal, 21* (18), 21.

Smith, D. D. (2004). *Introduction to special education: Teaching in an age of opportunity* (5th ed.). Needham Heights, MA: Allyn & Bacon.

UCLMRI Newsletter. (2003, Fall). *Has Proposition 227 reduced the English learner achievement gap?* Santa Barbara, CA: University of California Minority Research Institute.

Unz, R. K., & Tuchman, G. M. (1998). *Initiative statute: English language education for children in public schools.* Palo Alto, CA: Author. (Available: http://www.nabe.org/unz/text)

U.S. Census Bureau. (2003). *Statistical abstract of the United States: 2003* (123rd ed.). Washington, DC: U.S. Department of Commerce.

U.S. English. (2004). Retrieved August 5, 2004, from http://www.us_english.org/inc/

Wheeler, R. (Ed.). (1999). *The workings of language: From prescriptions to perspectives.* Connecticut: Praeger.

Wolfram, W., Adger, C., & Christian, D. (1999). *Dialects in schools and communities.* Mahwah, NJ: Lawrence Erlbaum Associates.

Wolfram, W., & Christian, D. (1989). *Dialects and education: Issues and answers.* Upper Saddle River, NJ: Prentice Hall.

If people learn to love and learn to share in early adulthood, they will be able to care for and guide the next generation effectively.

FERGUS P. HUGHES AND LLOYD D. NOPPE (1991)

Chapter 8

Age

M ark McKenzie was a tenth grader in an affluent school district in a Southwestern suburban community. The community is essentially a new town. The town, which 40 years ago had fewer than 50,000 residents, had grown to more than 250,000. Most homes in Mark's neighborhood were in the $300,000 to $450,000 price range. Some homes have sold in excess of $750,000. Crime in this community has been almost nonexistent. At least one fourth of the students in high school drive their own cars, including several late-model cars, two BMWs, and a Mercedes SUV.

Mark moved into this community with his family just two years ago. His father was an engineer in a large high-tech company, and his mother was a successful realtor. His brother was in the eighth grade and his sister in the sixth grade. Mark's parents were extremely fond of their children, but time commitments to their successful careers precluded extensive time and interactions with them. Mark had been promised a car for his next birthday. When Mark and his family moved from their previous home in the Midwest, Mark had begun to demonstrate occasional periods of depression. He had left two very close friends that he had grown up with, and he had objected vehemently to the move.

Since moving to the new home, Mark had made some casual friends, but none as close as the friends in his previous community. In the fall of Mark's sophomore year, he became more withdrawn, attended no school social events, and spent most of his nonschool hours in his room, behind closed doors.

In a conversation with two classmates the next spring, he stated that death brought people the ultimate peace and tranquility. He expressed the same sentiment in two poems written for his English class. His teacher considered the poetry good and passed off his expressions as a teenager's glamorization of death.

A month after writing the poems, Mark began giving away some of his prized possessions. He gave the baseball card collection that he had started 5 years before, and had always valued, to his brother along with his portable DVD player; he gave his stereo and CDs to his sister. When questioned by his parents, he replied only that he had paid for these out of his own money and thought it was his prerogative to do what he wanted with them. "Besides," he stated, "I'm no longer interested in the cards, movies, or music." Later, Mark gave his $300 guitar to his brother, along with his baseball glove. He gave other personal items to his sister and a few to friends at school.

Shortly after giving away his possessions, Mark's depression seemed to dissipate and his behavior was such that it could be described as euphoric. His parents were pleased, and his father remarked, "Mark's finally got his act together." A week later, Mark's body was found in a wooded area less than a half mile from his home. He had died of a self-inflicted gunshot wound. Mark had become one of more than 2,000 teenagers who would end their own lives that year.

Opportunities for Reflection

1. *Was Mark's death the fault of his parents who had forced the family move on their children?*
2. *Was it the fault of the parents who seemed to be too wrapped up in their careers to spend more time with their children?*
3. *What were some signs of Mark's impending action?*
4. *Why had he become euphoric when he was about to take such a drastic action on himself?*
5. *What should the school do after Mark's death?*
6. *Should a school memorial service be held? Why? Why not?*

To answer these questions online, go to this chapter's Opening Scenario module of the Companion Website.

Age and Culture

Each person who lives long enough will become a part of every age-group. Without choice, we must all go through the various stages in life and eventually join the ranks of the aged. Like other cultural groups, we feel, think, perceive, and behave, in part, because of the age group to which we belong. In this chapter, we examine the major age groups: childhood, adolescence, adulthood, and the aged. We examine how ethnicity, gender, social status, and other determinants of culture interface with these periods in an individual's life. We examine how peer pressure affects behavior in some age groups. Critical issues such as child abuse, adolescent substance abuse, and adolescent suicide are examined. Finally, we examine how an understanding of age-groups can affect the educational process.

An understanding of the various childhood and adult groups is helpful in understanding and providing appropriately for the needs of students. A student's classroom behavior may be a function of his or her relationship with parents, siblings, and significant others. As these family members and significant others move through various age stages in their lives, their behavior, as well as their relationship to the student, may change. Consequently, the student's behavior may, in part, be influenced by the age changes of the significant people in his or her life.

How we behave is often a function of age. Although many adolescents behave differently from one another, the way they think, feel, and behave is at least partly because they are adolescents. At the same time, age does not stand alone in affecting the way a person behaves or functions. Ethnicity, socioeconomic status, religion, and gender interact with age to influence a person's behavior and attitudes.

An African American woman in her 80s, for example, may eat the type of food she does partly because her age and related health condition require eliminating certain foods from her diet. But her socioeconomic status may determine, to some extent, the foods she can afford to buy, and her ethnicity may determine her choices in foods. Her gender, language, disability/nondisability status, and religious background may not influence eating habits to any significant degree. These other cultural variables, however, along with her age, may influence other types of behavior and functioning. From the time of birth through the last days of life, a person's age may influence perceptions, attitudes, values, and behavior.

In this chapter, we do not attempt to examine all developmental stages of the various age-groups. This information can be obtained through a human development text. Instead, we examine some critical issues related to various age groups. Because it is impossible to address all critical issues affecting each age-group, we selectively address issues affecting schools directly or indirectly.

SOCIAL CLASS AND POVERTY

One of the most critical issues that educators routinely face is that of social class and poverty. Today, more than one child in six lives in poverty (U.S. Census Bureau, 2004), and teachers in the inner city may find that nearly all of the children in their classrooms live in poverty. Poverty creates numerous problems for children. In many instances, children live with a single parent, typically the mother. When the father is absent, children often lack adequate male role models, and the mother often bears the entire burden of discipline and financial support. Single mothers living in poverty must often work outside the home to provide for their families.

Mothers from middle and upper socioeconomic groups may not need to work outside the home. Those who choose to do so can often be selective in their choice of a day care setting to ensure an environment congruent with family values. Day care settings are often important variables in the socialization process because many of a child's early behaviors are learned from peers and caregivers. Parents from less affluent groups, however, may have limited choices for their children's day care environment. In some instances, older siblings, themselves children, may be required to assume family child care responsibilities while their parents work at outside jobs.

In 2003, the percentage of the U.S. population living in poverty was 12.5%. The poverty rates for children and most racial minorities were higher, with child poverty rising from 16.7% to 17.6% in 2002. Estimates are that 12.9 million children in the United States live in poverty. They account for almost 25% of the homeless population (U.S. Census Bureau, 2004). With increasing cuts in programs for low-income children, an alarming number of additional children may be pushed into poverty.

Many of these children suffer from inadequate housing, nutrition, and medical care. Many of their homes have inadequate heating or cooling, which affects their sleep and physical well-being. Homes are often old and in neighborhoods where residents live in fear for their personal safety. The National Center for Health Statistics found that children living in poverty were 3.6 times more likely to have fair or poor health. They are also 2 times more likely to die from birth defects and 5 times more likely to die from infectious diseases (Free the Children, 2003). Children who suffer from physical problems are less likely to function academically at their highest potential. In addition, the pressures of poverty on parents may result in the likelihood of harsh and erratic discipline, thus contributing to child delinquency (Trojanowicz, Morash, & Schram, 2001).

For a more in-depth discussion of poverty, see Chapter 2.

One of the best sources for determining the conditions for children in the nation and each individual state is the Annie E. Casey Foundation. The Foundation publishes its *Kids Count* report annually, ranking states in 10 different at-risk areas:

- Low-birth-weight babies
- Infant mortality
- Child deaths rate

- Teen deaths by accident, homicide, or suicide
- Teen birthrates
- Teen high school dropouts
- Teens not in school and not working
- Children with parents without full-time, year-round employment
- Children living in poverty
- Children in families headed by single parent (Annie E. Casey Foundation, 2004)

By going to the Foundation's website (**http://www.aecf.org/**) you can see how your state compares to national scores and other states in the various at-risk categories. The nation's capital, Washington, DC, the center of power, leads the nation with children in poverty and in all but one of the other at-risk categories for children.

Pause to Reflect 8.1

After looking at the *Kids Count* data for your state on the Annie E. Casey Foundation report, think about the children in your state or the state you plan to teach in. Even if your state is among the highest ranked states, such as Minnesota, there are still too many infant deaths, teen deaths, children living in poverty, and so forth.

- *What should society be doing to make life better for these children?*
- *What do you want to do when you are teaching to make a difference?*

To answer these questions online, go to the Pause to Reflect module for this chapter of the Companion Website.

CW

As children enter school, they begin to recognize socioeconomic differences. Although the choice of friends may or may not be a function of socioeconomic levels, the type of playmates available may be. With the exception of children transported away from their neighborhood schools, most children in their earlier years attend schools that are somewhat homogeneous in terms of socioeconomic level. Neighborhood playmates are even more homogeneous. During this period, however, an increasing awareness develops regarding the differences in material possessions found in different homes. Children whose families lack financial resources are often unable to acquire clothing considered important to the peer group. Around the ages of 6 to 8, children begin to understand what is meant by rich and poor.

IMMIGRANT CHILDREN

The immigrant child who enters an American school for the first time may experience a culture shock resulting from losing all familiar signs and symbols for social interaction (Igoa, 1995). Igoa states, "Each time I encountered an unexplained cultural difference, I would feel awkward, confused, ashamed, or inadequate" (p. 16).

The beginning of school may also be a difficult time for an immigrant family. Children seeking peer acceptance may wish to become more acculturated than what is considered acceptable by parents seeking to maintain traditional cultural values. The conflicting values may emanate from teachers, as well as from peers. It is not uncommon to find immigrant children in their early school years resisting the language of the home, as well as family values related to dress and behavior. During the early school years, children begin to identify with significant adults in their lives who serve as role models. This identification allows children to strengthen, direct, and control their own behavior in such a way that it approximates the behavior of those they hold in esteem. Educators often serve as role models for children, and their influence can be profound. Educators who are sensitive to diverse cultural and family values can assist children from immigrant families in becoming bicultural, rather than in having to choose between the culture of the home and that of the school.

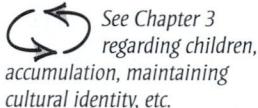 *See Chapter 3 regarding children, accumulation, maintaining cultural identity, etc.*

CHILDREN, ETHNIC AWARENESS, AND PREJUDICE

After years of work in improving race relations in this country, the 1980s and 1990s saw growing optimism that the United States had turned the corner on race relations. The hate crimes and racial violence that have emerged in recent years, however, remind us that the ugly head of racism continues to surface. Although we as educators expect to see racism among adults and, to some extent, adolescents, we are sometimes shocked and often dismayed when it is evidenced in the behavior of young children. Despite the overall improvement in race relations and the lower level of prejudice among parents, the level of prejudice among young children ages 4 to 7 has not declined in the last 40 years and continues to remain high.

Aboud (1988) defines ethnic awareness as a "conscious recognition of ethnicity in individuals or groups. . . being able to assign correctly the labels to the actual faces or pictures of various people indicates a basic form of perceptual ethnic awareness" (p. 6). Among young children, ethnic awareness and prejudice tend to increase with age. At some point, prejudice may decline but ethnic awareness may remain high. Although it may be necessary for a child to be aware of ethnic differences before he or she can develop prejudice, ethnic awareness in itself is not bad in a child. Attempts to discourage children from noticing that people are different, that they have different pigmentation, have different hair and eye colorization, or speak differently denies an accurate perception of reality in children (Aboud, 1988).

To recognize differences in others, a child must also be involved in self-identification because the child must be aware of what he or she is like before recognizing how another child differs. Children as young as 3 are able to identify with others of the same color or racial group and those who are different from themselves (Aboud, 1988; Sleek, 1997).

At 4 and 5 years of age, a significant number of children (about 75%) are able to correctly identify ethnic groupings. By ages 6 and 7, children are able to make the identification at close to 100% accuracy. Some children of color demonstrate

Between the ages of 4 and 5, a significant number of children are able to make ethnic identifications.

Opportunities for Reflection

an early preference for whites, and some white children indicate a preference for their minority group peers (Aboud, 1988). *How do young children develop racist attitudes at an early age when their own parents are open minded and non-racist in their attitudes?*

By the age of 5, some children have developed high levels of prejudice toward other racial groups (Bigler & Liben, 1993; Doyle & Aboud, 1995). It is often assumed that children who hold biased attitudes toward other groups are simply reflecting their parents' attitudes.

Prejudice is also discussed in Chapter 3.

VARIABLES AFFECTING ATTITUDES AND PREJUDICE

People assume that children who are prejudiced were taught these attitudes by their parents. Citing several studies (e.g., Aboud & Doyle, 1996a; Kofkin, Katz, & Downey, 1995), Aboud and Doyle (1996b) concluded that such assumptions are unjustified. There appears to be no strong evidence that children are influenced by the attitudes of parents or peers. Children under the age of 7 are often more prejudiced than their parents and often do not adopt the open and unbiased attitudes of their parents. Their parents to a greater extent influence children over the age of 7. However, others influence the biases they develop in addition to their parents (Aboud, 1988).

One proposed theory of prejudice in children is the social reflection theory. This theory suggests that the prejudice we see in children is a reflection of the values of society. Research studies, in general, have shown that the higher-status and in-groups in society are preferred by both white and some children of color. Whites are typically the higher-status and in-group in society. Where social stratification occurs in a community, young children develop negative attitudes toward the lower-status and out-groups. This tends to be true even if the parents hold positive or open attitudes toward minority groups who are typically the lower-status or out-groups (Aboud, 1988).

Tatum suggests (1997) that many whites never consider their own ethnic group membership, as they view themselves as the societal norm. White children, therefore, may grow up with this perception. If whiteness is the norm, then are those who are not white abnormal? Tatum states that white children are often unaware of their white privilege, which is conferred upon them by society simply for being white. In contrast, children of color often grow up aware that they are not perceived as part of this norm. Many if not most become aware of the institutional racism which exists, but to which most white children are oblivious. Children of color often observe or hear discussions by their elders regarding daily discrimination in employment, in being served (or inappropriately served) in restaurants, and in housing.

Opportunities for Reflection

Children are influenced by what those around them think, do, and say. Even when parents model tolerance, children may still be exposed to the racist behaviors of others. They observe how some individuals do not associate with members of certain groups (Anti-Defamation League [ADL], 2004). They may observe how some of the white teachers tend to sit only with other white teachers in the cafeteria. They may see that a particular teacher's table is filled primarily with individuals of color. Unwittingly, the teachers are modeling behaviors for the students. *Why are many Americans unable to grasp the concept of white privilege in which white individuals have benefits, privileges, or preferential treatment, which others do not?*

If students look through their books and notice the pictures of American Presidents, they can quickly observe how all are white and all are male. In some communities, their television news anchors may be primarily white, their school principal and their superintendent may also be white, and most often male. While we are seeing greater diversity in school leadership positions, there are still communities where diversity in management or administration is the exception. These same children may hear older children or adults putting down some groups in jokes. If no one addresses this behavior, the children may grow up believing that this is acceptable and normal behavior (ADL, 2004).

Children are greatly influenced by the media. They watch television and they observe their parents watching television. They have easy access to movies on television and those that family members rent on tape and DVD. They see pictures in newspapers and in the magazines their parents have in the home. There is hardly a day that goes by without children being exposed to stereotyping, misinformation, or exclusion of important information (ADL, 2004).

For the past few years, children have been exposed to the horrors of war in Afghanistan and Iraq, as well as bombings in Turkey, Russia, Spain, and other parts of the world. They have heard or seen the news of Americans killed daily by people of color, usually Arabs who are Muslims. They continually hear expressions of justifiable anger directed toward terrorists and suicide bombers, who are almost always described by race and religion.

The popular media has always had its villains. Many adults can remember when the American Indians were the villains. With the Second World War, the Japanese and the Germans became the villains of choice, and later the Russians. With the end of the Cold War there was a need for new villains, and Latin American drug lords seemed a good choice. Now the media has Arabs and Muslims as the villains. It is easy to see how children, particularly white children can grow up having prejudicial attitudes toward certain groups of individuals. This is especially so when there is so little effort to show that the majority of the people in these groups are good, law-abiding, loyal citizens.

The ADL (2004) suggests that children with poor self-images are prone toward developing prejudices. By targeting individuals they can put down, they may perceive this as a means to bolster their own self-worth. It enables them to feel more important and powerful than those they attack. At other times, children may exclude or ridicule other children because they perceive this to be a popular thing to do. They may feel that this behavior can enhance their standing among their peers (ADL, 2004).

Because prejudice appears to be somewhat prevalent among young children (ages 4 to 7) and because children are cognitively capable of becoming less prejudiced, it would appear to be very appropriate to develop activities that have been shown to reduce prejudice during the early years of elementary school. *Can you reflect back to a time when you observed a young child noticing someone who was racially different? What did the child do and/or say? What could you have done, or can you do in the future to help a young child to understand and accept, in a positive manner, racial differences among people?*

Opportunities for Reflection

CHILD ABUSE

Each year, hundreds of thousands of child abuse cases are reported. **Child abuse** is the physical or psychological mistreatment of children. Although the rate of victimization per 1,000 children has dropped from 13.4 children in 1990 to 12.3 children in 2002, the statistics are still alarming as shown in Table 8.1. In 2002, there were 896,000 victims of child abuse reported in the United States. More than half of these children (60%) suffered from neglect. Almost 20% were physically abused, 10% were sexually abused, and 7% were emotionally maltreated. More than one quarter of these young children (29%) were reported to have suffered from more than one form of abuse. It is estimated that 1,400 children died of abuse and neglect in 2002. This represents a rate of 1.98 deaths per 100,000 children in the general population. Of these fatalities 41% were children not yet 1 year old and 76% were children younger than 4 years of age (National Clearinghouse on Child Abuse and Neglect Information, 2004). Some experts believe these numbers are unrealistic and estimate that the number of children who die from abuse each year is three times greater than the number reported to authorities (Bartollas & Miller, 2005).

The incidence rates of child abuse vary from one ethnic/racial group to another. In 2002, the child abuse rate for Asian/Pacific Islanders was 3.8 per 1,000. The abuse rate for white children was 10.7 per 1,000, 10.6 for Latinos, 21.7 for American Indians/Alaska Natives, and 20.2 for African Americans. The majority (59.3%) of the perpetrators were women; and 80.9% of the abused children were victimized by one or both parents (National Clearinghouse on Child Abuse and Neglect Information, 2004).

Child abuse or maltreatment is usually categorized as physical abuse, physical neglect, sexual abuse, or emotional abuse.

Table 8.1 Child Maltreatment 2002: Key Findings

- 896,000 children are victims of child abuse or neglect
- Victimization rate per 100,000 in national population is 12.3 children
- More than 60 percent of child victims experienced neglect
- 10 percent are sexually abused
- 7 percent are emotionally maltreated
- Almost 20 percent are "other" types of abused based on state laws and policies
- Children birth to three years have the highest rates of victimization, at 16.0 per 1,000 children
- Girls are more likely to be victimized than boys
- American Indian or Alaska Native (21.7 per 1,000) and African American (20.2 per 1,000) children have the highest rates of victimization (compared to 10.7 per 1,000 for white)
- An estimated 1,400 children died due to abuse or neglect in 2002
- 76 percent of the children killed were under the age of four
- Infant boys (younger than one year) had the highest fatality rate at 19 deaths per 100,000
- One third of deaths are attributed to neglect
- More than 80 percent of perpetrators were the parents

Source: Adapted from National Clearinghouse on Child Abuse and Neglect Information. Retreived from **http://nccanch.acf.hhs. gov/pubs/factsheets/canstats.pdf**

Physical Abuse. **Physical abuse** refers to nonaccidental injury inflicted by a caretaker. There is often a fine line between physical abuse and discipline through physical punishment. In the United States, physical punishment is common in many families as a childrearing practice. Few states have prohibitions against corporal punishment in schools. Some state statutes consider corporal punishment abusive if bruises are visible after 24 hours. Others view an act as abusive if the person intends to harm the child. Physical indicators include unexplained bruises and welts, unexplained burns, unexplained fractures, and unexplained lacerations and abrasions (Tower, 1992).

Physical Neglect. Physical neglect involves the deliberate neglect or extraordinary inattentiveness to a child's physical well-being. When it becomes necessary for both parents to work, older siblings may be called upon to assume child care responsibilities. When the older siblings are considered by authorities to be too young to provide responsible care, this may by law be considered neglect. This is particularly problematic in cities with large immigrant populations. Some children who suffer from neglect may exhibit poor hygiene, may be inappropriately dressed for weather conditions, or may suffer from hunger. Children who suffer from neglect may have medical or dental needs that have not been attended to. At times, the practices of some religious groups can come into conflict with the law regarding parental decisions for addressing illness and refusing conventional medical care. The courts have, in some instances, intervened and overturned parental rights when children were considered to be at extreme risk.

Sexual Abuse.   **Sexual abuse** refers to the involvement of children or underage adolescents in sexual activities. It also includes practices that violate the social mores of one's culture as they relate to family roles. Sexual abuse is usually found in familial abuse or incest; extrafamilial molestation or rape; exploitation through pornography, prostitution, sex rings, or cults; or institutional abuse (e.g., day care centers). Children who are sexually abused may become withdrawn or secretive. Some may do poorly in school. While physical injury does not usually result from sexual abuse, research does indicate that the emotional impact is both serious and long term; including socioemotional behavior, low self-esteem, depression, and substance abuse (Lotz, 2005).

Emotional Abuse.   Children who are emotionally abused are chronically belittled, humiliated, or rejected, or they have their self-esteem attacked. **Emotional abuse** is a pattern of psychologically destructive behavior. "It includes acts or omissions by parents or caregivers that have caused or could cause serious behavioral, cognitive, emotional, or mental disorders." (National Clearinghouse on Child Abuse and Neglect Information, 2000). Children who are emotionally or psychologically abused may exhibit a low self-esteem by continually demeaning themselves. Some become self-destructive through the use of drugs, develop eating disorders, or even become suicidal. Some children exhibit withdrawal behaviors; others may exhibit destructive behaviors.

Abusive behavior can have a long-lasting effect on a child. The scars may persist into adulthood. Petersen (2004) reports that youth who are both physically and sexually abused are four times more likely to participate in a gang than youth who are not maltreated. Bartollas and Miller (2005) further assert that research continues to demonstrate that children who are victims of maltreatment are placed at a greater risk for arrest. More than one third of women in prisons reported being abused as children, as compared to 12 to 17% of women in the general population. Fourteen percent of male prison inmates reported abuse as children, as compared to 5 to 8% of men in the general population (Childhelp Inc., 2003).

Child abuse is everyone's problem. It is the responsibility of each teacher to report known or suspected cases of child abuse to the school supervisor. The supervisor, in turn, is responsible for reporting these problems or concerns to professionals who are mandated by state and federal laws to bring the matter to the attention of appropriate protective agencies. These professionals are referred to as "mandated reporters." Every state has mandated laws requiring the reporting of child abuse. State laws differ in that one state has no penalties for failure to report, whereas others impose fines and even jail terms. Some states stipulate that a report must be made if there is suspicion of abuse; others stipulate accountability for failure to report if there is "reasonable cause to believe." Beyond the legal mandates, educators have a professional and ethical obligation to make reports to protect children from abuse.

One of the newest concerns for parents and educators is the sexual predators who seek out children on the Internet. As children become increasingly computer literate, some begin to surf the Internet. Through this means, predators seek out potential victims and lure them into secret and illicit rendezvous. As educators train children to become proficient computer users, it is incumbent upon educators to train the children to be socially responsible in their use of technology.

Gay Student

Elizabeth Harvey is a 10th grade English teacher in a suburban middle class school, in a predominantly white, southern community. It is after school, the hallways are cleared of students, and she is on her way to the office from her classroom to check on mail, notices, and other things before going to her car. In a darkened, small hallway off the main hallway, she hears what sounds like sobs and whimpering. Investigating she sees John Cameron, one of her English students, curled up in a near fetal position, his face bruised and cut, with tears running down his face.

Harvey gets on her knees and carefully cradles his head in her arms. "What is it, John?" she asks. He shakes his head and replies, "nothing. I slipped and fell." "You and I both know that isn't true, John. I want to know who did this to you and why. We will get to the bottom of this and make sure that whoever did this will be punished." John, shakes his head and emphatically says, "No! It would only make it worse for me if you do something to them." "Who and why?" she asks. "It doesn't really matter who, Mrs. Harvey. It is everybody. They called me a dirty faggot, and said to get out of this school."

Gathering her composure, Harvey asks him in a gentle manner, "Is it true, John? I mean that you are gay?"

"Yes, I guess so. I've never even admitted it to my parents. My father would probably kick me out of the house if he knew. He is Mr. Macho and has always wanted me to be the same."

Elizabeth Harvey is a devout, Evangelical Christian. She believes that homosexuality is a sin, and a matter of choice. She believes that John can be cured through prayer and faith. Her first inclination is to tell him this and to tell him that she and others in her church love him, would welcome him, and will help him to change and to be normal.

Harvey, however, is also a devoted professional educator. The thoughts that are now racing through her mind are what is the appropriate thing for her to do for John in her professional role.

Questions for Discussion

1. *What should Elizabeth Harvey do with John at this time?*
2. *Should she take him into the principal's office and together with John discuss the incident with the site administrator in charge?*
3. *Should the school contact John's parents and tell them what has happened, informing them that their son is gay?*
4. *Should the school seek out and punish the students that attacked John?*
5. *Should the school seek out someone better qualified than they are in issues such as this to assist them in this matter?*

To answer these questions online, go to the Critical Incidents in Teaching module for this chapter of the Companion Website.

CW

Adolescence

Adolescence, approximately ages 13 through 19, is perhaps one of the most challenging times in the life of an individual and the family. It is a long transitional period (6 years or so) during which the individual is "suspended" between childhood and adulthood. During adolescence, emancipation from the primary family unit is the central task of the individual. It is a difficult period for the young person, who is attempting to be free from the role of a child but is not fully equipped to assume the responsibilities of adulthood.

In some cultures, entry into adulthood begins immediately after childhood. Adolescence as a stage of behavioral development does not exist. In Western culture, however, an individual is seldom allowed or expected to make an immediate transition from childhood to adulthood. It is interesting to note that the anticipated state of extreme disequilibrium associated with adolescence and the period of "storm and stress" does not exist in some cultures in which adolescence does not exist. Cultural definitions of the role of the adolescent, along with social attitudes, have created circumstances that cause this period of life to be what it is in Western culture.

RELATIONSHIP WITH PARENTS

As the adolescent shifts emotional ties from the family to peers, a restructuring may take place in the parent-adolescent relationship. Parents may be viewed more objectively. Parents may become more concerned about peer influence as they have increasingly less interaction with their child. These changes have the potential for turning the period of adolescence into one of dissonance and alienation from parents and other members of the family. One need only observe a few adolescent-family situations, however, to realize that the degree of dissonance and alienation varies greatly.

The attitude of the parents may contribute to the alienation. Parents who expect problems with their children in the adolescent period sometimes fall into the trap of a self-fulfilling prophecy. Their expectation of alienation generates a hostile attitude on their part. The adolescents quickly sense this attitude, and a vicious cycle is started. In contrast, parents who have confidence in their children may promote a feeling of confidence and trust. These children often develop sufficient self-confidence to resist peer pressure when it is appropriate.

Alienation is disturbing to families, to adult members of the community, and to the adolescents themselves. In their efforts to achieve autonomy, sexual functioning, and identity in order to become productive, self-sufficient individuals, some adolescents think they must turn away from the family. They exhibit considerable ambivalence because young persons are usually unprepared to yield family support systems in the quest for independence. As adolescents assert their rights to assume adult behaviors, they sometimes are unable to assume complementary adult-like responsibility. Recognizing this shortcoming, parents are understandably reluctant to grant adolescents adult privileges; this further adds to the alienation.

AT-RISK YOUTH AND HIGH-RISK BEHAVIOR

It is important to differentiate between the terms adolescent "**at risk**" and "**high-risk behaviors.**" At-risk youth are those who live in a disadvantaged status. This may be due to conditions such as poverty, discrimination, family instability, genetic or constitutional factors, parental neglect or abuse, or major traumatic events. High-risk adolescent behaviors are those that youth engage in that make them or others vulnerable to physical, social, or psychological harm or negative outcomes. Youth deemed "at risk" do not necessarily engage in high-risk behaviors. These categories of high-risk behaviors include the use of harmful substances such as alcohol or other drugs, and sexual behaviors leading to unwanted pregnancies or sexually transmitted diseases. These behaviors are initiated during adolescence, are frequently interrelated, and often extend into adulthood.

EXPLORE DIVERSITY Go to the *Exploring Diversity* CD located in the accompanying booklet to watch a science teacher engaging seventh grade students in a lesson on diseases in the case called *The Emerging Competence of Youth in 7th Grade.*

SUBSTANCE ABUSE

The use of harmful substances, primarily by children and adolescents, has been one of the most problematic areas faced by parents, schools, communities, and law enforcement agencies in the past two decades. It will inevitably continue to be a major problem in the next decade. **Substance abuse** is the use of banned or illegal drugs and substances or the overuse of legal substances. The problem is a national phenomenon, and many of the problems of adult substance abuse have their roots in adolescence.

Substances are abused to produce altered states of consciousness. The adolescents who use them often seek relief, escape, or comfort from stress. The social institutions, to which the adolescents must relate, including family and particularly the educational system, may be perceived as unresponsive or openly hostile. Their inability to focus on long-range goals, their desire for immediate gratification, and their lack of appreciation for the consequences of their behavior may contribute to some adolescents' misuse of substances.

Research over the years has established a clear relationship between alcohol use by adolescents and negative experiences with their families (Crowe, Philbin, Richards, & Crawford, 1998). The 2003 National Survey on Drug Use and Health reports that among youth 12 to 17 years of age, 17.7% reported drinking alcohol in the prior month. They also reported that for all youths, 10.6% were binge drinkers, and 2.6% were heavy drinkers (Department of Health & Human Services, 2004). Studies indicate that while motor vehicle accidents are the leading cause of death for youth 15 to 24, 75% of these involve the use of alcohol. In addition, alcohol is linked to the increasing incidence of date rapes and sexual assaults against women (McLoyd & Steinberg, 1998). Although alcohol is rarely given the attention focused on other drugs, it is the most readily available drug for teenagers and does frequently lead to

Experimentation with smoking, alcohol, and drugs often occurs during adolescence at the urging of peers.

violent behavior. Estimates are that alcohol takes a significantly greater toll on the overall health of the nation's youth than all other drugs combined (Prothrow-Stith & Spivak, 2004).

There are two broad categories of adolescent drug users: the experimenters and the compulsive users. Experimenters make up the majority of adolescent drug users. A few progress from experimenters to compulsive users. Although most experimenters eventually abandon such use, the fear of progression to compulsive use is a serious concern of parents and authorities. Recreational users fall somewhere between experimenters and compulsive users. For them, alcohol and marijuana are often the drugs of choice. Use is primarily to achieve relaxation and is typically intermittent. For a few, however, the goal is intoxication, and these recreational users pose a threat to themselves and others. This is particularly problematic among some groups of college students. Joseph and Taylor (2003) report that the results from several empirical studies have documented a strong association between alcohol abuse and sexual aggression on college campuses.

In a survey conducted of 48,467 students from 392 public and private schools, the 2003 Monitoring the Future Study reported an 11% decline in drug use over the past two years among 8th-, 10th- and 12th-grade students. This is the first substantial decline in youth drug use in over a decade. They estimate that this represents 400,000 fewer teen drug users (National Institute on Drug Abuse, 2003). However, the Department of Health and Human Services in their 2003 National Survey on Drug Use and Health reported that the actual rate of illicit drug use among youth (ages 12 to 17) had not changed significantly between 2002 (11.6%) and 2003 (11.2%). They further reported that the rate of actual substance dependence was

Table 8.2 Illicit Drug Use Among U.S. Youth

Racial Groups	Percent Using Drugs
American Indians/Alaska Natives	12.1%
Native Hawaiians/Pacific Islanders	11.1%
African Americans	8.7%
Whites	8.3%
Hispanics	8.0%
Asians	3.8%

Source: Department of Health and Human Services (2004). *Overview of findings from 2003 national survey on drug use and health.* Washington, D.C., Author.

8.9% for youth ages 12 to 17 (Department of Health and Human Services, 2004). The highest rate of illegal drug use has been reported in young adults ages 18 to 25 (Calhoun & Chapple, 2003).

Numerous problems related to substance abuse affect the community at large. Intravenous drug users are one group at high risk for AIDS. The spread of the deadly HIV virus among adolescents had, by the 1990s, affected thousands of the country's youth.

Substance abuse, while a concern among all youth groups, is no more problematic for minority youth than among their majority group counterparts. Table 8.2 shows that in 2003, the rate of illicit drug use was 12.1% for American Indians or Alaska Natives, 11.1% for Native Hawaiians or Other Pacific Islanders, 8.7% for African Americans, 8.3% for whites, 8% for Hispanics, and 3.8% for Asians (Department of Health and Human Services, 2004).

The problem of substance abuse is a national crisis and a national tragedy. Numerous research studies indicate that the abuse of alcohol or other drugs frequently has a detrimental effect on the normal development of adolescents, and contributes significantly to problems such as difficulty in school, absenteeism, and delinquent behaviors. And while there is a reluctance to state conclusively that drug and alcohol abuse causes delinquency, it is certainly evident that within the criminal justice system a substantial amount of activity is attributable to substance abuse (Calhoun & Chapple, 2003). Surveys further find that 60% of juveniles in institutions report regular drug use, and almost 40% report that at the time of arrest they were under the influence of drugs (Trojanowicz, Morash, & Schram, 2001). It is a complex problem that deserves more attention by educators than the brief coverage here. The problem can and must be dealt with through the home, school, and law enforcement authorities, as well as through social agencies and responsible media.

SEXUAL BEHAVIORS

A 2002 report on sexual risk behavior of high school students indicates that during the period from 1991 to 2001, students engaging in sexual intercourse decreased by 16%. The report also suggests that overall the number of high school students en-

Table 8.3 High School Students Sexually Active

Racial Groups	Percent Sexually Active
African Americans	60.8%
Hispanics	48.4%
Whites	43.2%

Source: Centers for Disease Control and Prevention (2002a). *Trends in sexual risk behaviors among high school students*— United States 1991–2001. Atlanta, GA: Author.

gaging in sexual risk behaviors resulting in pregnancy and sexually transmitted diseases, including HIV infection, has decreased substantially over the past decade. However, there was an increase in the number of students reporting the use of alcohol or drugs before engaging in sexual activity (from 21.6% in 1991 to 25.6% in 2001). African Americans (60.8%) were more likely than white (43.2%) or Hispanic students (48.4%) to be sexually active in high school as shown in Table 8.3. A disturbing statistic emerging from this study is that only 57.9% of these students reported using a condom during their last sexual encounter (Centers for Disease Control and Prevention, 2002a).

In 2003, the Centers for Disease Control and Prevention (CDC) also reported that while adolescent (under 13 years of age) cases of HIV/AIDS were but a small percentage of the total cases (9,300 out of an estimated 886,575), males with HIV/AIDS outnumbered female adolescents with HIV/AIDS by 2 to 1 (CDC, 2003b). HIV/AIDS has disproportionately affected African American and Hispanic adolescents. Although African Americans comprise only 15% of the adolescent population, they account for 61% of the youth AIDS cases. Latinos comprised 15% of the adolescent population and 21% of the newly reported AIDS cases reported in 2001 (CDC, 2002b). In 2002, African Americans accounted for more than half of the newly reported HIV cases in the United States. And 62% of children born to HIV-infected mothers were African American (CDC, 2004a).

Despite an impressive decline (30% over the past decade), the birthrate for teenagers in the United States is still significantly higher compared with other industrialized countries. Most impressive was the report that the teen birthrate for African Americans had been cut in half since 1991 (CDC, 2003a). However, the pregnancy rate for African American teens is twice the rate of white teens (CDC, 2003a).

Teen birthrates are closely linked to poverty. Consequently there is a higher birthrate among teens of color who are significantly impacted by poverty. When compared across poverty groups, teen birthrates among poor whites and poor African Americans are more similar. Children born to young mothers face a substantially greater risk of low birth weight, and of serious disabilities. A Johns Hopkins University study of 735 low-income black women suggests that poverty and associated stress are often linked to preterm births, the second leading cause of newborn deaths (*Midwifery Today,* 2001).

Pause to Reflect 8.2

It is quite obvious, whether we approve or not, that half or more of our nation's teenagers are involved in sexual activity. The problems are at least twofold. They are risking the possibility of pregnancies, and many (about half) are having unprotected sex and risking the possibility of contracting sexually transmitted diseases (STDs).

■ *Whose responsibility is this? The students? The parents? The school? Public health agencies?*

■ *Does providing free condoms to junior high and high school students encourage them to be sexually promiscuous?*

■ *If they are going to be involved in sexual activity anyway, should we protect both them and society?*

To answer these questions online, go to the Pause to Reflect module for this chapter of the Companion Website.

CW

ADOLESCENT SUICIDE

Although the overall rate among teenagers has declined since 1992, suicide remains the third leading cause of death among young people, surpassed only by car accidents and homicide. And it is estimated that each year in the United States nearly 2,000 young people commit suicide (CDC, 2004b). In addition to this alarming statistic is the estimate that approximately 2 million adolescents in the United States attempt suicide, with almost 700,000 receiving medical attention as a result of the attempt (National Alliance for the Mentally Ill [NAMI], 2004). In all likelihood, the actual number of adolescent deaths due to suicide is higher than that which is reported. Some suicides are likely reported as accidents; especially high-speed automobile crashes where no suicide notes are recovered. Some gunshot deaths may be reported as accidents as well.

The largest group of young people who attempt or commit suicide are 15 to 19 years old (8.2 per 100,000). However, the CDC reports that the suicide rate among children ages 10 to 14 has increased in the past decade, with 1.5 per 100,000 (CDC, 2004b). Alarming statistics suggest that some students of color may be at greater risk than previously thought. CDC statistics reveal that American Indian/Alaska Native adolescents are twice as likely to commit suicide as any other racial/ethnic group. Among high school students, 10.7% of Hispanics have attempted suicide. Female Hispanic teens in grades 9 through 12 (18.9%) have attempted suicide, compared with 7.5% for African Americans and 9.0% for white teens (CDC, 2004b).

In California, a state with large urban centers and many students from diverse backgrounds, there is a disproportionately high number of attempted youth suicides among some groups. Statistics indicate that 16% of Latino, 12% of Asian, and 12% of American Indian students have attempted suicide. These compare with the lower rates of 7% and 8% among African American and European American youth, respectively. These statistics can be puzzling because both Latino and African American students have disproportionately high levels of poverty, and Asians in California are, as a group, among the more affluent. One may question the effects of poverty and the stress of urban life, but these statistics may raise more questions than they answer (Nazario, 1997). Since 1980, the suicide rates for Asian American and Latino youth have been increasing. McLoyd and Steinberg (1998) speculate that this may be a function of the many pressures inherent in immigration and acculturation.

One encouraging statistic is that the CDC reported that the overall suicide rate for those ages 10 to 19 fell from 6.2 deaths per 100,000 in 1992 to 4.6 in 2001. Restrictions on the access to fire arms and decreased stigma over sexual orientation were suggested variables contributing to the decrease. Television programming today about gays and lesbians has increased. This, combined with increasing numbers of individuals including celebrities, who have acknowledged their sexual orientation, has likely saved a lot of lives (*Los Angles Times,* 2004).

Numerous theories have been advanced for the adolescent suicide phenomenon. Among the reasons offered are the decline in religion, tension between parents, the breakup of the nuclear family, and the competitiveness in school. Studies indicate that, in half of the cases of attempted youth suicide, the mother was reported to be depressed. Family tension and conflict were also reported in half of the cases (McKee, Jones, & Barbe, 1993). Because of their youth and lack of experience in making accurate judgments, depressed adolescents are more prone to respond to the suggestion of suicide than an adult. Adolescent depression is a function of a wide range of situations, perhaps involving failure, loss of a love object, or rejection. It can also be a function of biochemical imbalances in the brain or the loss of a parent through death, divorce, separation, or extended absence. Fewer than 38% of this country's children live with both natural parents. The loss of a parent may be viewed as parental rejection, which may lead to feelings of guilt in the adolescent. Some mental health professionals attribute adolescent suicide to the widespread availability and use of both legal prescription and illegal drugs. Some believe that the tightening of the job market along with the bleak prospects for the future among the less affluent is another contributing variable (Sidel, 1990).

Alienation in the family is cited as another major contributor to adolescent suicide. Where family ties are close, suicide rates are low; where families are not close, suicide rates tend to be high. Adolescent suicide victims come from all socioeconomic backgrounds, but many are from middle- and upper-income homes. The parents in these homes are generally high-achieving individuals, and they expect similar behavior from their children. Failure to conform to parental expectations may lead to alienation. McKee et al. (1993) suggest that adolescents at risk include those who have experienced a successful family suicide, adolescents who are very concerned about their parents (particularly unhappy parents), and those who are unable to conform to expected sexual behavior patterns. It is estimated that gay and lesbian youth constitute 30% of the completed suicides in their age-group. Approximately 30 of a surveyed group of gay and bisexual males indicated that they have attempted suicide at least once (American Academy of Pediatrics, 2004).

Risk factors for suicide completion include:

- Previous suicide attempts
- Mental disorders or co-occurring mental and alcohol or substance abuse disorders
- Family history of suicide
- Stressful life event or loss
- Easy access to lethal methods, especially guns
- Exposure to suicidal behaviors of others
- Incarceration (Youth Violence Prevention Resource Center, 2004)

Suicide attempts are often more of a desperate attempt to be heard and understood than a true intent to end life. Those who contemplate suicide but do not follow through with an attempt often report that their plans were changed by someone's simple act of concern.

YOUTH VIOLENCE

Violence is one of the greatest problems facing young Americans today. Although the violent crime rate in the United States has declined during the past five years, this trend has not been evident in the juvenile violent crime rate (Petersen, 2004). Champion (2004) reports that while youths ages 13 to 18 constitute approximately 10% of the population in the United States, this age-group actually accounts for 20% of all arrests. Between 1985 and 1991, the homicide rate among young males increased from 13 to 33 per 100,000. Between 1993 and 1997, there was an encouraging downward trend from 34 to 22.6 per 100,000. Despite the downward trend, the rates are still unacceptably high (CDC, 2000a). While official reports indicate that 1,402 children under the age of 18 were murdered in 2001, some estimates place the actual numbers between 2,000 and 5,000 children killed each year (Bartollas & Miller, 2005). In a study of the top industrialized nations in the world, it was determined that the United States was responsible for 73% of all child homicides (Prothrow-Stith & Spivak, 2004).

Due to media coverage, the nation has become well conditioned to school violence. In reality, less than 1% of all homicides among school-aged children (5–19 years of age) occur in or around school grounds or on the way to and from school. Since the 1992–1993 school year, incidents of school-related homicides (the majority of which involved firearms) have been on a steady decline. However the incidents involving multiple victims have been on the increase, with an average of five such occurrences per year (CDC, 2000b).

Even the most callous individuals were shocked and stunned when the images of the April 1999 shootings in Littleton, Colorado, reached their TV screens. In a few brief moments two outcast students shot and killed 12 of their classmates and a popular teacher/coach at Columbine High School, then killed themselves. The odds were certainly against such a scenario taking place at a school serving this comfortable community. Statistically black students are at greater risk at school than white students. Urban students are at greater risk than those from the suburbs, poor students at risk more than the affluent (Cannon, Streisand, & McGraw, 1999).

Columbine students are overwhelmingly white, and only one of the victims was black. The school served the affluent community of Littleton, and one of the assailants drove a BMW car to the school. Perhaps even more alarming was the intent of the two assailants, Eric Harris and Dylan Klebold, who had planted at least 30 bombs in the school with the intention of killing even more of their classmates. Fortunately the bombs never detonated.

The Littleton incident was but one of a string of violent attacks against students and teachers across the United States in recent years. Most of these high-profile shootings involved young white males, most of who are viewed as alienated individuals or outcasts. Often, their peers had ridiculed them, and they associated with other disaffected individuals in outcast groups. This was the case of the assailant in a Pearl, Mississippi, school who complained of "mistreatment every day." Another school killer allegedly hung around with individuals involved in the occult. One of the individuals involved in the Jonesboro, Arkansas, shootings boasted openly "individuals would die" (Cannon, Streisand, & McGraw, 1999).

Harris and Klebold had provided ample warning signs of their troubled lives and potential to do harm. Authorities apparently ignored or paid little heed when advised of a hate-filled website and death threats against another student. They intensely disliked the school athletes, who allegedly mocked and harassed them. Not unlike other suicidal teens, these were individuals who were troubled, and who gave out warning signs to those who would pay heed. Unfortunately no one who might have prevented the tragedy in this instance, and in so many other situations, paid heed.

Green (1999) indicates that some of the outcast students at Columbine may have been terrorized and harassed unmercifully by mainstream students. Whether or not these specific allegations are accurate, every educator knows that teasing and harassment, often unmerciful, takes place daily in the schools. Every teacher and administrator can remember seeing this done, having it done to him or her, or participating in some type of student-directed hurtful behavior. Educators must not allow such behavior to go on without intervention. The stakes are far too high. The problems associated with school violence are actually greater than the reported incidents. The CDC, in a national survey, found that in the 30 days prior to the study, 4% of students missed one or more days of school because of fears for their safety in or on the way to or from school. Of the students surveyed, 7.4% indicated that in the 12 months prior to the survey, they had been threatened or injured with a weapon on school property (CDC, 2000b). *Were you ever bullied or picked on? Teased unmercifully by other students? How did you feel? Did you want to get back at them?*

Opportunities for Reflection

The March 2001 school shooting in Santee, California, is particularly troubling since several friends and associates of the alleged shooter admitted that he had told them the weekend before that he was planning the incident. They did not report it because they said he later laughed it off as a joke, and as one said, he did not want to get his friend into trouble. It is essential that teachers, students, and the community be trained to take all talk of this nature seriously and to report it to the proper authorities.

Warning Signs. Many of these warning signs of potentially aggressive behavior overlap with the warning signs of individuals considering suicide. Whether or not the presence of these signs is indicative of suicide consideration or imminent danger

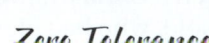

FOCUS YOUR CULTURAL LENS: DEBATE

Zero Tolerance

Because of the increasing violence in the schools, officials have instituted zero tolerance regulations in which specific behaviors and items are banned from the school. In general, violators are dealt with immediately and sometimes harshly (e.g., immediate expulsion) regardless of the intent, age of the offender, or the severity of the offense. Often administrators have no discretionary powers to make exceptions. The tough rules are designed to ensure that the schools will be safer, with every violation having a mandatory punishment.

FOR

- Seemingly harsh punishment for infractions is a small price to pay for keeping our schools and children safe.

- Students and their parents know what the rules are. If they break the rules then they must suffer the consequences.

- Zero tolerance means that there are consequences for every infraction.

- Good zero tolerance policies do not require the maximum punishment for every offense.

AGAINST

- Young children are expelled simply for forgetting some minor item.

- Zero tolerance has gone too far. Innocent children are treated like criminals, scarring them for life.

- Unless administrators are given more discretion, these ridiculous laws need to be scrapped.

Questions

1. *If we don't institute zero tolerance policies, then what can the schools do to make students and parents realize that they are serious in curbing violence?*
2. *Should there be more flexibility for administrators in dealing with grade school offenders than older students?*
3. *Is zero tolerance really zero tolerance if administrators have discretionary powers and can make exceptions?*

To answer these questions online, go to the Focus Your Cultural Lens: Debate module for this chapter of the Companion Website.

References: Cauchon, D. (1999). Zero Tolerance policies lack flexibility. *USA Today,* http://www.usatoday.com/educate/ednews3.htm; California Department of Education. (2004). *Zero Tolerance.* http://www.usatoday.com/educate/ednews3.htm.

to others, it is a potential warning of a troubled individual. Parents, teachers, and school authorities cannot risk taking such situations lightly.

Chua-Eoan (1999) suggests warning signs on "how to spot a depressed child":

- Difficulty in maintaining relationships
- Reduced physical activity
- Morbid suicidal thoughts
- Low self-esteem
- Problems at school
- Changes in sleep patterns

Warning signs for preschoolers:

- Frequent unexplained stomachaches, headaches, or fatigue
- Overactivity or excessive restlessness
- Sad appearance
- Low tolerance for frustration
- Irritability
- Loss of pleasure in activities
- Tendency to portray the world as bleak

Depression does not necessarily indicate the likelihood of violent behaviors; however, violent behavior is often the function of depression. If you have reason to suspect that a student is depressed, refer the individual to a school counselor or to an appropriate authority.

While the reasons for such untoward violent behaviors are multifaceted, the American Academy of Pediatrics (2000) reports that by the age of 18, the average American child will have viewed about 100,000 acts of violence on television alone. The level of violence on Saturday morning cartoons exceeds that of prime time. There are 20 to 25 acts of violence an hour on Saturday morning as compared with

 VIDEO INSIGHT

Girl Gangsters—The Queens of Armed Robbery

Few are surprised when they hear of urban street gang members involved in armed robberies. But what would possess four white middle-class girls from an upscale suburban community to rob several stores at gunpoint? In this segment, four girls in an affluent Houston, Texas, suburb apparently found themselves bored one summer. Between their boredom and their drug use, they turned a flippant remark about robbing a store into a crime spree that eventually ended in prison sentences.

It may be difficult to understand why children from privileged backgrounds would engage in such high-risk behavior that would leave an indelible stain on their lives.

1. *Does affluence provide more access to drugs?*
2. *How much does peer pressure shape behavior among teens?*
3. *Are teenagers too young to fully recognize the consequences of their behaviors?*
4. *Did their punishment fit the crime?*
5. *Should they have been treated more leniently because of their backgrounds and lack of prior criminal records?*
6. *Were they too young to be sent to prison?*
7. *What can we as educators do to help young people understand that there are consequences for almost every behavior?*

DVD

CW

To answer these questions online, go to the ABC News Video Insight module for this chapter of the Companion Website.

3 to 5 during prime time. With such continuous exposure to violence, is it possible that our children have become desensitized to senseless violent acts? Prothrow-Stith and Spivak (2004) argue that there is substantial evidence of the connection between exposure to violence on television and aggressive or violent behavior in children. Media violence affects children in the following ways:

- Increasing aggressiveness and antisocial behavior
- Increasing the fear of becoming a victim
- Making them less sensitive to violence and victims of violence
- Increasing their appetite for more violence in entertainment and real life

Bender, Clinton, and Bender (1999) suggest a number of factors that seem to influence youth violence:

- Easy access to handguns
- Early involvement with drugs
- Involvement with gangs or other antisocial groups
- Exposure to violent acts in the media
- Weak parenting
- Absence of a father or significant male role model
- Lack of connectedness
- Dysfunctional family life

Bender et al. (1999) indicate that connectedness in school is important because students need to be positively involved emotionally, academically, and socially in school and in the home environment. Bender et al. also indicate the importance of same-sex role models. They indicate that boys and girls learn to become successful adults by observing same-sex role models from their earliest years onward. This can be problematic in that 85 to 100% of the faculty in the lower grades is female, leaving a void in the area of male role models.

Palermo and Simpson (1998) suggest that the decline in the nuclear family is a contributing variable to the roots of violence. They indicate that half of the marriages now end in divorce, that one fourth of births are to single mothers, and that one in four Americans over the age of 18 never marry. Married couples with a child under the age of 18 have become a shrinking minority.

The Federal Bureau of Investigation (1994) reported that African American youth, who comprised 15% of all youth under the age of 18, accounted for 50.2% of those arrested for violent crimes. Latino youth were also more likely to be arrested for serious felony offenses than either white or Asian youth. Lotz (2005) argues that the higher rates are primarily the result of the social conditions in the daily lives of African Americans. They are more likely to live in neighborhoods with conditions that contribute to criminal activity. Joseph and Taylor (2003) suggest that drug violations account for the rise in arrests for young African Americans, noting that they account for more than 56% of the drug offenders in prison. However, Gibbs (1998) contends that African American youth receive differential treatment from the juvenile justice system. They are more likely to be arrested, convicted, and incarcerated than white youth for similar offenses. The poor typically have court appointed attorneys and the trial and subsequent incarceration is often a mere formality. Youth from middle-class backgrounds may have the benefit of privately retained attorneys who may be able to secure probation or reduced sentences. Incarceration severely impacts the future of these individuals, limiting educational opportunities, employment opportunities, and income.

Today, few children are cared for by one of their parents during normal working hours. Because of the need for two incomes in the nuclear family, both parents typically work out of the home. This is also the case even when two incomes are not an absolute necessity. Women often opt (rightfully) to pursue their chosen careers. This typically results in child care from hired sources, which is sometimes good and at other times marginal. The more affluent and professional parents often have the resources to pay for the highest quality child care. Others must accept whatever is available, and this is sometimes the crime-filled streets (Palermo & Simpson, 1998).

STREET GANGS

Juvenile gang activity in the United States can be documented as far back as the mid-1800s. Prior to the 1980s, gang activity and violence tended to affect only those in their immediate communities. Middle-class white Americans had few concerns with respect to street gangs. By the 1970s, however, and especially the 1980s, gang organizations had become more sophisticated and their activities had begun to affect a wider range of people (Kratcoski & Kratcoski, 2004). Because of the sensationalized portrayal of gangs on television, film, and in the news media, gangs and violence have become nearly synonymous with violent crime (McCorkle & Miethe, 2002). Research suggests that youth become involved in gangs for a variety of reasons. These include family stress, protection against victimization, and emotional fulfillment (Petersen, 2004). For many gang members, affiliation with a gang is their means of achieving status in a community. The gangs acquire power in a community through violent behavior and the fear that such behavior generates. Some of today's gangs are well armed, and in some areas either match or exceed the police with firepower. In Los Angeles County and in other Southern California communities, street gangs have grown in size much faster than the resources to combat them. In Los Angeles County there was an estimated 12,000 gang members in 1973. Today the estimated gang membership is 57,000. Neither the Los Angeles Police Department nor the Los Angeles County Sheriff's Department has come close to matching the growth of the gangs. In addition other resources such as gang prosecution, prevention, and intervention have been cut or have fallen short of keeping up with gang growth (Barrett & Browne, 2004).

With the expiration of the federal ban against assault weapons in 2004, law enforcement and other officials fear that gang members will have greater access to high-powered sophisticated weaponry. Even when gang members cannot legally obtain these weapons, they are readily available through other means. Gang members consider guns essential for passing through the turf of others. The problem of gun ownership is not limited to a few "bad apples"; rather, it is typical in the impoverished inner city and is spreading outward. For many, assault rifles are the weapon of choice. With weapons such as these, drive-by shootings have become commonplace among gang members struggling for turf, avenging an insult, or retaliating a rival gang's previous assault. Drive-by shootings claim the lives of almost as many innocent bystanders as intended victims.

In communities such as Los Angeles, the number of innocent bystanders injured or killed each year is in the hundreds. Los Angeles police estimate that members of street gangs are involved in more than 90% of all drive-by shootings (Petersen, 2004). These acts of violence generate the fear that, in turn, gives gangs power in the community. Although Petersen (2004) reports that only 10 to 15% of youths report being in a gang, and that this percentage has remained consistent over the past two decades, it is estimated that, in Los Angeles alone, more than 1,200 street gangs exist with more than 150,000 members (Jackson, Lopez, & Connell, 1997).

Howell (1998) summarizes the findings of several studies related to gang activities in the United States. While not all gangs are violent, violent gang activity is a growing problem in the country. These gangs draw the attention of the media, offenses have become more violent and more lethal weapons are being used, resulting in more serious injuries and death. While gangs are certainly a part of the problem, it is unclear whether the problems are primarily due to organized street gangs, law-breaking youth groups, or nongang–related youth. Gangs have moved eastward from the West Coast. Bloods and Crips have migrated from the Los Angeles area to 45 or more Western and Midwestern communities. It is uncertain if this migration is due primarily to family migration or deliberate gang relocation and expansion. Howell indicates that there is certainly ample evidence to indicate that some gang members are involved in drug use and have been involved in narcotics trafficking and drug-related killings. What is uncertain is whether the gang involvement is an organized effort, or primarily the acts of individuals who happen to be gang members. Most gang on gang violence is the result of turf disputes and some of the violence attributed to drug wars may be more related to turf wars.

The variables that contribute to gang membership and the reasons for the violent nature of many of the gangs are multifaceted. So too are the means to combat the problem. Either the solutions to ending gang membership have not yet been found, or the will to solve the problems has not yet been resolved.

Gang membership is usually structured by race or nationality. Actual estimates of gang membership vary, but indications are that whites comprise less than 15%, with the majority of members being African Americans or another group of color—usually Hispanic (Petersen, 2004). However, the racial/ethnic composition of gangs may vary depending on the area. For example, gang membership among whites was higher in small cities, but lower in large cities (Trojanowicz, Morash, & Schram, 2001).

Most visible among these gangs are Latino, African American, and Asian gangs, and Jamaican posses. Latino gangs tend to operate out of barrios and are some of the older gangs in existence. Some gang members belong to the same gangs that their fathers did before them. Among the best-known gangs are the African American Bloods and the Crips. The Crips began in the Los Angeles area as high school youth who extorted money from classmates and were involved in other violence. The Bloods are the primary rivals of the Crips. Both gangs have extended well beyond Los Angeles, spreading as far north as Alaska and as far east as Washington, DC, and making inroads in communities across the country.

Asian gangs are most prominent in Chinese and Vietnamese communities. Among the Chinese gangs, the Yu Li, Joe Boys, and Wah Ching are the most prominent. In Massachusetts, the Asian Boyz, Asian Crips, Asian Family/AR-Z, and Blood Red Dragons are comprised primarily of individuals with Southeast Asian backgrounds (Cambodian, Laotian, Vietnamese). Asian gangs are, by their own choice, less visible but capable of the same levels of violence as the other ethnic gangs. It is believed that some Asian gangs have ties to organized crime groups in Asia, such as the Hong Kong and Mainland China triads. They also have spread across the United States and Canada (Lindberg, 2002). These Asian gangs typically target other Asians who are distrustful of law enforcement and reluctant to participate in attempts to prosecute. Their typical activities include gambling, extortion, theft of luxury cars to ship overseas, and smuggling of illegal immigrants.

Gang members are identifiable by their clothing, communication, graffiti, and tattoos. Bloods and Crips often wear bandannas on their heads. The color of the Bloods is red; the Crips, blue. Clothing may identify individuals as gang members. Gang-specific clothing may include jackets or sweatshirts with gang names. Tattoos on the hands, arms, and shoulders are common among Latino gang members but are not usually displayed by African American gang members. Hand signs may identify an individual with a specific gang.

Graffiti used by gangs can provide considerable information. African American and Latino gang graffiti differ from one another: Black gang graffiti often contains profanity and other expressions that are absent from Latino gang graffiti. Latino gang graffiti has more flair and more attention to detail. Gangs use graffiti to stake a claim to turf. If the graffiti is crossed out and new graffiti written, another gang is challenging the former's claim to the turf. Through careful observation, law enforcement can determine the sphere of influence a gang has. Graffiti will indicate where the gang has unchallenged influence and where challenges begin and by whom.

Gang Violence and America's Schools.   In inner-city schools, gang members may be involved with student extortion and teacher intimidation. Violence occasionally erupts on school campuses. The presence of several gang members in the same class may be intimidating to teachers, as well as to other students. Discipline in such classes may be a considerable challenge. In addition, some gang members are involved in the sale and distribution of cocaine and crack cocaine. This has spread across the country, and the fight for drug turf is the cause of much of the violence.

The emergence of street gangs over the past two decades has become a major challenge for educators. In some instances, schools have become scenes of violence resulting in the installation of metal detectors and the hiring of security guards at the schools. If law enforcement is unable to stem the growth of gang violence, it is unlikely that educators are any better equipped to do so. As with other issues related to youth, gang participation is often a function of poverty. It disproportionately affects individuals of color because they are disproportionately affected by poverty. Calhoun and Chapple (2003) argue that poor family relationships frequently are one characteristic of gang youth. Compared to nongang youth, gang members are more likely to experience family conflict, live in single-parent homes, and to receive poor supervision. There are white gangs as well. Some of the white gangs are involved in hate groups, such as the "skinheads." Gang membership gives the disenfranchised perceived visibility and status. It provides a sense of acceptance and, at times, a substitute for family. It may even provide the individual an income from illegal activities. Somehow, society has failed to provide better alternatives than gang

Opportunities for Reflection

membership. Perhaps that is one of the major challenges for education. *How serious a problem is street gangs in your community? What is the attraction to a life of crime, violence, and possible early death that the gangs hold for the youth in your community? Has society and the schools done all that they can to provide a better alternative to this life? Is there anything that you can do to stop or minimize this problem?*

THE YOUNG AFRICAN AMERICAN MALE: AN ENDANGERED SPECIES

Gibbs (1992) has suggested that young African American males have become an endangered species and somewhat of an enigma in our society. "Miseducated by the educational system, mishandled by the criminal justice system, mislabeled by the mental health system, and mistreated by the social welfare system. . . . They have come in an unenviable and unconscionable sense—rejects of our affluent society and misfits in their own communities" (p. 6).

Although living in representative communities throughout the United States, young African American males live primarily in urban, inner-city neighborhoods. Disproportionately represented in the lower end of the socioeconomic continuum, and failing to become an integral part of society because of rejection and continued discrimination, many have become endangered, embittered, and embattled (Gibbs, 1992).

Gibbs (1992) suggests six social indicators or serious problems experienced by African American males (and some females) in our society: lack of education, unemployment, delinquency, drug abuse, teenage pregnancy, and mortality rates. Since the early 1980s, black males have sustained increases in all of these problems.

Dropout rates in inner-city schools remain disproportionately high. Among those who do graduate from high school, many are functionally illiterate and lack the basic skills necessary for entry-level jobs, military service, or postsecondary education. College enrollments for African Americans have been declining in recent years.

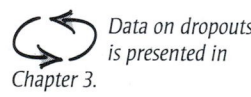
Data on dropouts is presented in Chapter 3.

The unemployment rate for African American males remains disproportionately high, typically at least twice that of the general population (Crockett and Coy, 2003). Those who are employed are frequently working in menial, low-paying jobs. Even these jobs have become increasingly difficult for African Americans to obtain because of increased competition from other groups, particularly immigrants. Coupled with this is the disposition of some employers to hire from groups other than African Americans.

Although African American youth make up less than 20% of the total youth population, they account for nearly one third of the arrests. They are arrested in greater frequency than white youth for robbery, rape, homicide, and aggravated assault. For example, New York University Law Student Drug Policy Forum's Fact Sheet (2004) states that rates of drug use and abuse are almost identical for all racial/ethnic groups. Among high school students, rates are lower for black students than for whites. However, the black arrest rate for all drug offenses is four times the arrest rate for whites.

The incarceration rate of black males is the highest of all groups. They were seven times more likely than white males to be incarcerated; and one in four black males between the ages of 20 and 29 is in the United States prison system (Joseph & Taylor, 2003). This finding suggests that African American youth are treated more harshly in the criminal justice system. The social and financial impact on black communities as a result of the numbers of African American males imprisoned cannot be accurately determined. Joseph and Taylor (2003) suggest that not only have crime control policies contributed to the social deterioration of African American communities, but they have also resulted in the "massive disenfranchisement of large numbers of African Americans and their exclusion from the political process" (p. 111). Estimates are that because of felony convictions, 13% of African American males have been denied the right to vote. "In states with the most restrictive voting laws, 40% of the next generation of black men is likely to be permanently disenfranchised. The rate of black voter disenfranchisement is seven times the national average" (Joseph & Taylor, 2003, p. 111).

With the exception of **inhalants** and **hallucinogens,** youth of color have an equal or higher rate of drug abuse than white youth. The related problem of AIDS among **intravenous drug users** is particularly problematic, with the sexually active too often infecting their partners. Although both a legal and a moral issue, drug use among African American youth is an even greater problem because of the destruction it creates not only physically, but psychologically and socially.

Young African American males have an alarmingly high mortality rate, primarily because of homicides and suicides. Homicide is the leading cause of death for all African Americans age 15 to 24. The rate is more than 700% higher for African American youths than white youths (Joseph & Taylor, 2003). A young black male has about a 1 in 20 chance of being murdered before the age of 25.

Gibbs (1992) suggests four variables that have contributed to the deteriorating status of African American males in the United States. The first variable is tied to historical factors, which include Roosevelt's New Deal, World War II's economic opportunities, Truman's postwar policies, and the civil rights and economic gains of the 1960s for African Americans. Throughout most of the 1960s and during some of the 1970s, liberal federal administrations were committed to increasing opportunities for persons of color. A conservative attack on these advances began in the 1980s, however, with a federal administration that dismantled or diluted many of the civil rights and social welfare programs. As the economy stopped expanding and as other disadvantaged groups began to compete with blacks for the scarce resources, African Americans saw many of their short-lived gains slip away.

Meanwhile, most middle-class African Americans moved out of the inner cities and into integrated urban centers or suburbs. This left the inner cities with a lack of strong leadership and the role models that its residents needed. This is the second variable that Gibbs says contributed significantly to the demise of many inner-city, young black males. Gibbs (1992) suggests that isolation from the black middle class and alienation from the white community turned the inner cities' ghettos into "welfare reservations" where black youth lack access to positive role models, quality education, recreation, cultural facilities, job opportunities, and transportation.

Another sociocultural factor that has contributed to the declining status of African American males is the loss of influence of the black church in the inner city. It has meant that, in many instances, the church is no longer the center of activity in the community and no longer exerts the high level of influence as the monitor of norms and values. Many inner-city residents no longer have the feelings of concern and responsibility for one another they once did. The sense of shared community and common purpose has been replaced by a sense of hopelessness, alienation, and despair (Gibbs, 1992).

Economic factors constitute the third of Gibbs' variables. Among the economic factors that contribute to the frustration and alienation of this country's black youth are the structural changes that occur when an economy that had a predominantly manufacturing and industrial base evolves to one with a high-technology and service base. With many manufacturing jobs moving out of the country and the new jobs located in the suburbs, African American youth are often at a disadvantage without adequate transportation or skills to compete (Gibbs, 1992). Many of the schools that serve poorer communities and students of color are not as well equipped with technology as the schools serving the more affluent students. Many low-income families, including African Americans, do not have computers in the home and are therefore limited in their ability to develop skills in technology.

See Chapter 2 regarding issues related to poverty and low-income families.

The fourth variable contributing to the problems of African American youth is the political climate of the country. A conservative political backlash gave the conservative federal administrations of the 1980s through the early 1990s what they believed to be a mandate to dismantle the antipoverty and affirmative action policies of the Kennedy, Johnson, and Carter administrations. In the mid-1990s, the anti-affirmative action efforts were continued at state levels. Major higher education systems in both California and Texas ended affirmative action efforts. Gibbs (1992) suggests that the goal of providing all Americans with a decent standard of living through federally subsidized health and welfare programs was placed on hold. At the same time, the low-income and disadvantaged were often characterized by their critics as lacking motivation and having dysfunctional family systems dependent on welfare programs. The resulting cutbacks on programs such as the **Comprehensive Employment Training Act (CETA),** the **Job Corps,** federally subsidized college student loans, and youth employment programs had a direct negative impact on African American youth. These cutbacks resulted in reduced training and employment opportunities and, in many instances, cut off the access of young black Americans to the American dream. The discontinuance or near elimination of these programs has been costly in civil unrest and in the deterioration of cities. Perhaps the greatest cost of all has been in the loss of human spirit and dignity.

By the beginning of the twenty-first century a new problem was seriously undermining the well-being of the country's working class. Outsourcing became a household word in much of U.S. industry. Manufacturing jobs have gone south of the U.S. border and to many countries in Asia. Major furniture manufacturing, historically centered in the U.S. southeastern states, has moved much of its activity to Asia. Many of the telecommunications jobs that handled business inquiries have been moved to countries such as India. One needs only to look at the labels of their garments to see where many of our manufacturing jobs have gone. Outsourcing may be good for the business profit lines, but is often devastating to African Americans and other Americans squeezed out of their jobs.

Adulthood

Adulthood, for our purposes ages 20 through 64, is of particular importance to multicultural education because adults, particularly parents, have such an important role in shaping the attitudes and behaviors of the students we see in our schools. Adulthood is a critical period in the life of an individual because it is the time when one's hopes and aspirations come into fruition or when one's dreams are shattered. For the millions of low-income and disenfranchised, the latter is often the case. In this section, we examine two major adult cohort groups: the baby boomers and the baby busters.

To some people, the adult years represent the best years of their lives. To others, it is a time of important decision making, coupled with stress and sometimes pain. Young adults are faced with some of the greatest decisions they will ever make in their lives. Some decisions are awesome because of the impact they may have on the rest of an individual's life. Decisions must be made about education beyond high school; vocational choices must be made; and decisions regarding a mate, marriage, and children are made during this period.

Physical vitality, the excitement of courtship and marriage, the birth of children, and career satisfaction can bring considerable pleasure to individuals during this period of life. At the same time, unwise choices in education or vocation along with frustration in courtship and failure in marriage can bring frustration and grief. To many Americans in poverty, adulthood brings the reality that they are among the disenfranchised in this country. If they are among the minority groups frequently targeted for discriminatory practices, life can be particularly difficult. Lack of financial resources may make the reality of a higher education elusive. Good jobs are particularly difficult to find because preference is often given to members of the dominant group and to individuals from more favored minority groups. During a recession, these individuals tend to be the most affected. They suffer from abject poverty, unemployment, and poor living conditions and are not likely to escape from this life. Frustration and anger appear to be inevitable, along with an intense feeling of impotence.

THE BABY BOOMERS

Baby boomers are those individuals born in 1946, immediately after World War II, through 1964. They were born during a time when the fertility rate for American women reached an all-time high (2.9 children per woman). The baby boomers, 76 million strong, are likely the most influential cohort group in the United States. The oldest of this group are now in their late 50s and early 60s. Together, the "boomers" set the moral and political tone of the country, as well as family styles and career patterns (Roof, 1990). President George W. Bush is part of this group, as are many of the advisors who surround him. Many boomers are in or approaching their professional prime and are therefore able to exert considerable influence on others.

The most educated cohort group in the history of this country, 85% of boomers have high school degrees and 36% have completed college. This generation was surrounded by the civil rights movement; issues related to the Vietnam War; and the changing moral, sexual, and familial values associated with the countercultural years. The boomers can be divided into two age-groups. Those born in the late 1940s tend to form a group that is different from those born in the early 1960s. The older group experienced or witnessed freedom marches, the Kennedy assassination, and the Vietnam War; they participated in or witnessed the political turmoil of the period. The younger group has experienced less social unrest and is more likely to have been affected by the gasoline shortages of 1970 and the incidents at Three Mile Island and Chernoble; they may, as a group, be more prone toward inwardness (Roof, 1990). Members of this group may have related more to the "me generation" of the 1980s than the older boomers.

Although many boomers dropped out of church involvement for two or more years, 43% of older boomers and 38% of younger boomers have returned to active involvement. The younger boomers tend to be more religious with respect to personal faith and practice. As a group, they adhere to traditional Judeo-Christian beliefs and practices more than the older group. They are more likely to be political conservatives and to hold more traditional views on moral issues than the older group (Roof, 1990).

More than most Americans, older boomers tend to endorse alternative religious beliefs, believe in reincarnation, practice meditation, and view other religions as equally viable alternatives to their own. Because more in this group are married and have children, they tend to be involved with religious institutions to a greater extent. Roof (1990) suggests that although married persons with children tend to be more involved with religious activities, the opposite is true for married persons without children. Those without children tend to have lower levels of religious involvement and to have views that are sometimes characterized as more liberal than those of singles on topics such as the legalization of marijuana, abortions, and the acceptance of alternative lifestyles.

Religion is discussed in-depth in Chapter 6.

It is apparent that the social and political views of one's youth often leave an indelible imprint that affects one's attitudes, beliefs, and religious involvement. The children in our schools today are, for the most part, those of the youngest baby boomers, and these attitudes and experiences are being communicated to them. Consequently, these beliefs are likely to become evident in our schools.

GENERATION X

Generation X represents the generation that follows the baby boomers. Born between 1965 and 1976, there are 41 million in this cohort group, tagged the "baby busters" or the "X generation." Whereas the average number of babies born during the 1946 to 1964 boomer years was 4 million per year, the average number of children born per year during the buster years was 3.4 million. It should be noted that some define the Generation X years through 1977, and some even as late as 1981.

Susan Mitchell (1993) of American Demographics described the busters as resentful of the boomers. These young adults believed that the boomers had a party and didn't clean up their mess. They ran the country into a huge deficit and job scarcity in the early 1990s. However, by the beginning of the new millennium, the U.S. economy had prospered, and the busters found a highly favorable job market.

Those with skills in technology found many opportunities, and some have become extremely wealthy in the high-tech industries.

Born into a more diverse world, the busters tend to be more accepting than older Americans in matters related to ethnicity, family structure, and lifestyle. They have grown up in an age of AIDS, latchkey children, divorce, economic decline, and increased violence. They realize that danger is always present and that stability may be difficult to come by (Mitchell, 1993).

Drury (1998) suggests some typical characteristics of this group. He indicates that the Xers have been burned by their parents' divorces and consequently have a higher view of marriage than the previous generation. As a group, they are willing to delay marriage until the "right person" comes along. They view sex as disconnected from marriage. They view living together prior to marriage, or safe sex, as normal. They are tolerant of almost everything except intolerance. They are more open to non-Judeo-Christian spirituality and are more prone than the earlier generation to embrace Hinduism, Buddhism, and New Age philosophy mixed with forms of Christianity. Some are contemptuous of organized religion.

Many of the Xers have been paying into the Social Security fund for 15 or more years. They see an unfair burden placed on them to maintain the system with minimal assurances that it will be there for them when they retire. The Xers account for 33.6% of the nation's work force. As a group, they tend to be self-confident, which was learned by fending for themselves. They have grown up in the age of information and technology, and are comfortable and function well in it. They have seen family and friends who were loyal to their work lose their jobs due to corporate downsizing in the 1990s. Consequently they tend to look for day-to-day dividends for their efforts (Tulgan, 1997).

Politically, nearly 50% of busters identify themselves as independent, compared with only 38% of other Americans. They are often more liberal on social issues than those who are older—including the boomers. They are less likely than others to support book bannings from libraries or the firing of gay teachers. They tend to be accepting of interracial dating and have a more positive view of the women's movement. They are more likely than other Americans to support affirmative action for persons of color (Mitchell, 1993).

GENERATION Y

Generation Y are the children of baby boomers, and the younger siblings of Generation X, who were born between the early 1980s and 1994. They are the largest generation since the baby boomers, and comprise nearly one third of the U.S. population. Martin and Tulgan (2001) describe members of Generation Y as the fourteenth generation of Americans. Some are still in grade school and some have already entered the workplace, where their presence will grow for several more years. In addition to being tagged Generation Y (Gen Yers, or Yers), they have been called Echo Boomers because they echo their parents' generation. They may also be called the Millennium Generation (*Businessweek,* 1999).

This cohort of young Americans has grown up in a society identified with crack cocaine, designer drugs, and an AIDS epidemic. While growing up, they watched on TV the Los Angeles riots following the Rodney King incident, the O. J. Simpson trial, the Branch Davidian standoff, the Oklahoma City bombing, Atlantic Olympic Park bombing, the Columbine shootings, the destruction of the World Trade Center, and a war in Afghanistan and in Iraq (Martin & Tulgan, 2001). While they have never been concerned about the Russians dropping a nuclear bomb on the United States, they have had to avoid areas of known street gang banging (activity), go through airport security, consider the threat of a terrorist attack, and be concerned that the draft may again be reinstated.

Martin and Tulgan (2001) describe the Generation Y group as more positive about their future than Generation X. Most have an optimistic outlook on life and work and expect to be better off financially than their parents. This is in sharp contrast to Generation Xers, who had been told that they would be the first generation in the history of the country to be worse off than their parents.

Martin and Tulgan (2001) describe the Yers as the "self-esteem generation." Because humanistic theories of childrearing permeated parenting efforts, this group reaped the benefits of greater involvement of both parents. In addition, this group has ended up the most technologically astute group that parents and educators have seen. Their ability to utilize technology and access information leaves many in the older generations in awe. They are the first generation to grow up with 500 TV channels, to design their own websites, and to have the ability to access people worldwide through their computers. They have become citizens of the world community (*60 Minutes,* 2004).

This group of young Americans may be the most education-minded generation in history. Between the influence of their boomer parents who tend to value education, and the workplace, which demands it, Yers generally have embraced education. Martin and Tulgan (2001) report that 90% of high school seniors indicate that they will attend college, 70% expect to have professional positions, 70% believe that a college degree is essential to meet their career goals, and 40% of college freshmen indicated that they plan to pursue a master's degree.

One of the most encouraging characteristics of Generation Yers is that they are perhaps the most tolerant generation in this country's history. Because they themselves are products of interracial or multicultural marriages or are friends of those who may be, they tend to rail against racism, sexism, and homophobia. Their icons are the Tiger Woods and Jessica Simpsons of the world and Martin and Tulgan (2001) suggest they are "struggling to define themselves beyond the traditional confines of race, worship or ethnicity."

A *60 Minutes* segment (2004) characterized them as overachieving, overmanaged, and pressured. Their parents have felt that they needed structure, so they were or are heavily programmed with organized activities. Because, as a group, they have been so highly valued by their parents, they view themselves as special. They in turn tend to be very close to their parents, and many consider their parents to be their best friends. Unlike some earlier generations they prefer rules to rebellion, and choose teamwork to individualism. Violent crime, substance abuse, and teen pregnancy are all down with this generation (*60 Minutes,* 2004). Levine (2004) suggests that they are used to instant gratification and grade inflation. They see themselves as the "now" generation, and will enter the real world of work naïve.

Beloit College Mindset List. Since 1998 Beloit College in Wisconsin has distributed its Mindset List to both the faculty and staff. The list identifies some of the characteristics, the mindset, or the facts of life, which distinguish the new incoming freshmen class from other students in years past who preceded them. The class of

2008 entered Beloit in 2004. Most were 17 or 18 years old. Most were born in 1986. The complete Mindset List can be accessed online at **http://www.beloit.edu/ ~pubaff/mindset/**. A sampling of the 50 items on the Mindset List includes:

- Photographs have always been processed in an hour or less
- Alan Greenspan has always been setting the nation's financial direction
- There's always been a Rock and Roll Hall of Fame (Beloit College Mindset List, 2004)

While most undergraduate students can easily relate to this mindset, their baby boomer professors will be reminded that they belong to another generation.

THE AGED

The aged are generally considered those individuals who are 65 years or older. All individuals who live into their mid-60s become members of the cultural group of the aged, along with their membership in other groups. Like other oppressed groups, the aged are often discriminated against. But unlike discrimination against minority groups, the individuals who discriminate will also someday become part of the aged group and may become victims of discrimination. Schaie and Willis (2002) describe ageism as "discrimination against the elderly simply because of their age" (p. 19). Bee (2000) suggests that the elderly "are routinely described or perceived as infirmed, cranky, sexless, childlike, senile or useless by both the young and old alike" (p. 8).

In U.S. society, little value is placed on nonproduction. Because of the decrease in some basic capacities (sensory, motor, cognitive, and physiological), aging does have a detrimental effect in a variety of professional fields (Schulz & Salthouse,

 VIDEO INSIGHT

A Closer Look

In this video segment you will see that according to the Census Bureau, 34 million people over the age of 65 are still working, and 50,000 of those are over the age of 90 and still cashing a paycheck. If medicine and technology continue at the rate they are moving now, by the year 2030, one third of our lifetimes will be spent in retirement. Right now, individuals who make it past the age of 65 can expect to live until they are approximately 83.

Often in our culture, the aged are seen as useless, noncontributing burdens for their younger family members and society to shoulder.

1. *How will the changing demographics and lifestyles of retirees alter the face of our country?*
2. *How might it alter our perception of the aged?*
3. *One of the misconceptions regarding the elderly is that most cannot be productive. Is this true? Why or why not?*

To answer these questions online, go to the ABC News Video Insight module for this chapter of the Companion Website.

DVD

CW

 # CRITICAL INCIDENTS IN TEACHING

Cultural Attitudes Toward the Aged

"That is really stupid!" exclaims Keith to Michael Wong. "You have the coolest room of anyone in the class, with your own stereo, DVD player, TV, and computer. Now you have to share it with your grandfather! Why do you have to share your bedroom with an old man? It isn't fair." "Because he's too old to care for himself, and he can't share my sister's room. She's a girl," Michael explains to his best friend, Keith.

"Why don't your parents put him in an old people's home as my parents did with my grandmother?" Keith protests. "When they get old, they're useless. They just get in your way. Old people just don't have the right to interfere with other people's lives. When I get too old, I want someone to put me to sleep permanently, to just help me go away—peaceful like. Old people are a pain in the butt to everyone. I'm not going to be a bother like that to anyone. Besides, it'll be a zillion years before I'm ever that old. Ha!"

Trying to explain, Michael says to Keith, "My grandfather really isn't a bother. He's a neat guy. He may be old, but he's very wise, you know. He's really smart. Besides, we Chinese don't like to put our parents and grandparents in nursing homes. It's kind of a disgrace to the family. Sure, I'd rather have my own room to myself, but it's okay. I really don't mind."

Hearing the discussion, Mr. Fitzpatrick, Michael and Keith's sixth-grade teacher, is trying to decide whether he should intervene.

Questions for Discussion

1. *Should Mr. Fitzpatrick intervene in the discussion or let the boys work it out themselves?*
2. *Should the teacher discuss attitudes toward the aged? If so, what should be discussed?*
3. *Should the teacher discuss how different cultures perceive old age differently?*
4. *Should the teacher address the ageist attitudes of Keith? If so, how?*

To answer these questions online, go to the Critical Incidents in Teaching module for this chapter of the Companion Website.

1999). Airline pilots, for example, are prohibited from flying commercial aircraft after the age of 60. Despite the passage of the Age Discrimination Employment Act in 1978, similar limitations are placed on occupations such as law enforcement and firefighting. It is understandable, then, why some individuals who view the aged as nonproductive may adopt an ageist attitude. Also contributing to the prevalence of ageism is the emphasis placed by U.S. society on physical beauty. The physical ideal is associated with youth, and the aging process only serves to move an individual farther from the accepted norms of physical beauty.

In 1900, 1 in 25 Americans was over age 65. Three million elderly lived in the United States that year. In 2002, one in eight Americans or 12.3% of the population, an estimated 35.6 million people, were 65 years of age or older (U.S. Census Bureau, 2003). Projections suggest nearly 70 million elderly by 2030, when all of the baby boomers will be over age 65 as shown in Table 8.4. The percentage of elderly will increase to an estimated 20.2% of the population in 2030 (Taeuber, 1993). People 85 years of age and older, one of the fastest-growing segments of society, make up 1.6% of the population

Table 8.4 Number of Americans 65 or Older

Year	Number	Percent of Population
1900	3,000,000	4.00%
2000	34,848,000	12.65%
2030	70,000,000	20.20%

Source: Taeuber, C. C. (1993). Sixty-five plus in America (U.S. Bureau of Census, Current Population Reports, Special Studies, P23-178RV). Washington, DC: U.S. Government Printing Office.

today, but that is expected to increase to 5% by 2050. The number of centenarians was estimated to be 59,000 in 2002 (Treas, 1995; U.S. Census Bureau, 2003).

The aged resemble other oppressed groups in that they suffer from prejudice, discrimination, and deprivation. As the aged increase in numbers and in percentage of the population, it is likely that resentment toward them will increase. As with immigrant bashing, segments of our society already perceive the elderly as a drain on resources. There are legitimate concerns regarding society's ability to pay for pensions, to finance health care for the chronically ill elderly, and to provide the personal assistance that the elderly with disabilities require. Will Social Security, Medicare, and Medicaid remain solvent given the increasing numbers of older adults? Providing adequate support for the aged will be a significant challenge in the future.

By 2011, the first of the nation's 76 million baby boomers will begin turning 65. The cost of Social Security benefits, Medicare, and Medicaid will be staggering. Already Congress is grappling with the problem of ensuring adequate resources to provide for Social Security. The retirement age to receive full benefits has already been raised and other possibilities such as reducing benefits and allowing for private investment of funds have been proposed. With the advances in medical science that are extending the lives of individuals, coupled with the increasing cost of health care, social services for the elderly, and nursing homes, the Congressional leaders and state officials are rightly concerned (Tanner, 2004).

The rest of society tends to have three basic misconceptions regarding the aged:

1. *Most elderly people are sick or infirm.* The reality is that only 20% of persons over age 65 are in this category and only 10% are unable to engage in normal activity.

2. *Most elderly people are senile.* The fact is that fewer than 10% of the aged have incapacitating mental illness or senility.

3. *Most elderly people cannot be productive.* The reality is that, as a group, the elderly are as productive as young workers, are less prone to job turnover, and have lower accident and absentee rates. (Schultz and Salthouse, 1999)

The aged are discriminated against in many areas that affect their well-being and lifestyles. For example, many employers discriminate against them in hiring and retention. In addition, many medical personnel admit that they prefer not to treat the elderly, while some younger people, because of their prejudices, appear to avoid the elderly.

As a cultural group, only some of the aged seem to have a sense of group identity. Some use chronological indices to determine the advent of old age; the remainder generally use functional criteria, such as retirement or health conditions. Some are

While many believe the popular misconception that most elderly are sick or infirm, only a few are not able to engage in normal activity.

Opportunities for Reflection

ashamed of old age and resist identification with the elderly. At the same time, some among the aged have adopted a militant posture, forming groups to protest and promote the rights of the elderly. *Can you envision yourself as an elderly person, with declining health, vision, and hearing? Do you think you will be concerned about financial resources for food, housing, and medical care?*

As a group, the aged make up a potent political force. As the federal and state governments move toward balancing their budgets, social and welfare programs have often been cut. With many of the elderly living on fixed incomes, they are rightfully fearful of cuts that directly affect the quality of their lives. Consequently, as a group, they typically exercise their right to vote to a greater extent than other age groups. The recognition of their voter influence has been evident in recent political campaigns, during which candidates openly courted the votes of this group, pledging to support their interests.

The aged are understandably concerned about voter issues related to the maintenance or enhancement of Social Security and health care benefits. They are more likely than other groups to support "taxpayer revolts" and to resist any efforts toward revenue enhancement that will affect their incomes. Because they typically are no longer involved in their education or that of their children, they often resist attempts to increase school revenues through taxes. Efforts such as California's Proposition 13, which rolled back property taxes but had a negative impact on education, have had wide support. As the ranks of the aged grow and as they successfully lobby for a greater share of available resources, they are at greater risk of ageist attacks. The working population is increasingly aware that larger amounts of their paychecks are being deducted to provide for Social Security benefits and other programs for the elderly. In addition, younger workers may perceive older workers who hold higher-paying supervisory positions as obstacles to their own advancement. They want the elderly to retire so that there will be greater opportunity for advancement for the young. Yet, when the aged do retire, younger workers may resent them because Social Security taxes must be deducted from their paychecks to fund their retired colleagues' pensions.

Poverty is a very serious problem with the aged. In 2003, the poverty threshold for a single individual 65 or older was $8,825, and for a couple in which the head of the household was 65 or older, $11,133 (U.S. Census Bureau, 2004). In 2001, 3,414,000 or 10.1% of the nation's 32,907,000 poor were 65 or older (Proctor & Dalaker, 2002).

Socioeconomic status tends to be a major factor in the adjustment to old age. As with the earlier years in life, income influences longevity, health status, housing, and marital status for the aged. Middle- and high-income individuals typically have Social Security, pension plans, savings, and medical plans that ease their transition into their retirement years. The pensions and Social Security incomes of low-income individuals tend to be limited and, in some instances, nonexistent. Many of these individuals must continue working well beyond usual retirement years in order to survive.

Socioeconomic status is discussed in greater detail in Chapter 2.

More than half of African American and Latino elderly tend to depend on Social Security as their sole source of income. Fewer elderly Latinos are eligible for Social Security benefits than their white counterparts. Social Security benefits of African American and Latino recipients tend to be lower than those of whites because of their frequently lower income levels during their working years.

Pause to Reflect 8.3

In general, most of American society prefers a capitalistic form of government as opposed to one that we might characterize as socialistic. We want the freedom to make our own choices and we, for the most part, do not want the government telling us what to do and how to do it. Yet when individuals grow older, and when some find that they do not have the resources to provide for a comfortable life in their old age, they want the government to step in, increase Social Security payments, and provide for their medical coverage and other services. For the individuals who reach their senior years in relative financial comfort, these are not major issues. They may be concerned with where they will take their next trip, or if they should buy a time-share condominium in their favorite vacation spot. Others are trying to determine how they will pay for their food and the medication they need. When the temperature reaches the 90s they must decide if they can really afford to run the air conditioner.

- *Do we as Americans have the responsibility to make sure that all residents, citizens and noncitizens, have adequate food to eat?*

- *Is every resident entitled to medical care and medication regardless of their ability to pay?*

- *What if they had decent jobs and chose not to save and set aside resources for the future? Does it matter?*

- *Is every older person entitled to at least a basic level of support?*

- *How do you feel about your taxes being used to support the elderly who did not prepare adequately to provide for themselves?*

To answer these questions online, go to the Pause to Reflect module for this chapter of the Companion Website.

CW

Elderly persons with high incomes have advantages associated with their greater financial resources. During their earlier years, they were able to maintain better living conditions and better health care, which often translates into better health in the advanced years. Their financial resources enable them to maintain these higher living and health care standards. This advantage, in turn, may result in extended, quality leisure activities, such as travel, which makes the retirement years more pleasurable. It is understandable, therefore, that individuals from high socioeconomic backgrounds tend to view old age more favorably than those from low socioeconomic backgrounds.

As people mature in age, they move through different age-groups and become members of different cultural groups. As individuals join new age-group cultures, they bring with them other aspects of culture, such as ethnicity, socioeconomic status, and gender. As these various cultures interface with one another and blend their individual, unique qualities, they add to the rich pluralistic nature of American society.

Educational Implications

As with other cultural groups, the various age-groups of the U.S. population contribute greatly to the pluralistic nature of this society. Some basic educational considerations should be examined in the study of age-groups as a function of culture. American society in general has not always been viewed as particularly supportive or positive in its perception of all age-groups. The discussion on adolescence noted that this period is often viewed as a time of storm and stress, whereas in some cultures this period passes with few crises. In American society, the former view tends to prevail. In addition, advancing age is not viewed by the U.S. dominant group with the respect or reverence that is found in many other cultures. Ageism does exist and is, regretfully, as much a part of our social system as racism and handicapism.

For these reasons, it is critically important that students be exposed to age as it relates to culture. Moreover, studying age and its relation to culture is important because students, if they live to full life expectancy, will become members of each age-group. Thus, unlike the study of different ethnic groups, students can learn to understand and appreciate cultural groups of which they have been members, are presently members, or will eventually become members. By addressing the issues of various age-groups in the classroom, educators can help students to better understand their siblings, parents, and other important persons in their lives. Knowledge can eliminate fear of the unknown as students begin to move into different age-groups at different times in their lives. It is important that issues related to age-groups be appropriately introduced into the curriculum because students need to understand the concept of ageism. Just as the school assists students in understanding the problem of racism, the school should be responsible for helping students understand the aged and dispel the myths related to this group. Field trips to retirement homes or visits to the class by senior citizens may provide useful experiences. As students become aware of the nature and characteristics of each age-group, they will develop perceptions of each individual, regardless of age, as being an important and integral part of society.

It is critically important for educators to understand age as it relates to both students and their parents. Understanding the particular age-group characteristics and needs of students can assist the educator in better understanding and managing age-related behavior, such as reactions or responses to peer-group pressure. Understanding the nature of parents, siblings, and other important individuals (e.g., grandparents) will assist the educator in parent-teacher relationships and in helping students cope with their interactions with others. For example, as an elderly grandparent moves into the family setting, this event may affect a child and his or her classroom behavior.

The school is perhaps in the best position of any agency in the community to observe the effects of child abuse. The classroom teacher is an important agent in detecting and reporting abuse and in all states is required by law to do so. To do this, the teacher must be aware of the problem of abuse, the manifestations of abuse, and the proper authorities to whom abuse is reported. If the teacher's immediate supervisor is unresponsive to the reporting of a potential abuse problem, the teacher should then continue to seek help until competent and concerned individuals in positions of authority provide it.

The single most important factor in determining possible child abuse is the physical condition of the child. Telltale marks, bruises, and abrasions that cannot be adequately explained may provide reason to suspect abuse. Unusual changes in the child's behavior patterns, such as extreme fatigue, may be reason to suspect problems. The parents' behavior and their ability or lack of ability to explain the child's condition and the social features of the family may be reason to suspect abuse. Although physical abuse or neglect may tend to have observable indicators, sexual abuse may occur with few, if any, obvious indicators. Adults may be unwilling to believe what a child says and may be hesitant to report alleged incidents. There is no typical profile of the victim, and the physical signs vary. Behavioral manifestations are usually exhibited by the victims but are often viewed as insignificant or attributed to typical childhood stress. Chronic depression, isolation from peers, apathy, and suicide attempts are some of the more serious behavioral manifestations of the problem.

The number of children and youth infected by the HIV virus and other sexually transmitted diseases is a national tragedy. Prevention efforts must be multifaceted if these diseases are to be eradicated. The school has a major role to play, and there are specific steps, which can be taken. School-based programs are critical in reaching youth before they engage in risky behaviors. Topics such as HIV, STDs, unintended pregnancy, and tobacco and other drug abuse should be integrated into the curriculum and should be an ongoing program for all students, kindergarten through high school. The development of these programs should be done carefully and should take into consideration parent and community values.

The majority of suicides are planned and are not committed on impulse, and most suicide victims mention their intentions to someone. Of adolescents who commit suicide, 80% make open threats beforehand (Griffin & Felsenthal, 1983). Often, a number of warning signs can alert teachers, other professionals, and parents. The following are some of the danger signals (Griffin & Felsenthal, 1983):

- Aggressive, hostile behavior
- Alcohol and drug abuse
- Passive behavior

- Changes in eating habits
- Changes in sleeping habits
- Fear of separation
- Abrupt changes in personality
- Sudden mood swings
- Decreased interest in schoolwork and decline in grades
- Inability to concentrate
- Hopelessness
- Obsession with death
- Giving away valued possessions
- Euphoria or increased activity after depression

If teachers or other school personnel suspect trouble, friendly, low-key questions or statements may provide an appropriate opening: "You seem down today" or "It seems like something is bothering you." If an affirmative response is given, a more direct and probing (but supportive) question may be asked. If there is any reason whatsoever to suspect a possible suicide attempt, teachers and other school staff should alert the appropriate school personnel. Teachers should recognize their limitations and avoid making judgments. The matter should be referred to the school psychologist, who should, in turn, alert a competent medical authority (psychiatrist) and the child's parents. Assistance can also be obtained from local mental health clinics and suicide prevention centers. Prompt action may save a life.

Our coverage of adolescent substance abuse has been brief. But the importance of the problem is such that every educator should be aware of the problem and work toward providing children at an early age with appropriate drug education. No agency, group, or individual can wage an effective campaign against substance abuse alone. Only with a united effort can an effective battle be waged.

Hafen and Frandsen (1980) indicate danger signs for drug or alcohol ingestion that may place an individual at life-threatening risk:

- *Unconsciousness.* The individual cannot be awakened or, if awakened, lapses back into deep sleep.
- *Breathing difficulties.* Breathing stops altogether, may be weak, or weak and strong in cycles. Skin may become bluish or purple, indicating lack of oxygenated blood.
- *Fever.* Any temperature above 100°F (38°C) is a danger sign when drugs are involved.
- *Vomiting while not fully conscious.* If a person is in a stupor or in a semi-conscious or unconscious state, vomiting can cause serious breathing problems.
- *Convulsions.* Twitching of face, trunk, arms, or legs; muscle spasms or muscle rigidity may indicate impending convulsions. Violent jerking motions and spasms likely indicate a convulsion.

In the event these signs are observed in the classroom, the school nurse should be summoned immediately. If none is available, then someone trained in CPR should be summoned. It would be advisable for a list of all personnel with CPR training to be made available to all teachers and other staff.

As parents hurry children into adulthood, educators may also contribute to the hurrying process. Teachers, administrators, and support personnel should be cognizant of the fact that the children they teach and work with are children, and not miniature adults. Children have but one opportunity to experience the wonders of childhood. In comparison with adulthood, childhood and adolescence are relatively short periods of time, and these young people should have every opportunity to enjoy these stages of their lives to the fullest extent possible.

Summary

The study of age as a cultural group is important to educators because it helps them understand how the child or adolescent struggles to win peer acceptance and to balance this effort with the need for parental approval. In some instances, the pressures from peers are not congruent with those from the home.

As each child develops into adolescence, we observe a growing need for independence. Adolescence for some is a time of storm and stress; for others, it passes with little or no trauma.

Young adulthood is one of the most exciting times in life. It is a time for courtship, marriage, children, and career choices. It is a time when individuals reach their physical and occupational prime. Young adulthood can also be a threatening time because choices made at this time often have a lifetime impact on the individual. Adulthood is the time when dreams are either fulfilled or become forever elusive. With the latter can come bitterness, resentment, and anger.

With life expectancy increasing each year, those in the aged cohort increase in numbers daily. More than half a million advance into the ranks of the aged each year. Like the ethnic minorities and those with disabilities, the aged face discrimination and prejudice in the form of ageism. Those who discriminate will someday become aged, perhaps to face the treatment that they themselves imposed on others.

QUESTIONS FOR DISCUSSION

1. Explain why child abuse is a problem, and cite some of the signs of child abuse.
2. When does ethnic identification begin in children, and how is it manifested?
3. Describe some variables that contribute to prejudice in children.
4. What are the sources of alienation between adolescents and their families?
5. What is the extent of substance abuse among adolescents, and what are some of the underlying causes of substance use in this age group?
6. What are the causes of adolescent suicide, and what are the warning signs?
7. What factors have contributed to some African American males being considered at risk in our society?

8. What are some primary differences between the younger and the older baby boomers?

9. In what ways do the baby busters differ from the baby boomers?

10. How does Generation Y differ from Generation X?

11. How does old age relate to ethnicity and socioeconomic status?

 ONLINE ACTIVITIES For additional questions and activities linked to the Exploring Diversity CD, and additional chapter exercises, visit this text's Companion Website at **http://www.prenhall.com/gollnick**.

 ## PORTFOLIO ACTIVITIES

1. Interview three teachers from three different schools and ask them what their school policy is in reporting suspected child abuse of their students. (INTASC Standard 10)

2. Interview teachers or administrators from schools to find out what their policy is on zero tolerance or if there is no zero tolerance policy, what measures are taken for students who carry weapons or drugs to school. (INTASC Standard 10)

3. Interview an elderly individual at least 80 years of age and ask them how they had planned for the future and if their life today is what they had anticipated when they were in their 20s and 30s.

SUGGESTED READINGS

Centers for Disease Control and Prevention. http://www.cdc.gov/.

This government website provides a wealth of information on issues such as adolescent sexual behaviors, suicide, child maltreatment and abuse, substance abuse, and so forth.

Schaie, K. W., & Willis, S. L. (2002). *Adult development and aging* (5th ed.). Upper Saddle River, NJ: Prentice Hall.

Provides an examination of young adulthood through aging. Includes a view on families and of men and women as they move through adulthood.

Trojanowicz, R. C., Morash, M., & Schram, P. J. (2001). *Juvnile delinquency, concepts and control* (6th ed.). Upper Saddle River, NJ: Prentice Hall.

A very good treatment of problems associated with juvenile delinquency.

REFERENCES

Aboud, F. (1988). *Children and prejudice.* Cambridge, MA: Basil Blackwell.

Aboud, F., & Doyle, A. B. (1996a). Does talk of race foster prejudice or tolerance in children? *Canadian Journal of Behavioral Science, 28*(3), 1–14.

Aboud, F., & Doyle, A. B. (1996b). Parental and peer influence on children's racial attitudes. *International Journal of Intercultural Relations, 20,* 371–383.

American Academy of Pediatrics. (2000). *Some things you should know about media literacy.* Retrieved September 3, 2004, from http://www.aap.org/advocacy/childhealthmonth/media.htm

American Academy of Pediatrics. (2004). Committee on Adolescence. *Homosexuality and adolescence.* Retrieved September 3, 2004, from http://www.medem.com/search/article_display.cfm?path=\\TANQUERAY\M_ContentItem&mstr=/M_ContentItem/ZZZUHJP3KAC.html&soc=AAP&srch_typ=NAV_SERCH

Annie E. Casey Foundation. (2004). *Kids count.* Baltimore, MD: Author.

Anti-Defamation League. (2004). *What to tell your child about prejudice and discrimination.* Retrieved September 3, 2004, from http://adl.org/what_to_tell/whattotell_intro.asp

Barrett, B., & Browne, P. W. (2004, September 27). Gangs outnumber police. *San Gabriel Valley Tribune,* A1, A6.

Bartollas, C., & Miller, S. (2005). *Juvenile Justice in America.* Upper Saddle River, NJ: Prentice Hall.

Bee, H. L. (2000). *The journey of adulthood* (4th ed.). Upper Saddle River, NJ: Prentice Hall.

Beloit College Mindset List. (2004). Retrieved September 3, 2004, from http://www.beloit.edu/~pubaff/mindset/

Bender, W. N., Clinton, G., & Bender, R. L. (Eds.). (1999). *Violence prevention and reduction in schools.* Austin, TX: Pro-Ed.

Bigler, R., & Liben, L. (1993). A cognitive development approach to racial stereotyping and reconstructive memory in Euro-American children. *Child Development, 64,* 1507–1519.

Businessweek. (1999, February 15). Generation Y. Retrieved September 3, 2004, from http://businessweek.com:/1999/99_07/b3616001.htm?scriptFramed

Calhoun, T. C., & Chapple, C. L. (2003). *Readings in juvenile delinquency and juvenile justice.* Upper Saddle River, NJ: Prentice Hall.

Cannon, A., Streisand, B., & McGraw, D. (1999, May 3). Why? *U.S. News and World Report, 26*(17), 16–19.

Centers for Disease Control and Prevention. (2000a). *Youth violence in the United States.* Retrieved September 3, 2004, from http://www.cdc.gov/ncipc/factsheets/yvfacts.htm

Centers for Disease Control and Prevention. (2000b). *Facts about violence among youth and violence in schools.* Retrieved September 3, 2004, from http://www.cdc.gov/ncipc/factsheets/schoolvi.htm

Centers for Disease Control and Prevention. (2002a). *Trends in sexual risk behaviors among high school students—United States, 1991–2001.* Atlanta, GA: Author.

Centers for Disease Control and Prevention–Division of HIV/AIDS Prevention. (2002b). *Young people at risk: HIV/AIDS among America's youth.* Atlanta, GA: Author.

Centers for Disease Control and Prevention (2003a). *U.S. pregnancy rate down from peak; births and abortion on the decline.* Atlanta, GA: Author.

Centers for Disease Control and Prevention–Division of HIV/AIDS Prevention. (2003b). *Basic statistics.* Atlanta, GA: Author.

Centers for Disease Control and Prevention–Division of HIV/AIDS Prevention. (2004a). *HIV/AIDS among African Americans.* Atlanta, GA: Author.

Centers for Disease Control and Prevention–National Center for Injury Prevention and Control. (2004b). *Suicide: Fact Sheet.* Atlanta, GA: Author.

Champion, D. (2004). *Juvenile justice system: Delinquency, processing, and the law* (4th ed.) Upper Saddle River, NJ: Prentice Hall.

Childhelp, Inc. (2003). *National child abuse statistics.* Retrieved September 3, 2004, from http://www.childhelpusa.org/pdf/stats2003.pdf

Chua-Eoan, H. (1999). Escaping from the darkness. *Time, 153*(21), 44–49.

Crockett, R. O., and Coy, P. (2003, July 14). Progress without parity. *Business Week.* Retrieved September 3, 2004, from http://www.keepmedia.com/pubs/BusinessWeek/2003/07/14/126670?page=1

Crowe, P., Philbin, J., Richards, M. H., & Crawford, I. (1998). Adolescent alcohol involvement and the experience of social environments. *Journal of Research on Adolescence, 8*(4), 403–422.

Department of Health and Human Services. (2004). *Overview of findings from the 2003 national survey on drug use and health.* Washington, DC: Author.

Doyle, A. B., & Aboud, F. E. (1995). A longitudinal study of white children's racial prejudice as a social cognitive development. *Merrill-Palmer Quarterly, 41,* 210–220.

Drury, K. (1998). *15 Characteristics of Generation X.* CompuCoach. Retrieved September 3, 2004, from http://www.churchsmart.com/compucoach/01056.htm

Federal Bureau of Investigation. (1994). *Uniform crime report: Crime in the United States, 1993.* Washington, DC: U.S. Department of Justice.

Free The Children. (2003). *Child poverty in the U.S.* Retrieved September 3, 2004, from http://www.freethechildren.org/youthinaction/child_poverty_usa.htm

Gibbs, J. T. (1992). Young black males in America: Endangered, embittered, and embattled. In M. S. Kimmell & M. A. Messner (Eds.), *Men's lives* (2nd ed.). New York: Macmillan.

Gibbs, J. T. (1998). High-risk behaviors in African American youth: Conceptual and methodological issues in research. In V. C. McLoyd & L. Steinberg (Eds.), *Studying minority adolescents.* Mahwah, NJ: Lawrence Erlbaum Associates.

Green, S. (1999, April 24). Trench coat mafia teen describes school life filled with taunts, abuse. *Denver Post,* p. A-01.

Griffin, M. E., & Felsenthal, C. (1983). *A cry for help.* Garden City, NY: Doubleday.

Hafen, B. Q., & Frandsen, K. J. (1980). *Drug and alcohol emergencies.* Center City, MN: Hazelden Foundation.

Howell, J. C. (1998). Recent gang research: Program and policy implications. In P. M. Sharp & B. W. Hancock (Eds.), *Juvenile delinquency* (2nd ed.). Upper Saddle River, NJ: Prentice Hall.

Igoa, C. (1995). *The inner world of the immigrant child.* Mahwah, NJ: Lawrence Erlbaum Associates.

Jackson, R. L., Lopez, R. J., & Connell, R. (1997, January 12). Clinton puts priority on curtailing gang crime. *Los Angeles Times,* pp. A1, A12.

Joseph, J., & Taylor, D. (Eds.). (2003). *With justice for all: Minorities and women in criminal justice.* Upper Saddle River, NJ: Prentice Hall.

Kofkin, J. A., Katz, P. A., & Downey, E. P. (1995). *Family discourse about race and the development of children's racial attitudes.* Paper presented at the meeting of the Society for Research in Child Development, Indianapolis, IN.

Kratcoski, P. C., & Kratcoski, L. D. (2004). *Juvenile delinquency* (5th ed.). Upper Saddle River, NJ: Prentice Hall.

Levine, M. (2004). Echo boomers. Interview on *60 Minutes* [Television series episode]. October 3, 2004, CBS, Steve Kroft, narrator.

Lindberg, R. C. (2002). *Spotlight on Asian organized crime.* Schaumburg, IL: Search International. Retrieved September 3, 2004, from http://www.search-international.com/WhatsNew/WNasiangangs.htm

Los Angeles Times [Associated Press]. (2004, June 11). Suicides among young down 25%, p. A31.

Lotz, R. (2005). *Youth crime in America: A modern synthesis.* Upper Saddle River, NJ: Prentice Hall.

Martin, C. A., & Tulgan, B. (2001). *Managing Generation Y.* Amherst, MA: HRD Press.

McCorkle, R. C., & Miethe, T. D. (2002). *Panic: The social construction of the street gang problem.* Upper Saddle River, NJ: Prentice Hall.

McKee, P. W., Jones, R. W., & Barbe, R. H. (1993). *Suicide in the school.* Horsham, PA: LRP.

McLoyd, V. C., & Steinberg, L. (1998). *Studying minority adolescents.* Mahwah, NJ: Lawrence Erlbaum Associates.

Midwifery Today. (2001, Autumn). Early births, poverty stresses linked, 65.

Mitchell, S. (1993, May 23). The baby busters. *San Jose Mercury News,* pp. 1L, 5L.

National Alliance for the Mentally Ill. (2003). *Suicide in Youth.* Retrieved from http://www.nami.org/Content/ContentGroups/Helpline1/Suicide_in_Youth.htm

National Clearinghouse on Child Abuse and Neglect Information. (2004). *Child maltreatment 2002: Summary of key findings.*

National Institute on Drug Abuse. (2003). *Teen drug abuse—Declines across wide fronts.*

Nazario, S. (1997, March 9). Children who kill themselves. *Los Angeles Times,* pp. A1, A28–A30.

New York University Law Student Drug Policy Forum's Fact Sheet. (2004). Retrieved September 3, 2004, from http://www.law.nyu.edu/studentorgs/lsdpf/factsheet.html

Palermo, G. B., & Simpson, D. (1998). At the roots of violence: The progressive decline and dissolution of the family. In P. M. Sharp & B. W. Hancock (Eds.), *Juvenile delinquency: Historical, theoretical, and societal reactions to youth* (2nd ed.). Upper Saddle River, NJ: Prentice Hall.

Petersen, R. D. (2004). *Understanding contemporary gangs in America: An interdisciplinary approach.* Upper Saddle River, NJ: Prentice Hall.

Proctor, B. D., & Dalaker, J. (2002). Poverty in the United States: 2001. *Current Population Reports.* Washington, DC: U.S. Census Bureau.

Prothrow-Stith, D., & Spivak, H. R. (2004). *Murder is no accident: Understanding and preventing youth violence in America.* San Francisco: Jossey-Bass.

Roof, W. C. (1990). Return of the baby boomers to organized religion. In C. H. Jacquet, Jr. (Ed.), *1990 yearbook of American and Canadian churches.* Nashville: Abingdon Press.

Schaie, K. W., & Willis, S. L. (2002). *Adult development and aging* (5th ed.). Upper Saddle River, NJ: Prentice Hall.

Schulz, R., & Salthouse, T. (1999). *Adult development and aging: Myths and emerging realities* (3rd ed.). Upper Saddle River, NJ: Prentice Hall.

Sidel, R. (1990). *On her own: Growing up in the shadow of the American dream.* New York: Viking.

Sixty (60) Minutes. (2004, October 3). Echo boomers [Television series episode]. *2004,* CBS, Steve Kroft, narrator.

Sleek, S. (1997, October). People's racist attitudes can be unlearned. *APA Monitor,* 38.

Taeuber, C. M. (1993). Sixty-five plus in America (U.S. Bureau of Census, Current Population Reports, Special Studies, P23-178Rv). Washington, DC: U.S. Government Printing Office.

Tanner, R. [Associated Press] (2004, July 19). Governors grapple with how to handle aging population. *Los Angeles Times,* p. A8.

Tatum, B. D. (1997). *Why are all the black kids sitting together in the cafeteria?* New York: Basic Books.

Tower, C. C. (1992). Child abuse and neglect. In N. A. Cohen (Ed.), *Child welfare.* Needham Heights, MA: Allyn & Bacon.

Treas, J. (1995). *Older Americans in the 1990s and beyond.* Washington, DC: Population Reference Bureau.

Trojanowicz, R. C., Morash, M., & Schram, P. J. (2001). *Juvenile delinquency, concepts and control* (6th ed.). Upper Saddle River, NJ: Prentice Hall.

Tulgan, B. (1997). *The manager's pocket guide to Generation X.* Amherst, MA: HRD Press.

U.S. Census Bureau. (2000). *Resident population estimates of the United States by age and sex.* Retrieved September 3, 2004, from http://www.census.gov/population/estimates/nation/untfile2-1.txt

U.S. Census Bureau. (2003). *Statistical abstract of the United States: 2003* (123rd ed.). Washington, DC: Author.

U.S. Census Bureau. (2004). *Current population survey, 2004* (Annual Social and Economic Supplement). Washington, DC: Author.

Youth Violence Prevention Resource Center. (2004). *Youth suicide fact sheet.* Retrieved September 3, 2004, from http://www.safeyouth.org/scripts/facts/suicide.asp

We must be the change we wish to see in the world.

MAHATMA GANDHI

Chapter 9

Education That Is Multicultural

Natisha Loftis had not said a word to any of her teachers since the beginning of school. It's not that she was a "bad" student; she turned in assignments and made Bs. She certainly didn't cause her teachers trouble. Therefore, the high school counselor, Mr. Williams, was somewhat surprised to hear that she was dropping out of school. He had been Natisha's advisor for more than two years, but he didn't really remember her. Nevertheless, it was his job to conduct interviews with students who were leaving school for one reason or another.

Natisha described her school experiences as coming to school, listening to teachers, and going home. School was boring and not connected at all to her real life, in which she had the responsibility for helping her father raise five brothers and sisters. She might even be able to get a job with the same cleaning firm that her dad worked for. For sure, nothing she was learning in school could help her get a job. And she knew from more than 10 years of listening to teachers and reading textbooks that her chances of becoming a news anchorwoman or even a teacher were about the same as winning the lottery. The last time a teacher had even asked about her family was in the sixth grade, when her mom left the family. The only place anyone paid attention to her was in church.

School had helped silence Natisha. Classes provided no meaningful experience for her. The content may have been important to the teachers, but she could find no relationship to her own world.

Opportunities
for Reflection

1. *Why has Natisha decided to drop out of school?*

2. *How can the curriculum be made more meaningful to students who are not white and middle class?*

3. *How can teachers make a student like Natisha excited about learning?*

To answer these questions online, go to this chapter's Opening Scenario module of the Companion Website.

CW

Initiating Multicultural Education

After learning the sociopolitical aspects that provide the framework for multicultural education in the first eight chapters of this book, you are probably wondering how you put it all together to provide education that is multicultural. There is no recipe book that indicates how to respond to students from different ethnic, racial, gender, language, class, religious, ability, and age groups. For one, differences within groups can be as great as differences among groups. Therefore, the recipe would work for some students, but not many of them. This chapter is designed to provide some suggestions for delivering multicultural education, incorporating the multiple identities of your students into your teaching, and becoming more multicultural yourself.

It is no easy task to incorporate cultural knowledge throughout teaching. In the beginning, you must consciously think about it as you interact with students and plan lessons and assignments. You should approach teaching multiculturally as an enthusiastic learner with much to learn from students and community members who have cultural identities different from your own. You may need to remind yourself that your way of believing, thinking, and acting evolved from your own culture and experiences, which may vary greatly from that of the students in your school. You will need to listen to the histories and experiences of students and their families and integrate them into your teaching. Students' values need to be validated within both their in-school and out-of-school realities—a process that is authentic only if you believe the cultures of your students are as valid as their own.

Educators are often at a disadvantage because they do not live, or have never lived, in the community in which their students live. Too often, the only parents with whom they interact are those who are able to attend parent-teacher meetings or who have scheduled conferences with them. In many cases, they have not been in their students' homes or been active participants in community activities. How do we begin to learn other's cultures? Using the tools of an anthropologist or ethnographer, we could observe children in classrooms and on playgrounds. We can listen carefully to students and their parents as they discuss their life experiences. We can study other cultures. We can learn about the perspectives of others by reading articles and books written by men and women from different ethnic, racial, socioeconomic, and religious groups. Participation in community, religious, and ethnic activities can provide another perspective on students' cultures. *How could you expand your knowledge about the cultural groups represented in the school in which you will teach or be student teaching? Which groups are you most interested in studying? Which ones do you have the least information about?*

Opportunities
for Reflection

Our knowledge about our students' cultures should allow us to make the academic content of our teaching more meaningful to students by relating it to their own experiences and building on their prior knowledge. It should help us make them and their histories the center of the education process in our effort to help them reach their academic, vocational, and social potentials. In the process, students should learn to believe in their own abilities and to become active participants in their own learning. Students should be able to achieve academically without adopting the dominant culture as their own. They should be able to maintain their own cultural identities inside and outside the school.

Teaching multiculturally requires the incorporation of diversity throughout the learning process. If race, ethnicity, class, and gender are not interrelated in the **curriculum** (that is, the content of courses), students do not learn that these are interrelated parts of a whole called self. Although Chapters 2 through 8 addressed membership in these cultural groups separately, they should be interwoven throughout one's own teaching. For example, if activities are developed to fight racism but continue to perpetuate sexism, we are not providing multicultural education. At the same time, we should not forget women of color and women in poverty when discussing the impact of sexism and other women's issues.

All teaching should be multicultural and all classrooms should be models of democracy, equity, and social justice. To do this, educators must do the following:

1. Place the student at the center of the teaching and learning process.
2. Promote human rights and respect for cultural differences.
3. Believe that all students can learn.
4. Acknowledge and build on the life histories and experiences of students' cultural group memberships.
5. Critically analyze oppression and power relationships to understand racism, sexism, classism, and discrimination against the disabled, gay, lesbian, young, and elderly.
6. Critique society in the interest of social justice and equality.
7. Participate in collective social action to ensure a democratic society.

Teachers and other school personnel can make a difference. Making one's teaching and classroom multicultural is an essential step in empowerment for both teachers and students. Now that you know about the multiple cultural groups to which your students belong, how can you put it all together to help students learn? Education that is multicultural incorporates the educational strategies described in Chapters 2 through 8, but moves beyond them to a holistic approach to teaching all students and confronting the barriers that prevent many students from being able to access the education that is so critical to their future.

Remember that multicultural education is for all students, not just English language learners or students of color. White students also belong to a racial and ethnic group and need to understand how their group has been privileged in schools. A strength of multicultural education is that we learn about our similarities and differences as we struggle to provide equity for all people. Students who are in segregated classrooms or in communities with little religious, language, ethnic, and racial diversity need to learn about the pluralistic world in which they live and the role they can play in providing social justice in their communities and beyond. Social justice and equity is part of our commitment to a democratic society.

FOCUSING ON LEARNING

Multicultural teachers care that all of their students learn regardless of the obstacles that many of them face because of their disabilities or economic conditions that limit their social capital. These teachers recognize when some students are not learning, reach out to them, and try different pedagogical strategies to help them learn. They do not allow students to sit in their classroom without being engaged with the content. They do not ignore the students who are withdrawn, depressed, or resistant to classroom work. They do everything they can to help students see themselves as learners and value learning.

The focus on learning is not limited to the basic literacy and numeracy skills that all people need to function effectively in society. Multicultural educators help students understand the **big ideas,** the concepts that undergird a subject. They encourage students to question what is written in textbooks and the newspaper and what they see on television and in movies. They do not treat students as receptacles in which knowledge is poured. They help students learn by doing through hands-on activities, community projects, collecting data from their neighborhoods, and testing their ideas.

The Center for Research on Education, Diversity, and Excellence (CREDE) (Viadero, 2004) at the University of California, Santa Cruz, has identified the following five standards as critical to improving the learning of diverse students:

1. *Teachers and Students Working Together.*   Use instructional group activities in which students and teacher work together to create a product or idea.

2. *Developing Language and Literacy Skills Across All Curriculum.* Apply literacy strategies and develop language competence in all subject areas.

3. *Connecting Lessons to Students' Lives.*   Contextualize teaching and curriculum in students' existing experiences in home, community, and school.

4. *Engaging Students with Challenging Lessons.*   Maintain challenging standards for student performance; design activities to advance understanding to more complex levels.

5. *Emphasizing Dialogue over Lectures.*   Instruct through teacher-student dialogue, especially academic, goal-directed, small-group conversations (known as instructional conversations), rather than lecture. (CREDE, 2004, p. 1)

Researchers at CREDE have tested and refined these standards in a number of schools with diverse populations. Lesson plans and multimedia resources for using the standards, as well as research reports, can be found at CREDE's website at **http://crede.ucsc.edu/.** These 5 standards will be discussed in this chapter as part of culturally responsive teaching.

A key to helping students learn is to connect the curriculum to their culture and real-world experiences. They should be able to see themselves in the curriculum to provide meaning for their own lives. Otherwise, they may resist the curriculum and learning, which are seen as the dominant culture's way of denigrating the culture of the students and their communities. The remainder of this chapter proposes **pedagogies** (that is, teaching strategies) that will help educators to deliver education that is multicultural education.

SUPPORTING DISPOSITIONS

Education that is multicultural requires teachers and other school personnel to have dispositions that support learning for students from diverse backgrounds. Dispositions are the values, commitments, and professional ethics that influence teaching and interactions with students, families, colleagues, and communities. An educator's dispositions affect student learning, motivation, and development as well as the educator's own professional growth. They are guided by beliefs and attitudes related to values such as caring, fairness, honesty, responsibility, and social justice (National Council for the Accreditation of Teacher Education, 2002). If a teacher's interaction with students is disrespectful and disparaging of the student's culture and experiences, the teacher will be incapable of delivering multicultural education. Educators with the dispositions outlined in Chapter 1 will be able to build on the cultures and experiences of students from diverse backgrounds to support and extend academic learning.

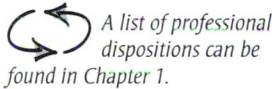

A list of professional dispositions can be found in Chapter 1.

One of the characteristics of teachers who are successful in working with students from diverse populations is caring. As part of their caring, they have high expectations for academic achievement and push students to achieve at those levels.

Culturally Responsive Teaching

Culturally responsive teaching is an essential component of education that is multicultural. This pedagogy affirms the cultures of students, views the cultures and experiences of students as strengths, and reflects the students' cultures in the teaching process. It is based on the premise that culture influences the way students learn (Darling-Hammond, French, & García-Lopez, 2002; Gay, 2000). It also moves beyond the dominant **canon** of knowledge and ways of knowing. "Students are taught to be proud of their ethnic identities and cultural backgrounds instead of being apologetic or ashamed of them" (Gay, 2000, p. 34).

In this section we will explore elements of the teaching-learning process that should be considered and developed to become a culturally responsive teacher. Begin now to incorporate these practices into your own lesson plans and work in classrooms. Look for evidence of these practices as you observe teachers in schools and identify others who support culturally responsive teaching.

MULTICULTURAL CURRICULUM

The curriculum defines the knowledge and skills that students are expected to learn in a course or program. It is also political. Whose story, whose culture, and whose values will be reflected in the curriculum being taught and the supporting textbooks and readings that are assigned? Will students be pushed to assimilate the dominant culture, making its stories their own? Or will the curriculum value the students' cultures and teach them their histories and experiences along with those of the dominant culture? A **multicultural curriculum** supports and celebrates our diversity in the broadest sense; it includes the histories, experiences, traditions, and cultures of students in the classroom. In classrooms with limited diversity, the curriculum introduces them to the major cultural groups in the state or nation. *How will you incorporate the cultures and histories of communities of color in the curriculum? How will you know that these communities are not represented in the curriculum or in the textbooks you have been assigned? Where will you find appropriate materials to supplement the curriculum?*

Opportunities for Reflection

Regardless of the grade level or subject being taught, the curriculum should be multicultural. The students in your classroom should be able to see themselves and their experiences in the curriculum. It is as important for students in a homogeneous setting as for those in more diverse settings to acknowledge and understand the diversity in the United States and the world. Because students in settings with limited diversity do not have the opportunities to interact with persons from other cultural backgrounds, they should learn to value diversity, rather than fear it. They should come to know that others have different perspectives on the world and events that are based in different experiences. The Internet could facilitate interacting with and getting to know persons from other cultures.

Although communities are not always rich in ethnic diversity, they all are diverse. Educators need to determine the cultural groups that exist in the community.

Schools that are on or near American Indian reservations will include students from the tribes in the area, as well as non-American Indians. Urban schools typically include multiethnic populations and students from different socioeconomic levels; inner-city schools have a high proportion of low-income and immigrant students. Rural schools include low-income and middle-class families. Teachers who enter schools attended by students from different cultural backgrounds than that of the teacher will need to adjust to that setting; otherwise, both students and teachers could suffer.

The current traditional curriculum is based on the histories, experiences, and perspectives of the dominant group. The result is the marginalization of the experiences of other groups. Multicultural teaching should tell it as it is. Diversity existed in the United States when Europeans arrived and became greater with each passing century. To teach as if only one group is worthy of inclusion in the curriculum is not to tell the truth. It suggests that only one group is important and that if you belong to another group, you are inferior to the one being taught. *How would you feel if you never saw yourself, your family, or your community in the curriculum? What groups discussed earlier in this book seldom, if ever, make it into textbooks or class discussions?*

Opportunities for Reflection

Instructional materials and information about different groups are available to students and teachers. It may be more difficult to find resources on groups where the membership is small or somewhat new to the United States, but it is not impossible. Both students and teachers can use the Internet to locate information, including personal narratives, art, music, and family histories. Although teachers cannot possibly address each of the hundreds of ethnic and religious groups in this country, they should attempt to include the groups represented in the school community, whether or not all of them are represented in the school.

For example, in western Pennsylvania, a teacher should include information about and examples from the Amish. This approach will help Amish students feel a valued part of the school and will signal to other students that cultural diversity is acceptable and valued. In schools in the Southwest, the culture of Mexican Americans and American Indians should be integrated throughout the curriculum. In other areas of the country, the curriculum should reflect the histories, experiences, and perspectives of Mormons, Muslims, Vietnamese Americans, Lakotas, Jamaican Americans, African Americans, Chinese Americans, Puerto Ricans, and other groups as appropriate. Students should find themselves in the curriculum; otherwise, they are marginalized and do not see themselves as an integral part of the school culture.

Educators are cautioned against giving superficial attention to cultural groups. Multicultural education is much more than food, festivals, and fun, or heroes and holidays. Even celebrating African American history only during February or women's history during March is not multicultural education. It is much more complex and pervasive than setting aside an hour, a unit, or a month. It should become the lens through which the curriculum is presented.

The amount of specific content about different groups will vary according to the course taught, but awareness and recognition of the nation's diversity can be reflected in all classroom experiences. No matter how assimilated students in a classroom are, it is the teacher's responsibility to ensure that they understand diversity,

Opportunities for Reflection

know the contributions of members of both dominant and other groups, and hear the voices of individuals and groups who are from cultural backgrounds different from the majority of students. *How could you incorporate diversity into the subject or subjects you plan to teach? What should white students know about people of color and non-Christian religions? Who are some of the women and persons of color who have made outstanding contributions to the subject that you will be teaching?*

Multiculturalism is not a compensatory process to make others more like the dominant group. As an educator integrates diversity into the curriculum, the differences across groups must not become deficits to be overcome. Teachers who believe that their own culture is superior to students' cultures will not be able to build the trust necessary to help all students learn. When one first begins to teach multiculturally, extra planning time will be needed to discover ways to make the curriculum and instruction reflect diversity. With experience, however, this process will be internalized. The teacher will begin to recognize immediately what materials are not multicultural and will be able to expand the standard curriculum to reflect diversity and multiple perspectives.

Reflecting Culture in Academic Subjects. Knowledge about students' cultures is important in teaching subject matter in a way that students can learn it. Culturally responsive teaching increases academic achievement because the subject matter is taught within the cultural context and experiences of the students and the communities served. In this approach, the subject begins to have meaning for students because it relates to their lives and what they know. It validates their experiences.

Teachers must know a subject well to help students learn it. Subject matter competence alone, however, does not automatically translate into student learning. Without an understanding of students' cultures, teachers are unable to develop instructional strategies that can be related to students' life experiences. Interviews with African American teachers who have successfully taught mathematics to black students who speak a dialect confirmed that the use of cultural context and students' prior experiences is essential in helping students learn. One teacher interviewed by Delpit (1995) reported:

> He found that the same problem that baffled students when posed in terms of distances between two unfamiliar places or in terms of numbers of milk cans needed by a farmer, were much more readily solved when familiar locales and the amount of money needed to buy a leather jacket were substituted. (p. 65)

Students' cultural backgrounds must be reflected in the examples used to teach academic concepts. Rural students do not relate to riding a subway to school or work, nor do inner-city students easily relate to single-family homes with large yards. If students seldom see representations of themselves, their families, or their communities in the curriculum, it becomes difficult to believe that the academic content has any meaning or usefulness for them. It will appear to them that the subject matter has been written and delivered for someone else. At the same time, they can still learn about other lifestyles based on different cultural backgrounds and experiences, but not as the only ones to which they are ever exposed. The teacher's repertoire of instructional strategies must relate content to the realities of the lives of students.

The teacher who understands the experiences of students from different cultural backgrounds can use that knowledge to help students learn subject matter. A teacher's sensitivity to those differences can be used to make students from oppressed groups feel as comfortable in the class as those from the dominant culture.

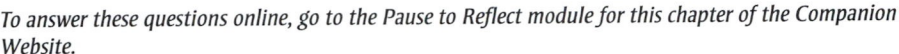

Pause to Reflect 9.1

Teaching that is culturally responsive requires changes in the curriculum to build upon the cultures of diverse groups, no matter the subject being taught. Think about a lesson you observed a teacher or professor in your discipline recently teach.

■ *How were the lesson and the teaching of it culturally responsive?*

■ *How might they have been culturally responsive?*

CW

To answer these questions online, go to the Pause to Reflect module for this chapter of the Companion Website.

Including Multiple Perspectives. It is important for students to learn that individuals from other ethnic, religious, and socioeconomic groups often have perspectives on issues and events that are different from their own. Most members of the dominant group have not had the negative and discriminatory experiences that people of color have had with schools, with the police, in government offices, or in shopping centers. They do not understand the privilege they experience based solely on their skin color. These experiences and the histories of groups provide the lens for viewing the world. Thus, perspectives vary for good reasons. Understanding the reasons makes it easier to accept that most other perspectives are just as valid as one's own. At the same time, perspectives and behaviors that degrade and harm members of specific groups such as those of the Ku Klux Klan and Nazis are not considered valid by the authors of this text.

CD
EXPLORE DIVERSITY Go to the *Exploring Diversity* CD located in the accompanying booklet to hear the perspective of one Native American on Thanksgiving in the case called *Majority Culture.*

Culturally responsive teaching requires examining sensitive issues and topics. It requires looking at historical and contemporary events from the perspective of white men, African American women, Puerto Ricans, Japanese Americans, Central American immigrants, Jewish Americans, and Southern Baptists. Reading books, poems, and articles by authors from diverse cultural backgrounds is helpful because it exposes students to the perspectives of other groups.

The community and students may view as untrustworthy teachers and others who are unable to accept alternate perspectives. An example is the inability of whites to see racism in almost everything experienced by African Americans. Even when African American students point out a racist action, many white teachers and students cannot see it, in part, because they have no experience of knowing or feeling racism. Instead of acknowledging it, they often argue that the reporter misinterpreted the action or that the action was not meant to be racist. As a result, many

CRITICAL INCIDENTS IN TEACHING

Teaching About Thanksgiving

Michele Johnson was observing a kindergarten class in a school near her campus during the fall semester of her junior year. She was taking a class in multicultural education at the same time and was expanding her knowledge base regarding groups of color. The week before Thanksgiving, the teacher she was observing gave her materials for students to color for their discussion of the meaning of Thanksgiving. When she looked through the materials, she discovered that the kindergartners were to cut out and decorate headbands that some of them would wear with feathers to give gifts to the Pilgrims for Thanksgiving. She was appalled that the teacher was perpetuating stereotypes of First Americans and their relationships with the European Settlers. She worried that the students were already learning stories about cultural groups that were inaccurate.

Questions for Discussion

1. Why does Michele think the project to teach about Thanksgiving is not appropriate?
2. How would you teach kindergartners about Thanksgiving? How would you project First Americans and the Pilgrims in relationship to each other?
3. Should she say something to the teacher who might later be evaluating her performance? Why or why not?

To answer these questions online, go to the Critical Incidents in Teaching module for this chapter of the Companion Website.

CW

African Americans learn that whites are really not interested in eliminating racism because they never recognize it or choose to ignore it (Tatum, 1997). Immigrant students, other students of color, students with disabilities, and girls and young women have similar narratives that are given little or no credit by many members of the dominant group.

HOLDING HIGH EXPECTATIONS

Unfortunately, some teachers respond differently to students because of the students' cultural identities. Some educators have low expectations for the academic achievement of students of color and students from low-income families. Low expectations are often based on negative generalizations about a group. When these generalizations are applied to all or most students from those groups, grave damage can be done. Students tend to meet the expectations of the teacher, no matter what their actual abilities are. Self-fulfilling prophecies about how well a student will perform in the classroom are often established early in the school year, and both student and teacher unconsciously fulfill those prophecies. Thus, educators should develop strategies to overcome negative expectations they may have for certain students and plan classroom instruction and activities to ensure success for all students.

Opportunities for Reflection

Cultural group membership cannot become an excuse for students' lack of academic achievement. Empathy with a student's situation (for example, being homeless) is appropriate, but we must prevent it from subsequently lowering our expectations for achievement. *What questions will you ask yourself if you find that low-performing students in your class are primarily African Americans, males, immigrants, or students with disabilities? What are the chances of your improving their academic performance?*

Not all expectations are low. Teachers often expect high achievement from Asian American students. Upper-middle-class students are placed disproportionately in high academic tracks, whereas low-income students are disproportionately placed in low academic tracks. Even when students have no differences in ability, academic tracks reflect race, gender, and class differences. Students who end up in the low-ability classes have limited academic mobility; they rarely are perceived to achieve at a level high enough to move them to the next highest level (Weinstein, 1996). Teaching behavior for high-ability groups is much different than for low-ability groups; middle-ability groups usually receive treatment more similar to that of high-ability groups. Students in the lowest tracks are often subject to practice and review drills. At the high end of the track, students are engaged in interesting and motivating intellectual activities.

To a large degree, students learn to behave in the manner that is expected of the group in which they are placed. Through tracking, educators have a great influence not only on directing a student's potential but also on determining it by their initial expectations for that student. The sad reality is that tracking does not appear to work, especially if the goal is to improve learning.

Heterogeneous grouping is more helpful in improving academic achievement for students from low-income and oppressed groups. Contrary to popular belief,

 VIDEO INSIGHT

Survival Lessons

Kids are faced with more and more violence and tragedy every day. To combat this, some schools across the country have set up full-time mental health programs to identify and help troubled children before the trouble gets out of control.

Francis Scott Key Elementary and the other schools mentioned in this video segment present models for helping troubled youth.

1. *What else can be done to help these children deal with some of the challenges of today's society?*
2. *What do you think the role of the teacher should be in helping students handle problems such as drugs, bullying, suicide, and violence?*

To answer these questions online, go to the ABC News Video Insight module for this chapter of the Companion Website.

DVD

CW

such grouping does not limit the academic achievement of the most academically talented students, especially when the instruction is geared to challenging them. The students who suffer the most from tracking practices are those from groups who are disproportionately placed in the low-ability groups. Compared with students in other tracks, these students develop more negative feelings about their academic potential and future aspirations. Educational equity demands a different strategy. It requires that all students be academically challenged with stimulating instruction that involves them actively in their own learning.

 *Tracking is discussed in more detail in Chapter 2.*

CARING

One of the complaints of students is that their teachers don't know them and do not care about them. Students indicate that they are more willing to work and perform better when they feel the teachers care about them (Cushman, 2003). However, caring does not mean that teachers are easy on students or permissive, letting them do what the students want. It is not enough to just like the students. A caring teacher has high expectations for students, and pushes students to meet those high expectations.

 EXPLORE DIVERSITY Go to the *Exploring Diversity* CD located in the accompanying booklet to hear one teacher's perspective on how teachers care for students in the case called *One Teacher's Influence*.

CD

Caring requires honoring the students and their families. Caring teachers have overcome their racial biases and do not stereotype students because they do not know their father, their parents are gay, their mother is on drugs, or they wear the same clothes day after day. They do not punish students because they do not conform to the dominant culture's expectations for normalcy. They do not label students or "find them unlovable, problematic, and difficult to honor or embrace without equivocation" (Gay, 2000, p. 46) because they are from different cultural groups than the teacher.

What are the characteristics of caring teachers? They are patient, persistent, and supportive of students. They listen to students and validate their culture. They empower their students to engage in their education. Caring teachers don't give up on their students. They understand why students may not feel well on some days or are having a difficult time outside of school. Nevertheless, these teachers do not accept failure.

"Uncaring [teachers] are distinguished by impatience, intolerance, dictations, and control" (Gay, 2000, p. 47). Natisha, whose story began this chapter, did not have teachers who tried to learn why she was silent. Her teachers did not care enough about her to reach out and engage her in her education. *What kind of teacher do you want to be? What can you do to overcome your biases and to reach out to students who are from different cultural groups than your own?*

 *Opportunities for Reflection*

CRITICAL INCIDENTS IN TEACHING

Caring

Apryl, a petite African American teenager, walks into an urban school's Spanish class 15 minutes late. The teacher, Mr. Roth informs her that she cannot sit with her friends. Apryl proceeds to seat herself in the corner with her friends. Mr. Roth declares that he is going to call Apryl's counselor to come to class and talk to Apryl, and that he will give Apryl none of the worksheets the class is required to complete until Apryl moves to her seat. As Mr. Roth circulates the room, he makes no eye contact with Apryl. Apryl freezes anytime Mr. Roth comes within earshot of her desk. Otherwise, she leans back in her chair, engages in conversation with the boys around her, and rearranges the papers in her backpack.

Apryl raises her hand to ask for the worksheets about 30 minutes into class, but is told she cannot have the worksheets until she moves. Apryl's conversation with the boys around her gets louder and more animated. She pulls food and drink out of her bag and starts eating and drinking. She gets out of her seat every 5 or 10 minutes to stand at the window to see what is going on outside. She starts a couple of exchanges with students across the room. Every once in a while, Mr. Roth shouts at Apryl, "You cannot talk in class." Apryl replies either that she "ain't talking, give me the work" or that she is "waiting for her counselor," and Mr. Roth starts ignoring Apryl again.

Fifty minutes into the 110-minute class, a boy near Apryl gets so disruptive that Mr. Roth starts filling out the paperwork to have security remove him from the classroom. Apryl starts packing her backpack. When security shows up at the door 10 minutes later, Apryl runs toward the door and begs the guard to remove her from the classroom. The guard cannot remove Apryl without a teacher request. Mr. Roth finally tells the guard to take both of them.

Questions for Discussion

1. *What are some reasons why Apryl may not be engaged in the assigned work?*
2. *How is the worksheet assignment, which was the assignment for the full 110-minute period, related to Apryl's world?*
3. *How did Mr. Roth's interactions with Apryl support or not support her learning of Spanish?*
4. *Do Mr. Roth's responses to Apryl suggest he has high expectations for her? Why or why not?*
5. *Based on this limited information, would you say that Mr. Roth has a caring relationship with Apryl? Why or why not?*

To answer these questions online, go to the Critical Incidents in Teaching module for this chapter of the Companion Website.

Source: Adapted from Anderson, L. (2003). Ain't doin' that: Why "doing good in school" can be so hard. In L. Darling-Hammond, J. French, & S.P. García-Lopez, *Learning to teach for social justice* (pp. 103–115). New York: Teachers College Press.

ENCOURAGING STUDENT VOICES

Teaching must start from the students' life experiences, not the teacher's life experiences or the experiences necessary to fit into the dominant school culture. Multicultural teachers seek, listen to, and incorporate voices of students, their families, and communities. Students are encouraged to speak from their own experiences, to do more than regurgitate answers that the teacher would like to hear. Teaching that incorporates the student voice allows students to make sense of subject matter within their own **lived experiences** or the realities that they know because they have themselves experienced them. Listening to students helps teachers understand their prior knowledge of the subject matter, including any misinformation or lack of information that suggests future instructional strategies. Student voices also provide important information about their cultures.

Most schools today legitimate only the voice of the dominant culture—the Standard English and world perspective of the white middle-class. Many students, especially those from oppressed groups, learn to be silent or disruptive, and/or they drop out, in part because their voices are not accepted as legitimate in the classroom. Culturally responsive teaching requires educators to recognize the incongruence between the voice of the school and the voices of students. Success in school should not be dependent on the adoption of the school's voice.

Teachers could use an approach in which instruction occurs as a dialogue between teacher and students' which is the fifth CREDE standard mentioned earlier in this chapter. This strategy requires that teachers have a thorough knowledge of the subject being taught. Rather than depend on a textbook and lecture format, the teacher listens to students and directs them in the learning of the discipline through dialogue. It incorporates content about the diverse backgrounds of students, as well as those of the dominant society. It requires discarding the traditional authoritarian classroom to establish a democratic one in which both teacher and students are active participants.

Introducing student voices to the instructional process can be difficult, especially when teacher and students are from different cultural backgrounds. The teacher may face both anger and silence, which in time will be overcome with dialogue that develops tolerance, patience, and a willingness to listen. Although this strategy increases the participation of students in the learning process, some teachers are not comfortable with handling the issues that are likely to be raised. Too often, teachers ignore students' attempts to engage in dialogue and, as a result, halt further learning by many students.

In addition to dialogue between students and teacher, student voices can be encouraged through written and artistic expression. Some teachers ask students to keep journals in which they write their reactions to what is occurring in class. The journals make the teacher aware of learning that is occurring over time. To be effective, students must feel comfortable writing whatever they want without the threat of reprisal from the teacher.

The dialogues developed through these approaches can help students understand the perspectives brought to the classroom by others from different cultural backgrounds. Multicultural education commits students and teachers to engage with others who come from different cultural groups than their own. The resulting dialogues can help students relate subject matter to their real world, encouraging them to take an interest in studying and learning it.

ENGAGING STUDENTS

Culturally responsive teaching encourages student participation, critical analysis, and action. Classroom projects focus on areas of interest to students and the communities in which they live. As they participate in these activities, they apply and extend the mathematics, science, language arts, and social studies that they have been learning. Teachers and students in these classrooms have developed a vision for a more egalitarian and socially just society. Projects often engage students in collective action to improve their communities.

EXPLORE DIVERSITY Go to the *Exploring Diversity* CD located in the accompanying booklet to listen to a teacher describe middle school students' engagement in a diversity club in the case called *One Teacher's Influence.*

After conducting research and collecting and analyzing data, students sometimes move their recommendations through the democratic processes of their local communities to make changes for improving conditions. In one Nebraska school, students and their teacher became very concerned about the treatment of new immigrants in the local community and businesses. They drafted a legislative bill requiring the study of race in social studies across the state. Facing opposition from some, they lobbied the state legislature on behalf of the bill and were successful in having it adopted. Students in this social studies class not only were able to affect school curriculum through their actions, but also learned the legislative process of their state through hands-on experience.

A group of teenagers from across the country shared their views of how teachers can keep students engaged, motivated, and challenged in the book, *Fires in the Bathroom: Advice for Teachers from High School Students.* These students from diverse cultural groups suggest that teachers get and keep students motivated by:

- Being passionate about your material and your work.
- Connecting to issues we care about outside school.
- Giving us choices on things that matter.
- Making learning a social thing.
- Making sure we understand.
- Responding with interest when we show interest.
- Caring about us and our progress.
- Helping us keep on top of our workload.
- Showing your pride in our good work.
- Providing role models to inspire us. (Cushman, 2003, p. 122)

Teaching for Social Justice

As a part of providing education that is multicultural, teachers and their students confront inequities in schools and communities. Then they take steps to eliminate existing inequities within the classroom and school and, sometimes, in the community. Teaching for social justice requires what the 2005 president of the American Educational Research Association, Marilyn Cochran-Smith (2004) calls "teaching against the grain." She identifies the dilemma for teachers who are trying to teach for social justice: "How to educate children who know about not only the canon of literature, language, and history, but also their own history, language, and literature; not only how to negotiate their way through the system's gatekeepers but also how to work to dismantle the inequities of the system" (p. 63).

Teaching for social justice requires a disposition of caring and social responsibility for persons who are not advantaged. Socially just educators believe that the country's resources should be somewhat equitably distributed. They also believe that all people have the right to decent housing, health insurance, education, and adequate food and nutrition, regardless of their ethnicity, race, socioeconomic status, sexual orientation, or disability. They confront inequity by critically analyzing oppression in society.

Socially just classrooms are democratic, engaging both students and teachers in learning together. Power relations between students and teachers are enacted in classrooms. Teachers and other school officials can use their power to develop either democratic settings in which students are active participants or autocratic settings controlled totally by adults. The problem with **authoritarianism,** which is the concentration of power in one person, is that it undermines democratic education (hooks, 2003). Establishing a democratic classroom helps overcome the power inequities that exist. It challenges the authoritarianism of the teacher and breaks down the power relationships between teacher and students. Students become active participants in governing the classroom and in critically analyzing school and societal practices related to equity and social justice.

DEVELOPING CRITICAL THINKING

As a result of being taught multiculturally, students learn to think critically about what they are learning and experiencing. **Critical thinking** challenges the status quo, encourages questioning of the dominant canon and culture, and considers alternate views to the inequitable structure of society. Students should be supported in questioning the validity of the knowledge presented in textbooks and other resources. They should be encouraged to explore other perspectives. Developing the skills to think critically about issues helps students make sense of the events and conditions that affect their own lives.

Multicultural teaching requires students to investigate racism, classism, and sexism and how societal institutions have served different populations in discriminatory ways. Even though we may overcome our own prejudices and eliminate our own discriminatory practices against members of other cultural groups, the problem is not solved. It goes beyond what we individually control. The problem is societal and is imbedded in historical and contemporary contexts that students must be helped to understand.

Most students accept the information written in their textbooks as the absolute truth. However, critical thinkers do not automatically accept the content of textbooks as truth. They understand that authors write from their own perspectives with their own biases. The presentation is usually from the perspective of the dominant culture rather than persons who have been oppressed because of events and practices supportive of the dominant culture. Teaching for social justice encourages students to question what is written in textbooks or appears in multimedia materials. Students are expected to conduct research that provides other facts and perspectives that might negate the content in the textbook.

Educators can help students examine their own biases and stereotypes related to different cultural groups. These biases often surface during class discussions or inci-

FOCUS YOUR CULTURAL LENS: DEBATE

Critical Thinking: At What Age Should We Teach the War?

The School Board in one school district passed a resolution that all middle level and high schools dedicate one class period and one after-school event to studying the war in Iraq. The resolution indicated that age-appropriate materials should be used by teachers and diverse perspectives presented. When the resolution was adopted, one teacher in the district was already discussing the war with her fourth-grade students. As part of social studies, these students were studying Iraq, "discussing what factors led to the current conflict, and listening to diverse perspectives on the impending war from people around the world." They were not limiting their discussion to one class period. Is it appropriate to discuss political issues with young children?

FOR

- Young children need to know the critical issues that are affecting the lives of their families (e.g., they or their classmates may have family members serving in Iraq).

- Young children should be helped to understand different perspectives on the political issues that they see on television.

- Without discussing war critically with younger students, they learn that war is an acceptable response to conflict.

- A critical discussion of war may help young students understand why they should not hate the Iraqis, other Arabs, or other Arab Americans.

AGAINST

- Talking about war may scare young children.

- Young children are not able to understand the complexity of war and other controversial political issues.

- Discussing war contributes to the development of extreme patriotism and hate against the citizens of another nation.

- Teachers should not be influencing students' perspectives on the Iraq War. It is the role of parents to help them understand the war.

Questions for Discussion

1. *Should teachers help students see the Iraq War from the perspectives of the Iraqi people and their leaders as well as the United States and its allies? Why or why not?*
2. *How old should students be to begin the critical study of political issues?*
3. *Why should teachers help students think critically about war and other political issues?*
4. *Thinking critically about issues fits naturally into social studies. How can teachers help students think critically about mathematics, science, and literacy?*

To answer these questions online, go to the Focus Your Cultural Lens: Debate module for this chapter of the Companion Website.

Source: Dawson, K. (2003, Summer). Learning from the past, talking about the present: A fourth-grade teacher reflects on her own schooling and poses hard questions to her students about the war. *Rethinking Schools, 17*(4), 17.

dents outside the classroom. They should not be ignored by the teacher. Instead, they should become one of those teachable moments in which issues are confronted and discussed. Accurate information can begin to displace the myths that many hold about others.

ADDRESSING INEQUITY AND POWER

Many teachers have a difficult time addressing the issue of race in the classroom. Yet, it affects the work of schools. Most white students probably don't believe that racism is a factor in their lives; they may even question its existence. Most persons of color, on the other hand, feel the pressure of racism all around them. They don't understand how their white peers and teachers could possibly miss it. To ignore the impact of racism on society and our everyday worlds is to negate the experiences of students and families who suffer from its negative impact. Can we afford to ignore it because it is complex, emotional, and hard for some to understand and handle? As teachers incorporate diversity throughout the curriculum, there should be opportunities to discuss the meaning of race in this country and the debilitating effect racism (as well as sexism, classism, etc.) has on large numbers of people in this country and the world.

There is value in racial and ethnic groups working together to overcome fears and correct myths and misperceptions. This healing cannot occur if educators are unwilling to facilitate the dialogue about race. Discussions of race often challenge the teachers and students deeply held beliefs about the topic. Some students react with anger; others are defensive and feel guilty. At the beginning, many white students resist reexamining their worldviews, acknowledging the privilege of whiteness, and accepting the existence of discrimination.

These changes do not occur overnight; they take months, and sometimes years, of study and self-reflection. Some people never accept that racism exists and needs to be eliminated. The dialogue about race and racism should occur in all schools, not just those with diverse populations.

Another difficult topic to analyze critically is poverty, especially its causes. Too often, families and individuals are blamed for their own poverty. It is difficult for many, especially those advantaged by the current economic conditions, to acknowledge that our system does not provide the same opportunities for all whites and persons of color. Chapter 2 described the growing gap between the incomes of the wealthy, the middle class, and persons in poverty.

 *Poverty and income differences are the focus of Chapter 2.*

Teachers can help students explore the contributions of the labor class as well as the rich and powerful. They can examine various perspectives on eliminating jobs in one area of the country and moving them to cheaper labor markets in another part of the country or world. Students could examine the changing job markets to determine the skills needed for future work. They could discuss why companies are seeking labor outside the United States for high-tech jobs as well as low-paying jobs in meat processing companies. They could critique different perspectives on seeking labor outside the country rather than ensuring that U.S. students have the necessary skills for the growing technology fields.

FOSTERING LEARNING COMMUNITIES

Numerous studies show that interactions and understandings among people from different racial and ethnic groups increase as they work together on **meaningful projects** inside and outside the classroom. In social justice education, these meaningful projects address equity, democratic, and social justice issues in the community.

As part of social justice education, teachers establish learning communities among students to encourage them to work together in the learning process. The learning communities with members from different cultural groups can also promote cross-cultural interactions and understandings.

Teachers should ensure that students are integrated in cooperative groups and group work. They can establish opportunities for cross-cultural communications and learning from each other. Teenagers who participated in the discussions about what teachers should do to engage students in learning support group work with members from different cultural groups to help them learn about each other.

Cooperative learning is a popular strategy for supporting learning communities. It is a strategy for grouping students to work together on a project to support and learn from each other. It minimizes competition among students and encourages sharing the work required to learn. One of the problems with cooperative learning is that students are often allowed to choose the members of their groups, which could prevent cross-cultural interactions.

WORKING WITH FAMILIES AND COMMUNITIES

After working in Alaska, in historically black and predominantly white universities, and in the South Pacific country of Papua, New Guinea, Delpit (1995) concluded, "If I want to learn how best to teach children who may be different from me, then I must seek the advice of adults—teachers and parents—who are from the same culture as my students" (p. 102).

Parents expect teachers to help their children learn academic skills. A well-known educational psychologist, Jere Brophy (1998) reports that:

> Most parents care about their children's success at school and will respond positively to information sharing and requests from teachers. Furthermore, one of the distinctive features of the teachers and schools that are most effective with students at risk for school failure is that they reach out to these students' families, get to know them, keep them informed of what is going on at school, and involve them in decision making. (pp. 240–241)

Children and Race

It has been more than forty years since school desegregation was mandated by the U.S. Supreme Court. Is this nation any closer to integrating children of different backgrounds in its schools? Do the generations of children who are growing up in schools today experience less prejudice than past generations? Is the nation any closer to melding relationships of racially and ethnically diverse people in this pluralistic society?

Do some independent reflective research by interviewing school-age children and recording their answers to the following question: "Have you ever had any good friends who are of a different race than you?" If the answer to this initial question is yes, ask, "What kinds of activities do you and this friend participate in together? How is this friendship the same or different from any of your other friendships? What do you value most about this friendship?" If the answer to the initial question is no, ask, "Would you be a friend to someone who is of a different race or ethnic background than you if you had the opportunity? Why or why not?" Consider the children's answers.

1. *What do your data reveal?*

2. *Using this knowledge, how will you make a difference by helping students develop as citizens in a global community who tolerate, respect, and accept all others?*

To answer these questions online, go to the ABC News Video Insight module for this chapter of the Companion Website.

Not all parents feel welcome in schools, in part because most schools reflect the dominant culture and language, rather than their own. Therefore, school personnel may need to reach out to the parents, rather than simply wait for them to show up at a meeting. A true collaboration requires that parents and teachers become partners in the teaching process. Teachers need to listen to parents and participate in the community to develop a range of teaching strategies that are congruent with the home cultures of students. Parents can learn to support their children's learning at home but may need concrete suggestions, which they will seek from teachers who they believe care about their children.

Educators must know the community to understand the lived cultures of the families. In a school in which a prayer is said every morning regardless of the Supreme Court's decision forbidding prayer in public schools, one should not teach evolution on the first day of class. In that school setting, one may not be able to teach sex education in the same way it is taught in many urban and suburban schools. In another school, Islamic parents may be upset with the attire that their daughters are expected to wear in physical education classes and may not approve of coed physical education courses. Jewish and Islamic students wonder why the school celebrates Christian holidays and never their religious holidays.

Adults in the community can be valuable resources in discussions of cultural differences. When community members trust school officials, they become partners with teachers in improving student learning.

Because members of the community may revolt against the content and activities in the curriculum does not mean that educators cannot teach multiculturally. It does suggest that they must know the sentiments of the community before introducing concepts that may be foreign and unacceptable. Only then can educators develop strategies for effectively introducing such concepts. The introduction of controversial issues may need to be accompanied by the education of parents and by the presentation of multiple perspectives that place value on the community's mores.

In addition, the community becomes a resource in a multicultural classroom. We can learn much about cultures in the community through participation in activities and by inviting community members into the school. Community speakers and helpers should represent the diversity of the community. Speakers also should be selected from different roles and age-groups.

School Climate

Another area in which commitment to multicultural education can be evaluated is the general school climate. Three factors were identified in a Metropolitan Life Insurance Company (1996) survey by students as having a positive role in promoting good relations among students and adults: (a) the quality of teachers' relationships with students, (b) the quality of education, and (c) the social skills that teachers impart to students. "When teachers support students by treating them with respect and caring about their futures, and encourage students by helping them to succeed, students are more likely to respect and get along with one another; when taught how to be more tolerant of others, students exhibit greater tolerance" (p. 3). A disturbing finding of the survey was that a majority of students do not think that teachers, parents, and other adults treat students of color and low-income equally.

Visitors entering a school can usually feel the tension that exists when cross-cultural communications are poor. They can observe whether diversity is a positive and appreciated factor at the school. If only students of color or only males are waiting to be seen by the assistant principal in charge of discipline, visitors will wonder whether the school is providing effectively for the needs of all of its students. If bulletin boards in classrooms are covered with only white people, visitors will question the appreciation of diversity in the school. If the football team is comprised primarily of African Americans and the chess club of whites, they will wonder about the inclusion of students from a variety of cultural groups in extracurricular activities. If school administrators are primarily men and most teachers are women, or if the teachers are white and the teacher aides are Latino, the visitors will envision discriminatory practices in hiring and promotion procedures. These are examples of a school climate that does not reflect a commitment to multicultural education.

Staffing composition and patterns should reflect the cultural diversity of the country. At a minimum, they should reflect the diversity of the geographic area. Women, as well as men, should be school administrators; men, as well as women, should teach at preschool and primary levels. Persons of color should be found in the administration and teaching ranks, not primarily in custodial and clerical positions.

When diversity is valued within a school, student government and extracurricular activities include students from different cultural groups. Students should not be segregated on the basis of their membership in a certain group. In a school where multiculturalism is valued, students from various cultural backgrounds hold leadership positions. Those roles are not automatically delegated to students from the dominant group in the school.

If the school climate is multicultural, it is reflected in every aspect of the educational program. In addition to those areas already mentioned, assembly programs reflect multiculturalism in their content, as well as in the choice of speakers. Bulletin boards and displays reflect the diversity of the nation, even if the community is not rich in diversity. Cross-cultural communications among students and between students and teachers are positive. Different languages and dialects used by students are respected. Both girls and boys are found in technology education, family science, calculus, bookkeeping, physics, and vocational classes. Students from different cultural groups participate in college preparatory classes, advanced placement classes, special education, and gifted education at a rate equal to their representation in the schools.

The school climate must be supportive of multicultural education. When respect for cultural differences is reflected in all aspects of students' educational programs, the goals of multicultural education are being attained. Educators are the key to attaining this climate.

The school climate is an indicator of whether diversity and equality are respected and promoted in a school. Take an inventory of: (a) a school that you may be observing; (b) the school, college, or department of education that is responsible for preparing teachers at your college or university; or (c) the college or university itself.

- *What is the diversity of the faculty? How diverse is the student body?*
- *How does the diversity differ between administrators and faculty?*
- *In what activities do white students and students of color participate?*
- *How reflective of diversity are displays on the walls and in display cases?*
- *What is the diversity of students on the honor roll or dean's list?*
- *What positive and negative characteristics do you observe?*

To answer these questions online, go to the Pause to Reflect module for this chapter of the Companion Website.

CW

HIDDEN CURRICULUM

In addition to a formal curriculum, schools have a hidden curriculum that consists of the unstated norms, values, and beliefs about the social relations of school and classroom life that are transmitted to students. Because the hidden curriculum includes the norms and values that support the formal curriculum, it must also reflect diversity if education is to become multicultural. Although the hidden curriculum is not taught directly or included in the objectives for the formal curriculum, it has a great impact on students and teachers alike. It includes the organizational structures of the classroom and the school, as well as the interactions of students and teachers.

Students must take turns, stand in line, wait to speak, wait for the teacher to provide individual help, face interruptions from others, and be distracted constantly by the needs of others. They must develop patience in order to be successful in the school setting. They must also learn to work alone within the crowd. Even though they share the classroom with many other students, they usually are not allowed to interact with classmates unless the teacher permits it. These same characteristics will be encountered in the work situations for which students are being prepared. They are not part of the formal curriculum but are central to the operation of most classrooms.

MESSAGES SENT TO STUDENTS

Opportunities for Reflection

Unknowingly, educators often transmit biased messages to students. For example, lining up students by gender to go to lunch reinforces the notion that boys and girls are distinct groups. *Why not line them up by shoe colors or birth dates? What messages do students receive when girls are always asked to take attendance and boys are asked to move chairs; when upper-middle-class students are almost always asked to lead small-group work; or when persons of color are never asked to speak to the class?* Most educators do not consciously or intentionally stereotype students or discriminate against them; they usually try to treat all students fairly and equitably. We have learned our attitudes and behaviors, however, in a society that is ageist, handicapist, racist, sexist, and ethnocentric. Some biases have been internalized to such a degree that we do not realize we have them. When educators are able to recognize the subtle and unintentional biases in their behavior, positive changes can be made in the classroom.

Traditionally, teachers have been part of the socialization process that teaches different male and female behaviors based on gender. Although boys are often more aggressive than girls, many of the differences observed in the way teachers treat the two groups are based on their own beliefs about male and female behavior.

Students of color are often treated significantly different from white students. Because many white students share the same European and/or middle-class culture as the teacher, they also share the same cultural cues that foster success in the classroom. Students who ask appropriate questions at appropriate times or who smile and seek attention from the teacher at times when the teacher is open to such gestures are likely to receive encouragement and reinforcement from the teacher. In contrast, students who interrupt the class or who seek attention from the teacher when the teacher is not open to providing the necessary attention do not receive the necessary reinforcement.

As a result of the teacher's misreading of the cultural cues, ethnic or racial boundaries are established within the classroom. This situation is exacerbated when students from the dominant group receive more opportunities to participate in instructional interactions and receive more praise and encouragement. Low-income students and students of color receive fewer opportunities to participate, and the opportunities usually are of a less-substantive nature. They also may be criticized or disciplined more frequently than white students for breaking the rules.

Opportunities for Reflection

Unless teachers can critically examine their treatment of students in the classroom, they will not know whether they treat students inequitably because of cultural differences. Once that step has been taken, changes can be initiated to ensure that cultural identity is not a factor for automatically relating differently to students. Teachers may need to become more proactive in initiating interactions and in providing encouragement, praise, and reinforcement to students from cultural backgrounds different from their own. *How can teachers begin to cross racial and poverty borders?*

Teachers usually evaluate students' academic performance through tests and written and oral work. Much more than academic performance is evaluated by teachers, however. Student misbehavior occurs when classroom rules are not adequately obeyed, which usually results in some sort of punishment. Discipline varies by the infraction and student, but sometimes is influenced by the gender, race, and class of the student. Similarly, students who have been assigned a low-ability status often receive negative attention from the teacher because they are not following the rules, rather than because they are not performing adequately on academic tasks.

In addition to evaluations based on academic performance and institutional rules, teachers often make evaluations based on personal qualities. Students are sometimes grouped according to their clothes, family income, cleanliness, and personality, rather than academic abilities. This practice is particularly dangerous because most tracking perpetuates inequities; it does not improve academic achievement.

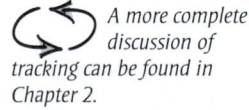

A more complete discussion of tracking can be found in Chapter 2.

Another aspect of the hidden curriculum is that of unequal power. In many ways, this is a dilemma of childhood. By the time students enter kindergarten, they have learned that power is in the hands of adults. The teacher and other school officials require that their rules be followed. In addition to the institutional rules, teachers may require that students give up their home languages or dialects to be successful academically or at least to receive the teacher's approval. Instead, students should be encouraged to be bicultural, knowing both their home and dominant cultural language and patterns.

How can the hidden curriculum reflect multicultural education? A first step is to recognize that it exists and that it provides lessons that are valuable in life. However, the rules are known to the members of the dominant culture. They don't have to think about them. Students' curiosity must be valued and encouraged. Too often, the requirements of the classroom place more value on following the rules than on learning. Our interactions with students should be evaluated to ensure that we are actually supporting learning, rather than preventing it.

STUDENT AND TEACHER RELATIONS

Although the development and use of culturally responsive materials and curricula are important and necessary steps toward providing multicultural education, alone they are not enough. The interactions between teachers and students determine the quality of education. Teachers send messages that tell students that they have potential and that they can learn. Teachers who know their subject matter, believe that all students can learn, and care about students as individuals can have a great impact on students and their learning. Teenagers recommend that teachers show respect, trust, and fairness by:

- Letting us know what to expect from you and from the class.
- Knowing your material.
- Pushing us to do our best—and push us equally.
- Doing your part.
- Making sure everyone understands.
- Grading us fairly.
- Understanding that we make mistakes.
- Not denigrating us.
- Keeping your biases to yourself.
- Not treating us like little kids.
- Listening to what we think.
- Caring what's going on with us.
- Not betraying our confidences.

The teacher who is enthusiastic about culturally responsive teaching will be more likely to use multicultural materials and encourage students to develop more egalitarian views. Research studies have found that warmer and more enthusiastic teachers produce students with greater achievement gains. These teachers solicit better affective responses from their students, which leads to classrooms with a more positive atmosphere. Students from low-income families and students of color "do especially well with teachers who share warm, personal interactions with them but also hold high expectations for their academic progress, require them to perform up to their capabilities, and see that they progress as far and as fast as they are able" (Brophy, 1998). Teachers need to carefully assess the needs of individual students in the classroom, however, to develop effective teaching strategies.

Teachers do make a difference in student learning. They can make students feel either very special or incompetent and worthless. After reviewing the research on teacher interactions with students of color, Gay (2000) concluded that

> students of color, especially those who are poor and live in urban areas, get less total instructional attention; are called on less frequently; are encouraged to continue to develop intellectual thinking less often; are criticized more and praised less; receive fewer direct responses to their questions and comments; and are reprimanded more often and disciplined more severely. (p. 63).

These factors are critical in promoting students' learning. When teachers respond to students of color in this way, they are limiting their possibilities for high achievement.

To provide the greatest assistance to all students, teachers cannot provide the same treatment to each student, because they should be working toward meeting individual needs and differences. Teachers must be sure they are not treating students differently, however, based solely on students' membership in a cultural group. With the elimination of bias from the teaching process and the emergence of proactive teachers who seek the most effective strategies to meet the needs of individual students, the classroom can become a stimulating place for most students, regardless of their cultural identities, abilities, and experiences.

EXPLORE DIVERSITY Go to the *Exploring Diversity* CD located in the accompanying booklet for a discussion of how white teachers connect with students from other racial groups by viewing the "Empower the Student" section in the case called *One Teacher's Influence.*

How can teachers analyze their own classroom interactions and teaching styles? If equipment is available, teachers can videotape or audiotape a class and then systematically record the interactions as they view or listen to the tape later. An outside observer could be asked to record the nature of a teacher's interaction with students. An analysis of the data would show teachers how much class time they spend interacting with students and the nature of the interactions. These data would show any differences in interactions based on gender, ethnicity, or other characteristics of students. Such an analysis would be an excellent starting point for teachers who want to ensure that they do not discriminate against male or female students or students from different ethnic or socioeconomic groups. *How do you plan to analyze your interactions with students when you student teach? What are the advantages and disadvantages of videotaping your teaching during the first week of student teaching and several times later in your student teaching?*

Opportunities for Reflection

Every effort must be made to ensure that a teacher's prejudices are not reflected in their interactions with students. Teachers must continually assess their interactions with boys, girls, and students from dominant and oppressed groups to determine whether the interactions provide different types of praise, criticism, encouragement, and reinforcement based on the culture of the students. Only then can steps be taken to equalize treatment.

STUDENT AND TEACHER COMMUNICATIONS

Lack of skill in cross-cultural communications between students and teachers can prevent learning from occurring in the classroom. This problem is usually the result of misunderstanding cultural cues when students have cultural identities different from that of the teacher.

Just as cultures differ in the structure of their language, they also differ in the structure of oral discourse. Moves made in teaching-learning discourse, who is to make them, and the sequence they should take vary from culture to culture. These rules are not absolute laws governing behavior; in fact, they are learned in their interactions within their own cultural groups. But when these patterns differ from the culture-of-teacher to culture-of-child, serious misunderstandings can occur as the two participants try to play out different patterns and assign different social meanings to the same actions.

These differences are likely to prevail in schools with large numbers of students from oppressed groups. Miscommunications occur when the same words and actions mean something different to the individuals involved. When students are

Effective cross-cultural communications between students and teachers promote student learning. When the cultural cues between students and teachers are not understood, communications and learning often are affected adversely.

not responding appropriately in the classroom, teachers should consider the possibility that their communication cues do not match those of their students.

Direct and continuous participation in cultures that are different from our own can improve our competency in other communication systems and should help us be more sensitive to differences in cultures with which we are not familiar. Teachers who are aware of these differences can redirect their instruction to use primarily the communications that work most effectively with students. At the same time, the teacher can begin to teach students how to interact effectively in the situations with which they are uncomfortable. This approach will assist all students in responding appropriately in future classroom situations that are dominated by interactions with which they are not familiar.

Developing Multicultural Proficiencies

Educators should undertake a number of actions to prepare to deliver education that is multicultural. First, they should know their own cultural identity and the degree to which they identify with the various cultural groups of which they are members. The degree of identification will probably change over time. Second, they should be able to accept the fact that they have prejudices that may affect the way they react to students in the classroom. When they recognize these biases, they can develop strategies to overcome or compensate for them in the classroom.

KNOW YOURSELF AND OTHERS

One of the first steps to becoming multicultural is knowing your own cultural identity. Many white students have never identified themselves as ethnic nor racial (Weinstein, Tomlinson-Clarke, & Curran, 2004). They have not thought about their privilege in society. Students of color may have thought little about their multiple identities because their race or ethnicity has been the center of their identity. *What is your ethnic background? How important is your religion in your identity? What impact has your family's socioeconomic status had on your identity? What other cultural group memberships have been critical to your cultural identity?*

Opportunities for Reflection

 *Refer to Chapter 3 for a more in-depth discussion of ethnicity.*

In addition to knowing yourself, you need to learn about cultural groups other than your own. You might read about different cultural groups, attend ethnic movies or plays, participate in ethnic celebrations, visit different churches and ethnic community groups, and interact with members of different groups in a variety of settings. If you enjoy reading novels, you should select authors from different cultural backgrounds. The perspective presented may be very different from your own. Novels may help you understand that other people's experiences may lead them to react to situations differently from the way you would. It is often an advantage to discuss one's reactions to such new experiences with someone else to clarify and confront your own feelings of prejudices or stereotypes.

You should make an effort to interact with persons who are culturally different from yourself. Long-term cultural experiences are probably the most effective means for overcoming fear and misconceptions about a group. You must remember, however, that there is much diversity within a group. You cannot generalize about an entire group on the basis of the characteristics of a few persons. In direct cross-cultural contacts, you can learn to be open to the traditions and ways of the other culture in order to learn from the experience. Otherwise, your own traditions, habits, and perspectives are likely to be projected as better, rather than as just different.

Teachers also should take a critical look at their own interactions with students and communities of color. Many teachers have not critically examined the meaning of race and racism and their role in maintaining the status quo. If educators are unable to acknowledge the existence of racism and understand the effect it has on their students, it will be difficult to serve communities of color effectively and nearly impossible to eliminate racism in either schools or society.

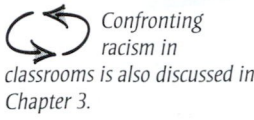
Confronting racism in classrooms is also discussed in Chapter 3.

If you can learn to understand, empathize with, and participate in a second culture, you will have a valuable experience. If you learn to live multiculturally, you are indeed fortunate.

REFLECTING ON YOUR PRACTICE

Opportunities for Reflection

To provide education that is multicultural, professional educators need to continually reflect on their practice in the classroom. *Are students learning? Why not? What can you do differently so that those students do learn? Do you have high expectations for all of your students? Are you incorporating the histories and experiences of your students in the curriculum? Are you relating the content to the realities of students' lives? How engaged are students in their schoolwork?*

Multicultural educators question the content of textbooks and district-wide curriculum for its accurate portrayal of diversity and perspectives beyond the dominant culture. They ask questions about school practices that lead to disproportionate numbers of students of color who are suspended from school; the disproportionate numbers of Asian Americans and upper-middle-class white students in gifted and talented programs; and the disproportionate numbers of low-income males and English language learners in low-ability classes. They recognize racism, sexism, homophobia, and ablism and confront students and colleagues who are not treating others with respect. They correct their own behavior when they learn that their prejudices are showing.

As you begin working with students and other professional educators in schools, continue to observe how you and others interact with students, parents, and colleagues who are from different cultural groups than your own. Think about ways you can use the students' cultures to help them learn the subjects and skills you are teaching. By reflecting on what works and does not work in the classroom, you can continuously improve your teaching for all students.

TEACHING AS A POLITICAL ACTIVITY

Teachers who have made their teaching multicultural confront and fight against racism, sexism, and other discrimination in schools and society. They develop strategies to recognize their own biases and overcome them. They use their knowledge and skills to support a democratic and equitable society.

Politically active teachers become advocates for children who have been marginalized by society. They may become active in political campaigns, supporting candidates who have a positive agenda for children, and for adults with the greatest needs. They become involved in local political action to improve conditions in the community. They are teachers who work for equity, democracy, and social justice.

Summary

Multicultural education is a means for using cultural diversity positively in the total learning process. In the process, classrooms become models of democracy and equity. To do this requires that educators: (a) place the student at the center of the teaching and learning process; (b) promote human rights and respect for cultural differences; (c) believe that all students can learn; (d) acknowledge and build on the life histories and experiences of students' cultural group memberships; (e) critically analyze oppression and power relationships to understand racism, sexism, classism, and discrimination against the disabled, young, and elderly; (f) critique society in the interest of social justice and equality; and (g) participate in collective social action to ensure a democratic society.

Culturally responsive teachers help students increase their academic achievement levels in all areas, including basic skills, through the use of teaching approaches and materials that are sensitive and relevant to students' cultural backgrounds and experiences. The voices of students and the community are valued and validated in the process. No longer can we afford to teach all students the same knowledge and skills in the same way. Teachers must make an effort to know all of their students, to build on their strengths, and to help them overcome their weaknesses.

The curriculum must incorporate the culture of the community and students in the classroom. Students should learn to think critically, deal with the social and historical realities of U.S. society, and gain a better understanding of the causes of oppression and inequality, including racism and sexism. Multicultural education starts where people are, builds on the histories and experiences of the community, and incorporates multicultural resources from the local community.

Positive student and teacher interactions can support academic achievement, regardless of gender, ethnicity, age, religion, language, or exceptionality. Oral and nonverbal communication patterns between students and teachers can be analyzed and changed to increase the involvement of students in the learning process. Teachers must be sure, however, that they do not treat students differently solely on the basis of the students' membership in a group. Teachers should regularly evaluate their academic expectations for students and their biases to ensure that they are helping all students learn.

One of the first steps in becoming a multicultural educator is to examine and clarify one's own cultural identity. In addition, teachers should become familiar with the cultures of others through studying them and participating in them. To provide education that is multicultural throughout one's career will require continuous reflection on one's teaching to determine what is working and what needs to be changed to help all students learn.

QUESTIONS FOR DISCUSSION

1. How do multicultural education and culturally responsive teaching interact?

2. How can a student's culture be used to teach academic content? Give examples that apply to the subject area that you plan to teach.

3. If the textbook you have been assigned to use includes no information or examples pertaining to groups other than European, what can you do to provide a balanced and realisitc view of society to students?

4. How can you incorporate student voices into the subject that you plan to teach?

5. Identify teacher behaviors and attributes that should positively support the delivery of education that is multicultural.

6. How might you structure group work in your class to facilitate cross-group interactions?

7. What are the characteristics of socially just classrooms and why are most classrooms not supportive of social justice?

8. Why is teaching for social justice controversial in some school systems?

9. What characteristics would determine that a school is committed to education that is multicultural?

10. What do you need to do to prepare yourself to understand and use the culture of students in your own teaching?

 ONLINE ACTIVITIES For additional questions and activities linked to the *Exploring Diversity* and additional chapter exercises, visit this text's Companion Website at **http://www.prenhall.com/gollnick.**

PORTFOLIO ACTIVITIES

1. Select a school and write a case study of its multicultural orientation. Describe the diversity of the students and teachers in the school. Describe the inside and outside of the school. Describe how the school addresses multicultural education based on interviews with selected teachers and students. (INTASC Standard 3)

2. Develop a lesson plan in your subject area that relates the subject to a real-life community issue (for example, social services, care of the elderly, or environment issues). (INTASC Standards 3, 7, and 10)

3. Write your own biography, describing your multiple cultural identities and the impact they have on who you are. (INTASC Standard 3)

4. Develop a personal plan for increasing your knowledge about and experiences with cultural groups that are different than your own. How will you assess your progress at becoming more aware of cultural differences? (INTASC Standard 3)

SUGGESTED READINGS

Banks, J. A., & Banks, C. A. M. (Eds.). (2004). *Handbook of research on multicultural education* (2nd ed.). New York: Macmillan.

This major reference document includes chapters on the history, goals, status, and research issues related to multicultural education. Drawing on the expertise of national leaders in the field, it addresses knowledge construction, ethnic groups, immigration, language issues, academic achievement, intergroup education, and international perspectives.

Bigelow, B., & Peterson, B. (Eds.). (2002). *Rethinking globalization: Teaching for justice in an unjust world.* Milwaukee, WI: Rethinking Schools.

This collection of articles on globalization and linkages from one country to another includes articles, lesson plans, student handouts, role plays and simulations, interviews, poems, cartoons, and teaching ideas. It is a wonderful resource on inequity around the world.

Christensen, L. (2000). *Reading, writing, and rising up: Teaching about social justice and the power of the written word.* Milwaukee, WI: Rethinking Schools.

The author describes how reading and writing are political acts. This practical, inspirational book offers essays, lesson plans, and a collection of student writing, all rooted in an unwavering focus on language arts teaching for justice.

Cushman, K. and the Students of What Kids Can Do. (2003). *Fires in the bathroom: Advice for teachers from high school students.* New York: New Press.

Forty teenagers provide advice to teachers on building mutual understanding and respect, classroom behavior, group work, language difficulties, and homework.

Darling-Hammond, L., French, J., & García-Lopez, S. P. (2002). *Learning to teach for social justice.* New York: Teachers College Press.

Student teachers share the dilemmas they faced as they tried to teach for social justice and social change. The book includes case studies, lessons, and projects used by the student teachers.

Gay, G. (Ed.). (2003). *Becoming multicultural educators: Personal journey toward professional agency.* San Francisco, CA: Jossey-Bass.

These fourteen stories by educators from different cultural groups with years of experience in schools describe how they became multicultural teachers.

Gay, G. (2000). *Culturally responsive teaching: Theory, research, & practice.* New York: Teachers College Press.

This book includes detailed descriptions and examples of the key components of culturally responsive teaching, including teacher caring, expectations, formal and informal multicultural curriculum, culturally informed classroom discourse, and cultural congruity in teaching and learning strategies.

Ladson-Billings, G. (1994). *The dreamkeepers: Successful teachers of African American children.* San Francisco: Jossey-Bass.

This ethnographic study describes the differing dispositions, philosophies, and practices of eight teachers who were identified as successful by parents of African American students. Culturally responsive pedagogy becomes meaningful with the examples from the group of teachers.

Menkart, D., Murray, A. D., & View, J. L. (Eds.). (2004). *Putting the movement back into civil rights teaching: A resource guide for K–12 classrooms.* Washington, DC: Teaching for Change and the Poverty & Race Research Action Council.

This book challenges the typical story of the Civil Rights Movement that describes it as a spontaneous movement led by a few inspired orators. It presents the stories of the many ordinary people who performed heroic acts in the name of social justice during this period. The articles, instructional materials, and lesson plans provide an action-oriented history of the time.

Multicultural Perspectives. (Published by the National Association for Multicultural Education, 733 15th

Street, NW, Suite 430, Washington, DC 20005; nameorg@nameorg.org).

This quarterly magazine features articles by scholars and practitioners in the field of multicultural education. It also includes promising practices, multicultural resources, and book and film reviews.

Nieto, S. (2003). *What keeps teachers going?* New York: Teachers College Press.

Experienced teachers who have been successful with culturally diverse students in urban schools identify the challenges of helping these students learn. The book offers an alternative vision of what's important in teaching and learning.

Rethinking Schools. (Published by Rethinking Schools, 1001 E. Keefe Ave., Milwaukee, WI 53212; www. rethinkingschools.org).

Advocating the reform of elementary and secondary schools, this quarterly newsletter promotes educational equity and supports progressive educational values. Teachers, parents, and students are the regular contributors.

Teaching Tolerance. (Published by the Southern Poverty Law Center, 400 Washington Ave., Montgomery, AL 36104; www.tolerance.org/teach/).

This semiannual magazine provides teachers with ready-to-use ideas and strategies to help promote harmony in the classroom. Contributions address politics, race, economics, abilities, culture, and language.

REFERENCES

Brophy, J. E. (1998). *Motivating students to learn.* Boston: McGraw-Hill.

Center for Research on Education, Diversity, and Excellence. (2004). *Five standards.* Retrieved November 2, 2004, from http://crede.ucsc.edu/

Cochran-Smith, M. (2004). *Walking the road: Race, diversity, and social justice in teacher education.* New York: Teachers College Press.

Cushman, K. and the Students of What Kids Can Do. (2003). *Fires in the bathroom: Advice for teachers from high school students.* New York: New Press.

Darling-Hammond, L., French, J., & García-Lopez, S.P. (2002). *Learning to teach for social justice.* New York: Teachers College Press.

Delpit, L. (1995). *Other people's children: Cultural conflict in the classroom.* New York: New Press.

Gay, G. (2000). *Culturally responsive teaching: Theory, research, & practice.* New York: Teachers College Press.

hooks, b. (2003). *Teaching community: A pedagogy of hope.* New York: Routledge.

Metropolitan Life Insurance Company. (1996). *Students voice their opinions on: Violence, social tension, and equality among teens.* The Metropolitan Life Survey of the American Teacher: Part 1. New York: Louis Harris.

National Council for the Accreditation of Teacher Education. (2002). *Professional standards for the accreditation of schools, colleges, and departments of education* (2002 ed.). Washington, DC: Author.

Tatum, B. D. (1997). *Why are all the black kids sitting together in the cafeteria? And other conversations about race.* New York: Basic Books.

Viadero, D. (2004, April 21). Keys to success: Researchers identify methods to help 'nonmainstream' pupils make academic gains. *Education Week,* 28–31.

Weinstein, C. S., Tomlinson-Clarke, S., & Curran, M. (2004, January/February). Toward a conception of culturally responsive classroom management. *Journal of Teacher Education, 55*(1), 25–38.

Weinstein, R. S. (1996, November). High standards in a tracked system of schooling: For which students and with what educational supports? *Educational Researcher, 25*(8), 16–19.

Glossary

accent Refers to how an individual pronounces words.

acculturation Adoption of the dominant group's cultural patterns by a new or oppressed group.

acting white Taking on the behaviors, values, and attitudes of the dominant white culture when the individual is not a member of a European group.

additive bilingualism Additive bilingualism occurs when two languages are of equal value and neither dominates the other.

adequate yearly progress (AYP) A minimum level of improvement—measurable in terms of student performance—that school districts and schools must achieve within specific time frames specified in the law *No Child Left Behind*.

adolecence Approximately ages 13 through 19.

adulthood For the purposes of this book, ages 20 through 64.

afrocentric curriculum Curriculum centered on or derived from Africa.

aged, the Generally considered those individuals who are 65 years or older.

agnostic One who believes that the existence of God can neither be proven or unproven. An agnostic does not believe in a God or Goddess.

alienation Estrangement or disconnected from oneself or others.

Allah Allah is God in Arabic. It is the term used by Muslims for God, and it is also how Arab Christians refer to God.

American Sign Language (ASL) A natural language that has been developed and used by persons who are deaf using a system of manual gestures.

Americans with Disabilities Act (ADA) Public Law 101–336 passed on January 26, 1990. ADA was designed to end discrimination against individuals with disabilities in private-sector employment, public services, public accommodations, transportation, and telecommunications. It was intended to complete what Section 504 was unable to do. The greater accessibilities in buildings, in public transportation, sidewalk curbs, etc., can to a great extent be credited to ADA.

argot Somewhat secret vocabulary of a co-culture group.

ascribed status Characteristics such as ethnicity, race, socioeconomic level, and gender that are assigned at birth by families and society.

assimilation Process by which groups adopt or change the dominant culture.

at risk youth Youth who live in a disadvantaged status.

atheist One who positively does not believe in the existence of a God or Goddess.

authenticity Relates the curriculum and activities to real-world applications with meaning in the lives of students.

authoritarianism The concentration of power in one figure, usually the teacher or principal in schools.

baby boomers Individuals born between 1946, immediately after World War II, and 1964.

basic interpersonal communications skills (BICS) Basic, everyday conversational skills, which English Language Learners can develop in approximately two years.

bi-dialectical An individual who is bi-dialectical has the ability to speak in or utilize two or more dialects.

biased assessments Assessments that tend to be biased toward a particular group or against a group. Many assessments are culturally biased and in the past tests were typically developed and normed on white middle class children. Children of color, particularly African American and Latinos, have been and often still are at a disadvantage in testing because test items are more familiar to white middle class children. The bias may be in the instrument, the administration of the assessment, or the interpretation of test results.

big ideas The concepts that support a subject.

bilingual education "Bilingual education is the use of two languages as media of instruction" (Baca & Cervantes, 2004). It accepts and develops native language and culture in the instructional process to learn English and to learn academic subject matter. Bilingual education may use the native language, as well as English, as the medium of instruction.

bilingualism The ability to function in two languages. While some contend that bilingualism implies native-like fluency, others measure competency in two languages as adequate to be considered bilingual.

Black English A dialect which is also known as vernacular Black, African American Vernacular English, and Ebonics. It is the form of communication for the majority of African Americans and is used by working-class African Americans.

Black Muslims Black Muslims in the United States likely had their early beginnings in the late 1800s, but at that time had little in common with traditional Islam. In the 1970s Elijah Muhammad led the Black Muslims into national visibility. While now aligning themselves primarily with the Sunni form of Islam, American Black Muslims form a unique identity of their own.

blue-collar Jobs or workers characterized by manual labor that is usually mechanical and routine.

Buddhism The fourth largest religion in the world. Founded in 535 BC by Siddhartha Gautama, who was believed to be a prince of India. Buddhists believe in reincarnation and emphasize virtue, good conduct, morality, concentration, meditation, mental development, discernment, insight, wisdom, and enlightenment.

canon The principles, rules, standards, values, or norms that guide a Western European education.

caste A distinction imposed at birth to justify the inequitable social distribution of power and privilege on a group.

child abuse The physical or psychological mistreatment of children.

civil rights The rights of personal liberty guaranteed by the 13th and 14th Amendments to the U.S. Constitution and by acts of Congress.

class A group sharing the same economic or social status.

classism The view that one's class level (e.g., middle class or upper class) makes one superior to members of classes perceived below one's own.

co-cultures Groups of people who exist and function apart from the dominant culture (e.g., street gangs, drug dealers, prostitutes).

cognitive academic language proficiency (CALP) The higher levels of proficiency required in highly structured academic situations.

colloquialisms The informal or conversational speech in a community (e.g., Texas colloquialism, "I like to got hit by that car" meaning "I was almost struck by that car").

color blindness Claim that one does not see a person's race and treats everyone equally regardless of race.

cooperative learning Strategy for grouping students to work together on a project to support and learn from each other.

critical thinking An effort to see an issue clearly and truly to judge it fairly. It usually involves not adopting the status quo without questioning it.

cultural borders A boundary based on cultural differences that limit an individual's understanding of persons from a different cultural background.

cultural capital Endowments such as academic competence, language competence, and wealth that provide an advantage to an individual, family, or group.

cultural pluralism The maintenance of cultures as parallel and equal to the dominant culture in a society.

culturally responsive teaching A pedagogy that affirms the cultures of students, views the cultures and experiences of students as strengths, and reflects the students' cultures in the teaching process.

culture Socially transmitted ways of thinking, believing, feeling, and acting within a group. These patterns are transmitted from one generation to the next.

curriculum A sequence of courses offered by educational institutions.

de facto segregation Segregation that occurs by the choice of the participants.

de jure segregation State-mandated segregation.

deductive A way of thinking and reasoning that begins with the general and moves to the details.

democracy A government in which power is vested in the people and exercised by them directly or indirectly through elected representatives.

developmental disabilities Refers to mental or physical impairments during birth or by the adolescent years. Typically, functional limitations in at least three areas of major life activities such as self-care, language, learning, mobility, independent living, etc.

dialects Variations of a language usually determined by region or social class (e.g., Southern drawl).

discrimination The arbitrary denial of the privileges and rewards of society to members of a group.

dispositions Values, attitudes, and commitments that guide the work of teachers and other school personnel.

Ebonics (see Black English)

egalitarianism A belief in social, political, and economic rights and privileges for all people.

enculturation Process of acquiring the characteristics of a given culture and becoming competent in its language and ways of behaving and learning.

endogamy Marriage within the same ethnic or cultural or religious group.

English as a Second Language (ESL) English as a Second Language instruction relies exclusively on English for teaching and learning the English language. ESL programs are used extensively in this country as a primary medium to assimilate English Language Learners (ELL) into the linguistic mainstream as quickly as possible.

English Language Learners (ELL) Is the term used for students who have limited or no English skills and who are in the process of learning English.

equality State of being equal in that one cultural group is not inferior or superior to another and that all groups have access to the same benefits of society regardless of their group memberships.

ethnic group Membership based on one's national origin or the national origin of one's ancestors when they immigrated to the United States.

ethnocentrism View that one's cultural group is superior to all others.

feminists Persons who actively support the rights of women.

formal standard The acceptable written language that is typically found in grammar books.

freedom Not being unduly hampered or constrained in choice or action by others.

full inclusion Refers to serving students with disabilities and other special needs entirely within the general classroom. This is an important difference from inclusion, as students in full inclusion do not receive any of their education in segregated settings.

fundamentalist Fundamentalism is one of the most controversial terms used in religion. It is generally used to refer to the most conservative wing of a religious group, whether Protestant, Catholic, Jewish, Islamic, etc. These are often groups that dig in their heels to protect their faith from external forces they perceive as attacking their faith and morality. Some use the term *fundamentalist* to denigrate particular groups, implying that they are intolerant and will use terror to accomplish their goals.

Generation X The generation born between 1965 and 1976.

Generation Y The children of baby boomers, and the younger siblings of Generation X, who were born between the early 1980s and 1994.

gifted and talented Refers to students with very high intelligence or such unusual gifts and talents in the arts that they require special educational programming to reach their full potential.

high-risk behaviors Actions such as drug use or premarital sex, which could lead to alcohol or drug dependancy, teenage pregnancy, sexually transmitted diseases, etc.

Hinduism The major religion of India and the third largest religion in the world, with over 750,000 adherents and as many as 1,000,000 in the United States. Unlike Christianity and Islam, Hinduism does not limit itself to a single religious book of writings, or to one God. Hinduism relies on a number of sacred writings and a number of gods. They believe that the goodness of an individual's life will determine how he or she will be reincarnated.

homophobia An irrational fear of or aversion to homosexuals that leads to prejudice, discrimination, and sometimes violence against gays, lesbians, bisexuals, and transgendered persons.

homosexuality Sexual attraction for persons of the same sex.

inclusion Refers to the placement of special education students in general education settings. (*See also full inclusion*)

income Amount of money earned in wages or salaries.

indigenous Population that is native to a country or region. In the United States, Native Americans, Hawaiians, and Alaska Natives are indigenous populations.

individualism Dominant feature of Western culture that stresses the rights, freedom, and importance of the individual over groups.

Individualized Education Program (IEP) A written program required for all children with disabilities under IDEA. It includes statements of the student's present performance, annual goals, short-term objectives, specific educational services needed, relevant dates, participation in regular education, and evaluation procedures. Parents should participate in the development of the IEP and sign the document.

inductive A way of thinking and reasoning that begins with the details to figure out the general.

inequality Marked distinctions in economic success, educational achievement, educational credentials, and power among groups of people.

informal curriculum Rules that guide the expected behaviors and attitudes of students.

informal standard The language considered proper in a community.

involuntary immigrants Immigrants who did not choose to emigrate from their native countries, but were forced to or conquered by others.

Islam The second largest religion in the world and it is still growing in numbers and influence. "Islam" means to submit to the will of Allah or God. Islam is derived from the same Arabic word as "peace." Islam offers hope and salvation to the righteous and God-fearing individuals of all religions. Muslims believe that the Quran (Koran) is the final message delivered to his prophet Muhammad. The holy writing contains laws,

moral precepts, and narratives guiding the lives of nearly one fifth of the world's population.

Jihad The Arabic word for Muslims, which means the struggle in the path of Allah or God. It can mean the struggle against human passions and instincts, which inhibit one from doing the work of God. It can also mean an armed struggle against forces of injustice. Muslim scholars teach that only defensive wars are truly jihad. It is often mistakenly interpreted by non-Muslims to mean a holy war, evoking images of terrorists.

Jim Crow laws Legal restrictions on persons of color sharing public accommodations with whites.

language Written or spoken human speech. It is a system that enables people to communicate with one another and to share their thoughts and ideas with one another.

least restrictive environment (LRE) The educational setting closest to a regular school or general education setting in which the child with a disability can be educated. For many children, this may mean a general education classroom. Others may require a less inclusive setting to best meet their needs.

lived experiences Realities that individuals know because they have themselves experienced them.

maintenance programs Maintenance programs in bilingual education teach the ELL student to function effectively in both the native language and English. The student becomes bilingual and bicultural in the process, with neither language surfacing as the dominant one. The student's native language and culture are taught concurrently with English and the dominant culture.

marginalization Relegation to a position that is not part of the mainstream or accepted by most people.

McKinney-Vento Homeless Assistance Act The federal legislation that outlined the education rights and protections for homeless children and youth.

meaningful projects Student projects that address equity, democratic, and social justice issues in the community.

median income An equal number of persons, families, or households earn more than this number as earn less than this number.

Mennonites Protestants who adhere to a simple life style and simple forms of worship. They base their beliefs on the Bible, particularly the New Testament, and place much focus on the Sermon on the Mount (Matthew 5-7). They believe the Bible forbids them from going to war, swearing oaths, or holding offices that require the use of force. Their origins were in Switzerland in the early 1500s. Some settled in Pennsylvania in the late 1600s and early 1700s and became part of the group known as the Pennsylvania Dutch. In the 1870s some moved to Canada and the Great Plains States.

meritocracy A system based on the belief that an individual's achievements are based on their own personal merits and hard work and that the people who achieve at the highest levels deserve the greatest social and financial rewards.

middle class Group whose members earn annual incomes that allow them to have a standard of living that includes owning a home and car. Members are usually white-collar workers, professionals, and managers.

mild mental retardation Refers to individuals with limited intellectual or cognitive abilities, which often inhibit their academic functioning and socialization. Those with mild mental retardation are the highest functioning of those individuals with mental retardation and can generally master some basic academic skills.

miscegenation Marriage between persons of different race.

monolingualism The ability to speak only one language.

multicultural curriculum Coursework in schools that incorporates the histories, experiences, traditions, and cultures of students in the classroom and supports and celebrates diversity in the broadest sense.

multicultural education An educational concept that addresses cultural diversity and equity in schools. It incorporates the different cultural groups to which individuals belong, with an emphasis on the interaction of race, ethnicity, class, and gender in students' lives.

multiethnic curriculum Curriculum that reflects accurate and positive references to ethnic diversity.

Muslims (or Moslems) The adherents of Islam. Estimates of Muslims are as high as 1.3 billion in the world, and the highest estimates of Muslims in the United States are approximately 7,000,000. Only about 20% of the world's Muslims live in the Middle East. India and Indonesia have the largest numbers of Muslims, with about 175 million each.

nationalism Identity and membership based on a common language and culture in a nation that includes loyalty and devotion to the nation.

nativism Policy favoring assimilated ethnic groups in a country over immigrants.

net worth Amount of money remaining if all owned property was converted to cash and all debts were paid.

New Age Movement that began in the early 1980s. New Age has roots in nineteenth-century spiritualism and in the counterculture movement of the

1960s, rejecting materialism and favoring spiritual experience to organized religion. New Age emphasizes reincarnation, biofeedback, shamanism, the occult, psychic healing, and extraterrestrial life. The movement is difficult to define, as there are so many variations of followers.

nonsexist education Education that attends to the needs of girls and boys equitably by incorporating women as well as men in the curriculum, ensuring that girls and boys achieve at the same levels in all subjects, and encouraging girls and boys to choose subjects which they traditionally would not have selected.

nonstandard dialect A dialect of the same language, but a different dialect than that which is considered standard (e.g., Black English).

Nordic race Germanic people of northern Europe who are white with a tall stature, long head, light skin and hair, and blue eyes.

normalization Normalization means "making available to all persons with disabilities or other handicaps, patterns of life and conditions of everyday living which are as close as possible to or indeed the same as the regular circumstances and ways of life of society" (Nirje, 1985, p. 67).

official English A position supported by U.S. English, a citizens action group, which is seeking to have English declared by Congress as the official language of the United States. Individuals who support this movement believe that all public documents, records, legislation and regulations, as well as hearings, official ceremonies, and public meetings should be conducted solely in English.

Old Order Amish Also referred to simply as the Amish. They had their origins with the Swiss Mennonites but broke away in the 1690s because of disagree-ments over church discipline. Like the Mennonites, they are forbidden to go to war, swear oaths, or hold any public offices (Mennonites will not hold any office, which requires use of force.) They require their members to maintain themselves as separated from the rest of the world as possible. Men wear dark clothes and wide-brimmed hats, and women wear plain long dresses and bonnets. They prohibit the use of electricity, telephones, and mechanical equipment in their homes and farms. They farm with equipment drawn by horses, and they travel by horse-drawn carriages. Children are allowed to attend school only to the age of 15.

Orthodox Jews Orthodox Judaism is the oldest, most conservative, and most diverse form of Judaism. Orthodox Jews look upon every word in their sacred texts as being divinely inspired. They adhere to a strict dietary law (kosher), which requires the use of special ingredients and preparation. Kosher usually refers to food, but may refer to anything ritually fit or proper by Jewish law.

otherness/others Cultural groups that are different than our own.

over-referrals Typically related to the practice of excessive or disproportionate referrals to special education of particular groups of children. Typically, over-referrals involve children of color, particularly African American, Latino, and American Indian students.

patriarchal Social organization in which the father controls the family, and the wife and children are legally dependent on him. It also refers to men having a disproportionately large share of power in society.

pedagogies Art or science of teaching, which includes instructional strategies or methods.

prejudice Negative attitudes about a group of people.

proficiencies Knowledge, skills, or dispositions that students or teachers acquire to meet standards.

Proposition 227 An initiative passed by voters in 1998. Now a California law, Proposition 227 requires all language minority students to be educated in sheltered English immersion programs, not normally intended to exceed one year. Although it has not completely succeeded, Proposition 227 was designed to eliminate bilingual education from California's schools.

Protestants The general name given to an extremely diverse group of Christians, who may differ slightly or greatly from one another. Together, they form the second largest Christian group in the world after Roman Catholics. Protestants are centered primarily in Europe and North America. The hundreds of Protestant groups evolved out of the Reformation in the 1500s led by Martin Luther against the Catholic Church. Protestants share some important beliefs and values with Roman Catholics, such as the belief of only one God and the Trinity (God the Father, God the Son, and God the Holy Spirit). They differ in their views of the authority of the Pope and the ways that people relate to God.

Public Law 94-142, Education for All Handicapped Children's Act A comprehensive legislation signed into law in 1975. It guarantees all children ages 3–21 with disabilities a free and appropriate education in the least restrictive environment.

Public Law 101-476, Individuals with Disabilities Education Act (IDEA, 1990) Emphasized the individual first and the disability second, and forever changed how individuals with disabilities are referred to in the literature (e.g., *students with mental retardation* took the place of *mentally retarded students*).

Public Law 105-17, Individuals with Disabilities Act Amendments (1997) The IDEA Amendments of 1997 consolidated the law from eight parts to four parts, strengthened parental roles, encouraged parents and educators to resolve differences through mediation, gave schools more latitude in discipline of students with disabilities, and set funding patterns.

racism The belief that one race has inherent superiority over all others and thereby has the right to dominance.

Reformation A religious movement in the early 1500s, which led to the formation of Protestantism. In 1517, the German monk Martin Luther protested alleged abuses and certain practices of the Catholic Church. Within 40 years, Protestantism had spread through half of Europe.

refugees Persons recognized by the U.S. government as being persecuted or legitimately bearing persecution in their home country because of race, religion, nationality, or membership in a specific social or political group.

regression to the mean A statistical phenomenon that implies that scores at the extreme ends of the statistical distribution move toward the population average (mean), with low scores moving higher and high scores moving lower.

Roman Catholics Members of the Roman Catholic Church are often referred to simply as Catholics. They comprise the largest Christian church in the world with over one billion adherents. Most believers live in Europe, South America, and North America. The numbers of Catholics in Africa and Asia have been growing in recent years. Catholics believe that Jesus founded their Church and that the Apostle Peter was the first in the line of bishops leading to the current Bishop of Vatican City. The Pope is the spiritual and political leader of Roman Catholics.

Sabbath (or Shabbat) A day of rest and holiness; observed by Jews and a minority of Christian denominations (e.g., Seventh Day Adventists). It is observed from sunset on Friday night until nightfall on Saturday. Most Christian groups observe Sunday as the Sabbath.

Section 504 of Public Law 93-112 Part of the Rehabilitation Act of 1973 designed to be a counterpart law for individuals with disabilities to the Civil Rights Act of 1964. It requires reasonable accommodations for those with disabilities, and prohibits the denial of participation in any program receiving federal funds solely on the basis of one's disability.

secular humanism A non-religiously based philosophy promoting man as the measure of all things. Typically rejects the concept of a personal God and regard humans as supreme. Secular humanists tend to see God as a creation of man, rather than man being a creation of God.

self-fulfilling prophecy In education, the projection of the teacher's expectations for student achievement being realized in the student's performance in the classroom, whether or not it matches the student's academic potential.

sexism The conscious or unconscious belief that men are superior to women that results in behavior and action to maintain the superior, powerful position of males in society and families.

sexual harassment Unwanted and unwelcome sexual behavior that interferes with the victim's life.

sexual orientation One's sexual attraction to persons of the same or opposite sex or both sexes.

sheltered English immersion Refers to an instructional process in which English language acquisition is structured so that nearly all instruction is in English. This is the instructional method mandated by California Proposition 227 and is normally limited to one year.

signed English A system that translates the English oral or written word into a sign.

Sikhism Founded by Guru Nanak during the fifteenth or sixteenth century B.C.E. in India. He drew from the elements of Hinduism and Islam, and stressed a universal single God. Union with God, he said, is accomplished through meditation and surrender to divine will. He believed in reincarnation, karma, and the destruction and rebuilding of the universe, but he rejected the Hindu belief in the caste system.

social justice A philosophy that expects citizens to provide for those persons in society who are not as advantaged as others.

social role valorization Refers to giving value to individuals with mental retardation.

social stratification Ranking of persons and families based on specific characteristics such as income, education, occupation, wealth, and power.

socialization Process of learning the social norms and expectations of the culture.

socioeconomic status (SES) Composite of the economic status of families or persons on the basis of occupation, educational attainment, and income.

standard English The English spoken by a particular group of individuals in a community. Typically this group is the professional educated middle class and the group with a high degree of influence and prestige in the community.

stereotypes Exaggerated and usually biased views of a group.

stereotyping Application of generalizations, many of which are negative, about a group without consideration of individual differences within the group.

structural assimilation Assimilation of groups to the point that they share primary relationships, intermarry, and have equality with the dominant group.

subcultures Subsocieties connected to cultural group memberships such as gender, race, ethnicity, socioeconomic status, religion, exceptionalities, language, and age.

subsocieties Systems of values, attitudes, and behaviors of social groups within society. Examples are gangs, groupies, and skinheads.

substance abuse Use of drugs or alcohol to a level of addiction or other at-risk behaviors.

subtractive bilingualism Occurs when a second language replaces the first.

Title IX Legislation passed by Congress in 1972 to provide girls equal access to all aspects of education.

tracking The practice of separating students based on their perceived academic abilities to receive instruction that is supposed to be most appropriate to their abilities.

transition Transition plans became a requirement for all children with disabilities by the age of 14 years in IDEA 1990. A transition plan includes a needs assessment and planning to transition from student into adulthood.

transitional programs Transitional programs emphasize bilingual education as a means of moving from the culture and language most commonly used for communication in the home to the mainstream of U.S. language and culture. The native language of the home is used to help the student make the transition to the English language. The native language is gradually phased out as the student becomes more proficient in English.

under-referrals Disproportionately low referrals by teachers of children for specific programs or activities. These often include the disproportionately low numbers of children of color (particularly black, Hispanic, and American Indian) in classes for the gifted and talented or advanced placement classes.

Unification Church Founded in Korea in 1954 by the Rev. Sun Myung Moon. Individuals outside of the faith refer to the group's adherents as "Moonies," considered derogatory by its members. Members refer to themselves as Unificationists. Rev. Moon moved to the United States in 1972 and began a major effort to proselytize members into his church. A decade later he performed the first of many mass arranged marriages in which 2,000 couples exchanged vows.

upper class Group whose members earn high annual incomes and have wealth.

upper middle class Group whose members are the affluent middle class. Members are highly educated professionals, managers, and administrators.

values Qualities or principles that are considered desirable and important.

vernacular A native language, dialect, or speech (e.g., Black vernacular or Black English).

wealth Accumulated money and property such as stocks, homes, and cars that can be turned into money.

white-collar Jobs or workers characterized by nonmanual labor in offices, retail stores, and sales.

working class Group whose members work at manual jobs that do not usually require higher education. The more skilled jobs may require specialized training.

Zoroastrianism One of the oldest religions still in existence; a relatively small religion with about 140,000 adherents. It is significant because it may have been the first monotheistic religions, and had a great impact on Judaism, Christianity, and other later religions with respect to beliefs in God and Satan, the soul, heaven and hell, resurrection, the final judgment, etc.

Author Index

King, S. S., 168
Klinger, S., 51, 52, 66
Kofkin, J. A., 313
Kosmin, B. A., 237, 238
Kratcoski, L. D., 331
Kratcoski, P. C., 331
Kuper, A., 22

Lachman, S. P., 237, 238
Ladson-Billings, G., 11
Laine, R. D., 84
Lee, C., 131
Lee, V. E., 74
Levine, M., 340
Liben, L., 313
Lincoln, C. E., 237, 250
Lindberg, R. C., 333
Lindner, E. W., 230
Lindsay, D. M., 221–224
Lopez, R. J., 332
Los Angeles Almanac, 275
Los Angles Times, 325
Losen, D. J., 186, 199, 200, 201
Lotz, R., 317, 330
Lucas, S. R., 79
Luxembourg Income Study, 74
Lyons, L., 222, 257

Madsen, R., 27
Mamiya, L. H., 250
Martin, C. A., 339, 340
Marty, M. E., 242
Maslow, K. W., 202
Mastropieri, M. A., 206
McCall, L., 161
McCorkle, R. C., 331
McDonald, J. J., Jr., 86
McGraw, B. A., 235, 237, 240, 241, 243, 244
McGraw, D., 326, 327
McKee, P. W., 325
McKinney, W., 252
McLoyd, V. C., 320, 325
Mehring, J., 297
Mercer, J., 197
Metropolitan Life Insurance Company, 376
Meyer, P. A., 199
Midwifery Today, 323
Miethe, T. D., 331
Miller, S., 317
Mishel, L., 66, 67, 68
Mitchell, Susan, 338, 339
Montalto, N. V., 8
Morash, M., 310, 322, 332
Mowder, B. A., 198
Murdick, N., 184–189
Murray, C., 128
Musial, D., 21

National Alliance for the Mentally Ill (NAMI), 324
National Association for Bilingual Education (NABE), 291
National Association for the Education of Homeless Children and Youth (NAEHCY), 58

National Board for Professional Teaching Standards, 15
National Catholic Reporter, 224, 230, 241
National Clearinghouse on Child Abuse and Neglect Information, 315, 317
National Coalition for the Homeless, 60
National Coalition for Women and Girls in Education, 171
National Commission on Teaching & America's Future, 83
National Conference for Community and Justice, 109, 114
National Council for the Accreditation of Teacher Education, 359
National Federation of State High School Associations, 171
National Gay and Lesbian Task Force, 145
National Institute on Drug Abuse, 321
National Low Income Housing Coalition, 60
Nazario, S., 325
Nee, V., 29, 30
New York University Law Student Drug Policy Forum's Fact Sheet, 334
Newport, F., 230
News-Medical.Net., 285
Nieto, S., 270
Nirje, B., 205
Nix, M., 297
Noguera, P., 78
NYC Mayors, 272

Office of Civil Rights, 198, 283
Ogbu, J. U., 130
Olson, L., 97, 120
Ontario Consultants on Religious Tolerance, 255
Orfield, G., 58, 131, 186, 199, 200, 201
Orr, J. E., 292
Ortner, S. B., 143
Owens, R. E., Jr., 273, 278, 280, 281
Oxtoby, W. G., 236

Palermo, G. B., 330, 331
Pang, V. O., 109
Patton, J. M., 195
Peach, L. J., 247
Persell, C. H., 66
Petersen, R. D., 317, 326, 332
Philbin, J., 320
Phillips, C. B., 102
Polakow, V., 61
Porter, R. E., 273, 274, 287

Portes, A., 30, 97, 130
Potok, M., 118
President's Committee on Mental Retardation, 179
Privetz, T., 199
Proctor, B. D., 345
Prothrow-Stith, D., 321, 326, 330

Radziewicz, C., 206
Rank, R., 62, 74
Reschly, D. J., 198, 296
Ribeau, S., 281
Richard, M. H., 117, 320
Riley, R. W., 131
Rivers, J. C., 129
Robinson, B. A., 240, 245, 262
Robinson, F., 236
Roof, W. C., 252, 337, 338
Rose, S. J., 51, 53, 57, 58, 63, 65
Rosen, R., 156
Rossell, C., 293
Roth, W., 191
Rothstein, R., 75
Rumbaut, R. G., 30, 97, 130

Salthouse, T., 342
Samovar, L. A., 273, 274, 287
Sandall, S. R., 198
Sanders, J., 169, 170
Sanders, W. I., 78, 129
Schaie, K. W., 341
Schechter, S., 295
Schmitt, J., 66, 67, 68
Schnaiberg, L., 282
Schoonover, J., 199
Schram, P. J., 310, 322, 332
Schulz, R., 342
Schwartz, M., 163
Scruggs, T. E., 206
Sears, J. T., 145
Seifert, M. W., 286
Shank, M., 206
Shapka, J. D., 169
Shipler, D. K., 63
Shulman, B., 63
Sidel, R., 325
Simpson, D., 330, 331
Singer, C., 297
Singer, D., 224, 232
60 Minutes, 340
Slavin, R., 84
Sleek, S., 312
Sleeter, C. E., 7, 9, 11, 39
Smith, D. D., 270, 285
Smith, Dan, 53, 96
Smith, S. J., 206
Solomon, R. P., 130
SoundVision, 238
Southern Poverty Law Center, 116, 118, 119
Spencer, R., 68
Spivak, H. R., 321, 326, 330
Spring, J., 11
Steinberg, L., 320, 325
Stone-Romero, E. F., 286
Streisand, B., 326, 327
Sullivan, W. M., 27
Swanson, C. B., 69
Swidler, A., 27

Taeuber, C. M., 342
Tafoya, S. M., 110
Takaki, R., 98
Tanner, R., 343
Tatum, B. D., 112, 121, 314, 364
Taylor, D., 321, 330, 335
Thompson, M., 143, 144
Thurlow, M., 199
Tiegerman-Farber, E., 206
Tipton, S. M., 27
Tower, C. C., 316
Treas, J., 343
Trojanowicz, R. C., 310, 322, 332
Tuchman, G. M., 291
Tulgan, B., 339, 340
Turnbull, A., 206
Turnbull, R., 206
Tyack, D., 8, 11, 169

UCLMRI Newsletter, 292
U.S. Census Bureau, 4, 51, 52, 54, 55, 58, 62, 64, 67, 68, 69, 70, 71, 72, 73, 74, 92, 95, 96, 97, 106, 109, 111, 119, 120, 151, 158, 159, 160, 163, 164, 272, 310, 342, 343, 345
U.S. Conference of Mayors, 59, 60
U.S. Department of Education, 4, 11, 55, 61, 74, 119, 159, 163, 164, 166
U.S. Department of Labor, 160
U.S. English, 290
U.S. State Department, 234
Unz, R. K., 291
Urban Institute, 58, 60

Viadero, D., 358
Viskel, F., 52, 62

Wehmeyer, M. L., 163
Weinstein, R. S., 365
Welner, K. G., 79, 80
Wesson, C., 199
West, P., 255
WestEd, 293
Wheeler, R. D., 282, 283
Widerstrom, A. H., 198
Williams, D., 132
Williams, P. W., 234
Willis, P. E., 130
Willis, S. L., 341
Willoughby, B., 99
Witt, D., 290
Wolfensberger, W., 205
Wolfram, W., 271, 273, 278–283, 296

Yell, M. L., 184–189
Yoon, I., 131
Young, R. L., 109
Youth and Hate, 118
Youth Violence Prevention Resource Center, 326
Ysseldyke, J. E., 199

Subject Index

Equal Pay Act, 154
Equal Rights Amendment (ERA), 154
Equality, 6, 36–37
  and educational curriculum, 81, 83
  obstacles to, 39–41
ERA; See Equal Rights Amendment (ERA)
ESL; See English as a Second Language (ESL)
Ethnic awareness, and children, 312–313
Ethnic group, 92, 103, 105
Ethnic identity, 103, 106
Ethnic inequality, 68–70
Ethnic and racial diversity, 92–102
  civil rights, 97–102
  immigration, 94–97
  introduction to, 92–94
  U.S. history, 92–94
Ethnic and racial group identity, 102–113
  ethnicity, 103, 104–107
  introduction to, 102
  race, 107–113
Ethnic studies, 123–125
  and multicultural education, 9
Ethnicity, 103, 104; See also Race and ethnicity
  ethnic identity, 106
  and gender identity, 153
  group assimilation, 106–107
Ethnocentric curriculum, 125–126
Ethnocentrism, 19–20
Eugenic sterilization, 181
Eurocentric curricula, 270–271
Eurocentrism, 270–271
European settlers, and U.S. ethnic and racial diversity, 93
Exceptional children; See Exceptional people, Special education
Exceptional people
  acceptance, 204
  and Brown v. Board of Education of Topeka, 182–183
  communication needs, 204
  defined, 178–179
  educational implications, 202–205
  freedom to grow, 204–205
  historical antecedents, 180–181
  and IDEA mandates, 188–189
  introduction to, 178–179
  labeling, 179–180
  legislation, 184–188
  litigation, 181–184
  and Mills v. Board of Education, 184

normalization and inclusion, 205–210
and PARC v. The Commonwealth of Pennsylvania, 183–184
socialization of, 181, 191–195
Experiences, and multicultural education, 368
Experimenters, and drug use, 321

Family, and multicultural education, 374–375
FAPE; See Free and appropriate education (FAPE)
Farrakhan, Louis, 237
Favored status, 96
Female; See Gender; Gender differences; Women
Feminists, 153–155
  anti-, 155
Financial support, and education, 83–84
Fires in the Bathroom: Advice for Teachers from High School Students, 369
First language acquisition, 287–294
Fiscal resources, and special education resources, 206–207
Formal standard, 280
Free and appropriate education (FAPE), 189
Freedom, 27
Fundamentalists
  and multicultural education, 10–11
  and religion, 220

Gandhi, Mahatma, 354
Gangs, 331–334
Gay, Lesbian, and Straight Education Network (GLSEN), 147–148
Gebhart v. Belton, 98
Gender
  cultural influences, 143–144
  defined, 143
  differences, 140–142
  educational implications, 163–172
  ethnicity, race, and religion interaction, 152–153
  identity, 148–153
  and mathematics, science, and technology, 166–169
  and religion, 246–247
  sexism and discrimination, 156–163
  sexual harassment, 161–163
  sexual orientation, 144–148

teacher and student interaction, 168–169
and Title IX, 100, 138, 169, 171–172
women's movement, 154–156
Gender differences
  biological determinism, 140–142
  introduction to, 140
Gender discrimination, defined, 157–158; See also Discrimination; Gender
Gender identity, 148–153
  ethnicity, race, and religion interaction, 152–153
  introduction to, 148
  socialization, 148–151
  stereotyping, 151–152
Gender inequality, 70–73; See also Women
Gender role, expectations, 149
Generation X, 338–339
Generation Y, 339–341
Geographical regions, and religion, 217–218
Gifted and talented, 179
GLSEN; See Gay, Lesbian, and Straight Education Network (GLSEN)
Gong Lum v. Rice, 99
Grammatical differences, 278–279
Grant, Madison, 108
Group assimilation, 106–107
Group homes, 194–195
Grouping
  and exceptional people, 192–195
  low-ability, 79–80
  and teacher expectations, 77–78
  and tracking, 79–81
Guadalupe Organization, Inc. v. Tempe Elementary School District No. 3, 296

Hate groups, 117–119
Hearing impairments, and cultural groups, 193–194
Heaven's Gate, 245
Hendrick Hudson School District v. Rowley, 188–189
Heterosexuality, 144
Hidden curriculum, 377
High-risk behaviors, 320
Hinduism, 240–241
Hispanic
  identification of race, 108–109
  and race relations, 116
HIV, and adolescence, 323
Homeless, 58–62

Homosexuality, 144–148
  acknowledgement of, 145–147
  classroom interaction, 168–169
  homophobia, 147–148
  and religion, 247–248
Homophobia, 144, 147–148
Hostile Hallways: Bullying, Teasing, and Sexual Harassment in School, 161
Hughes, Fergus P., 306

IDEA Amendments, 188
IDEA; See Individuals with Disabilities Education Act (IDEA)
IEP; See Individualized Education Program (IEP)
Immigrants
  and assimilation, 30–31
  and children, 311–312
  education of, 97
  location of, 96–97
Immigration
  changing patterns, 95–96
  ethnic and racial diversity, 92–94
  favored status, 96
  location of immigrants, 96–97
  U.S. history of, 94–97
Immigration Reform and Control Act, 94
Inclusion
  defined, 206
  normalization and inclusion, 205–210
Income
  defined, 51
  and gender discrimination, 158
  inequality, 67–68
  and middle class, 63–64
  and socioeconomic status (SES), 51–52
  and working class, 62
Income inequality, 67–68
Indigenous, 92
Individualism, 27, 34–35
Individualized Education Program (IEP), 186
Individuals with Disabilities Education Act (IDEA), 187–188
  amendments, 188
  and language, 298–299
Inductive reasoning, and girls, 142
Inequality, 36
Inequity and power, addressing of, 372–373
Informal curriculum, 22
Informal standard, 280
Inner-city schools, and teacher expectations, 78–79

INTASC; *See* Interstate New Teacher Assessment and Support Consortium (INTASC)
Intergroup relations, 114–116
and desegregation, 131–133
Internet, and hate groups, 118–119
Interstate New Teacher Assessment and Support Consortium (INTASC), 12
teacher standards, 13–15
Involuntary immigrants, 30
Islam, 234–238
Black Muslims, 237–238
diversity, 236–237
and education, 238
extremists, 235–236

Jainism, 243
Jewish Holocaust, 233–234
Jihad, 235
Jim Crow laws, 98, 154
Job Corps, 336
Johnson, President Lyndon, 154
Johnson-Reed Act, 94
Jones, Jim, 245
Judaism, 231–234
anti-Semitism, 233–234
diversity, 232–233
and education, 233
Orthodox Jews, 233
political influence, 233
Reformed Jews, 233

Ka'ba, 235
Kentucky Industries for the Blind, 193
Kentucky School for the Blind, 193
Kids Count, 310
Kinsey, Alfred Charles, 145
Koran, 235
Koresh, David, 245

Labeling, 179–180
Language
acquisition of first, 287–294
acquisition of second, 287–294
and culture, 19, 270–273
defined, 270
dialect, 277–284
differences, 275–284
diversity, 272
educational implications, 294–301
English only, 290–294
nature of, 273–275
sign, 284–285
and socialization, 271–272
and special education placement, 200–201
Language diversity, 272

Language proficiency, 288–290
Larry P. v. Riles, 200
Latter-Day Saints, 241
Lau v. Nichols, 99, 297–300
Lead poisoning, and special education placement, 199
Learning communities, 373
Learning disability, and labeling, 180
Least restrictive environment, 206
Lee v. Weisman, 254
Legislation, 184–188
Americans with Disability Act (ADA), 187
Education for All Handicapped Children Act, 185–187
Individuals with Disabilities Education Act (IDEA), 187–188
Public Law 94-142, 185–187
Section 504 of Public Law 93-112, 184–185
LEP; *See* Limited English proficient (LEP)
Lesbian, gay, bisexual, and transgender (LGBT), 148
LGBT; *See* Lesbian, gay, bisexual, and transgender (LGBT)
Limited English proficient (LEP), 287
Litigation, free and appropriate education (FAPE), 189
Lived experiences, and multicultural education, 368
Lower class, 48

Mainstreaming, 206; *See* Inclusion; Normalization and inclusion
Maintenance programs, and bilingual education, 299
Malcolm X, 237
Male; *See* Gender; Gender differences
Male stereotype, 144
Managers
and middle class, 64
and upper middle class, 65
Marginalization, 29
Masculinity, 143–144
Maslow, Abraham, 202
Mathematics
and gender, 166–168
and single-sex education, 169
McCollum v. Board of Education, 252
McKinney-Vento Homeless Assistance Act, 61
Mecca, 235

Media
and prejudice, 314–315
and stereotyping, 151–152
violence affecting children, 330
and women's movement, 156
Median income, 52
and age inequality, 74
and middle class, 64
race and ethnic inequality, 68
and upper middle class, 65
and women, 72
and working class, 62
Mendez v. Westminster, 99
Mennonites, 218
Mental disabilities; *See* Exceptional people
Mental retardation; *See also* Exceptional people
and labeling, 179–180
and socialization, 181
Meritocracy, 34–35
Messages, biased, 378–379
Mexican Americans, and U.S. ethnic and racial diversity, 93
Middle class, and class differences, 63–64
Mild mental retardation (MMR), 179
Millennium Generation, 339
Mills v. Board of Education, 184
Miscegenation, 108
MMR; *See* Mild mental retardation (MMR)
Monolingualism, 275
Moore, Roy, 216–217
Mormon; *See* Latter-Day Saints
Muhammad, Deen, 237
Multicultural curriculum, 360–364
Multicultural education, 6–16; *See also* Culturally responsive teaching; Education; Teachers
culturally responsive teaching, 360–369
current practices, 10–12
defined, 5
evolution of, 8–9
focus on learning, 358–359
history of, 8–9
initiating of, 356–359
introduction to, 6–7
proficiencies, 382–384
school characteristics, 7–8
school climate, 376–381
social justice, 369–375
strategies for, 7
supporting dispositions, 359
teacher proficiencies, 12–16
Multiculturalism, 24

Multiculturalists, and multicultural education, 10–11
Multiethnic curriculum, 126–127
Multiracial backgrounds, 110
Murray v. Curlett, 254
Muslims, 235–237
and hate crimes, 117–118

NAEP; *See* National Assessment of Educational Progress (NAEP)
Nation, defined, 103
Nation of Islam, 237
National Assessment of Educational Progress (NAEP), 12
National Organization for Women (NOW), 155
Nationalism, 94
Native American, 242–243
and U.S. ethnic and racial diversity, 92
Nativism, 94, 108
Naturalization Law, 98
NCLB; *See* No Child Left Behind (NCLB)
Negative expectations, prevention of, 78
Net worth, 52
New Age Spirituality, 243–244
Nguyen, My Lien, 90
No Child Left Behind (NCLB), 11–12
Non-Hispanic, identification of race, 108–109
Nonsexist education, 156, 165–169
Nonstandard dialect, 270
Nonverbal communication, 285–287, 300
and culture, 19
Noppe, Lloyd D., 306
Nordic race, 108
Normalization, defined, 205
Normalization and inclusion, and exceptional people, 205–210
NOW; *See* National Organization for Women (NOW)

OAAU; *See* Organization of Afro-American Unity (OAAU)
Oakland Unified School District, 281–283
Occupation
and socioeconomic status (SES), 54
10 fastest growing, 54
and women, 71
and working class, 62